Out of my comfort zone

Out of My Comfort Zone

The Autobiography

Steve Waugh

MICHAEL JOSEPH
an imprint of
PENGUIN BOOKS

MICHAEL JOSEPH

Published by the Penguin Group

Penguin Books Ltd, 80 Strand, London WC2R 0RL, England

Penguin Group (USA) Inc., 375 Hudson Street, New York, New York 10014, USA

Penguin Group (Canada), 90 Eglinton Avenue East, Suite 700, Toronto, Ontario, Canada M4P 2Y3

(a division of Pearson Penguin Canada Inc.)

Penguin Ireland, 25 St Stephen's Green, Dublin 2, Ireland (a division of Penguin Books Ltd)

Penguin Group (Australia), 250 Camberwell Road,

Camberwell, Victoria 3124, Australia (a division of Pearson Australia Group Pty Ltd)

Penguin Books India Pvt Ltd, 11 Community Centre,

Panchsheel Park, New Delhi – 110 017, India

Penguin Group (NZ), cnr Airborne and Rosedale Roads, Albany,

Auckland 1310, New Zealand (a division of Pearson New Zealand Ltd)

Penguin Books (South Africa) (Pty) Ltd, 24 Sturdee Avenue,

Rosebank, Johannesburg 2196, South Africa

Penguin Books Ltd, Registered Offices: 80 Strand, London WC2R 0RL, England

www.penguin.com

First published in Australia by Penguin Books Australia 2005
First published in Great Britain By Michael Joseph 2006

1

Copyright © Steve Waugh, 2005

The moral right of the author has been asserted

Set in 11.25/16 pt Garamond
Typeset by Post Pre-Press Group, Queensland, Australia
Printed in Australia by McPherson's Printing Group, Maryborough, Victoria

A CIP catalogue record for this book is available from the British Library

ISBN-13: 978–0–718–14833–1
ISBN-10: 0–718–14833–9

*For my lifelong friend and partner, Lynette, who has
endured and shared the best and worst times with me,
whose nurturing ways, wisdom and unconditional
love have comforted and inspired me.*

*And for our children, Rosalie, Austin and Lillian –
you are life's most precious and greatest gifts. Your love
of life, unique character and spirit make each
and every day an adventure.*

*Of all my achievements, nothing matches the feeling of
returning home to my family and the sight of you guys
running up the hallway, trying to be the first
to jump into my arms.*

CONTENTS

FOREWORD BY RAHUL DRAVID

I was 14 years old – sweating at the nets and dreaming, like schoolboys do, of playing for my country – when I first saw Steve Waugh. It was the 1987 World Cup in India, which Australia won, and while Steve was in his early twenties he had already caught my eye. This was not merely because of his ability with bat and ball (his slower deliveries bowled with various actions would soon be replicated in nets around India), but also for his grit under pressure. Steve appeared to relish the big occasion, seemed to thrive in such situations, but I had no idea back then that it would be this characteristic that would become his signature or that years later I would be privileged to see it first hand.

Greatness is a label easily bestowed in these 'exaggerated' times, but Steve earned such high praise. History will remember him as one of the game's finest practitioners. He averaged over 50 in Test cricket, the mark of a superb batsman, and played a significant role in two World Cup victories, 12 years apart. As captain, he inherited a gifted Australian team from Mark Taylor and forged it into an even more aggressive and successful side. He was influential beyond his shores, a man looked up to.

Steve was a hard man and respected because he had done it the hard way. Greatness was not handed to him; he pursued it diligently, single-mindedly. Dropped from the team, he worked his way back. The story of his resolute journey, among other things, makes for interesting reading.

With 32 Test centuries, there is no shortage of impressive innings to remember, but the one that stands out for me is the 67 not out in 273 minutes he made against us in a one-off Test in Delhi in 1996. On a turning wicket, alive with uneven bounce, he constructed an innings that was masterful in both its technique and its complete concentration. Watching it from silly point as he fended off gifted

spinners like Anil Kumble was an education, a lesson for a youngster like me playing in his first season of international cricket.

For me, when Steve batted, a couple of things stood out. There was the infinite
care he put into his defence, each ball carefully watched and played as if his life
depended on it. The acceleration of his bat was interesting as well, for sometimes
you thought he was going to be late for the ball, but then his bat would descend
at tremendous speed to meet it. Most of the time we left him alone, not speaking
to him on the field, for we knew he fed off any conversation, and enjoyed confrontation and the challenge that came with it. Australia was never beaten while
he was there at the crease.

On the field, his manner was introverted, his emotions tightly locked. He
appeared to live the cliché of 'No quarter given and none asked'. But off the field,
if you sought him out for a chat, he was never reluctant to share his thoughts.

On Australia's 1998 tour to India I was keen to pick his brain on batting and
cricket in general, and Steve promised to let me do so once the series was over.
But Australia lost the series and he was injured and missed the last Test, in Bangalore. I would have understood if he had forgotten about this eager youngster,
and I thought it was inappropriate to remind him, but on the third day of the Test,
unprompted, he called me and we met for dinner. It was a discussion that would
have a lasting influence on me.

His ruthless style, combined with a passion for the game, has won him a staggering, almost unrivalled, following in India. But this is a reverence that does not
stem only from cricket but also from a generosity of spirit. Steve's work with the
children of Udayan in Calcutta has been widely admired, and he has also sought
to discover India, to learn about us and go beyond the tired, stereotypical image of
this beautiful country that so many visiting cricketers carry with them.

Steve's legacy is hard to define, but I will remember him because he gave grit
a good name. He proved that it is not only the pretty player who can capture the
imagination, but also the tough and determined. Suddenly these qualities became
as vital, as spoken about, as silken grace and sublime timing. He was leathery
tough, played the game aggressively, and would do whatever it took within the

rules to win. He built a team that has achieved legendary status, raised the level of young cricketers who played under him, and also embraced the traditions of the game and highlighted their importance.

I will remember the pain of not beating him in that last Test of his, in Sydney in January 2004, but also recall fondly his final innings in cricket against us, for it was a typical Steve Waugh innings: mind over matter, a man not in form but soldiering on, taking his team to safety. I will remember, too, that when I hit the winning runs in the Test in Adelaide in that same series, Steve found the ball and handed it to me. I have it still and it is signed by him.

Steve Waugh is an interesting man who has lived an interesting life; a man of cricket but not just of cricket. For 18 years he has travelled the world, won and lost and learnt and led. He has faced cameras, critics and fast bowlers, and he has brought to it all a commitment to excellence.

FOREWORD BY TIM MAY

The Australian cricket team in the late 1980s was an evolving and revolving team, with the majority of players trying to establish themselves within the side. The captain was not entirely comfortable with being captain; the squad was not entirely comfortable with the idea that they were up to international standard. The first priority, it seemed, was survival.

Indeed, the squad of players that set off to represent Australia in the 1987 World Cup were described by Pakistan cricket legend Zaheer Abbas as being no better than club cricketers.

This was the environment in which I made my international debut. I had played with or against all my teammates, with the exception of Stephen Waugh. I had no idea what to expect from him as a bloke – all I knew of him was what I had seen on television. It seemed like he didn't smile a great deal. He seemed like a 'stiff'. I silently hoped I wouldn't have to room with him.

It's not my intention here to write of Steve Waugh, the cricketer. We all know about that, we've seen it. He doesn't smile. He is a 'stiff'. It's my goal to try to paint a picture of Steve Waugh the person, the bloke away from cricket – perhaps the Stephen Waugh you don't know.

From early in 1988 Steve Waugh was my roommate in the Australian side. You can room with a teammate and never get to know him. A typical tour around Australia or to one of the more 'Western' countries basically sees you entertained and out of your room during downtime. However, because of the limited entertainment options, a tour of the subcontinent involves plenty of time doing nothing and gives you ample opportunity to mix with your teammates.

They say you don't really know what makes a person tick until they are under pressure or facing adversity. It was the Pakistan tour of 1998. Stephen had a stinker of a tour. I got to know him well. The temptation when you are down is to retreat to your room, brood and become a reasonably ordinary bloke. Stephen did not do this. I could tell that this competitive and determined man was hurting inside and was down, frustrated, but that mindset did not affect his role as a teammate. He would not bring the team down.

Instead, a relatively unknown side of Stephen was exposed – the humorous, the risk taker, the generous unselfish man. And, even in social surrounds, the incredibly competitive man.

I lost count of the times we stayed up laughing uncontrollably as we recounted the day's activities and the characters we had met and nicknamed, whether it was 'The Fly', 'The Frog' or 'Spud'. There were the plain stupid times – nights spent crawling and hiding in corridors and fire-emergency stairwells in Pakistan hotels as detectives May and Waugh investigated alleged prostitution rackets involving air hostesses. There were nights/mornings that left us running late for the team bus as Stephen tried pathetically and unsuccessfully to beat me at 'Othello', the game that takes 'a minute to learn – a lifetime to master'.

Yet among all this immaturity was the realist – a bloke who was able to see beyond the cocoon international cricketers live in. It is so easy to get carried away with the trimmings that come with the international cricketing life, to the point where you lose perspective of what is reality and what is really important in life.

Stephen provided that perspective.

He is a leader, able to educate and influence both young and old team members about the balance needed in life and the relevance of the plight of others. He has an ability to assist and offer encouragement to those in need. He is a person who inspires and invites mateship, respect, unselfishness and loyalty.

He is smart, he is a street fighter, he is seriousness, he is damn funny, he is incredibly determined and confident. Yet the bloke can't play Othello for nuts.

I trust that the pages that follow give you a further insight into Stephen Waugh 'off the field'. But if he mentions that he ever beat me in Othello, you can add a description of 'liar' to the characteristics I have provided above.

INTRODUCTION

The catch of a lifetime

Nestled among the sun-stealing skyscrapers of Hong Kong lies a small cricket ground. In 1988, this speck of greenery was the venue for a friendly match between the Australian touring team, en route back to Oz after a disastrous tour of Pakistan, and a Hong Kong XI. It was here, on perhaps cricket's most expensive piece of real estate, where I reached the point where something had to give. They say that the darkest hour is before the dawn and that this is when the great avenger is born. Well, I was experiencing what every sportsperson goes through at least once in his or her career – that deep, disturbing inner voice of negativity, the one that says, *You aren't good enough, stop wasting your time, no more torture, take the easy option. Just fade away and be happy to lead a normal, controlled and relaxed life.*

In truth, I just wanted someone to recognise that I was suffering, to tell me it was all going to work out okay in the end. I needed someone to explain that, occasionally, it is normal to feel trapped and inadequate.

After all, this was only an exhibition match. Nevertheless, it was as if a jagged stake had been driven through my heart. In my mind, I was trying to justify what had become of my cricket career: *I can't believe my bad luck . . . Why is it always me? . . . Just give me a break once in a while.* These and other worthless and hollow excuses soothe for a second but scar for much longer.

It wasn't the fact that a local merchant banker had snaffled the catch of a lifetime to dismiss me; it was the certainty that it was going to happen. Bad body language is a bit like smelly underarms in that you don't really sense it, but those around you pick up on it in an instant. I had been walking out to bat like a man who hadn't tubbed for a week. With the doomsday cloud hovering above my shoulders, even this fielding side sensed a kill. I was the weakened prey. The end result was a top-edged slog that spiralled high into the polluted atmosphere. Then a flailing fieldsman at backward point leapt high and backwards with his right hand outstretched to its fullest length, more in hope than expectation, to cling onto the ball. Unfortunately, there was no elaborate celebration for the fieldsman; instead he lay prostrate on the turf, having seriously damaged his torso when he tumbled awkwardly to finish up in a classic crime-scene 'human chalk-outline' position.

We trudged off, he carried by two teammates, thronelike, to the waiting medical staff, me not having troubled the scorers. I thought I heard muffled laughter coming from the spectators, and pretended it didn't really matter because, after all, it wasn't a real match. Wrong. I was representing my country and the laugh was on S. Waugh. I felt like the game was having a lend of me. I wanted to shrivel up and disappear; this whole business of playing for my country seemed too demanding and pressurised for me to continue, or to even begin to fight against the momentum that was engulfing me and suffocating the life out of me . . .

Fast forward the best part of 11 years, to Lord's, London, and to the aftermath of the 1999 World Cup Final. Pure ecstasy, elation, relief and overwhelming contentment raced through my veins, together with a healthy measure of adrenaline as the realisation hit me that a dream had come to fruition.

My teammates and I made our way out onto the fabled, sloping turf, where we gathered together in a huddle on the playing pitch. Arm in arm, still dressed in our garish yellow uniforms, a vibe like a current ran through us; we were experiencing cricket nirvana. Swaying back and forth as one, we felt impregnable and bulletproof while the rest of the world was being held hostage by the pause button. Suddenly, Ricky Ponting was whisked high into the air by Tom Moody and placed like a scarf around his neck. It was time for Aussie cricket's ultimate feeling of togetherness, a snapshot of cricket life that each member of the squad knew would always stay in the memory bank. As was the custom, Ricky went into his summation of the game and the tournament, with all the lads encircling him. Each personal and team highlight was celebrated by dousing either your closest buddy or the guy who had earned Ricky's accolade. A brief pause ensued after each, before it came like a tidal wave, each player's complexion turning crimson red, the veins bulging to the maximum, faces contorted with the ferocity of intent, muscles flexed to confirm our brotherhood and a touch of extra personality thanks to Mr Booze: 'Underneath the Southern Cross I stand . . .'

Our team song echoed with enormous passion around the empty stadium as players and support staff soaked up the uniqueness of the occasion. Instead of stopping after the usual two verses, we instinctively launched into a third as the beer spewed out and sprayed around like an out-of-control fire extinguisher. *It doesn't get any better than this* was all I could think. I wanted time to stand still – this was the moment that underlined the fact that all the sacrifices, hard work and dedication had converged to deliver a perfectly finished product.

Another round of high-fives and backslapping confirmed that it was reality and not an illusion. Then we walked slowly back to the legendary red-brick Lord's pavilion, reminiscing as we meandered, trying to soak up as much of this life experience as we could. A final look back over my shoulder to the middle filled me with pride: we were cricket's world champions and I had the honour of being the winning captain.

★

From Boxing Day 1985 to January 6, 2004, my life as an international cricketer featured moments of exaltation and times of brutal introspection. Self-denial, self-belief, pity, anguish, joy, relief, satisfaction and myriad other thoughts and emotions were what ultimately made my journey so fulfilling and stimulating. I was fortunate to be exposed to both ends of the emotional spectrum, because I've come to believe that you have to experience the depths of the valley to appreciate the views from the peak. Strength of character and the will to prevail and ultimately succeed are forged by the trials and tribulations experienced along the way.

I have come to learn that life wouldn't be as enjoyable if it was always easy, and that personal growth comes from having to move out of your comfort zone. What I didn't know in Hong Kong was that it is the challenge itself that provides the environment in which you can fight and struggle – and ultimately prevail.

I

All in the family

Picnic Point Road, Panania, sounds exotic, somewhat upper class. In reality, it is in the heart of Sydney's suburbia. Back in the 1960s, when I was born, it was 'fibro' territory, that tag coming from the cheap building material that was the basis of many of the homes in the area, a place where mums and dads had to work long and hard to make ends meet. The Waugh boys never wanted for anything as kids, but then our needs were pretty simple. All we required was a place to play sport and some basic equipment to make it happen.

My twin brother, Mark, and I were born four minutes apart at Canterbury Hospital, maybe 30 minutes' drive south-west of the city centre, on June 2, 1965. We arrived much to the shock of the nurse on duty, as this was not only the first time she had delivered a set of twins, but her first birth of any kind. Afterwards, I imagine there was relief all round: Mum was only a frightened, nervous teenager, the doctor hadn't made it for our arrival and if we had been female a danger existed that the Waugh name would cease to continue, for Dad was an only child.

Childhood memories can sometimes fade over the passage of time but many of mine remain vivid to this day. The first thing I can remember is the sweet taste of the sticky, pink polio vaccine coaxed down my throat with a miniature white plastic spoon by the baby-health nurse. Growing up in the same bedroom as Mark for 16 years meant we were in many ways like Siamese twins, especially as it wasn't the biggest room ever. A positive was that we always had each other to rely upon, a crutch to lean on if we felt insecure in any situation or threatened by outsiders.

Mum used to make a lot of our clothes. At the time, we didn't really mind because fashion wasn't a priority, but looking back there were some pretty hideous outfits (or perhaps they were a reflection of the fashions of those days). We always had matching attire, right down to the accessories, and there was never any doubt that we were twins.

Competition and comparison were our endless companions. Whose turn is it to bat first? Who gets to kick off? Who gets the extra piece of steak for dinner? Who gets to wear the soccer socks without the holes in them? Who received the highest marks in the spelling test? Whose turn is it to ride up to the shop on the scooter to get the Sunday papers? Everything seemed to need a result. As most twins will tell you, always being compared can at times be damaging. Jealousy is a direct consequence of everybody expecting a winner and a loser, and Mark and I certainly had our times of conflict. These increased as we began to clearly exhibit our cricket, soccer and tennis abilities, and, to a lesser extent, in our scholastic endeavours.

More than anything, though, our childhood was fun. We always had the support and encouragement of Mum and Dad. Dad worked for the National Bank in their telex communications department, and Mum fluctuated between being a swimming instructor and a school-teacher. Both were also part-time tennis coaches, and eventually the parents of four boys. Dad's work ethic set a great example – he refused to take days off, even if he was physically unwell, for fear of letting down the team and organisation around him – while Mum always displayed compassion for those less fortunate and took the time to listen and help them as much as she could. As juniors, they had both been outstanding tennis prospects, playing against future legends like Tony Roche, John Newcombe and Evonne Goolagong, but the birth of twins before their 20th birthdays put paid to their sporting ambitions. In a funny sort of way, knowing that Mum and Dad had relinquished their personal sporting dreams drove Mark and me to achieve as much as we could. We felt that our parents were part of our journey, that our success was theirs, too.

Arriving three years after Mark and me was Dean, who had to endure hand-me-downs such as the homemade purple-and-white 'Sunday best' strip that came in duplicate and couldn't be avoided. Becoming the outgoing comedian of the family, in later life Dean also achieved success as a sportsman; as such he was inevitably compared with Mark and me and the sometimes harsh comments from observers could make his life difficult. Seven years after Dean, Daniel entered the world, and his elder brothers doted on him. I couldn't wait to hold and look after him, and as soon as Mum gave me an opportunity to do so I cradled his newborn head and poured milk into his mouth faster than I'm sure he wanted it. I felt a strong urge to protect Danny, which hasn't dimmed over the years; if anything, it has intensified with time. We were a close family in that we looked out for each other, but as brothers we never showed a lot of emotion towards one another. In those days, this was the 'macho' boy way.

Certain images from my childhood have stuck with me. I can't recall being in any life-threatening situations, but as the mischievous twin my curiosity often got the better of me. Once, my love of confectionery and all things sweet nearly left me minus a tongue. After one particularly hectic battle in the backyard, I came racing inside to quench my thirst and decided to grab an iceblock from the freezer. Standing on a stool to reach the freezer box I peered inside to find that, as usual, we had already gulped the lot down. Wanting to salvage something from a hopeless cause, I scoured the frosted box and came across a patch of green ice that had formed courtesy of an earlier cordial spillage. However, I instantaneously realised my error when my tongue became one with the floor of the freezer box; to make matters worse, I had my head at a 90-degree angle to my shoulders because the lime-flavoured ice was located towards the back of the freezer. Thankfully, Mum grew bored with playing backyard soccer with Mark and Dean and my speech was eventually saved, but only after a few ungainly attempts to prise me loose.

Walking into a barbed-wire fence on a relative's property is another memory of my youth that hasn't faded over time. While it was pitch dark and there was a fair distance between the house and our aqua-blue Holden Kingswood, the real problem revolved around me pretending I was Pele, scoring goals from every angle using cowpats in the paddock as imaginary soccer balls. With my mind on curling one into the top right-hand corner of the net, I waltzed into the property's boundary fence and felt a grabbing sensation on my neck. Believing my jumper to be the culprit, Mum began yanking me back and forth until she realised it was skin and not my collar that was entangled. An ambulance was summoned and eventually I was free again to score many more goals (though mindful of not booting a 'hot' one because they tended to explode on impact).

Accidents are part of anyone's childhood and we had our fair share, but amazingly none was too serious. I'm not sure how Mark and I survived our scooter races down the driveway, because they were incredibly competitive and, at times, physical. They would always begin at the top of our block's driveway, which led steeply down the side of the house before the track bent sharply to the left in order to miss the garage door that sat directly ahead. The finishing mark was Mum's washing hanging on the line, which either acted as a parachute or blindfolded us before we crashed into the above-ground pool. It was crucial to get the inside lane or be ahead entering that decisive bend, or else you were doomed to a dispiriting loss. Leg speed and 'ticker' were the other factors needed for bragging rights, while foul play was another variable that occasionally determined the outcome of the race.

I must admit to one particularly nasty occurrence that saw Mark unable to continue the contest when he came to serious mental and physical grief, his scooter reduced to a mangled wreck. As usual, it was full tilt down the concrete driveway, heads down, thighs pumping, each with an eye on the other. It was a tight affair and we both knew something had to give, as only one scooter could fit comfortably as we exited the driveway. There was no way I was letting Mark dive across me from the outside lane, especially as we would have to swap starting spots in the next round and the advantage would be his. A quick sideways nudge to the ankle connected sufficiently to send the younger twin's pristine scooter off in a very unwanted direction. For a split second and for the first time, I saw genuine fear on Mark's face – and for good reason, as he slammed into the painted diamond on the garage's timber door before his frantic attempts to engage the brakes could retrieve the situation. Victory was mine, but it didn't feel quite the same as I came back to inspect the wreckage. No doubt Mark got me back later on, because we always kept each other honest and neither of us ever had the upper hand for too long.

Occasionally we would both get ourselves in serious trouble, never more so than the day in Year 5 at Panania Primary School when, having been assigned the task along with two other pupils of gathering the school's one and only television set for an afternoon lesson keenly anticipated by the rest of the class, we had a major mishap. It was little wonder we came to grief – daydreaming as we weaved our way across the playground, thrashing the trolley around like a racing car while the brand-new TV stayed precariously balanced on top. Our confidence in our manoeuvring skills proved to be our downfall, when one of the wheels unexpectedly wedged itself into a groove on the concrete just as we were about to enter the classroom. The sudden shift in weight meant there could only be one conclusion to our adventure – four bodies diving for cover as the school's pride and joy plummeted to the concrete, smashing into pieces on impact. Thirty heads spun around from the school desks in total shock as we began to apportion the blame. Somehow we survived that one, and for Mark being in trouble was a new experience. He was always the more attentive, studious one, handing in beautifully illustrated projects on time, while I tended to run with the pack and find strife on a much more regular basis.

★

Sport was our life. Every waking hour was spent playing, watching and discussing anything that had a ball in it. Our first foray into competitive sport came via tee-ball, an endeavour so popular there were only two teams in the competition: a Red side and a Green side. We were regularly trounced by the dominant red outfit, but the lack of variety actually did us a favour because we had no choice but to improve. Soccer and tennis were a huge part of our childhood, but it was cricket that was our great love. Today, I am constantly reminded of the influence cricket has had on my life. The smell of Aerogard, the insect repellent, takes me back to the Under 10s, Saturday-morning cricket, where the coach or mums would ask us to close our eyes while they doused us with the foul-tasting spray, always managing to get some into our mouths. The scent of freshly mown grass, the aroma of freesias in spring, the whiff of linseed oil, the taste of green cordial, even hearing a Bee Gees number on the car radio – these are all things I associate with cricket and that take me back to a time of blissful innocence.

Every Saturday morning Mark and I would hop into the back of the coach's white ute as he made his way around the local area, picking up all his players. We froze as we huddled together on the metal tray with the icy chill of the morning air blasting our unprotected legs, but our excitement and anticipation of the battle ahead had us forgetting the numbness. Friday night's sleep was restless as I dreamt of fours and sixes, and of wickets to be taken. I couldn't wait for the sun to come up. It was like Christmas Day every Saturday – except when it rained. Then it was instant misery. *Surely we can still play, it looks like the clouds are lifting, here comes the sun* – but then it would hit you like a sledgehammer between the eyes. Ring . . . ring . . . ring . . . Mum would pick the phone up and you'd hear those dreaded words: 'That's a shame, I'll tell the boys . . .'

Our early days of playing against kids two to three years older than us allowed Mark and me to develop our fielding skills, because that's all we did. Each team, including ours, had one or two stars and we weren't it, so like the other seven 'also-rans' we watched the prodigies do all the batting and bowling. Mind you, we didn't care; we were on an adventure and there was no other place we'd rather have been.

Our very first official game of cricket was in many ways a disaster, and over before we realised what had happened. Not having a coach wasn't a promising start, and it was left to a group of mothers to guide the debutants of Panania–East Hills Under 10s. Not only did we collapse to be all out for the grand total of four, which included three wides, but the Waugh boys lasted a meagre three deliveries. Mark had his stumps knocked over first ball, while I was fortunate that a full toss landed on my bat first up before I lost my stumps to the very next delivery. But it wasn't the pair of ducks or the pitiful total that hurt us the most – it was the embarrassment of wearing our only pad on the wrong leg and the placement (by our parents) of our protectors on our kneecaps.

As we became more involved and started to learn about the game, we, like all our mates, wanted to have the latest and most popular cricket bat. During our first couple of years the team had two kit bats, to complement the prized possession of our No. 11 specialist batsman and back-door neighbour, who had a brand-spanking-new Slazenger Polyarmour Five-Star bat. It was so impressive that everyone used to squabble over who would use it in the match. The boys would be constantly picking it up to play imaginary hook shots as they admired the 'cherries' that had already stained the bat's face and edges. By the end of the season it was smothered in dirt and ball stains, the grip handle had perished and the toe of the bat had worn away significantly. We all prayed that Robert Hall would make Santa's good-boy list and find the newest model under his tree next year.

My special wish was granted a few seasons later, when the bat of the day, the Greg Chappell-autograph Gray-Nicolls Steel Spring with the maroon stripe down the back, arrived. It was the greatest gift possible and duly received the utmost love and attention. There's nothing like owning your very own bat. I must have counted the number of grains across the face a thousand times after I read in the *Calling All Cricketers* coaching manual that between seven and nine grains was the ideal number. Further joy was mine when I spotted a butterfly knot in the wood – this was supposedly another good sign because it meant the timber was solid and wouldn't split.

Preparation of the bat was the absolute key to its longevity. I wanted mine to last as long as possible, and used an old rag dipped in linseed oil to wipe down the front and back of the blade with an even application; to get too much oil in one part would affect the pick-up of the bat. Critically, you could under no circumstances spread oil around the splice of the bat, where the handle met the blade, as this would weaken the glue and loosen the handle. Perhaps an even greater crime was to stand your bat in the oil and saturate the bottom, which would ruin the balance.

Once the bat's face was sealed, it was time to 'knock it in'. This was done by spending countless hours banging an old, soft cricket ball against the face, to gradually condense and toughen the wood in readiness for the harsher confrontations of a real match. I must have driven everyone in the family mad with the constant clunking sounds that went with me as I paraded around the house for hours on end.

As the years went on, Mark and I progressed to whatever was the latest craze – the single red-scooped Gray-Nicolls, the double scoop with pink grooves, and so on – until the age of 16, when former Test player Ian Davis awarded both of us a personal sponsorship to use County cricket gear. I couldn't believe that we no longer had to pay for our kit and could even choose more than one bat. This was our first taste of the commercial benefits associated with the game. Around the same time, after we'd begun our association with Bankstown Cricket Club, Test fast bowler Len Pascoe, who'd opened the first-grade bowling at Bankstown with Jeff Thomson before Thommo moved to Queensland in 1974, began mentoring us. Once a week we'd talk all things cricket. Len would offload some of his used handcrafted boots and I'd wear them even though they were two sizes too big. To me, they had magic in them because Len had played for Australia.

Competitive instincts might be genetic, but in my experience they can be accelerated and brought to the surface if stimulated. Duelling with Mark, Dean and Danny over the years provided a perfect learning environment for the battles that lay ahead. When we wanted a game, we had three separate venues to choose from. The front yard offered a real test of hand–eye coordination for the batsman, with the pitch situated across a slope far more pronounced than Lord's, with a sharp drop-off from the off side to the leg side. Bowlers could produce massive off-cutters at will, so as a batsman you had to counteract this excessive sideways movement by going with the angle and flicking it off the stumps in the direction of midwicket. This shot ended up being Mark's trademark stroke, and would also prove a productive area for me throughout my career.

However, this was a pitch that needed at least one other player, a wicketkeeper, to stop the ball flying into the property of our next-door neighbour, who didn't really appreciate our enthusiasm and whose unkempt garden swallowed errant missiles quicker than we could flog them from the basket of tennis balls Dad used during his coaching classes. Consequently, Mark and I had to wait for Dean to grow up and fill that need, which meant that, early on, the driveway was our favourite hunting ground. Again, we had to improvise and use our imagination to devise special rules and playing conditions. The bowler had a distinct advantage, running downhill and delivering to a batsman who had nowhere to back-pedal. On the leg side, close to the pitch, was a tangled mess of intertwining plants and vines, while the garage door acted as both wicket and backstop. Further adding to the batsman's woes were stationary objects like the clothesline and back end of the house, which, together with strategically placed moveable objects like scooters and toys, doubled as fieldsmen. If any of these 'catchers' was struck on the full, that was the end of your dig. The tennis ball was taped heavily on one side, enabling the bowler to deliver prodigious movement through the air that required close watching to avoid dismissal. Perhaps even worse, a wicked late in-swinger could cannon into exposed flesh and cause degrading tears to be spilled on the concrete.

The third and perhaps the most defining and influential venue was the backyard. I describe it this way not because it was our favourite place – in fact, it was usually our last option because of its confines and the awkward positions of the clothesline (especially when the bed sheets were hanging out to dry) and the above-ground pool. That latter obstacle ended many a game, particularly in winter, when the ball landed in the middle and couldn't be reached. However, it was here that a dream was launched. I remember clearly listening to legendary cricket commentator Alan McGilvray as he described Test-match action, his voice emanating from the portable radio positioned on the back veranda. McGilvray's dulcet tones transported us to another place. The 1974–75 season stays with me still. There was one more problem, though, and it was simple: no one wanted to be the Poms when we re-enacted the action. We wanted to be one of the Chappells, or Lillee, Thommo, Dougie Walters or Rod Marsh, never Greig or Edrich or Willis. I'd been to the Sydney Cricket Ground to watch a Sheffield Shield match, and knew that I wanted to one day play at the great ground, with the seagulls lolling around on the outfield beneath the huge, glorious scoreboard at the back of the Hill, but getting there seemed so far away. A seed had been planted.

For me, there were never enough hours in the day to practise and compete. I was always looking to hit another cricket ball in the summer, kick an extra goal in winter and serve more tennis balls all year round.

Being so keen invariably meant I ran out of opponents to take on, and the garage door could only take so much punishment, so I had to be innovative to satisfy my insatiable desire to be active and improve. Mum's stockings provided the solution. A tennis ball was placed inside an old pair, which was then hung from a beam in the garage. To make it more realistic, electrical tape was bound around the ball to give it hardness. Later, the tennis ball was replaced by an old cricket ball, with the tape now used to reinforce the stocking. To adjust the height of the ball, all I had to do was wind the stockings around the beam a few times to simulate shorter-pitched deliveries. The trick of the whole exercise was to play as straight as possible, so the ball would crash into the tiled roof and then fly down at good pace directly back to where I was waiting. If I got it slightly wrong, the angle would be accentuated by the ricochet and the sequence would be broken, much to my frustration. I believe I learnt patience and perseverance from the thousands of hours I spent alone in the garage. I would keep trying until I could hit 10 in a row, then 20, eventually 100. I loved the challenge I would set myself to maintain the pleasure I gained from playing the perfect shot, the one that 'pinged' off the bat. Without knowing it, I was enthusiastically searching for the perfect technique and developing routines that would later form the basis around which my game could evolve. The only downsides were that the expenditure on Mum's lingerie increased, occasionally a roof tile was broken, and once or twice I suffered the shock of a broken window after the ball flew out of a frayed stocking. But overall, I think Mum and Dad approved because it kept me out of potential trouble. It was healthy exercise, and they knew I loved it; it would have been self-defeating trying to stop me.

Another illustration of my youthful love of cricket is the detailed diary entries I made after each innings I played, whether it be for school or in a representative game. I'd record the length of each innings, how I was dismissed, how many fours I hit and, of course, my score. It was always easy to remember the latter, as Mark and I had learnt from an early age that we needed to keep our own score when batting out in the middle, after being mixed up by scorers too many times. As soon as we got out we'd go and check the scorebooks, and have them altered if they'd got it wrong. If there were disputes, we'd quickly recall each run we'd made and where it had been struck, much to everyone's disbelief. Runs were important to us and neither of us wanted our rival twin to poach a couple here and there.

I'm constantly amazed at how clear my recollections of sporting encounters from my youth are. Recently I drove past Arncliffe Oval, the scene of the Waugh twins' first representative match – as seven-year-olds playing for Bankstown in the Under 10 Foster Shield. We batted numbers 10 and 11, but gave the team two very enthusiastic fieldsmen who wanted every ball to come their way.

As I slowed down in my car that day, to concentrate on reliving the memories that came flooding back to me, one shot I played became so clear it felt like it had happened only yesterday. It was a straight drive that sped past the bowler and had enough power to reach the boundary ropes. I'll never forget that feeling of accomplishment, of doing something no one expected. It was a sensation I wanted to replicate time and again. The thrill of dominating a bowler – and being good enough to do so – was already a part of my character.

2

A matter of survival

When it came to sport, being twins certainly gave Mark and me the advantage of being noticed, but as we began to dominate junior rep cricket our uniqueness also accelerated the debate about which of us was better. Being a double act, with a reputation that preceded us, saved us on one occasion, when our school sports master forgot to tell us about the Liverpool Region high-school cricket selection trials. Such was the power of the Waugh name that the officials decided to restage them, even though they had already selected a squad. Our eventual selection was nice, but I couldn't help wondering about the feelings of the two players who'd been omitted as a result.

I did miss out on the New South Wales Under 15 side once, which led to Dad having a major run-in with the coach about the issue. I hid from that argument, knowing that the old man had overstepped the boundary, but I did feel a sense of pride because he was protecting me and fighting for me. Like any parents, Mum and Dad were one-eyed and often couldn't see the logic in decisions that went against their progeny, and in this case the coach's line that I 'scored too quick, played too many shots and didn't build an innings' seemed a little thin on commonsense. Standing out was something I never coveted, but I also wanted to be the best I could be, so my success often caused me internal conflict. I loved being successful but hated being the centre of attention.

In 1978, Mark and I were selected as two of 50 lucky kids to take part in a week's intensive coaching at the flash Cranbrook School in Sydney's eastern suburbs. Legends of the game would be there to give us coaching sessions and mentoring. This was an iniative of World Series Cricket, the rebel series that had been born out of the game's best players' dissatisfaction with the way the sport was run. We stayed at the school for a week, a couple of kids to each room. No one knew much about anyone else, though we had become accustomed to the whispers that were around concerning who the gun cricketers were. The Waugh twins were top of many lists. On the first night, after the introductions had been made and expectations for the week had been announced, we made our way to the mess hall for dinner. Meat and three veg were served in production-line style, and it was with a trayful of food that I ensured *everyone* knew I was at the camp. In full stride and with my head down, I didn't spot the spilled juice on the floor, and before I could regather myself I took a nasty tumble, spilling food and drink everywhere. My act of clumsiness created a dead silence, with heads turning en masse as if watching a tennis match. This wasn't the impression I had wanted to make, and my natural shyness didn't allow the memory of that fall to be easily erased from my thoughts.

I was hoping that my cricket would nullify the embarrassment of that evening, but my first net session the next day left me in a state of shock and utterly deflated. The famous South African batting maestro, Barry Richards, who was part of WSC's World XI team, was our coach for the day. I desperately wanted to impress him, so I pulled out the full array of shots, including a few that sailed off into the far corners of the playing field, ensuring the deflated bowler would experience a lengthy absence as he went off to retrieve his ball. However, this obviously wasn't what the coach wanted, judging by the tone of his voice when he said, 'Keep it in the nets. Hit them along the ground.'

Good advice, but with youth comes the need for expression and the urge to do what comes naturally. So when a juicy half-volley came my way not long after, I didn't think twice about the outcome. High and long it sailed, and in my mind there was no need to run for that one, for surely it would have been a six in any game. I settled back into my stance in preparation for the next delivery, but when I looked up I saw a very agitated Mr Richards moving purposefully towards me. Perhaps he was going to tell me what a great shot I'd just played? However, as he got closer, my optimism diminished.

'That's it – get out. You don't listen. You've faced your last ball today.'

I was frozen to the spot. *Surely he doesn't mean me? This isn't happening.* Yes, it was, and out I skulked, not knowing which way to look. Such a dressing-down is not easy to digest for a 12-year-old, and neither is the torment of having to watch the action rather than take part in it. Come next morning, I banked on redeeming myself. Again, we worked under the examining eye of Barry Richards, who I was sure had me in his sights but who in reality had probably already forgotten yesterday's young upstart. Suddenly, the arts of concentration and discipline were a part of my game. These two attributes form the nucleus of mental toughness, and it was at Cranbrook School's oval that they surfaced for the first time when the pressure was on. I had learnt my lesson and it was one that stuck with me throughout my career.

The week was a real eye-opener in cricketing terms, and gave me the chance to rub shoulders with some greats of the game. It was also my first taste of freedom and a chance to express myself as an individual. I made new friends and we talked about strange things such as girls, who seemed to us to be highly overrated. I wondered what impression I had made on the coaches during the camp and whether or not they thought I could make it in the years ahead.

★

At this stage of my young life, soccer was an equal love with cricket, while I also couldn't practise and play tennis enough, idolising the likes of Jimmy Connors and Bjorn Borg. The painted blue diamond on the garage door copped a hammering all year round as I kicked, threw or hit various balls in its direction. In summer it acted as the stumps to enhance the accuracy of my bowling and throwing, while in winter it was the spot to which penalty kicks had to be directed. And when time permitted, I tested my tennis volleying skills, trying to hit as many consecutive shots as I could into the zone.

Talent-wise, soccer was probably the sport where I was most gifted, but in the end it gave way to my real passion. I played soccer for Revesby–Milperra Lions, who regularly ran second to the highly credentialled Panania Soccer Club. It was almost a case of the fibro lads verses the silver-spoon boys, or at least that's the way I saw it. I couldn't wait to take on the red-hot favourites and seemed to always lift for the occasion, relishing our underdog status and the prospect of taking them down a notch.

Representative honours came to Mark and me in all three sports, but it wasn't until I reached the age of 13 that I experienced my first taste of what it was like not to be a part of the inner sanctum. In many parts of Australia in the 1970s and '80s soccer was known as 'wog ball' or a game for 'pansies', but I only ever saw it as a fantastic team sport, even if many clubs and organisations were ethnic-based and -influenced. Travelling interstate with the NSW Under 15 side was a huge honour and a pretty fair achievement considering I was only 13, but with my youth came unfamiliar territory. I wasn't used to not being the star, or to not knowing anyone else in the squad. Whether it was intentional or not, I was left alone, without any friends and feeling totally isolated from the other guys, who all seemed to know each other well. Being Anglo-Saxon was a major hindrance, because I couldn't speak Greek or Italian or whatever language was the basis for their conversations. I kept to myself and played as well as I could, but there was something missing – my heart wasn't totally in it. I didn't feel an attachment to the team and no one made an effort to ease the apprehension and uneasiness I felt as an unfamiliar face. It wounded me. I didn't want to ever again feel so isolated and unwanted in a team environment and I didn't want to see it happen to anyone else, either.

Something had to give during my final years of school at East Hills Boys High. Study, albeit still a lower priority than sport, needed attention, while the levels at which I was playing soccer and cricket meant that the seasons were now overlapping and a decision had to be made. Being the only player at Sydney Croatia without 'vic' on the end of my surname wasn't the major problem, but the fact that the coach had made it clear he wouldn't promote me to first grade unless I stopped attending the cricket training sessions that had encroached on his schedule certainly was. When I was selected for the Australian Schoolboys cricket side a year after being selected for the equivalent soccer squad, a choice had to be made. My football career was suddenly all over. Deep down,

I was content that the path I had chosen was the correct one because my decision had come from the heart.

★

School to me was always a vehicle through which I could try my hand at as many sports as possible. The correlation between my exam results and whether or not my teacher was a sports enthusiast was quite obvious. I considered myself street-smart rather than intellectual, and could manage to put together a decent essay to bail myself out of the many tricky situations I found myself in. I was one of a group of hecklers who used to sit in the back row and cause the teachers a bit of grief, practising my throwing accuracy by picking off fellow students in the front rows with paper aeroplanes and anything else I could lay my hands on. Mark, on the other hand, was more of a teacher's pet, rarely getting into trouble and always sitting up the front, obeying each order to the fullest and handing assignments in on time. I fell victim to the dreaded cane for my indiscretions on more than one occasion. It was an unforgettable stinging, numbing pain that lasted for at least the duration of the next lesson, and was hard to hide from my buddies, who wanted a detailed account of how hard the blows had come down and what the pain was like. Later on, I would experience exactly the same numbness when fielding in the slips in England during April, after interrupting a flying outside edge in the freezing conditions.

I was rarely at the top of the class academically, but nor was I at the bottom; to me it was a matter of survival – don't excel because you'll stand out, and don't fail because the dunce tag is a tough one to shake and the stigma is long-lasting. I was content to roll with the punches and lift when need be.

I did, however, pull off one minor miracle in Year 8, during the second year of studying compulsory German. Why the school authorities deemed this language valuable is still a mystery to me. Counting to 10 was the summit I had climbed after 18 months of confusion, so I wasn't feeling all that confident when Mr Gordon, a teacher with a wild Afro hairdo who made the subject seem even weirder than it was, handed out the half-yearly test of 25 multiple-choice questions, each worth four marks. The following week we were informed that one pupil had achieved what no other student in the history of East Hills Boys High School had ever done before in this subject – a perfect score. *There's always one smartypants in every class*, I thought. Then Mr Gordon began reading out the results, from worst to best, and I was quite shocked when my name wasn't read out early on. But as he got past halfway, I started thinking, *Surely he's lost my paper*. Finally, there he was, standing in front of the lot of us, about to introduce who he now believed to be his star pupil. When he began walking towards me I realised I'd won my lottery early in life, because the odds against guessing 25 correct answers in a row were astronomical. I was somewhat stunned, although nowhere near as much as the class 'brains', who were gob-smacked at my meteoric ascension. The unfortunate aspect of my one-off piece of brilliance was to allow my heart to rule my head: I chose to continue German as an elective subject for a further two years, stumbling from one disaster to another. The end result of those four years of 'study' is that I now possess an amazing repertoire of fluent German amounting to 'Ja' and 'Nein' and the valuable skill of being able to count to 99.

The Higher School Certificate at the end of Year 12 was, for most of us, our first taste of the real world. It was a period of time that shaped many lives and altered others, depending on whether or not the results went as hoped. It was hardly fair, but the fact that the HSC came down to a series of mainly essay-based exams suited people who could memorise well and write essays that might be appropriate to a broad range of topics. Helping me in a major way were my good buddies, one of whom, as luck would have it, was repeating his final year.

I spent most of my time photocopying his book reviews and lesson plans, and homework that I'd been unable or unwilling to do myself because it clashed with my sporting endeavours.

Expulsion was never really on the cards, but I ran into serious bother on more than one occasion. Having the whole Biology class bar one – the class 'nerd' – around to my place to enhance our knowledge of anatomy courtesy of an R-rated video was a solid plan, except for the fact that the deserter revealed our whereabouts and I then made the ultimate error by answering the home phone. Attempting to establish an imaginary world record by having the most people inside and out-side of a car was another appealing idea I came up with, but it ended in near disaster when one of the boys opened the door that happened to be providing an anchoring point for another clinging on to the boot. The ensuing fall and stuntlike tumbling routine was impressive and comical to watch until we heard the screeching of brakes and saw that a startled driver behind us had stopped his vehicle within inches of our mate's melon. Some serious negotiation amid a constant stream of apologies eventually enabled me and the gang to remain a part of the school and to sit our imminent tests. Six exams, each worth two units totalling 12, were to be sat, but only the top 10 units would count.

From early in Year 11 I'd gambled on doing five subjects well and ditching the other, as this would give me some freedom and clear my sport-filled calendar somewhat. Mathematics, to me, was irrele-vant – after all, how many times can cos, tan, πr^2 or other ridiculous signs and equations come in handy in the real world? I could add, sub-tract and divide with the best of them and my need for adventure was a much greater calling. A couple of hours of possum hunting along the Georges River, a visit to KFC or Macca's, or a midday movie, was the stuff to recharge the batteries and sustain me for the challenges ahead.

Every year, Year 12 students talked excitedly about the annual trip to Jindabyne. We'd heard tales from previous excursions of girls, smoking, drinking and fun times, and eagerly waited for our chance to live through the adventure of a lifetime. But then, in the week leading up to this huge event, Mark and I were selected to make our first-grade debuts at age 17, for Bankstown against Western Suburbs. 'What to do?' was an agonising decision.

I believe we made the right one, but I also look back with a tinge of sadness and regret, because the many experiences my mates enjoyed led to a distancing of relationships in the following weeks. Making the tough choice and sacrificing opportunities was difficult, but staying home was a step along the path I wanted to travel. I knew even then that the bigger picture must always be seen.

Earning money was alien to Mark and me, but once we took control of the family cars during Year 12 we had an obligation to fill them with petrol and look after their maintenance. Our one source of income came from umpiring indoor cricket matches, and it wasn't much fun being perched high up on a plastic chair, freezing to death and being constantly abused by pretenders amped up on alcohol. To earn 10 bucks a match was reasonable, but the physical threats and constant tirades we copped left a sour taste in my mouth.

Mark and I are both A-to-B men and to me the definition of a good car was a decent radio, a loud horn, and not too thirsty. We didn't want to waste any more of our hard-earned cash on petrol than we had to, so it was never more than a couple of bucks at a time into the tank. Consequently, the family's prized possession, the crème-coloured Ford Falcon station wagon, was never out of the red zone on the gauge at any stage. Whoever last put 'juice' in the tank had the right to drive around until he deemed it appropriate to hand over the beast. The transition was always fraught with danger, however, because quite obviously the thing was running on the smell of the proverbial oily rag. At least once a fortnight we'd have to walk to the nearest 'servo' with a jerry can to purchase another two bucks' worth and revive the stranded vehicle and its occupants. On one memorable day I managed to get marooned in two cars. After running home from the first mishap, I urgently needed to get to soccer training, but that didn't happen because the old aqua-blue Holden also spluttered to a stop not more than a kilometre from home, much to my disgust.

High school 'muck-up day' signifies the end of school life, a chance to let your hair down and cause a bit of chaos without overstepping the boundaries. As usual, I was in the thick of it, at the local park running around spraying foam, dousing people with buckets of water and throwing food at whoever appeared in my field of vision. Then I copped it – a bucket full of cold spaghetti from one of the girls at East Hills Girls High School, the school directly across the road from ours. She was an innocent-looking, freckle-faced, blue-eyed, petite-framed girl who caught my eye in that split second. Sport, all of a sudden, took a back seat and I wanted to know who she was. Not long after, at the schools' disco night, I convinced a friend of mine who was 'in the know' to introduce me to the mystery girl after I accidentally-on-purpose bumped into her on the dance floor. It needed to be subtle, because I didn't want a big fuss and feared she'd notice my limited routine on the boards, which amounted to a slight sway of the arms, left and right, accompanied by each foot moving in a similar direction. I was no John Travolta. In fact, I had modelled myself on the old man, who, like all the boys in our clan, has two left feet and very limited rhythm to work with.

Fortunately, the introduction went well and I knew instinctively that this was a person I wanted to spend a lot of time with, although Lynette Doughty probably didn't have reciprocal ideas. Having never had a girlfriend meant I had no experience asking Lynette out for a date – not that I would have known where to take her, but my school's farewell formal gave me the opportunity. Ringing her from a phone booth, I began to sweat as soon as the coins dropped and her voice resonated from the other end. Somehow I managed to extend an invitation, which was courteously responded to in the affirmative, much to my relief; especially as she had asked twice who it was she was talking to.

There's nothing like meeting the girl of your dreams – and her parents – for the first time. In retrospect, both experiences were a bit like facing Curtly Ambrose without a helmet – you couldn't afford to make a mistake because you wouldn't get a second chance.

Falling in love opened my eyes to a new world of opportunities and discoveries. And it meant I inherited a second set of parents, Phil and Ethel, who treated me like a son from the very beginning, even if they must have had their doubts initially, particularly after I answered their question about what job I was going to do in the future. My response – 'I want to be a professional cricketer and play for Australia' – created one of those uneasy silent moments . . .

When in January 1984 Mark and I called home from a phone box in Melbourne during the Australian Under 19 cricket carnival, Mum gave us our HSC results. My 305 was a top 30 per cent ranking and was more than I expected or deserved, while Mark's total fell well below his estimations. For a second or two I felt a tinge of guilt, but then I thought, *Don't stress – the numbers don't lie*. Mark, however, thought they did and convinced himself that the examiners had mixed our papers up and that the error would eventually be rectified.

The highlight wasn't the last-to-first surge I'd executed in Geography, but the ingenuity I'd shown in dealing with a mathematics question that may as well have been in Chinese. On being asked to calculate the circumference of a circle drawn on the exam paper, I hadn't seen the need for a detailed equation. The answer was obvious: all I needed was a hair long enough to wrap around the circle and hey presto, Bob's your uncle! After I plucked one long enough from my head, I carefully laid it along the length of my ruler to reveal what was really a quite obvious answer. Only one thing foiled my plan – the drawing wasn't to scale – but at least I had fun getting the question wrong.

I now had a decent HSC result, but no idea what to do with it. After consultation with the school's career advisor and a chat with Mum and Dad, I went for what I considered to be the easy option: teachers' college. Unfortunately this plan soon came unstuck, as my selection in the Australian Under 19 side directly coincided with the first three weeks of first semester. In my naivety I believed I could juggle the joint demands of college and cricket successfully – until I was informed on my arrival at the Milperra campus that my absence had already ensured failure in a number of subjects. This wasn't the welcome news I was after; nor did the first two lessons I encountered make me feel at home. I was straight into drama class, which for me made translating German a piece of cake. Digesting Shakespeare had my head in a spin as I stumbled into lesson No. 2: Music.

My musical expertise to that point revolved around mastering the plastic recorder in primary school and an aborted attempt at the harmonica in high school, so I was seriously out of my depth when the lecturer started talking about notes, chords and symbols and the correlation they had to one another. Enough was enough! I slid my chair out, gathered my doodled-on notepad and bag of pens, and headed out the door. It didn't seem that big a deal to me, but it was apparently serious enough for three girls to pursue me and try to persuade me not to ruin my life by walking out. However, I strode from freedom into trouble when Mum and Dad were told the news of how the first day of the rest of my life had gone. In my mind, my future was crystal clear. I wanted to be a cricketer and nothing was going to get in the road of that vision – least of all a primary-school teaching degree.

3

Showing a bit of promise

Selection in the Australian Under 19 cricket team was something I desperately wanted and worked hard for. When it was achieved, I could for the first time visualise the backyard dream materialising.

Being picked in the same team as Craig McDermott gave all of us that link to the next level – Sheffield Shield cricket – because the red-headed demon was already an established Shield player for Queensland. Craig, or 'Billy', as he became known, was always much stronger and quicker than anyone of his age, even at primary school where he terrorised Mark and me at the Australian carnival just by his imposing physical presence and aura. He and Victorian paceman Denis Hickey formed a lethal duo at Under 19 international level and in February–March 1984 traumatised a talented Sri Lankan side that featured a number of future Test players, including captain Aravinda de Silva, Roshan Mahanama and Asanka Gurusinha. Being on the road together for three weeks, coming under the management of the Australian Cricket Board, and playing at the alluring Adelaide Oval and the cauldron of the Melbourne Cricket Ground were all part of an education process that would produce future Test players in Mark Taylor, Mark Waugh, McDermott and myself.

Scoring 187 in the 'Test' at Melbourne gave me enormous self-belief. There were only a few scattered spectators there that day, and I couldn't help wondering what the ground would be like when it was packed. Would I be able to concentrate? Would the pressure be suffocating? Was I good enough to get to the top level? My form was excellent throughout the series, but what I most treasured was my baggy green cap, which wasn't a replica but the *same* as what was given to the fair dinkum Test players. I'm not sure why we were given the real thing, but I couldn't believe I had that almost mythical possession in my hands. It is the one I played with throughout my entire Test career and that became known for its tattiness and character. I loved what it represented and the history attached to it, and that passion has never diminished, only heightened with the passing of time.

Playing grade cricket for Bankstown was now serious business for me and by the start of the 1984–85 season my name was beginning to get tossed around in higher selection circles. I was scoring runs on a regular basis and bowling first change, but because I was a teenager, some of the old guard thought I was still too young and needed to have a couple of solid grounding years under my belt. I felt ready. My attitude was – in my mind, at least – professional, the results were on the board and I was certainly getting more comfortable in my own skin and clear in my mind about what I wanted to achieve: a blue NSW cap.

The culture at Bankstown wasn't always one I felt at ease with; it was a working man's cricket club whose priorities were blurred between socialising and winning. I debuted as a 13-year-old in fifth grade, filling in at the last minute for an injured player. The captain of the day, Ted Baker, obviously didn't rate my junior performances or my reputation, because he slotted me in at No. 11, from where I managed 16 not out. After I was forced to follow on, he again showed faith in the top 10 by slotting the young buck into the same position in the batting order, as if to say, 'Do it again, just to prove it wasn't a fluke.' Being the new boy and not knowing anyone, I stuck to one of the old man's favourite sayings, 'You should be seen but not heard', and followed the advice of Mum, who had instilled in her boys the ethic that actions speak louder than words. I went out and made 30 not out to ensure a promotion next time around.

The culture of the club was very much a good-time, man's-man environment. Drinking after a match in the change rooms with guys twice my age who were reliving tales of the past and had different interests to me was at times uncomfortable. However, I also realised that in order for the team to be successful everyone had to make an effort to fit in, that we needed to all try to enjoy each other's company, and that many lessons and experiences could be passed on in the change-room environment. Getting to know your teammates often starts there. But peer-group pressure was certainly evident, with alcohol consumption encouraged. Partying the night before a game wasn't unusual, and after-match celebrations usually revolved around drinks in the clubhouse followed by a pub outing. I felt uneasy with this, but looking back, I can understand that weekend sport was a stress-release valve after a week's hard work. The guys were amateurs seeking fun and enjoyment as well as possible success, and also a sense of belonging to a team.

I should also stress that my arm wasn't totally twisted to get involved in any of these activities. But I wanted more and knew it had to be done differently if I was to take the next step up. Being extremely shy gave me the advantage of being able to hang back and allowed me to be my own man to some extent. I can still remember the way I'd respond to any senior player or official who asked me how I was going – all I could manage was 'Good', and then I'd slide off to avoid further conversation. Friendships and memories did come, but the fire within was burning fiercely and it wasn't the time or place for me to fritter away opportunities that might never present themselves again. They were all good guys and the club had (and has) many great volunteer workers, and over the years developed a production line that has seen many players represent NSW and Australia. However, in some ways it was a breeding ground for unfulfilled promise if the 'system' got hold of you. You needed to have the strength of your convictions, and in the 1980s there was a fine line between learning sport 'the Australian way' and moving with the times.

Trying to earn a few bucks, I began working one day a week with what was known at Bankstown Council as the 'Tree Gang'. These knockabout guys knew how to work the system and lived by their own motto, 'lazy but obedient'. They knew all the cul-de-sacs to hide in for a little siesta so their bosses didn't spot them, but they were disciplined when they had to be: one slip-up while feeding a tree branch into a shredder would have the offender instantly eligible for a disability pension. Keen to make a good impression on my first day, I began removing the trees from a large tract of land that incorporated a couple of soccer fields. I was tearing into my work with great enthusiasm and was feeling pretty happy with myself, especially considering

I'd retired from mowing lawns after being offered 10 bucks to cut the next-door neighbour's grass only to be confronted by a minefield of dog droppings that detonated on impact with the blades. Suddenly the section leader signalled with a frantic motioning of the arms for me to stop. Instead of offering me a bit of encouragement, he sternly said, 'What the hell do you think you're doing? Slow down, buddy – this is a two-day job!' I now knew they were committed to their mantra. Who was I to take it on?

The passage to the ultimate goal of wearing my baggy green in a genuine Test match became clearer when I was called to the phone by Harry Solomons, my boss at the Kingsgrove Sports Shop, where I was masquerading as a part-time employee – looking busy, doing little – to supplement my Tree Gang income. My association with the store had come about through a bat sponsorship with Symonds, for whom the owner was the agent. On the other end of the phone was the chairman of the NSW cricket team's selection panel, and the instant I was told who it was, I felt my legs go to jelly, because this surely meant that the whisper that had been doing the rounds about my likely inclusion in the team to take on Queensland at the Gabba in Brisbane was true.

The first couple of minutes after finding out about my imminent entry into first-class cricket were surreal. I was on a natural high and bursting with pride, but my natural reaction was to keep it all contained. Many thoughts floated through my mind, both teasing – *Am I ready? How tough is it going to be? There's no place to hide now* – and exciting – *I'm going to play with guys I've seen on TV. Now I really have a chance to test myself.*

The only unnerving part of my selection was that it was based largely around my bowling ability. My role was to come on first change and restrict the scoring by bowling line and length, while I was pencilled in to bat at No. 9 in the hope of bolstering the middle-to-late order. Deep down, I knew the selectors had undervalued my batting and overrated my bowling – but the bottom line was, I was in the team. I'd only really taken up bowling a few years earlier to stay involved in the action; I was a batsman first and foremost. Now I had the chance to show it, even if I wasn't placed exactly in the order I had hoped for.

The long-time CEO of the NSW Cricket Association, Bob Radford, wanted to make my first trip away with the boys an experience to remember. With the idea being that I could learn and listen to one of cricket's best-ever all-rounders, my roommate for the six-day trip was the great Imran Khan, who was playing his one and only season for NSW. However, after our time together ended, I wondered if I had been chosen as a promising all-rounder or a potential secretary. Imran really was a legend, to the point that I was so busy answering inquiries about his availability that I didn't have time to get nervous about the match. Looking back, I wish I had picked his brains and gathered some know-how from him, but at the time I was too nervous and intimidated. This, plus the aura he exuded and the respect I held him in, added up to me being tongue-tied and unable to hold a conversation. He was using his time with the Blues to work his way back to full fitness after a long layoff due to stress fractures in his left shin, and I wasn't a priority for him. It's a strange sensation sleeping less than a metre from someone you idolise, listening to them snore, sharing a toilet with them and making small talk as you watch TV before falling asleep. It is not a normal everyday occurrence and I wasn't mature enough to feel relaxed, so I just observed and kept to myself.

The match itself was a real eye-opener for me. The intensity of the contest, the verbal interrogation, the mental fatigue and the quality of the players involved made it live up to and surpass my expectations. I wanted it to be tough and a thorough examination, but at the conclusion of the game I had serious doubts as to how long I was going to last. Walking out to bat, I passed the retired-hurt Mark O'Neill, who had just broken a finger and had a face to match, as contorted as a cabbage-patch doll's. The sky was a menacing gathering of black, tightly congested clouds with that grey–green tinge that often precipitates hail, and the pitch was a dreaded bright green, signalling moisture and meaning extravagant movement and a real examination of one's technique. It was ideal for the threatening pace quartet of John Maguire, Jeff Thomson, Carl Rackemann and Craig McDermott. Greg Ritchie in the slip cordon immediately got my attention as I began to scratch out my middle-stump guard, saying, 'Get ready, champ – you ain't playing with the schoolboys any longer.'

Before I reached double figures my ribs, collarbone and helmet had been picked off in a show of strength by the big quicks, and I hadn't done much to suggest the momentum was going to swing the other way. Then it changed. At this stage of my teenage cricket life I'd never suffered a major setback, so I didn't worry about consequences, nor was I inhibited by expectations or blinded by overanalysing. I was a batsman who loved playing shots, no matter the situation of the game. I fancied taking anyone on. Technically I was sound, but I played with my eye and not the position of my feet. Instinctively, I clipped a delivery from Craig McDermott off my toes; it sailed high over the fine-leg fielder's head and landed for six on the dog track that in those days ran around the ground. McDermott was horrified and I was amazed it had carried so far on the fly, but in those couple of seconds I discovered that I could mix it with the best of them – and I sensed my opponents understood it as well. It's akin to unlocking a secret code. I'd been granted rights to an invitation-only club that meant being treated on equal terms and afforded respect. But scoring 31 was not enough to confirm I was good enough. Nor was it a failure: the jury was still out.

Being a skinny kid of just over 70 kg, I relied on a 'whippy' action to generate my pace with the ball. No one could say that I muscled it down with an imposing physique. I had modelled my action on my boyhood buddy Brad McNamara, who went on to play many times for NSW, and while it was technically a little unstable, the quickness of my shoulder rotation and changes of pace enabled me to catch a few players by surprise. The selectors were hardly popping the corks of the bubbly stuff, but I managed to do the job required of me, sending down 23 overs for 34 runs. I craved a wicket, but was denied the breakthrough when Greg Matthews spilled a sitter in his eagerness to celebrate with me. 'Mo' (short for 'misère', which he always called when we played five hundred) was apologetic and disappointed with himself, because he wanted to share in the special event that is someone's first wicket. It would have been fitting, too, as from day one Greg was a real support to me, providing positive reinforcement and offering advice in his left-field way. He naturally gravitated towards the younger guys, and saw himself as a mentor of sorts. We were at opposite ends of the spectrum, but so intrigued by each other's differences that we actually got on very well. He was the complete extrovert, dressing to shock; I was the introvert, shockingly dressed.

★

There is a fine line between luck and fate. Many things can get you in the right place at the right time, but I'm a true believer in the adage that hard work and preparation get you in a position where opportunities present themselves. The late withdrawal of our Test paceman, Geoff Lawson, who failed a fitness test on the morning of the match, elevated me into the starting XI for the 1984–85 Shield final against arch-rivals Queensland. I was told the day before the game that I'd be carrying the drinks, so I didn't really have time to think about or properly prepare for the start of play. In hindsight this was a good thing, as the nerves didn't have a chance to dominate my emotions. The start of the game was like a scene from a movie set, with the grand old Sheridan Stand imploding, spewing dust and debris in all directions, as we walked out onto the field. No one had told the players the stand was to be levelled to make way for another structure, so the savagery of the explosion took us all by surprise.

It also captured pretty well the intensity of the battle that lay ahead over the next fours days. The fantastic match fluctuated from session to session, with neither team holding sway. In the end, it came down to our last pairing of Dave Gilbert and Peter Clifford, who formed the match-winning partnership. The heartache and distress for the 'banana benders' was evident, with Carl Rackemann bowling himself to a standstill and crying uncontrollably at the conclusion due to a mixture of exhaustion and emotions that were swirling out of control. Our opponents were emotionally spent, their quest to break a Shield hoodoo and claim the prestigious trophy for the first time eluding them again. They carried a curse that was self-perpetuating for years, caused by a 'hard done by' attitude. Only a new breed with a fresh outlook could break it.

Three incidents from the match are etched in my personal archives. One is the sight of the combative Kepler Wessels shoulder-charging Peter Clifford on the pitch as the players moved between overs. It was a good solid hit and took me by surprise. I was only a couple of metres away. It was a very rare moment where aggressive talk had led to physical contact, directly resulting from a perceived incorrect decision. If it happened today, someone would be handed a lengthy holiday. Back then, we just laughed it off and moved on.

Second, I was privileged to see an outstanding piece of instinct, skill and gamesmanship all rolled into one during Queensland's second innings. With the game delicately poised, an intriguing personal battle was unfolding between Imran Khan and Allan Border, with the victor's impact probably swaying the match in his team's favour. You could see they both loved the duel. Imran had been probing for a leg before wicket or a possible catch behind for a couple of overs without luck; then he decided to make a very obvious and inflammatory change to the field. He stopped mid-pitch, held up play and said to our captain, Dirk Wellham, 'Third slip, just move him that way.' He then motioned for John Dyson to move across, readjusting him a couple of times until he was exactly on the blade of grass he wanted. Border obviously took it all in, but in his own trusted way he pretended not to be too impressed with Imran's obvious ploy. The very next ball was delivered from wide of the crease and angled away from AB, who half-heartedly fended at the rising ball and steered it straight to 'Dyso', who didn't have to move an inch from that 'floater' position. It was a wonderful piece of brinkmanship that united us and fractured them. It demonstrated that while cricket is a team game, with a flash of brilliance any individual can stamp his authority and lift those around him.

As I celebrated a great team victory in an outstanding match, I took comfort from my own performance. It wasn't the fact that I had scored 71 after coming in at No. 8 with the side facing a big first-innings deficit, but the way I had done it. During this game, the pressure had seemed to invigorate me and I'd played with a clear mind and just let it happen. The big names in the opposition hadn't fazed me – they'd actually motivated me to lift to their level. It was fun. I was earning about $300 a game and where else in the world would I rather be? To top it all off – and this is the third moment of the match I'll never forget – the captain of the Australian team, Allan Border, had come running up to me after my dismissal, shaken my hand and said, 'Well played.' Initially I'd thought he was jogging off so he could get ready for their innings, but for him to stop and congratulate me was a significant moment. He was a hero to me and a role model for all aspiring cricketers. I felt a foot taller and my confidence level doubled in that very instant.

My world was changing very quickly. During the after-match party held at Imran Khan's palatial city apartment at the Connaught, I saw for the first time people using marijuana. Recreational drugs were something I'd never considered, or even laid eyes on, and they didn't interest me in the slightest – in contrast to a few of my teammates who joined the constant flow of people moving in and out of a secluded room. Alcohol, on the other hand, and specifically Southern Comfort and Coke, had reacted favourably with my tastebuds and I had tangled with the after-effects more times than I cared to remember.

Soon after, it was time for Mark and me to spread our wings and spend the off-season playing league cricket in the north of England. Jack Simmons, of Lancashire County Cricket Club fame and a trusted go-between, organised for the two of us to play for Egerton in the Bolton League. We were to earn a few pounds as the overseas professionals, the only sticking point being our lack of accommodation. An advertisement was placed in the local Bolton rag saying that a set of twins were coming from Australia, they'd never been far from home, would be lonely and homesick, and needed some good home cooking and care. It was a desperate plea and it worked, because Peter and Iris Greenalgh, who had a few spare rooms after their daughters had moved out, took up the challenge.

The instant I hopped on the KLM flight and found my dreaded 'B' seat I knew it was going to be a testing journey. I was already in a contemplative frame of mind after saying goodbye to Lynette, Mum, my grandmother and assorted friends at the terminal. My relationship with Lynette was now serious to the point of spending a part of every day in each other's company and talking about moving in together, and the goodbye tears suggested this separation would be a real test for us.

Sitting in economy class wasn't a problem, except for the fact that my window-side buddy would have struggled to squeeze into a luxurious first-class seat. A generous proportion of his girth rolled over into my personal space and I knew my first great aeroplane adventure was about to become an ordeal of sorts. Meanwhile, Mark lounged back quite comfortably before dozing off in his spacious aisle seat in readiness for our 30-hour trip to Manchester via Melbourne, Colombo, Dubai and Amsterdam. It was during the next day and a quarter that I wished I was a lover of novels instead of someone who had never even been guilty of dog-earing pages. I sat like a stunned mullet, unable to sleep, move or amuse myself except for the two in-flight movies, *The Man with the Golden Gun* and *Supergirl*, which were more punishment than entertainment. Conversation between Mark and me was never a priority growing up – our lack of communication stemmed partly from always having a sense of knowing what the other was feeling and thinking, but primarily from immaturity and a lack of depth in our relationship. I really believe that being so competitive and unable to be seen as individuals drove a wedge between us that took years to remove.

A late arrival in Amsterdam left us a window of only 45 minutes to recheck our bags for the final British Airways leg of the trip. The nerds from Panania were way out of their depth, but one of us had to take charge. Being four minutes older may seem insignificant, but it still means you're the older brother, so I took on the role of organising the final flight, with Mark two steps behind. *Do we need to get our passports stamped? Do we have to collect our luggage? Does departure tax need to be paid? Have we got enough time to make the plane?* We were like two cavemen walking around in a dazed state, communicating via grunts and hand signals, until we found the counter we were looking for and headed off to Gate 25 with a few minutes to spare.

Finally, we were greeted by a typical northern-England day – grey, lifeless skies and a continual drizzle that seemed to suck the life out of everyone. We couldn't locate our luggage and there was no welcoming party to ease our anxiety. We were stranded for over two hours until our hosts turned up full of apologies after being informed that we weren't going to make our connection. Fortunately, the Greenalgh family made us extremely comfortable and relaxed with their friendly, warm demeanour, and we knew we'd landed on our feet.

Just five days into the trip, I received a phone call from Mum saying, 'PBL Marketing is going to contact you in relation to a contractual interview.' I had no idea what that meant or what they wanted from me, but was interested to know what they had in mind. The next morning I received a call from a bloke named Austin Robertson, on behalf of himself, PBL and the Australian Cricket Board. He was offering $15 000 a year for three years in return for a guarantee that I would stay and play in Australia and that I would be managed by him. I was stunned. They were willing to pay me in return for trying to live out my boyhood dream. With $100 in my bank account, I thought there must be a catch. This was too good to be true.

I was aware of the strong rumours that were circulating at the time of a possible rebel tour to South Africa, but never once imagined I'd be drawn into the episode in any way. I seriously doubted that anyone would want me on that tour and even if they'd offered me a million bucks I would have said no. Money and material possessions had never played a big part in my life and while I had needs, the greatest at the time was to snare a baggy green.

I put in a hurried phone call to Mum, who then consulted our mentor of sorts, Harry Solomons, who in turn advised me of his thoughts. After Mum called back, I could see only positives out of the whole deal and quickly told Austin Robertson of my decision. Within hours, a representative of PBL had flown up to Manchester and was knocking on the front door with a contract in her briefcase. Forty-five thousand bucks for showing a bit of promise was massive money for me back in

1985. I know now that I have Tony Greig to thank for it. On behalf of Kerry Packer, it was he who had chosen a small group of players he earmarked for longevity in Australian cricket; these were players who, in his eyes, needed to be contracted away from the sights of the rebel tour organisers. Mike Veletta, Dean Jones, Robbie Kerr and Peter Clifford were the others to fall on their feet, while Dave Gilbert rejected his offer, in conjunction with his father, after meeting Lynton Taylor from PBL and being unimpressed by his 'gruff manner' and the uncertainties of the time. It was a decision he would regret.

More drama followed four days later when an ACB official rang to tell me I'd been elevated to one of the prestigious Esso scholarships, replacing Dave Gilbert. An original recipient of that award, Dave had been called up to the 1985 Ashes touring party after seven players had withdrawn because they'd secretly signed up months before for the rebel South African tour. Australian cricket was in a real mess, with four rebel players jumping ship back to the official set-up amid strong information that three of them had been financially enticed into the fold. Looking back, it is clear that the air was thick with deception, and trust was virtually non-existent. It was a testing time and vision was needed by those in decision-making positions.

Dave's scholarship was with Essex, so after only a short time with Bolton, I left Mark and headed south. My time at Essex saw my cricket take a giant step forward. I revelled in the responsibility of being the overseas guest with potential. Cricketwise I blitzed them, my best efforts including an unbeaten double hundred against Sussex in a one-day game and 100 off 28 balls playing for Ilford in the Essex League. My body, however, wasn't used to the workload and I suffered my first serious injury: a couple of stress fractures to my right shinbone that required me to wear a plastic cast for three weeks. This was a cruel piece of timing, as Essex were about to select me to play against the touring Australian team; if I'd known at the time they were planning on promoting me I wouldn't have bothered consulting the doctors. It was also a lonely time, being away from home and trying to fit into teams where I knew no one. The lodgings for my duration were with Essex's perennial 'nearly man', Alan Lilley, and his wife. Alan didn't ease my anxiety upon arrival when he only half-jokingly said, 'We only put our hand up to look after you for the 50 quid a week we're getting. That'll pay for our new kitchen.' I had one home-cooked meal in three months and sometimes became extremely homesick, penning letters every day to Lynette – who more than matched my efforts, most notably, with a 53-page mini-novel that further confirmed our love. Postcards to family and friends and calls from the local phone booth helped to keep the spirits up when I wasn't engrossed on the field.

I took every chance I could to catch up with familiar faces such as my lifelong buddy Brad McNamara, who was plying his trade for Teddington Cricket Club in London and learning how to skol pints of 'mudslides' (vodka, Kahlua and Bailey's), a skill essential for his survival at the legendary club. With Essex being close to London and the Australian team preparing for the Lord's Test, I was able to make contact with the two blokes who had been almost 'father figures' to me in the NSW squad, Greg Matthews and Dave Gilbert.

There was no way I was going to bypass the opportunity to see an Ashes battle at Lord's, and Greg was able to leave an envelope at the players' entrance containing a ticket for a couple of days' play. Once inside, I was immediately taken aback by the outrageous slope of the ground, which was much greater than I had ever imagined or than it appeared on television. I couldn't take my eyes off it. Why hadn't someone levelled it out? Surely there was a piece of flat land available when they decided they were going to build the old ground all those years ago? But then it just happened – I fell in love with the ground's shortcomings, because somehow everything seemed to be right. I'd seen the famous pavilion and players' balcony many times on TV, but when I noticed a couple of Aussie team tracksuits fluttering on the iron railings I saw them in an entirely different light. In many ways Lord's is a real assortment of structures, but they somehow gel together, the glue being the intimacy and sense of history that consumes the venue.

I was transfixed for two days as Australia clawed its way to the ascendancy. Allan Border's match-winning 196 provided a short-cut lesson for anyone studying body language, concentration, technique and application to the task at hand. His performance certainly impacted on me, particularly his will to just keep on going, never altering his processes and always having the toughness of mind to wear his opponents down. He was like a gladiator, repelling everything the Poms could dish out and inspiring his team by his deeds. The large Aussie contingent in the crowd seemed assured by his very presence; we knew that if he could stay in, we'd be a real chance of winning, but if he fell cheaply we'd be in trouble.

A few weeks later another Aussie icon, Midnight Oil, were in the UK playing the pub circuit. Hanging out with Greg and Dave was pretty cool – even if by this stage I had a cast on my leg – and going to a concert together with all the other Aussies in London made for a pretty wild night. My enduring image is of a pumped-up Peter Garrett, the Oils' amazing and intimidating lead singer, launching himself off the ground and cleaning himself up on the roof of an 'underground' venue that was only a bit more than 2 metres from floor to ceiling. Garrett had such energy and life. Being so far from home I felt like I'd entered into another world, mixing with Test cricketers and seeing a side to life that I never knew existed when I was growing up at 56 Picnic Point Road.

★

At season's end, I returned to Sydney with a wider view about what was happening in the world. I was certainly a much better cricketer, purely because I'd met the responsibilities that had been imposed on me. And I had grown up, having survived the reality of needing to look after myself for the first time in my life. I was looking forward with relish to putting my new-found maturity to the test, not only in sport but also in my relationship with Lynette, which had grown immeasurably stronger during our separation.

The rollercoaster ride continued when news came through of my selection in the Australian Under 25 team to tour Zimbabwe in September–October. I was off to a country that I didn't know existed and about to receive my first contract from the ACB – and a tour fee! Nine months earlier I'd been playing grade cricket, and now I was only one step away from the ultimate prize.

Zimbabwe was stunningly beautiful in parts, with the majestic Victoria Falls justifying their status as one of the natural wonders of the world. However, Zimbabwe was desperately pathetic in other ways, with shanty towns and plenty of destitute and homeless people living on the streets, not knowing where their next meal was coming from.

The cricket played was outstanding, even if the 5–0 result in favour of Zimbabwe suggested otherwise. We had eight present or future Test players in our squad – captain Robbie Kerr, Simon Davis, Tony Dodemaide, Dave Gilbert, Dean Jones, Bruce Reid, Mike Veletta and myself – but were outplayed by a Zimbabwean side that during this period won an incredible 18 one-day games in a row against international touring teams. A young Graeme Hick was as good as any 18-year-old has ever been in the history of cricket; to my mind, he was at his peak back then. They had a real toughness and sense of fun about their play, and won at least three games in the final overs to further emphasise their sense of team. It's such a pity when you see the state of Zimbabwe's game now and the standard they are at, because back in 1985 those guys would have given any nation a really tough match. Not to mention a hiding in the drinking stakes!

Dad and Mum, Rodger and Beverley, at the christening of their eldest two boys. I'm the twin on the right.

Cuddling up with Dad before he sets off for another day's work at the National Bank in the city. I'm at left, showing my fondness for the dummy.

Quality time with Mum. You've got to love the cheesy smiles and, as always, the matching outfits.

It looks like just another Christmas at Picnic Point Road, Panania, but the truth is this photo was snapped in January 1968. When the presents were first handed out someone forgot to put any film in the camera, hence the re-enactment.

With our grandfather Edward who, sadly, died the night Australia won the 1999 World Cup.

Edward's father, 'Gampie', and everyone's favourite billycart.

As kids, we were easily pleased. All we needed were a couple of boxes and our imaginations.

Dress-up time – with Mum's clothes.

The 'loving twins' pose.

Dean (centre) with his elder brothers on the famous Waugh driveway, where many a scooter race was won and lost, and cricket 'Tests' were played using the blue diamond on the garage door as the wicket.

Saturday mornings in summer were an adventure, which began and ended with a ride in the coach's ute.

The three older Waugh boys with youngest brother Danny in the front yard, winter 1976.

The batting stance looks okay, but the big worry was the bird-of-paradise plant at first slip that ate any ball that came near it.

Wearing my Bankstown C.S. Watson Shield cap, 1979–80. Getting picked for rep teams like this was fantastic; the acne on my face was not.

Mark and I appeared in the *Sydney Morning Herald* in 1981; this photo was part of a story about our run-getting feats in junior cricket.

The Australian Combined High Schools soccer team of 1983. I'm standing, fifth from right.

Year 12 muck-up day at East Hills Boys High, 1983. The other larrikins are (from left) Andrew Goodchild, Danny Stanley and Richard Lane.

My first date with Lynette Doughty. I was wearing my blue NSW Under 19s jacket and a tasteful apricot-and-white-striped shirt that Lynette talks about to this day.

A pull shot during my first innings in the 1984–85 Sheffield Shield final. I scored 71, batting eight.

The Waugh boys before the 1995–96 Sydney first-grade cricket final, which Bankstown lost to Sutherland. This was the only time all four of us played in the same match. Dean (front left) was captain and Mark refused to wear a cap for the photo, arguing that such a move would mess his hair up.

4

The young fella

I entered the 1985–86 Australian domestic season confident in my abilities but without the comfort and leeway naturally given to a 'new boy'. With the rebels in South Africa, NSW now had in its side my great mate from schoolboys cricket, Mark Taylor, and my 'Siamese twin', Mark. We immediately formed a tight unit on and off the field and inspired each other to outperform one another.

However, both Marks nearly sabotaged their careers in their debut match, in Hobart against Tasmania. The dual mistakes of not asking for a wake-up call and not setting an alarm clock were always going to end in mayhem. When a call from coach Bob Simpson on the first morning of the match broke the silence of their hotel room, it was perceived as a gee-up by the new boys and fobbed off with the comment, 'Yeah, sure pal, we're not falling for that one.'

'You'd better get up, get dressed, and get down here, because the boys are ready to go!' 'Simmo' replied.

The debutants felt pretty proud of themselves for not yielding to the prank call, but their satisfaction soon turned to horror seconds later when the phone rang again and the boys decided they'd better actually have a glance at the clock. 'Sorry, Simmo,' were the next words to emanate down the line.

It was a match I'll never forget, because I scored my first first-class hundred. Such landmarks are always special because they free you from the 'promising' tag and give you credibility. Even better than getting the century was the knowledge that I had achieved it against an attack spearheaded by the former West Indian quick Winston Davis. West Indian cricket was held in such a revered state at that time that any success against anyone from that part of the world was considered a real achievement, and because of that it commanded the attention of people in influential places.

A first-up positive performance can prove a catalyst for the whole season, in the same way that a failure can be your downfall because you immediately begin to chase your tail. I've never been a big goal setter or ever focused on what numbers I wanted to achieve for a season, simply because if you fall behind your expectations, the added pressure of getting back to where you want to be can compromise the way you play and what you have to do. For me, the formula was uncomplicated, easy to execute, and allowed me to stay in the present. All that was required was the mental toughness to carry out my plan.

I tried to play the next ball as well as I could and devote my concentration entirely to playing it to the best of my ability. If I could do that, then all I needed to do was to replicate the routine over and over, and the odds in the success stakes were in my favour.

For a young buck like myself, it was exciting to come up against a tough, seasoned campaigner to gauge where I was at. Occasionally, such a player would pull me into line or deflate my tyres a bit, which is exactly what the South Australian captain, David Hookes, did during a McDonald's Cup one-day match at the SCG in December 1985. 'Hookesy' was a maverick, full of gamesmanship, innovation and banter. He liked to test the boundaries of sportsmanship and wasn't afraid to push them. He had used five different bowlers in the first five overs of the previous year's McDonald's Cup final without success, but at least he'd had the courage of his convictions to follow through on his ideas – even if they had bemused all around him. During this 1985–86 match, when rain looked like intervening and with his side in real trouble, he reverted to subtle time-wasting tactics that he couldn't be pinned for. With the match one over away from being a 'live' one, he threw the ball from first slip in the direction of mid-off to make it look like he was trying to get on with the game. But with a high degree of skill and cunning he managed to make the ball sail over the fieldsman's head – only by a short distance, but with sufficient power for it to run all the way to the boundary. In doing so he soaked up valuable time, and in such a way that the officials couldn't chastise him. But they knew what he was up to.

The game continued, and my game began to flow. As my confidence and run tally increased, I was ready to express myself and improvise a little by premeditating a lap sweep. It didn't quite come off: I bottom-edged it for an unconvincing two runs, and in the process raised the ire of the opposing captain. Just as I thought I'd got away with my cheeky upstart of a shot, Hookesy moved in from midwicket to give me his thoughts on my stroke selection. Without attracting too much attention, he quipped, 'You've got too much talent to be playing those dicky, muck-around cricket shots. They'll wreck your career.'

At the time, I thought, *Why don't you worry about your team and stay out of my business?* However, on reflection he probably did me a favour, because it made me stop and think, and realise that it was indeed a high-risk shot and that it would have been a real waste of my ability to get out like that. I needed to be more professional in what I was doing, and David had provided me with a lesson that he had probably learnt the hard way from his own experiences over the years.

Another century against South Australia in the Sheffield Shield and the coat-tuggers were beginning to whisper my name as a chance to wear the baggy green. 'Tubby' Taylor scored his first Shield hundred in the same game, further strengthening our bond and friendly rivalry. Upon passing my then-highest first-class score of 107, he signalled to the dressing-room to gain my attention. When I snuck past his 116 a few hours later, I returned the favour.

With Australian cricket in a mini-crisis after losing three greats of the game in Dennis Lillee, Rod Marsh and Greg Chappell through retirement in 1983–84 and the sudden exodus of 16 others to the rebel South African tour, a huge window of opportunity suddenly presented itself. I was attracting plenty of attention with the help of Bill O'Reilly's thunderous endorsements in his newspaper columns and Greg Matthews' constant stream of encouragement whenever he was speaking to the media. Once, Greg commented, 'Steve Waugh's got more talent in his little finger than I've got in my whole body.' Such extravagant backing was great for my confidence, but in some ways it didn't sit as comfortably as it could have. While my form in Shield and domestic one-day cricket had been encouraging, I was learning that I didn't really know my own methods and mechanisms all that well. I'd always survived on talent alone and until reaching first-class level had never had my technique seriously challenged. Now I wondered whether or not I had a solid enough base to cope at the next level. Furthermore, I didn't know how I would work through such shortcomings, because failure had never really been an issue for me in the junior ranks.

Change was in the air at the top level. Geoff Marsh, Bruce Reid and Merv Hughes had all made their Test debuts in Adelaide against a highly credentialled Indian line-up that included Kapil Dev, Sunil Gavaskar, Ravi Shastri, Dilip Vengsarkar and others. It was a time that called for cool heads in the selection room. People with vision and intuition were needed and, thankfully for Australian cricket, Lawrie Sawle, a former West Australian opening batsman of patience and perseverance, was in charge. Over the following two seasons he would need both of those traits and a belief that he and his fellow selectors, Greg Chappell, Jim Higgs and Dick Guy, were on the right track.

An epic Gavaskar century was the feature of that Test at the Adelaide Oval, the first of a three-match series. The match ended in a draw, with India clearly having the better of the game. Earlier in the summer, the New Zealanders had won a three-Test series 2–1, so Australia were desperate for success. The all-rounder position was being talked about in the media and my name, along with that of Simon O'Donnell, was at the forefront as the looming Boxing Day Test match appeared on the radar.

Instinctively, I knew that one more good performance would push me close to selection and that thought both excited and terrified me. One moment I was imagining how sensational it would be – a dream realised, fame, fortune and everything associated with representing your country. In the very next instant I'd be thinking, *I'm not ready to be exposed and have my life changed forever, nor is my cricket at the level required.* It was like having a boxing ring inside my head with two contenders, pessimism and optimism, and no clear winner. As NSW's next match, against Victoria, began, I decided not to force the issue but to just let it happen as instinctively and naturally as possible.

At the end of the third day of the four-day game, December 22, we were making our way back to the hotel on the team's hired minibus when I overheard a quiet conversation between two blokes, the kind of hushed chat that makes you oblivious to the world around you. Sitting two rows in front of me was the respected long-time sports journalist Phil Wilkins, talking to the team's manager as secretively as you possibly could in such a cramped and confined area. One sentence was all it took for my heart to skip a beat and a hot flush to sweep through my body.

'I think they're going to pick the young fella for Boxing Day,' Phil said.

For the next five or so minutes of the trip I was in a state of internal panic, flickering between disbelief, denial and excitement. Initially, I wasn't sure what to do about the comment I had heard on the bus, and eventually decided not to share it with anyone. Instead, as the junior partner assuming the butler's role, I bunked down for a fitful night's sleep in my single bed while my roomie, 36-Test veteran Geoff Lawson, enjoyed the benefits of seniority and stretched out on the double bed. Early next morning, around 6 a.m., the phone rang and was answered by 'Henry', purely because the phone and all the relevant switches to utilities were next to him as the 'boss' of the room.

Henry had missed the first Test against India but had been the spearhead of the Australian attack since Lillee's retirement, so, like myself, he might have been anticipating good news. The conversation that followed after he picked up the phone was not a long one. I eavesdropped as discreetly as I could from my pretending-to-be-asleep position, the sheet half-covering my face. As best as I can recall, he said, 'Okay . . . He's in . . . I'll pass it on.'

Down went the receiver and back to bed went the big quick. The next hour or so was torturous for me. A million different thoughts ran around in my head while I waited for the requested wake-up call to liven up the place. I must admit I was a little surprised Henry hadn't woken me up, but then again he was renowned as a 'tough' roomie, one who took control and ruled the roost. Greg Matthews found this out the hard way in one of his first games for NSW, when he challenged the 12 o'clock curfew the room's elder statesman had put in place. A knock on the door sometime after this deadline was met with a 'find another room' answer, which the young eccentric, whose mantra was 'Live each day as if it's your last', couldn't really argue about. Looking back, though, it was an extra-tough call on Mo, because these were his socialising hours and the time he came to life.

Finally the operator broke the suspense and the world's worst mathematician on a golf course turned to me and said casually: 'Well done, young fella, you've been selected in the Test team.'

Life would never be the same again.

5

Good enough?

I was about to become the 335th player to don the baggy green, but I wasn't sure exactly how to act or feel. I kept my emotions concealed, but underneath I was proud of myself and knew my family and friends would be ecstatic. The final day's play in the Shield match was a bit of a blur, although I found enough composure to score 41 not out and was thus able to take some good form into the upcoming Test.

The next morning, the first day of my new life, started with a young

Melbourne journalist carrying out his first-ever interview . . . with me. I'm not sure who was the more nervous or unsure, but both Eddie McGuire and I would get plenty more practice over the years to come, with Eddie going on to become just about Australia's biggest media identity. All I could think of during that interview in the summer of '85–86 was all those people on the other side of the camera lens who were staring at me, waiting for me to make a mistake. The red light was hypnotic; I was like a rabbit in the headlights, drawn in but unable to do anything about the outcome. Media training for cricketers was non-existent in those days and my answers were short and straight out of the pro-sportsman's cliché manual, featuring plenty of 'hopefullys', 'dreams come true' and 'one game at a time'.

Christmas morning was spent back in Panania at the family home with most of my relatives, enjoying our traditional mix-and-match buffet lunch. This was the usual 'dig in and don't wait' affair, particularly with so many males in the midst. My mind was all over the place, wondering what the next week or so had in store for me. It was a leap into the unknown, and the uncertainty had me both uneasy and excited about what might occur. I knew very few of my teammates. Having to play out of my age in junior sport had now become an excellent preparation for what was ahead of me, because I was, again, the youngest kid on the block.

My shyness was without doubt the greatest barrier I needed to overcome. It hindered my ability to communicate and consequently starved me of information and input. I was a guy who needed time to feel comfortable in a group situation; only when I reached that point would I become open and relaxed with people I considered friends. Loyalty and mateship are essential for me and I pride myself on those two traits once I form relationships.

Growing up always presents challenges. I'd had more than my fair share of knee and back injuries, but the 'ailment' that had caused me the most angst was acne. No matter what creams, lotions or tablets I used, the problem was perennial. It made me extremely self-conscious, particularly as Mark never looked like getting a blemish while I looked like a pepperoni pizza. Keep the head down, avoid eye contact and sustain a 'fold-over' hairdo – these were my answers to a problem that derailed my social activities and destroyed my confidence with girls.

Becoming more worldly and approachable was always going to be a gradual process for me, but the predicament I now faced was that it needed to happen overnight.

Travelling down to Melbourne, I was almost certain I'd be 12th man for the Test, as I couldn't see myself forcing out any of the incumbents. I figured I was there for the experience, to soak up the atmosphere and become familiar with the environment and treat it as an investment for the future. However, that line of thinking was short-lived. Upon arrival at training, I was told that Greg Ritchie had dropped a wooden sleeper on his big toe while doing a spot of gardening on Christmas morning, and had been ruled out of the match.

I can't recall much of that training session or the Christmas-night team meeting. I focused on getting to know my new teammates and exchanging some form of communication. I wish someone had pulled me aside and told me what to expect, given me a few short cuts that might have allayed my doubts. It was a team that revolved around Allan Border, who had more Tests next to his name than the rest of us put together. The other 'elder' players were unsure of their positions, teetering between a secure spot if they were consistent and being jettisoned if they didn't perform. They were all walking a tightrope without a safety net, and courage was needed to maintain focus and encourage belief. The rest of the team was a gathering of new boys starting out, guys looking to make an impact, to ensure they were more than just a gut feeling of the selectors. They, like me, were very unsure of how things were going to pan out.

AB, by his own admission, wasn't a natural leader. He'd been made

captain the previous season following Kim Hughes's tearful resignation after the West Indies had tormented him and muddled his mind
with their relentless pursuit of his wicket and mental state. Allan was
still growing into the role, which quite obviously he needed time to
devote to. With no coach there to assist in the planning of strategies
and the mentoring of players, it was a 'sink or swim' environment. The
enormous need for a coach to be appointed had finally been recognised, because Bob Simpson had been invited into the mix for this and
the next Test with a view to getting him on board full time.

Through no one's fault in particular, I felt relatively alone and isolated. The reality of the situation was that I had to look after myself
and try to adapt as quickly as I could. Otherwise, I'd become another
casualty of the system. As is the case with most teams struggling to
match ambition with results, we were a group of players working individually in the hope that positive results for the team would follow on
from solid one-out efforts.

Lynette and Dad made their separate ways via car to Melbourne,
arriving early on 26 December 1985, to see my Test debut. The first
morning of the match couldn't really go quickly enough for me;
I wanted the game to start so I could get into it and immerse myself
in the action and stop thinking about all the possible outcomes. Quite
often for sportspeople, centre stage is a place where they feel at ease,
because that's what they are most comfortable with – performing. The
isolation of their profession very often gives them a clear perspective
on what needs to be done. Waiting around can be a breeding ground
for negativity if the inner voice of doom overcomes the one of confidence. If I'd had a choice I would have opted to field first, in order to
give myself a chance to settle in, relax the nerves and get a feeling for
the intensity of the contest before having to perform the task for which
I had been chosen: batting. However, it wasn't to be, and we were sent
in to bat first. I was really on edge. There was no place to hide.

When you're the next batsman in, there's nothing that can compare to the adrenaline surge that follows a confident appeal or the roar of the crowd. From my first Test to my last, my senses were always on high alert and my emotions heightened by the unfolding events. At the precise moment the batsman was confirmed as out, I would experience the purest form of exhilaration and the clearest type of terror all at once. But, as quickly as the conflicting emotions swamped me, it would always be over before I got out of the dressing-room. It was like a surge of electricity through my entire body, and a wake-up call to signify the start of action.

Walking to the crease on day one of my Test career, I firstly had to brush past the members seated on either side of the walkway leading out onto the ground. It's a journey of about 25 metres. Every comment made by the well-wishers and the hecklers is taken in, but they are heard in a muffled way, not really analysed or digested. The next comment quickly consumes the previous one. I was glad to get out of the ever-narrowing corridor of asphalt and onto the pristine surface of the MCG. I didn't have the benefit of a routine that ensures peace of mind, so I stretched, hopped and strode out in a nervous fashion before meeting up with Geoff Marsh on the fringe of the pitch square to engage in a bit of small talk.

As you become more familiar with one another, there is a greater understanding of each other's needs, and this little ritual, which has its roots in junior cricket, is generally dispensed with. However, on this day I needed it, because I was basically reintroducing myself to the tough-as-teak wheat and sheep farmer, whom I'd met for the first time the night before. I had visions of making a complete goose of myself and calling him 'Rodney' or 'Graham', but thankfully the right name came out. 'Good luck and enjoy yourself,' are the only words I can remember from my senior partner, who himself was playing in only his second Test.

It's amazing how much a pitch can change its appearance in a short period of time, especially when you put 11 fielders and a couple of umpires near it, together with the stumps and marked creases. It was greener than I had noticed during the warm-ups. When I did the usual 'gardening' of the surface, I felt the top level give way under the toe of the bat, signalling it contained moisture and lacked the Melbourne pitch's normal baked solidity. Nothing to fret about, but still it raised my antennae for the task ahead, especially as I was hoping to do okay, rather than being confident of going well. I could feel the tension all around the ground and sensed that everyone was wishing me positive thoughts, but at the same time holding their breath and transfixing their sights on how I was going to cope.

As I had always done, I took guard on centre, for no other reason than my first cricket coach had told me to stand in front of the stumps and ask the umpire at the other end to tell me where the middle one was. I scratched a nervous mark in the soil and saw the sticky, thick mud cling to my half-spikes as I glanced around to get my bearings. I tried to avoid eye contact with the eager Indian fielders who had gathered around me like seagulls after a greasy chip. The keeper, Syed Kirmani, and Gavaskar, Kapil Dev and Mohinder Armanath seemed relaxed and expectant in their semi-crouched positions, while the 'smiling knife', Ravi Shastri, steadied himself at the bowler's end. My legs were weak, my breathing was shallow and my mindset was survival. *Don't get out first ball in your first innings – just get something in the road of the ball.* A hush went across the arena and I was about to experience one of those moments in life where you say, 'What will be, will be' and then just hope for the best.

Somehow I kept it out, and the relief was immeasurable. It's funny how cricketers place so much emphasis on statistics when, in the overall scheme of things, many of them are basically irrelevant. A duck is a duck, but to get a 'golden duck' is somehow deemed to be much worse – even if it is a term used in the backyard or school ground to stir up your mates.

With this mini-mission completed, I desperately wanted to get a run next to my name on the scoreboard, one that could never be taken away. An unconvincing half-forward defensive push into the covers off Kapil Dev and I was away. The seed that had been planted by Alan McGilvray's commentary during our backyard cricket matches had sprouted. Standing at the non-striker's end, the pent-up tension drained away. I was actually enjoying where I was and what was happening.

The baggy green was fitted so tight it left a telltale indentation on my forehead and verged on giving me a headache; my first serious sponsor, Symonds, had me well protected; and my personally hand-crafted shoes made of kangaroo leather felt comfortable and ready for some work. Emphasising how much cricket is played in the head, that one run had altered my thinking and expectations. Immediately I thought to myself, *There's no reason why you can't start off with a century; it isn't so hard after all.* By the time I reached double figures I'd settled down into a relaxed state of mind and had visions of bigger things, particularly as I'd seen off both Shastri and Kapil Dev and was now up against a young slither of a man bowling unpredictable leggies, Laxman Sivaramakrishnan.

Later on, I would learn the benefits of clear and precise thinking. Concentration is about thinking only one thought at a time and staying in the present. But here I was ahead of myself, thinking of possible outcomes, and I fell for the ultimate sin: not giving the bowler enough respect. A juicy half-volley floated up outside the off stump and I instinctively threw my hands at it to smash an easy four through the covers. However, instead of crashing into the pickets, it squirted off the outside edge and was plucked out of the air by second slip Kapil Dev as if it was a warm-up drill. It was a phenomenal piece of reflex-action catching, achieved with minimal movement – so special that first slip Gavaskar didn't even react when the ball took the outside edge of my bat. It was over, way before I wanted it to end, and with 13 next to my name the jury was certainly uninformed as to my credentials to succeed at this level.

I cursed myself inwardly, as most batsman do when they let themselves down through poor thinking. But on the positive side, I now knew that Test players weren't that much different to the Shield players I'd become used to playing against. It was more the expectations that I'd created in my head that had to be overcome next time.

Bowling to me was always a bonus; I placed less emphasis on it and didn't expect too much in return. That's not to say I didn't practise or have ambitions; it was just that I used it as an outlet for frustration and a pressure-release valve. And it gave me an opportunity to stay involved in the action. Coming into the attack after our frontliners had bowled poorly gave me the chance to make an impression, and my return of 2/36 was better than I'd envisaged. Accuracy, cunning and the element of surprise with my pace were my main weapons – if you could call them that – and they accounted for Shastri and Kirmani, thanks to the silky hands of our keeper, Wayne Phillips, who was very confident and capable when standing back but lapsed into self-doubt when keeping to spinners.

My second innings was a real battle, both technically and mentally. Just smashing the spinners in the junior ranks and showing them scant respect hadn't exactly allowed me to become proficient in judging length and overcoming the various subtleties that quality spinners possess, so against the Indian slow men I moved as if kitted up with a spacesuit and cement boots. I feared the unplayable ball and retreated into my shell, shackled by hesitation. Never at any stage did I gain the ascendancy or look comfortable, and my misery was ended when I was bowled around my legs, sweeping in ungainly fashion, for five. As soon as the bails fell off, I heard Kapil Dev from second slip say, 'See ya in Sydney.'

When you play a scratchy innings like that, all you can think of upon dismissal is *Get the hell of out of here, as quick as you can.* That's exactly what I did. Somehow, we managed to escape with a draw after brilliant centuries from Greg Matthews in the first innings and Allan Border in the second, but the press didn't miss in their summation of events. The *Sydney Morning Herald* described us as the 'worst team in the world', hardly a boost for one's ego. It was a tough initiation and I only had two days to gather myself before a home Test at the SCG.

That whole Test turned out to be a disaster for me and further sapped my confidence and that of a team already firmly on the back foot. I was again somewhat of a surprise inclusion, with Greg Ritchie returning, but even the experience of David Hookes couldn't prevent the man who had taken to Tony Greig so famously in his first Test from carrying the drinks. Years earlier, I had been among the crowd at the Sydney Showgrounds during a World Series Cricket match in which the feared West Indian quick Andy Roberts pinned Hookesy with a cleverly disguised quicker bouncer that made a sickening noise as it shattered his jawbone. Now the spectator had become the player, in what was David's last involvement with the Australian squad. I think I was saved from being dropped because of my purposeful attitude when bowling in the Boxing Day Test, even though AB hadn't used me until our 99th over.

You can always judge a team and how well they're travelling by their efforts and execution in the field. A strong unit will hunt together in a pack. Fielding is a true test of players sacrificing themselves for the interests of the team, because it's the only facet of the game where you don't get statistically rewarded for your efforts. You give yourself up for the team's benefit and often your work goes unnoticed. In Sydney we were slipshod and uninspired, missing countless chances and being reactive rather than proactive. And the opposition made us pay dearly. Batting-wise, I was all at sea on a turning pitch against quality spinners and laboured for eight from 38 balls in the first innings followed by a torturous nought from 20 balls in the second. While I was 'fired' by the umpire in the second dig after being struck on the pad by a ball that was clearly missing leg stump, the ump probably did me and the crowd a big favour. My batting wasn't going to get any better. I had stage fright and was unable to play any shots; it felt like I was using someone else's hands and my coordination had been stolen.

It was depressing to sit down after my first two Tests and realise how large the gap between promise and fulfilment seemed. I wasn't sure if I could 'cut the mustard' and didn't really know where to turn. I imagined I'd let the selectors, the fans and my family down because so much was expected of me; 'the next Don Bradman' (as I'd been hyped in sections of the media) certainly hadn't delivered. Fortunately, I'd never been one to dwell on things for too long and soon enough my natural competitiveness and stomach for a battle took over and I committed myself to training hard and overcoming my deficiencies. I'd had a taste of life at the top level and, even though the results weren't what I'd hoped for, deep down, I knew I wanted more. Good times were still a possibility. And now I really had something to prove – which is how I wanted it, even though I didn't know it at the time.

6

My natural game

Thankfully, the 1985–86 Test season ended in Sydney and three days later the one-day World Series Cup began. I was selected to make my limited-overs debut, and saw it as an opportunity to open up a bit and play more naturally in this less revealing form of the game, instead of being inhibited as I had been in my first two Tests.

One-day cricket to me is in some ways akin to soccer and the rugby codes in wet weather. The skill element is somewhat reduced and consequently the sides become closer, because you can't be as expansive or divulge the full range of your repertoire as much. Time is obviously the major factor in one-day cricket and the game's over restrictions don't allow batsmen to show off their stamina, patience and opportunism. The batsman has to do everything in a hurry and can only bat for 50 overs at the most, while in Tests you can be in for two days or longer if your temperament and fitness are in line with your technique. The bowlers' roles are very much defined, limited as they are to a maximum of 10 overs, with each bowler appearing at roughly the same stage of each game, with similar field settings and unable to bowl short or down the leg side. Test cricket is like a game of chess, whereas the one-dayers are over as quickly as a hand of blackjack.

Fielding is probably the one facet of the one-day game that allows for scope and improvement. Agility and an instinct for where the ball is going to be are the attributes that allow natural fielders to stand out and excel and influence outcomes.

Having a clearly defined role in one-day cricket certainly gave me added confidence, because I knew what was expected of me and that I was an important cog in the Australian team's wheel. Batting at No. 6 or 7 usually meant I would come in during the innings' final 10 overs, play my shots straight away, run between wickets without worrying about the consequences, and often take high-risk runs to get us to a decent total by swinging wildly in the last two or three overs. It wasn't until Michael Bevan came along that batting at the death became an art form based on sound logic and clear planning. Bowling-wise, I would come in around the 20-over mark and send down five or six overs in tandem with another bowler, with the prime aims of being as restrictive as I could and establishing a partnership with the other bowler.

In the field, I generally occupied a catching position in the first 15 overs and then reverted to being a 'boundary rider' for the rest of the innings, utilising my pace and strong throwing arm. Fielding on the fence for me was always tougher than inner-circle work, for a number of reasons. Communication was often by way of hand signals, especially at the big grounds like the MCG and the Adelaide Oval, rather than by voice. This meant that concentration was essential, because I certainly didn't want to miss any of AB's field changes, especially if it was me he was after. Occasionally, the spectators would play on this aspect and yell at me to turn around because the captain wanted my attention, which I promptly did only to hear muffled laughter from behind me. Regular sledges would rain down on me during my stints on the fence:

'Nice undies, pal.'

'How much did you pay for your haircut? Four bucks, one for each corner?'

'Have a shave, buddy.'

'Sign the kid's autograph, you mongrel.'

'You wouldn't get a bowl in a Chinese restaurant.'

And various other pieces of character-building advice. I certainly found it hard to respond to the fans when things weren't exactly going to plan on the field and always considered it hard to be both entertaining and interactive with the crowd between balls and then suddenly switch into gear and concentrate on the on-field action. Players like Merv Hughes and Greg Matthews used their interaction with the crowd to burn off nervous energy and to relax, immersing themselves in the spirit of the day and the mood needed to get the spectators on side. They used it for motivation and to lift themselves to a level where their senses were heightened and primed for action.

One of my most embarrassing moments came in this 1985–86 season, during a match in Perth. I had a premonition that a catch was coming my way on the fence at deep mid-off during the 'slog' (last 10) overs and so could the crowd, who kept saying, 'Get ready, one's coming your way, Waughy.' Everyone's instinct was right and the chance came hard, fast and at a catchable height above my head. You know almost immediately whether or not you've made the correct move on an outfield catch. Unfortunately, this time I had misjudged the trajectory and taken a couple of steps forward instead of holding my ground, thus putting myself badly out of position and in real trouble of muffing the opportunity. Scrambling backwards, arms fully stretched in the style of a soccer goalkeeper, was my only hope and when I managed to get two hands on the ball I thought I'd done enough to redeem myself. But against the clear blue sky, which prevented a depth of field, I misjudged how quickly the ball was travelling and allowed it to burst through my grasp. It ricocheted off my fingertips and went over the fence for six. For a bowler, this is the worst possible result for his figures *and* his ego. As the source of vexation, I was looking for a hole to disappear into. Dusting myself off after my awkward tumble, I now had to retrieve the ball, which was in the hands of the animated spectators. I didn't have to look long, because the very instant I turned around and got to my feet I was smacked on the top of my skull by the returned ball, giving the crowd a double dose of comedy within the space of 30 seconds. All I could do was pretend it didn't hurt and pray that another chance didn't come my way before the innings finished.

My first international one-day series was full of learning. Dealing with the media and peer-group pressure and getting to know my game were all part of the process. Not only was I on that learning curve, but so were the team and the selectors, and it was always going to take time for things to settle and for it to become clearer which path we all needed to take. The selection of Simon Davis as a medium-pace opening bowler capable of containment ahead of strike power was a forerunner to future selections. Simon was a specialist one-day bowler who had a designated role to fill and who wasn't considered to have enough strike power to be a long-term option in Test cricket. He proved to be an inspired choice, leading the way, restricting the opposition's initial onslaught and providing opportunities for the rest of our attack to profit from his defining opening spell, which was usually 10 overs straight. He owned the concept of line and length and was the 'banker' for Allan Border, a guy the team built its game plans around. Essentially, we believed that restricting the opposition's batsmen was the key to winning, and as such, AB normally had at least six bowling options to call upon in our quest to keep teams under 220, which was considered a par score. It was left to each batsman to work out the modus operandi best suited to themselves, based on the premise that we wanted the top three to create a platform that would allow the rest of us to go in and play shots pretty much straightaway. Fifty runs from the first 15 overs was our objective, but we would be happy if we lost only one wicket for 30 or 40 runs if their bowling was good enough to restrict us.

Our fielding was one area that needed immediate attention. When I joined the Australian team, I quickly noticed the massive difference between the way the Test team worked and the NSW set-up run by Bob Simpson. For the Blues in my first two seasons of first-class cricket, Simmo was a brilliant fielding coach with the priceless ability to recreate game intensity in all his practice drills. He combined tough physical work-outs with technical enhancement in a competitive but always fun environment. After each session, most players felt like they'd achieved an improvement and were better off because of Simmo's innovative yet simple routines. I couldn't wait to get to NSW training and test myself out against the mercurial bat skills of Simmo, who would always judge high catches to perfection, inevitably requiring me to stretch full-length every time to haul them in. Nine times out of 10, his slip catches headed for the gap between the men in the cordon, and close catching required lightning reflexes to avoid a toe injury or a trip to the dentist. But the terrific part of all these exercises was that Bob would, without exception, explain if your technique wasn't quite right and what you needed to do to rectify it. If you caught well, the praise was equally forthcoming.

I remember Simmo worked with me on developing what he called 'soft hands'. Being relaxed and giving with the ball when it came was the key, while getting your feet and head in the right position to allow you to turn your body with the ball gave you an extra split second to complete the catch. Endless hours of practice, focusing on anticipation, feet position, balance and throwing methods, were incorporated into hitting-the-stumps competitions and slip-catching contests, and it all combined to give me increased confidence on top of my natural ability. Anyone who wanted to improve under Simmo had enormous scope to do so, but the pay-off was hard physical work; I knew I'd much rather do that chasing a ball than have to resort to a running track or a treadmill.

★

My first one-day international was severely rain-affected and abandoned after only 29 overs, but I took a couple of positives away that enabled me to look ahead with genuine belief. The wicket of New Zealand's captain, Jeremy Coney, ensured my name entered the end-of-season averages, but it was my catch of John Bracewell off Craig McDermott that really lifted my confidence. A wild swipe sent the ball spiralling into the dull grey sky where it was virtually camouflaged in the clouds, but straightaway, from my fielding position at point, I knew it was my catch. With Simmo's words echoing in my head – 'Take off when you see a high ball, then reassess later in order to give yourself a little bit of extra time' – I darted backwards and then tried to focus on the scuffed white ball that was harder to find than 'Where's Wally'.

Ideally, you want a backdrop with both clouds and clear sky to give you perspective when catching a high ball, because that enables you to time your movements better. A uniform backdrop makes it extremely difficult to judge the speed of the ball and whether or not it's swirling about. In such circumstances, a skied ball can drop on you unexpectedly and make you look like an idiot if you don't prepare well. Making this type of catch even harder is the knowledge that all eyes are on you, and the longer you have to wait, the more chance that sniping little inner voice has to do his damaging work. Legs will often go to jelly, giving you a wobbly platform, in direct opposition to your top half, which tends to tighten up in anticipation. Past success makes these catches relatively simple, but previous failures can often lead to mind games you don't want to play – and an epidemic of grassed chances.

Eventually the ball appeared in my line of vision. Once it does, it's a bit like a car crash in that everything happens in a split second, but in slow motion. There's not much you can do now to change the outcome except hope and pray it's going to be okay. I ended up having to slightly compensate, taking it Australian-football style over my head and landing flat on my back with arms outstretched. I was inwardly ecstatic with the outcome and so were my teammates, who came rushing in to congratulate me, which is always a sign you've done something special.

Speaking of special, receiving your first 'man of the match' award is exactly that – a time to celebrate and later look back on fondly. Mine, however, wasn't all smooth sailing and came about in highly unusual circumstances. Being on the losing side virtually guarantees you not becoming man of the match, especially when your team has been demoralised with almost 10 overs to spare. Somehow, the judges thought my 73 not out from a dismal total of 161 in Melbourne was noteworthy enough to upstage any of the Indian performances, so a very red-faced, 74 kg, hungover youngster embarrassingly accepted the gold tray and four matching goblets.

The previous evening had somehow managed to get away from the young punks – Glenn Trimble, Craig McDermott and me – before we realised what was happening. I'm not sure we had any reason to go out looking for a quiet beer or two; maybe it was to celebrate Glenn's selection in the one-day squad, but in all probability we didn't need one.

Using the safety-in-numbers theory, we headed off and away from the unwanted prying eyes of management and the team hierarchy, but what started out as a tame affair at a restaurant soon got out of control. We had our bulletproof security blankets on and our 'invisible pills' at the ready to give us immunity against trouble. A subdued meal turned dramatically when the owner found out it was a celebration of sorts and offered us free port for the evening. Subscribing to one of Tim May's theories on life – 'The more you drink, the more you save' – we began investing heavily. Now, port had never touched the lips of one S. Waugh before and I quickly developed a liking for its sweetness and burning aftertaste. After four or five, the fact that we were playing a one-day international tomorrow was conveniently forgotten. Losing face wasn't an option for me, even though it was quite obvious I was up against two highly seasoned campaigners, so I soldiered on. From sipping to skolling and finally racing, the 'grandfathers' slid down as easily as our brain cells were being obliterated. It wasn't until a dozen or so later that someone twigged onto the notion that maybe we'd better get home. An open taxi window, a dodgy hotdog, and as much water as I could force down my throat were my anti-hangover tactics, but when I woke up the next morning I felt like I'd gone 12 rounds with George Foreman. This was not a scenario I wanted to be part of, especially as there were only a few hours left before the start of play.

Plan B had to be executed, and very swiftly, if I was to bluff my way through this ordeal and come out with an international cricket career still a possibility. A cold shower followed by a couple of sizzling

Beroccas would surely do the trick – after all, I had the restorative powers of youth on my side. That notion was quickly squashed when the orange liquid came gushing out both nose and mouth along with the acidic remnants of that deadly port. As the pregame minutes dwindled away, I spent more and more time getting acquainted with the bathroom facilities. I was in uncharted waters, with a splitting headache, continual vomiting and constant nausea, and an imminent international cricket match to be played.

With no viable alternative after exhausting all possible known remedies, I took the last option: calling for outside help. The team's physiotherapist, Errol Alcott, had probably heard it all before, but he was still both mildly amused and concerned about my state of health. Upon closer inspection, and with time being a major factor, he decided to call for the doctor and go with a sure-fire and quick-acting needle in the stomach to settle things down. To a point, it had the required effect, until I had to run a warm-up lap around the world's biggest cricket ground an hour and a half before the 2.30 p.m. start. Once in motion I was confident I could beat this demon that had taken over my body, but as soon as I stopped and begun my hamstring stretches, I felt as if I had just hopped off a wild amusement-park ride. My head was spinning and my balance was askew. Toppling to one side, I gained the unwanted attention of my fellow players, in particular the captain, and I knew I was in serious trouble.

It was at that precise moment that I found a hangover cure – pure fear! It's quite incredible how strong one's mind can be, because that day I certainly played from memory and out of self-preservation. In between balls, I suffered from nausea and a parched mouth, but I refused to call for drinks so as to not draw further attention to my precarious state. Once I immersed myself into the battle ahead, I began to dismantle the self-imposed barriers and was clear-headed enough to bat through the innings after coming in at 4/40. I knew I'd dodged a bullet that day, and vowed never again to put myself in such a perilous position.

★

Australia's form leading up to the final series was patchy and unpredictable, with a couple of solid wins promptly followed by a dismal showing. As a team, we couldn't quite put our finger on the reason for our inconsistency, but looking back I think it was very simply a case of poor concentration and a lack of commitment. No one was prepared to put his hand up and lead the way on a regular basis. The record 206-run loss to New Zealand in Adelaide prompted the *Herald* to say: 'Let's pick the park cricketers.' It was a game the Kiwis needed to win to stay in contention for a finals berth, while we had already qualified, but the intensity and hunger should still have been there.

Chasing a massive one-day total usually has one of two outcomes: a famous victory or a crushing defeat. This is because the team doing the pursuing is forced to play at a pace that can throw its equilibrium out. A flying start gives their batsmen a chance to consolidate and then surge later on for a victory, but a poor start leaves no option but to continue on in a haphazard, reckless way. At least, that's how we went about chasing an imposing target – and we completely lost our way, disintegrating to a meek and mild 70 all out. I muffed my chance to score heavily from the pivotal No. 3 position, getting ahead of myself and thinking about what might be rather than defusing the human bowling machine Ewen Chatfield, whose remorseless advances found a friend in my hard hands and resulted in an edge to the waiting slip cordon. We were soft, and I was ordinary, going down without a fight – a sportsman's greatest sin. And we all knew it as we skulked around the dressing-room, trying to avoid eye contact with our captain.

It's often said when referring to sport that a loss before a final can be a good thing, because you get your one bad game out of your system before it really counts and it also provides you with a wake-up call that makes you reassess and reminds you to work that little bit harder. To me, this has some merit, but I'll always argue that there is no need to lose to find out what it's going to take to ultimately win a trophy. Perhaps because we were an inexperienced side, this ugly reminder did jolt us into action, because we went on to win the one-day finals 2–0 over India, and I got my first taste of David Boon getting up on the table to lead us in the team victory song, 'Underneath the Southern Cross I Stand'. I just followed along, yelling as loudly as I could, revelling in the unity and satisfaction of my first taste of success in the 'canary yellows'.

I finished the tournament looking like an Aussie player and no longer questioning my right to be part of the squad. My 'natural game' had surfaced and it was nice to be written and spoken about in a positive fashion. 'Playing my natural game' was a phrase I used often when reporters asked me what my expectations were during that season. It is a fall-back cliché that really means nothing more than 'I'm hoping I don't take the gas and choke with nerves'. At least now when I was interviewed during the 1985–86 season, I could use it with some degree of certainty.

7

A sinking ship

In many ways, the Australian team's tour to New Zealand in February–March 1986 marked the beginning of a new era. The squad featured a batch of inexperienced players and for the first time included an assistant manager/coach in Bob Simpson, who had been invited by the then chairman of the Australian Cricket Board, Fred Bennett, to oversee the New Zealand tour and at the same time see if he wanted to take the job full-time. Simmo's love of the game and ability to pass on his extraordinary cricket knowledge were, no doubt, crucial factors in this 'semi-formal' appointment, and I noticed immediately how Allan Border appreciated having another voice of wisdom around, someone who would ease his burden and put a more structured set-up in place.

I'm not sure who got the bigger shock during the first couple of training sessions on that tour: Simmo, due to the team's low-intensity work ethic, or the players, who had never been exposed to his level of passion at practice. Bob is a great believer in simulating the intensity of match situations when training, and for a lot of the guys such a philosophy was 'straight between the eyes' stuff. No longer was it your mate who was tapping straightforward catches in a predictable one-catch-each-along-the-line-and-back-again mode, but the new coach hitting random half-chances that often necessitated self-preservation kept on coming until you had taken enough good ones or improvement had been demonstrated. Early on, there was a lot of complaining about sore hands, but under Simmo that was an irrelevant excuse and not what he was searching for. As a player, you had two choices: embrace and enjoy, or disregard and disappear.

After failing in the first Test of the series, at Wellington, albeit thanks to a diabolical umpiring decision, my confidence was at best teetering. If your body language exudes negativity, then it's amazing how that follows you around and infiltrates everything you do. Accentuating this, I was discovering that umpires find it easier to make the tough calls on younger, no-name players or guys on the way out because by making a decision they are seen to be backing themselves; if they get it wrong, it won't affect the game quite as much or be as damaging on the report card. If you have been around for a while or are an influential player, then decisions seem to go your way. Perhaps I was suffering from a siege mentality, but I couldn't get the rub of the green to go my way.

So walking out to bat on the first day of the second Test, at Christchurch, with our total reading 5/74 after being 0/57 and with

The first ball I faced in Test cricket, at the MCG on Boxing Day 1985, was from Indian left-arm spinner Ravi Shastri. Geoff Marsh is the other batsman, Syed Kirmani the keeper, Sunil Gavaskar is at first slip, Kapil Dev to his right, Mohinder Armanath at silly point.

My maiden Test innings ended on 13, when Kapil Dev took this phenomenal reflex catch.

My first man-of-the-match award in one-day internationals came in unlikely circumstances – I was nursing a massive hangover, but somehow managed to score 73 not out.

One of the more critical moments in my early Test career: New Zealand's John Bracewell spills a sharp chance in Christchurch. I went on to make 74. Had the catch been taken, I'm sure I would have been dropped from the Australian team.

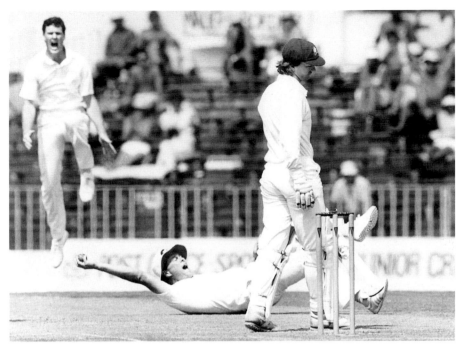

The first of twin failures, caught close in off Bracewell during Australia's humiliating third-Test defeat at Auckland in 1986.

With Allan Border (centre) and Wayne Phillips in Wellington, after 'Flipper' inspired us to a brilliant one-day win.

The end of cricket's second tied Test, at Madras in 1986. I'm at far left, racing in for a souvenir, while India's No. 11, Maninder Singh (obscured), complains about the umpire's verdict and (from left) Allan Border, Bruce Reid and Tim Zoehrer go crazy. The autographs are those of me, AB and Greg Matthews.

The Aussie squad after the tied Test. Back row, from left: physio Errol Alcott, Craig McDermott, Bruce Reid, coach Bob Simpson, David Boon, Allan Border, me, Greg Matthews, Greg Ritchie, Geoff Marsh, Dave Gilbert, manager Alan Crompton, Simon Davis. Front: Greg Dyer, Mike Veletta, Tim Zoehrer, Ray Bright, Dean Jones.

Allan Border is overjoyed, while Geoff Marsh (in helmet) and I are the first to congratulate Peter Sleep, who took the final wicket in the fifth Ashes Test, 1986–87.

The clothesline in the back courtyard of our home at Nelson in Lancashire in 1987 was wide enough for a couple of pairs of cricket pants and not much else. Of course, the size of the place made the task of vacuuming a relatively simple one.

With one ball remaining in the Australia–India match that opened the 1987 World Cup, India needed two runs to win, one to tie and I was bowling to the home team's last man, Maninder Singh. The result was a perfect yorker, and his off stump went flying through the air.

The celebrations that followed were as animated as any I was involved in during my career. First to reach me was Allan Border, rushing in from short cover.

Soon we were joined by (from left) keeper Greg Dyer, David Boon, Tom Moody, Simon O'Donnell (with back to camera) and Geoff Marsh. The looks on the faces of Allan, Tom and Geoff capture how much this victory meant to us.

England's Allan Lamb loses his off stump to my bowling in the 1987 World Cup final.

The full house at Eden Gardens stayed to watch Dean Jones and Tom Moody chair Allan Border around the ground after the game.

With Hunter 'Stork' Hendry, a wonderful man and at the time the oldest Australian Test cricketer, in the SCG dressing-room late in the 1987–88 season.

Mike Veletta, Peter Taylor, Tim May and Tony Dodemaide take a break during a mostly unsuccessful crab-fishing exhibition on Karachi Harbour in 1988. The only bloke to catch anything on this voyage was the one holding the camera.

my previous Test scores being 13, 5, 8, 0 and 11, I knew I needed to reveal whatever it was that had made the selectors pick me at such an early stage of my development. Out in the centre, I met a resolute and fiercely determined Allan Border, but only after waiting anxiously to see whether or not Greg Matthews, who was permanently shadowed by controversy, was to be recalled after he'd been quite obviously caught on the first bounce by the Kiwi keeper, Ian Smith. Further testing my resolve was the fact that the great Richard Hadlee was bowling in front of his home crowd. Hadlee invariably tested a new batsman out from the very first ball, scrutinising his body language, gauging his temperament and determining how watertight his technique was under pressure. I was batting on the only pitch in New Zealand that remotely resembled an Australian wicket with regard to pace and bounce, and the master of the corridor of uncertainty was exploiting the sideways movement it offered. Anyone without 100 per cent belief in his own game and calmness under interrogation was in serious danger of failing. It was no coincidence that AB, with his steel-trap mind, was standing resolutely while others came and went at regular intervals. Through more good fortune than skill, I managed to squirt a four through the slip cordon when the ball hit the bat rather than the other way around, followed by a clip off the legs for three to be seven not out after two balls.

I was away to every batsman's ideal start. Often, you'll see a batsman start recklessly, but once his safety barometer has been reached, normally somewhere between 10 and 20, he will settle down and consolidate for the long task at hand. My 'trigger' was always 15, because by that point I'd usually faced at least 30 balls and felt very settled at the crease. I would have adjusted my shot selection according to the pace and bounce of the pitch, probably faced most of the opposition's attack, and been familiar with what they were trying to achieve. Footwork and judgement of singles were sharper and more precise, and I was looking to capitalise on any scoring opportunities. I also felt that unless I played a poor shot through a lapse in concentration, I was likely to go on and get a decent score. At the end of my career I saw a statistic that showed that for innings where I got to 20 I averaged around 90.

Three hours after I played those first two shots, and for the first time since I'd been selected for the Boxing Day Test, I sensed that I did belong in Test cricket and wasn't an impostor languishing with the dreaded 'potential' tag. I was walking off the ground at the end of the day's play undefeated alongside my revered captain. AB was a man who used an economy of words, and I hung on every one, so when he said, 'Great Test-match batting today', all my debilitating self-doubts instantly evaporated. However, thoughts of a first Test hundred were short-lived, because early the next morning Hadlee had me stranded in 'no man's land', stuck on the crease and plumb lbw. The two steps forward of yesterday had frustratingly been followed by a backwards one today.

It's amazing how that elusive first Test hundred somehow equates to a graduation; until it is achieved a batsman can't quite be deemed the 'genuine article'. Likewise, a bowler doesn't believe he's made his imprint on the game until he has taken five wickets in a Test innings. Rightly or wrongly, these benchmarks define you among your peers and, although it's never openly said, this hurdle can become one of the toughest to overcome. It's why you see extreme emotions from players when they complete their 'rite of passage'. I would come to know all this only too well.

Another failure in the second innings in Christchurch, when I was deemed to have snicked one into Smith's gloves even though he hadn't appealed, really ticked me off, quickly had me cursing my ill-fortune and made me disillusioned once more with how events were unfolding. I've heard people say cricket's a great character builder and a great revealer of character, too, and I was certainly learning about myself, and how painful the game can be, as my journey continued. Still, watching Allan Border make back-to-back hundreds, both remarkable rearguard actions that saved the game, was a short-cut manual to success. I tried to digest and analyse the professional way these innings were constructed and the self-discipline that characterised both of them. Watching from the non-striker's end, I was amazed at AB's shot selection and the risk assessment he applied to each ball he faced. Often, especially early on, it appeared to me that he had passed up a good scoring opportunity, but in sacrificing a couple of wide, short deliveries he was summing up the pace and bounce of the pitch. Once he satisfied his curiosity and felt at ease with the conditions, he allowed his natural instincts to take over. This method was also used by David Boon and Geoff Marsh, but neither at that stage had the focused mind of his leader.

I was caught between wanting to learn this method and being the shot-a-minute Doug Walters-like prodigy that the press had built me up to be. I was having trouble with my style, because like a lot of players who don't know their game, I ended up playing to other people's expectations and consequently lost my originality. I was a work in progress, which was okay, bar the fact that I was doing my apprenticeship with all the world watching on.

The final Test of the series, at Eden Park in Auckland, was akin to a terrible recurring nightmare. As a team, we squandered a number of opportunities to dominate the Test before capitulating to 103 all out in our second innings, with 'Boonie' scoring more than half our runs and carrying his bat through the debacle. Afterwards, I was not game to show my face or make eye contact with anyone else as I sat with my head down between my legs in the silence of a depression-drenched change room. I had lasted roughly 10 minutes out in the middle for a return of one run, having been unable to come to terms with either John Bracewell's highly underrated off-spin or his hostile verbal barrage and imposing body language. He was all over me like a cheap suit and I wasn't equipped to repel him in any way. I was a soft target.

A losing dressing-room is a lonely place, often with only your own thoughts for comfort. An experienced squad can use past encounters to put things in perspective and then move forward. An inexperienced unit doesn't have the benefit of a storeroom full of archives and often can only see the damage directly in front of them. It's hard to look forward with any sort of optimism when you think your base has been eroded. I had now had nine digs in Test cricket and surpassed 15 only once, and seriously doubted whether I was good enough. I also genuinely wondered if we were ever going to win a Test match. I hated how worthless I felt after being crushed by our arch-rival neighbours and knew it was a pain only I could correct.

Some quickfire redemption was possible, because a four-match one-day series was due to start two days after the conclusion of the third Test. Our playing squad remained the same for the impending clashes, while the home team had the advantage of adding in-form players and dropping struggling ones. Making our quest for some limited-overs success even more challenging was the mindset of our captain, whose emotions spilled out like a dam bursting its walls in his press conference after the first of the one-dayers.

A team meeting was called in the room of our manager, Bob Merriman, before the second one-dayer, in Christchurch. This was normal procedure except for one aspect: our captain didn't turn up. Vice-captain Ray Bright delivered the news to a stunned squad: 'AB won't be joining us tonight, but I think we had better listen to this.' And then he put a black dictaphone on the table and hit the play button to reveal what Allan had said at the day's press conference. We all sat transfixed, without a sound being uttered. I believe Allan had nothing but admirable intentions when his interrogation by the media began, but he ended up laying everything on the table – probably through sheer frustration at our ineptness. Of course, his sad and angry words provided quotes reporters loved, because they came from the heart and not the manual and they were quite rightly used extensively the next day in the media. All of what he said had relevance, but I believe at least some of his words should have been communicated to his players face to face, rather than through the media. Looking back, it was an appeal for help from AB, but saying that it meant more to New Zealanders to play for their country than playing for Australia meant for us was a captaincy style that involved inspiring players by embarrassing them. AB had retreated after the Test series was lost, unable to extinguish his overflowing emotions and unsure of the way ahead. He was no doubt thoroughly unhappy with the team's lack of professionalism and, as captain, was aware that it reflected badly on him. We players were aware we needed to improve and perform, but our captain's depressed demeanour had created a barrier and the mood of the team was tense and subdued.

The five minutes of dialogue left us stunned, and I didn't know what to say or think. I was on my first voyage and the ship was sinking. His barrage included words such as these: 'I've given up speaking to them. I've said everything that possibly can be said to this bunch. I'm basically leaving it up to them now. They are going to show me if they really want to play for Australia and whether they really want to play under me. I will resign if there is not a victory over the next three games.'

'Spotty' Bright then hit the stop button and said, 'Well, boys, what are we going to do about that?'

I felt like I'd been taken hostage and had to negotiate my way out and justify my existence on the tour. Here I was struggling to survive, and now the captain was threatening to resign – this was as far as pos-sible from how I had imagined it would be to play cricket for Australia. The 90-minute meeting was torturous. We went round in circles with no real, clear direction, except for a pact we made to lift our games and to give it our all. We desperately needed AB and wanted him to be our captain, but for it all to work someone had to step forward and lead by example. During the 'honesty' element of our discussion, Greg Ritchie took a lead and decided to debate the question of whether there was a 'senior and junior' split within the team. Immediately he turned to me and said, 'Tugga, what do you think? Is there a junior/senior divide in the team?'

'Yeah,' I replied. 'I think there is a senior player, junior player mentality.'

Greg quickly returned fire by saying, 'No, there's not', which might have proved my point. Back into my box I went, and I took very little part in the rest of the proceedings for fear of recriminations. I didn't know how to feel at the conclusion of the meeting, but I did want to prove to AB that I was good enough to play alongside him and that I wanted him as my leader. I think we all wanted more commitment and needed a bit of tender loving care to turn things around.

Another loss followed in the second one-dayer, but there were signs of an improved effort and commitment. This didn't go unnoticed by our captain, who said as much to the media and thus eased our tensions a little and gave us a glimmer of confidence. Unfortunately, the following game, in Wellington, was heading down a familiar path until that sporadic genius, Wayne Phillips, joined me at the crease with the equation having ballooned out to a near-impossible 88 runs off 11 overs with only five wickets in hand. 'Flipper' was always upbeat and great fun to be around – except when he was driving the team bus, in a style that on occasions bordered on maniacal and broke most of the known road rules – but I could never quite work out whether his casual, laid-back attitude was genuine or a disguise for uncertainty and self-doubt. He and 'Fat Cat' Ritchie were always the life of the party and together could have easily made a living as stand-up comics. Flipper's quick wit could hold an audience captive and provided many humorous nights on tour, while Fat Cat's 'Three Stooges' routine was always a showstopper. Greg was also a deft hand at offloading canapés into the pockets of unsuspecting invited guests at official functions.

He loved to shock but couldn't quite find the balance between fun and pushing the boundaries too far. On one occasion in India, he burnt cigarette holes into the safari suit of a serial pest who had a million and one questions and couldn't be shaken off discreetly. I also fell victim to Cat's scheming ways, making the schoolboy mistake of hanging my breakfast order on the outside door handle of my hotel room before one Test match. This was too good to be true for the ever-alert prankster, who thought I'd severely under-ordered and generously rectified my mistake with extra bowls of prunes, a couple of mushroom omelettes, the complete complement of pastries and a full English breakfast.

In Wellington, Flipper strode to the middle as if he owned the ground. Here we were, needing eight runs an over with not much batting talent in the shed to come (a target of anything more than six runs an over is considered to be to the bowling team's favour), and though I felt in reasonably good touch I needed help. So I said to Wayne, 'What do you think?'

In a blink, he quipped, 'Simple, young fella. With my talent and your youth, we'll get these with an over to spare.'

Great stuff! Following that mid-pitch chat, I stood back and marvelled at the brilliance of Flipper's placement and improvisation. He demoralised their attack, scoring 53 from 32 balls. From one Ewen Chatfield over he produced a stunning display of inside-out hitting: four consecutive lofted boundaries, each executed with a geometrical flair, hit in an arc between point and mid-off. We ended up needing two from the last over and managed to scramble home for our first win against the Kiwis on the tour, after six weeks of occasional highs and frequent lows.

Afterwards, we celebrated as if we'd won a series, with AB, Flipper and me smiling like synchronised swimmers for a happy snap in front of the media. The release of the accrued stress from AB's face was clearly visible, and for the first time I experienced a genuine connection with my revered captain, as we stood arm in arm.

A win against the odds has a major effect on a team. All of a sudden, anything seems possible, everyone is more relaxed and content, and the bar has been lifted as regards the team's expectations. We carried with us a newfound confidence and levelled the series in the final match to take home some positives from a cluster of matches that were evenly contested, except for one disastrous day in the Auckland Test.

It was a noteworthy tour in regard to the direction Australian cricket was about to take. Simmo had analysed the behaviour and levels of professionalism of the various players, and saw huge potential in many guys and a curtailing of involvement for others. To be fair, AB was probably the only member of the squad at that time who was a genuine world-class player, which was no fluke, because his preparation and dedication far exceeded anyone else's. As a tour debutant, I got caught up in the 'Every day is Christmas Day, every night's a bucks night' mentality and didn't fully respect the responsibility I needed to assume. The culture of the day was 'Play hard, party hard', but in truth we weren't good enough to deserve the latter. There was certainly a drinking culture among the group, as there was in most other teams in world cricket with the probable exception of the West Indies, who had a fitness trainer as part of their support staff. I would learn soon enough that the Windies were, without doubt, at a different level to everyone else fitness-wise, which, when combined with their strength of mind, intimidated all opposition and made them unbeatable.

Changes needed to happen within the Australian team. Simmo and the selectors had a vision for the future: people with poor attitudes would be left behind, while those selected needed to respond to the faith placed in them by committing to hard work and getting accustomed to stepping out of their comfort zone, in order to get to the level required to compete on a regular basis.

Simmo was quite upbeat at the conclusion of the New Zealand tour. He talked up the prospect of an emerging young team, which for a new member like me was encouraging. He was quoted in the press as saying, 'In retrospect, the New Zealand tour will play an important part in the recovery of Australian cricket. One disastrous day does not make a tour a total failure, which is now being suggested.' Further good news for me was that our interim coach had decided to take up a two-year deal to help get Australian cricket back on track. It was going to take a lot of hard work, but I for one was excited at developing my game and also helping to make the Australian team more than being sometimes competitive and often unpredictable.

8

Another world

Constant, continual vomiting; uncontrollable liquid bowel motions; a raging fever; involuntary shaking; a migraine-intensity headache . . .

I was cursing myself for letting my guard down after basically being the last man standing at the end of seven weeks of touring around India in August–October 1986. We'd been to cricketing out-posts such as Rajkot, Baroda, Gwalior, Srinigar and Hyderabad – not exactly salubrious locations with top-class hotels or where standards of hygiene are a priority. Yet I'd survived the dreaded 'Delhi belly' and thought I'd celebrate with my first milkshake of the tour – an icy-cold vanilla one with an extra scoop of ice-cream – and a hamburger that didn't seem entirely cooked . . . but the Taj Mahal Hotel's reputation quelled any reluctance to gorge it down. Big mistake all round. I woke up on the morning of our last Test, in Bombay, feeling decidedly unwell. If mine was a nine-to-five job I'm sure I would have rung in crook for the day, but here I was with a Test match about to begin, so I stacked up on Imodium, Panadol and a couple of electrolyte drinks to enable me to get on with what had to be done. It didn't occur to me that my condition could get dramatically worse. It wasn't allowed to – I had a Test match to play.

Australia batting first gave me temporary respite, and I lay prostrate on the dressing-room floor, praying the stomach cramps would dissipate and the nausea would subside before I was required. But as the day's play unfolded, my health unravelled to the point where I had to dash off to the toilet, wearing pads and protective gear, at least eight or nine times in the 20 minutes before I went out to bat. Indian toilet paper isn't too kind at the best of times and by the end of my torment it felt like sandpaper and I had the gait of a cowboy looking for trouble. Walking out to bat, my main concern was not to mess up my pants or topple over with dizziness, and I was no match for the cunning off-spin of Shivlal Yadav. In fact, my sole means of survival was through a revival of my junior soccer skills, rather than via any form of batsmanship. I couldn't clearly focus on the ball; instead, I relied entirely on instinct. I felt cheated by this unfair turn of events, because I genuinely wanted to leave an exclamation mark rather than a question mark next to my name in reviews of the tour.

After I was dismissed for six, the remainder of the Test was spent convalescing in my hotel room, fighting off a raging temperature, vomiting bile, passing a vile green fluid and being injected with antibiotics. I was suddenly very homesick and lonely, trapped in my four-walled prison, unable to assist my teammates. Eventually, by day three, I couldn't take the strain of being a passenger any longer and managed to field for a short time and even bowl a couple of overs. In the dressing-room, the boys had erected a memorial in the place I had briefly occupied and I must admit there were moments when I thought I was going to need one. For the next 12 months, my life revolved around frantic dashes to the toilet, frequent stomach ailments and a constant feeling of being unwell, I was a sickly yellow colour and I lost 6–8 kilos I couldn't recover. India was a place that tested my patience and resolve, and I swore that next time around I would come with a more understanding attitude in order to be successful. It was a challenge I looked forward to, especially as the 1987 World Cup was to be held on the subcontinent.

Touching down on foreign soil is always an exciting moment for a touring squad. Everyone has aspirations to play well and secure a position in the team, and has a vision of being a part of a squad that wins away from home. Back in the '80s, the fact that the major matches at the start of a tour would be controlled by two 'home' umpires was perceived to be a major stumbling block. At the end of the tour, it was regularly used as a reason for failure.

The first thing that hit me about India as I took my initial step off the aircraft was the damp, musty smell, which suddenly made my breathing very noticeable. It was hard to get in enough good air to satisfy my needs and it took a minute or two to adjust, which was just enough time to notice that if staring was an Olympic sport, India would be a certainty for the gold medal. I'd only been in India a short time and couldn't believe what a bombardment to my senses the place was. I knew I was in for a life-altering adventure.

Trying to work our way through customs at Bombay Airport proved to be a difficult exercise, with a succession of officials promising us a speedy progression but in reality all they wanted was an autograph book full of Aussie signatures. Camera flashes were going off in all directions and a general state of chaos engulfed the tour party. Finally, all the customs officials fulfilled their relatives' requests, and we gathered our mountain of baggage before being greeted by a plethora of cameras, microphones and journalists all pushing and cursing each other in their desperation for a prime position. A sturdy but ageing bus with an air-conditioning system that spewed out chilly, grubby air caught our attention, as did the mosquitoes that greeted us from behind the paisley curtains that clung to the grimy windows.

An overnight stop at the Centaur Hotel, adjacent to the airport, gave us our first real taste of things to come. This was no Melbourne Hilton. The rooms smelled as if kerosene had been poured all over the mouldy carpet, while the pillows could have doubled as sandbags in a flood emergency and the water pressure from the shower heads made shampooing an impossibility. Looking to christen our tour, we all agreed to meet downstairs in the bar for a beer before attempting to convert our clocks to Indian time. But just as we were beginning to settle in and get a taste for the local drop, Kingfisher, the ever-alert Ray Bright spotted a rat that could have doubled as a cat scampering through the doorway and into the adjoining kitchen. Now we were all decidedly edgy about drifting off to sleep back in our rooms, for fear of being nibbled at. Room service was not an option, particularly the meat dishes. Meanwhile, showing his 'You can't buy that off the shelf' touring experience, Spotty explained how to drink the Kingfishers and wake up hangover free the next day. Indian beer, unlike its Aussie counterpart, has a high glycerine content that helps its shelf-life. The downside to this method of preserving the beer, he explained, is the diabolical headaches it generates the following morning. The solution to this dilemma proved quite simple and was demonstrated with a degree of skill by our left-arm 'tweaker'. A glass of mineral water, filled three-quarters to the top, was used to extract the demon ingredient. The bottle of Kingfisher was turned upside down as quickly as possible, immersing the neck in the water, which almost magically extracted the swirling, rhythmically rolling glycerine. When there appeared to be no more, you again quickly turned the bottle upright and were left with a decent-tasting and less damaging beer.

My first on-field involvement on the tour came in the lead-up to the first two one-dayers – a three-day match in the ancient city of Gwalior. But before the game started I savoured a visit to the ancient part of the city, high on a hill, surrounded by walls built to stop invaders hundreds of years ago; this was better than any history lesson at school. The sight of buffalos, cows, donkeys and monkeys roaming the streets freely, among vehicles that had been mixed and matched and then soldered together, had me straining not to miss any of the action.

The highlight of the official function held in our honour at the city's Old Fort was the sporadic explosions of our locally acquired firecrackers. These were of the 'Tom Thumb' variety, going off like gunfire and scaring the daylights out of our media contingent, who became an early target. The skill lay not just in discreetly dropping the cracker under a seat, but also in setting up unsuspecting targets such as the Aussie scribes on tour by offering them a chair and then waiting for Greg Ritchie's ingenious system to fall into place. A Benson & Hedges was partially inhaled before inserting the wick of a row of Tom Thumbs halfway up the cigarette, which was then placed under the appropriate chair. All we had to do then was wait for the fuse to ignite and enjoy the startled reaction as the journo ducked for cover, not knowing what was happening.

The ground itself was bereft of grass and, for that matter, facilities up until 72 hours before the start of the game. However, by the time we won the toss and elected to bat we were sitting in a new concrete change room with walls that were still damp, but nevertheless standing. Unusually, the field was surrounded by a barbed-wire fence, perhaps to keep out the wandering cows, but on the day before the game began it nearly left us a player short for the remainder of the tour.

Catching practice for us had escalated in the 'Simpson era' to that of a personal battle between player and coach. Nine times out of 10 there was only one winner, with each player taking on Simmo in high-ball practice, taking endless catches until the fielder either dropped one or was exhausted. Bob had a gift for making every catch one for which you had to stretch and strain every sinew of muscle in your body. Tim 'Ziggy' Zoehrer, our new wicketkeeper, had the God-given gifts of soft hands and an incredible natural catching ability, and when he decided to make the most of these assets he attained a level others could only dream about. During this particular workout, he was obviously out to impress Simmo, because he was making it look easy, even as a succession of balls edged ever closer to a stationary pitch roller situated in the outfield. Seeing Tim unfazed by this obstacle, our coach cajoled him backwards towards a mentally tougher examination. Not wanting to show weakness with the final catch of this 10–15 catch routine, Ziggy leapt high and backwards to take what would have to be classed as a 'screamer' of a mark. 'Out' it was, but his joy was very brief, because seconds later he realised he was suspended a few centimetres off the ground, entangled on three rows of barbed wire. Simmo, I'm sure, was impressed with his commitment, while we were stunned by the outcome and Ziggy was in shock – at both his catch and his perilous position. The session was terminated after we extracted him, but a benchmark had been set. Whatever it was going to take, we were prepared to sacrifice ourselves in order to better our results and impress our influential coach.

Cricketwise, the game in Gwalior provided a satisfactory result, with the prodigiously talented Greg Ritchie scoring a century and the human Energiser bunny, Greg Matthews, playing beautifully before charging India's quick and getting caught on the point fence for 99 in a dismissal only he could justify. That was Greg summed up to perfection: expect the unexpected. He was always excellent for the shock-value element, but also a guy who could play better than he probably ever realised and whose record as an all-rounder for NSW is unrivalled.

A dinner invitation to the Maharaja of Gwalior's palace was a real treat, especially as we later learnt that across the country many similarly magnificent mansions were now derelict or run by government authorities. Few regal families were still in residence, so it was a rare privilege to eat with sterling-silver cutlery and sample Indian delicacies while admiring the antique chandeliers and mounted tiger heads that adorned the grandiose rooms. This was as far as imaginable from the tiny room I had shared with Mark in our fibro house in the western suburbs of Sydney. I could only wonder how long this caper had been going on!

Flying into Srinigar for the second one-day international, I was overwhelmed by the beauty of the Himalayas. Standing on the tarmac, flanked by security guards, it seemed unreal to be viewing snow-covered mountains that disappeared gracefully into the clouds. Like most people, the name 'Everest' immediately conjures up exotic images for me, but until you stand before its prodigious girth and elevation, you can't fully appreciate its magnificence. Being in a hot-bed of political conflict, the crowd for the game included more police than paying spectators, ensuring it was packed to capacity. It was here that I claimed my first spectator 'victim', when I overhit a catch to Tim

Zoehrer during the warm-ups and hit a casually chatting fan straight between the eyes. My initial thought was *Please don't keel over and die – I don't want to spend time in an Indian jail*, so I was mightily relieved when he just shook it off and settled for an autograph. Judging by his facial expression afterwards, you'd have thought he'd just won the lottery, not head-butted a rock-hard Kookaburra six-stitcher.

The scheduling for the tour was a dog's breakfast. Tests were intermingled with one-dayers and three-day tour matches at venues all over the country, which often meant we were backtracking or enduring onerous multi-stop trips. In the one-day series we ended up on the losing end of the equation, going down 2–3 with a washout at Hyderabad, but the signs were encouraging nevertheless. A poor piece of sportsmanship cost us victory in Delhi, when Greg Dyer and I put on a record seventh-wicket partnership. As we aimed at a huge total, the Indians slowed down their over rate to ridiculous levels so that we ended up receiving only 45 of our originally allotted 50 overs, which allowed them to keep control of the match by terminating our momentum and adjusting their batting tactics in the knowledge that they would be receiving the exact number of overs we received. No fines were in place for these underhand tactics, so only strong ethics acted as a deterrent.

Luckily for us, the Hyderabad match was washed out after we batted, because no one could stomach the fare on offer at lunch. It was a selection of the hottest curries imaginable, with even the rice spiced up with flavours we'd never seen or heard of before. I can still recall chomping into a cardamom pod and gagging with my first mouthful; the way I did with my first taste of a black sambuca. Neither cardamom nor anchovies have since been afforded a second chance. Confirmation that this was the worst lunch ever came when the cold sections of roast chicken were lifted off the plate to reveal plump maggots clinging to the bones and crawling among the undercooked flesh.

Out came the Vegemite and Vita-Weat from the emergency supplies, and away went any willingness on my part to be adventurous with the local cuisine.

The accountability of the catering staff was saved by the ineptness of the match authorities, who had a counterfeit black-market ticket scandal on their hands. The 20000-capacity venue had 40000 people stacked in, queued up and overflowing out onto the ground. It was mayhem, and a minor miracle that we didn't end up with a riot as tempers flared, though this was exactly what occurred at Ahmedabad, another new experience and one that both enlivened and frightened me. It was a strange sort of buzz to see the crowd go wild after a policeman incited trouble by throwing a bottle back into the capacity 60000 crowd. Anarchy reigned for a good 20 minutes, during which time we left the field and took refuge in the change rooms. Sanity was restored and the match resumed, only to end with us losing the series.

Staying in the satellite cities meant a fairly average standard of accommodation, which wasn't such a big deal. To me the basics, such as a good pillow, shower and bed and dark curtains, were the real issues, rather than tasteful decor, a minibar and nice towel rails. However, one item that was in all the rooms but didn't ever work properly was a telephone. Often, I would wait for hours on end, desperate to talk to Lynette, only to lose the connection and be unable to make contact due to all the lines being busy. At other times, we would be having a deep-and-meaningful and the operator would interrupt and tell me, 'Your time is up' or 'Would you like to continue, Mr Wog?' (It was 'Wog', not 'Waugh' – the locals always had trouble with my surname.) Privacy was not an option, and when the homesickness kicked in I had periods of utter frustration and moments of acute loneliness. Touring life can be like that: a real rollercoaster of emotions where you sometimes can't distinguish between what's real and what's not. Your mind can trick you, especially when it's idle, and contemplation often turns to torment.

Leading into the first Test, in Madras, we had a game at Chandigarh where I took seven wickets, which almost doubled my career first-class total. In reality I was a novice with the ball, but here I was looking for a Test spot and the wickets I was taking gave me a huge boost at the selection table. Signing autographs was also good for the ego, and having nervously waited at Bankstown Oval for over an hour before plucking up the courage to sneak up and get Tony Greig's autograph when the then England captain played a season of Sydney grade cricket back in 1975–76, I was more than happy to sign for anyone who wanted my average-looking scribble. I made the most of my spare time after failing with the bat by sitting by myself on the steps leading up to the main grandstand and signing for well over an hour. I was quite enjoying the interaction with the kids when AB came back from a catching session with Simmo and said, 'Jeez, Tugga, you'll soon get tired of doing that!' Perhaps he was speaking from experience, particularly in the subcontinent, where they will keep coming as long as you want to sit there. For me, though, it was just the right thing to do, and in a funny sort of way I was humbled by their respect.

The final selection for the first Test team came down to a duel for the No. 3 spot between Dean Jones and Mike Veletta, with 'Jonah' getting the nod on a gut feeling more than anything else. I was thankful for that, because Dean was my roomie and consequently the vibe was really positive once we both found ourselves in the starting XI. The MA Chidambaram Stadium in Madras is a bit like a poor man's MCG, with stands of half the height and bereft of seats. Clearly there hadn't been much rain, because the outfield was bone dry and in parts as hard and shiny as an ice rink. The humidity stole the air from your lungs and forced you to conserve energy that would be needed later on. Sweat streamed off every part of my body as if I was in a weight-loss sauna, and that was without any exertion – it was blindingly hot and agitatingly uncomfortable. Making life almost impossible to bear was the stench that wafted over the ground from the adjacent canal, which was full of green slime that moved as a single leaden mass of bubbling gases of God-knows-what and was escorted by swirling masses of mosquitos. If you can imagine a toilet that hasn't been flushed and is left for a couple of days, and then has the lid lifted, that's what we had to deal with. Buffalos and cows grazed lazily on the creek's banks while the local kids chased kites and played their version of hide-and-seek on the squelchy-mud banks amid scattered human and animal faeces. I'm sure doctors would have argued that walking around the block in such conditions was dangerous to the health, yet here we were about to embark on a five-day duel.

At the end of our first innings we had almost lost a player due to severe dehydration, but added another chapter in the story of 'greatest Test innings ever played'. Dean Jones's double century combined courage, determination and skill to produce an epic performance. I'll never forget how, after more than eight hours at the crease, his physical appearance had changed. He was gaunt and pale in the face and had a vacant expression that suggested he was in serious trouble, his body bordering on completely shutting down. At tea on day two he came in, on 202 not out, to rapturous applause from his teammates and enthusiastic backslapping, but none of it registered – he was like a walking corpse. Sitting next to Dean in the dressing-room, I could see first hand how serious his condition was. He had lost control of his bodily functions, and was slumped in his chair saturated in urine, shaking uncontrollably and virtually incoherent.

He was, however, aware of his predicament, because he asked AB to retire him through sickness, but his request was met this way: 'No way. You can throw your wicket away if you want, but I'm not retiring you hurt.'

This stern rebuke was all that was needed to swing us into action. A couple of us managed to undress Jonesy and give him a fresh set of gear, in the hope it would reinvigorate him, and he did manage to score another eight runs purely on memory before he was bowled by Yadav. Immortality and a saline drip in the hospital awaited our star that evening and I had our room to myself.

Throughout the Test, both teams toiled away to the point of exhaustion. I can still see the distressed state of Ray Bright after he made 30 after coming in late on the first day as a nightwatchman. He basically gave his wicket away, and such was his physical and emotional state that back in the physio's room he was crying with pain as he sat, head bowed, draped in an ice-soaked towel in the hope of lowering his body temperature, and consumed a bottle of Bisleri water with quivering hands. He then remained motionless under a cold shower for the next hour until he came back to life. I had my own demons to ward off during the game, vomiting at regular intervals due to heatstroke. But considering I only scored 12 not out and two not out and bowled 15 overs, I tried to keep my state of health to myself.

The match itself ended up being only the second tied Test in history, which was great for the game on the subcontinent and in many ways a saviour for both teams, because the match was at times extremely spiteful. I'm sure the 50°C-plus temperatures stretched the players' patience to the maximum and played a role in the ineptness of the umpires, but even without these factors there was a real edge and quarrelsome element to both teams' play. It all seemed to boil over on the last day, which began with India needing 348 to win. At drinks in the final session, I'm sure I saw a sly head butt after Greg Matthews and the Indian keeper, Chandrakant Pandit, came together, while Tim Zoehrer and Chetan Sharma held play up at one point as they offered animated advice to each other. AB was threatened with a send-off by umpire Dotiwalla after a debate over whether our captain was taking too long to set his fields during the final 15 overs. AB sought advice from vice-captain David Boon as to the legitimacy of this threat, and Boonie, in his usual unruffled manner, said, 'Don't know. I don't think he can.'

There were many heroes throughout the exhausting five days of play, but without doubt, the most unsung of them was Matthews, who scored 44 and 27 not out and took five wickets in each innings. His stamina and resilience were absolutely staggering, especially on the last day, when he bowled 39.5 overs just about consecutively to keep us in the game and then ultimately tie it. Making his feat all the more noteworthy in the eyes of his fellow players was the fact that he wore two sleeveless sweaters throughout the day. Actually, he gave one to the umpire when he fielded and only wore them both when he was bowling. We just shook our heads in disbelief, because it was so hot with 90 per cent humidity, but as usual Greg had a theory. He explained that nomadic herders in the desert wore woollen coats because they kept the cool air in, thus acting as a kind of air-conditioner. Sounds fair enough, plus we all needed a good laugh in the trying conditions that were testing everyone to the limit. More likely, though, it was Greg's way of saying to everyone, 'It's not that hot – let's just get on with it and do the job.'

The last over of the match was as tense as Test cricket can get, with the result quite possibly hanging on one mistake. You know someone is going to crack under the pressure, you just pray it's not going to be you. In such situations, the one thing you can't do as a fieldsman is say to yourself, 'I'm not going to play a part in this, the ball's not going to come to me!' Because it always will. I was stationed three-quarters of the way to the boundary at square leg to protect against the four that would have spelled disaster. India needed four to win when the final over started; we required one more wicket. Unfortunately for me, no matter how much I tried to talk myself into being positive, I was so nervous at the thought of costing my team the match that I couldn't totally swipe away the nagging doubts. The crowd were delirious and incredibly noisy, so much so that from where I was fielding, with the commotion on top of me, I felt strangely detached from the action. Then, second ball, I saw it – a flick off his legs by Ravi Shastri – and it was coming my way. My heart missed a beat as I set off in a hurry to try to stop the all-important second run and thus keep India's No. 11, Maninder Singh, on strike. Just as I bent down to gather the ball, I got a lousy bounce and the ball bobbled off my wrist, enabling Shastri that split second's grace to make it back safely. The catcalls and whistles rang in my ears, but there was nowhere to regroup or hide; in fact, the stakes had been raised. India now needed two to win from four balls.

God, I hoped that ball wasn't coming my way again. If it did, I was going to need some help. Thankfully for us, Shastri took the conservative option of a single from the third ball to ensure that a tie was the home team's worst result. Maninder crudely defended the next ball, so with two balls to go and a recognised 'bunny' on strike we still had a chance, but we all thought it would have to be either bowled or caught for history to be made.

The nine Australian fieldsmen made their way into close proximity to the batsman, to either take a catch or execute a run-out. The moment Greg delivered the penultimate ball, time became irrelevant, because while it was all over in a flash, it felt like everything had been put in slow motion. The well-flighted delivery hit Maninder's pads as he jabbed indecisively at the wrong line, and all our close-in catchers and the bowler went up in unison . . . but it was a wasted appeal because umpire Vikram Raju had beaten everyone to the punch. His finger was already up; like us, he wanted to be a part of history, and not even the possibility of arriving home to a smouldering house was going to deny him.

Greg was off and he was going to be hard to catch. We all ran in different directions, whether through relief or exhaustion I'm not sure, but I do know we were all mentally drained, as much as you could ever be playing sport. I swiped a couple of stumps on the way through before we all caught up in the change rooms. As soon as I could catch Mo I gave him a souvenir stump, because without his effort the result would have been vastly different. We celebrated proudly, as if we'd won, which was a totally different response to our opponents, who I learnt later sat quietly, suggesting they thought they'd lost an opportunity to win. Meanwhile, in the scorers' booth, chaos reigned for a good half an hour, with both the ground scorers manually collating their totals after the two had different winners in their books straight after the game.

For Australia the result was a triumph, not only because we'd made the running for the whole game and declared twice (7/574 in the first innings, 5/170 in the second), and not even because a number of players had shown Allan Border-type traits in their performance, but because Simmo – and, with some coercing, AB – had believed in the team enough to set up the final day's play by offering India the chance to chase a reasonable target. In his brief post-match speech to the boys Simmo said, with a wry smile on his face, 'There you are, guys, I told you they wouldn't get 348!' We were doing the dictating and not being dictated to – that was the vital change of tack for us as a side.

A presentation ceremony of farcical proportions was squeezed in between us celebrating, showering and catching a flight to Hyderabad that was put back an hour so we could all catch it. The man-of-the-match award was shared between Dean Jones and Kapil Dev (who had scored 119 in India's first innings), which was a real home-towner but expected, as two Indians and our manager, Alan Crompton, had picked it. Feeling perhaps a little guilty, the powers-that-be then decided some 10 minutes later to announce Greg Matthews as the 'all-rounder of the match'. But by that time we were busy packing our bags and well past being sensitive to their political offering.

★

The much-anticipated follow-up Test in Delhi was destroyed not by the amount of rain on the days leading up to the Test, but by ineffective plastic covers. There was no protection for the bowlers' run-ups and they became boglike but, worse still, when the main covers were rolled back, a myriad of holes and rips had let the rain drench the pitch. Days of sunshine followed, but nothing could be done to retrieve the situation, which only emphasised how behind the times cricket can sometimes be. No 'super-sopper' was available to soak up the excess water, and lack of foresight and reluctance to spend money meant that cheap plastic was expected to save a Test that was to be watched by thousands of people and generate big dollars in income and sponsorship.

A tied series was probably a just result, but it felt like unfinished business for both squads. From my perspective, I averaged over 50 but only because I didn't spend enough time at the crease to get out more than once. It was a series that provided almost no opportunity for me to judge where I was at in my career. Two 'mini' not-outs in the tied Test, a non-event 39 not out as the game petered out in Delhi and then that six in Bombay that was a total blur thanks to my illness. On the flight home I didn't feel as if I'd advanced as a player or achieved anything that would give me some degree of comfort for future battles. I still didn't know if I had it in me to make the grade, and that bugged me.

My one significant achievement was that – for the first time, really – I had been able to put myself a little outside my comfort zone. I had tried to get out and see as much as possible, to sample the culture and embrace it as much as I could. Standing in front of the majestic Taj Mahal, visiting the ancient city of Delhi, and doing the tourist thing in Jaipur had set me apart from most of the lads, who preferred a game of cards or a swim in the hotel pool.

I had a desire to experience the places I was playing in, and loved to see them, warts and all. Taking a taxi by myself, or maybe with one or two others, was my way of seeing what life was really like for the majority, not the minority. Hotel concierges or a team liaison guy would always point you in the direction of the touristy spots, where your photos would turn out nice and lovely. That was okay, but I wanted to sample the *real* India, the vibrant, swarming mass of humanity, and get amongst it. While it was at times disturbing, particularly seeing young children living on the footpath with little or no clothing, there was a sense that everyone simply got on with their lives and survived the best they could. I had to admire their resolute nature and inner strength to battle on, though I couldn't help but wonder how families dealt with ailments as simple as a toothache or common cold, let alone something more serious.

Without a doubt the image that stays with me the clearest from the tour is the beggars in Bombay, who would appear from nowhere and, desperate for cash, begin tapping on the cab's window. Generally, they'd have a baby who quite often had been rented out by the local mafia for the day, to prick the conscience of their 'target'. Most often, these poor kids were badly malnourished and sickly-looking, with their minder/parents pointing in the direction of their mouths and bellies to further emphasise their plight. On one occasion, I wound my window down to offer a few rupees and was stunned by the scene that unfolded in front of me. A tiny, lifeless arm dangled on the window frame. I hesitantly looked up and saw an almost certainly dead baby swathed in bandages. I wanted to see whether it was still alive, but the taxi dashed off amid the mass of converging vehicles that encircled us. I felt like throwing up on the spot; the helplessness of the whole situation was so numbing. I didn't really know how to compartmentalise it.

This was India. I both loved and hated it.

9

The Ashes

Thank God that's over! The Poms had finally decided to end the torture at 8/592, with not much of the second day of the second Ashes Test of 1986–87 remaining. I hadn't exactly blitzed them either, managing a poor return of 0/90 from 24 overs, and was reflecting on how the half-chances and appeals weren't happening for me. Then AB came rushing up alongside me just before we entered the players' tunnel at the WACA. Very matter-of-factly, he said, 'You're batting three this dig.'

All I could manage to say was, 'Okay, thanks, that's great.'

It didn't really bother me whether or not I was a nightwatchman or that perhaps he wanted to see if I had the temperament to handle the situation. I was just thankful for the opportunity after batting at No. 8 and then No. 7 in the first Test, at the Gabba. A bonus about batting in the top order is that I would pretty much know when I was going to get into the action, in contrast to the middle-order and lower-order guys who often had to sit around for long periods burning up mental energy, watching every ball and often becoming fatigued in the process. The degree of certainty that comes from being in the top order can help focus the mind on the task at hand, and I experienced a new sense of being ready for the occasion. My thought process suddenly was far different from the one I'd had as a No. 7 or No. 8, where I imagined my runs were considered almost a bonus. At No. 3 runs are expected, and that degree of extra responsibility brought out a level of self-confidence in me that had been missing.

Even allowing for my upbeat state of mind, I was still incredibly nervous at the thought of taking on Ian Botham and Graham Dilley in fading light. I didn't have to wait long, as David Boon perished very early on and I was suddenly in a situation that I sensed was the real deal. *Be strong, back yourself and don't play these guys on their reputations* were the themes running through my head. Easier said than done when a cricketing colossus with a golden touch – Botham – has you in his sights.

The Perth pitch is unique in world cricket, with its trampoline-like true bounce and express pace off the wicket. If you can see out the first 30-minute 'adjustment phase', it suddenly transforms into the flattest batting track of them all. The key to this transition from perilous to paradise is patience, but when you are a 21-year-old with plenty to prove this is easier said than done, and that was for tomorrow, as there was only time for Geoff Marsh and me to get as far as 1/19 at stumps.

I'd survived my first examination and called home that night to talk to my parents and Lynette, telling them, 'I'm about to play the most important innings of my life.'

By lunch the next day I was 71 not out and staring down at my first Test hundred. At least that's what I was thinking to myself as I made my way back to take centre and face up to off-spinner John Emburey on the resumption of play. Seconds later, I couldn't believe I'd succumbed so easily to an innocuous warm-up delivery, which was no more than a straight half-volley I managed to nick to slip. 'What a bloody waste, you imbecile,' was all I could mutter to myself as I walked off. I was livid at this lame dismissal, which came from a cocktail of poor concentration, lack of respect and absence of routine. I had faced up without being quite ready, but then again the way I faced up was different every time I came out to bat. I didn't have a method that automatically made me switch 'on', as I know now that the consistent players do. Just when I'd done the spadework and felt certain of a big score, I'd wasted a chance that was never coming back.

Spurred on by my batting and propelled by an equal sense of frustration, I surprised everyone, including myself, by taking 5/69 in England's second innings to give me a fifty/five-for double. The Test ended in a draw, but I was invigorated by my results and the sense of belonging that had finally surfaced.

The third Test, in Adelaide, was for me the first time that the *real* Steve Waugh turned up to bat and deal with the media. Tossed away were the standard quotes, such as 'I just want to take it one game at a time', 'I just want to play my natural game' and 'Hopefully, things will go well'. Instead, I went on the offensive after sharing an unbroken stand of 146 with Greg Matthews, saying to a group of journos, 'I've had a gutful of all that speculation.' I was answering a question about whether my place was still in jeopardy. The need to be myself and play naturally saw me attack on instinct in the middle and then respond with emotion to the press. Something had ignited a spark that no longer lay dormant within, burdened by other people's expectations. My spirit had been unleashed.

★

My first Ashes campaign had begun in Brisbane amid intense media interest, highlighted by the huge influx of both tabloid and broadsheet journalists from the United Kingdom. It was exciting to be part of an atmosphere that was definitely much more upbeat than my previous series. The history of Ashes conquests and the legacy left by past legends from both sides added to a lead-up that featured plenty of hype and headlines. One English paper ran the memorable line, 'Can't bat, can't bowl, can't field', in reference to the English team, and the general consensus seemed to be that the Poms had little chance of winning. This was ridiculous when you consider they had players of class such as Allan Lamb, Mike Gatting, David Gower, Ian Botham and Graham Dilley, while we really had only one proven performer in Allan Border.

The decision by the Australian selectors to leave the highly credentialled Geoff Lawson out of our final XI was a surprise and a big gamble, considering the inexperience of our attack, and, adding to our confusion, most of us didn't find out he was the one who'd missed out until word filtered around the change room. In those days, the 'twelfthy' was generally told in the final warm-up of his omission, while everyone else hoped they weren't going to get the tap on the shoulder. We didn't know for sure whether we were in or out until AB went out to toss and someone in the know let us in on the mail.

That toss was ours, but it was about our only win for the Test, as we ended up being pulverised by seven wickets, largely due to Botham's murderous 138, which saw a particularly savage assault on Merv

Hughes on the second day. As a teammate, this was hard to watch. A mauling like that can ruin a career if the guy on the receiving end isn't tough enough to come back and be prepared to fail again in his quest to succeed next time around. Making it even tougher was the knowledge that Merv, like a lot of us, was playing for his place in the team. We all felt that one shocker could signal the end.

Sometimes one incident can become the turning point in a match or even a series, and I believe the dropping of David Gower on nought by our Test debutant, left-arm quick Chris Matthews, was such an example. Going on gut feeling is, to me, a captain's greatest weapon, because he is, after all, the leader and expected to make decisions – most of which are based on fact but some, often the critical ones, on intuition. Sending Chris into the slip cordon without any prior warning or formal practice in the lead-up to the Test was a bold move, to say the least, but obviously AB had seen something he liked. Whatever the reason, it was a huge show of faith that went horribly wrong. A 'sitter' in the slips is never really as easy as it appears considering you have barely half a second to coordinate the hands in the right place before the ball arrives, but this was as simple as they come, carrying at a comfortable waist-height and at a predictable pace. Down it went, and so did our heads. We knew this was a crucial mistake, because Gower's form leading into the Test had been patchy, but being a touch player he was only ever one good stroke away from being back in form. And he certainly didn't need us to help him get there. His elegance and manner seemed to have a knock-on effect on his teammates and his 51 was the catalyst for their big total and subsequent seven-wicket victory.

To play against guys like Botham and Gower was to see class of a different level. According to the press, these were a couple of guys who were having a fun time, drinking wine and champagne and pulling off pranks whenever they pleased. They, like all great players, have the 'X factor', that indefinable quality that sets them apart from the rest. It is a combination of charisma, aura, presence and match-winning ability. Whenever they walked to the crease or had the ball in hand they demanded respect, and our antennae sprung into action, sensing danger ahead. Duelling with such quality can bring out either a positive reaction, with a player wanting to challenge himself and lift to the occasion, or a negative one, with him retreating for fear of what might happen. I loved to test myself out against them. Even if I didn't win the battle, at least I was in the contest.

Despite better showings in Perth and Adelaide, that 1–0 lead was one we could never make any inroads into, and we eventually lost the series with an abysmal showing in the Boxing Day Test in Melbourne. The worst part of our inept display was that Botham took five wickets on his reputation alone. His strained intercostal muscle was only partially healed and he had missed the third Test, but though he ambled in off about half his normal run and rolled his arm over at slow medium pace, we somehow managed to self-destruct. Long hops were nicked to the keeper or chopped onto the stumps; it was the presence and aura of a great cricketer that had us spellbound. I'm sure he couldn't believe his figures, which eventually read 5/41 from 16 overs as we crashed to 141 all out on the first day. Considering his mindset would have been to do a job for the side and avoid further injury, the end result must have been beyond even his wildest expectations.

Compounding our woes was the battering we were receiving from the media and our supporters over not only our performance but also some of the guys' behaviour on the field. Tim Zoehrer, who as a player had a feisty streak, and Craig McDermott, the team's 'enforcer', came in for criticism over their appealing and mannerisms. You can sometimes gain an insight into a player's make-up when they are under pressure, because they have to dig deep and rely on the character that defines them. The truth was we all needed an injection of 'ticker' after such a spineless showing, which we all knew wasn't good enough.

Half an hour in a house of mirrors to have a good look at ourselves might have been a good option.

One of the beauties of sport is that an individual or a team can reverse results quickly. Nothing is ever guaranteed. Changes were made to our team for the final Test, in Sydney, with Boon, Matthews and McDermott making way for Greg Ritchie, Dirk Wellham and Peter Taylor. The call-up of 'PT' created a media storm, with many journos keen to pursue the line that the selectors had mistakenly picked the wrong Taylor. Their theory had some credibility, because Boonie was out but no specialist opener had come into the squad to replace him. Meanwhile, Mark Taylor was in pretty good form in his second season for NSW. Adding to the intrigue, Peter Taylor had played only six first-class games in total and just one in 1986–87, but Greg Chappell had suggested to his fellow selectors that his temperament and type of bowling would be up to the assignment. In truth, Dirk Wellham's selection was tougher on the team dynamic, because there was apparently still plenty of lingering tension between AB and Dirk over my NSW captain's decision to sign for the rebel South African tour and then renege on that move so he could go on the 1985 Ashes tour. The suggestion was that Dirk had been looked after by Kerry Packer, which didn't sit well with Allan. Furthermore, AB must have been threatened by Dirk's captaincy credentials, and the fact that he was now there to help direct proceedings and pass on his local knowledge. I must say, though, that I never saw anything to back up or deny the rumours of a split between the two.

In the end, things worked out well, primarily because we wanted to finish the series on a positive note. I had played 12 Test matches without tasting success and needed to know what victory felt like.

Failing any time is disheartening, but in cricket not to last even one ball is embarrassing. On the opening day of this fifth Test, it happened so quickly that I didn't even realise I was gone, given out, caught down the leg side to a ball that jumped off the pitch and grazed my glove on the way through to keeper Jack Richards. As it happened, I wasn't totally certain what the ball did, but the umpire's finger went up and the long, lonely walk began. It was one of those where the umpire had to be partly guessing, and I dared not look up for fear of appearing guilty. In such situations you never need to look, because you can tell the outcome by the reaction of the fielders, and when they started running towards the bowler, Gladstone Small, I knew my fate.

Dean Jones was the best non-walker I've ever seen because his reaction never gave any inkling as to his guilt. He just scratched centre, adjusted his pads and carried on in a 'business as usual' fashion. His method worked beautifully in this innings, as he quite obviously nicked one before he'd scored a run, but was given not out by umpire Steve Randall and went on to make 184 not out. He was one tough cookie mentally: most guys find it hard to settle down after not walking because of the nagging guilt. The really good players seem to be lucky, but if you analyse it more closely, they just make the most of their good fortune while less-equipped players don't capitalise on theirs.

It was just me and my thoughts on the way off, plus I could feel the eyes of the world homing in on me. I knew that every emotion I showed would be seen and scrutinised if need be. For me, the hardest part about not doing well was that I began to think I was a failure not just as a player but as a person, too. Cricketers will often equate their overall worth with their on-field performance, because that performance rules and dominates their lives and feeds their egos.

A valuable 73 in the second innings gave me belief in my ability to overcome adversity and to fight back. I knew I had a fierce competitive streak, but the skill lay in displaying it when it counted. Again, though, I fell into an amateurish piece of cricket, holing out to fieldsman Bill Athey at deep mid-off after he had been positioned out there. *You've blown another century* was my instant reaction, and it was a spot-on assessment. This was a clear-cut display of getting ahead of myself and not concentrating on the here and now, and it was a habit I needed to address before the selectors lost patience with me.

With two overs of the match to go, we were within one wicket of a victory with Peter Sleep bowling to John Emburey. AB seemed a little unsure at the start of this over as to who should bowl, so a mini 'team summit' was called with four or five players consulted. We were on the brink of a breakthrough, and I think AB in particular knew how important a win was for the guys who hadn't been successful before, so he wanted to get the decision-making process right. The genial South Australian skidded a top-spinner past the defence of England's premier spinner and we all lost the plot. The gorilla was tossed off our backs, and a huge amount of tension and pent-up stress that had come from being labelled a poor cricket side was expelled from our systems. All of a sudden, I didn't consider myself to be part of a team that was a failure. I was experiencing the winning vibe and it was great to share it with others who, like me, were virgins in the success stakes. Before this game, only AB, Greg Ritchie and Dirk Wellham of the XI who took the field for Australia had been involved in a Test-match win, so we carried on a bit for a team that had actually lost the series. The usual couple-of-dozen beers ended up on our heads and surrounding cricket kit, amid back-slapping and mutual congratulations, which was special, though in the pit of my stomach it didn't seem entirely right. We had lost and, worst of all, it was to the Poms – a fact that was immediately embedded in my personal archive, to be remembered whenever needed at later dates.

Losing to England was not all that stayed with me from the education that was this series. Before the Adelaide Test, I turned one of my nightmares into a reality: I missed the plane! Regrettably, I couldn't even come up with an original or worthy excuse, except the old favourite, 'The cab turned up late.' My mistake was the tight timeline I always worked to, because there wasn't too much margin for error and no Plan B to fall back on. I can't think of a worse feeling than waiting on the footpath at home, dressed in the Australian team blazer and with a massive kitbag and suitcase, sweating profusely. After making numerous calls to the taxi company, I was finally told that my booking from the previous night had been lost in the system. I was now in more trouble than Burke and Wills on a hot day; even if the cab was on its way I'd need either a plane delay or a bomb scare to get me out of trouble. Trying to look cool while running full pace towards the Ansett counter and then pushing in wasn't easy, so when the check-in representative uttered the words, 'I'm sorry, sir, the gate's already closed', I not only experienced a hot flush, I also saw my career path suddenly dissolve. *What the hell do I do now?* There was no one to hold my hand and I had a training session in three hours' time. How best to make a call to Allan Border from an airport pay phone wasn't a scenario that had been taught at school; all I could do was plead guilty and hope for the best. He was actually quite understanding and just said, 'Get here as quickly as you can.'

I eventually arrived at the hotel and tried to slink into the team environment without drawing too much attention to myself. I knew the guys would be thinking, *I'm glad it's him and not me.* Simmo gave me a pretty severe dressing-down, saying 'There is no excuse. It is not acceptable. If it happens again, there will be severe consequences. Make sure you get organised in the future.' I just swallowed my medicine and for the rest of my career booked a limo-type service.

The America's Cup was staged off Fremantle in Western Australia in 1986–87, and as part of the celebrations a one-day series involving Australia, England, Pakistan and the West Indies was staged in Perth. The competition began after the fourth Test. We were the party poopers, losing three straight and crashing out with a massive 164-run loss to the Windies in our final match. Earlier, Ian Botham's mauling of our opening bowler, Simon Davis, was the most brutal batting I'd ever seen. It was pure strength as he bludgeoned 20 runs in one over to swing the game in his team's favour. As this carnage unfolded, we knew we couldn't stop him because he had complete control of the situation. Shrewd field settings or well-thought-out deliveries weren't going to matter. It was his time and things were only going to change when he started to think too much about what he was doing. It was clinical and instinctive, unaffected by thought processes and uncluttered by expectations. Perhaps this is the key to being in the 'zone' – sporting nirvana.

Household names such as Javed Miandad, Imran Khan, Viv Richards and Michael Holding all had that special presence, and battling against and matching wits with them was enormous fun. Perhaps the reality that one-day cricket doesn't expose you in the same way as Test cricket gave me the added confidence to have a real go. There is more time to dissect a Test failure than to worry about a setback in the hustle and bustle of one-dayers, and mistakes don't usually have the same impact in the shorter game as they can in the five-day matches. I could let myself go and I did, and the results were pretty good – I scored 82 against Imran and Wasim Akram and top-scored with 29 (of 91) against the Windies. Playing a hook shot against Michael Holding at the WACA is a treasured memory, even though he was probably only in third gear. It's the feeling of instant respect that came with the stroke that lingers in my mind – the Windies loved to intimidate, but they also had time for and seemed to want the challenge of guys who took them on.

Elton John became a friendly face throughout the summer as he followed his beloved England around the country and supported his good mates Gower, Botham and Lamb. He was always respectful around the change rooms, remembered everyone's name, including wives and partners, and took the lot of us out (and fixed up the bill!) after our loss to England in this tournament. His openness and compassion belied his superstar status, and were traits that endeared him to all of the cricketers. He was also the only person I saw with whom the players actually wanted to swap memorabilia; the most sought-after items, not surprisingly, were his hats.

★

A whistle-stop tour to Sharjah in the United Arab Emirates followed soon after England left Australia with the Ashes, the America's Cup Challenge trophy and the World Series Cup in their possession, and success eluded us again in matches against Pakistan, India and England. Even though we gave ourselves plenty of chances to win, our self-belief on the slow, flat, turning pitches left us floundering at crucial stages. In truth, England and Australia were the ugly sisters during this event, while the Indian and Pakistani teams were showered with gifts of gold bars and jewellery from the obscenely wealthy oil-rich sheiks. A final between these two was almost a formality, given the heavy one-sided support they received from the crowds and the pitches that were specifically tailored to their requirements. From our point of view, we were hoping for success, but without the steeliness and ability to overcome obstacles out of our control we were not tough enough to be a threat to the two subcontinent teams.

Once again, but in a very different way to India, visiting the gold-filled shops of Dubai was a world away from places like Panania's all-you-can-eat buffet at the Star Lake Chinese Restaurant or the one-price-for-all haircuts at Roger's barber shop. I revelled in observing a different culture and the way the people lived. This was my second trip there; 12 months earlier, straight after the New Zealand tour, we had flown to the desert to lose the only match we played. My strongest memory of that trip was of its very beginning. Just before leaving for Sharjah I caught up with my school buddies, who wanted to know all the ins and outs of my 'glamorous' life – a welcome break from the fishbowl existence I was then trying so hard to come to terms with. Being a 'normal, average guy' was a nice role to take on and our regular after-school haunt of the Revesby Workers' Club gave me the relaxed, friendly atmosphere I desperately needed – so much so that the lethal cocktail of time-enhanced tales of school life and a generous alcohol intake left me in a poor state, with my bags not yet packed, my passport proving elusive and a plane to catch to cricket's newest and most exotic venue. In my haste to pull it all together I made a very large mistake, one that I couldn't hide or make an excuse for later. I will never forget coming face to face with stand-in captain Ray Bright after passing through customs at Sydney Airport (Allan Border had been given a break between his stressful time in New Zealand and a stint in county cricket with Essex). Here I was, on my second overseas tour, casually attired in my domestic 'travelling' one-day uniform of beige slacks and bottle-green open-neck shirt while everyone else was wearing their Australian team touring blazer. All I could muster was: 'Sorry, Spotty – I'll pay whatever fine the team thinks is right.'

During the '87 Sharjah tour there was an incident that attracted more headlines than our efforts on the park. It revolved around the free-spirited Greg Matthews. Apparently, Greg took umbrage at the guy running the barbecue at a function early in the tour, after the chef gave his specially cooked steak to another player. Even today, versions of the event vary from a friendly slap on the cook's body to a punch, but I can't believe it was anything vicious – I was unaware of the incident, even though I was maybe 20 metres away having my dinner. However, the affair became a major issue when Bob Simpson and the team's manager, Ian McDonald, fined Greg $1000, which represented a large proportion of his tour fee.

I didn't think it should have become such a big issue, but my intuition told me that Greg was being punished largely for previous infractions and perceived attitude problems. This was a message to all of us that off-field behaviour was now considered a major part of being a full-time professional cricketer and that we had to be accountable for our actions. It also showed us the power Simmo now wielded and that he was a guy you didn't want to get on the wrong side of – particularly as he had just been co-opted onto the selection panel. This change was announced by Ian McDonald on the team bus on the way to the airport to come home, and straight away you could sense that a couple of guys felt their careers might be over. This was especially true of Tim Zoehrer, who never warmed to Simmo, and vice versa.

Hero or villain?

During the 1980s, whenever it was time for a touring party to be named I made sure I was busy, to take my mind off the impending announcement. Often, I found myself taking a drive in the car and tuning into the radio to discover whether or not I'd made it. But when it came to this, having a surname that started with W was an inconvenience, as the team was always revealed in alphabetical order.

But in the case of the Australian squad for the 1987 'Cricket for

Peace' World Cup, there was one guy who had an even longer wait than me to hear his name. Unless he had been tipped off he probably wouldn't have even considered himself a chance, although he had that season become the youngest Australian bowler to reach 100 first-class wickets. He'd been preferred to Simon Davis, who had played eight World Series Cup matches in Australia in 1986–87 and then toured Sharjah. The new man's name was Andrew Zesers, and his shock selection emphasised the fact that this was a young squad, with only two guys – Allan Border and Peter Taylor – aged over 30. It was to be a vibrant and enthusiastic group who wanted to achieve and not just compete. Tim May had been preferred to Greg Matthews, Greg Dyer had tipped out Tim Zoehrer, and Tom Moody and Mike Veletta had come in for Greg Ritchie and Dirk Wellham. It was a team that had the look and feel of Bob Simpson stamped all over it.

Our first port of call was Madras, and the vivid and enduring image of the previous year's tied Test made us feel comfortable there. Immediately, we were training, preparing and working harder and more professionally than we'd ever done before. Errol Alcott, alias 'Hooter', the team physiotherapist, began our first training session by weighing each player in his jockstrap – in order to discover how much fluid we'd lost individually in a two-to-three hour session. Of course, everyone was different, but generally the lads who tipped the scales with force needed more fluid replenishment than the slight-of-frames such as S. Waugh. Neither was on this tour, but the two greatest sweaters in my time were, firstly and predictably, Merv Hughes, who had an all-over 'rug' that wasn't designed to cool things down, and, more surprisingly, Michael Slater, whose high metabolism and energy levels revealed themselves through perspiration.

Monitoring fluid loss was a large step forward for cricketers, who normally kept a tally of intake, but only of the after-match variety. Errol's was a well-thought-out blueprint that took into account factors such as the type of food eaten the night before a game. What might or might not dehydrate us during play? Chinese and Indian spices went out, pasta and protein came in. Likewise, our alcohol consumption was restricted and the drinking of bottled water encouraged. Cooling 'neckties' were made available and sweatbands were talked about, as were the benefits of fielding in long-sleeved shirts to prevent skin abrasions when diving for the ball. Our training was incredibly intense, reflecting a desire to simulate match conditions so we could acclimatise to the heat and be technically sharp and peaking at the right time. Time and time again, we were told by locals, liaison officials and observers that we were crazy to use up all our energy on the training paddock, that we needed to be fresh to win. There were occasions I doubted the wisdom of what we were doing, especially when the session was over and AB and Simmo would call us back out for an extra session of 'high ball catching', or 'cutting down the angles in the outfield' to create run-out opportunities. But we would always jump to attention in our sweat-soaked, dust-covered training outfits – the dirtier the better – which were for the first time complemented with shorts rather than track pants. We loved what we were doing; there was already an inkling that something special was brewing. Laughter at a training session is generally a precursor to success on the field, and while practice was physically taxing it was fun, too, even if the humour came from Simmo hitting someone on the foot, which he desperately tried to do during every close-catching routine.

I thought I was ready to do well. I'd invented a slower ball back in Australia, bowling in the nets to Greg Matthews who, after he first saw it, said, 'Man, that's a winner. That's going to be a real wicket-taker for you.' The delivery came out the back of my hand, a bit like how a leggie would bowl a wrong 'un. Just before the point of delivery, instead of keeping my wrist cocked, I'd flip it backwards and deliver the ball with my fingers pointed skyward instead of pulling down.

It came out very much delayed but with the same seam position, and quickly I realised it was extremely hard for a batsman to detect, especially a batsman who had never seen it before. The key for it to work well was for me to never grip the ball too tightly because otherwise I'd drag it down and deliver a 'half-tracker'. To further reduce the chances of this happening, I'd take a smaller last step to curtail my momentum at the crease and let the ball go a fraction earlier to gain more loop. When it came out well, it dipped, drifted fractionally like a spinner would want his best deliveries to, and finally bounce unexpectedly higher. I spent plenty of time trying to land the ball on a handkerchief or spot on the ground, perfecting the length needed to make the delivery dependable under pressure. This new, extra component to my game had a flow-on effect confidence-wise; now I believed I could make an impact in one-day cricket in all three disciplines – batting, bowling and fielding.

★

The choice of who should room with whom on tour is part of the man-managing role of the captain, coach and manager. Getting the right combination can be a very important factor in a team's harmony. Generally, the opening batsmen will be put together, as they need to know each other well and can form a strong bond that will show itself when they walk out and give the opposition a glimpse of how tight a unit the whole side is going to be. A new boy might be put with a veteran to give him some insights and help him learn a few short cuts. Perhaps two close mates might have their request to share a room agreed to. What you usually don't want is a non-smoker and a chain-smoker together, or a guy who likes to sleep and a party animal; but such cases can teach you to accept others' little habits and traits and get on with it.

Quite possibly the least compatible duo to share accommodation during my career were Brad Hogg and Stuart Law, whose early-morning routines were so contrasting that the pairing was doomed from the beginning. 'Hoggy' was up with the crow of a rooster, pumping out push-ups, sit-ups and stomach crunches by the hundred at the foot of their adjacent single beds, counting and grunting with each exertion, while 'Lawey' dozed away in the hope that his roomie would soon release all his pent-up energy. But just when equilibrium appeared to have been restored, the dumbbells would materialise and the arm-curls-in-front-of-the-mirror routine would commence with the same intensity. At night the roles would be reversed, with Stuart relaxing with a few cold ones while Brad was tucked up and ready for lights out after downing a couple of lime and sodas, even before the evening movie began. It was Oscar and Felix stuff.

On this tour, I bunked up with a good mate of mine, a bloke with whom I'd duelled in my junior rep days. The only downer to sharing with 'Moods' was that if there was a double bed and a single, I was always going to get the smaller one. Tom is 6 ft 8 (195 cm) and needed a bit of room to stretch out. On the flip side, his mother had thought-fully hidden bags of lollies throughout his suitcase just so the poor little fella wouldn't get too distressed on his first big tour away from home. The strawberry creams and milk bottles didn't see out the first day, but every zipper had a new surprise and the Saladas and water crackers with Vegemite on top proved a masterstroke, particularly with my unadventurous diet. Touring India 12 months earlier, I'd ordered a two-egg omelette with chicken every morning for 55 days because it was safe and non-spicy, and I saw no reason to be more adventurous this time around and risk a week of dashing to the toilet.

What a game of fluctuating momentum shifts and swings our open-ing match of this World Cup turned out to be. In the end, we won the game on the penultimate ball after India lost eight wickets for 62 runs from their final 12.5 overs. Even more remarkable than that collapse, I found myself bowling the last over with two options available to me: hero or villain.

I'm not sure to this day whether or not AB had planned to bowl me last up, or if he was forced into it. Our frontline bowlers, Craig McDermott and Bruce Reid, had bowled their allotted 10 overs earlier to try to get us back in the game, which they did magnificently. When I was thrown the ball by Allan for that final over, I really wanted to bowl, as opposed to pretending I did. Since I had come into the Australian team, my role in one-day cricket had been defined and repetitious, which was comforting in that I knew what I had to do, but I also longed for anything out of the ordinary that stimulated my competitive juices. Some players like to know exactly what their roles are, but I liked to have scope in my play and wanted to meet the unexpected head on. On this occasion, bowling to a No. 11, Maninder Singh, the plan I had in my head was simple: *Don't bowl a no-ball – get it on target, and preferably make it a yorker*. The odds were that he'd miss one trying to heave it to the leg side, or just crack under the weight of expectation.

I didn't get it quite right with any of the first four balls, instead delivering half-volleys in my eagerness to get the execution spot-on. A couple of twos and we were one run away from another potential tie in Madras, with India two away from achieving a memorable win. My composure was about to be tested to the max. Putting myself momentarily in the batsman's mind, as the great Alan Davidson had once advised me, I imagined Maninder would just want to get bat on ball and sneak the single that would gain at least a tie for his team. I tried to counter that strategy with the best straight yorker I could muster, so that any air swing would be fatal. Running up to bowl, I was aware the eyes of the world were on me, but I tried to concentrate purely on what I needed to do. I felt strong and somehow destined to deliver a killer blow. Two steps out from the crease I focused not on the batsman, but his crease line, because that's where I wanted to land the ball. My vision was clear and my mind was homing in on the intended target. Perfect. The ball came out like a dream and right on cue the No. 11 played a trademark wild slog that wouldn't have connected if I'd delivered him a basketball. Out of the parched soil flew the off stump. The sight was pure bliss for me and incited wild celebrations for our team. At that precise moment our hopes turned into genuine belief.

The first person to hug me was my captain, who was overwhelmed with emotion. He knew the value of winning such a close match, while I was ecstatic at having been able to repay the captain's faith in me, though I remained somewhat composed considering the gravity of the situation. What I was most pleased about were my own high expectations in such a situation and the enjoyment I got out of having everything hanging on how I performed under pressure. I loved the adrenaline rush and the tenseness of the circumstances. I actually craved the pressure, because it channelled my thoughts and gave me only one choice: to do the job and do it well.

Our manager, Alan Crompton, was an unsung hero in our victory at Madras. During the change of innings he'd gone to the umpires' room to query whether a shot by Dean Jones that had been signalled a four by Ravi Shastri after it had cleared his head in the outfield was actually a six. It had been quite obvious to all the Australian contingent who were directly behind the flight path of the ball that it had landed a couple of metres over the boundary. Umpire 'Dickie' Bird, whose initial reaction was a six, went to the Indian change rooms after Alan's inquiry, to ask Shastri, who remained noncommittal. However, when the bowler, Maninder Singh, also said he thought it was six, the umps changed our innings total from 268 to 270, giving us what proved to be a very crucial extra two runs. This was a courageous decision by the best umpire in world cricket and a noteworthy piece of sportsmanship from Maninder. Dickie was an eccentric, colourful character from Barnsley in Yorkshire, who loved his home comforts to the point of being obsessive. He didn't trust 'foreign' food, water or hygiene, and didn't venture outside his hotel in the six weeks he was in India. He ate one gingerbread man specially cooked by the local bakery in Barnsley each day, plus cans of baked beans, and didn't like shaking hands for fear of catching an infectious disease. He ingested his daily malaria tablets with great enthusiasm until he started to feel off colour and was told by Errol Alcott that he was actually consuming a weekly dose by the day. Now he was in trouble, he didn't even trust himself. But still he remained his affable, chatty self, always discussing a day's play with a boyish innocence and love for the game that rubbed off on the people he came into contact with.

Normally a win in a one-day international would be celebrated with a few quiet beers in the change rooms, but this time we felt compelled to take it a step further. This was a chance to reward our professional and hard-working approach, and also a chance to blow off some steam and let our guard down a bit with each other. Alan Crompton was kind enough to make his hotel suite available, while the Australian High Commission provided Aussie beer, which didn't touch our sides. The consensus among the group was that we were on the verge of doing something very special – everyone seemed to notice it, and I knew right there and then that we were going to win the World Cup. Proceedings ended with Mike Veletta's head coming into contact with a chandelier as he sat atop Tom Moody's shoulders, which at least gave him an excuse for his sore head the next morning.

The 16–1 outsiders tag we had been assigned before the tournament had diminished to 8–1 overnight, but by this stage my bet was safe.

A good mate of mine, Michael Welch, had called me before our opening match and told me that he had seen us quoted at odds better than 16s in one of the local betting shops. I can't remember exactly what price I got, but I definitely told him to put £50 on for me.

The game plan we had developed for these matches was quite simple and one that we all agreed could work if we maintained discipline and patience. Geoff Marsh would be the anchorman and try to bat through the innings as others accelerated around him. Simmo highlighted the fact that nine times out of 10 the team scoring the most singles in one-dayers wins, so we quickly realised that running between the wickets was an area in which we could dominate and give ourselves an advantage. In normal circumstances, after 15 overs we'd look to have our innings total at about 50 or 60 runs and at the halfway stage wanted to be around 100. Then it was six runs an over from the 25th over to the 40th and, if we had wickets in hand, 80 or 90 from the last 10, when that fine line between heightened aggression and agricultural slogging blurred. Wickets in hand was crucial to our success, because if we did achieve this we could then capitalise on a solid foundation if batting first or make an assault if we were chasing a target.

From a bowling perspective, we sought to be aggressive in the first 10 overs, trying to disrupt the opposition's rhythm. From there, we could either push hard in the quest to break their backbone or settle into a containment pattern. In the final overs, we aimed to bowl yorkers and changes of pace to keep the batsmen guessing. The quick fielders would patrol the boundaries late in the innings, running at the ball rather than around the boundary rope to minimise twos and threes, while AB would lead the way in the circle with his deadly throwing at the stumps. It was actually pretty simple stuff, but I believe we had a better idea of how we wanted to play than most other sides, who appeared to be relying heavily on individuals rather than working as a team.

After playing each of Zimbabwe, India and New Zealand twice, we finished second on run rates in our group, good enough to qualify for the semi-finals but meaning that we faced a clash with Pakistan, the No. 1 ranked side from the other half of the draw. Making the assignment much tougher was the fact that it was to be played at Lahore's Gaddafi Stadium in front of 40 000 cricket-mad fans.

Our only lapse as a team came against India at the Feroz Shah Kotla stadium in Delhi, an intimate but ugly venue with mismatched stands, poor seating, polluted air that stung the eyes, and a bumpy outfield. The home team had the momentum from ball one and we were never really in it, swamped by the heady atmosphere, but we took solace in the notion that it was good to get a bad performance out of the road early, rather than in the knockout second stage – even if we weren't sure the old adage had any validity.

Countering this loss, we pulled off a second miracle win, this time against the Kiwis in a rain-affected match. Again, I had the task of bowling the last over and with a bit of good fortune and cool-headedness managed to take two wickets and complete a run-out to snatch the game away from the side we considered most likely to stop our journey to the semi-finals. Despite my success in our opening match, I had not been an automatic choice to bowl at the death in this game, but again circumstances developed in such a way that it was me who was left as the best option. Once might be considered a fluke, but now I was convinced I was the man for the job.

★

Passing the hours away on a tour when there are days between one-day matches needs some inventiveness, especially for guys who aren't schooled in the art of card playing. Not to be outdone on this trip, the ones of us not addicted to 500 or euchre began a quest to find the Uno champion in each place we visited. I can still see Tom Moody sitting as proud as punch in the hotel garden with a 'crown' (a pair of Boonie's undies) on his head as the Uno King of Bhubaneshwar, which is located outside of Cuttack on the Indian east coast.

Eleven days earlier and 1100 km west of Bhubaneshwar, the hotel in Indore wasn't waterproofed too well and when an unexpected storm hit town, all our rooms sprang leaks and left us congregated in the hallway. Someone suggested a putting competition, which became competitive enough to catch the attention of New Zealand's Martin Crowe, who joined in to fill in time before our game due to start the following day. Throughout the six weeks of seemingly endless plane and bus journeys, Tim May and I engaged in a 100-game marathon of Othello, a game with the catchcry 'A minute to learn, a lifetime to master'. It requires foresight and concentration because one false move of the discs on the chequered playing surface means you're snookered and a goner. Trivial Pursuit was another crowd pleaser, but with the exception of Maysie's all-round knowledge, the rest of us could generally only manage to collect the orange sporting cheese and maybe the odd blue one for geography.

We arrived in Lahore to the headlines that we were 'a bunch of schoolboys', thanks to comments from Zaheer Abbas, one of Pakistan's greatest former batsmen, but the controversy didn't distract us and only helped to unite us further. The first thing that struck me about this, my first visit to Pakistan, was the lack of people compared to the situation that had confronted us in India: Lahore was a clean city with beautiful gardens and plenty of parklands. It was also my old NSW teammate Imran Khan's home turf, and the semi-final was supposed to be another leg in his grand farewell journey towards collecting the World Cup before retiring. Meanwhile, we were the underdogs and revelled in the tag. We felt like the mangy cross-bred 'mutts' that roamed the streets in the eternal hope of a good feed, up against the pampered poodles living on gourmet tinned food.

We were acutely aware that keeping the crowd noise down during the game would be a major factor, because the vociferous local support would lift them and distract us. We also knew that the only way to achieve this was to dominate the action on the field. And so it proved: after we won the toss and batted pretty much according to our usual plan, the hero of the nation, Imran, threatened to derail us with a magical spell of reverse swing bowling. The squealing and screaming coming from one particular stand situated square to the pitch was reminiscent of what I'm sure the Beatles would have copped everywhere they went back in the '60s. This particular enclosure was not only the loudest, but also the most colourful, with a strikingly brilliant array of red, orange and blue saris belonging to the female fans, who appeared to be losing the plot, delirious at the sight of their demigod cutting a swathe through the opposition.

My impression from the game was that a day out for the girls in Lahore was a rarity. Clearly, they intended to cash in and have the time of their lives as they played their part in lifting the home team's spirits. Every time Imran touched the ball they screamed hysterically, giving the match a truly 'big game' atmosphere – and he gave them plenty to cheer about. In contrast, when I managed to take 18 off the last over of our innings, which was bowled by Saleem Jaffer, there was complete and utter silence – except for the Australian team and support staff, who were going berserk.

In my view, a key to batting in one-day cricket is to pick a couple of areas that you know you can hit fours to. I set myself to hit across the line to the boundary either side of the fieldsman at deep mid-wicket. I was banking on full-length balls, so I stepped back in my crease to enable me to get up and under them; and I didn't want my intentions to be obvious – subtlety is the key to catching the bowler unawares. Saleem Jaffer was 18 months older than me and had been a regular member of the Pakistan one-day team for the previous year, but his nerves got the better of him and he was unable to bowl his intended yorkers. Instead, he dished up a series of good-length balls that I was able to have a full swing at, and when Pakistan's pursuit of victory finished precisely 18 runs short, he was the fall guy and consequently copped it. Cruel as it may seem, this young man hardly represented his country again, proving just how fickle professional sport can be. After all, any of my slogs could have gone to hand if he'd had an ounce of luck, but they didn't and his career was all but over. The implications of this 'blame game' didn't sit well with me for a long time, with the thought of this poor guy and the stigma of that loss he would always have to carry around. The truth was that we finished in a flurry, thanks to the earlier superb work of Geoff Marsh, David Boon and Dean Jones at the top of the order, and the inventive batting of Mike Veletta, whose premeditated shots and innovative footwork caught most people by surprise as he raced to 48 from 50 balls. Mike's batting during the Cup was a forerunner of future one-day batting methods, and is a legacy he can be proud of.

That deflating last over for Pakistan seemed to badly unsettle them, while we came out on a high. Poor Mansoor Akhtar not only ran out his opening partner, Rameez Raja, in the first over but then struggled for half an hour before being bowled by Craig 'Billy' McDermott. Worse was to follow, though, because when Mansoor returned home, his house was stoned and he was beaten up by his family and neighbours in retaliation for his part in Pakistan's loss. Billy showed his class, taking five wickets in conditions he generally didn't enjoy; his effort and attitude reflected our overall hard-nosed approach of hanging in and fighting like terriers when the defining segments of the game revealed themselves. We were all loving the closeness and tenseness of the battles and our team spirit kept shining through. Attention to detail and putting the interests of the side first were best exemplified by players diving on rock-hard outfields, players running in to offer encouragement for the bowlers and the reserves constantly running out drinks for the guys on the field were all signs we were a tight unit, made up of players who were going to support each other no matter what.

The streetfighter and the silver-spooner, Javed Miandad and Imran Khan, threatened to take away our dream, but still we kept our composure, knowing that our fitness levels and tough preparation were the deposits we'd made that could be withdrawn when required. The crowd began to disperse as soon as keeper Greg Dyer held the final chance, and 90 minutes later we were on a charter plane for Calcutta that almost everyone had expected the Pakistanis to be on. I hardly had time to let it all sink in: in four days' time we were to play either India or England in front of maybe 100 000 people for the chance to be world champs.

★

When we landed back on Indian soil we quickly discovered that the Indian people loved us, because we had knocked over their arch-enemy on their home turf. Twenty-four hours later, and our popularity was like a tsunami gathering up anyone and everything – thanks to England's shock victory over the host nation. Our support base had now gone from 20 million to one billion.

Calcutta certainly provided a magnificent spectacle for the final, with an estimated 90 000 people turning up to Eden Gardens even though India hadn't made it through. (*Wisden* consistently records that there were around 70 000 there, but I have no doubt that there were many more than that.) The only aspect I didn't like about the whole extravaganza was the cosmetic changes made to the city itself in the three days leading up to the final. In order to give the city a facelift in the eyes of the world, beggars were evicted from outside luxury hotels, street vendors usually situated around the stadium had their goods confiscated, and quite a few traders had their fast-food stands demolished. I heard stories that beggars had been threatened with the lock-up if they didn't leave town (mind you, the lock-up would probably have been a step up). Otherwise, the occasion was perfect. Walking out onto the billiard-table-like playing surface on match morning for warm-ups, with the crowd already settled in and eager for action, was a real 'goose-bump' moment. Here we were on the threshold of achieving a minor miracle, and the atmosphere was buzzing to the point of charging us up with even more energy.

For some reason, the toss in a big game always seems to take on extra significance. So we all peered out from the change rooms and watched intently as Allan Border bent down to pick the coin up; we knew straightaway we'd won it and would be batting. Billy McDermott gave his customary cheer and ran around mauling everyone in a gorilla-like hold; that was his way of getting rid of the nervous energy he'd built up in readiness for perhaps bowling the game's first over. Marsh and Boon began to arrange their gear, hold back on dialogue and retreat into their own world, cocooning themselves until they went out, while Dean Jones, our No. 3, was his usual upbeat, chirpy self. I sat quietly, confident I'd play an important role sometime during the game. As our trusty openers walked out to bat, there was an enormous roar and I felt a crazy adrenaline rush surge through me. *Jeez, there's no place to hide here* was all I could think. *You've got to stand up and enjoy the occasion as much as you can.*

Fifty overs later, we had 253 to defend, an even-money bet. Mike Veletta again played a gem of a cameo, using all of his crease to dance and manoeuvre around, prima ballerina-like, almost to the point of distracting the bowler. He finished 45 not out, made from just 31 balls of mayhem and madness, and perhaps the key partnership was the 73 for the fifth wicket put on in just 10 overs by him and AB. Mike and

I also managed to squeeze 11 from the final over, leaving us five down and satisfied after we'd been 4/168 in the 39th over.

I don't think any of us could eat much at the interval. Perhaps a piece of naan bread and rice, maybe some chicken and sweetcorn soup. Our anxiety levels were high, but it was a positive form of tension; we were ready and just wanted to get out there. A few last words from the captain and coach reaffirmed our plan to be aggressive early on, then settle in and be patient, and always pressure them in the field. I made some last-minute adjustments to my two large white sweatbands, retightened my laces on my boots to the point of being uncomfortable, reefed up two pairs of socks on either foot to iron out the creases, applied a liberal splash of sunscreen and finally put on the baggy green. Strange as it was, that was the headgear we had to wear. There was no special one-day cap, perhaps a reflection of the scant regard many had for the shorter game, and of its lack of tradition and history. I didn't need an invitation to wear the fabled felt but, looking back, it doesn't seem right that we were wearing Test caps in such an important limited-overs game.

The whole 50 overs went by in a blink. The match seesawed back and forth, with neither team able to grasp opportunities that presented themselves. England captain Mike Gatting's reverse sweep off Allan Border's first ball has been assigned to folklore as the shot that sank his team, but from my close vantage position, at backward point, the shot was only a few centimetres away from entering legendary status. It was obviously premeditated, because he was in position early and in fact hit it almost perfectly – but he finessed it with not quite enough blade, meaning it caught his own shoulder on the way through and popped straight up for a 'caught-behind' dismissal that both sides knew would be influential. 'Gatt' was like that: a player of enormous talent, an innovative mind and competitive juices, but often with a doomsday cloud hovering above him that seemed to drop bad karma on him from time to time.

I was heavily involved in the action from about midway through the innings until the conclusion and I loved every second of it. Well, almost . . .

Fielding at long-on to Tim May's bowling, I took what I thought was a match-winning catch off Gatting, until I looked down and saw the boundary rope between my legs. I could hardly bear to tell my great mate Maysie that despite his wild celebratory punching of the air a six was going to be recorded against his name. I don't think I could have had a worse experience as a fieldsman than that, and I tortured myself for the next couple of balls wondering whether or not I could have prevented the outcome. However, I knew I had to snap out of it, so I decided I'd done everything positive to make the catch and that was the end of the matter.

Not long after, I engineered the crucial run-out of Bill Athey, who was past his 50 and anchoring the England innings as David Boon had done so well for us earlier in the day. As soon as Athey hit the ball past me at wide mid-on, I said to myself, *Run-out chance.* The shot was struck well, but not hard enough to reach the boundary: certainly an easy two and perhaps a tight three. I sped after it, thinking all the way, *Run-out, run-out, he'll look for three.* The ball seemed to gather speed across the rock-hard outfield, and I kind of 'lassoed' it, knocking it back and throwing myself off-balance for a split second. In my peripheral vision, I saw Athey set off for the bowler's end and I immediately regained my balance and let the return rip. I banked on a low, flat throw that would skim off the even surface and into Bruce Reid's waiting hands. As soon as I threw it I knew Athey was gone, and for a fielder there is no greater thrill, especially in a Colosseum-like stadium filled with so many screaming fans.

Bowling at the death with the final in the balance was a real 'buzz' and knocking over the dangerous Allan Lamb and Phil DeFreitas ensured our victory. The only time I thought that maybe it wasn't meant to be was during the 49th over, which began with England needing

19 to win. Second ball of the over I had DeFreitas caught behind and given not out, and then he smashed me next ball to deep long-off. As soon as he hit it, I thought it was going to be tight, but as fate would have it, Bruce Reid at 6 ft 10 (208 cm) stretched out to haul the ball in before it sailed over the ropes. Again, someone was looking after me! Throughout these final overs I concentrated solely on hitting the stumps if the batsman missed, knowing that often a batsman trying to win a big game loses his clarity of thought because he's thinking too far ahead. I was in the 'zone' and knew there was only going to be one winner in these duels. I wish it was easy to replicate that state of mind, but if it was, everyone would be a champion. How to find that mindset remains one of the great unknowns in sport.

We were mentally drained and physically exhausted, but the victory lap was a joy, and so rewarding, especially as the majority of our supporters stayed to cheer us on. Our celebrations took place amid an expansive fireworks display that signalled the end of a tournament that was really something of a beginning for us. The look of contentment on AB's face was obvious to all of us; after the immense burden of captaining a losing side for the previous three years, he seemed so happy and relieved to be leading us around the ground. Right there and then, we knew this triumph could be the catalyst for an Australian cricket revival. But instead of crazy, over-the-top celebrations, we all but collapsed in the dressing-room, totally spent after six weeks of intense commitment. Even the team's ringleader, 'Scuba' O'Donnell, could only punch out one verse of 'his' song, the ol' Paper Lace classic 'Billy, Don't Be a Hero', on top of the physio's bench. Only weeks later did we find out that he'd been diagnosed with cancer and had played the entire World Cup suspecting he had a serious problem with one of his ribs but not knowing how potentially life-threatening the ailment was. Only Bob Simpson and Errol Alcott knew of his condition, as he didn't want to appear to be making excuses.

Overall, I'd describe the mood as a subdued one of complete sat-isfaction, with each of us trying to come to terms with what we'd achieved. There weren't a lot of extras in the room, but one comment from the ACB chairman, Malcolm Gray, who showed a lack of tact on occasion, confused those who didn't appreciate his humour. Turning to Tim May, who was quenching his thirst with a Kingfisher, Gray quipped, 'Do you reckon you deserve that?' It wasn't the icebreaker he'd envisaged, and continued the distrustful relationship between players and officials that was the order of the day.

My last recollections of the night of the World Cup final are of being mesmerised by the rotating metallic disco ball on the ceiling of the Oberoi Hotel and watching in amazement as Tim licked the well-trodden carpet after dropping an expensive bottle of 'champers'.

Earlier, at the official presentation, we were called up one by one to receive our individual winner's prize: a cheap medallion atop a paltry plastic base. A kid getting such a 'trophy' for being the most improved in the Under 10s would have felt ripped off. However, the organiser's cost cutting didn't dampen our spirits as we responded to Scuba's calls for impromptu versions of 'Billy, Don't Be a Hero', and Peter Allen's 'I Still Call Australia Home'. The prim-and-proper, well-to-do-end-of-town folk stared in stunned silence as we butchered our renditions.

None of us cared. It was our time.

11

Destination unknown

I felt from the start that the 1987–88 home season was going to be a true test of both the team's and my own improvement. I needed 'starts' to turn into hundreds, while Allan Border's attention had quickly and clearly been averted away from our one-day triumph to improving the team's credibility in the Test arena. The World Cup win had lifted our expectations, but with New Zealand our first opponent of the summer, it was time to deliver and we all knew it.

Allan and the team hierarchy decided before the first Test in Brisbane that there would be an alcohol ban, starting the day before each Test and ending at the conclusion of the match. For a social drinker like myself this wasn't any big deal, but for guys like AB, Boonie, 'Swamp' Marsh and Peter Sleep, who used the odd drink as a relaxant on an everyday basis, it was a big sacrifice and a good example to all of us. Times were changing and this was the sort of thing we needed to do to improve. Usually on the night before a Test, after a team meeting, the boys would go back to their rooms, take off their casual team shirts and head out as a big group for dinner. My roomie, 'Sounda' Sleep, said he'd pass on this particular team feed and catch up with a few mates instead. We made sure we took separate room keys, and then headed off in different directions. But not more than 15 minutes later, and less than 500 metres from our hotel, the bulk of our walking group's attention was diverted to some raucous goings-on at the Post Office Hotel.

Concealed among the office workers letting their hair down was Sounda, comfortably propped up at the bar blowing the froth off a couple of cold ones. Rather than ducking for cover, he ushered us over and asked, 'Who wants a beer?' Our stunned looks gave him a clue as to the seriousness of the situation, and he sheepishly asked, 'You guys weren't serious, were you?' Sounda was one of only two members of the Australian squad for this Test who hadn't been part of the World Cup (Merv Hughes was the other). Times might have been changing, but obviously there were going to be some teething problems along the way.

A series win against New Zealand confirmed our new-found self belief and growth as a unit, particularly as the Kiwis had probably their best bowling attack ever in Richard Hadlee, Danny Morrison, Ewen Chatfield and John Bracewell. To be totally honest, though, the series should have been drawn. After we won the first Test by nine wickets and the second was drawn, the outcome came down to a cliffhanger of a climax in Melbourne, where Mike Whitney and Craig McDermott somehow survived for 29 deliveries in a last-wicket salvation act. Thanks to sheer will and determination, especially from 'Whit', who if you threw him 10 balls in the nets would miss five, AB finally had his first Test series win as captain after 30 Tests in charge.

Good decisions from umpires are accepted and forgotten just as quickly as bad ones cause angst and linger in the memory. Morrison's lbw shout on McDermott was as 'plumb' as there ever was in the history of cricket, and considering the importance of the decision the Kiwis kept their composure remarkably well. They were robbed, but it didn't stop us from running onto the field and greeting the boys as heroes. Being a devout 'Bluebagger', Whit quickly grabbed NSW teammates Greg Dyer and me and dazzled us with his magnetic personality and already-exaggerated tales of his batting prowess.

From the dressing-room, we headed pretty much straight to the airport because, as always seemed to be the case, we had to catch a plane straight after the match. For most of the team, this somewhat killed the emotion and desire to unwind, but not to be deterred, our happy little trio embarked on a crusade to drink the Ansett aircraft dry of its alcohol contents before we hit Perth airport. We pursued our goal with vigour, setting a cracking pace, and I was mightily relieved to look at my watch upon arrival and see it was just after midnight. I was imagining a solid meal, a couple of bottles of water, then lights out and a chance to sleep it off.

How wrong could I be? Due to the time difference it was only 9 p.m., and my Blues comrades' plans contrasted vastly with mine. A pillaging of the hotel's liquor bar was followed by an evening on the town. Few things remain unclouded from the ensuing frivolities, except for the suicidal mission we set ourselves of drinking the bar from left to right, top to bottom. Greg's tactical chunder upon advancement to the middle row of the bar was seen as a moral victory to Whitney and Waugh, but as we were later to find out, it was in fact a clever byplay that paid handsome dividends later on. My next and final recollection of the evening are the needle-like bristles of Whit's five-day growth stabbing my face as he embraced Greg and me in an affectionately aggressive bear hug. Balance was a hurdle that couldn't be overcome, and as soon as Whit's power took control we became mobile, and our stumbling rotations became a whirling dervish. Down we went, scattering tables, patrons and drinks everywhere before we were escorted to a nearby taxi rank. Some hours later I awoke with no idea where I was or how I got there, but cognisant enough to recognise the vibrant orange colour of carrots and to inhale the sharp pungent odour of the vomit my head was nestled in as I lay 'starfished' in my underwear. The next two days were a struggle for survival, with my roommate, Tim May, supplying cups of water, headache tables and bread rolls to keep me in the land of the living. My only saving grace was that the day after the Test was an off day as far as training was concerned, but even the day after that I was cursing my stupidity and promising myself 'Never again'. Again!

Two days after the bender, Whit walked up to reception to enquire as to his room number, which had slipped his mind.

'You're in room 227, Mr Whitney,' said the guy behind the counter immediately.

'How do you know that?' Whit replied.

'I carried you up there two days ago, Mr Whitney.'

Upon reflection, Richard Hadlee's comments about my cricket before the Melbourne Test probably weren't too far off the mark. He had said I was overrated and still had a long way to go, but then admitted he might be wrong when I was 55 not out at the end of day one in our first innings. Feeling buoyed by the retraction that appeared in his newspaper column, I went out and proceeded to pop up the first ball of the day, from 'Cement Head' Bracewell, to bat-pad on the off side. It was a doubly disappointing way to get out, particularly after I had thrown a century away in the previous Test, in Adelaide, falling lbw to Martin Snedden for 61 on a wicket that Allan Border batted on for 599 minutes while scoring 205. Besides being a lazy shot to a guy who was a steady bowler at best, on the world's flattest pitch, I was dismissed by the first ball I faced after a drinks break. As I struggled to come to terms with my wasted chance, I saw how a great player made the most of an opportunity. AB looked immoveable, unwavering in his concentration and shot selection, frustrating the Kiwis into eventually bowling to the areas he wanted them to by constantly ignoring their attempts to get him to play a loose shot.

'Switching on' is a key element to batting, but unless you realise that your method isn't working to its full potential, you'll keep making the same mistakes. My focus wasn't as sharp as it could have been or as clear as I'd imagined. Looking back, I think sometimes my mind was tricking me into thinking that everybody would be easing their way into things after an interval. Certainly, the need for total and utter devotion to each and every ball wasn't being met. I was being hampered by a lack of attention to detail. The lights were on, but the dimmer switch needed to be turned up.

While the umpiring of this time was widely agreed to be rarely up to standard under pressure, the biggest controversy of the series came on the opening day of the third Test, when Greg Dyer tumbled down the leg side in a diving attempt to claim the wicket of New Zealand's No. 3, Andrew Jones. Greg went one-handed with his left glove, but came up holding the ball in his right hand. At the time he seemed unsure if he'd completed the catch, but the umpire had given it out and the boys rushed him in the excitement of a key breakthrough. Unfortunately, a slow-motion replay can make a split-second incident look embarrassingly bad, and as soon as Greg saw vision of the dismissal at the end of the day he knew he had made a mistake in not calling the batsman back. He desperately wanted to call a media conference and apologise, but was hamstrung by the board's player code, which prevented comment on umpiring decisions. Commonsense was passed over and a tricky situation that could have been diffused instead escalated by the minute. Greg withdrew into his shell and played without emotion or intensity, racked with guilt and frustrated by the lack of cooperation from team management and the board. He was on a slippery slope from that moment; in the following off-season he was dropped from the Australian side and within 12 months of the Melbourne Test was out of the NSW side as well, despite the fact he'd been the Blues' captain. As fate would have it, that latter sacking came about after he was a victim of circumstances again, though his lack of authority and desire to avoid confrontation did cost him. When Geoff Lawson got tangled up with the South Australian batsman Darren Lehmann at the Adelaide Oval as Lehmann and Andrew Hilditch attempted a quick single, the laws of the game clearly stated that Lehmann was short of his ground and technically out. I wasn't there, as I was involved in the World Series Cup, but it seems to me that sportsmanship should have dictated that the appeal be withdrawn. But the battle-hardened Lawson, with steam coming out of his ears, apparently demanded that his captain not recall the rising star from SA. Of course, Greg, as the man in charge, was the one to cop it in the neck afterwards and that he did, ensuring that his tertiary qualifications as an accountant were about to become very useful. Henry, ironically, was his replacement as NSW captain.

Greg should have got more support from everyone associated with both the Australian and NSW teams, including his mates. But again, when individuals are desperately trying to develop their careers, the compassion that gels all great teams isn't always what it should be. Neither Australia nor NSW were as successful as they could be at that time, and Greg fought his battles pretty much alone, partly due to his inner strength and strong character, and gave an 'Everything's okay' impression, which, of course, it wasn't. The bottling-up of his anger ate away at him to the point where his on-field play started to deteriorate. The controversy and innuendo that he was a cheat followed him, and must have been torture for such an honest, decent guy.

By the conclusion of the '87–88 summer, I was still treading water. I had the skills and willpower but not quite that steely self-belief that was going to take me to the next level. Simmo continued to counsel me as best he could, but I knew I had to improve myself through hours in the nets and patience in everything I was doing. Scores of 21, 61, 55, 10, 27 and 20 from the five Tests were promising but far from satisfying; something was stopping me getting to a century. It was really very simple. I wanted it too much and each time I began to think, *This is the innings*, I perished. The destination had become the focus, not the journey. Until I could better break down my thoughts, there was always going to be a tug of war in my mind.

Strangely enough, my bowling had developed at a greater rate than my infinitely stronger suit of batting. Further emphasising how much cricket is played between the ears was my totally relaxed state of mind when I was bowling. I didn't feel the constraints I felt when batting – being able to mess up one ball and immediately get another opportunity is a tremendous safety valve to have as a bowler. I could let my natural aggressive style loose, sending down bumpers when I wanted to and enjoying the one-on-one confrontations.

At the same time, I was proud of my advancements in the NSW team. At season's start I had put my hand up to bat at No. 3 when no one else wanted the job – I saw it as a chance to step out of my comfort zone, improve my cricket and give me more flexibility in the eyes of the Australian selectors. I also believed that I needed to show everyone that I was a Test-class player capable of accepting a challenge when the team needed me.

After scoring 170 against a Victorian team that included Merv Hughes and Tony Dodemaide, who both played Test cricket during the season, I gave the press a bit of a spray when I said, 'I think that will keep a few people quiet for a while.' Deep down, I knew the journos were fair in their criticisms, but in getting my frustrations out I felt more comfortable because some excess baggage had been shelved.

The signs of a revival in Australia's fortunes were certainly there. This progress was due largely to Lawrie Sawle, a chairman of selectors who kept himself away from the headlines, but whose foresight was a driving force at the selection table. A gentleman who matched his cricket knowledge with a commonsense approach, Lawrie had a great eye for talent and also, more importantly, for strength of character, and he possessed an intuitive feel for the type of player who was going to be a long-term proposition for the Aussie side. With Simmo and AB, he started to form a solid triumvirate, each man with an eye not only for the present but also with a view to the future. Allan's style had begun to loosen up, as one would expect with some success on his captaincy résumé and the fact that Dean Jones, Geoff Marsh and David Boon had all taken responsibility with the bat.

By 1987, Lynette and I felt that it was time to spread our wings and take our relationship to the next level – living together away from home. A contract was secured in the Lancashire League, playing for the old mill village of Nelson. Each side had an overseas professional to lift the standard and draw patrons through the gate. Viv Richards played at Rishton and was obviously a huge drawcard, while Dave Gilbert lined up at East Lancashire and the South African pace bowler Fanie de Villiers at Todmorden to make it one of the strongest group of pros ever assembled in that league.

As the only paid player in the Nelson side, I quickly realised that there were high expectations to be met, not least because the money I was on was roughly the same as the town butcher earnt in a year. I remember that fellow well: Paul Garrety batted three, gave us quality cuts during the week and used a bat heavier than Sachin Tendulkar's on the weekend, which he wielded with ease.

Arriving at our digs for the first time was a bit of a shock for both of us, even though we hadn't set out sights too high. We stood in front of a mill house used by the workers in the early 1900s, into which had been built a terrace house not more than 4 metres wide. Our front yard was about a square metre of concrete. Adjoining our new home were endless replicas, forming a Lego-like row fronted by a cobblestone street. On the other side was an identical row of houses in mirror image to ours.

But the real concern for Lynette and me was the seven different latches and accompanying bolts that covered the door. This wasn't exactly a reassuring sight, and when all our washing was stolen from the clothesline in the back courtyard two days later we knew the neighbourhood wasn't about to throw a party to welcome us. Having to put pound coins into an archaic gas heater to thaw us out quickly went from having novelty value to being a pain in the butt when we ran out of coins and had to sit frozen in front of a TV choosing between *East-Enders*, a re-run of *Neighbours* or the world snooker championships. A month of continual rain in June led to a nasty discovery when the damp environment of our 'digs' and the abysmal weather combined to create a mouldy growth that sealed shut our kitchen drawers. It didn't fill us with confidence about our future health.

However, first impressions aren't always the right ones, and it became a wonderful life experience to live in such a closed environment, where the local cricket club was the centre of everyone's social life. The guys trained, played and drank there most nights, and the wives and girlfriends organised fundraising activities and catering on match days. Many of the people I met hadn't been to London in their lifetime, with Manchester being as far away as they'd ventured. As soon as the temperature got anywhere near 20°C, our neighbours would be sunbaking on the cobblestone streets while we contemplated taking off the jumper.

Time off during the week between matches allowed Lynette and me to day-trip to places like London, where we did the tourist thing on the red bus, York and the Lake District. A visit to Paris was a big cultural step for the boy from Panania, who had never dreamt of taking the elevator up the Eiffel Tower or being astonished at the small size of the *Mona Lisa* in the Louvre.

Living together gave us a chance to see whether we were compatible; for the first time we had to rely on one another instead of family and friends. It was a big change from living at home, having your meals cooked, washing done and everything catered for. I had to take another person into account rather than just worrying about myself, and further, for the first time I was the breadwinner. We had fun burning pots and pans, interacting with other couples and learning about each other's habits, but most of all we loved the freedom and companionship that enabled us to explore new horizons together.

It was to be a very wet summer, with most games being played in conditions where the bowlers couldn't take a full run-up and on pitches that were difficult to play shots on. As a young pro keen to make an impression and give value for money, I nearly always bowled half the team's allotted 46 overs each week, but would pay the price when stress fractures in my back revealed themselves the following year.

Collections at the game for a batsman who scores 50 or a bowler who takes six wickets are traditions of the Lancashire League and hotly sought after by the amateurs. For an international player, scoring 50 against a 'chippie' or 'sparky' wasn't exactly a momentous feat, so my collections regularly ended up on the bar for the guys to have a drink. Mind you, to get a decent collection you had to capture their imagination or play entertainingly. My NSW teammate of the mid-'80s, John Dyson, recounts the tale of a laborious 50 he scored in one league match that so enraptured the crowd that the collection box came back with an assortment of rocks and bottle tops as marks of their appreciation.

Without doubt, the highlight of my on-field action was the battle against the legendary Vivian Richards, in a game that went down to the last over and in which I stuffed up – getting out for 93 in reply to Viv's earlier century. That mistake, however, is not my lasting recollection of the encounter, rather the serious bouncer I let rip that ended up hitting him right between the eyes. As usual, Viv had just waltzed out and assumed ownership of the ground, taking control of the tempo and mood of the game from the first ball he faced, playing whatever shot he felt like whenever he deemed it appropriate. But as the opposition pro I couldn't let it be seen that I was bowing to him, so when he kept on planting his foot down the pitch and hoicking me across the line, I decided it was time for some 'chin music'.

A bit of extra run up speed and a fuller retraction of the wrist and shoulder gave me a yard more pace and the great one was a split second late with his shot, taking the full impact flush on his forehead. I was more shocked than he was, as I waited for him to crumble under the impact. Instead, he just shook his head, regathered his composure and replied to my 'Are you okay?' with 'No problem, man. It got me in the hard spot.' Now, that's impressive body language and strength of character, to dismiss such a blow so lightly, because I know it definitely hurt him. His sense of pride was never going to allow him to show pain.

One of my reasons for playing league cricket was to gather experience in English conditions with an eye to the 1989 Ashes series. So when Somerset's captain, Peter Roebuck, called up and asked me to fill in for their injured overseas pro, Martin Crowe, I jumped at the chance. In 1987, this involved only four first-class games, but the month developed into one of the most influential periods of my whole career. I came up against some feared West Indian quicks – Hampshire's Malcolm Marshall, Gloucestershire's Courtney Walsh and Surrey's Sylvester Clarke – and their pace was something I hadn't confronted in a first-class match. This was particularly true of the ferocious Clarke, who bowled the most awkward and nastiest spell I ever encountered in a match at the Oval. All week in the lead-up to that match, the Somerset boys had been talking about the ferocity and 'strike rate' of Clarke. By strike rate, they were referring not to the wickets he took but to the number of helmets he cracked per game. As the contest drew nearer I could see the determination of the players disintegrating, and by the time we pulled on the whites half the boys were already out. Pace and bounce of the kind Clarke could muster is something you can't prepare for; it's an assault both physically and mentally and the moment you weaken and think about what might happen, you're either out or injured. I think this was the first time I experienced a genuine awareness that if I didn't concentrate there would be serious implications.

I now know that in confrontations like this, the initial onslaught either hypnotises your state of mind or accentuates your senses. Facing Clarke, I felt good fear, in that it made me sharp and alert, instead of bad fear, which would have clouded me in sluggishness and doubt. After the first barrage, which was a bit like being thrown into a freezing cold pool, I gradually got used to the conditions and came to life. I began to really enjoy the challenge of trying to avoid his steepling bouncers, which were generated by a supposedly double-jointed shoulderblade. This guy was a one-off, a mountain of a man, who bowled in half-spikes off about 12 paces at close to a hundred miles per hour. Scoring a century was not in my thoughts during the time it took me to score my first 20 or 30 runs, but I could feel myself getting off on the danger aspect of the duel. It was the raw element of the battle, the one-on-one tussle, that made the adrenaline kick in. I loved it, and knew afterwards, as I reflected on an innings of 111 not out, that I'd made a huge breakthrough in my game. I could score runs against the quickest of bowlers. And he was a West Indian. To succeed against one of the fast men from the Caribbean was a great notch to have on my belt in an era in which they pretty much did what they liked.

With my confidence rocketing, two weeks later I made an equally difficult hundred on a dodgy pitch at Gloucester against Courtney Walsh. But perhaps more significantly I got a close look at the psyche of English cricket. Chasing 282, we had reached 8/251 and I was dominating the attack, unbeaten on 137. Neil Mallender and I had put on 113 when suddenly Roebuck began clapping on the player's balcony, signalling his intent to declare. I couldn't believe my eyes. We'd battled our guts out to get on top of Walsh and just when we looked like getting a first-innings lead, our team was taking the soft option of declaring behind in the hope of being set a reasonable fourth-innings target. Perhaps immaturely, I threw my bat down in disgust and reluctantly walked off, to find a somewhat startled captain who most likely was thinking, 'Who does this young upstart think he is?' Immediately, Peter and I agreed to disagree, but the captain is ultimately always right and soon after I gave myself an upper cut and got on with the job.

I'm sure the confidence gained during my county experience in 1987 helped me throughout the World Cup. In 1988, I was lucky enough to again share overseas import duties with Martin Crowe. I wanted to study Martin at close quarters, and this swayed my decision to sign with Somerset rather than Middlesex. The chance to observe him didn't eventuate because he once more succumbed to injury, but Martin was still a master technician and a role model. When he batted, everything seemed to be in the perfect position. He carried himself well at the crease, always appearing in control and rarely, if ever, looking out of form.

Besides the bonus for me of playing most games in Martin's absence, Lynette and I also went up a few grades in the pecking order, moving into his digs when he returned to New Zealand. A 425-year-old thatched cottage with four fireplaces and crammed with priceless antiques, perched on 25 hectares, gave me a glimpse of life at the top level. While I appreciated the comforts, I resolved not to lose touch with the everyday members of the club and cricket community, as had reportedly happened to a few senior players at Somerset in years gone past.

By the end of the 1988 English season, I knew I had evolved into a much better player, one who was confident and thrived under pressure and responsibility. But I still had to overcome what had become a major hurdle: a Test century. It was something I was now beginning to crave, not for the critics' sake, but for my own peace of mind.

Death by silence

Perched atop an old wooden stool sipping a Budweiser after wolfing down a pizza and nachos was like finding an oasis in the desert. The Australian team were in a buoyant mood, revelling in some home comforts at the bar of the American embassy in the troubled city of Peshawar, located on the Pakistan–Afghanistan border. The strength of alcohol in the foreign beer had an immediate effect on me and I opened up to the guy sitting next to me, team veteran Graeme Wood.

'I'm not sure I'm ever going to score a Test hundred,' I said. 'I just can't seem to make the breakthrough with the bat.'

'You'll get there one day,' he responded. 'You'll get a hundred and it will all seem worthwhile. You'll look back on this time and wonder why you were worrying so much.'

Woody's words stuck with me for some reason – probably because he was the first senior person in the Australian team to actually tell me I *could* do it. Others, I guess, had just assumed I would progress naturally. Woody wasn't the greatest mentor around, but he was experienced, and his reassuring voice was what I needed as I struggled through a tough time that bordered on despair. In the two diabolical Tests I had played to that point on this controversial tour, I'd scored 33 runs in four innings. I was no fun to be around, I'm sure, blaming everything except the true cause: my attitude.

The other good news from that night came when we were informed that we didn't have to sign a form saying we were alcoholics in order to get served any type of alcohol. In this land of prohibition, the only way you can get a drink is to admit to having a problem, then sign a document and receive a limited supply in return. Normally the team manager would vouch for all of us and sign one form on our behalf. The other way was to get a consignment from the Australian High Commission and drink it in the manager's room, but, of course, they didn't want to provide us with their entire quota.

A tour of Pakistan was always seen by Australian cricketers of the '80s as the worst to go on – little beer, no social life, poor hotels, dodgy food and dubious umpiring. These were the thought processes we took with us, and the moment our pessimistic expectations came to fruition in the slightest way we cocooned ourselves from the voice of reason. Instead we preferred to indulge in a siege mentality and let the negativity snowball out of control. We were fighting a sombre atmosphere from day one, with the country in mourning after the death of their leader, General Zia, in a plane crash. Before we left Australia, ACB chairman Malcolm Gray addressed the team at a training camp in Brisbane, expressing concerns about the instability in Pakistan and the need for us to make sure there was no repeat of the controversial finger-pointing verbal clash between England captain Mike Gatting and umpire Shakoor Rana the previous year, which soured relations between the two countries involved.

Talk among the Australian team from the very beginning of the '88 tour revolved around horror tales from previous trips. We expected to get ripped off in the first Test, on a dustbowl of a pitch and plagued by home-team umpiring, then be dealt two flat wickets to ensure draws and soothe relations tarnished by the opening Test debacle. Of course, we'd still be a 0-1 series loser. Things were out of kilter from the very first morning of the tour, when Woody said it was 'so-and-so' day, in reference to a well-known Aussie Rules player who wore a number that corresponded to the days left on tour. Trying to find a famous VFL or rugby league player to match every number was sometimes difficult, but invariably a name came up. Unintentionally, a negative trend had started, as we counted down days as if it was a relief that a day was gone rather than taking each day as a challenge and not looking too far ahead.

For a new boy like Ian Healy, whose selection as the only wicket-keeper had been a complete shock, it was the toughest possible place to start your international career. Although extremely inexperienced, Heals exhibited composure in his dealings with the media and professionalism in his training work ethic. You could tell he also had a larrikin, mischievous streak lurking beneath the surface. It was also the first Test tour for Tim May, who I had met at the World Cup the previous year. Once again the strong bond between Tim and me was evident and we spent a lot of time together, enjoying each other's humour and sense of adventure.

The second of two lead-up games before the first Test was played in Quetta, and while it wasn't memorable from a cricket point of view, it was because of my toilet troubles. Invariably, each player would go through a phase of adjusting to the local food. Generally it's not too serious and a couple of Imodium tablets counter the bugs and parasites and 'clog up' the system enough for normal activities to eventually resume. It's almost an initiation ceremony for first-time tourists to each country of the subcontinent. A problem is that the onset of loose bowel motions can catch you off guard initially, and it was a left hamstring stretch on the fence during warm-ups before training that left me in an awkward predicament. An extra lunge to touch the toes left me prone, and once that irretrievable impulse took over all I could do was to try to prevent the damage as best I could. I snuck off to the dressing-sheds, holding the contents in and hoping the boys hadn't noticed my little mishap but equally sure someone would have spotted it, to be brought up at the next team fines night.

Still, my stomach problem was a minor ailment compared to what happened to Jamie Siddons on his first and what proved, unluckily, to be his only overseas tour. Breaking one of the golden rules – 'Don't drink anything you haven't personally opened or taken the top off' – Jamie dropped a couple of cubes of ice into his lukewarm beer to chill it up a bit. That might have been okay if they'd been bottled-water ice cubes, but being at the private residence of one of the ambassadors the ice might have been made from tap water or could have been handled by bare hands. The next day the poor bloke was 'death warmed up', unable to move except to throw up, and in constant pain. Within days, his gaunt appearance meant he looked like tennis champion Ivan Lendl and his aspirations of a Test berth, most probably mine, were lost. For the following 12 months, 'Spanner' suffered a succession of medical problems and couldn't eat much at all. While he went on to establish some Sheffield Shield run-scoring records, his whole international career evaporated as quickly as those dodgy ice cubes. Thankfully, he at least appeared in the final match we played in Pakistan – the only one-day international of the tour, which we lost on a countback, having lost eight wickets to the home team's seven when the innings totals finished level – and he played the spin with a real touch of class, hitting the magician, Abdul Qadir, inside out through the covers in a manner that left everyone in awe. He and Darren Berry, the Victorian and South Australian gloveman, were the best Australian players I've seen not to have had the privilege of having the baggy green bestowed upon them.

Not long before the first Test came a rare opportunity to get out of the team hotel and have a day out on Karachi Harbour. Tales from guys who had been to Karachi before of a fantastic day catching crabs meant this was too good an opportunity to pass up, especially when the other options available were to watch the local TV stations, get sunburnt around the pool, or go to the markets and buy a couple of cheap leather coats you'd never wear again or perhaps a silk Persian rug you'd find was actually wool when you got home.

Five of us – Tony Dodemaide, Peter Taylor, Tim May, Peter Sleep and I – took up the challenge. A garishly decorated taxi – internally lined with carpet on the walls and roof, and with religious ornaments dangling from the rear-vision mirror that partially obscured the driver's line of sight, and with a horn that was continually being shoved and prodded – dropped us at a wharf where we rendezvoused with our contact. From here we set off on an obstacle course, jumping from boat to boat and scurrying down alleyways until we found our craft for the day: an old fishing boat that looked well used but, to my uneducated eye, quite sturdy. Plenty of shady characters were lurking among the vessels we'd just clambered over, and in one case I spotted a couple of large knives and a revolver protruding out of the top of some tattered trousers.

Just being out of the hotel room on the harbour, with fresh air and the whiff of sea salt, made for a great day. Only one blue swimmer crab committed suicide by taking the chicken-gut bait, and that unfortunate crustacean was to be mine. Thus I was crowned the 'Crab King of Karachi'. On the homeward leg of our cruise, Maysie, in his 'master of disaster' guise, began to suffer from either a touch of sunstroke or an overdose of salt water from his frolicking on the harbour and was in desperate need of fluid replacement. The bad news for him was that his quota of soft drink had been gulped down with the naan bread, onion mash and secret stash of mud crabs the crew had cooked up for us for lunch. With half a bottle of Pepsi left to myself, I became the target of 10 minutes of pleading, leading up to the point of complete desperation where Tim offered me 100 US dollars for a mouthful of the 'truckies' toothbrush'.

I milked the situation as best I could, always knowing that Maysie might be handy for the upcoming Test, until finally I relented and handed him the remainder. His dehydration problem was fixed, but his head still shone like a beacon: the sunburn issue looked a far greater menace than his parched throat. Even so, we all agreed that the day had been worth the effort, because we'd had a few laughs and, in my case at least, a taste for adventure had been satisfied.

Our state of mind after the first Test debacle was best summed up by one particular penalty awarded at the postmatch fines meeting. It was decided to fine Graeme Wood for kicking a Pakistani fieldsman's helmet that had been lying unused on the ground behind the keeper. This was obviously an uncivil act, but there was a slight twist in that Graeme wasn't relieved of his rupees because of his boot but because there hadn't been a head inside the helmet. We all had a good laugh and, of course, it was in jest, but still it provides a glimpse of the attitude that had developed.

It's hard to know where to start when describing the debacle of the Test played in Karachi. It was the stuff of a horror-movie script. A shockingly underprepared pitch that resembled a parched creek bed with cracks and fissures running through it and not a blade of grass in sight, made the toss a must-win affair. But a despondent outlook in a team will often be reflected in the outcome of the coin toss, so AB was odds on to get the call wrong. Which, of course, he did.

Pakistan went in minus their captain, Imran Khan, who refused to play cricket in Pakistan in September–October because of the oppressive conditions that he considered dangerous to players' health. In his place came the people's hero from the Karachi backblocks, Javed Miandad, whose fierce competitive spirit had few equals, not to mention his trait of brazenly sledging bowlers and fielders while he batted.

We had the perfect start when Bruce Reid accounted for Mudassar Nazar in the first over with an in-swinger. Bruce could have been a legend had the gods been kinder to him. His frame resembled a stick insect and couldn't do his rhythmical flowing action justice over any extended period of time. This stunted his right to be cast alongside the likes of Glenn McGrath and Dennis Lillee in the pantheon of fast-bowling greats. Not long after Mudassar's dismissal, Heals, on his Test debut, took a stunning catch, diving forward, to dismiss Rameez Raja, and give us the impetus we had so hoped for. I'm sure our new wicketkeeper would have been relieved to take an early catch to settle his nerves, because he was an unknown quantity to the rest of us. When he snared that one to get Rameez, we immediately thought, *We've got a beauty here.*

Sadly, these were our last fond memories of the match. The arrival of the prickly Javed in the middle had everyone on edge. We knew he was the player the Pakistanis all loved to bat with, and as usual he strutted around like he owned the place. Consecutive unsuccessful lbw shouts when he was on 15, both from the bowling of Tim May and both of which we thought were quite obviously out, not only set the tone but dramatically altered the course of the match. Javed was a brilliant watcher of the ball, leaving it as late as possible off the pitch before playing his shots, particularly against the spinners. But it was like he was having a game of French cricket in the backyard – except he wasn't going to be given out lbw. Most frustrating of all, he knew it and would tell you so whenever he got to the non-striker's end. I recall him saying to me just out of earshot from the umpires, during one of my fruitless spells in the debilitating heat, 'What are you doing? Don't waste your time. This is my turf.' He was referring to an earlier appeal for leg before. Javed's wry smile and ultraconfident body language conveyed the belief that we were never going to get him out. He basically did as he wished, even to the extent of wearing a white half-mesh, half-polyester, cheap-and-nasty tourist-souvenir cap with the 'I ♥ NY' logo instead of his national cap. Finally, he gave us a chance on 211, but the damage had well and truly been done both on the scoreboard and through the mind games he had played.

By the time we had a chance to bat the pitch had started to crumble, and although it played okay once a batsman got used to its pace and turn, the initial stages of an innings came down to a mixture of skill and good fortune. Patience was the basis of my plan to score runs, but after 11 balls of uncertainty the umpire imagined there were six stumps instead of the usual three and sent me on my way for a big fat zero. I was livid, especially as I'd been 'sawn off' in both lead-up matches as well, adding further fuel to the already-ignited conspiracy theories I'd consumed myself with.

A tray full of drinks in plastic cups was my first target, and then anything and everything else was swiped off the bench in the dressing-room as I screamed, 'Get me out of this fucking place!' I had to let go of the pent-up anger and frustration, but the ferocious way I did so surprised even me. Seconds later, as I contemplated my actions, only the room attendants remained in the room. My teammates had seen the dark mood I was in and had left me as quickly as possible to wallow in self-pity at my wretched luck. Then just as quickly, I snapped out of it, totally embarrassed at my trail of destruction and the poor attitude I was carrying around. I cleared the results of my 'Babe Ruth home run' off the floor and went out to watch the strength of character Peter Taylor and Ian Healy were now displaying out in the middle.

Meanwhile, an international incident was brewing. Bob Simpson and team manager Col Egar were complaining to the press about the pitch and umpire Mahboob Shah's officiating. Bob and Col felt compelled to stick up for the team, but because of their status in Australian cricket – Simmo as an ex-captain and current coach and selector, and Col as one of the game's most respected former Test umpires – their actions virtually gave the rest of us a green light to air our grievances. Perhaps the most inflammatory remark came from our manager when he said, 'The umpiring is totally unacceptable. We have to let the world know what is going on!'

Such was our sense of injustice that we held a team meeting at the conclusion of day three of the Test to discuss our position and the options available. At the time we were 7/116 in our first innings in reply to Pakistan's 9 declared for 469. We vowed to fight hard and to salvage a draw if possible, but also – dangerously – we openly canvassed the idea of abandoning the tour if the umpiring didn't improve.

After a rest day, controversy just kept on coming, peaking with the farcical dismissal of Peter Taylor in our second innings. Having showed stubborn resistance in the first innings for 54 not out, he was told by AB to keep his gear on and go straight back out to open the batting with Geoff Marsh after Javed enforced the follow-on. Again, Peter looked the goods, leaving as many deliveries alone as possible and kicking away balls he didn't have to play at, until he was 'undone' by their designated shine remover and wicket scuffer, Aamer Malik. Bowling around the wicket, Malik got one to jump off a length, but PT withdrew his bat and allowed the ball to bounce off his thigh guard and loop into the hands of Ijaz Ahmed at short leg. The umpire met the inevitable orchestrated appeal from the Pakistanis with a shake of the head – we'd finally got one to go our way – but then, under the intense pressure of a continued shout from the fieldsmen and bowler, suddenly the finger went up. This sent our viewing room into meltdown. Even the mild-mannered, clear-thinking Taylor remonstrated with Malik for having the temerity to appeal and then to carry it on until the decision was reversed.

Only the calmest of temperaments and clearest of thinkers could hope to do well now, for the atmosphere in the room was charged with negativity and distrust. I waited for my turn in the middle as if I was about to be summoned to the electric chair. Appropriately, I made 13, and for the second time in the match felt like a prop on a movie set. I was given out stumped, but by the time the keeper took the ball I had retreated to the crease with plenty of time to spare, which to the umpire was totally irrelevant, as he sent me on my way. Obviously, my attempted resilience was slowing down proceedings; they wanted to move onto the next 'scene'.

This time my reaction was in complete contrast to the 'toys out of the cot' dummy spit of day three. I just walked in and sat down, numb. *Surely Test cricket isn't meant to be like this* – that was all I could think. I needed to hear my girlfriend's reassuring voice of reason and get comfort from my parents. Instead, I was stuck in an ordeal that was spiralling out of control.

The massacre ended in an innings and 188 runs defeat, but the mayhem was just about to begin. Comments from the Australian camp at a spiteful post-Test press conference left no one doubting our beliefs and led to a split in the journalists' camp. On the sympathetic side were Rod Nicholson and Terry Brindle, while Mike Coward and Phil Wilkins aligned themselves with the 'bigger picture' argument. AB certainly didn't hold back when he said, 'This was a conspiracy from the word go. We are not going to be allowed to win. We will talk long and hard about the rest of the tour, because the ramifications of us going home now are huge and we understand that, no matter what was said, it would look like sour grapes after losing. But, ultimately, somebody has to take a stand, because this sort of thing has been going on for too long. If we are the ones who have to cop it, then so be it.'

Later that evening, back at Karachi's Pearl Continental Hotel, we held an urgent crisis meeting that ultimately led to a vote on whether or not we should immediately abandon the tour. I'm not sure we were fully aware of the consequences of our actions. I certainly saw it only from my point of view – that I'd been ripped off and didn't want any more of it. In the end, the captain, coach and manager took the brunt of the criticism we copped; it was a courageous if not wise move to encourage a boycott. A show of hands was called and only two players – Tony Dodemaide and Jamie Siddons – were seemingly unaffected and had the strength of character to want to stay on. Being first-time tourists and not wanting to jeopardise future selection chances may have influenced their vote, but it was a brave stance nevertheless.

I can't recall any words of caution from the tour hierarchy, only confirmation that we had taken the right decision. In my mind, we were going home and all I could think was, *Thank God it's over!* Col Egar had the task of passing on the information to Malcolm Gray.

In Faisalabad the next day another emergency team meeting was called and Col informed us that there was no way we were going to be allowed to abandon the tour: it must progress as scheduled. We felt let down, but deep down we also knew that, cricket politics being what they are, the ACB had no alternative but to deny our request. In many ways, it was good to know that our only option was to just get on with it.

As a break from all the conjecture, I took off to the Faisalabad markets, which were a real eye-opener. The unrefrigerated meat, covered in flies and dangling from huge silver hooks, the goat's heads for sale piled up haphazardly on the sidewalks, and fashion items such as fake beards being sold for as little as $2 reminded me that I was a long way from home, but also intrigued me in a way that suggested that being in a foreign land wasn't necessarily a disastrous thing.

But then, just when we thought things had settled down, came the arrival from home of a *60 Minutes* crew headed up by reporter Mike Munro, there to do a yarn about our threat to cancel the tour. Any chance of a balanced account of events was scuttled by the ACB gagging players and management from making any comment, and death by silence was our sentence. AB, as captain, was put in the nightmarish position of being ambushed by Munro at a press conference during the second Test. He could only deflect questions until Simmo intervened and put an end to the ad hoc nature of the proceedings. The board's theory was that if we didn't say anything the storm clouds would pass over, but instead we became an easy target and were made to look like prima donnas and bad sports.

Former Australian captain Ian Chappell didn't miss his chance to slip the boot in, accusing us of 'lacking the "digger" spirit'. This, I thought, was drawing a pretty long bow, particularly when it came from a bloke who had never toured Pakistan with an Australian team during his playing career. I would later learn that Ian's style of commentary was to never deal in shades of grey but always be very clear in his intent. Often, though, I found there was no constructive element to his criticism to balance his views.

When a tape of Munro's story arrived during the third Test, in Lahore, we all squirmed in our seats at the bleak picture that had been painted of the whole squad. Again, like the Greg Dyer incident from the previous Australian season, our version of events was suppressed. Only half the story was told – and it was all bad!

★

I look back on this Pakistan experience as a battle of mind over matter. It was a place that could make or break you. At tour's end, I left for Hong Kong and then home clinging to the precipice, but fortunately I was willing to absorb the lessons I'd learnt from a tour full of negative headlines. I'd played every game, copped at least five poor umpiring decisions, been jettisoned to third man after dropping catches at second slip, and allowed my own and the collective disillusionment and depression of the squad to consume me. The fallout came in a plethora of bad articles, and I was shocked to see later just how the tour had been reported. I couldn't quite understand some of the commentary – bits of it I still don't – but I realise that when you are involved in an argument, seeing the other side isn't always an option you want to explore.

A couple of moments above all the others capture my misery. One came late in the at times dull and boring Faisalabad Test. When you are struggling, it's amazing what half an hour out in the middle at the end of a match that's winding down can do to your confidence. A dig of 15 or 20 not out can provide a massive boost. It's not really about the runs; it's the fact you've lasted 30 or 40 balls and spent time in the middle sharpening up your technique and learning to trust yourself again.

On this occasion the match was petering out and we all knew stumps would be drawn half an hour early. I was 19 not out and had survived 45 minutes, enough to give me some sort of encouragement. The umpires had consulted with Javed Miandad and given us the word that there was only one over left. For many captains, this is the perfect opportunity to throw the ball to a 'joke' bowler, someone who at training gets told to swap nets when they pick up a ball because to face them is to waste your time.

In this instance, Pakistan's opening bat, Shoaib Mohammed, was thrown the ball, much to his delight. He was eager to impress. My consuming thoughts were threefold: *Don't get out, this is the last over, block it out.* Blinded by this line of thought, I simply forgot to bat and paid the ultimate price. A ragged long hop that should have come back with passport stamps on it was instead unconvincingly bunted back straight into the bowler's hands. As is the case when a totally unexpected wicket materialises, all hell broke loose, with high-fives, demeaning laughter and an extended celebration. I just stood there, stunned, almost pretending it hadn't happened.

Walking off was a blur. I didn't even notice the unfortunate Graeme Wood walking past me to face the last two balls of the match. Resembling a zombie, I sat down among my usual mass of entangled gear and felt like bawling my eyes out. I wanted out, this was all too much. I would have dropped myself if someone had asked my opinion right there and then.

By the time the final Test came around my game was in a real mess. However, the belief Simmo had in me persuaded the other selectors that I was worthy of another chance. I had to bluff myself into believing I was good enough, and after I scored 59 in our first innings I got onto the front foot with the press when I said, 'The wheels fell off in Karachi, but the disappointments have made me a tougher cricketer. It can only be good for the character to come back and do well here.' After all, I'd made runs against an attack led by Abdul Qadir, and duelling with a great wrist-spinner like Qadir was no different from coming up against a champion paceman like Richard Hadlee or Malcolm Marshall. These bowlers were at a different level to everyone else. Indeed, my view is that Qadir wasn't far behind Shane Warne as the complete package. He didn't possess a 'flipper' of Shane's quality, but his wrong 'un was exceptional. He was quick through the air and had a real flurry of arms at the point of delivery that made his variations hard to detect. His temperament sometimes let him down – his performance depended on his mood – but like Shane he was a match-winner and a guy with charisma, who always lifted the intensity of the contest simply by his presence. To score runs here, after going into the match with such a gloomy and jaundiced attitude, was to learn that I could prevail through willpower once the actual duel in the middle began, which was comforting to know.

This tour provided me with valuable lessons for the future on how not to think and act, which became a sort of checklist for the remainder of my career. Things are never as bad as they appear, for the mind can overcome anything if you tell yourself enough times, and excuses are for losers while winners make it happen. The worst example of my resolve caving in also came during the Faisalabad Test, when the home team was batting. Standing at second slip, I missed an Exocet of a nick from the bowling of Bruce Reid when we were standing way too close in the slips cordon. I couldn't even get a hand on the chance because of the speed it came at, and the ball thudded into my left collarbone and immediately gave me a 'dead arm'. It was double embarrassment: a dropped catch coupled with me carrying on like I'd been shot by the guy on the grassy knoll. I'm not proud of what I thought next. Hunched over in agony, I said to myself, *Hang on, this could be broken. End of tour! Qantas flight back to Oz!* That's where my mindset was at. But then came the bad news . . . The squashed nerve kick-started back to life while the captain's patience had been exhausted, and I was dispatched to field on the boundary, to lick my wounds and pray the pill didn't come my way. It was to be the last time I thought that way. Such a mentality was pitiful and pathetic, and deep down I was ashamed of it.

13

An eye for an eye

I knew 1988–89 had to be the season where I showed that I was going to be a reliable, consistent cricketer. It was also a summer in which the mighty West Indies were to arrive for a five-Test series. After the last home Test I'd played, against Sri Lanka in February 1988, Allan Border gave me a heads-up on how he saw my progress when he said: 'Steve is the first to admit that he hasn't played as well as he would have liked in Test-match cricket. He says he tends to freeze a fraction.

When he's playing for NSW he tends to go out and play his shots; if the ball is there he hits it over the top. He needs to do that in Test cricket as well, be almost as brash in his batting as Ian Botham, who always takes up the challenge. Waugh might not be as awesome as Botham, but if he can develop the confidence that Botham exudes, he will be more successful than he is at the moment.'

There was a lot of truth to what he said, because during my first three years in international cricket I had felt restrained and shackled by the expectations of being the new 'wonder kid'. Playing for NSW was much less stressful. I had a greater sense of team with the Blue-baggers, in part because I'd known the players longer, but it was more than that. They played with passion and enjoyment, while the 'Baggy Greeners' had more of the moments of failure that tend to split up and disorientate the team ethic that is critical in all great sides. I hoped Australia would eventually be as united as NSW, but that could really only happen in conjunction with team stability.

This was also a time that, as a Test cricketer, I didn't feel entirely comfortable in my own skin. At the start of the '88–89 Australian season, I was still suffering from the fallout of my disastrous Pakistan tour and also from an even more ruinous performance in my first outing as a public speaker. Just thinking about getting up in front of a group of people gave me sweaty palms, and with no media training or any experience in school debating, I was terrified of the prospect. Being honoured by the local Bankstown Council at a civic reception for my achievements in the Australian cricket team was a function I couldn't avoid, as it was specifically organised to fit in around my cricket commitments. I was nervous enough at the prospect of saying a few words, but in the minute preceding my acceptance of the honour my mind went walkabout. I couldn't remember who to thank, what to say, or how long I should speak for. My body experienced that hot-flush sensation, coupled with excessive sweat beading on the forehead and a thumping chest. By the time I got to the microphone, I thought the invisible man had me in a 'sleeper hold', because my breathing was laboured due to anxiety and after 30 seconds of muddling, I just walked off to the side of the stage, unable to complete the task, clutching my cobweb-collecting plaque for comfort. That was it: my first and last speech. I was shattered. Not even Lynette's and my family's well-meaning words could soothe the embarrassment and feeling of total ineptness that consumed me.

As a team, I don't think we ever expected to beat the Windies. Our meetings were often based around the word 'competing'. To me, this said, 'Let's have a go and you never know what might happen', rather than believing we could actually control parts of the match and be in charge of our own destiny. But maybe it was realistic. Part of me had 'competing' as a goal, though I didn't want to be a passive competitor but an aggressive one.

Our first innings in Brisbane went according to the script, with Courtney Walsh, Malcolm Marshall and Curtly Ambrose dissecting the Australian batting order with clinical precision. Not even the loss of an injured Patrick Patterson, who could bowl only 3.1 overs, slowed them down. I felt intimidated the moment I set foot on the ground. These guys had a very real aura about them and they moved around with a mixture of grace and arrogance. They seemed relaxed yet filled with purpose, and, above all else, were certainly much more impressive physically than I was. I felt like a boy on a man's errand and played accordingly, missing a straight one from the great Marshall to be out lbw for four. I was mesmerised by his explosive run-up, his systematic and beautifully balanced front-on action and his speedy arm, and in all honesty I don't even think I watched the ball, for the man was too impressive to ignore. He was a martial-arts work in full flow, with a wrist that could eliminate you in one swipe. Walking back to the pavilion, I knew my career was hanging by a thread and that with such a

meek offering I'd let myself and the selectors down. As I sat contemplatively in my gear back in the rooms, it suddenly hit me like a bolt of
lightning: *For God's sake, back yourself and have a bloody go! Go out
and walk the walk.* It was the way I'd always naturally played sport but
now, once I'd reached the ultimate, my mantra had been forgotten.

By the time I got the ball in my hand, the dominance of Windies
openers Desmond Haynes and Gordon Greenidge had well and truly
set the tone for the match. I believed we hadn't given them anything
that neared the physical interrogation they'd dished out to us. I was
consumed by the notion of not backing down, getting right among
them and not worrying about the consequences.

From 0/135, they crashed to 3/162, with two wickets falling my
way. Out strode cricket's equivalent of the great heavyweight champion Joe Frazier – Viv Richards. The swagger was unmistakable, the
coolness unimaginable. Running in to bowl that first ball to Viv,
I thought about making sure he had to at least play a shot, possibly
across the line, in the hope of an lbw. I knew he would want to play a
shot to establish his authority. But then, two steps from the delivery
point, the urge to bounce him and let him know he was in a contest
where he wasn't going to dictate terms took over. I mustered all the
effort I could and gave him a pretty useful short one that certainly got
his attention, and also the interest of my teammates. I was enjoying
the buzz that the crowd was now giving off and couldn't resist another
bouncer, which again was on the money. Viv got under it with a certain
degree of ugliness that I could tell didn't sit well with him. I'm sure he
was thinking, 'Okay punk, you've had your day in the sun, let's see if
you've got the balls to do it again.'

I knew I was smashing up a hornets' nest, but I also needed to
express my natural instincts, and they told me to go even harder.
A third bumper had the crowd loving it and Viv fuming under his
beloved red cap with its badge of a swaying palm tree. I had achieved

Gordon Greenidge is on his knees and despondent while I'm mightily relieved after the Windies third slip spilled a regulation catch during the first Test, at Brisbane, in 1988–89. I always looked upon a let-off like this as being not so much a stroke of 'luck' as an opportunity.

Here's proof, from that same innings at the Gabba, that I once tried to hook fast bowlers.

Geoff Lawson has
his jaw broken by
the West Indies'
Curtly Ambrose at
the WACA in Perth
in 1988–89. Soon after,
Gordon Greenidge is
out lbw first ball of
the Windies second
innings (BELOW), which
gave Merv Hughes
a sensational hat-trick
spread over three overs
and two innings.

In the 1988 Boxing Day Test I managed to dismiss Viv Richards in both innings, to the delight of keeper Ian Healy, Merv Hughes and Dean Jones. What I like most about this photo is our body language, which suggests that the dominance the West Indies had over Australia through the 1980s was finally on the wane.

This was confirmed in the final two Tests of the series, when we won in Sydney and had the better of a draw in Adelaide. At the SCG, I found myself in a blue with their great fast bowler Malcolm Marshall.

I've just taken perhaps the most famous catch of my career, a skier from the bat of the Windies' Roger Harper that saw me sprint from the edge of the circle at mid-off towards the boundary and then, after I held the chance, run behind the sightscreen with the ball held aloft. The full house at the MCG loved it!

Thirteen days later, I enjoyed the rare experience of hitting Curtly Ambrose for six off the last ball of our innings in the deciding final of the World Series Cup. Dean Jones, as good a batting partner as you could find, was as excited as I was.

This was one of a number of photographs taken to support XXXX beer's sponsorship of the Australian team in England in 1989. From left: David Boon, Geoff Marsh, Allan Border, Dean Jones, Merv Hughes, Terry Alderman and me.

The Queen is introduced to the 1989 Australians at Lord's. From left: me, Tom Moody, Tim May (obscured behind Allan Border and the Queen), AB, Dean Jones, Mike Veletta, Trevor Hohns, Greg Campbell, Merv Hughes, Terry Alderman, Geoff Lawson, Carl Rackemann.

This defensive shot at Lord's in 1989 captures the confidence and balance I felt during the series. Jack Russell is the keeper, 'Dickie' Bird the square-leg umpire.

David Boon leads the Aussie team in song after we regained the Ashes at Old Trafford.

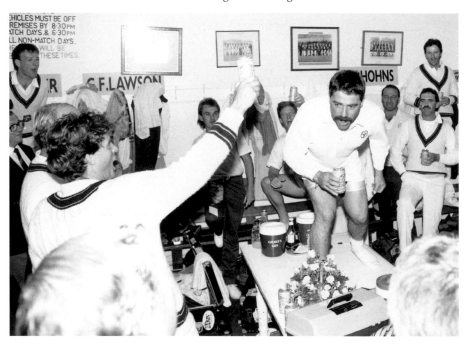

Lynette and I got engaged in Hong Kong in 1989, on the way back from the Ashes tour. We weren't quite sure what to make of the fact that this was front-page news.

With Nigel Websdale, the fitness guru who gave me a new sense of focus after he contacted me during the 1989–90 season.

Merv Hughes, Ian Healy (with broom) and I survey what organisers in the Bronx, New York, planned to use as a pitch before our game there against Pakistan in 1990.

Celebrations in the SCG dressing-room after Australia retained the Ashes in 1990–91. For me, this was a bittersweet experience – it's always good to win, but I wasn't scoring enough runs and sensed I was about to be dropped.

something, because I'd unsettled their pillar of strength, and when, in the next over, I gave him my out-of-the-back-of-the-hand slower ball, he ducked into a full toss that to my impartial one eye would have hit the middle stump three-quarters of the way up. Sadly, my greatest piece of bowling went unrewarded by an umpiring decision that I can only guess was motivated by the desire to get a positive match appraisal from the visiting captain or was perhaps thrown by the unusual trajectory of the ball.

Viv dodged his bullet and went on to score 68, and I had the whole artillery after me when I strode out with intent in the second dig. The words that Geoff Boycott had passed on to me during Somerset's visit to Scarborough in Yorkshire in August 1988 (a lesson I'd ignored in Pakistan and in the first innings here) – 'Walk out there with purpose, don't wander out there like you're half-asleep, the opposition will pick up on it' – rang 100 per cent true with me now. I took centre from the umpire in complete silence, but knew that brief lull was like finding refuge in the eye of a cyclone. I began to prepare for the onslaught, concentrating on getting my bearings right, memorising their field placements without making any eye contact, going through a few random stretches and hoping for a bit of divine intervention.

Finally, with a perfect piece of timing, Viv chirped up from first slip: 'Let's see how he likes it, let's give him some back, boys. Let's get stuck in, don't take too long.' At 4/65, having conceded a first-innings lead of 227 and with my future on the line, this was truly the meaning of *Test* cricket. I tried to look calm, but internally I was churning up, knowing this was an innings that had to be played more in the mind than with skill. Making it tougher was having that 'loader of bullets' Desmond Haynes smiling at me from a very adjacent short leg to ensure he was in my peripheral vision, laughing to himself and saying, 'You're gonna cop it now!' Often Dessie would go up to the bowler and fire him up by saying something like, 'He thinks you aren't that quick any more!' He was a real competitor who loved the gamesmanship angle that cricket can provide.

My lucky break came when Greenidge spilled a straightforward chance in the slips early on in my innings. I must admit I was shocked to see him smash his fist into the turf after missing the chance. After all, I didn't have a track record of getting hundreds and had hardly looked convincing to that point. Maybe Viv had wanted my scalp too badly and had created tension among his team, or perhaps Gordon's perfectionist nature was coming through. Whatever – his reaction gave me a little rev-up to know they were disappointed and valued my wicket so much. To prove how much cricket is played in the mind, my first thought was, *I've been dropped now – I can relax a bit, because as a Test batsman I should be able to capitalise on my good fortune.* That slight shift in thinking allowed me to open up and play much more aggressively, and it was only a delayed bad-light call from the umpires that stopped me reaching that elusive Test ton. After consulting each other at least three or four times in vague speculation, but apparently unable to make a call to go off, I ended up making the decision for them when I smashed one from Marshall off the back foot to Haynes at cover in the eerily encroaching darkness, allowing everyone else to escort me off the park. I was 10 runs short of that key breakthrough, annoyed at the umpires' indecisiveness but pleased we had at least forced the Windies to bat again before they finished us off.

Having played the first Test on the green-tinged Gabba, the ACB then further enhanced its relationship with its players by serving up to the quickest quartet of fast bowlers in the world the marble-topped trampoline of the WACA for their second Test feast. At least a second successive ninety proved to me that the one I had scored in the first encounter wasn't just an apparition. This is an innings I remember for the fact that I really enjoyed running between the wickets with the much-maligned Graeme Wood, who had a reputation for being unpredictable at times when calling singles but totally predictable if he needed to get off the mark or was nearing a milestone. He used to tell John Dyson to get ready, because if he hit one he was running, but I found him to be helpful and a good communicator. Our 200-run partnership is something I'm proud to look back on.

The pitch dried out more than expected and by the time we batted, having watched Viv take us apart for 146 out of 449, the cracks had widened to an almost alarming point. Standing at your crease, watching the Windies quicks charge in, knowing they might land one smack bang on a crack, is a situation you should not fret about, but of course it's human nature to focus on that danger rather than worry about the fundamentals of batting. Very rarely do such cracks affect the trajectory of the ball, but if a quick bowler is closer to seven than six feet tall and does get it to catch a soft edge or a ridge on the pitch, sometimes the result is taken out of the batsman's control.

Our No. 10, Geoff Lawson, for a reason only known to him, batted in a helmet that had earpieces but not the full protective grill. Ambrose could smell the kill and see the fear and let go a ripsnorter that leapt off a length and zeroed in on vulnerable flesh and bone – as soon as Geoff recoiled his head and turned away, he was an accident waiting to happen. The sickening sound of leather on jaw echoed around the WACA as Henry crumpled to the ground and tried to reclaim his face by cupping his hands around the affected area. Errol Alcott was already on his way to collect his medical kit and inspect the damage, which he later said was consistent with an injury sustained in a car crash.

Meanwhile, our last man had gone deathly pale. He asked AB three times, 'Do you want me to bat?' before finally hearing the words he desperately wanted: 'Okay, Merv, don't worry. I'm declaring.'

In the change rooms, we awaited the arrival of Geoff on the stretcher. We could tell he wasn't far away by the commotion outside and the moaning noises that were getting louder. A glass beer jug was grabbed by Errol on the way in to give Geoff something to spit clots of blood and saliva into, and we saw that his jaw had an indentation as if it had been struck with a large mallet. To me, it looked like the whole side of his face might collapse. Seeing one of our team in this terrible state got us into such a mindset that if we were playing a contact sport we would have instigated an all-in brawl straight after kick-off. Merv was enraged, and when he took Greenidge's wicket with his first ball he gave the batsman the biggest send-off ever as we embraced each other in an emotion-charged huddle. It was an eye for an eye. Even though Merv's fast-bowling partner would be eating blended meals through a straw for the next six weeks, we had salvaged some pride.

Greenidge was also the third part of a miraculous hat-trick that spread over three overs and two innings. When I heard news of the feat announced over the public-address system I passed the information onto Merv, who said, 'Are you sure?' Feeling remorseful for the gobful he'd given Greenidge on the field, at the end of the day's play Merv went into the Windies' dressing-room and tried to make amends face to face. But his olive branch was snapped when Greenidge refused to accept the apology, and our big quick wasn't a happy camper.

We thought we'd find respite going into the Boxing Day third Test, but someone forgot to tell the curator to cross-roll the pitch. It had a corrugated appearance, giving the tall quicks a massive advantage because it was going to provide up-and-down bounce. It must have helped the shorter medium-pacers, because I took my second Test five-for and claimed eight wickets for the match, including the king, Viv, twice.

Successful batting on this wicket required courage and patience, and a large amount of ice afterwards. I scored 42 and 4, and my hands were red raw from taking endless balls on the gloves, including one from Ambrose that clipped my thumb before crashing into my jawbone, which had been fractionally exposed when I threw my head backwards. I couldn't eat steak for a couple of days, and the after-innings look of two hessian bags full of ice on each cheek, encased by a towel, wasn't a great fashion statement. Mind you, I'd rather have a freezing head than a frozen groin, which is what Heals had after being struck flush on his protector on three occasions. The first time provided a good laugh in the change rooms that only guys can fully appreciate; second time, the boys were falling down, clutching their stomachs at his poor fortune; but by the third time our eyes were watering in sympathy for our keeper. When he peeled off his kit as he lay on the physio's bench, we were happy for him that all was accounted for, but shocked to see the dramatic colour transformation.

The physical nature of the contest stepped up to a ferocious level at the conclusion of day four. Sticking to my plan for the series, I was bouncing all of their players because I figured they couldn't target me any more anyway. I even let their No. 11, Patrick Patterson, have a couple of bouncers, which went down as well as cough medicine to a sick child. Making the situation escalate somewhat was the fact that my bowling partner at the time, Big Merv, was bellowing his support from fine leg, saying, 'Great stuff, Tugga. He doesn't like it.'

AB, who had weathered the storm so many times in the past, many times single-handedly, seemed to be enjoying the exchanges, because he threw in some 'encouragement' of his own, which heightened the tension. I was fielding at square leg for the following over when Merv was bowling, and between balls I could see Patterson eyeing me off with a deadpan expression as he craned his neck in my direction. With that five-for next to my name, I thought I was Sir Garfield Sobers for a split second and gave the giant quick a smart-arse wave that served the same purpose as waving a red rag at an enraged bull. Patterson obviously didn't see the funny side to our antics. When we got back to our respective dressing-rooms, which were then located next to each other under the old Members Stand, separated only by a short walk and two doors, the fireworks began. Moments after we sat down, Patterson burst through our door and said, 'You guys are going to pay for that tomorrow . . . I'm going to kill you.'

Our jovial mood was suddenly terminated; a restless night awaited us. The fast man was as good as his word, taking 5/39 and bowling with real anger and physical presence, slamming down his front leg with incredible force and following through to such an extent that it seemed like he was bowling from halfway down the pitch. Whoever described Patterson at his peak as being like 'an apartment block tumbling down on you' when you faced him was right on the money. To score runs or survive required complete devotion to the task at hand, which was difficult when the very real prospect of injury was consuming a great deal of your thoughts. I was by this time already feeling the strain of the intense mental requirements that back-to-back nineties and a first-innings 42 had taken out of me. These guys had the skill and aura to extinguish all but the strongest resolve, and once they had a player at their mercy, I never saw anyone come back and reverse the trend. You had to make sure that the first Test of any series against these guys was a positive experience, or else they'd come looking for you and it wouldn't be long before one mistake suddenly became a new-found weakness. They had the ability to create a vulnerability in you that you didn't know was there, and on occasion made you believe it even when it wasn't true. The battle, of course, remained in large part between our ears, but with their stellar reputations, the adoring media attention and their relentless assaults on the field, it was exceptionally hard to compartmentalise the issues at hand. Instead, they became blurred.

Even though we ended up losing, there were some resolute Australian performances in that Melbourne Test that brightened the mood of an at times overwhelmed unit. For example, Peter Taylor's heroic 18 not out against the fury of Patterson was a magnificent morale boost for the side and showed everyone what application and concentration could achieve, even in the toughest of environments.

Finally, in the Sydney and Adelaide Tests, we got pitches that the Windies didn't give each other high-fives about when they saw them. A resulting win and a draw gave us credibility and a genuine belief that better things lay ahead. The best part about playing against great sides is that they can drag you up a level when you compete with them, but you don't really notice that improvement until you play a team of lesser capabilities. Facing a champion like Marshall had to be good for tightening up my defensive technique, because he interrogated my every move, probing for a chink in the armour, waiting for that split second of indecision that proves fatal. For that reason, my 55 not out in Sydney, on a dry and dusty pitch that enabled him to swing it 'Irish', was as tough an examination as I'd experienced to that point in my career. (To swing it Irish is to get the ball to move the opposite way to conventional swing due to excessive wear and tear on the ball aided by extra polishing and wetting it.) These guys played it hard, and when Gus Logie claimed a bat-pad catch off me, then half-heartedly said, 'I don't think I caught it,' I refused to walk. Instead, I waited for him to tell his celebrating teammates that there was too much doubt to claim the dismissal. That he did, but Marshall wasn't best pleased and disdainfully told me to do the batting and let the umpire do the umpiring. It was a lesson well learnt, because I didn't walk when on nought in the next Test after feathering one through to Jeffrey Dujon off a decidedly unhappy Marshall. Thankfully, I managed to inside-edge one to get off the mark soon after, though that run brought me down to the non-striker's end. After delivering the next ball, the great fast bowler stopped on his walk back to his mark, did some superficial work to the crease with his spikes, and quietly said to me, 'You convicts are all the same.'

I thought that was a pretty fair call. It was part of the game and really, when it's all said and done, something that was worth a chuckle or two, rather than having people get uptight about it.

A sense of humour was very much an essential element when playing these guys, because we all needed a release from the constant barrage that rained down on us. Tim May was almost always in the thick of things. Laughing at others' misfortune is part and parcel of being in a team, as long as the chuckling doesn't cut too close to the bone and cause a rift. Standing with camera in hand over a petrified man with a phobia about needles while a very large pain-killing injection was being prepared by the doctor provided some good mirth. The crowd of caring teammates that gathered to witness the injection kept on remarking about the impressive size of the syringe and how it would probably come out the other side of Maysie's foot. With cameras clicking, our offie was tensing up to the point of seizure, a serious sweat on his brow. The cries of, 'There it goes . . .', 'Jeez, that's gonna hurt . . .' didn't help and the succession of desperate pleas from Maysie was the icing on the cake.

Only a best friend can get away with destroying another man's entire kit. I must admit I didn't expect the damage to be so great – how much grief could one small prawn head stuffed in the end of a bowling shoe cause? I now know that the answer clearly depends on how long it remains there. Tragically for Tim, we had a break in the program after the Adelaide Test, and the offending crustacean didn't appreciate being in the damp, humid environment of a sweaty shoe inside a fibreglass 'coffin' (kitbag) for a number of days. I learnt later that the stench was so revolting when the coffin was opened at the start of his next game for SA that everyone in the room had to flee, leaving Maysie no option but to ring his sponsors up and plead for some new gear. I now formally apologise for my mistake.

Elsewhere, Merv was always up for a laugh and was a vital ingredient to pep up the spirits and mood of the team when things weren't going well. But this, of course, also left him open to the occasional prank. Before he went out to bat against the Windies in Adelaide, I procured a life-size cardboard cut-out of the team's cult figure and told him we'd put an 'X' on the matching spot every time he got hit. By the time he walked off, with an excellent 72 not out next to his name (his previous highest score in first-class cricket was 47; in Test cricket it was 21 not out), the Texta was just about empty. Merv could always see the funny side of things, and could also get away with more than most because everyone just loved him. During a routine weigh-in designed to monitor body fat and to make sure the kilos were coming off, Errol Alcott said, 'Okay, Merv, your turn. Jump on.' Jump on he did, with a massive leap that shattered the scales, ending the session immediately.

Merv also played a part in probably the best catch I ever took. It came about during a day/night game against the Windies in Melbourne, when I was fielding on the edge of the inner circle at mid-off. A slower ball from Craig McDermott partially deceived the big-hitting Roger Harper, who followed through on a lofted drive and sent the ball incredibly high into the night sky. As a fielder, I knew instinctively if I had time to look up and check the flight of a skied ball, but on this occasion that split second would have cost me the couple of metres I desperately needed: I knew it was going to take a full-tilt sprint to haul the ball in. When I sensed that time was against me and that I was nearing the boundary, I looked up and saw the descending white ball against the black sky and quickly extended both hands in anticipation. It landed perfectly, as if someone had dropped it in from half a metre away, and softly dropped straight into my right hand. It was only then that I realised how close I was to running into the sightscreen or, perhaps worse, into Mervyn Hughes, who had come in searching like a bear after a salmon. I continued on and ran around the sightscreen as the crowd had erupted, before being swamped by my teammates. This was the best single feeling I'd ever experienced in cricket, because it was a match-altering moment that lifted everyone. I discovered later that technically Harper wasn't out, because the umpire wasn't able to see if I had control of the ball as I ran behind the sightscreen. However, it would have been a brave call for the ump to give it not out.

It was a catch that in this case even the batter might have appreciated, as he was the greatest all-round fieldsman I'd ever played against. I recall him coming on as a substitute during the '88–89 Boxing Day Test and being immediately summoned to the slip cordon. There was only time for Harper to adjust his cap and settle into his crouched position before Dean Jones tried to work Ambrose behind square on the leg side. However, the delivery seamed off the pitch and forced a leading edge to fly off at an unexpected angle. The entire slip cordon and keeper remained focused on the intended leg-side trajectory of the ball except for the freak Harper, who dived full length to his left at third slip to take a stunning one-handed grab. It was a breathtaking piece of athleticism and a remarkable piece of anticipation from a guy who could almost have been selected solely for his fielding. He had the silken hands of a Mark Waugh, the agility of a Jonty Rhodes, the hunger for involvement of a Ricky Ponting and a throwing arm a baseballer would dream of. It was worth the admission price just to watch him appraise and survey a situation before imposing himself on the match.

I mentioned earlier how Allan Border became involved in that on-field battle with Patrick Patterson during the third Test. This was the match in which AB became the first Australian to play 100 Tests. As a captain he was a guy who didn't like confrontation with his own players, and would sometimes keep it all in until he eventually exploded. Fortunately, I only copped one spray from him in all my years under his leadership, and I probably deserved it after messing up a crucial run-out chance and in the process nearly knocking out Graeme Wood during our opening one-dayer against the Windies. Back-pedalling to take an outfield throw over the stumps at the non-striker's end to complete a run-out on an attempted third run, I leapt high to take the return but only managed to get my fingertips on it and in the process deflect it flush into the face of Woody, who was perfectly positioned over the stumps. Down he went like a sack of spuds, and off went AB: 'You idiot! What the hell are you doing?' Point taken and agreed upon by all – especially my dazed colleague, who lay prone, clutching at a possibly fractured jaw.

This might have been one of the most embarrassing incidents in my career, but I had better luck during the third and deciding final against the Windies at the SCG. Batting with the one-day maestro, Dean Jones, we put on 74 from the last eight overs, which culminated in me hitting a last-ball six off the emerging greatness of Ambrose. Batting with Jonesy was always great fun, as I fed off his energy and vibrancy. He had the ability to drag you into his whirlpool of activity and lift your game merely by his presence. When Ambrose began his languid, lengthy run-up for this delivery, I was already thinking it was going to be a yorker and that I would back away to leg and then step back into my crease and smite him over cover. The danger would be a leg-side bumper – which might find me being assisted from the field by the St John Ambulance men. The ball came exactly as I had envisaged it, allowing me the luxury of having time to rock back and smash it over the cover fence. The crowd went into a frenzy, while Jonesy leapt on top of me as we ran off together, believing we had altered the sway of the match enough to take the competition decider and confirm our status as world one-day champions. It's such a natural high for a batsman to pull off a shot like that, and utterly deflating for the bowler.

Unfortunately, in those days a mid-innings rain delay was a virtual death sentence for the team that batted first. We had scored 226 from 38 overs (the match having been cut back from 50 overs per side after two hours were lost to the weather in the afternoon) and the Windies' target was reduced still further, to 108 from 18 overs, after another storm hit when they'd reached 2/47 in 6.4 overs. They needed 61 from 11.2 overs with eight wickets in hand, which amounted to little more than a walk in the park for Richards and Haynes.

I didn't mind the loss so much, because the result was basically out of our control. However, I took offence at the way Dessie ran off with his arms aloft, and without shaking hands, as if he'd pulled off a miracle win. Maybe I was slightly cheesed off because the winning shot was a six off my bowling, but still, our opponents' lack of humility was an image that stuck with me. It was one I knew would motivate me at a later date.

14

'When's he going to get a hundred?'

There's nothing quite like it for an Australian touring team – touching down at Heathrow Airport at the start of an unrivalled cricketing odyssey featuring the entrenched traditions of Ashes battles, the chance to create your own piece of cricket folklore, travelling around together in a team bus for four months and, to cap it off, a chance to play at the home of cricket, Lord's.

I couldn't wait to set foot again on English soil and have my breath taken away by the icy chill of a spring breeze. Some of the other lads were just plain happy to stand without aid after a marathon journey that saw our Qantas plane run out of alcohol. The very instant we pulled up at our allotted gate, Tim Zoehrer lurched forward and filled up the sick bag to christen our tour. Boonie, after downing 52 cans of beer, didn't appear to be in too bad a shape . . . until he tried to walk. Thankfully, Geoff Marsh realised his great mate's predicament and grabbed his arm and, *Weekend at Bernie's* style, escorted him through customs and onto our bus to begin a recuperation that included a couple of days of sleep.

Whichever seat you grabbed on the bus first up was yours for the whole tour, so it was crucial to get the one you wanted. Card players generally went to the back, movie watchers to the front, while book readers assumed the middle.

I arrived in the UK fresh and ready to test out the gear I had received from my new sponsor, Gunn & Moore. The remuneration players were receiving for using one company's gear exclusively had skyrocketed since Dean Jones gained a 'landmark' deal from Kookaburra and I was now receiving around $70 000, triple what I had earnt previously. Furthermore, the reputation of my new, English sponsors made me feel like I was just starting out on a new phase of my career.

For me, one of the highlights of the tour, whose memory remains with me, was our first couple of days training at Lord's before the start of the one-day series that preceded the Tests. That place is something special: I will always recall fondly its uniquely sloping playing surface, the then men-only members' pavilion, the old wooden scoreboard with its Father Time weathervane, the fact that we had to wear predominantly whites to training. I felt sorry for the MCC playing staff, a collection of aspiring young cricketers who weren't quite good enough to get a county contract. They were at the whim of the MCC members, so if a 70-year-old gentleman fancied a knock before his midday nap these guys had to haul themselves away from whatever they were doing to send down some nice juicy half-volleys. The temptation to slip in a quick bouncer must have been hard to suppress as they went through the motions. At least when a touring side arrived these tyros could test themselves out, but still they had to keep bowling until they dropped. I'm sure most of them, by the end of their stint, hated the game and were looking elsewhere for employment.

From ball one in those nets I believed this was going to be *my* tour. It probably needed to be, because when we landed at Heathrow I'd played 26 Tests and was averaging 30.52 runs per innings. For Dean Jones, Merv Hughes and me, and, to a lesser extent, Geoff Marsh and Ian Healy – guys who had played a number of Tests without ever truly cementing a place in the side – this shaped as a make-or-break tour. For our captain, it was also a special trip: after the victory in the World Cup, AB had made it quite clear that winning back the Ashes was a priority. With that in mind, he decided we would put a 'freeze' on the Poms. Basically, this meant there would be no friendly banter on the field, in direct contrast to the attitude taken by the highly unsuccessful Australian team of 1985. On that tour, David Gower and company had a picnic as our boys made them feel welcome at every opportunity.

Strategically, it was a good move. The English county championship is very much a competition where guys have grown to know each other extremely well over a long period of time. Opposing players are also good mates, and being approachable and friendly is the normal code of behaviour. In such an environment, I believe at times you can lose that edge or killer instinct from your game, often without noticing it, and AB saw a chink that we could exploit. This time there would be no 'How are you going, Both?' or 'G'day, Lamby' when Ian Botham or Allan Lamb came out to bat. Instead, a snarling, fire-breathing Hughes would welcome them to the crease with a bumper and a gobful of choice phrases.

Before the first Test, at Headingley, we came back from a convincing loss in the first one-day international by salvaging a tie in the second game and successfully chasing a big total in the third to have some impetus in our favour going into the six-Test series. Hitting successive sixes off Neil Foster in our winning match at Lord's had me in a positive state of mind for the Test match. However, not everyone was so keen in their appraisal of our chances, and it was Jeff Thomson who led the charge (although with Thommo it's always hard to know how many of his comments are tongue in cheek and what his real opinion is). Merv came in for a bake when Thommo wrote for a London tabloid: 'I am ready to bet Merv all the XXXXs he can drink that he doesn't bag 18 wickets in the series. I reckon the English batsmen could play him with a walking stick.' He also didn't have much faith in the team when he stated: 'I wouldn't give you a XXXX for Australia's chances of regaining the Ashes this summer.' Really, it was all about Thommo making a few fast bucks out of a rag that was using his name. His couple of big statements were definitely of much more use wrapping the greasy hake and chips down at the local 'chippy' than a realistic assessment of our chances.

Going into the series, the Poms obviously thought we were vulnerable against a seaming ball. This and the reputation that Headingley was a bowler-friendly wicket caused them to send us in, a move they must have regretted as we compiled 7/601 declared. Mark Taylor played a tremendous innings in his first Test on foreign soil and finished 96 not out at the end of the opening day when we scored 3/207. Watching him play well was significant for me, because I knew if Tubby could do it, so could I. This was not because I considered myself a better player, but because we'd played a fair bit of under-age and state cricket together. We knew what the other was capable of.

His effort had the effect of relaxing me; after all, we'd mirrored each other's work plenty of times before. Also helping me get into the groove was my good mate Tom Moody, who was the best giver of 'throwdowns' in the business. After a day's play it was often good to get out and do something physical, especially when I had six hours intently watching every ball in readiness for my turn at the crease. The fresh air, combined with some practice shots on the outfield, livened me up and relieved the tension of an engrossing day. My game was based a lot around feeling good beforehand, making sure I was hitting them out of the middle. Often, I wouldn't have a full-on practice-net session before or during the game, preferring a teammate to toss me 20 or so balls. I always made sure I finished with a couple hit out of the middle of the bat, so I could walk away with a positive note as my last memory – which would then be what I'd take with me to the crease. Obviously, the quality of throwing was a key. Bad throwing could be frustrating and lead to scrappy shots, rendering the exercise useless. But with Moods throwing them down and handing out compliments I was primed and went to bed dreaming of big things, while Tubby, I'm sure, didn't sleep a wink searching all night for those four runs he needed for his maiden Test hundred.

Possibly the shot that had the most impact on the series was AB's cut shot for six off Phillip DeFreitas on the first day of the series, because it signalled our intent and the type of cricket we wanted to play. The following day, I edged my first ball, off Foster, to second slip but fortunately it landed short of the fieldsman. Soon after, a front-foot defensive push took me from 10 to 14 as it sped away down the slope, and I was away. From that moment on, I knew that all I had to do was concentrate and not get ahead of myself. This sense of tranquillity seemed to release my natural game and the shots just flowed. I timed the ball so well it pinged off my blade and I pierced just about every gap I sought. When batting happens like that, you get a real surge of power almost to the point of feeling invincible, but to me the ultimate compliment comes when you catch a glimpse of one of the opposition batsmen mimicking one of your best shots in admiration.

I saw a couple of their guys practising my back-foot drive, which had got a workout from same wayward bowling, and I felt I'd arrived as a Test batsman.

A fair proportion of my innings was in partnership with Dean Jones, a guy who played cricket in a similar way to me. He was always aggressive with his running between the wickets, liked to give and hear encouragement from his batting partner and, like me, playing shots was his natural game. We fed well off each other and there was a point in this innings when Jonesy even took a back seat, which was unusual for him as he thrived on holding centre stage. I remember during one of the lead-up games, a one-dayer at Sussex, he top-edged a hook onto his face and fractured a cheekbone, forcing him to retire hurt. By the time he returned to the ground after his hospital visit, I had moved into the 80s, but we lost eight wickets in the process before, unbelievably, 'Jonah' made his way out to the middle with a black eye, swollen beyond recognition, under his helmet. My first words to him were, 'Don't be silly, mate, it doesn't matter to me whether or not I get a hundred. You don't need to risk any more damage.' With typical Jones defiance he replied, 'I'm not worried about you – I want a hundred myself.' Optimism was his strong suit, but I doubted he could get the 86 more runs he needed for his century in the eight overs remaining with only one eye working. But I loved his attitude.

Back to the Test. Almost cruelly, when I reached 99 there was one last hurdle to overcome. I was so dry in the mouth my breathing was shallow, and all I could think was *Don't stuff it up now! Just get bat on ball*. If I'd got out then I may have never got a Test hundred, because the insecurity and self-doubt I was carrying had accumulated to such an extent that getting a century wasn't a target but a barrier. The shot that finally got me there was one I played on automatic pilot, a back-foot push out to the deep-cover fieldsman, who for some unknown reason wasn't in the 'circle' sweating on a single. Absolute joy and relief swept over me. I was so glad that I had the baggy green on and not a helmet. Most of the top order, without talking about it, had decided to wear caps as often as possible during the series. It was a positive statement that gave us a slight edge psychologically. I know I felt an extra bit of pride if I wore it when I batted. I also got an edge from knowing that I needed to be sharp because the security blanket of a protective helmet wasn't there as a backstop.

A huge weight had been lifted off my shoulders. No one could keep saying, 'When's he going to get a hundred?' I'd always wondered how I'd celebrate my first Test ton, but when it came I was so happy I almost forgot to acknowledge anyone. Finally, I gave a low-key response to the squad on the balcony, who all seemed genuinely happy. I thought of Lynette and how she had been there through all the dark, doubting times and I thought, too, of my parents and hers, who had all played their part in this success. Each failure I suffered wounded Lynette more than me, because the solution was out of her control – she could only watch and hope I could turn things around.

The first person I thanked was our team manager and chairman of selectors, Lawrie Sawle, who I bumped into on the stairs leading up to our dressing-room during the next break in play. I just said, 'Thanks for sticking by me and giving me the chances.' Lawrie was a source of inspiration; he was humble, self-effacing and considerate, but a man of substance. He also suffered from a bad stutter, but never shirked the responsibility of making a speech – which was different to AB, who point-blank refused to do so many times. Incredibly, Lawrie would always talk at the most prestigious of occasions and somehow do it without a mistake or his stutter. He lifted under pressure, which couldn't have been easy, and I was inspired by his courage.

We went on to win the Test, despite the fact that our first priority on day five was to make sure we couldn't lose. That was why AB didn't declare until just before lunch, when our lead was more than

400. When England were just three wickets down with Gower and Gooch looking comfortable, a draw still seemed the most likely result. But then Terry Alderman, Merv Hughes and Geoff Lawson combined to take the last seven English wickets for 57 runs.

A surprise victory invariably leads to an animated celebration, and we certainly had one of those. Boonie got up on the table to lead the team in an impassioned version of 'Underneath the Southern Cross', and then, as our Tasmanian paceman Greg Campbell had done six days earlier, the iconic Cold Chisel song 'Khe Sanh' made its debut to mark our victory. Why 'Khe Sanh'? I just grabbed it out of my CD case and thought it was the song to play, because every Aussie worth his salt knows the words and we needed something to remind us of home.

The bus trip down the motorway from Leeds to Manchester was as close as you can get to bonding through alcohol and the mesmerising melodies of Roy Orbison. By the time we rocked up to our new hotel there was no way the festivities were going to end sedately, so off to a cocktail bar and nightclub we marched.

The dunderheads who drew up the tour program had decided that a county match would begin the day after each Test match finished, but to tell you the truth most of us forgot we had a match to play. Sporting massive hangovers, we decided a quick knock in the nets was enough, with only Swamp interested in a decent hit, as he was the captain for this game and trying to set the standards, and a 'bataholic' who dreamt nightly of getting the handle in his hands. We all stood there, temple veins bulging, mouths parched and then wide open when we saw a sight that terrified us all – Lancashire's two overseas professionals warming up off their long runs, which meant they were playing instead of resting as overseas pros normally do for matches against touring sides. In one net was our good buddy Patrick Patterson, and in the other the deadly Wasim Akram. We immediately prayed for Swamp to win the toss, because batting less than sober against guys bowling 90-plus miles per hour would require our physio to know the number for the local ambulance service. There is a god, because we sent them into bat – and proceeded to drop eight catches in the first session, mostly off the team's only teetotaller, Geoff Lawson. To his credit, Henry could see the funny side of Boonie slipping over and crashing head first into the ground as he tried to haul in a simple, looping, bat-pad catch that he didn't even touch.

Swamp put one down at first slip because he couldn't see through his tears of laughter after a dropped catch the ball before had set off the entire slips cordon. But the ineptness of the locals meant that, despite all the missed chances, we still had to bat later in the day. While we couldn't have driven legally, we managed to steer a couple through the covers and end the day in a dominant position.

For any cricketer touring England with a national team, the Lord's Test is a special occasion. For England players, in contrast, a game at Lord's is a regular occurrence, with county cricket and internationals happening every season, so consequently the mystique for them is diluted. The change rooms are huge and give you a fantastic view of the match – I managed to snare a position in a corner, which was handy as it allowed me a bit more space to distribute my gear and came with the added bonus of a window that provided a fairly direct line of vision down the pitch. The shower-room facilities are worth remembering, with long, deep baths to soothe the aches, and shower heads the size of dinner plates that blast away the worries of the day. And the Lord's lunch is quite astonishing, offering so much variety and quality that it borders on being cruel because there's no way you can do it justice with only 40 minutes allocated. But I always gave it my best shot. Soups, salads, salmon, steak, chicken, pasta, desserts and fruit were lined up, and when it was a batting day the bowlers would cash in, stacking up on the carbohydrates and then just sitting back and (hopefully) watching the batsmen do their thing for the rest of the day.

Walking out to bat at Lord's during a Test match is an experience in itself. After going down two flights of stairs, you have to force your way through a swarm of mostly elderly members, all resplendent in their egg-and-bacon ties and many in top hats. Then you turn right and make your way through the Long Room, past the portrait of W.G. Grace looking down on you from a wall. The members make a tunnel for you to get through amid a waft of cigar smoke that lingers, but almost every time I played there at least one ageing gent didn't hear the footsteps or was incapable of moving quickly enough and I would be held up for a few seconds. Their politeness borders on being irritating, as they offer well-used lines such as, 'Good to see you. Good luck, but not too much.' Of course, it is well intentioned, but on my way out to bat I just want to get there, not exchange pleasantries.

My first-ever outing at Lord's had occurred in the previous season, in a one-day match for Somerset. Without a crowd to shepherd me out to the middle, I went straight ahead at the foot of the stairs instead of turning right to enter the Long Room, and ended up jumping the fence when the gate I went to wouldn't open. I was sufficiently embarrassed to make sure I scored a few runs, but even 140 not out didn't prevent my Pommie teammates from serving it up to me back in the rooms.

In the 1989 Test match, Lynette's arrival in England coincided with me being 35 not out at the end of day two. We were six down, 10 runs behind England, with Merv on 2 and Trevor Hohns, Geoff Lawson and Terry Alderman still to come. I had started with such authority and assurance in all my movements that a second Test ton felt almost inevitable, as long as my batting partners did their part. Lynette had decided to travel with David Boon's wife, Pip, and their seven-month-old daughter, Georgina, to help on the long flight over. Wives and girlfriends were arriving spasmodically, with the lucky ones having relatives or friends to stay with and take care of them. For the rest, it was fend for yourself until the tour rules allowed partners to move into the team hotel for the last two weeks of the tour. Up until that point wives and partners couldn't set foot in the team hotel; instead, they had to find alternative accommodation and modes of transport to keep in touch with us. It was a strange situation, with the single guys able to entertain female company at our digs, but the partners shunned. Henry's wife, Julie, wouldn't have a bar of it and was known to even climb the fire ladder to avoid detection in her quest to see her husband. It was all our own doing, because we had voted on this rule at the beginning of the tour, but with AB and Simmo very strong in their views on the matter it wasn't exactly my place to take them on. Boonie and Swampy were probably in the toughest situation, with their families in England while they also occupied senior roles within the side, but neither wanted to rock the boat so the ban was put in place to ensure we maintained a clear focus on our cricket with as few distractions as possible.

It would take nearly 10 years for this line of thinking to vanish. Back in '89, our hierarchy didn't have the benefit of a winning culture within the squad, or players who knew their games and were clear in their thinking as to what it took to win. So I understand where they were coming from, even if I wasn't in total agreement with them.

The life of the partner of a cricketing professional can be rewarding but it is equally difficult. After Lynette had flown for 24 hours in economy and then checked into a not very salubrious hotel, I popped in to have a meal and reacquaint myself with her before heading off to get a good night's sleep. Peace of mind is a sportsperson's most important asset, for it allows greater clarity and focus. The next morning I went out and played technically one of my best innings. Not at any stage did I think I was going to get out, and I don't mean that in a cocky way.

I was in the 'zone' of complete relaxation and enjoyment. The sun was shining, it was the fabled turf, an enthusiastic crowd containing plenty of Aussies created a passionate atmosphere, and I was playing to my full potential.

One crucial indicator that I was playing well and the point that was forever at the top of my 'checklist' was the bending of my front knee. If that was falling into place then my balance would follow suit, my head would be still and straight, and there wouldn't be any gaps in my defensive armoury. Simmo kept on reinforcing this message until it became my maxim. Besides feeling like I'd opened my personal floodgates, in this game I initiated a method of batting with the tail that I would use throughout my career. I assumed that the bowlers all wanted to score runs, but often didn't get much encouragement to make it seem worth the effort. When Geoff Lawson came to the crease with the score at 8/381, he was still experiencing Ambrose 'aftershocks' and needed a lot of reinforcement to get some belief back into his batting. I said to him, 'The wicket's flat, their bowlers are buggered – let's have some fun and get a partnership.' Henry responded in such a way that with 20 minutes of the middle session left he was 74 not out and came up to me and said, 'Do you realise I could score a hundred in a session at Lord's?' Big mistake. He started to think ahead and not in the present and two minutes later his crucial cameo was over. We finished 528 all out and I gained a valuable insight into the make-up of the tail and what was needed to get the best out of them.

For me, life was great. Back-to-back hundreds, two Test wins and being in the middle with Boonie when he hit the winning runs at Lord's was so far away from where I had been when I was totally exasperated with cricket in the dressing-room at Faisalabad just nine months before. How did it all turn around? I don't really have an answer; perhaps it was just meant to be. Maybe I'd had enough of being an average player and personal pride had taken over. Whatever it was, I wanted to bottle it.

An unfortunate aspect of being a professional sportsperson is that your perspective on the world is so influenced by how well you are playing. Failure can lead you into a deep dark abyss of gloom and depression, while success can elevate you into a world that doesn't really exist either. The great players have balance and recognise both these outcomes as impostors, seeing that the bigger picture is what it's all about. Family, friends, ethics, values and lifestyle sometimes become lost in the quest to be as good as you possibly can be. Success at sport can be a selfish aspiration, in that total commitment is all-consuming.

Celebrating a Test win was something we quickly took a liking to and we wanted to share it with the massive Aussie contingent who were supporting us. But before that could happen, we'd have a couple of hours in the dressing-room soaking up the winning feeling with just a few visitors. If you had a mate you wanted to invite in, it was courtesy to ask the captain for permission, because it was seen as 'our turf', a place to be ourselves away from the prying eyes of the media and eagerness of the public. Even with this system in place, we didn't always know everyone.

I remember a time on a later tour when one of the boys said, 'Who's the old grey-headed bloke over there in the corner?' Someone else responded, 'Buggered if I know, probably just a freeloader.'

Brendon Julian nearly fainted. 'Are you guys kidding?' he said. 'That's the legendary Stones drummer, Charlie Watts!'

It's amazing how a 'celeb' can change your opinion very quickly. In a flash the lads were saying, 'G'day Charlie, great to meet you.' I had the guilts and gave him a training cap, which I'm sure he cherished . . . Well, maybe not!

In 1989, the Lord's Test finished in the late afternoon of the fifth day, and eventually we headed to the pub next door to the ground, accompanied by no security, and got among the fans. I sensed our supporters loved the fact that we were just like them and not full of airs and graces. Of course, our wives and girlfriends had to put up with our extended celebrations, which went long into the night under the guise of team bonding. It was a tough ask on them but, like the rest of the guys, I wanted to enjoy the win after the struggles we'd been through over the previous few years, even if that meant putting our families second. On reflection, we had a right to celebrate, but so did the partners – they are often the pillars of strength in a crisis but forgotten straight after a triumph.

One of the strongest indicators of how tough touring life can be for families are the bonds that can be temporarily lost due to time apart. After one tour, Boonie knelt down to greet his daughter after six weeks away but she wouldn't go to him because she wasn't sure who he was. I'm certain this is a normal reaction at that stage of life, but at the time it made me think that when I had kids I wanted to be around as much as possible and ensure nothing was taken for granted.

At the other end of the spectrum, there's no better feeling than waking up after a big Test win and going down to scoff a huge English breakfast and read the flattering articles in the morning's papers. It's a wise move to pick them up when you are playing well, and an even smarter one to avoid them if you're not. The tabloids were having a field day with my surname and the plays on words they could come up with, and stinkers of headlines greeted me during the first two Tests. Maysie would delight in reading them out each morning on the team bus: 'Waugh Lord', 'Waugh Blimey', 'Waugh of the Roses', 'Waugh Tour', 'Waugh Declared' and 'Oh What a Lovely Waugh' are samples of the shockers they came up with. At least it was good press and not anything that created too much embarrassment.

★

Proving cricket is a continual learning process, I strayed away from my mode of batting with the lower order at Old Trafford during the fourth Test and paid the price for lacking faith in my teammates. I was eight runs short of my third Test century but had only Lawson and Terry Alderman left to bat with. My summing-up of the situation led me to believe that No. 11 Terry wouldn't last long against Angus Fraser and Neil Foster, so I was left with only Henry, who I decided had already had his day out at Lord's. I panicked and tried to premeditate a hook shot off Fraser when there were two balls left in an over, my plan being back-to-back boundaries. A brilliant right-handed catch by Tim Curtis at square leg finished me off and rightly foiled my ambitions. I was dirty on myself for throwing my wicket away, and for not showing faith in my teammates.

This was the Test in which Australia regained the Ashes. When Boonie swept the four that gave us a nine-wicket win and a 3–0 series lead, the whole squad, plus the bus driver, baggage handler and travel agent, stood on the balcony and embraced each other, amazed that we'd wrapped the series up with two Tests still to be played (the third Test at Edgbaston was drawn). The unity of the group was the strength behind our victory – we used only 12 players during the campaign, while by series' end the English had jotted down 29 different names on their team sheets – and we had beaten an English team that boasted heavyweight names like Botham, Gower, Gooch, Gatting, Lamb and Dilley. Emphasising the English selectors' scattergun approach was the incredible statistic that during the series Merv Hughes took 19 wickets involving 17 different batsmen. No wonder the champagne didn't touch any lips but was sprayed over the mostly Aussie crowd and each other in a celebration in our Manchester dressing-room that lasted for hours.

I can still remember singing in the showers for at least an hour. There were half a dozen showers in a row, none with a door, and we punched out the national anthem, 'I Still Call Australia Home', 'Khe Sanh' and countless other songs we only knew the choruses of. When AB held the replica Ashes urn up to his face, we knew we'd achieved one of his dreams, lengthened our careers and helped put Australian cricket back on track.

We went on to win the series 4–0 and only rain prevented it being a 6–0 result. When you consider we had been labelled 'the worst team to leave Australia' at the start of the tour by Thommo and others, you can put into perspective what an era-changing adventure the four months were. A key factor in our win was that during the series AB's captaincy went from being solid to flamboyant as he employed tactics and field placements he'd learnt off his former Essex captain, Keith Fletcher. The experience of Terry Alderman, who had played a lot of county cricket, was invaluable and proved a huge asset for the team. Similarly important was the contribution of Geoff Lawson, who among other things plotted the downfall of David Gower a few times by deliberately getting him caught down the leg side, flying in the face of commonsense.

Unusual moves like having fieldsmen in catching positions at short cover and short midwicket threw a lot of the Englishmen's regimented games into turmoil. Graham Gooch couldn't come to grips with AB placing two fielders in the short midwicket area; he kept trying to hit straight balls squarer but only succeeded in getting himself regularly trapped lbw. To me, this showed their lack of flexibility, that over the years they had fine-tuned their game to the point that they couldn't play any other way. I was stunned and felt let down when Gooch pulled out of the fifth Test, saying that he needed to go back and get some form in county cricket. He could get runs blindfolded for Essex, but his country needed his quality and experience, especially after a number of senior players revealed they had signed up for a South African rebel tour and were thus out of the final two Tests. Gooch was a guy the others looked to for guidance. His presence should have given others peace of mind, but he walked away when he was needed most, showing that lack of total commitment which is one of the primary reasons England never won back the Ashes during my career. Another prominent player, Neil Foster, who obviously had South Africa on his mind, had pulled out of the third Test, at Edgbaston, because of what amounted to no more than a blood blister on his right index finger. I remember him showing us the affected area the day before the game. The damage was hardly visible and he probably summed it up perfectly when he said, 'I'll still get paid the same [if I don't play] – insurance will cover it.' Maybe he said it tongue in cheek, but where there's smoke there's fire.

In total contrast, our regular benchies, especially Tim May, Carl 'Mocca' Rackemann and Tom Moody, were absolutely phenomenal, never complaining, always supportive and very much a part of our success. They gave themselves and put aside personal aspirations for the benefit of the team and that made our unit tougher and tighter. My favourite Mocca story centres around his relaxed attitude to getting ready for the start of play. Carl would invariably be just gathering his gear together when the umpires walked in to tell us they were on their way. At this point all the guys should have been ready to take the field, but on one particular occasion Mocca was frantically searching for a second sock to put on his left foot, needed to aid in softening the impact as he landed his giant frame at the crease in his delivery. Refusing to believe the sock lost or misplaced, he insisted on the 12th man taking his place for the first over while he found it. It was a sheepish-looking quick bowler who eventually made it out to the middle, explaining that he'd put three socks on his right foot, hence the confusion.

David Gower was a laid-back England captain who seemed to let things just evolve in due course, without trying too much to influence the direction of the game. But perhaps his worst error came before a ball was bowled in the series. During our lead-up match at Worcester we played with 'Reader' balls, which had elevated seams that enabled certain bowlers to gain exaggerated sideways movement off the pitch. Phil Newport was unplayable and captured 11 wickets in a bowling display that was simply too good for us. We preferred the 'Duke' ball, which was similar to the 'Kookaburra' we used in Australia and far more friendly for the batsman. It was agreed before the Headingley Test that if both captains wanted the same brand of ball, then that one would be used, but if they didn't agree then a toss of the coin would decide the outcome. Gower didn't push for the ball that could have helped his bowlers, instead agreeing to the Duke and in the process wiping out Newport, Foster, DeFreitas and Derek Pringle's chances of success. Of course, a ball still has to be put in the right areas, but the Poms hadn't done their homework. It wasn't until the fourth Test that they decided to argue the choice of ball, but by then the momentum was so seriously in our favour that it made no difference when Gower won both tosses that took place before the match.

Not only was the England captain accommodating, so too were the hometown umpires. I'm not sure why, but we certainly seemed to get the better of close decisions during the series. Terry Alderman seemed to be shouting for something every over he bowled – and it was little wonder, up against the suspect techniques of batsmen such as Tim Curtis, Kim Barnett, Martyn Moxon and Tim Robinson (who all batted in the England top three at some point during the series). These guys batted in a manner that allowed them to cash in on flat pitches against journeyman bowlers in county cricket, but on closer examination and under intense pressure they melted like a chocolate bar in a hot saucepan. The extent of Alderman's dominance was probably best summed up in a billboard we saw which read 'Thatcher Out' and under which was written, in a graffiti scrawl, 'lbw Alderman'. Similarly, the local media certainly didn't help the English team by their merciless attack and constant 'mickey-taking' jibes. Probably the most personal attack came after the Old Trafford hiding, the story of which was headlined in one paper with regard to the English team: 'No Pride, No Guts, No Good!'

England players making their debut during this summer, such as Mike Atherton and Devon Malcolm, must have felt like retreating from the all-consuming barrage rather than restoring the imbalance on the field. It seemed like they were all fair game for the poison pen, but our attitude was if it wasn't them it sure would have been us. Especially sweet was the fact that the Botham bogey that had afflicted Australian teams for the previous decade or more had finally been put to rest, even if we were still obliged to watch the 'miracle of Headingley, 1981' every time there was a rain delay. And maybe I played a part in this. At our first team meeting, AB had kept on saying, 'Botham this, Botham that, what are we going to do?' Eventually, as discreetly as I could, I said, 'Why are we worrying about him? That was the team's problem back in 1981, it's not a problem now.' At this point of my career I wasn't the most vocal of team members at a team meeting, but I could see us going down the Windies path of paying too much respect to the opposition when the key element should be always worrying about your own game.

After the final Test, at The Oval, we further celebrated our success at the exclusive Park Lane Hotel, courtesy of two of Australian cricket's best supporters, and the prime architects of the World Series Cricket revolution of the '70s, Austin Robertson and John Cornell. The wives and partners came along and we all got kitted up in our best gear. Every player stood up and made a speech and then proposed a toast. My words of wisdom were brief, as usual, but hopefully to the point: 'It was a great tour, one I'll never forget, and I'm glad I was part of it.' Then we went home to a ticker-tape parade that astounded us all in its size and emotion, with Sydneysiders jam-packing the city centre to salute us. I'll never forget gathering in a room at the Regent

Hotel, near Circular Quay, where we discussed the day's schedule and what we had to do. There hadn't been too many people around when we entered the hotel, and the general consensus was that the event was going to be a bit of a fizzer. Then we walked out the front doors and the whole of George Street was packed with screaming supporters who showered us in confetti and some well-directed unused 'dunny' rolls. At the Town Hall the team was handed the keys to the city, and certainly the mood of the moment suggested that Australia's resurgence back to the top was well and truly under way.

I was at ease with my game. The real Steve Waugh had finally broken through the self-imposed constraints caused by 'paralysis by analysis' and my constant worrying about other people's expectations. I felt good about my tour, except for the last couple of Tests, where I dropped off intensity and lost the momentum I'd built up during the first three months. I had peaked in the 'live' Tests and faded in the 'dead rubber' ones, a habit the Australian team would find difficult to shake in the coming years. I wanted to believe this was the start of something big for me, and at that moment could not have believed that within 16 months I'd be out of the Test XI.

My education wasn't complete just yet. And the cause of that sharp pain in my back when I bowled had not yet been identified.

With Lynette after I scored one of the more important centuries of my career, against the West Indies in Sydney, 1992–93.

Three images from
my first tour of the
Caribbean, in 1991.

Beach cricket in
St Vincent.

On the bus in
Antigua with (from
left) Mark Taylor, Geoff
Marsh, Peter Taylor,
Mike Veletta, Terry
Alderman, Mark Waugh,
Craig McDermott and
Merv Hughes.

Enjoying the Dunn's
River Falls, made famous
in the movie *Cocktail*,
with Ian Healy, Peter
Taylor, Bruce Reid and
Mike Whitney. This was
the rest day of the first
Test, in Jamaica.

Viv Richards is caught and bowled in the second one-dayer of our 1991 tour, at Bridgetown in Barbados, a match we won to clinch the series. This was my 100th wicket in limited-overs internationals.

The Waugh twins in the dressing-room at North Sydney Oval after we both scored hundreds in an FAI Cup match against Victoria in 1991–92.

Mark and me in Adelaide in late 1992, helping to promote Mark Gately's biography of us, quaintly titled *Waugh Declared*.

Michael Slater and me in London at the start of the 1993 Ashes tour, wearing our new business suits.

The 1993 Australians at Bristol for the game against Gloucestershire where we donned plastic ears as a 'tribute' to Craig McDermott.

Matt Hayden (LEFT) in the infamous 'Daktari' outfit during the '93 trip, with Ian Healy looking on, and me with fellow nerd Tim May (RIGHT) on the same tour.

Michael Slater (left) and Tim May celebrate a catch by the headless S. Waugh that dismissed Graham Thorpe at Trent Bridge in 1993.

In 1994, the ACB finally introduced media training for its elite cricketers, and Mark Taylor, Shane Warne, Ian Healy and I learnt plenty. Long-time ACB media manager Ian McDonald is at far left.

This crowd stampede during an aborted one-dayer at Gujranwala in Pakistan in 1994 was one of the most potentially horrific things I ever saw. Yet the man smiling near the front still had time to yell out, 'Steve Waugh, you are my favourite cricketer!'

Here are the results of the facial growth competition we amused ourselves with on the same tour. From left: Bob Simpson, Justin Langer, me, Ian Healy (at the back, near the light so you can make out his 'moustache'), Damien Fleming, Jo Angel, Michael Slater, David Boon, Tim May, Glenn McGrath, Gavin Robertson, Craig McDermott, Michael Bevan.

By 1994, as the worlds of sport and entertainment slowly merged, cricket's
highest-profile players became as much celebrities as cricketers. No one personified
this evolution more than our new superstar, Shane Warne. Here, Shane (catching
Alfred E. Neuman), Michael Slater and I pose for a shot that appeared on the
cover of *MAD* magazine.

15

Lofty expectations

There were nights during the '89 Ashes tour when I had to sleep on the floor or take painkilling tablets to alleviate lower-back pain that had that 'catchy' nature about it. If I got myself into a certain position the pain would be searing. Bowling was definitely out of the question. The quicks used to say you weren't a bowler until you'd had 'stressies' (stress fractures) in your back and had torn your 'grunt' (intercostal) muscle. After having X-rays that showed nothing of consequence,

I underwent an MRI (magnetic resonance imaging) scan and, sure enough, it revealed a pars defect and a stress fracture in the fifth lumbar vertebra (L5).

An MRI can be a very daunting experience if the medical staff hasn't briefed you beforehand on exactly what is going to happen. I was placed on a sliding table the width of my shoulders, with cushions underneath me. In a 'mummy' position, arms crossed, hands on opposite shoulders and knees slightly bent, I was pushed into a round opening before being gently lifted up towards the ceiling on the machine, which totally enclosed me. Unable to move and feeling incredibly claustrophobic, I panicked and broke out in a cold sweat a split second before the machine stopped and left me cross-eyed and staring at the roof just centimetres away. Trying to relax in that machine for 45 minutes was the closest thing to torture I have experienced, but the knowledge gained made it worthwhile. In lay terms, an injury to one side of the spine that I had suffered as a young kid had calcified and healed itself to an exaggerated level but in the process made the other side vulnerable. Under the stress of constant sport, it had finally cracked.

The L5 is down near the base of the back. The only cure was a complete withdrawal from the bowling crease, which was a devastating piece of news for me because bowling was not only an outlet for frustration, it also allowed me to stay involved in the game and express myself rather than drift out of it. It would be 12 months before I could get back into the action with ball in hand.

A positive was that I now appreciated the fact that I needed to improve my fitness if I wanted longevity in the game. It was the beginning of a relationship with the medical fraternity that would continue throughout my career, as I finally realised how important they were in keeping guys on the park through correct diagnosis and rehabilitation programs. During this first experience with stress fractures, I needed medical intervention to help get me as close to pain-free as possible. A relatively new procedure, proposed by Dr Phil Hardcastle from Perth, involved injecting cortisone into the aggravated and highly inflamed area under the guidance of an ultrasound to make sure the needle found its required mark. The worst part of this procedure was played out in my head. A first-up injection was easy to handle, but my bravery quickly subsided when the doctor said, 'That's just to deaden the area for the next one.' It wasn't the vague sensation of the second injection entering the flesh between the joints but the size of the needle and the distance it went in that had me tensing up as I watched with clenched teeth all the action on a nearby monitor.

As soon as the fluid surged from the needle, the pain subsided instantly, but once the bone had mended with rest the ailment needed a long-term remedy, which would come via a totally unexpected phone call. I can only put it down to fate. On the other end of the phone was Nigel Websdale, a guy I'd never met, who had read about my problem in the newspaper. He told me I was soft but that he could fix me if I was prepared to work hard and listen to him. It was a leap of faith, but as no one else had offered me a solution, beyond rest, I agreed to meet him.

Trying to label Nigel is almost impossible. He is a free-spirited fitness- and lifestyle-obsessed 'guru' with a love of the surf and an acquired knowledge that has come from listening to and observing those around him. When I met him I found that he walked with a limp, his hair was untamed and he had fathered many children, but he looked as fresh-faced as a 25-year-old – nothing like a guy in his mid-40s, a result that came, he reckoned, from an 'alternative' diet and a belief in his workout regime. Two things we all need in life but often don't get are direction and discipline. Here was a chance for me to improve that I wasn't about to let slip, even though I knew nothing of the guy. It was a gut-instinct decision on my part to work with

Nigel, and I made a commitment to follow his out-of-left-field ideas as part of my quest not only to bowl again but also to become leaner and stronger than I'd ever been before.

Out went all the junk food, including my eternal weakness for choco-lates, fried food and takeaways. In came buckwheat, steamed vegetables, miso paste and ginseng tablets. The miso paste was a test of my will-power. Each day before breakfast I would roll up 20 ball-bearing-sized pieces of this black, tar-like substance and swallow them with water. They had a bitter taste 100 times more biting than Vegemite and when they stuck in the throat the aftertaste lingered long into the morning. A half-dozen tablets of ginseng followed to lift the energy levels, and then buckwheat cooked like rice gave me an extra boost to put in the hard yards at the gym – though it had the unwanted side-effect of dam-aging the ozone layer. This diet, while bland and boring, was bearable; the real life change came from sticking with the strengthening routines, which could only be described as unique. They revolved around giving me 'core stability', which would act as the base that muscles surround-ing the spine could rely on and alleviate the stress and strain placed on my lower back.

At least once a week Nigel would come down from the central coast, more than an hour's drive north of Sydney, and we'd train at the Bondi Surf Life Saving Club, an equidistant journey for me. At first, the work was so demanding and different from what I'd seen or done before that the results weren't very encouraging, but the thought of a new body to match a tougher mind was very appealing. Nigel had me on the chin-up bar doing lateral raises, chin-ups and leg raises. The leg raises weren't your average knees-to-chest stuff, but straight legs up to the bar and back down again, with the goal of not swinging on the bar but stabilis-ing myself using core stability. The first day I managed to do three of them; three months later I was doing 10 repetitions of 20 and for the first time in my life had a real base of strength. 'Roller work' initially involved using a hand-held wheel, then a bar and weights, and finally the bumper bar of a car parked in neutral, which I would grab and roll back and forth while in a kneeling position.

Nigel always had something new to keep the sessions lively and fun. He believed my fingers needed strengthening, so he brought along a pair of gardening gloves that had large lead sinkers tied to each finger with thick string. I would don the gloves and curl my fingers up and down. A motorbike helmet had a 10 kg free weight welded to it and was used to work my neck muscles. Each week I became stronger and eventually, and for the first time in my life, I looked forward to visiting the gym. The discipline required was to prove a blessing in disguise – I could fall back on the lessons I had learnt and put them into action when in early 1991 the selectors made their judgement call and dropped me. I was the type of guy who struggled to train alone but revelled in rivalry and a companion to measure up against, so Nigel would call every day and demand logbooks of the work I had done, which was exactly the influence I needed. There were plenty of days when I'd get to 17 or 18 leg raises and think, *That's enough – no one will know I haven't done 20.* But something told me these were the little battles that needed to be won for the bigger picture to become clear. The only person I needed to impress was myself.

In 1989–90 we faced three different countries in six Tests over eight weeks, with one-day games in between. It was a jumbled program and difficult to adapt to. I carried my excellent Ashes form and confidence into the New Zealand and Sri Lanka legs of the summer, but lost my way against Pakistan's world-class attack, which featured Imran Khan, Wasim Akram and Waqar Younis. Maybe it was the fact that I was in commanding form against the lesser-quality attacks that started the dominos tumbling that would eventually lead to me losing my place in the side. I was given a somewhat false snapshot of where I was at and how good I was.

At this stage of my career I was a very good player of average bowling and an average player of very good bowling. The wake-up call Wasim, Waqar and Imran gave me was another part of my overall cricket education, which had to be learnt and earnt before I could consider myself the finished product. I became distracted, believing my game was in great shape, which led to a drop-off in intensity at cricket training. This was ironic, given that I was working harder than ever on my fitness. As far as my batting was concerned, instead of realising the journey had just begun, I sat back and admired the view. Further, having struggled for so much of my first three years of Test cricket, I still didn't trust myself enough and subconsciously kept thinking that my excellent run of form was going to have to end shortly. And relations with Bob Simpson had stalled somewhat after I rejected his offer to become my manager. He'd made Greg Matthews a wealthy man by securing him a range of endorsements, and obviously saw me as the natural progression after he fell out with Mo. I'd never had a manager before and, besides not really needing one, I thought having the coach in charge of my affairs would represent a conflict of interest.

The upshot of all this was that I was hardly ready when my mind began playing tricks on me whenever the two great 'Ws' from Pakistan had the ball in their hands. Watching opposition quick bowlers can be helpful in assessing their pace, bounce and body language, but it can also be terminal if you take too much in. This is especially so if they are taking wickets or beating the bat regularly, because you start to build up an image of it being impossible to do well out there when your turn comes around.

The Adelaide Oval is the worst venue for this suffocating line of thought to develop. The players' viewing room is parallel to the pitch, with open windows that give you the feel of being an extension of the crowd while also being much closer to the action than at any other ground owing to Adelaide's modestly sized square boundaries. By the time you watch the ball out of the bowler's hand and then swivel around to see the batsman play it, only a split second has elapsed, but the illusion of speed and the apparent lack of time in which to counter it are magnified. During the second Test against Pakistan in 1989–90 I should have moved from my seat to break the trancelike state I had assumed, but I didn't want to look flustered or unsettled and instead stayed put and was drawn further into a dilemma that clouded my judgement.

By the time I arrived at the crease, all that had to be done was for the scoreboard attendant to reach down and grab another sign to put next to Wasim Akram's wicket column. Some days out in the middle, starting in such a fragile way can change, but only if you have recognised the mediocre psyche you've immersed yourself in. It may be a blow to the body or your partner saying, 'Come on, sharpen up, get yourself going.' On this occasion I didn't escape, and ended up missing a yorker because I had my eye on the man and not the ball. Wasim had a jet-propelled run-up that exploded out of a casual walk back to its starting point. He was equally adept at over and around the wicket, could sense fear in a batsman and instinctively knew when to up the ante. He was a cunning competitor, especially around the wicket because he ran in directly behind the umpire and only appeared a split second before delivery, as if he was trying to win a game of peekaboo. A batsman needs that extra bit of concentration to focus on the ball at the point of delivery. His deceptively broad shoulders, incredibly fast shoulder rotation and beautiful wrist position gave him the ability to change his pace at will and catch batsmen by surprise.

Wasim was a guy who was at his most dangerous when he appeared to be struggling through tiredness, injury or lack of form. Most often he was foxing, and when a batsman fell into the trap he'd swoop and finish off the unsuspecting in an instant. Both he and Waqar would 'verbal' batsmen as part of their armoury and had the pace and skill to back it up, making them a formidable combination.

My form slump wasn't helped by a 'Clayton's' Test in Sydney, where more than two-thirds of the match was lost to the weather and S. Waugh went wicketless, runless and catchless. Luckily, I wasn't playing on incentives.

As the season went on, I felt my strength somehow draining, particularly after having such a poor run in the one-day World Series, where I lost my place (to Mark) for the second final. Often a player can't identify why things are going well, and the same can be said when a downturn in fortunes presents itself. A niggling injury, mental fatigue, family issues, negative press articles, homesickness and complacency can all play their part; they may not seem damaging at first, but like a leaking ballpoint pen in your pocket they get away from you quickly without getting your attention until someone finally has the boldness to tell you about the damage they have caused. I'm not sure what precipitated my downward spiral. Perhaps being in the limelight was something I still wasn't entirely comfortable with, nor did I enjoy the lofty expectations that now escorted my every exploit. I was in a similar position to when I first started – the 'wonder boy' who saw himself as an average guy and just wanted to play the game he loved.

★

While I was struggling with life in the public eye, the Australian team had become one of the better Test and one-day outfits in world cricket. By the time we travelled to Wellington for a one-off Test in March 1990, we had strung together 14 Tests in a row without defeat and fancied our chances against anyone bar the litmus test, the West Indies.

The Basin Reserve in Wellington would probably rate as one of my least favourite venues for international cricket, purely because it's invariably freezing cold and howling a gale, which makes playing both uncomfortable and very challenging. It's uncomfortable no matter where you are, with concrete floors in the change rooms and no trees or enough grandstands to halt the icy winds, which all adds up to a venue that lacks that special character that brings the best out of players. Leading up to the Test we endured two days of consistent rain, which continued on the morning of the match. As a group we fell for the oldest trick in the book, believing the match officials' verdict about the chances of a start in the match without ever questioning the guy with the best knowledge of local conditions: the groundsman. We left the ground not long after arriving, having been told there was no chance of play before lunch and probably not much of a chance all day, so we returned to our hotel to await further instructions. Half an hour later, a frantic message was being relayed around our rooms: 'Get down to the ground – we're starting in 45 minutes.'

A couple of the guys were nabbed just before getting into the lift for a spot of shopping, while others had their nap interrupted. We were chaotic in our warm-ups, with AB going virtually straight from one of the two minibuses we used to travel to and from the hotel each day out to lose the toss, and as if to further punish us for our unprofessionalism we were 4/12 after 25 minutes of play. The pitch had the consistency of plasticine, with the ball coming off with a sluggish bounce that was incredibly hard to time and caused us enormous anxiety. The Kiwis, on the other hand, were loving it, especially Richard Hadlee, who like Glenn McGrath today was an owner of line and length, a bowler with the class to land *everything* on the seam. Hadlee got me with the perfect ball just as I looked set with 25 to my name. It pitched middle then deviated past my technically correct forward defence and took the top of off-stump, leaving me without an intact set of bails and a pose worthy of a bronze statue. It was one of the very few times I felt utterly helpless to defend myself; quite simply, he was too good for me. I would have defied even Don Bradman to have laid bat on that ball, though perhaps he would have stepped back and pulled it though midwicket.

My second innings was one that lingers in my memory, not for the fact that I made 25 again, but for the ferocity of the send-off I copped from the fieldsman at point, Mark Greatbatch. It's fair to say that 'Batchy' and I didn't see eye to eye, but for that matter he didn't rate too many of us Aussies, believing we were too cocky and arrogant. We thought he was an evenly balanced guy, with chips on both shoulders. Hadlee did me with the 'pea and thimble' trick: a couple of searching deliveries followed by a nice juicy wide one that had boundary written all over it, except for the undetected fact of it being a slower ball. Like a chocoholic in Willy Wonka's factory, I couldn't stop myself and awkwardly spooned the ball out to point. The humiliation of being deceived doubled when I was shown exactly which way to exit the field in tandem with a 'Fuck off!' that reverberated around the ground. Batchy was immediately struck off the Christmas card list – as later would be Arjuna Ranatunga and Salim Malik – and he also went straight into the memory, in the file marked 'every dog has its day'.

Our eventual nine-wicket loss was severe, but we had at least been taught a valuable lesson: don't leave the ground until the day's play has been officially declared 'washed out'.

There was just one more game to be played in the Australian season before a short tour of Sharjah and then, finally, a break from the game. That one more game was the grudge Sheffield Shield final against Queensland at the SCG. For the second time in his career, Geoff Lawson was a late withdrawal on the morning of the final, this time throwing us into a state of upheaval as he was the captain. I assumed

I would get the job, having been in the Australian team for four years and having being told by Henry during the season that I'd probably be next in line if the chance came around. At the same time, Mark Taylor was in the middle of a sensational run of form, having scored six hundreds in his first 14 Tests since his debut the previous season, and three out of the four NSW selectors had a connection with his grade club, Northern District. Tubby got the nod and they probably made the right choice, as I was struggling with the bat and looking a bit jaded. It's history now that Mark hit a century in each innings for the winning side and was immediately pencilled in as not only Henry's successor, but AB's too.

In many ways the fact that this path was now pretty much set was a relief to both of us, and being good mates we accepted the course that had been decided. Tubby was ready and looking for more say in team mechanics, while I needed more time to get comfortable with the media and my game. Not having the state captaincy would allow me to work on a number of things I needed to get right: oratory skills, the mental aspect of the game, a better understanding of my style of play, and a full appreciation of the requirements of being an international cricketer.

Our form in Sharjah was again largely forgettable, probably best explained by our fear of playing on grassless pitches that favoured spin over pace. Most memorable was an unexpected invitation to the Australian team from Imran Khan during the tournament, to take the place of late withdrawal India in two exhibition matches in America. As players we jumped at the chance, but I'm sure our partners weren't too thrilled with the 12-day junket, and neither was Bob Simpson. He didn't believe we deserved the reward of such an appealing tour and told us flatly, 'This is the last freebie you blokes are getting.'

But the opportunity was too attractive for us to turn down. The first match was played in the Bronx in New York and threatened to turn into a complete farce when the organisers tried to lay coir matting on top of sand. Needless to say, we refused to face Wasim, Waqar and Imran on such a treacherous pitch and successfully had it moved to the adjoining grass, which was the lesser of two evils.

We somehow managed to win despite playing with little or no discipline, but rather with a free spirit and carefree attitude. 'Exhibition' to us meant exactly that, but to Pakistan's supporters the result was a killer blow, as I think they had backed their side for plenty. Promoting the game wasn't easy. I recall one American, when asked what he thought about 'cricket', replying succinctly, 'Isn't that a bug?' Merv Hughes, being the most gregarious and possibly the closest thing we had to an American, became our spokesperson for promoting the game, but he sometimes struggled to get his message across in the way the organisers wanted. During an interview with Aussie ex-pat Gordon Elliott, Mervyn's answers were subtitled so the New Yorkers could understand what he was gibbering on about.

Ten days of partying, seeing Madonna at Madison Square Garden, watching the New York Mets baseball team at Shea Stadium, a drive through Harlem at 3 a.m. in a taxi with Darren Lehmann, a second match with Pakistan at the Los Angeles Coliseum (main venue for the 1984 Olympics and then home to the Los Angeles Raiders NFL team), and being paid only half the money owed to us – these are the events that have stayed with me from this unique tour.

I've always loved the element of adventure that touring different countries provides, and if a hint of danger is involved, the more likely I'll be attracted to it. The adrenaline rush of being in one of the world's most energetic cities, combined with the relaxing effects of a couple of Southern Comforts and Coke, gave me the idea of taking a first-hand look at Harlem, one of the world's most feared precincts. 'Boof' Lehmann, just past his 20th birthday, was a willing ally, so we commandeered a cab and gave the driver $50 to show us the rough end of town. It was stuff straight out of a movie set – fire-riddled apartments, graffiti everywhere you looked, gangster types ducking and weaving on every corner, drug deals openly taking place and groups of youths in street clothes huddling around 44-gallon drums of open flames. Only once did we actually stop and look someone in the eye, and the intent aimed at us was unmistakeable. We weren't welcome and the taxi driver shouted, 'Don't look at them, let's get out of here!'

It was a real buzz, but we read in the next morning's paper a story of a cabbie who had been killed the previous evening in the area we'd been scouting around in. We were probably irresponsibly misguided in our belief that alcohol gave us an exemption from vulnerability, but I've always believed that to grow as a person you have to live your life and experience what the world has to offer.

16

Attitude

I had been playing cricket consistently since the tour of India that began in August 1986, while the Australian team had not had a break since the start of the Pakistan adventure in 1988. Now, finally, it was time to stay at home during the winter of 1990, to build a house and prepare for my wedding to Lynette the following year. Subcontracting a house from scratch was a job I had no idea about, and certainly I underestimated how much time and effort was needed to make it all come together, but at the time it seemed like an exciting concept that would open up my eyes to a whole new experience. Thankfully, Lynette's father, Phil, took control of the site as the foreman/project manager and guided us through a process which became a two-year exercise. I was a willing and able worker, with eagerness overcoming my lack of skill as a carpenter, painter and labourer, and it was stimulating to do something that wasn't associated with sport. Mind you, the novelty of painting cedar windows three times over, together with the whole inside and outside of the house, wore off after 18 months!

Our purchase of the block of land had been a direct result of Mr Packer's $15 000-a-year-for-three-years loyalty contract that I'd signed back in 1985. Every dollar went towards the acquisition of the land. Sport can give you a privileged lifestyle, but I never wanted to see cricket as a job because that would have taken away its very essence – that it was a game to be enjoyed and one that can reveal your character and let you express yourself. The word 'job' to me conjures up images of *having* to do it rather than *wanting* to do it, and increased the importance of earning money from it. For professional cricketers, the money should be an end product of the process, not the starting point.

I'm not sure why, but I went into the Ashes campaign of 1990–91 experiencing a mixture of emotions. I knew that I could score runs against the Poms, but the previous season's results had me in a fluctuating state of mind. A failure in my only innings of the first Test in Brisbane, followed by another at the MCG in the Boxing Day Test, gave me the sinking sensation that bad news was just around the corner. No doubt my lack of Test runs was due to the space between my ears, because domestically I was playing brilliant cricket. In the lead-up to the Melbourne Test, Mark and I assembled a world-record partnership for the fifth wicket of 464, both of us making chanceless double hundreds against an attack that featured Bruce Reid, Terry Alderman and Chris Matthews on a WACA pitch that had chewed up and spat out many a helpless Bluebag batting line-up before (and has since).

This innings gave me an insight into what made me tick. I had been dropped from No. 3 to No. 6 without explanation by captain Geoff Lawson, which I thought was fairly ordinary considering I had stepped into the breach under Greg Dyer's leadership to fill the problematic 'first drop' position. Now I'd been flicked and not told why, which I saw as a slap in the face for a guy who was in the national side as a batsman. Anger can never be used as a motivator, because its poison seeps in almost unnoticed until it rots you to the core, by diluting your focus on the task at hand. However, it can strengthen your resolve so that when you are not playing well you don't back off the accelerator and become satisfied with your work. Instead, your focus becomes increasingly narrow and your desire intensifies. Good form must be capitalised on, not admired.

I was driven, to the extent of feeling unleashed, and wanted the massacre to keep going, but of course a declaration had to happen eventually. Half-jokingly, in the dressing-room after Henry called us in, I mentioned to Mike Whitney, 'Jeez, we could have put on 600!' As time goes by, stories get more elaborate, and I often hear now how I cursed the fact that we hadn't kept going and was dirty on the declaration. The truth is that I reckon we could have made that many if we'd been given the chance, but obviously the right decision had been made. Maybe Henry made the correct call in changing the order, too, and I'll always abide by the captain's decision, but I disagreed with his lack of man-management skills. From a brilliant, uninhibited display of batsmanship I metamorphosed into a lead-footed block artist in the space of a week, and on the third day of the Test I missed a straight one from Angus Fraser. I was burdened by the weight of expectation and a loitering pessimistic train of thought that I'd peaked for NSW and consequently failure must be imminent.

★

A home Test is meant to be a special experience, but I generally found it to be a distracting one. Numerous requests for tickets came in from people I barely knew, and there were family commitments and countless offers to catch up with people I hadn't seen recently, which all contributed to a rushed and hectic lead-up to the game. In 1991, something had to give; the whispers that this was my last chance had now gathered enough impetus for teammates to say to me, 'Good luck in this Test – hope you play well.' While this support was appreciated, in many ways it worsened the situation because it made me think about my predicament more. Frailty of mind can easily be detected by the opposition: it may be exposed by how you walk to the wicket, a lack of animation in mid-pitch conversations, the avoidance of eye contact with fielders, or perhaps the amount of 'air' batting you do between balls. (Incidentally, if I had to pick my favourite and all-time top-scorer in Tests in this specialised art form it would have to be Chris Harris of New Zealand, who was poetry in motion, with shots all around the park . . . until the five and a quarter ounces of leather came his way, when batting suddenly became much tougher.)

Just as I had batted my way through to within two runs of a potentially career-saving half-century, I got a faint edge to a spiteful delivery from Devon Malcolm. The ball crashed into my ribcage at 90 miles an hour, and looped to short leg to end my fightback. It was a double blow, the termination of my dig and the stinging, searing pain of a couple of crushed ribs. It's amazing how, when you're in a battle, adrenaline inhibits pain, but as soon as you break out of that cocooned world of match play the agony surges and homes in on the damaged area. Further punishment awaited me once I'd thrown off my gear and undressed, because the only way to treat cricket ball-impact injuries is by applying ice in a hessian bag to the tender areas. The initial contact of the ice with the skin takes your breath away, but it's the constant dripping of water droplets that tortures and torments and acts as punishment for your dismissal.

I always found facing Devon Malcolm a difficult assignment, largely due to his unpredictability and genuine pace. He was a match-winner, but throughout his career he didn't fit the mould required by the English selectors. He was poorly managed, plagued by inconsistent selection and hampered by team strategies. Australia, as a team, breathed a sigh of relief whenever a steady medium-pacer was picked in front of him, because we knew what we were going to get, unlike with Devon who was either hot or cold but invariably kept you anxious about what might happen. He could plant that seed of doubt in your mind in the lead-up to a game, and got the bowler at the other end plenty of wickets through his unsettling methods. He had a loose action that relied on his imposing physical attributes, going wide of the crease and slinging it into right-handers as a genuine rule, but unbeknownst to him, if the seam came down right – as it did occasionally – he could move it away with alarming curve. On his day, he was as quick as anyone I'd ever faced. But setting him back were his 'Tufnell-like' qualities in the field and a complete lack of coordination with the willow in hand. It was as if he was allergic to the bat, which just wouldn't sit comfortably in his hands, and his stance was somewhere between that of a baseball slugger and a rabbit caught in the headlights of a Mack truck.

At the other end of the scale was the stereotypical English professional, Eddie Hemmings, whose bowling was all bells and whistles disguised as 'powder puffs'. He was a nice enough guy and was always looking for a lovely friendly chat in the middle, but he didn't realise international cricket was a serious business and not just the 'another day, another dollar' grind that some county players had grown accustomed to. Getting out to the bowling of Hemmings wasn't a crime, but playing for spin was. The very instant I nicked the ball through to the keeper in our second innings I thought, *That's it, pal – time to take a breather!*

I had already resigned myself to being axed, and when Bob Simpson rang a couple of days later at my soon-to-be in-laws' home to tell me the news that I'd been dropped, it was relief, not sadness, that enveloped me. It had more of an impact on Lynette, who was visibly upset, while Phil and Ethel, who had treated me like a son from the very beginning, didn't really know what to say. It was a bonus to get the news straight from the coach, as often players learn of their demise second-hand, via a journalist or a report on radio or TV. Simmo's message was simple but targeted: work hard and make sure you come back a stronger, better player. Telling Mum and Dad was always going to be a lot more difficult than hearing the news myself, and so it was. Instinctively, Mum knew there was something amiss when she opened the front door on my return home. Straightaway, she said, 'What's wrong?'

'I've just been dropped.'

She was pretty upset, with tears welling up. 'Look it's all okay,' I said. 'It's the right time. I'm not too concerned.'

Mark was in the background with Dad when Mum inquired, 'Who's your replacement?'

Pointing towards Mark, I said, 'He's over there. Congratulations – you're in the Test side.'

Of all of us, I think I was probably the most comfortable with the situation, because I knew the decision was right. Mum was in a state of simultaneous elation for Mark and distress for me, while my brother couldn't fully show his joy at being chosen, even after such a long apprenticeship.

It didn't take long for Mark to reveal his class at the highest level, peeling off an effortless Test hundred at the first opportunity, while I went back to Bankstown Oval to start my rehabilitation. Mark's confidence in his own ability was best summed up when, after walking off with that initial Test century next to his name, he looked up to the players' enclosure from the steps leading up to the rooms at Adelaide and said to AB, 'I told you so. You should have picked me earlier!'

That is pretty much Mark to a tee – offering opinions full of dry humour that border on being outrageous but are often underlined with the truth. Generally in team meetings Mark would bring a clear, concise perspective to an issue that was going back and forth, by saying exactly what he thought. 'We're talking rubbish,' he might say. 'It's as simple as sticking to the basics.' Or, 'Let's enjoy what we're doing.' At times the team would get themselves into a bit of a bind in search of meaningful ways to handle the Windies quicks' constant barrage, until Mark would put a spin on the normal wisdom of playing each ball on its merits by saying, 'Hang on – their strength is also their weakness. They have no variety. Once you get used to the pace, there aren't any surprises or variations to upset your rhythm.' Quickly, he turned a negative into a positive.

The impact of being dropped doesn't really hit home until it dawns on you that you're not on the next plane with the team heading to another Test-match venue. Listening to Mark cruise to his debut hundred in front of 20 000 people while I tussled at the local oval in front of 20 devotees of grade cricket underlined the reality of the situation and a plan of attack began to stir in my mind. I knew if I never made it back into the national team that I wouldn't have done my talents justice. And that fact would haunt me – I didn't want to join the 'could have, might have, should have' club of former players gradually eroding through regret. I wanted to make the most of my abilities, so that I'd feel complete with the slippers on and the pipe glowing in front of an open fire.

You'll often hear commentators and analysts utter the phrases, 'It'll make him a better player, he'll come back stronger next time around.' Sounds fantastic in theory, but most players who get dropped either don't make it back or are no better prepared when they get their next chance. Only the iron-willed and fiercely determined ones who are prepared to work harder than they have ever done before will fulfil this furphy of a prophecy. Being dropped is psychologically damaging for most, because the discarded player sees himself as surplus to the requirements of the team and unwanted for the tasks at hand. The first thing I had to do was get over the self-pity. Once my mind was clear of this booby trap, the path back was set out in front of me. I had to be honest about my faults, and needed the help of trusted advisors. I came to the conclusion that I was suffering from an inconsistent method of concentration and the lack of a common routine while preparing for an innings and while at the crease.

And technically there was my troublesome 'Achilles heel'. The absence of a consistently bent front knee when I played forward was causing a chain reaction in which various appendages were out of alignment as I played many of my shots. These included the key to good balance, the head, which was often in motion when it needed to be dead still. When this happened, my eyes were tilted and outside the line of the ball while my weight swayed towards the off side, making me an easy lbw candidate and a regular giver of chances to the keeper from the outside edge of my angled bat. Bob Simpson also tipped me off as to why I was getting all congested when the quicks aimed their short deliveries at my body: I had to stop tucking my left (front) elbow into my body as I tried to play the short ball, he explained. Doing this would free up the elbow and allow me to 'go with' the momentum of the ball, to ride it to safety rather than having to take it on the body or pop it up to a close-in fielder. The correction was simple, and once perfected it gave me a mechanism to repel the short stuff. This was vitally important because I had been tagged as having a serious weakness against the quicks. I needed to have a plan of defence against short-pitched deliveries, as I had made up my mind to put the hook shot away for good after seeing our guys continuously fall victim to it while trying to take on the Windies' fast bowlers. Taking an attacking shot out of the armoury wasn't the 'Australian way', but it would make the fast men bowl to *me*. In these circumstances, I theorised, I would feel more in control of the situation, having forced the quicks to change their plans. I didn't mind being a target for 'bodyline-type' bowling, as it heightened my alertness and activated my combative qualities.

I decided to step up the training with Nigel Websdale, carefully monitor what I was eating and get back in the nets to tighten up my defence. Without doubt, the biggest change I made was in the way I conducted my net practice sessions. I wanted to simulate match conditions every time I walked in. I had probable field placements in my mind depending on who was bowling to me and what type of pitch I was on, and I played each ball on its merits rather than premeditating. Every imaginary innings was built up as if I was in a real contest. I tried not to get out, I wanted to get into the habit of winning the one-on-one battles, and rehearse concentrating when the stakes weren't that high. If I could do this in the nets or playing for Bankstown, the big occasions would seem relatively easy and flow naturally. In a way, I was acquiring mental toughness because I was not giving in to myself or taking the easy option. Top-level cricket is a game that is won between the ears and not necessarily by the most aesthetically pleasing techniques. To me, peer-group pressure and ego are the two greatest dangers to a professional sportsperson, because they take you away from being yourself and playing in the present. I wanted to reach a different level of mental toughness from everyone else. And as is the case in all big things we try to achieve in life, my success or failure in this quest came down to one word: attitude.

Surprisingly enough, I was thrown an unexpected lifeline when the team to tour the West Indies in early 1991 was announced and I was in it. Being on tour but not being in the starting XI was a totally new episode in my sporting life, but I figured that being in the top 16 was infinitely better than being judged the 17th-best option in the land.

The experience would enhance my admiration for the guys who regularly toured during their careers but were rarely selected in the games they craved. No matter what anyone says or does, being a 'benchie' or 'dirt tracker' is tough work. The drain of watching all day and being attentive to everyone else's needs is consuming and tiresome. On tour, the 12th man, for some unknown reason, must shoulder the burden and almost act as a 'gopher' for the needs of the starting XI. I'll never forget the 12th man's nemesis, Greg Matthews, badgering the unfortunate Merv Hughes during a Test match to the point where Merv ended up bringing Greg's entire kitbag onto the field to save running out on future errands. Really, it isn't much of a reward for being the next in line for a starting spot, and in no other sport is a reserve expected to do so much. While the other benchies help out with bits and pieces like getting drinks and towels for the guys, the designated one needs to commit to every ball. It's almost a test to see if he wants it badly enough to break free of the subservient role.

Later on in my career a more united group effort on tour from the reserves gave the 12th man some respite from these monotonous tasks and gave him a chance to practise in the nets or even have a day off. At home in Australia, he can sometimes go back and play state cricket to gain match practice rather than hamper his chances by continual watching, and hence have an opportunity to push his claims when the opening arises. This resolution came about after talks with chairman of selectors Trevor Hohns, coach John Buchanan and me, when certain players who didn't have much game time on tours ended up falling behind the chasing pack, who had the big advantage of actually playing four-day domestic matches while the 12th man was in the dressing-room. Andy Bichel was the guy in my experience who suffered most from carrying the drinks for an extended time. During the 2003–04 season he hardly bowled a ball in anger and eventually lost his impressive form, to the point that he had to rebuild his stocks again in other forms of cricket.

One of the biggest dangers of being a reserve is the fact that there is an abundance of food around the dressing-room. Whether it's nervous energy or boredom, often the remedy is dictated by your stomach. Frustration is a natural response to wanting to be out in the middle, and all guys need to be able to channel their energies somewhere, usually through fitness work or a session in the nets. When I was out of the side I found my practice workouts gained a new level, because they were my only lifeline to the real thing – action out in the middle. From a coach's point of view, a fair degree of insight can be gathered from these sessions. Something as simple as asking for an extra 10 minutes of catching practice, perhaps the way in which you treat the local net bowlers in terms of attitude and respect, or maybe the purpose with which you go about your work can offer clues to your state of mind and how you are reacting to the situation you are in. I found that being upbeat and enthusiastic was largely a matter of personal pride and my desire to make it into the starting side.

I've seen guys lose hope and fall victim to the seductions touring life can offer. A young, wide-eyed Wayne Holdsworth was picked for the 1993 Ashes tour when he was in the prime form of his career, having just taken 7/41 for NSW in the Shield final. On tour, 'Cracker' was knocking over everyone in the nets, including captain Allan Border, with a mixture of raw pace and prodigious late away swing. He was primed to go in the first Test, but missed out to Brendon Julian, whose left-arm swing gave the attack more variety. Stung by his non-selection, Wayne basically went off the required pathway, suffered from a lack of match play and too much social time and wasn't ever again considered seriously for selection in a Test team. He did, however, have the consolation of ending up with three baggy greens when tour manager Des Rundle gave his spares to Wayne at the end of the tour, apparently because he wanted to clear out his excess supplies. The subsequent sale of these iconic symbols at testimonial functions led to a tightening of the ACB's generosity in handing them out. Today, each player receives only one and must sign a statutory declaration explaining why a substitute is needed before it can be replaced.

Our tour of the Caribbean in 1991 was always going to be a stern examination of the team's mettle and a measure of how far we'd come as a team. Our first trial came via an arduous flight seated back in 'cattle class', which spanned a couple of days, and by the time we touched down in the postcard-pretty St Kitts, Bruce Reid had basically seized up. Six weeks earlier, in one of the finest bowling performances of my experience, Bruce had taken 13/148 in the Boxing Day Ashes Test. Now, having been unable to move for most of the trip to the Caribbean as his knees were up near his chin, he literally couldn't get going for the first couple of weeks of the tour. Here was an example of poor business practice by the ACB. We had our prime asset handicapped because they wouldn't pay for upgraded airfares, which hindered our chances and in turn impacted on the board's commercial outcomes. The big picture was cast aside for the pragmatic snapshot that blinded their vision. The time spent together in our cramped confines did, however, give us a chance to get to know one another that little bit better, and for me, it provided a chance for a conversation I needed. Bob Simpson and Errol Alcott both offered their thoughts on my past and present and what I needed to change to fulfil my potential. In their view, it simply came down to a combination of hard work and discipline, with the underrated 'enjoyment factor' thrown in. This wasn't rocket science – in a large part it mirrored my own view – but the fact that they had me in their thoughts and took the time to advise me gave me a real lift as I prepared to take some major steps into the unknown.

★

The Caribbean is the one place where expectations meet reality. It's an invigorating cocktail of laid-back people and carefree lifestyle, sparkling aqua water and pristine sand beaches, steel drums that give off the sound of vitality, rum so smooth that teetollers begin to waver, swaying palm trees that mesmerise in the balmy breeze, the contagious beat of reggae music and a love of life that greets you as soon as you disembark from the plane. The people are so passionate about cricket that it has the ability to both unite and divide the islands, depending on results. Walking through customs the first time is like entering a lion's den, with the locals laughing as they say, 'You boys going to get some good licks', or 'Amby's going to get you good'. Translated, this means: 'You're in for some pain and we're going to enjoy it!' They have a charming way of stating the hauntingly obvious.

Courage and an ability to block out pain were needed if you wanted to succeed against the Windies' imposing pace attack of the '80s and early '90s. Craig McDermott became the first casualty in the second four-day game of the tour, against Jamaica, when he had an eyebrow opened up by a Courtney Walsh bouncer that squeezed between Billy's visor and helmet, leaving a trail of claret and marking the resumption of hostilities. Craig was never the same at the crease after this incident. Geoff Lawson had been similarly scarred after Curtly Ambrose flattened him at the WACA in 1988–89, with the demons taking hold no matter how hard he tried to block them out. Being sconed is like being in a car crash: you know it's about to happen, and even though it materialises almost at a leisurely pace, there's still nothing you can do to stop it. You also know it's going to hurt, but hope the impact won't be too damaging, and then it rips into your flesh and bone and numbs you for a split second before the searing pain takes over. Gus Logie was the Windies' first victim, during the first Test – ironically at the hands of McDermott, with the ball again finding its way through the gap between grill and helmet. Such was the shock of hearing her son being struck and reeling away that Gus's mum had a heart attack and died as she listened on the radio.

Before he learnt of his mother's death, Logie came back from the hospital and batted intelligently with the tail, playing a most courageous innings in scoring 77 not out. The entire encounter was a brutally tough one, with Boonie copping one on the chin that required stitches during the lunch break (repair work he had done without any anaesthetic due to a lack of time and his insistence that it wasn't needed). Mark Waugh was also clouted on the helmet in a game that was more like trench warfare. My position as a reserve gave me the chance to better appreciate what was needed to survive – ticker, and plenty of it. The faint-hearted had no place to hide out in the middle and were picked off as a vulture would attack a dead carcass. I wanted a piece of the action, but knew I was a fair way behind the six batsmen in the side and in all probability would only play if someone suffered an injury or totally lost form.

Sabina Park at Kingston, Jamaica, provided as hostile an environment as you could ever imagine as a cricketer; even the trip on the bus down to the ground every morning stung you into action. Only about a kilometre away was the notorious St Catherine's Prison, full of serious offenders, and each day as we drove past they would stand on benches near the fence line and give it to us, mimicking the slashing of throats and flicking their wrists and fingers to give off a cracking noise that signified the licks we were about to get. The tension and our combative instincts would always kick in when passing these guys, because it was as if we had passed the point of no return. The spectators on the hill would regularly be boozed up with Cockspur rum, while the waft of local 'weed' permeated the air. With their love of the game and the expectation of a physical encounter, the fans gave the match an atmosphere more in keeping with a fight night, and they loved nothing more than seeing local boys Patrick Patterson and Courtney Walsh crack a few heads.

The intoxicating mood could sidetrack certain players, most notably Mike Whitney, who had been down in the change room putting
on his whites when two wickets fell to consecutive balls from Patterson. We had to tell Whit he was required out in the middle ASAP. As
a benchie, I lent a hand as he tried to locate his arm and chest guards
while desperately arranging the rest of his protective gear. Eventually
our No. 11 arrived at the wicket, just a couple of minutes late, to be
met by the thunderous chant of 'Hat-trick! Hat-trick!' booming from
the crowd. Whit later recounted to the boys how loud the locals were
and the bloodthirstiness of their 'Patrick! Patrick!' call. Never at any
stage did he realise he'd survived a hat-trick until we told him after his
gutsy little cameo came to an end.

A drawn Test ended up being a deflating outcome for us, because
we held the balance of power for most of the game, only to mess it
up with one or two crucial dropped catches. The Windies capitalised
on this mini-escape by rising up a couple of gears to pulverise the lads
in the second Test, in Guyana. In many ways it seems strange that a
country that borders Venezuela, Brazil and Suriname in the north of
South America forms part of West Indies cricket. Apparently it was
a beautiful place when under British rule, but it is now a run-down
country with Third World problems. The local dollar has vaporised
against all currencies and the capital and main port, Georgetown,
is basically run by the local mafia. Water in the showers is a murky
brown concoction and leaves a lingering rusty smell on your body that
you can't seem to escape, while restaurant and entertainment options
are very limited.

In 1991, however, I had a chance to experience a life lesson when
Greg Matthews, Mike Whitney and I visited the mafia-dominated slum
of Tiger Bay. We had been befriended by the 'top dog', who went by the
name of Big Daddy. He had helped Greg retrieve part of a gold neck-
lace that had his wedding ring on it, stolen while Mo and Whit were

strolling along a lane that was on Big Daddy's turf. The following night, he took the three of us into his quadrant of town and introduced us to a community worlds away from ours. We entered through alleyways and secret passages and ended up having a beer with his mates in a seedy pool hall called Sagony, where everyone was either drugged out or anticipating trouble. I'd never been so uncomfortable with my lack of a suntan and was eternally grateful we were enjoying the hospitality of the main man. I was also intrigued just watching the interaction going on around the tables, but wary of the potential threats that lurked in my thoughts. Never in my wildest dreams could I have imagined I'd be standing where I was, sipping a Carib beer, mixing with the dark forces of the underworld.

During the second Test I again attended to the cordial requirements and tested my throwing arm out in the nets, allowing the batsmen to find rhythm and confidence. Out in the middle, Richie Richardson was absolutely unstoppable, brutalising the attack for 181 on a barren pitch and taking advantage of a lightning-fast outfield that was as small in all directions as the square boundaries at the Adelaide Oval. I can recall coming on as a substitute fielder and being placed straight into the gully, which is a tough ask when you've been half-asleep watching for hours not expecting any action. I received my wake-up call first ball, when the heir to Viv's throne pinned his ears back and launched a square drive that scorched the turf before crashing into the wooden planks that protected the ball from the polluted canal encircling the ground. The guy was in the zone – you could see it in his eyes – and our bowlers were rendered almost helpless by his assault. Richardson was the most fearless batsman I ever played against, hooking quicks with no regard for personal safety and no second thoughts. He was instinctive and athletic, and had a brooding intensity that menaced opponents. To me, he was a guy to look up to.

Animosity seemed to go hand in hand with the Windies and us, and the controversial run-out of Dean Jones off a no-ball heightened the tensions once more. Dean was bowled by Walsh but didn't hear the call due to the crowd's wild reaction to the stumps being uprooted, and – as you do – he began to walk off. But then the non-striker, Allan Border, started screaming, 'Get back, get back, it's a no-ball!' In the meantime, Carl Hooper had run in from gully, picked the ball up and extracted a stump before Jonesy's frantic attempt to regain his ground could be completed. He was then incorrectly given out by the square-leg umpire, Clyde Cumberbatch. No one seemed to know what the relevant rules said, but our whole squad believed an injustice had occurred. Simmo had the bit between his teeth, but by the time we had the laws clarified a new batsman had taken strike, the tea adjournment was being taken and any chance of a recall had evaporated. We were livid that Jonesy had been run out while not attempting a run, and the mood of the series was now set in stone.

AB returned fire in a symbolic way during his innings by smashing a ball that slipped out of the bowler's hand and lobbed embarrassingly halfway down on the adjacent strip. He was within his rights to hit it for four, though normally sportsmanship would have dictated that the batsman leave it alone. However, after Dean's dubious dismissal our captain wasn't going to show any sympathy towards this gift offering. There had been pre-series pledges about the teams having the occasional drink together, and these had been followed through in Kingston, but now the gloves were off. Windies keeper Jeff Dujon was as welcoming and affable as ever after this match, but no one else from his team shared his enthusiasm.

The atmosphere was bordering on intimidation, at least in my mind – or maybe I was overawed. Guys like Viv, Dessie Haynes and Gordon Greenidge seemed to revel in the concept of 'Black Power'. They knew they were a great team, but I believe that by 1991 they also knew that the balance of power had begun to shift, that the West

Indies team wouldn't always be so dominant. While they were still 'in charge', they were going to make the most of it.

★

This Windies tour saw two of my close friends and teammates, Ian Healy and Mike Veletta, become first-time fathers. To me, to be on tour while your first-born came into the world back home was a huge sacrifice for these guys to make. But such is the commitment and focus that top-level cricket requires that often it takes precedence over family issues. Of course, the game was our job, and planning the birth of a child was each player's responsibility. In 1991 even thinking of going home mid-tour wasn't an option. Later on, in the age of full-time professionalism and with a greater recognition that family involvement is crucial to a player's success, those attitudes were relaxed somewhat. In Jamaica, Heals celebrated the arrival of Emma with teammates, a beer and cigars, and first laid eyes on his daughter via a faxed picture, then Mike celebrated the arrival of Timothy shortly after.

I'm sure Heals felt helpless not being there for the birth, but at least he had the consolation of playing in the Tests and achieving his ambitions. 'Waggy', on the other hand, couldn't get a run in the starting side and must have been agonising over his predicament – unable to be with his wife and new son *and* unable to take on the might of Ambrose and company on the field. Moments like these seemed much more acute to me than some of my colleagues, perhaps because I was to marry Lynette in a few months' time and would then in all probability be faced with a similar circumstance in the not-too-distant future. Would I be willing to miss a Test match or even a tour to be at the birth of my first child? I wanted to think I would, but if it came to destabilising my spot in the team . . . then maybe the answer would be one that favoured the game. It was an event that I decided needed to be planned as best as possible, though luck would still play a big part, of course. Lynette, I'm sure, like the other girls, would have urged me to play cricket, but deep down she would have wanted me to be there, too. Such is the strength of character and sense of independence needed by a cricketer's wife; the ones that manage just get on with life and cope the best way they can.

Between the first and second Test, the two teams played a five-match one-day series, which Australia won 4–1. My form in these games was quite encouraging, and featured my 100th wicket in one-day internationals, achieved when I dived full length to take a one-handed caught-and-bowled to snare Viv Richards in the fourth match, in Barbados. Coming on top of some excellent form in the early tour games, my efforts were rewarded with a recall to the starting XI for the third Test. However, while being eternally grateful for the chance to play in Trinidad, I couldn't help but think I didn't really have a role to play. As Greg Matthews had been unable to break through in the first two Tests, I came into the side in his place to bat at No. 7 and bowl a few overs if the frontliners couldn't make an impression. Still, becoming the first twins to play a Test together was a proud moment for Mark and me, though we both just wanted to get on with the game and bypass the sideshow that developed once the new line-up was announced. No doubt Mum and Dad back home were excited, doubly nervous and extremely proud at seeing their boys making it together.

As I'd learnt early in my Test career, batting at seven or below when you are used to going in earlier can result in your mentality changing; expectation and responsibility when batting in the top six bring a focus that can otherwise be lacking. There is a hesitancy that comes with uncertainty when your role or place in the side is unclear. Batting at seven was tough for a player such as me who liked to build an innings, because from the outset I'd be thinking that time and partners were going to run out. In contrast, an Adam Gilchrist or Ian Healy type can hop straight into their work with the freedom of attacking and not worrying about the consequences as much, because they haven't got that 'specialist batsman' tag on them. My form wasn't an issue, but getting accustomed to the bits-and-pieces function I had to perform left me feeling I'd gained a sympathy vote rather than earnt my spot.

I participated in the third and fourth Tests, making little impact, with my fears coming to fruition in the fourth Test, in Barbados, as I was left four not out at the completion of our ill-fated second innings. Merv Hughes, Craig McDermott and Bruce Reid as a bowling combination could match Glenn McGrath, Jason Gillespie and Brett Lee for class and skill, but with the bat they certainly didn't pose too many problems for the Windies quicks, who saw them as easy kills. 'Chook' Reid was brutally honest when assessing his style of batting, which often had him playing from the adjoining strip. 'I'm no hero – I've got two kids and a family to think of,' he'd say.

It was back to the bench for the final Test, so I kept busy as part of the tour fines committee alongside Heals and Boonie. Not playing also gave me a chance to drop a few postcards to the family, indulge in playing Pass the Pigs with the other reserves and keep up the fitness program Nigel had devised for me. I longed for success out in the middle, but by the time my Caribbean odyssey ended I wasn't any closer to making it back into the team than I had been at the start of the tour. A win for the guys in Antigua failed to hide the disappointment that came with losing the series; we'd again come up short against the world champions. However, we all felt the gap was closing and to a man hoped that we would be among the ones to end their domination in the near future.

★

After a long, arduous tour most of the guys couldn't wait to get home, but we had a mini-tour of Bermuda to complete first. This wasn't exactly hard work; in fact, the place had a mystical, magical quality about it and we looked on the three games as an unwanted intrusion to our holiday, even though they were the reason we'd lobbed on the shores of this picture-perfect tax haven. Besides scoring an eminently forgettable four and two in the two matches I played in, which was ironically appropriate considering the emphasis placed on the golf duels we had while we were there, my favourite recollections of the week came thanks to my roomie, Mike Whitney. Whit was a guy I always loved to see on my side – he played with passion, pride and unrelenting purpose, overcoming crippling injuries and doubting critics and milking every drop of his potential. He was the ultimate team man: loyal, courageous and a great raconteur, with a story for every occasion.

With narrow lanes and speed limits of about 30 kilometres an hour in place across the island of 53 square kilometres, mopeds were the main mode of transport and in our hands they were destined for trouble. One early morning, during a big night on the town, I jumped on the back of Whit's machine and we headed back to our hotel, only to be pulled over by the local constabulary. The policeman's words quickly sobered us up: 'Do you guys know that you're speeding? Twenty miles per hour over the limit, travelling on the wrong side of the road, the driver's helmet is illegal, and the passenger hasn't got one.' Claiming innocence by ignorance of the local laws got us a reprieve *and* some strict instructions: 'Don't do it again!'

As you do with the extra injections of courage we'd consumed earlier in the evening, we sped off twice as fast once we were around the very next corner. We were quite a sight as we began descending the 50 steps leading to our bungalows, with Whit's golliwog hair flowing out from under his Australian team helmet and me clinging on frantically as each step was driven over *Italian Job* style. This was bad news for our next-door neighbours, Mark Waugh and Peter Taylor, because we were in no mood to call it a night just yet. A succession of knocks on their front door failed to entice our teammates out, so we went to Plan B. An open bathroom window was just the lucky break we needed, and in I popped, aided by a leglift from my partner in crime, to open the front door. With that, Whit rushed in at Evel Knievel pace, stopping on a sixpence right next to the boys in their beds. Mark jumped up in a flash while PT, believing his maturity would defuse the situation, played a cool hand, saying simply, 'Don't be silly, Whit. Just go away.'

Undaunted by our off-spinner's calm exterior under pressure, Whit revved the bike as hard as he could, chucked a wheelie and mounted the bed, leaving tyre marks on the sheets. It was then things went pear-shaped, with Whit toppling over backwards and taking the television off the bench with him. I'm not sure how the boys explained the burnout on the carpet or the treadmarks on the bed sheets, and I also doubt that the next person to use the TV in that room would have been too happy with the reception.

PT was stunned by the stupidity and the fact that he was now in possession of damaged goods, and demanded that we leave immediately. But he and Mark hadn't learnt the error of their ways, because no sooner had we been bundled out of the room than I was again scaling the bathroom wall and sliding back in through the window to give Whit a chance to redeem himself. This passed without major incident bar a few more burnouts, but obviously the subsequent two hours' kip I managed wasn't enough, because when I went out in the morning for a spin on the moped, I immediately came to grief. Attempting a kick-start, I had an air swing and both bike and I toppled over from the patio into the prickly bushes below. I was pinned by the weight of the bike, and embarrassed by my predicament and the joy Whit got out of the incident.

Having PT as a roomie was like living with your granddad. He loved his cuppa and complimentary biscuits, would always have a brew in his hand or on the boil, and hated rooms without an electric jug. It was lights out early for the man also known as 'Boat' (as in 'PT 73' from the television show *McHale's Navy* – although I reckon he was the long-lost twin brother of Dr Zachary Smith from *Lost in Space*), which was fairly uncommon among cricketers – as were his preferred topics of conversation, which could include world affairs, local politics or the price of wool in the market. He loved to be intellectually challenged, but could mix it with the best in dressing-room banter and less mature conversation. PT didn't let his guard down much and his quick wit didn't have a genuine challenger, but deep down he loved the change-room environment because it kept him on his toes, alerting his mind for the battles ahead.

I only ever saw one player spit the dummy at PT during his time in the Aussie side, and I have to take some of the responsibility for that. Dean Jones's suitcase went missing for the entire duration of a Test match in Adelaide, and he told just about all of Australia how disastrous it was and how valuable the contents were. Ansett employees were on red alert for days, trying to avoid a PR disaster while Jonesy filled out insurance-claim papers for thousands of dollars in replacement kit. With team blazers on, PT and I did a quick last-minute reconnaissance of the room to make sure we hadn't left anything behind (mostly for my benefit, as I'd regularly leave my toiletry bag on the basin). Satisfied we'd accounted for everything, we wheeled our bags towards the door before checking out of the hotel and heading back to our home ports. Thinking I was doing my roomie a huge favour, I said, 'Hey PT, what about your other bag – the one between the wardrobe and television?'

The quizzical look on his face said it all. 'What? I thought that was yours.'

A guarded peek at the name tag and we both said, 'How dirty is Jonesy going to be?' before nearly wetting ourselves with laughter.

As PT was the 'brains' of the group I figured responsibility for the mistake should fall on his shoulders, but Jonesy gave us an equal barrage of abuse for the next couple of weeks, probably because we'd cost him a couple of grand on the bogus claim that was about to give him a nice new wardrobe fit-out.

While in the Caribbean, I quietly told Whit that I had received an offer from Queensland to move north for the following Shield season. Barry Richards – the same Barry Richards who had thrown me out of the nets during that World Series Cricket coaching camp 12 years earlier – was working for Queensland Cricket, and not long after getting home, I received a call from him to formally ask whether I had any interest in playing for them. A follow-up meeting lasted only a short time, and we never made contact about such a transfer after that. The lure in the approach was that Barry was offering me a chance to bat at No. 4. It was good for the ego to be sounded out in this way, but loyalty, the urge to win back the No. 3 position and a sense of belonging to a team that had always been a priority to me won out. I couldn't imagine myself playing for anyone other than Bankstown and NSW in Australia. My heart wouldn't be in it.

17

Speed bumps

On the afternoon of August 16, 1991 I married Lynette at Curzon Hall in Sydney, surrounded by best man Brad McNamara and Lynette's younger sister, Sharon, as matron of honour. In keeping with a fine Aussie tradition, groomsman Mark Taylor and schoolboy mate Tony Fort, aided by the best man, liquid-papered the heel of my left shoe with an 'H' and an 'E' and the heel of my right with an 'L' and a 'P'. It was a caring touch that the congregation appreciated when I knelt during the service. Further proving their worth, the groomsmen managed to cover my car in shaving cream and Vaseline, forming a giant phallic symbol on the bonnet, which was a classy forerunner to the jet of flour that doused us when we put the air-conditioning on, and the ashtray full of Parmesan cheese that we eventually tracked down a few days later, in contrast to the rancid prawn heads that were strategically placed in the hub caps and escaped detection for weeks.

Waiting for Lynette to walk down the aisle with her father was to see a dad who truly loved his daughter and was both proud she was about to embark on her own journey and saddened by the fact that from this moment she would take another name and no longer be his little girl. I felt nervous, young, ready and, above all else, convinced I was marrying my soul mate and first love. The day went by in a condensed blink, but I can recall how Mum told me on the dance floor that after 27 years of marriage she and Dad had decided to separate. The swirling emotions of bliss and bleakness had to show themselves, and so it was that I found myself unable to stem a flow of tears that had a mind of its own the next time Lynette and I came together, tripping over each other on the boards.

The next shock came with my selection for an Australian XI to tour Zimbabwe. This team was supposed to represent the promising youth of Australian cricket, but three relatively experienced players – tour captain Mark Taylor, Tom Moody and I – were picked as mentors and quite possibly to assess our leadership qualities. It wasn't exactly the 'honeymoon' Lynette and I had envisaged (I left my new wife behind three weeks after the wedding), but my career was in the balance and I needed to score some runs against whomever I had the chance to play. Scoring hundreds against teams that included amateurs and part-timers wasn't exactly earth-shattering news, but it kept my name at the forefront with the national selectors and provided an opportunity for me to test out my template for future success: to always play with purpose and to respect every opposition player. And the early signs were encouraging – three hundreds in six matches.

Tubs had been a member of the bridal party at the wedding, and we further strengthened our bonds of mateship over a urinal at the Bulawayo Athletic Club when he casually turned towards me and said, 'Tugga, I'm going to be a father.' This moment struck me not only for its timing but also because it underlined the fact that time was waiting for no one.

In many ways, my entire cricket career was standing still. It was an honour to be a member of the Australian one-day team, and I loved the mateship and challenges that the abbreviated form of the game could often provide, but at the same time I felt stuck in cement, firmly entrenched in the No. 6 role, usually coming in during the final overs to play a dashing cameo or perish with a wild slog. Being the 'all-rounder' had the obvious benefit of my being in the action regularly, but this tag restricted my advancement up the order to play more meaningful and satisfying roles with the bat. I craved a chance to show what I could do, but the form of those above me was consistently good and it seemed that the well-worked way the team played didn't really need to be tinkered with. I envied the batsmen in the top order, who could build an innings before taking risks and in the process develop their game, but to get such an opportunity myself I needed to prove my worth. Probably the best way to do that would be in the Tests, but now I wasn't even there.

I'm sure the Zimbabwe tour was looked upon as a talent-spotting exercise by the national selectors, but even they couldn't have imagined the gem they were about to discover. A little-known blond-headed kid with a mullet, who looked like the love child of new PGA golf champion John Daly, blew everyone on tour away with his freakish ability and enthusiasm for a battle. I can still hear the ball fizzing as it flicked out of his fingers, and he had such a simple, economical action that it belied the enormous revolutions he imparted on the ball. He really ripped it, and didn't seem to have the frailties that most wrist-spinners have. Instead of worrying about bowling a long hop or a full toss, it appeared to me that this guy didn't even contemplate such a delivery; instead, he could land it on a 10-cent piece complete with drift, subtleties of pace and flight and prodigious turn. After one over, I knew I'd seen a superstar in the making. This guy had it all and I decided that Shane Warne would look better in a NSW cap than in a Victorian second XI one.

Weeks later, and the deal was nearly done. A job had been lined up at the Bankstown Sports Club and a spot virtually guaranteed in the NSW side if things fell into place as expected. Shane was all set to come, but in a piece of quick thinking before a state trial game in Victoria, Dean Jones gave the rising star an ultimatum along the lines of 'Commit yourself to Victorian cricket today or else you won't be playing in this trial'. A poignant dose of reality hit Warney hard and the move north was scuttled; looking back, rightly so, because he was a talent Victoria had nurtured and invested in and to have taken him away would have been tantamount to stealing.

The 1991–92 season was a strange one for me. I was a Sheffield Shield and one-day international player, but not a Test one. I still felt as if I was a professional cricketer and knew that in some ways the pressure was off – which wasn't necessarily a bad thing, as I think I needed time to recharge my energies and work on my game while I still had a lifeline to the top. Shield cricket is the toughest domestic competition in the world, but it is many miles away from the intense focus and media scrutiny of a Test match, where the detailed analysis wears down all but the consistent performers. The hunger and desire within me to make it back to the Test side was simmering, but I also knew I needed time to consolidate my game and allow my confidence to be rebuilt to a point where it would be hard to dismantle in the future. I was somewhat hamstrung in my season of limbo (because of my involvement with the one-day team, I played in only seven of NSW's 12 fixtures, averaging 46 with two centuries), but remained fairly relaxed about my Test future, even if it was hanging in the balance.

High expectations were held for us in the lead-up to the 1992 World Cup. The tournament was being held in Australasia, we were the defending champions, and both the Test and one-day Australian teams had been in commanding form. We had lost only two of 10 matches in the just-completed World Series, and the Test boys had won four of five matches at home against India. Unfortunately, though, the closest we came to realising our dream in front of our home crowd came from the newspaper articles and commentators, who had installed us as short-priced favourites. Looking back, maybe we believed in our own minds that making the semi-finals was a given, and then we could switch on and do the business when it counted. However, our Cup ambitions were quickly extinguished, as we lost three of our first four games.

We could point to any number of excuses: the foolish scheduling that saw Australia play two Test matches immediately before the game's most important one-day tournament; the controversial omission of proven all-rounder Simon O'Donnell; even our tough draw, which saw us playing New Zealand at Eden Park in the Cup's first match. But none of these could hide the fact that we had come up short. As far as that opening game was concerned, the reality was that we didn't assimilate to the known conditions of a slow, low, clay-based pitch and the Kiwis' 'dinky' bowlers. Martin Crowe's strategy of opening the bowling with the off-spinner, Dipak Patel, followed by short two-over spells from part-time slow–medium bowlers – who local park cricketers would usually have been raring to have a crack at – was brilliantly conceived and carried out. We caved in, confused by Crowe's tactics and unable to break the regimented ways that had been successful for us in the past. So established were we with our mode of play that we lost the instincts of inventiveness and improvisation that are so crucial in this shortened form of the game.

The 37-run loss was tough to take and danger signs were radiating like a Hong Kong neon advertisement, but we failed to confront them or take them seriously. Our usual hustle and energy were replaced by a run of flat, lifeless displays in which we relied on individual brilliance rather than contributions as a unit. South Africa overcame us with passion and the Poms strangled us with pressure, leaving the dream of back-to-back Cups all but dissolved. A one-run victory over India in between was to prove our only highlight; the decisive win over the West Indies in our final match meant no more than that we missed the semis by a single point. Pakistan, who finished just in front of us, had managed to salvage that point from a rain-affected match against England after being bowled out for 77.

The win over India by the narrowest of margins saw me take a lead role in the outcome. With India needing four to win off the last delivery, I was fielding on the deep mid-on boundary and I knew I was a special to have the ball come my way. India's tail-ender, Javagal Srinath, slogged the delivery from Tom Moody high and wide of me towards the boundary, and in my eagerness to take the match-winning catch I overran the chance and grassed it, to everyone's horror. I had too much time to take the catch, which gave me 'jelly legs' and unhinged my composure. I scrambled to retrieve the ball and then, in a split second and out of the corner of my eye, saw Venkatapathy Raju pump his fist in the air as he grounded his bat for a second run and set off for the third that would tie the match. Fuming from my clumsiness and driven by the cockiness of Raju's gesture, I launched a bounce throw laced with anger to our stand-in keeper, David Boon, with all the force I had in me, and ran the batsman out.

I performed okay in our other matches, playing in all eight games and finishing fourth in the Australian batting aggregates (behind Boon, Jones and Moody) and equal second in the wicket-taking stakes (level with McDermott, one behind Whitney). But reasonable form and an early exit for the team wasn't what I'd hoped for, especially because without Test cricket this was my pinnacle for the season. Mind you, at least I had the chance to determine the outcome of games – unlike Mark Taylor and Merv Hughes, who renamed themselves 'Con' and 'Tiki' in reference to the fact that they became almost permanent reserves. Tubby played in two games, Merv in one. They might as well have been on a drinking holiday.

My spare time outside of the one-dayers and the Shield through 1991 and 1992 was channelled into areas outside of cricket, into experiences that taught me the value of diversifying and following other options I have a passion for. In previous years I'd dabbled in negotiating a couple of my contracts – with Dunlop shoes and Ellesse watches – which gave me a taste of the business world and excited my entrepreneurial urges. Setting up a series of coaching clinics with Brad McNamara and Greg Matthews also gave me an appreciation of the 'real world'. Encouraging and gathering sponsors, advertising and then administering the exercise and, crucially, providing a quality product gave me an outlet away from the closed environment of professional sport.

This and putting together the house with Lynette and her father, with the help of mates, gave me a grounding that formed the basis of everything that lay ahead. Value your true friends and work on the relationships, because that core group will always be there, in the good *and* bad times. Never having much money as a teenager was a blessing in disguise, as had been watching Mum and Dad earn every cent through hard work and diligence to the task, for it ingrained in me the benefits of respecting money and never taking it for granted. I hated owing money to anyone and believed in being debt free, so I paid for each new part of the house as I earnt the money. Lynette had put her potential career as a preschool teacher on hold after graduating with honours, in order to make our relationship sustainable – with me likely to be regularly away we wanted and needed to have as much time together as we could.

★

There's a wise old saying: 'You don't know what you've got till it's gone.' That's exactly how I felt in August 1992 as I watched the sports news and saw the Australian squad flying out of Sydney bound for a tour of Sri Lanka. My career was at the crossroads. That 13-man touring party had included seven batsmen, so logically I was behind all of them; I assumed I was still in the picture but knew that another year in limbo would see my image fade into the background as others clambered over me to make the most of a chance. I didn't want to keep reading about Tests in the newspapers (as I had to with the team in Sri Lanka) or watching them on television (as I'd done throughout 1991–92), wishing I was there, but that niggling query in my mind as to whether I could achieve what I wanted blurred my sights. I know now that just about every sportsperson on the outer suffers from these ambivalent thoughts, and it generally takes time and life lessons to work through the speed bumps that you place in front of yourself.

Merv Hughes certainly didn't help my chances of a recall to the national team. Our opening game of the Shield season was against Victoria at the SCG. This was Mark Taylor's first match as full-time NSW captain, Geoff Lawson having retired after we lost the previous year's Shield final. I was batting at No. 3 and eager to prove that I deserved this promotion up the order. Unfortunately I came off a distant second-best to Merv, whose first ball to me reared off a short length and crushed the pinkie of my top hand against the bat handle. Both pride and flesh were wounded as I trudged off with a first-ball duck, caught at short leg, against my name, but somehow someone was keeping the faith at the selection table and I found myself lining up against the touring West Indies in Hobart for an Australian XI team captained by Ian Healy in what was seen as a crucial lead-up to the first Test. A double of 95 and 100 not out, batting at second drop, galvanised my spirits and helped reinforce to me the benefits of my work since the West Indies tour, and especially my renewed efforts in the 1992 off-season. Playing technically proficiently against quality pace bowling from Ian Bishop and Kenny Benjamin, against the backdrop of competition for a Test spot, meant to me that I was moving in the right direction. Having the awareness to lift at the appropriate time is something that is hard to teach, because it needs to come from within. No matter how many encouraging words I received – though they did play a part – the ending needed to be conjured up by me. And being able to *continue* to lift was the key to longevity.

Handling the short ball was a topic that was never far away from my name when it came to reports about my batting against the quicks. As a junior cricketer and in my early years as a Shield player I was almost a compulsive hooker, but as I've mentioned earlier I gave the shot away when I saw the Windies pace quartet destroy all who took them on. For my new policy to be successful, I needed to be technically stable and devoted in concentration. Instinct had to make way for routine and I needed to overcome my natural urges, the doubts of my wisdom and the extra blows I would take on the hands and body. In a way, it was like retraining a Formula One driver to venture back to go-karts.

I had also been working on a shorter backlift, the idea being to minimise the impact of any flaw in my downswing. As well, I opted to instigate a set routine when walking out to bat and throughout my innings. Crucially, though, I began developing my own method of constructing an innings and forcing the opposition to bowl to me the way I wanted them to. At the peak of my powers, I believed I could wear my opponents down so they eventually bowled to my strengths. Inevitably, my patience and shot selection forced them to bowl straight and onto the pads in search of a chink in the armour, which is when I capitalised.

In the lead-up to the first Test I received a phone call from selector John Benaud, asking me what I thought about taking up the challenge of batting No. 3 against the Windies. This was a question that didn't need to be asked. I'd bat anywhere in the top XI, I quickly confirmed, because it meant I would be playing and not be 12th man or, worse, out of the squad completely. David Boon had been batting three since Mark Taylor came into the side to open with Geoff Marsh, but with Swamp having been omitted and the selectors struggling to find a new opener to replace him, Boonie was moving to the top of the order. With Test debutant Damien Martyn also coming into the starting XI, there was no room for Dean Jones, even though he was coming off a reasonably solid series in Sri Lanka. A theory was doing the rounds that Jonesy performed better in 'dead' Tests than 'live' ones, which to me seemed a tough call, particularly as I saw every match as being of equal importance.

The memory of my first innings back in Test cricket after nearly 20 months out of the team stays with me. Crossing over the old greyhound racing track at the Gabba and down onto the field I passed a departing Mark Taylor amid conservative applause, my heart racing. I found the environment I strode into both surreal and threatening. The pitch was lively, as expected on day one, and I knew all eyes were on me as the jury was definitely split on my selection at first wicket down. I tried to appear calm and relaxed, but the Windies had a knack for reading body language and I knew what they were thinking: I sensed they didn't see me as too much of a threat. Scores of 10 and 20 in this game, followed by 38 and one in the second Test at the MCG, didn't convinced anyone, including me, that my promotion was wise or long-term.

Time was running out. The media had written me off after Brisbane, with Phil Wilkins wording me up before the Boxing Day Test that without runs I'd be a state cricketer again. It seemed that being comfortable and established in the team was a far-off notion; instead, I'd been condemned to a nagging uneasiness about what might happen if I failed again. The more negatives and pessimistic voices I heard, the greater the unsettling effect it had upon me. As my nature would have it, I kept my concerns and fears to myself and soldiered on, with only Lynette really being privy to my inner thoughts, which at that time were primarily based on not succeeding. Time and time again she would reinforce her belief in my ability and the destiny she believed I could attain. She gave me strength and the will to find the intestinal fortitude required to battle on. I didn't need a long spiel, just an injection of faith, and suddenly the noose eased up. Ian Healy was supportive in his own way, telling me at the team's family Christmas function, 'If you get 20 or 30 each time batting at three, the team will be happy, because you will have done your job.'

I appreciated his compassionate attitude, but it also made me say to myself, *Jeez, their expectations of me are pretty low*. I didn't want to just play a minor role and surely I could be better than that. He didn't mean to, but Heals underlined the point that I needed to get a bit of 'shit' in my game or face the prospect of being considered a lightweight.

I wasn't sure whether Phil Wilkins was being polite or trying to fire me up by mentioning the 'dropped' word again during an interview before the start of the Sydney Test. Phil didn't have to reiterate the point, which had been made in most newspaper stories in the lead-up to the match; I knew where I stood.

Taking centre and knowing that it may be the last ball of your career is both terrifying and stimulating. All senses are aroused, each one battling for supremacy at a moment when you know tranquillity needs to be the driving force. Fortune is often needed in these split seconds before equilibrium can be restored and a clearer focus convened. Four hours later, I was saluting the crowd and gesturing aggressively towards the press box in a flimsy display of defiance. I'm not really sure why I did that, because it wasn't premeditated; perhaps it was the easiest way to discard the personal baggage I had been accruing. Whatever possessed me, I then paid for it almost immediately as I was caught freakishly by Phil Simmons off my nemesis, Curtly Ambrose, from a hip-high delivery that I clipped as sweet as any shot I had played all day. Karma is part of the X factor for me, along with character, culture and camaraderie – the game will always get you back if you don't show it or the people involved due respect.

Professional sportspeople do become self-absorbed, can take criticism to heart, and do exaggerate the importance of someone else's opinion. Often it feels as if everyone has read and formed a view about you on the basis of one unflattering comment, or drawn a common negative from what was actually a constructive piece. Like others, I often equated my overall worth with my performances on the field. Foolhardily, I believed I was a lesser person if I failed and more worthy if I did well. For the five weeks from my selection in the first Test to my hundred in Sydney, the cricket headlines seemed to dominate and my field of vision narrowed to a point where all I could see was my name and personality being dissected piece by piece. Gradually I became more and more agitated, and the jaundiced views I formed began to eat away at every aspect of my life. But if I was to have had a good look in the mirror leading up to the Sydney Test, I would have acknowledged that I hadn't reached 50 in my previous 17 Test innings, a statistic that clearly needed some investigation.

★

By the time we reached Adelaide for the fourth Test, we were one win away from the series victory we all craved. Draws in Brisbane and Sydney had been split by a commanding Australian win in Melbourne that featured the arrival of a genius when Shane Warne claimed 7/52 on the final day, his first major impact on the international scene. It was a massive breakthrough for the team to know we now had a match-winner – it was as if a crucial piece of the jigsaw had been found. Noteworthy also was Mark Waugh's century in our first innings, not only for the milestone, but also for the inventive 'backing away' system he employed that allowed him to lift many of the bumpers over the slip cordon to the boundary. The Windies quicks were incensed, claiming cowardice and perceiving it as an insult to play this way, but it was an effective if not sustainable solution to their brutal assaults on the body.

We were happy then, but a month later, on Australia Day, our mood had changed. The pent-up anger with which AB threw his 'worry ball' into the viewing-room floor, causing it to bounce up and crash into the roof, became a symbol of the depression that engulfed our room; it was a good 15 minutes before anyone uttered a word. The hurt in our captain's eyes was evident – the realisation of his vision to defeat the arch-enemy and tormentor of every Australian side he'd played in had been cruelly snatched away.

We'd needed 186 to win, which was roughly a 50/50 bet considering we were against four quicks on a pitch that had 'opened up' and featured a hotchpotch of small plates, independent of each other, that were uneven and crumbly on the edges. The loss of Boonie without scoring was the first of many tremors before the big one – one wicket doesn't normally set the tone, but the manner in which the ball shot through at a low height didn't go unnoticed by the whole team as we sat and watched the first over of the day. Debutant Justin Langer, who'd come into the side after Simmo accidentally poked Damien Martyn in the eye during a fielding drill the day before the Test, was thrust into the cauldron at No. 3 to test his credentials, and he needed all the courage he could muster. In our first dig, a sickening blow crashed into his helmet before he'd scored and gave him dizziness and headaches for the whole match, yet here he was three days later giving us a solid first look at his make-up and love of a contest. I wafted at an Ambrose loosener first ball after lunch, giving the momentum back to Richie Richardson and company, triggering off a steady succession of wickets. By the time last man Craig McDermott joined Tim May, we needed an improbable 42 runs to win.

Initially, a few of the boys started to sort their gear out and prepare for the end, but as the partnership began to take shape it became increasingly obvious that Maysie wasn't going to get out and Billy was feeding off the confidence of his partner. Twenty to go and we were tensing up, unable and not allowed to move from our designated seats for fear of changing our luck. AB was a stickler for this superstition, having set the tone back at Lord's in 1989 when he stayed in the shower for over an hour while Boonie and I completed the game-winning partnership. One run to go and the ordeal was nearly over, but we all knew that when you start to concentrate on the ending the focus can be lost, especially if you are a tail-ender. A possible single to mid-off was turned down, but then a sweetly clipped leg-side shot from Billy had us out of our seats, until we realised it had been stopped by Haynes's leg guards at bat pad. The way we cursed our misfortune suggested we all knew fate was about to deliver a mortal blow, and so it did when a Walsh bouncer brushed the bat or glove with Craig's head swaying away from the ball making umpire Darrell Hair's decision a gut-feel one but also a correct one.

There was no catching Walsh as he mimicked a Tiger Moth at an air show while our last pair remained stunned out in the middle, devastated to get so close and be consigned to history as the duo who *nearly* did it. Maysie said there wasn't a night in the next six months when he didn't have nightmares about the outcome, and every time he managed to knock back a few of his favourite Mexican beers, Sol, he gave us all a full replay of his dig . . . except for the last ball, which instead he put away for the winning boundary.

Only once in my career did I face up and say to myself, *I don't know how I'm going to score any runs. This is too hard.* That happened at the WACA, four days after Maysie's heroics in Adelaide, on a pitch that was as hard as a cat's head and came complete with a green tinge and bounce that reared off a length like a cobra striking at a mongoose. My first delivery was a good-length ball that I jabbed at, only to catch a glimpse of it as it steepled over the shoulder of the bat and carried through to keeper Junior Murray, who took the ball above his head while standing where the inner circle for a one-day game would have been. In Perth, you usually have that extra split second to turn around and watch the flying ball before it thuds into the keeper's mitts. This time, I couldn't believe the trajectory that continued to defy gravity as it continued on its way. I was 'cooked' mentally, like a pulverised boxer awaiting the death knell. No escape seemed possible, particularly as the howling of a particularly vibrant 'Fremantle doctor' further complicated the issue.

Ian Bishop's high side-on action accounted for me in both digs. Viv has said of Bishop that but for his serious back injury he would have been the greatest of them all. If I hadn't been part of such a carve-up that featured Amby slaying us with an unbelievable spell of 7/1 from 32 deliveries, and instead been a spectator, I would have marvelled at the athleticism and skill of Bishop, Ambrose and Walsh, who were simply poetry in motion. Border bagged his only Test pair, Mark Taylor won the lottery and mixed the drinks, and umpire Steve Randell warned *our* paceman, Jo Angel, for intimidatory bowling. I couldn't help but have a crack at the normally jovial Randell, who always offered Minties and jelly babies between balls when standing at square leg, about his hypocritical stance on the short-pitched stuff. 'Are we playing that rule today?' I facetiously asked him.

★

Randell's reprimand of Jo Angel is one of a number of incidents I've put away in the 'Did it really happen?' file. The name Asif Mujtaba isn't exactly a household one, but he's also in that file in bold print, after a World Series game in Hobart from the 1992–93 season. As Pakistan needed six to tie off the last ball, we had all but won as I ran in to administer the last rites. I had only one delivery in mind: a yorker, or at least a low full toss. But not a half-volley. The success I had enjoyed in the past bowling the final over of one-day internationals had given me a belief in my ability to get the job done, but I rushed the whole episode and served up a waist-high full toss that Mujtaba hammered over the midwicket fence, narrowly missing a mountaineer atop an advertising billboard that said: 'Come to Tassie!' The ball was never retrieved and I wanted to get out of Tassie as fast as I possibly could.

The Windies won that World Series final after we'd topped the qualifying table. It was that sort of season. Before we could get back to England for another Ashes adventure, we were scheduled to travel to New Zealand, and the tour nearly got under way minus our rising star Shane Warne, who forgot his passport but somehow had another one organised in the hour before our flight left. Then Boonie's father passed away on the second day of the tour; I can recall coming down to the bar to see Boonie obviously distressed but being looked after by his new roomie, Justin Langer. He might have been on his first tour, but Lang was already showing the soft side of his nature and displaying the qualities that have enhanced every team he's been a part of. Compassion is one of the keys to a tight unit, and appreciating someone else's plight or point of view needs to be a priority. Viewing each other as not just cricketers but also mates with families and a whole range of interests and passions gives a clearer perspective and allows a genuine connection with one another and a better balance to be attained.

Likewise, injuries are part and parcel of cricket, with each player having a different pain threshold and view on what he can deal with and play through. I always saw a missed Test match as one I could never get back, and unless the injury was so debilitating that it affected my standard of play and consequently jeopardised the team's objectives, I made myself available. Merv Hughes and Allan Border would play until they dropped, as does Glenn McGrath today. I'll never forget Merv bowling through the '93 Ashes tour with a hole in his knee that degenerated to the size of a 10-cent coin. His career was curtailed as a direct result not long after. NSW wicketkeeper Phil Emery made his Test debut in Lahore in 1994 filling in for the equally tough Ian Healy, who because of a badly broken thumb was missing a Test through injury for the only time in his career. In what proved to be his only Test innings, Phil also badly broke *his* thumb, but carried on because he wanted to make the most of his chance. Upon returning home, he had the busted digit surgically pinned and played a Shield game with the ends of the screws protruding from each side of the thumb in his quest for another Test match, which was due to begin just 22 days after he was hurt. Heals recovered in time, but to all those who heard the story a new benchmark in determination had been set.

My own constitution was examined before the third Test match, in Auckland, when a local net bowler keen to make an impression had me cursing as I held my right index finger in agony. As is often the case, to ease the burden on the curator (and because it isn't really necessary for them to be full length) the practice pitches were only half the normal length, and this tyro dropped in a short one that landed in the unprepared grass and shot off at me quicker than expected. Instinctively I withdrew my hands, but I still copped the ball flush on the end of my finger with nothing but the thin leather of the palm of the glove to absorb the impact. It felt ugly, and the telltale ring bruise around the swollen digit meant only one thing: a break. Ice and more ice was followed by an X-ray to confirm the crack and a damaged ligament, and then came the usual advice: 'I can't recommend you play.'

I understand doctors have to say these things, but if I'd always taken their advice I would have missed about 20 per cent of the Tests I played. If a specialist said 'two weeks off' then I rated myself a 50/50 proposition to play. In this case, after consulting Errol Alcott we decided to give it a go during warm-ups and then make the call.

Time got away from me. After a disjointed and indecisive session in the nets, I reluctantly decided to head back to tell AB I was unable to bat without a fair degree of pain, but as I walked into the change room I heard our skipper say to the boys, 'I've won the toss, we're batting.' My line of thinking needed to change, and quickly. Having a master physio certainly helped, and I got through with ice followed by near-boiling water, which was then followed by having a piece of string wound agonisingly tight and then unwound to stimulate blood flow and aid the healing process, added padding in the gloves, and a double hit of the last resort, Panadeine Forte. Losing six wickets for 10 runs after being 38 without loss further helped redirect my thoughts to the task in front of me and, as often is the case, a handicap made me concentrate better than anything else I know. If you can convince yourself it's only going to hurt for a split second, you're on your way. Adrenaline is an amazing pain inhibiter, as is the pressure of the situation, and the 41 runs I scored didn't translate into pain until I had cooled down.

Player behaviour was a big issue on this tour. In New Zealand's second innings of the third Test, Merv spat in the direction of Mark Greatbatch and from a certain camera angle it looked diabolical. The image of the side suffered and so did Merv's wallet as he was slapped with a secret $500 fine by the ACB, which subsequently became public, as they always do. The media generally get the gossip or inside stories from what they term 'sources', which is another word for 'bignoters' – who are generally management or administrators, but might even be fellow cricketers looking for a sympathetic ear or simply trying to upset the equilibrium of a rival or opponent.

The home side also suffered, with Martin Crowe at a press conference confronting a journalist who had inferred certain things about his sexuality. 'Do you think I'm gay?' Martin said straight to him. Apparently the confrontation was a showstopper. We all knew that the game was changing rapidly, that nothing was off the record any more and nothing was unreportable. The old wink-wink, nudge-nudge, look-after-each-other relationship between touring journalists and players was well and truly over. Television networks and fans wanted more and more to get a greater insight into the players' mindsets and personalities. Stump microphones and cameras were seen by us as being intrusive and unnecessary. It was agreed they wouldn't be used once the ball was deemed to be 'dead', but the reality was that this was never going to happen. Celebrating a wicket had to be done away from the stumps and we were constantly reminding each other that we were within earshot of the microphone.

The series was drawn one-all, and a pair for Lang in the third Test saw him become a scapegoat and miss his dream tour to the UK. It was a tough call for a guy who'd repelled the Windies only weeks before to now be told, 'Bad luck.' Someone else was going to get a crack against the medium-pace Pommie attack.

One last memory of this New Zealand tour concerns a gentleman we had first met during the 1986–87 Ashes series. I was amazed at Elton John's memory when the team caught up with him backstage before a concert in Auckland. I don't know whether he was nervous meeting up with the Australian cricket team (doubt it!), but I certainly was, and struggled to get more than a few words out. Suffice to say, I was stunned when he engaged in a conversation with me and then finished our chat with, 'Say hello to Lynette and pass on my love to her.' More than six years earlier, during our Boxing Day massacre at the hands of Ian Botham and company, Elton had tried to lift the spirits of our partners by sitting among them, offering words of encouragement. Quite obviously, he had a photographic memory – an impressive skill to have and one I can't say I have mastered.

In contrast, I still get hot flushes recollecting my complete memory blank when introducing the Australian team to the Queen at Lord's before the 1999 World Cup final. Over and over, I kept on telling myself, 'Don't forget anyone's name.' For some peculiar reason I kept focusing on Damien Martyn and Damien Fleming, and suddenly I realised we had two Damiens in the team. I'd never taken much notice before. The suggested greeting choice is 'Ma'am' or 'Your Majesty' and after that you're advised to speak only when spoken to. All was going nicely until Flem's goatee and unusually serious look threw me and I couldn't for the life of me remember his first name. I'm sure the Queen has seen it all before, and she carried on as if nothing had gone amiss, much to my relief.

18

Not how, but how many

An overwhelming sense of anticipation on top of the comforting knowledge that this was an Australian cricketer's ultimate sporting adventure stirred me as we gathered at Sydney Airport in readiness for my second Ashes tour. I couldn't help but think that in four months' time some careers would have hit a brick wall while others would be blossoming. I was hoping for another step forward in my desire to never again be dropped, but more importantly for a series where I would improve as a player and look to mentor and guide the younger guys. Experience is invaluable on tour. Senior players can provide information on the nature of certain pitches, conditions likely to be encountered and options for getting away from the insularity of the cricket world, warn which journalists might be divisive and trouble-some, and give tips on touring life and the little short cuts and tricks needed to make a long tour an enjoyable experience.

Within the first two weeks, I achieved a cricketing ambition when I struck a six off what proved to be the last ball of a match to secure victory in a first-class game. The generosity of the flighted left-arm orthodox delivery from Richard Illingworth would have been frowned upon in Australia, and rightly so, especially as his county side, Worces-tershire, only had one option – a draw. Surely Illingworth should have speared a quicker ball in to cut my options down. But no, it was a juicy half-volley, which disappeared out of the ground. Strangely, the Worcester players didn't seem too upset; nor did they realise they had done their national team's chances in the upcoming Test series abso-lutely no favours by allowing us to kick-start our tour.

Good vibes, positive results and camaraderie seem to be ampli-fied in the confines of a bus zigzagging all over England. Bonds of friendship are formed quickly and cemented as guys get to know each other's habits and intricacies while overlooking their faults. A losing environment, conversely, accentuates the negatives and divides a group of people who can't escape each other. This had apparently happened on the 1985 Ashes tour. A losing team tends to split into small fac-tions and grumble about things, while winners stay a tight unit. To me, that 'X factor' that all winning teams and organisations exude and others try to emulate is best defined by the culture, character, cama-raderie and karma that the group exhibits. It can't be manufactured easily – which is why the people involved are the critical ingredient. Individuals who can, if needed, put aside personal aspirations for the benefit of the team set examples that motivate and inspire, and ensure that the bar is raised in terms of attitude. For them, nothing below this level is acceptable. Helping a struggling teammate get through a fitness test by joining in or shouting encouragement, organising a team barbecue, staying after training to help another player work on a weakness, remembering each other's birthdays or just inquiring how the kids are going at school are all examples of that little bit of extra effort that can make a world of difference.

Often one innings or match can dramatically alter the course of a career. Michael Slater's double of 91 and 50 not out against Leicestershire, in contrast to Matt Hayden's two and 15, set them on diverging paths for the next few years. It was for both their last chance to push for the spot to partner Mark Taylor in the opening Test match, as the game had literally come down to a 'bat-off' for the position. As a teammate watching them walk out together, I imagined what was going through their minds. Cricket, like very few other team sports, has a highly individual component, yet still relies totally on team commitment. This is one reason why it evokes fervent passion and such a variety of comment from observers, because often these two factors can clash and become blurred, depending on what spin is placed on a moment or segment of play. In this case, I'm sure both guys were well aware of the situation and were desperate to do well, but ultimately their partnership would be the aspect that would sustain them against 11 opposition players who would much rather face two individuals than a strong, united combination.

Focus and clarity from each batsman in a partnership form the basis of individual success, but the strength of solidarity further cements the platform. Slater got the nod and went on to form one of Australia's great opening combinations with Taylor. Opposites seem to get better when in alliance, and the excitable, flighty dasher in Slater was beautifully complemented by the resilient, grounded accumulator in Taylor.

'Slats' and Tubby knew each other's games and personalities well, and could spot danger signs in each other's body language. Batting three for NSW allowed me the opportunity to watch them at close quarters and appreciate their games. The Bentley and the Ferrari managed their fair share of road kill over the years, starting with this commanding tour of the UK that laid the foundations for a prosperous long-term partnerships.

With Taylor on strike and in prime form, I could relax because there was little chance I was going to be needed in the first session. He was technically sound, temperamentally rock solid and totally in command of his game. He was also not the most enthralling player to watch, but an opener's job description doesn't include aesthetics. By contrast, Slater was like a balloon that had just escaped before being tied up. He was all over the place – an improvising, thrill-seeking daredevil who was oblivious to risk and had me out of my chair every couple of balls.

As a batting partner, Slats was always energetic and keen to get at the opposition. He was a Rottweiler trying to break free of the leash and liked to be amped up with positive talk and the notion that you were in the battle together. Tubby was completely different, using the break between overs to get all the niggling issues off his back, complaining about his terrible bat and the fact that the bowler was giving me all the bad balls and he the 'jaffas' (unplayables). He was generally clearing his head for the next over. Tubs expected his partner to be as single-minded and temperamentally strong as he was, and was never big on the hype factor.

While Slater's career took off, Hayden had to bide his time. Matthew and Damien Martyn both had very limited opportunities in England in '93, but have since become regular top-liners. At the same time, the career of Craig McDermott was severely tested as he succumbed to a fate that would regularly befall him on overseas trips – he wouldn't see out the tour.

Billy was an obvious talent from a very early age, when he was always the main man and the spearhead of the bowling attack. I can still see him charging in, this big, red-haired bully boy, physically dominating the landscape and terrorising us – the NSW primary school side – with his presence and pace. It was rumoured that he'd have a whole chicken and three chocolate milkshakes for lunch before going out to crack a few heads with his blistering pace. Over the years we would discover that he was blessed with an imposing physique and exceptional skills that could plaster over the cracks in his make-up. Craig was a guy who didn't tour well: he was constantly homesick and worrying about his family and insecure about his place in the team. On occasions he carried injuries that had the medical staff scratching their heads and teammates wondering where he was coming from. Get a ball in his hand, though, and he was dynamite, combining a menacing run-up, textbook side-on motion and late outswinger to regularly dismiss top-order batsmen as only quality bowlers can. He could be a match-winner, but away from home, he was like Superman with kryptonite.

During our marathon first innings in the second Test, at Lord's, Billy disappeared out the back, heading for the amenities block clutching his stomach but not attracting that much attention. Shortly after, he was in Emergency having a section of his large intestine removed, which had become infected by the staples and mesh that had been inserted to fix an earlier hernia operation. It was a devastating blow for him and the team, but was followed by one of our best away Test-match wins ever. Such was the stranglehold we were beginning to exert over the Poms that we lost only four wickets for the match and won by an innings and 62 runs, despite being without our main strike weapon.

By the end of the series, scars had been etched onto the likes of Michael Atherton, Graeme Hick, Alec Stewart, Robin Smith, Andy Caddick, Phil Tufnell and Nasser Hussain, and old ones reopened for Graham Gooch and Mike Gatting. Ashes cricket in the '90s would be a psychological battle that curtailed many English careers and frustrated others. They were all quality players in their own right, but didn't have sufficient bond as a team to instil any fear in us. Under the blowtorch they seemed to buckle while we held firm. Often it felt like they were happy to do well individually in order to get a run in the next Test but were not as concerned about the team's outcome.

Anyone who has played in a losing team for an extended period of time can relate to that state of mind. I certainly could, because I could see a lot of my early experiences in the Australian Test team being repeated by our opponents and stunting their growth. Insecurity, and the fear not of failure but of success, assume control. It takes courage to be the guy to stand up and break the mould. Entering uncharted waters can be daunting.

Seven and a half years after my Test debut I was still learning about my own capabilities and strength of mind. Perhaps the most influential innings of my career came in the third Test, at Trent Bridge. I was still not a certain selection after my time on the sidelines and yearned for the respect a regular spot commands. I needed to play an innings of substance, not so much for the attention of others, but to satisfy the high expectations I imposed on myself.

Thirty-two overs remained in the match as Brendon Julian and I walked out to bat at the start of the last session, England needing four wickets for a come-from-behind win. I knew this was the challenge I'd been craving, a chance to accomplish something I hadn't done before: save a Test match. Our change room was tense in an unsettling way and the team were reliant on our partnership, as only the bowlers were left in the shed after us. It's a strange sensation to leave a room full of well-wishers, many of whom are hopeful rather than confident of your survival. Repelling the opposition in these circumstances would give me a great deal of personal satisfaction, and the joy of attaining a team objective and inspiring and motivating others in the process. I had made up my mind not to play any shots except defensive ones and had a willing ally in 'BJ', whose natural attacking instincts had to be barricaded away for the plan to come off. Up until this point of my career, I hadn't fully appreciated the satisfaction that comes with being technically sound in defence. Now I was getting off on defusing England's advances, and as each over passed BJ and I challenged each other to commit to more of the same. The end result was an honorable draw, and for the second straight Ashes series in England we went to the fourth Test with a 2–0 lead.

It takes enormous self-control to defend a half-volley or let a long hop go through to the keeper when the normal thought process is to look for a boundary. Doing this successfully was for me a new experience and meant my mind was now the strongest facet of my game. If I could harness the power of my mind to block out an entire session and suppress my natural instincts to save a game, then anything was possible in the future. I had completed a task I'd been unsure I could perform, and because of that I would never again doubt myself. Instead, anything was possible. The penny had finally dropped; that old saying that cricket at the top level is '90 per cent mental and 10 per cent skill' now had validation with me!

Getting runs 'ugly' is an art that all but the geniuses of the game need to master, so they can attain consistency. Not only is it a learnt trait, it is one that some players find hard to come to terms with. It can go against the grain for the guys whose style of play is easy on the eye and who don't want those 'good looks' diminished. Brother Mark was one who couldn't let his ego suffer the ignominy of scratching around, mistiming shots, playing and missing. His way of solving the problem was to hit out instead of battling through, which gained him an unwanted tag of having too many 'soft' dismissals. It was only towards the last third of his career, when others were pushing for his spot, that he recognised the need to develop this mechanism. It's a fine line between compromising your natural game and making the most of your abilities. Allan Border, David Boon and Mark Taylor were all outstanding examples of 'not how, but how many' in order to maximise their potential. From 1993 I believed it was a key element of my repertoire, because the odds were that it wouldn't be every day that you would walk out and feel on top of your game.

Buoyant about the new level my batting had reached, I put on 332 with AB in the next Test, at Headingley, contributing 157 not out, most of which were hard-earned runs. Again, I didn't play a startling, eye-catching innings, but I could feel my mind strengthening and my focus developing. Spending time in the middle with Allan was invaluable in terms of seeing how a guy could will himself to do well. His words were always simple: 'Great stuff, keep working hard', 'I'm here for the long haul' and 'Don't relax, let's keep the physical and mental disintegration going!'

AB never allowed himself the liberty of relaxing too much or taking the situation for granted. He was always looking ahead to make sure we ended up in a better position. I think his years of early struggle and torment as captain shaped his outlook, and it wasn't until the side started to be consistently successful that he backed his judgement and instincts as a leader. I certainly enjoyed batting with him, because he subdued opposition by his intensity and his reputation for taking on every challenge.

Not only was Headingley an intimate learning experience for me, it was also the venue where the 'red rag' was born. Having been sweating profusely during a long, hot day at the crease, I signalled for the 'twelfthy' to bring out a cloth so I could wipe away the perspiration that had begun to drip annoyingly from the foam inserts of my helmet over the eyebrows, obscuring my line of vision. A signal like this is a 12th man's nightmare, because he has no idea whether the item required is in your kitbag or a new one needs to be found. Further complicating the issue is that he has only six balls to get it right or face a 'please explain' from the batsman. A piece of red cloth from the players' quota of towels made its way out two overs later after being cut up into a pocket-size portion. It would accompany me to the crease for the next 10 and a half years, becoming a security blanket and somehow easing my mind whenever I pulled it out to wipe the brow. At times it became a cloak to conceal my worries because it gave me a few seconds' grace to gather my composure. Occasionally I'd see strands of it littered around the crease line and think, 'That's a good sign – I've marked my turf.'

You learn to almost trick yourself into believing things like that really count and will make a difference. Another omen I was pleased to see was a ladybird landing on me or if I spotted one on the ground. I'd always pick it up and place it on my shirt and hope it would cling on for a couple of balls. Shane Warne would pull out his lucky bowling pants if he was going through a lean trot. Needless to say, they weren't often required. Other 'old wives' tales' could take on significance, too, like a seagull pooping on you being good luck – when Ian Healy copped one smack in the middle of his keeping gloves in an Adelaide Test match and then took a catch next ball, we were all believers.

Routine and feeling comfortable are part of all top players' make-ups, but when it becomes obsessive and the main focus of your approach, it makes a simple game complicated. The two guys who took superstition to the absolute limit in my experience were John Wright of New Zealand and Neil McKenzie of South Africa. John was always signalling the crowd to stop moving behind the bowler's arm even if there was no one there, or to have the sightscreen moved a centimetre or two either way. While I'm sure it was just habit and almost became part of his routine, it was his gear that gave him the most grief. He would regularly change bats, to the point of often using a new one in each innings, and once produced one of the most bizarre examples of overanalysing one's game: while trying to settle on the perfect grip, hoping for the consistency he craved, he superglued his top-hand glove to the handle so that it wouldn't change!

McKenzie was so obsessed with his little idiosyncrasies that he often appeared agitated at the crease, trying to pull all the elements together but never gaining focus because there was too much going on in his brain. He would touch his gear in a certain way before every ball, not allow himself to step on any lines, and always meet his batting partner in the other half of the pitch at the conclusion of an over, then turn around and walk back on the adjoining pitch. Being so obsessive gave us an opportunity to have some fun and play with his mind. We'd say to each other within his earshot, 'I think he just walked on the creaseline.' Or, 'He didn't make it past halfway last over. I hope he doesn't start thinking about it.'

Victory in an Ashes contest is as good a sensation as an Australian cricketer can have. Even though during the last 15 years of my career the series were dominated by one side, it was still a huge thrill to win, because it linked you to the great teams of the past and meant you hadn't handed the urn back to the old foe. Going into the last day of the fourth Test in 1993, at Leeds, we needed six wickets before the celebrations could begin. In such a situation the weather is constantly on your mind as you pray it won't intervene. This later played a role in my strategies as a captain: if I could take rain out of the equation, then that was one less thing to worry about.

At lunch we needed two more wickets, which was just about perfect timing for it allowed us to prepare for the 'onslaught'. Bags were packed and zipped up tight to avoid a dousing in beer and champagne, a bottle of Southern Comfort was placed next to my seat, the winning CD, 'Khe Sanh', was inserted into the team's ghetto blaster and the beers were put on ice. The danger of a victory so early in the day was the amount of time we would then sit and reminisce in the change rooms and the alcoholic consumption that would go with it. By the time we got into the a.m. at a seedy establishment, Tubby and I decided our kebabs and pizzas had soaked up enough fluid, so we set off for home on a sobering-up walk. Twenty minutes later, a passing police van inquired as to why we were wandering around aimlessly in a dangerous part of town. Would we like a ride? Into the cage we hopped, two future Australian captains.

The word 'fun' is one that resonates with successful teams. It binds the guys together and doesn't always have to occur off the field; it's probably more crucial if it comes during the heat of battle. I remember Tim May taking a swirling high ball from a Graham Gooch top edge at fine leg on the hallowed turf of Lord's. Now Maysie was a guy who hated fielding and his perfect day was to not touch a ball at all except when he was bowling. We only fully comprehended his terror at having been under a high ball with the world and his parents in the adjacent grandstand watching when we heard his first words as we gathered in a group: 'Which fellow did I get out?'

For much of my career it was hard for me to imagine what went through a fieldsman's mind when he was petrified of stuffing up. Fielding was always a part of the game I looked forward to – except when my knees were troubling me to the extent that bending down caused sharp enough pain to make me anxious every time I got into a compromising position. I hated the thought of letting the bowler down and the negative effect it had on me, and also the way missing a ground ball I'd normally field with my eyes closed teased my mind. To be constantly doubting yourself and hoping you won't figure in the action must be like slow torture, and I'm sure the more you want to avoid the action, the more you become involved.

Taking the mickey out of each other was a favourite pastime and the team's 'fines nights' were an ideal time to give it to your mates. At the conclusion of each meeting of the fines committee, nominations for the stupidest act of the week would be called for. The winner in 1993, decided by a show of hands, would get to wear the Daktari on a designated team night out. The Daktari was a hideous jungle-type camouflage round-neck top and shorts, topped off by long white socks and a wide-brimmed hat that Tom Moody and I had procured in a shopping mall in Harare in 1991. Tragically for Tubby, many thought it was the best outfit in his touring attire when he paraded it as the week's winner.

The idea that originated on this tour, of dividing the squad into two groups – the 'Julios', named after Julio Iglesias, and the 'Nerds' – also gelled the unit. A series of events between the two teams, including touch footy, trivia nights and tenpin bowling, was played out over the four months we were in England. A rough summation of the criteria for being a Julio would be this: talented but lazy, fond of using mirrors and beauty products, walk as if they're carrying a watermelon under each arm and act as if the world revolves around them. On the other side were the Nerds: unappealing to the eye, hardworking, possessing poor dress sense, usually good drinkers and representatives of the average guy on the street. There were certainties for each side, most notably Errol Alcott, the Julio of all Julios and a role model to be admired by protégés such as Shane Warne, Mark Waugh, Brendon Julian and company. We Nerds all looked up to the 'king', Tim May, a natural if ever there was one, who received promising support from Merv Hughes, Mark Taylor and David Boon.

There were others in later years who couldn't make up their mind who they were or what they wanted to be. Justin Langer was a Nerd trapped in a Julio mindset. Adam Gilchrist was a born Nerd who metamorphosed into a role-model Julio.

Clashes between the groups were eagerly awaited affairs and each team would go to extraordinary lengths to prepare for battle. Reading glasses with Coke-bottle-thick lenses and checked western shirts were our team issue, while the pretty boys often donned flash jacket tops and Ray-Bans in an attempt to show their class. The tenpin-bowling tournament leading up to the first Test was seen as a near-certainty for the 'Joe Average' boys, for bowling alleys are the breeding ground for all aspiring Nerds and a wouldn't-be-seen-dead venue for 'Fancy Dans'. But we went down by 706 pins to 691, largely due to Merv's quest to land the ball as far down the alley on the full as he could, thus sacrificing accuracy. These tussles not only gave us a vehicle to let off some steam, but also to build a portfolio of stories that would provide entertainment value during the tour. I can't imagine the England team having as much fun as we did, judging from their complete lack of a celebration after they beat us at the Oval in the sixth Test. Instead of reminiscing and rewarding themselves, they all set off down the motorway to play the next day for their respective counties – it was the counties who provided the players with the security of a contract, not the English Cricket Board, and as such they basically held the players to ransom to play every day possible. Our unwritten motto was 'Play hard, party hard', while the Poms' seemed to be 'Compete, then disappear'.

I always believed that hanging out together was important for an emerging side, because you got to know one another on a personal level rather than just seeing each other as cricketers. Through the '90s, this broadening of relationships strengthened us in times of need and made us want to achieve for each other. Regularly on tour we would walk into a restaurant as a group of 10 or 15 and make eye contact with two or three English players having a quiet meal together. You could tell they were uneasy about our team spirit and their contrasting lack of togetherness. It may not have really been an issue, but for us it further galvanised what we wanted to be like – a collection of guys from different backgrounds and interests who'd bonded as one.

The spirit of a guy like Merv Hughes was a standout example for the rest of the squad. Playing through an injury to his knee that required painkilling injections and ultimately shortened his career was courage and sacrifice of the highest order. Merv also gave the team great humour and vibrancy, often at his own expense. Trying desperately to lose weight, he employed a dietician to harness his healthy appetite and quench his unquenchable thirst. Unfortunately for him, Merv left his food-intake diary lying around the change rooms at Durham during a rain delay. Word of its discovery quickly spread and the lads all huddled around as if listening to a ghost story as his diet for the day was revealed. You had to give him 'A' for effort, for it couldn't have been easy consuming only half a hamburger (probably not his), or one and a half racks of ribs rather than two, let alone *six* pints of Diet Coke instead of the real thing!

Merv was larger than life, as gentle as a teddy bear off the field and a grizzly one on it. He had the ability to intimidate batsmen and was relentless when he pinpointed a weakness. He single-handedly accounted for the precocious talent of Graeme Hick, verbalising and scheming against him to the point where Hick was rendered a liability. Merv was all heart and soul with a fair element of bluff, and he had a priceless asset: character.

I often roomed with Merv, and it wasn't the most pleasant experience to be accosted by a naked man whose five-day growth bristled up against your face every morning. He was generally bored in the confines of a room, so I became a substitute for one of his toys, always at his mercy in his desire to liven up proceedings. While the minibar was tough competition, particularly if it stocked ice-creams, he had a caring nature that saw him on more than one occasion collect my dirty gear and go down into the hotel basement to use the washing machine. Merv was an invaluable tourist, lifting those around him and lightening moments that had the potential to ignite. However, on the field he used humour to detonate tricky situations, such as when AB told him to bowl a consistent line and length. Our captain simply said, 'Pick a spot out on the wicket and aim for it.' Quick as he could, Merv replied, 'Why would I do that? I couldn't hit it!'

Merv and I would regularly go to the movies and it was never dull. If he was bored, the screen would invariably have little indentation marks all over it from high-velocity Maltesers. On one occasion, while watching *Nightmare on Elm Street* in a jam-packed cinema, he further terrorised fellow movie-goers by imitating Freddy Krueger and clawing at them from the row behind. Previously, his love of Freddy had nearly turned into a nightmare at the SCG when, in one of his skylarking moods, he taped all the fingers of his left hand up with our luncheon knives extending out. A surprise knock on the door moments later and Prime Minister Bob Hawke strolled in, surrounded by a swarm of security, eager to press the flesh. I don't think I ever saw Merv so obedient and well behaved as he stood upright with his left hand well hidden behind his backside.

The odd prank or two not only provided much mirth, but also gave us plenty to talk about on the sometimes lengthy motorway trips. Meals were often quick takeaways at a motorway services centre, even if we'd originally had noble intentions of using the microwave on board our bus. Back in '93, Big Macs were seen as healthy because they had lettuce in them; 10 years later, cricketers' attitudes to diet had evolved to the stage where sushi was the quick takeaway.

Enthusiasm needed to be coaxed out of us sometimes, usually in games against the counties, who regularly put up second-rate teams who were a waste of time and achieved very little. Cold, windswept days didn't help, so when Tim May and I spotted a set of large plastic novelty ears in a Leeds market stall on a day off we immediately thought, 'McDermott!' As luck would have it, the vendor had 11 sets left and all that was required to relieve him of the lot was 22 quid. An opportune time presented itself shortly after, in the tour game against Gloucestershire. On a slow, low pitch the hosts crawled along at two runs an over. By teatime, needing a lifeline to stay awake, we decided it was time for the 'sting' to materialise. Craig was diverted outside by the physio for some stretching, while the boys tried on their ears, giggling like a bunch of naughty schoolboys. When our quick returned, he found an unexpectedly animated group, with one-liners coming from everywhere, including: 'Let's 'ear a bit of chat out there.' Merv told the captain, 'I'm all ears as to how you want me to bowl.' And then he turned to the team and said, 'C'mon lads, it will be 'ears and 'ears before we come back 'ere, so let's put on a good show.'

Billy seemed genuinely warmed by our improved outlook for the last session and fired up to join in on the spirit. Shortly after, it was showtime. As Billy made his way back to his bowling mark, the signal went out and the ears were slipped out of the pockets and attached, amid laughter from the cordon, who looked like they'd lobbed in from a Star Trek convention. It wasn't until Craig was a couple of steps from delivery that he noticed the 'Andy Caddick autographs' and lost his momentum, nearly tripping over in the process. A half-paced ball that just landed on the mown strip set us all off, including Billy, who appreciated the moment but vowed revenge on the perpetrators if he could identify them. The twelfthy capped off the sting perfectly by running out onto the field with a huge black garbage bag to collect the ears amid solid applause from the crowd.

The most audacious prank ever performed would have to be the one by the tour-group supporter who ended up fielding for Australia during a first-class match in the Caribbean in 1995. During a drinks break in the last session, this sports fan managed to secure a pair of creams from our reserves that allowed him the chance to serve the drinks. Without concern for repercussions, we all thought, *Why not give the guy a run and fulfil his dream?* So off he went down to fine leg for the next over, followed by a stint at mid-on, then back to fine leg, before scampering off, with the umpires none the wiser as to the identity of our mystery substitute.

The Ashes of 1993 broke one jinx for the Waugh family, but also created one for the Australian team. Father Rodger flew over for the fifth Test, at Edgbaston, to see Mark score a fluent 139 and the older twin an unconvincing 59. It was a proud moment for all of us, but particularly for Dad, who had always seen himself as a jinx, his slightest involvement in a game being the prime reason we'd get out. Whether it was turning up at a junior rep game after he'd been tennis coaching, tuning into the radio or walking into the SCG to catch some Shield action, he'd convinced himself he was always the reason for our demise. Seeing us succeed broke the hoodoo, exorcised the demons and made the old man's trip a lifetime highlight.

Losing the 'dead rubber' Test at the Oval was the start of something we would find hard to shake in years to come. It took a little of the gloss off a wonderfully successful series, but we also knew we'd lifted when the stakes were highest – and as any sportsman would say, 'That's what it's all about.' Of course, we tried to reinvigorate and finish off on a winning note, but the lure of home and having already completed a series win, together with fatigue and a level of mental tiredness, saw us fade away. It was to become an issue that needed correcting, and that quest became one of my goals when I was appointed captain.

Sledging also reared its ugly head and culminated in a stinging article by John Thicknesse in the 1994 *Wisden*. The senior cricket journalist wrote, 'That Border will be remembered in England with respect rather than affection stemmed from his condoning, not infrequently his participation in, the sledging of opponents and umpires during play in open violation of the International Cricket Council's code of conduct.' The tag of 'Ugly Australians', first acquired by the Australian team under Ian Chappell's leadership, was to prove a hard one to shake and came up whenever an on-field issue arose. Admittedly, we bordered the fine line between gamesmanship and sledging, and no doubt we 'pushed it' in many people's minds. Direct abuse to me is sledging and should never be allowed, while putting doubts in batsmen's minds by encouraging each other and indulging in banter is all part of the game. Occasionally abuse did arise, and it was an area we needed to clean up as we were aware kids were copying our every move and such an example was not the one we wanted to set.

19

The fires are here!

The images on television startled me and diminished my appetite as the two teams sat together for lunch on the final day of the Shield match between Tasmania and NSW in Hobart in January 1994. I was the Blues captain, returning from injury in state cricket while the Australian team was involved in the World Series one-dayers, but at this moment match tactics were far from my mind. Sydney was ablaze!

The breaking news was of a major outbreak of intense fires, with

walls of flame and rampaging fireballs jumping roads and threatening houses. The suburb of Heathcote, located in the Royal National
Park on the southern outskirts of Sydney, was the hot spot and, as the
crow flies, only kilometres away from my family home. I'd spoken
to Lynette earlier that morning and she sounded anxious, telling me
there was a deathly stillness and a burnt smell in the air while a hazy
pink–grey sky encircled the city. With the help of her parents, she had
plugged the downpipes with tennis balls and then filled the gutters
with water to stop stray embers causing damage, filled four or five
garbage bins full of water, and stocked up on face masks, wet towels
and appropriate clothing in case they were called to action.

I naturally assumed that if there was to be a fire close to our house
it would have the courtesy to wait until I got home that night. As a
professional sportsperson, the one thing you don't want to hear down
the line is bad news. It makes you feel vulnerable, worthless and guilty
because you aren't able to deal with or solve the problem. My natural
reaction would be to fix it, and because I couldn't I didn't want to hear
anything negative. This, I'm sure, was a burden Lynette had to carry
for a lot of years, holding it together so I could fully concentrate on
the business of professional cricket. She coped with severe morning
sickness, protected me from negative press, dealt with issues aris-
ing at school and kindergarten, and did the day-to-day running of a
household and a business. I would talk myself into believing all major
concerns would do me the favour of waiting, so I could be there and
help solve the issue face to face.

My worst nightmare was realised an hour after lunch, when our
12th man and my best buddy, Brad McNamara, made an impromptu
dash onto the field, singling me out for attention. The tone of his voice
suggested it wasn't easy news to pass on and it hit me straight between
the eyes. 'Tugga, I think you had better go off,' he shouted. 'Your
house is about to burn down.'

I just said, 'OK, I'm off. You stay on and get someone else to do the captaincy.'

I went straight into the match office and tried to call home, while our team manager booked me on the next available flight out. Not being able to get through the first three times I attempted to call was incredibly frustrating and must have seemed like a real-life 'soapie' to the staff, who were going about their business as usual. Eventually Lynette answered in a hurried, agitated voice, saying, 'The fires are here! I've got to go.'

The phone clicked dead and I experienced the ultimate in helplessness, stunned at the news. *Shit, what's happening? Will everyone be safe? Will the house burn down? Why aren't I there? How is everyone going to cope?* 'The fires are here!' kept tormenting me. What did that mean? Were they in the valley below, at the back fence, on the back veranda? Was it a ground fire or was there a full-blown wall of flame approaching?

I needed more information, but I also knew I shouldn't hassle Lynette again, as clearly she had other priorities. I had to trust that her father, Phil, my dad, Rodger, my mother Beverley's partner, Darryl Webster, and Bankstown Cricket Club president Brian Freedman, who were all there, would somehow manage and survive the situation.

I waited for what seemed like an eternity, around 10 minutes, before trying to make contact again. Two things people take for granted in a bushfire situation are water and communications, but both are usually unavailable and it wasn't until about the sixth call that I got through. Brian answered and assured me everything was okay. Lynette then came on and said, 'The fire's gone. It came through and burnt the back veranda and the fences, and a fireball dashed across the roof line, but it's now safe as there was no ground fuel left to burn.' She added, 'Stay there and finish the match and we'll see you later tonight. Love you.'

'Love you too – see you later.'

A few hours later, flying back home, I was invited up into the cock-pit by the captain to have a look at Sydney ablaze, as he'd heard what I'd been through during the day. An eerie pinkish-red light hovered over the horizon and there was a dusty grey layer of ash and smoke in every direction. Down below, I could see our suburb surrounded by a ring of smouldering fire and knew it must have been a terrifyingly close call. The reality of that sight and the subsequent news that six houses had been destroyed in the street next to ours, on the same ridge of ground, were almost too shocking to take in.

★

During my career there were two other major outbreaks of bushfire in our area, and both times I was returning from interstate when the danger was at its peak. On the first of these occasions I was trapped in a cab on the Alford's Point Bridge about 4 kilometres from home, in a state of panic because no one was being allowed through. This was one time I was glad to be Steve Waugh, the Australian cricketer. I jumped out of the cab, sent it with my gear to the in-laws' place and signalled to a passing police car, which was making its way through the road-block, to stop. Thankfully he loved his cricket, so he waved me over and said, 'Jump in quick – I'm not supposed to do this.'

Again potential disaster was averted thanks to family and friends, including Brad, who answered Lynette's call for help. I was dropped off at the top of our steep block and ran past a crew of volunteer fire-fighters going the other way with hoses in hand. A quick 'Your house is okay' was relayed to me, as if they'd read my mind, before they dashed off into the murky light.

This was also the time when I realised that there is no clear delinea-tion between private and public life for someone like me. News crews were waiting at the front and back of our house, while a telescopic lens was aimed at the house from a vantage point on the fire trail below our block of land. I saw this as a bit macabre, but recognised the news value of a prominent cricketer's house being under the threat of fire. However, even if I understood it to a point, I still didn't like it. If the emphasis was purely on me I wouldn't have had an issue with it, but when they began to focus on my family, who had no say in the matter, I found that bordering on exploitation.

The third emergency, in 2002, saw me trapped in a massive traffic queue at Padstow, some kilometres from the Alford's Point Bridge. It must have been quite a sight for onlookers to see Steve Waugh jogging 5 or 6 kilometres in the Australian team uniform before cutting across a steep hill into our suburb and then flagging down a car to reach home. I had never been a long-distance track star, but it is amazing what fear and adrenaline can do when they take control. Help from mates again made the battle a winning one, with Glenn McGrath entering the fray as he came from a part of Sydney that had access to our suburb, and Gavin Robertson going the extra yard to help out. Robbo had received the distress call and, like me, had run into a dead-end in the traffic jam. Not to be deterred, he'd lifted his young daughter's pink Barbie Dragstar out of the back of his car and begun to pound the pavement. It must have been quite a sight with Robbo's knees around his ears and him digging deep as he climbed the substantial incline into the cordoned-off suburb. It was an inspiring effort and a true reflection of our friendship. But the lactic acid that had flooded his lower limbs caused him so much grief that the simple act of walking was a big ask for the next week!

A New Zealand side without Sir Richard Hadlee didn't really capture the imagination of the public, but for Australia the three-Test home series against the Kiwis in 1993–94 was noteworthy because a future all-time great in McGrath entered the fray. Although dropped after one Test before later returning, the young quick from Narromine in outback NSW showed considerable promise. He was wafer-thin and decidedly uncool, and a dead ringer for Shaggy out of *Scooby-Doo* with his short-of-a-length trousers, cumbersome boots and prisoner-of-war haircut, but you could sense something simmering beneath the surface – he had a quiet inner core of strength and a willingness to listen and learn, and there was a purpose about the way he played.

Early on, Glenn, like others before him (notably Merv Hughes), suffered from a lack of security about his place in the side and struggled to feel comfortable until enough faith in his potential was shown by the selectors. An axe hanging over the head plays on anyone's mind and restricts the endangered one's natural talents. Tenseness acts like a short circuit in the system and dilutes a person's ability to let go and enjoy the experience. Glenn seemed stiff and unnatural at first, but it wouldn't be long before he elevated himself to the apex of the attack and even worked out that long pants need to drop further down than the top of your ankles.

Meanwhile, consistency – that trait all cricketers crave – was beginning to become a feature of my game. Knowing my own game and what I was capable of helped me to be reliable and allowed me to develop a calmer approach. Having a routine before the contest was a process that took years to develop, but one that had to evolve. Going with the flow and being spontaneous is fine and needed to be a part of what I was about, but the solidarity of preparing in a similar way in the lead-up to and especially the day before a match helped me to be ready for the tasks ahead and think with a clear mind. It almost became a ritual in the 24 hours before a Test, starting with a solid net session that featured a heavy emphasis on quality over quantity. If I was struggling for form, I'd have a demanding workout against the net bowlers followed by 20 or 30 throwdowns with an emphasis on concentration and execution of shots. If I was in good shape, it might be a low-key net in which I'd pinpoint and work on a shot I wanted to improve – or sometimes I might even bypass a structured workout and simply face throwdowns until I could walk away feeling good about the way I was hitting them. With facets of my game that were going well, I always found the smartest way to keep them going was to leave them alone or just top them up. I'd regularly see players in outstanding form suffer from 'paralysis by analysis', overpractising to the point where things started to go amiss because of the quantity of time they were putting into it. Good intentions aside, the simple fact of the matter is that the longer you overdo something, the more likely it is that things will begin to dismantle.

It wasn't only me who was at ease with my own game: the top seven of the Australian batting order – Taylor, Slater, Boon, M. Waugh, Border, S. Waugh and Healy – were enjoying a streak of nine Tests in a row where the line-up had remained unchanged. It was only my injury, a torn hamstring I suffered in a one-day international at the MCG, that broke this run. Damien Martyn came into the side for our first two Tests against South Africa, which followed the New Zealand series.

The structure was now in place for our climb to the top of the cricketing world. We had the skill and the spirit; all we needed was that unblinking self-belief. While we crushed the Kiwis in the second and third Tests, in hindsight we didn't push hard enough for a win in the first Test, at Perth, which was symbolic of our 'Let's have a go, but only when the coast is clear' attitude. We were 90 per cent there, but needed to fully release the handbrake.

★

To my mind, the word 'great' is the most misused word in the English vocabulary and particularly so when describing a cricketer or his feats.

The word should refer to a person who challenges or changes the expectations and perceptions of the game or creates memories that will stand the test of time. For example, Shane Warne's greatest legacy may well be the fact that he introduced spin bowling to one-day cricket at a time when it was widely thought that in the shortened form of the game a containment role was the most you could hope for from a slow bowler. There were many who believed Shane's selection in the Australian one-day team in 1993–94 was a risk and not worth experimenting with, but it soon became apparent that he could not only restrict run rates but also swing the momentum Australia's way and win matches.

Before Shane, the two best spinners in limited-overs cricket were Abdul Qadir – who didn't recognise any method other than full-out attack, which won Pakistan a few games but probably cost them as many through his poor economy rate – and our own Peter Taylor. PT didn't worry so much about turn, and even told Ian Healy to concentrate on outside edges rather than the ones that turned back in towards the pads. Instead, he used subtle changes of pace, varied his angle at the crease and hurried the batsmen between balls, never affording them the chance to find rhythm and balance. Between 1988 and 1992 he was the 'banker' for AB, because we knew he'd do the job, never go for more than 40 runs in a match and regularly take 'big' wickets.

I might have been comfortable with my own form and my place in the side, but my career was about to hit a snag – one of those setbacks that you never imagine will happen to you – in the shape of that hamstring tear. The whole nature of one-day cricket is based on one word: 'hustle'. Everything is attempted in fast motion – suicidal runs, impossible diving saves, no respite between overs that need to be finished in a tight time frame. I loved the thrill of turning an easy two into a daring three or stealing an improbable single, especially in conjunction with Dean Jones and, later, Michael Bevan – the two guys I fed off best and competed with to get the most out of one another.

Coaches and commentators always say, 'Don't turn blind', when talking about running between wickets, but the art of brilliant running sometimes involves backing your instinct and sacrificing convention to maximise opportunities. The good runners between wickets know as soon as they hit the ball how many they can get; the great runners always challenge that first thought. If you're alert and fit, you can sniff out an extra run here and there, but as the overs tick away the line between poaching and speculating blurs and the chances of a mix-up multiply. It was in the quest to negotiate a tight two that I experienced a spasmlike 'grabbing' in the back of my hamstring, like a squash ball materialising in the belly of my muscle. Initially I thought it was a cramp, like the ones I used to get in the back of the family's Holden Kingswood after playing three games of soccer in a row for Auburn's Under 14s, 15s and 16s. Back then, a bump in the road that tossed me off balance, in conjunction with having little or no room to move with three or four of us packed together, would send my groin or hamstring into what felt like an electric shock that would only dissipate over time. This was different: I didn't have a lump in the troublesome area, rather a grabbing sensation each time I tried to move quickly.

Fixing the tear would be the first of many intensive treatment programs I embarked on during my career. I was totally committed to rehabilitation and always got back on the park as quickly as humanly possible, but I'd let myself down with my base of fitness. While I had actively participated in team sport from the age of six, I had done no other substantial physical work to ensure durability over the long term. I had length in my muscles, but not strength, which meant I could get into any position I wanted to but under duress the chances of something going wrong were increased. Fortunately, I was blessed to have the professionalism of NSW cricket physio Patrick Farhart ('The Smiling Melon') to help me get the hamstring right. He even cancelled his Christmas holidays to supervise the crucial first week of healing and treatment. Patrick always made me feel as though my injury and comeback regime were the most important he'd ever overseen, and for that I, like many others, am indebted to him.

Missing two Tests (the first two of the series against South Africa that followed the New Zealand series) because of injury was something I did only once in my whole career. It proved to be a valuable time for learning. The often-used statement 'One door closes and another door opens' is very true if you keep a positive outlook and are aware of the opportunities – some more obvious than others – that present themselves. The first realisation to strike me was how quickly I was forgotten once I was detached from the group, as if an umbilical cord had been severed. I was now on my own. Contact with the Australian squad was occasional and I felt left behind. *Surely*, I thought, *I'm worthy of some follow-up.*

The reality is that the caravan moves on, the team focuses on the present and not the past, and in the tightly controlled environment a team lives in, priority is given to the next game. It's nothing personal; life as a full-time professional teaches you to be selfish in many ways. Once you are at the top, everything you do seems to be exaggerated, magnified and overstated and the world becomes smaller, seemingly revolving purely around whether or not you are successful on the cricket field. People such as your manager, fellow players and members of the media are telling you how great you are on a regular basis, which inflates your self-importance. You have to acquire a fallback mechanism to avoid these trappings of stardom, and I was lucky to have rock-solid mates from my school days, guys I'd played with and against in sport since I was 10 years old, and a wife, in-laws and family to keep me grounded.

Injuries can also be a wake-up call. Not only do they provide a warning that changes need to be made, they also offer a chance to reassess, clear the head and recharge the batteries. When injured I always made the trek to the NSW Central Coast to a sleepy fishing hamlet called Patonga, to smell the salty air, fish on a rocky outcrop in isolation and rehabilitate in the water or on a mountain bike. For me, a couple of days without access to phones or newspapers is the best stress-reliever available, and afterwards I'd always return to the game feeling like it was my first match of the year.

In early January 1994, as I drove home from Patonga, I listened intently to the radio as Australia began to unravel in the second Test, at the SCG, against a fiercely proud South African side led by Hansie Cronje in the absence of Kepler Wessels. It was to be a devastating loss for the team as they failed to reach the small target of 117, and for one player the ramifications would be far-reaching and over the top. Damien Martyn, who had replaced me, was the most visible player at this crucial time and therefore the one to cop the brunt of the criticism. Having faced 58 balls for six runs, and with Australia eight down and seven runs from victory, Damien was caught driving hesitantly on the up on a faltering surface against the bowling of Fanie de Villiers. One run later, the calamity was complete, and the Proteas were celebrating one of their greatest-ever Test wins. From that moment on, that 'loose shot under pressure', which had been no different from those of his more senior teammates, plagued and haunted him to the point of almost becoming a barrier too large to overcome. Damien paid the price for doing the hard work early then tripping up with the finish line in sight. As the last visible top-order player, he became the scapegoat.

Greg Norman was a notable sufferer of this curse of being almost *too* good. Many golfers never got themselves into a position where their moment of weakness was noteworthy. In effect, they weren't good enough to be found out, because their race had already been run and no one took any notice. To succeed, you must be willing to face failure and its consequences. Not to know the depths of despair is to live in a bubble of safety and never test yourself. 'Marto' would wait more than six years for another crack at Test cricket and during this time he must have felt abandoned, but sport can be cruel. Yet sometimes an early episode of 'unfairness' may work in a player's favour, because he can either tackle it head on and allow the struggle to strengthen his resolve, or turn away and acknowledge that playing at the top level is not what he is looking for. Most people take the latter option, because it's easier and less painful, but nearly all those who make it to the top have to work through dark periods and push themselves harder than they ever imagined they would have to.

Back in 1993–94, injuries were divided into two categories by the physiotherapist: 'external' (such as a broken finger) or 'internal' (such as a pulled muscle). The category of his injury was the sole determinant of a player's path back into the national side. With an external injury, the player did not have to pass a fitness test or do a required amount of match play to prove he was right to play. An internal injury necessitated playing at least one Sheffield Shield game to alleviate concerns about a recurrence. I only ever slotted into the 'internal injury' category, so missing games became a frustration until, seasons later, Errol Alcott amended the policy and began judging each case individually. I thus not only enjoyed a rare Christmas at home, but the honour of captaining NSW came my way. With little experience of being in charge besides skippering schoolboy sides, I led NSW purely by instinct and intuition, and found I loved the challenges and stimulation that captaincy provided. It was a lot easier when I only had the job for a short period of time, and therefore didn't have to look at the big picture as much. Furthermore, no one had preconceived ideas about me. The slate was clean and I could experiment more because I knew that the consequences wouldn't be as severe if any of my moves didn't work. That I didn't yet know my own style was also a bonus, because fear didn't hold me back. Sometimes experience cuts down a captain's options because he has been undone by previous events and caution takes over the reins.

I was leading via the first thought that came into my head as we gathered together in the change room before walking out onto the Adelaide Oval, with SA needing 268 to win in a little more than four hours. I'd seen what effect Tim May had managed to have on a deteriorating fourth-day pitch at his home ground, and linked that realisation with the thought that opening batsmen wouldn't be expecting a spinner with a new ball in his hand. Gavin Robertson was the man I had in mind, and when I said, 'Robbo, are you right to take the new ball?' his look was a mixture of 'Are you serious?' and 'How good does that sound!' I told the team we were going to try a few different things, with Robbo taking the new ball, and that I expected us to win even though the odds were realistically in SA's favour.

A wrist spinner like Warney has trouble imparting his turn with the shiny surface of a new ball and the discomfort of a protruding hard seam on his fingers. A finger spinner has these troubles to a lesser degree, but can overcome them more easily because the revolutions imparted aren't as severe. On this occasion we ended up blitzing them, with Gav doing the damage, and my captaincy career was up and running. Seeing Robbo surprise even himself gave me enormous satisfaction, because he was performing as a result of me beckoning him and, critically, because he had been taken out of his comfort zone. He was asked a question and responded in a manner he didn't really know he was capable of – until he found himself at a point where he had no option but to back himself.

For me, the real challenge of captaincy wouldn't come until later, when an unconventional move mightn't come off and then would be picked to pieces by the fans, media, players – everyone. I would later learn, though, that I much preferred to do things my way rather than by consensus or to please some ex-captain who had, all of a sudden, improved after retiring.

The toughest aspect of recovering from an injury was that I invariably wanted to get back into the action sooner than the medical experts advised. I would look back later and realise that maybe what the experts were saying had relevance. Taking a couple of extra days is probably a good safeguard, but when you are out of the team and someone has your spot, it feels like time can't wait and you must get back as quickly as possible. Consequently I resented the notion that I needed *another* first-class game for NSW after the win in SA to prove to the national team's hierarchy that I was over the muscle tear. It seemed as if I wasn't being trusted and that not enough reliance was being placed on my judgement. I responded with a score of 190 not out against Tasmania, which vindicated my thoughts – and probably those of the selectors, too, who wanted me to show them I was 100 per cent okay. In the overall scheme of things they did me a real favour, as I was now confident about my body and my form and both would be needed in the crucial third Test against South Africa, in Adelaide, which Australia needed to win to level the series.

In terms of pure placement of the ball, the 164 I scored in our first innings at the Adelaide Oval was as good as it ever got. Some days, fielders seem to be magnetised and you're playing with a steel ball bearing. But during that innings, everything funnelled into the gaps. Children's coaches will often say, 'Make sure you know where all the fielders are so you can hit the gaps', but, like most things you're told not to do, being told to watch where the fielders are only increases your focus on them and you end up not achieving the desired outcome. I found it much better to be aware of fielding positions but to *target* the gaps and prioritise the open spaces. It certainly worked for me on this occasion.

Getting a hundred against a quality side in a crucial Test match gave me enormous satisfaction, and the disappointment I showed when gunslinger umpire Terry Prue fired me, caught off the thigh pad, was probably over the top. But it bugged me because I'd worked my butt off to make it back into the side, then come out and played a near-faultless innings, only to be given out to a half-hearted shout by an umpire who obviously wasn't concentrating enough to see the obvious or gauge the genuineness of the appeal. Standards had to improve, umpires had to be paid more to make them professional and, in turn, accountable for the quality of their decision making. I'm sure the South Africans would have concurred after umpire Darrell Hair had a shocker, two of his disputed decisions being lbws off my medium-pace skidders that Andrew Hudson (who looks like Prince Charles' long-lost twin) and Brian McMillan believed they should have survived.

So the Australian summer ended, but one question kept on resurfacing: 'Allan, are you going to retire?' No matter what AB said, his denials didn't dampen the media's insatiable appetite to break down his tough veneer and get at his innermost thoughts. I would later learn that this is all part of the cycle that comes with achieving longevity in a sport. Inevitably the question has to come, and once someone throws it out at a press conference, there's no stopping the momentum. For Allan, it was a tedious distraction, especially when the usual suspects threw in their two bob's worth. I'm sure negative comments from a guy like Neil Harvey would have stung AB, especially as Harvey was a player Allan had looked up to as a kid.

I didn't know what AB was thinking, because I never asked and he never mentioned what his intentions were. Nor did I expect him to. He kept his cards close to his chest, but we all sensed that the impending decision was causing him a lot of angst. My gut feeling, like many in the side, was that he would retire after the South African tour scheduled to begin immediately after the Adelaide Test. We thought this because he'd publicly stated he didn't want to tour Pakistan again. And, after South Africa and a quick trip to Sharjah, Pakistan was next on the agenda.

20

Under guard

In 1994, probably for the first time in my career, I left Australia for an overseas tour as an established member of the team, a 'mini-leader' of sorts, privy to more of the goings-on and internal workings of the side. I was on top of my game, technically sound and mentally toughened, and couldn't wait to get among the first official sporting tour of South Africa by an Australian sporting team in 24 years.

The fanfare surrounding our arrival was overwhelming, with the white community thrilled about the resumption of international sport while the country seemed to be sitting on the brink of civil war. I'll never forget the scene after we left the airport on our first day on tour. Within 60 seconds of heading down the motorway en route to our hotel, we saw a trail of carnage on the opposite side of the road, the result of an awful traffic accident. Bodies were strewn across the lanes for some 50 metres, some moving, others motionless. The sight of a large woman slumped against a minivan that had been ripped open like a can of sardines by the steel railings that divided the traffic is something I have never forgotten. I can still see her propped up against the mangled wreck, either dead or unconscious.

Wherever we went we were feted like rock stars, receiving free meals at restaurants, drink cards at bars and instant recognition. Being such a showman and an outrageous talent, Warney had the status of an Elvis Presley. The public couldn't get enough of him, particularly as the South African team were quite conservative on the field and many of the players avid churchgoers off it. Warney was a superstar with all the trimmings, and our team of assigned bodyguards took special care in supervising his safety after cricket hours.

The most obvious difference between Australian and South African culture surfaced on one of our first nights out, at a sports cafe-bar in Johannesburg. Instead of being a storage area for patrons' coats and jackets, the cloakroom housed an assortment of hand guns left by patrons for safekeeping. This, we were told, was normal: most people carried a 'piece' for safety, because nearly everyone had been touched by crime at some stage in their life. Stopping at a red light in certain parts of town was 'asking' to be carjacked, and every time we wanted to go out it had to be as a large group accompanied by our security people, and to a designated safe zone. Arguments that in Australia might be solved by a few 'haymakers' and a black eye were, we were told, over here resolved with guns.

Our security team was headed by Rory Steyn, a mate I still keep in contact with and a guy who was Nelson Mandela's personal bodyguard for many years. Our guards were highly skilled and had undergone intensive training with pistols, assault rifles, shotguns and submachine guns. They also had considerable expertise in unarmed combat, identification of explosives, close-quarters protection and defensive driving techniques (which would come in handy if their vehicle was ambushed). They were with us at all times, travelling on the team bus, sharing meals with us at restaurants, always armed with a couple of well-disguised weapons. I felt both safe and vulnerable, knowing we were well protected but obviously in a country where many people didn't value life as highly as Australians did.

Fostering team spirit is something most Aussie squads do well, and in our case, presenting an award for the week's silliest act was an excellent way to have a few laughs and build momentum as a strong unit. The perfect trophy stood out like a beacon as I strolled through the Sandton Sun shopping mall – a life-sized baby doll that sucked its thumb and wore a nappy. The team resolved that each week's winner of the 'bub' would have to take it out with them on a designated excursion, which might be a plane journey, a restaurant meal or the trip to the ground for a day's play. Penalty served, each 'owner' had to autograph the baby's large melon before passing it on. McGrath, on his first tour, won the award first up for his removal with the bat of the remaining stumps after being bowled in a net session. Seeing the leg and middle stumps flying through the air further than the ball had been coming off his blade provided good humour for the boys.

Mind you, it wasn't always a barrel of laughs. When an alcohol-filled Springbok winger named James Small walked up and put his face centimetres from mine and threatened to kill me because I had been talking to his girlfriend (who had initiated our conversation), I needed to think quickly to avert a front-page headline. I figured the best way to pacify him was to massage his enormous ego, so I mentioned how good his try was against the Wallabies in Sydney a few months earlier. That, together with a couple of his gorilla mates pulling him away, ensured my tour progressed, but I'll never forget the crazed look in that guy's eyes and how he really wanted to make a name for himself. He probably achieved that, because a couple of police cars awaited his exit – apparently not for the first time – to give him a stern warning and tell him what an A-grade goose he was.

Much more enjoyable was the coaching clinic we conducted in Soweto, a place worlds away from the comforts of home but exactly the same in other ways. The children had vitality, life and energy but quite obviously would need a lucky break to get out of the cycle of poverty and crime they would eventually be caught in. Opportunities are what kids need, and with that gift anything is possible. It's a credit to South African cricket supremo Ali Bacher and the United Cricket Board of South Africa that players from disadvantaged backgrounds – like Makhaya Ntini, who developed into an opening bowler of genuine Test class – have prospered and developed under their programs.

It was good to get a taste of this side of South Africa, because almost invariably touring sides are escorted to the nice tourist spots and diverted past the harsh realities of life on the streets. I have always been much more interested in seeing how people live from day to day, the hurdles they have to overcome, the different lifestyles and cultures they embrace. Everyone has a story to tell and often you can see their story in their faces and expressions, which is why I love to take as many photos as I can. The thrill of getting back a photograph that captured the moment is something that sustained me as I walked through back streets and townships during my overseas tours.

★

One of the highlights of my time in the Australian team was the opportunity to meet and shake the hand of a man who in my view has had more of a positive influence in the world in recent times than probably any other individual. Seeing Nelson Mandela close up and clasping his hand was almost surreal, and was over so quickly that it seemed like it hadn't really happened.

Leaders have immense power. They can inspire or deflate those around them. Mandela obviously fits into the former category, to his eternal credit showing unbelievable forgiveness towards his captors for his 27 years of incarceration by advocating peace and harmony. Being the captain of a cricket squad doesn't carry the same credibility, but the leader's mood is often reflected in the team's disposition and attitude. We were a keyed-up, anxious side going into the first Test, at the imposing 'bullring' in Johannesburg, because that's how Allan was feeling. I don't think I've ever been as worried about getting out as I was in our first innings after being involved in a run-out mix-up with AB that was largely my fault. I knew he would be fuming about the circumstances, as we'd talked about being cautious when running between the wickets whenever Jonty Rhodes was in the picture. It's amazing what you can achieve when you've been backed into a corner and have no option but to lift and funnel your energies into the task at hand, and I managed to bat through the innings, which alleviated the tension somewhat. One of Allan's major strengths was his ability to compartmentalise, to put aside incidents. He never held grudges, unceasingly staying focused on the present and what needed to be done, but not everyone was as good as he was at just getting on with the job.

The edgy atmosphere that had infiltrated the team came to a peak during the third morning of the match. For some reason Shane Warne wasn't introduced into the attack until after lunch, by which time South Africa had reached 1/123 from 43 overs. Success soon followed, with Shane taking the wicket of Andrew Hudson, but in tandem with a virulent barrage of abuse that stunned everyone. Hudson was simply in the wrong place at the wrong time, copping the wrath of a temper tantrum that was out of character for Shane and had obviously been building up well beforehand. With the benefit of hindsight, it had been brewing during our morning stretches and warm-ups. Warney had been distant and evasive, and quite obviously something was troubling him. However, the cues to intervene were all but ignored by us as we figured he'd settle down by the start of play. It's a fine line between stepping in and probing for information, and letting the player work his troubles out of his system without disrupting his routine. One of the mistakes that was made in this instance was Shane's prolonged absence from the action, which allowed his mood to darken and culminated in the brain explosion that ended up with the then chairman of the ACB, Alan Crompton, and its CEO, Graham Halbish, imposing an additional hefty fine on Shane of $4000 on top of the match referee's original penalty of $400.

Merv Hughes was also thrown into the mix after a confrontation with an abusive spectator on his way off the field near the end of the Test, and he needed to earn an extra $8000 to pay off the penalty. It was an issue that caused a division between the team and the board, with coach Bob Simpson and the board representative and manager, Cam Battersby, aligning themselves with the players. We all thought the board's response was a kneejerk one, that they wanted to make an example of these guys for previous perceived or genuine bad behaviour by other members of the side. Not for the first or last time, the board was in a no-win situation. They were struggling to stem a flow of negativity about the team's behaviour and many critics wanted them to show some authority, but in doing so they lost the faith and support of the players. We felt let down to some extent, sacrificed for the sake of the board wanting the public's sympathy, but we were also aware that the behaviour was unacceptable.

Whoever was right, the ACB's actions did have the desired effect of letting the players know that a line had been drawn in the sand. The standards expected had been spelled out in no uncertain terms. It must be said that from a player's point of view it's always embarrassing to watch a teammate abuse another player, and we all felt sorry for Hudson and cringed when we saw the replay of the incident.

In my time as a player, the most public displays of sledging invariably occurred when a player was frustrated at his poor form and wanted to show how much he was trying and how much he was annoyed with his performance. It is a cheap way of getting attention, and no different to a batsman trashing a change room after getting out. Deep down, all players know what is acceptable behaviour and what isn't, and to me that's what it's all about: individual players accepting responsibility for their actions. No one should hide behind lines such as 'It was the heat of the battle' or 'It was out of character'. If a player oversteps the line, he has to accept the fine or do the time – simple as that – unless exceptional circumstances arise.

Dressing-room tantrums are rare and scary, but once the dust has settled the yarns that can be retold are pure gold. One year at Eden Park in Auckland, a bag Santa Claus would have struggled to carry, full of locally grown apples, was lovingly given to us by our room attendant. Unfortunately, it sat smack-bang in the middle of our change room and became the No. 1 frustration-valve release for Ian Healy after his dismissal. It quickly became pulped apple cider, with chunks spewing out in every direction, and Heals had to clean the mess up to avoid further embarrassment. Not long after, the 'roomie' came back and couldn't believe how popular his fruit had been, saying, 'Jeez, you guys have eaten all the apples already! I'll bring another bagful tomorrow.' No one had the heart to tell him the apples had been splattered to all corners, so instead we just said, 'Yeah, they were really tasty.'

Stories of Michael Bevan's behaviour after being dismissed are legendary, with showers being taken still fully kitted up, and overs full of bumpers being bowled in the nets off the long run with no batsmen at the other end. However, my favourite came during a one-day international at Eden Park. 'Bevo' came into the room looking disconsolate after getting out and quietly sat down to gather his thoughts. It was an unusually passive reaction, and for a good reason that we were about to find out. A security guard entered the room minutes later looking for Michael, as he had something he might be interested in – his bat! On the way off, Bevo hadn't appreciated the razzing the members were giving him and decided to offer them a souvenir: a flying cricket bat that apparently sailed high and long, missing the intended targets but sobering them up pretty quickly.

Michael Slater once valiantly tried to flush his entire kit down the toilet after a soft dismissal, only to see his bat sticking up like a periscope amid a couple of soggy pads and gloves, and a team that had to find alternative facilities to relieve themselves. I also had the good fortune to witness Matt Hayden tussling with a plastic chair during a Sydney Test and coming off second best by a long way. With an almighty heave, the brooding hulk let rip a right-legged kick that found his goofy foot become wedged in the oval-shaped hole where the base of one's back would normally rest. To see him hopping around, unable to extricate himself, was priceless and only topped by the fact that he had to swallow all dignity and ask me to prise the chair off his crushed toes.

We ended up copping a comprehensive hiding in the first Test, and needed desperately to revive our spirits. This came in the form of a road trip to the fantasyland, Sun City, a two-hour drive from Johannesburg. With a couple of attitude adjusters consumed, the atmosphere became much lighter and more welcoming than during the dramas of the previous few days. Then it was down to Cape Town for the second Test and to probably the only time in my Test-match career when I thought, *Hey, I'm a genuine all-rounder!* A double of 86 and 5/28 came only two Tests after my 164 and 4/26 in Adelaide, and helped us achieve a comprehensive victory against the stunning backdrop of Table Mountain.

However, the win wasn't completed without a little more tension between the players and the captain along the way. Being able to lighten up a tense situation has always been one of Heals' assets; often he'd use this ability to hold things together. But after AB and Boonie dug in for a grinding middle session together to set up an important base for the rest of us to capitalise on, Ian presented a bucket of ice to AB and placed the captain's Duncan Fearnley bat in it to extinguish the 'heat' out of a 'smoking blade'. It was a piss-take, but our captain obviously wasn't in the mood for a laugh at his expense and blew his top, lashing out at Heals and the rest of us and calling us 'party boys', among other things. The severity of the attack stunned us and a prickly silence hung in the air, with Heals standing there 'holding the baby' and the rest of us slinking out as discreetly as we could. It was an unusual way to motivate us, but it did spur us on for the remainder of the match.

When South Africa went back in for the second innings, for some reason they refused to play any shots against my bowling, and the more they respected me, the greater my confidence grew. In truth, my bowling could best be described as well-controlled and investigative: steady on flat wickets and dangerous on low, bouncing, cracking surfaces, mixed with good body language and a fair dose of 'huff and bluff'. I enjoyed engaging in a one-on-one battle, matching wits and probing for an opening while relishing batsmen who either searched for the ball, played across the line or didn't like combativeness. Hansie Cronje, Jonty Rhodes and Carl Hooper were opponents whom I also felt I had the wood on, that they could sense my level of optimism, which threw them off balance. In my case, I was uncomfortable facing bowlers who hit a consistent length and might expose my footwork, which could be minimal at times. Names that spring to mind include Gladstone Small, Angus Fraser and Curtly Ambrose.

What turned out to be Allan Border's final Test, in Durban, could best be described as a waste of time for five days. Neither side pushed for victory, preferring to settle for a drawn series. It seemed such a shallow way to end one of the most anticipated series in Test-match history. It must be said that South Africa's captain, Kepler Wessels, was the prime culprit, allowing his side to meander through 205.2 overs to accumulate 422 runs in their first innings and essentially kill off the match. It was an attitude that was to cripple South African cricket for the next 10 years. They were a well-drilled, highly skilled but regimented team, who lacked flexibility and the flair for improvisation needed to take them to the next level. There was no doubting their professionalism and commitment, and they were fierce adversaries, but I believe that sometimes they wanted the outcome too much and neglected the various processes along the way. Precision planning has a part to play in Test matches, but so does the need to take control and dominate a match rather than allowing it to run its own course. Every so often, I felt the computer analysts around the South African team were having too much of a say rather than the 'gut instinct' perceptions of the guys in the heat of the battle. Playing it safe and by the book will make you competitive, but it won't win you the defining games that allow you to ascend to the top.

A sombre mood engulfed our rooms at the conclusion of the match as AB walked in undefeated on 42, defiant to the end, giving 'crowd entertainment' bowler Rhodes the utmost respect, watching the ball like a hawk and guarding his stumps like a crocodile would her nest of eggs. AB's legendary mental toughness was still there, but the light within had dimmed and Test cricket had seen the last of a man who earnt the respect of all those he played with and against.

Without an admission from the man himself, it still wasn't a foregone conclusion that he wouldn't be back. I think he knew what he was going to do, but quite rightly wanted some time to himself to think through the issue. Finally he set things straight via an exclusive interview after a round of golf with his good mate Pat Welch of Channel Seven. At the end of the interview, AB said, 'It's like a part of me has died by making this decision to retire.' It was an honest, straight-from-the-heart admission, but a shame that such a glittering career hadn't culminated with a positive line. As I listened to it on television, I remember hoping that when my time came to retire it would be a happy moment and one that signalled a new chapter in my life. But maybe that was being a bit too idealistic.

At the end of the tour I felt totally satisfied with my efforts in both forms of the game, but I experienced a weird sensation that things would never be the same again. I had more than enough great memories of Allan Border to reflect on and digest, and also a prized possession – the sweat-stained helmet he wore during his last Test innings – to keep proudly as a lasting reminder.

21

'Are you going to tell Stephen?'

'To lose patience is to lose the battle.' This was the theme the Australian team of 1994 decided to try to adopt in our quest to master a challenging tour of Sri Lanka and Pakistan. To succeed, we'd decided, we would need to be able to work together, have a laugh at our triumphs and misfortunes and slide sideways out of our usual ways.

Wanting to create that special something that can often lead to bigger things, for the Pakistan leg Gavin Robertson and I decided in

1994 to produce a weekly magazine titled *The No Whinge, No Whine Tour* to hand out on the team bus in the hope that a few laughs would be had and a better understanding of each other could be achieved. We put plenty of hours into its production, writing articles and featuring guest writers in each issue, with the final document of photocopied pages being stapled together. Each week we 'profiled' one player – with my favourite answer to the question 'Favourite hobby?' coming from West Australian fast bowler Jo Angel, who replied: 'Collecting rock-star T-shirts from concerts'. He wasn't joking, either – the big fella had nothing but black T-shirts in his luggage.

Mark Taylor had assumed the captaincy and slotted in with ease, comfortable with communications and willing to guide the agenda. It wasn't an easy transition for Bob Simpson, though, for his power base had certainly been eroded. His relationship with AB had been mutually satisfying, with each allowing the other space and a separation of responsibilities that enabled both to showcase their strengths. In contrast, Tubs wanted to be the main factor from ball one, including finishing off meetings, something that had previously been Simmo's brief. It was to be a battle of wills to some degree, with both guys wanting the commanding role, which to my mind should always remain the domain of the captain. Mark was a guy who liked to have meetings with the senior players to get a feel for what was happening within the team environment and what issues needed addressing, and to explain how he saw the team functioning on and off the field. He enjoyed the authority and wanted the responsibilities that came with the job.

Tubby's resolve and temperament were to be tested immediately in the ill-fated and historically significant first Test, at Karachi. Our new captain's first Test in charge featured a debut pair with the bat; the loss of our spearheads, Craig McDermott and Glenn McGrath, through an infected toenail to Craig before the match and a thigh strain to Glenn during the game; and to cap it off Ian Healy missing a stumping chance when the home side needed three runs to win. The ball went for four byes, and we lost after Pakistan put on a 57-run last-wicket partnership. And then the match was tarnished forever by the discovery that Pakistan captain Salim Malik had offered $US200 000 each to Tim May and Shane Warne to deliberately bowl poorly on day five of a match that at the time was balanced on a knife's edge.

★

It was movie-script stuff, with villains, heroes, surprises at regular intervals and a finale that had everyone biting their nails. The night before the final day's script played out, October 1, at the Pearl Continental Hotel, a phone call from Pakistan skipper Salim Malik, 'the rat with the gold tooth', had set the wheels in motion for the destabilisation of the very fabric of the game, precipitating a chain of events that exposed cricket's dark side: match fixing, information sharing and a plethora of other devious activities. In time, players would be banned, fined, stigmatised, traumatised and tarnished, but many would also escape through lack of evidence and a force too powerful to control: the criminal underworld. Crucially, too, much information was recalled from memory and not from documented notes; it was here that inaccuracies, discrepancies and conflicting information led to a clouded picture.

What is certain is that unscrupulous individuals had been operating in and around the sport for longer than many people wanted to recognise or explore. Like many, I was naive about what was going on and had absolutely no idea that players were giving anything but 100 per cent in every game they played. It has been said often that low player payments, endless meaningless one-day games and greedy administrators created an environment of frustrated, undervalued players. This might have been the case, but I still find it almost unbelievable that some players sold themselves out, sacrificed their teammates, betrayed the trust of millions of cricket supporters and devalued the very essence of the sport.

It was to be the most infamous stain on the game in history, with no definitive solution introduced to cause these activities to cease. The International Cricket Council did eventually deal with the problem as best they could considering their limited powers, but with so few players paying the price for their deceitful ways and with such large sums of money rumoured to have changed hands, it would be fool-hardy to believe the slur on the game has been eradicated.

Hindsight allows me to put together some of the story, but unfortunately the match-fixing puzzle is made up of a thousand obscure, difficult-to-link pieces. Some have been lost and the search for others has been abandoned. The first sign for me was an out-of-the-blue phone call from Pakistan's former Test captain, Mushtaq Mohammad, to Allan Border at Trent Bridge during the fifth Ashes Test of 1993. AB was summoned from the viewing area as we commenced our run chase of 120 to go 4–0 up in the series. Soon after, Allan came back with a stunned look on his face and told us that we had been offered a large amount of money to lose the match. Such an idea was so ridiculous to contemplate that we literally laughed it off. We didn't think about it or discuss it again. If we'd only known what this insidious behaviour would lead to, our assessment of the offer would have been much more serious. As it was, we just said, 'What a twat. Tell him to piss off.'

A bit less than a year later, in a one-day international in Colombo, Pakistan were chasing a modest total of 180. They got off to a flyer to reach 2/80 before their opener, Saeed Anwar, retired hurt with cramp. It was roughly the time I came into the attack, and I ended up taking 3/16 from 10 overs. I remember thinking during my spell, *Why are these guys blocking everything? Am I really bowling that well that they can't get me off the square on such a flat, batsman-friendly pitch?*

Salim Malik was particularly watchful of my non-deviating medium-pacers, and we ran out surprise winners by 28 runs. Of course, we were consumed with our victory against expectations and I was rapt with my man-of-the-match award, a ghetto blaster that was appropriately cheap and nasty, but this masked the fact that, deep down, we didn't feel entirely satisfied with the outcome.

The Pakistan manager at the time, Intikhab Alam, was reportedly telephoned at his hotel room by a caller who refused to disclose his name but stated that he had lost money on the result and that four players had colluded to deliberately surrender the match. Saeed Anwar later told investigators from the inquiry instigated by the Pakistani Cricket Board and led by Justice Malik Qayyum that he had also sensed during the day that the match had been fixed. This interpretation was independently supported at the Qayyam Inquiry by a Lahore bookmaker, Salim Pervez, who told investigators that he had paid a total of $US100000 to Salim Malik and leg-spinner Mushtaq Ahmed to ensure Australia won the game.

Once the match-fixing story broke, there was a mass of rumour, gossip and information swirling around. Names, games and considerable amounts of money were mentioned, and every player became entangled in the web in some way. This happened even though I'm sure 95 per cent of players had absolutely nothing to do with what was going on.

About as close as I got to the 'coalface' was at a function at Rawalpindi on our tour in 1994, where both teams were being feted the night before a one-day international. As usual, most of the guys formed a huddle as a safeguard to prevent too many unwanted interlopers barraging them with repeated questions. Into our group came Mark Waugh and Shane Warne, with body language that suggested something was amiss. Warney pretty much came out with it straight away: 'Well, Junior, are you going to tell Stephen?'

Mark said, looking at me, 'Malik just offered $200 000 to be split up among Maysie, Warney and us two if we play poorly tomorrow.'

My first reaction was disgust that this low-life of a prick would even consider my name as a candidate for his vile plan. 'Tell him to fuck off,' was my only response. This was the consensus among the others, too, and the matter was never aired again.

When I was questioned for the O'Regan Report, which was commissioned in 1998 by the ACB to investigate the rumours that mentioned the Australian team, I'm sure the answers I gave were short on detail. The only way I can explain this now is to say that the notion of not letting a game of cricket run its natural course was so far removed from the way I'd been brought up, and so against my grain, that the offer in Rawalpindi and the rumours that were now surfacing had been immediately diverted to a 'safety box' in my mind that needed a key to unlock it. It is difficult now to accurately catalogue all the events, comments and incidents that took place; what you are reading here is how I remember them. Initially, I know I wanted to believe it wasn't really happening and that the guys making the offers couldn't find any takers. I just wanted to play cricket and minimise the distractions.

The situation became very real, however, when, on the eve of leaving for the West Indies in 1995, Tubby Taylor gathered Heals, Shane, Mark and me together for a chat that took me completely by surprise and stunned me with its ramifications. I learnt that Mark and Shane might not be making the tour – the board had decided to fine them for giving information to bookies about pitch conditions, weather and so on. Surely this wasn't happening! What the hell were Mark and Shane thinking? I perceived the anguish and embarrassment of the guilty pair and felt angry about the potential success of the tour being in jeopardy, but I wasn't sure who to direct that anger to.

People would often laugh about the fact that Mark and I are twins, saying we don't talk much to each other and aren't close. However, I'm sure we have a hotline to each other's feelings, and I knew how hard this was hitting Mark. Yet, strangely, because we had often been seen as a unit and not as individuals, I experienced a sensation that part of me was now involved, too.

Straight from this bombshell we went into a pretour briefing in the manager's hotel room at Sydney Airport, which finished with the Warne–Waugh story being detailed to all present. ACB CEO Graham Halbish and chairman Alan Crompton concluded by making it very clear that this was an in-house issue that had been dealt with. No one else had to know about it.

A little less than four years later, during the 1998–99 Ashes series, the story would surface with all the drama of a Loch Ness Monster sighting. During our pregame team meeting before the third Test, in Adelaide, we learnt that Malcolm Conn from *The Australian* was onto the fines that Mark and Shane had incurred. Conn is a journo who isn't afraid to ask the tough questions and who has strong views that have often gained him enemies among the players. He is a man who tends to hang on to his line of thought no matter what, and who at times refuses to be swayed or admit he is wrong, but the bottom line is that he is a thorough and diligent professional who is damn good at what he does. Conn knows he isn't there to be liked or make millions of friends; his job is to provide breaking stories and give strong opinions. In 1998–99 he did just that.

For Conn, breaking such a newsworthy story was like winning a World Cup was for us. As a team, we braced ourselves for the onslaught. Mark volunteered his side of the story to us in a calm and insightful manner and by the conclusion we had all agreed as a unit that we were 100 per cent behind both him and Shane, who at the time was out of the side through injury. I'm sure the backing we gave the two provided some comfort as they fronted the world's media the day before the Test. We recognised that they had been naive in accepting money, but also believed they were bearing the brunt of a more serious attack largely because they were the first Aussies to be embroiled in the match-fixing controversy. As such, they were easy targets.

It wasn't until that night that I had a one-on-one conversation with Mark about the whole affair. He talked me through the chain of events and clearly regretted what had transpired, especially the stigma forced on Mum and Dad and on our three grandparents, three of whom were still alive but didn't have much of an idea as to what was going on. It all seemed so simple, yet unbelievably complex at the same time. I assured Mark that I believed him totally and that, if he needed me, I would be there.

Before we parted, we had one of those moments where you know you should let your guard down and just do something. I'm sure we both sensed it – the notion that we should embrace and reassure each other it was going to be okay. But we didn't. Instead, we left it to our extrasensory perception to transmit the message. Being stoic and afraid to totally let go can occasionally be useful, but more often than not it creates a blockage that is difficult to clear. Storing emotions had been our way as we grew up, so even in the most trying of times it was hard to break the mould. Knocking down the brick walls you surround yourself with is one of the hardest things to do in life.

How could giving information that is readily available at the toss, during a media conference or in general chitchat become so damaging? The answer, of course, lay in where it was going to lead. There is no doubt in my mind that the unseen dark forces chose their potential victims well. An inclination to gamble, being a free spirit, a guy who likes his money or is self-absorbed were characteristics that made some people prime targets. With Mark's love of horse racing and Warney's attachment to casinos and love of roulette being well known, they would have gone straight to the top of a list of potential candidates. Once enticed, forever trapped.

Seeing Mark walk out to bat amid a chorus of boos was one of the toughest couple of seconds of my cricketing life. I can only imagine what he was feeling. His on-the-surface laid-back attitude was at times a safety mechanism for his insecurity and lack of confidence, and to be publicly vilified would have been like putting salt on an open wound. Of all his achievements, the 51 not out he scored in the second innings of that game was the most courageous segment of play he put together. As his brother, I was proud of his will to get on with the task at hand.

One member of our family who couldn't escape the innuendo and public opinion surrounding Mark's involvement was our father, Rodger, who ran a newsagency at Revesby in south-west Sydney, a sports-mad working-class suburb. He couldn't avoid the newspapers or many of the discussions the stories on their front and back pages generated. Of course, it was tough on everyone in the immediate family circle, because answers were expected of them. Trying to explain the complexities of what was being reported to the ladies at a local church gathering or at bingo in a nursing home proved to be enormously stressful for both our grandmothers. Our mother, Beverley, also had nowhere to turn and often called me to find out the latest rather than hassle Mark, who had more than enough to deal with. It wasn't the opinions offered or whether they were negative or positive that was the problem, more the fact that there was no escape. The frustration of knowing very little about what was going on gnawed away at and often frayed their nerve endings.

Dad embodies the definition of a one-eyed supporter, always showing blind faith in his boys. He is also a pretty good judge of a cricketer, often picking up subtle hints as to their promise, probably as a result of his own sporting upbringing. Because he couldn't contemplate any type of media criticism of Mark or me, there were many days when he refused to sell a paper that had a negative comment – a practice that was, of course, to his own cost. Regularly in 1998–99 *The Australian* would be picked up from the front door at 6 a.m. and moved straight out to the storeroom, where Malcolm Conn's stinging rebukes would be unavailable to the public. Other days, Mark's other main detractor, Robert Craddock in the *Daily Telegraph*, would suffer the same fate. It may have been a futile attempt at stemming the onslaught, but Dad was doing the only thing in his power to protect his boy.

★

Only once was I ever mentioned as being involved in colluding to affect the outcome of a match. Pakistani wicketkeeper Rashid Latif, on his own web site, accused more than half our side of performing inappropriately in the questionable one-dayer against Pakistan in Colombo in 1994. Latif saw himself as a lone crusader in cleaning up the game and regularly, consistently and to his great credit pointed the finger at his teammates. However, the exposure went to his head and extra little 'porky pies' began to surface. I'm not sure whether he was being pressured by outside influences, but he accused me of throwing my wicket away in Colombo. It was years later before he and I came face to face in a Test match, and because of political unrest in Pakistan it was, ironically, at the neutral venue of Colombo. Latif was a real contradiction at times – one minute knifing you in the back, the next your best mate. As I scratched out centre, he said to me in a genuine tone, 'Good luck today, captain, I hope you score plenty of runs.'

My reply probably wasn't what he was expecting: 'Don't you ever put that shit on your web site again, or I'll wrap this fucking bat around your head.'

The message sank in, for he didn't say another word, except, 'Nice shot, captain', for the remainder of the series.

Two guys who I would never have imagined being involved in match-fixing were India's Mohammad Azharuddin and South Africa's Hansie Cronje. That they were seduced by the easy cash and sold themselves out shocked me to the core. Azharuddin was a shy, quiet, modest man blessed with extraordinary gifts for cricket and a common touch that enabled him to relate to the average guy in the street. It was rare that a Muslim made it into the Indian side, let alone led the national team, so he became a role model for all castes and religions of the second most populous nation on earth. His only vice seemed to be a penchant for designer clothes, and it would have taken Scotland Yard's best to sniff out that he would end up being a cricketing pariah. I always found him good company, polite and courteous.

Similarly, Cronje was unceasingly friendly, warm and keen to talk about cricket, especially the Australian way of playing. In 1997, when he was the overseas professional for Ireland and the Australian team were touring England, he would often call me out of the blue to say hello and see how the tour was going. As an adversary he was tough, uncompromising and obsessed with beating us, but I saw him as thoroughly professional, if sometimes too intense to enjoy himself and let his own and his team's talents flourish.

Cronje sometimes wanted success too much, and I'll never forget him going for the practice nets straight after scoring 251 for Orange Free State in a tour game against us in 1994. Such was his desire to leave no stone unturned that he continued to smash the net bowlers for another hour before his hunger was satisfied. Physically he was a fitness freak, but mentally he pushed himself so hard that, like a piece of pottery in a kiln when the heat became too much, he cracked. He was thought to be the cricketing prototype for the future, but had an underlying fragility that at times could be exposed.

On the field, we enjoyed facing South Africa because they played hard, didn't mind giving and taking verbal banter, and made an effort to get together and have a beer at the end of the day. Cronje and I would tease one another about the outcome of matches and often used to have a friendly $50 wager on the result, although payment was never forthcoming. It was all about whether we could get one up on each other.

Looking back on our relationship, the familiarity levels dropped away quite dramatically during the 1999 World Cup, which I assumed was a tactical manoeuvre along the lines of the one Allan Border had employed on David Gower during the 1989 Ashes tour: to be distant and send out the 'Don't mess with me' attitude. Instead of having a chatty conversation on the way out to the toss, Cronje gave me the cold shoulder, only uttering 'heads' or 'tails' before heading back to the change rooms. I generally tried to engage with opposing captains, even if it was about how their hotel was, whether they were enjoying the tour, how their form was or how good the ground was looking. As we went our separate ways, I would always say, 'Play well' before switching into game mode and lifting in intensity.

Mind you, with all that was plaguing Cronje's mind, I'm sure every relationship he had would have been affected. Somehow this proud man had entangled himself so badly that I'm sure a vicelike grip of guilt was strangling him every waking second. In April 2000, just as we were about to board a plane to head off to South Africa for a three-game one-day series, the unthinkable came to light. Cronje, among others, was named by Indian police, who claimed hard evidence of links to match-fixing. I honestly didn't know whether it was true, but hoped it wasn't for the sake of the game. Like the chief of South African cricket, Ali Bacher, I was a big Cronje fan, so as we waited for our customs forms to be processed at Johannesburg Airport, I asked Bacher a few questions to clear up my understanding of the situation.

One comment worried me like a late-night phone call to a parent with a teenager. Ali Bacher told me that Hansie had said that, as had been alleged, he did have people in his hotel room talking about cricket, but he didn't know that they were bookmakers. Immediately I thought that didn't sound like the guy I knew, who was wary of strangers, careful to pay attention to detail and experienced enough to know who to trust. As an international cricket captain, you need to have your antennae tuned and to keep plenty of issues close to your chest. To me, Cronje having strangers from backgrounds unknown in the confines of his hotel room was a cause for concern.

Being something of a mentor to Cronje put Bacher in a delicate position. He desperately wanted to believe his protégé, but he was finding his trust dissolving as the evidence mounted. Soon after, Cronje cracked in the early hours of the morning, disclosing more of the facts than he'd previously volunteered to our mutual friend, top security guy Rory Steyn. South African cricket was in turmoil, the fans' belief in and love for their leader had been destroyed, and a chain of events was about to unfold that would lead to a questioning in many people's minds of the legitimacy of every game of cricket played over the previous few years.

Some mysteries were solved, but many questions remain unanswered. Was it just players involved, or did umpires and administrators play a role? Perhaps only time and someone's conscience will tell.

The best part about touring Pakistan is the unexpected random incidents, such as having the opportunity to take the team bus up the fabled Khyber Pass, fire a few rounds from an AK47 with the Khyber Rifles and mingle with the locals in this territory ruled by the tribal owners and not by the government. Anything and everything goes through this passage between Afghanistan and Pakistan. To the locals, buying guns and drugs is as simple as ordering fish and chips is for us, and as we strolled among the counterfeit video and CD shops, every second alley wall had a cache of enough guns to satisfy anyone's needs. It had the feel of an Indiana Jones movie set and I imagined life here to be a tough, dog-eat-dog world.

Rooming with the amicable giant Jo Angel in a minuscule dogbox of a room in Peshawar was a challenge to say the least. Our 200 cm (6'6") Corona-bottle replica had to sleep with his ankles protruding from the bed and his arms dangling ominously close to me on the neighbouring mattress. My worst nightmare appeared to be materialising when, in the early hours of the morning, I thought the big fella was in the middle of a sleep-walk. I woke to find my bed shaking, and initially believed Jo had picked up the end of the bed and was taking out his hallucination on me. However, a quick glance sideways revealed that Jo was still in his bed and was similarly startled, and I realised we had just experienced an earth tremor. Where to go and what to do? The fear of a larger, bigger quake saw us scuttle downstairs to the foyer, where we caught up with most of the other guys. They, like us, had no idea what to do. Fortunately the tremor wasn't a precursor to a major quake.

Another totally new situation confronted the team when we arrived for a one-dayer at Gujranwala, about 90 minutes' drive from our base in Lahore. Preparing at 5.30 a.m. didn't go down that well with the players, some of whom took their pillows on board the bus in an attempt to stick closer to their normal hours of sleep. After a night of torrential rain, most of us thought even going to the ground would be a waste of time, but we were assured by the local cricket association that all was in readiness for a big day out. Games in these satellite cities are the big event of the year for the locals, and many save their money 12 months in advance for what is both a major social outing and an escape from the rigours of their tough everyday existence. They expect to be entertained, and nothing gets in the way of that objective.

Local knowledge is always a handy asset, as we found upon arrival at the ground that the Pakistan team had only just left their hotel back in

Lahore. It's not the quantity of information you get that matters, but the quality. Quite obviously there was going to be no game, judging from our pitch inspection, which revealed that half the pitch was under water and gumboots would be more useful on the outfield than spikes.

When you know the game won't be called off early, because no official wants to be accountable for informing the spectators, 'Sorry, the game has been cancelled', boredom invariably sets in. Some of the guys settled into a hand of five hundred, others tinkered with their equipment, while quite a few of us continued to survey the conditions and interact with the ever-expanding crowd. The ground was full, but there were further thousands desperate to get in. Unfortunately, no one told them the game was to be called off – not that they would have been interested. Eventually large rocks began raining down from outside the ground, courtesy of the throwing arms of potential spectators who most probably were in possession of opportunistic scalpers' counterfeit tickets. A confrontation was inevitable, and when a mass of fanatical supporters squeezed into a tunnel between two stands, a stampede developed. The sounds of bamboo lathis smacking into exposed flesh, the shrieks of trampled individuals and the desperate pleas of the under-resourced police summed up a potentially life-threatening situation. Further complicating matters was the fact that a steel-barred fence with skewerlike barbs had collapsed and settled in a position where it could become a torturous deathtrap. Luckily sanity was eventually restored. Many people were ushered out of the ground minus their sandals, which had become embedded in the mud during the chaos. The scattering of people mimicked a collection of slaters seeking refuge after fleeing from beneath an overturned rock.

It wasn't until later on that I realised I had a scoop inside my camera. The tour photographers hadn't been picked up at the hotel by their pre-arranged transport, and I had the only photographs, albeit no more than the three shots remaining on my roll, and they had been hastily taken.

Proving that cricketers assume godlike status in this part of the world, a guy at the front of the crush who saw me line up the camera in his direction changed his anguished, pained expression to a glowing smile for a couple of seconds just before I clicked the shutter as he shouted, 'Steve Waugh, you are my favourite cricketer!' Once the camera eased down away from my eyeline, he returned from fantasy land to the battle of trying to extricate himself from the mass entanglement. Moments like these made me realise how out of proportion and distorted our importance could become. While there was no denying it was nice to be liked, even revered, such status sat uncomfortably with me and made me feel somewhat of an impostor.

The Test series was a source of real frustration for us. Australia had not won a series in Pakistan since 1959–60, and the drought continued by the barest of margins – that one ball that ended the Karachi Test. Personally, the tour offered a real rollercoaster of emotions and fluctuating fortunes that culminated in me suffering a serious injury. A shoulder dislocation and a tendon that tore off the bone during the final of the one-day tri-series saw me join Ian Healy, who broke a thumb, on an early plane home. Three and a half weeks earlier, I'd been dismissed for 98 in the first innings of the second Test, and of all the nineties I scored through my Test career – and there were 10, including two not-outs – this was the most soul-destroying. I had weathered probably the most brutal, all-consuming assault of my career from Wasim Akram and Waqar Younis to get as close to the hundred as I did. On this occasion it was all-out warfare, or at least as close as you could get to that in a cricket match.

As usual, Waqar had greeted me with his in-your-face style that centred on verbal and physical intimidation. (I always had a laugh whenever the Pakistanis claimed innocence at match-referee hearings, claiming they didn't understand English, for their grasp of certain four-letter words was very competent.) Waqar was a guy we all respected for always putting in, never shirking any task, and this combined with his blistering pace and wicked reverse swing made him the complete package. While he and I had our fair share of 'conversations' out in the middle, he would always have a chat at the end of the day's play.

During this innings Wasim had been off the field with a supposed back injury and had to wait until he'd done his 'penance' as a mere fielder, according to the rules, which he obviously didn't agree with. As soon as his time was up, on he came and bowled one of the quickest, meanest spells I'd ever seen. Wasim either didn't like me or I was in the wrong place at the wrong time. Nothing was in my half of the wicket and it was all genuinely quick, the ball leaping off the pitch with spite and venom. At the same time, the danger heightened my faculties and I fought fire with fire against the two bowlers, including this brief conversation with Waqar:

Waqar, as he followed through after a venomous bouncer narrowly missed the grill of my helmet: 'I'm gonna kill you today.'

Me: 'I thought you were supposed to be quick.'

Of course, the next ball was 2 metres quicker and the ensuing glare between us was like two heavyweights at a weigh-in ceremony. This environment was one in which I flourished, because it drew out my competitive instincts and the will to never back down. I enjoyed the battle and expected no less of my batting partners, hoping that my intensity levels and combativeness would be contagious. I would try to lift those I batted with, especially if they were tail-enders.

Having two all-time greats like Waqar and Wasim using you as target practice takes courage when your expertise is taking wickets rather than defending on the back foot. On this occasion Warney tried to take them on, backing away and hitting over the cordon, but to me that strategy sent out the wrong message – that their tactics were working. I knew they couldn't go on too much longer due to fatigue, so I took a gamble and chastised Shane. My advice went along these lines: 'C'mon Warney, let's get stuck in and get behind it. I haven't busted my balls all day for you to throw your wicket away.'

A nod of the head and, to Shane's great credit, we were both singing from the same hymn sheet. However, on 98, I experienced another Waqar short ball, which thudded into my ribs, then ricocheted off my left elbow before bouncing off the back of my left heel, trickling onto my leg stump and dislodging a single bail. I looked down in disgust at the weakness of that pathetic bail. Surely it could have clung on. Hadn't it been watching the game and appreciated how tough it was to get so close? It was a cruel blow, but would later serve as a nice reminder of how sweet future hundreds would be. Disappointment definitely is the breeding ground for desire.

Two days later, the team's inner strength was severely tested. Tubs had enforced the follow-on after superb bowling from Craig McDermott and Test debutant Damien Fleming had given us a first-innings lead of 261. But this decision led to us enduring a marathon in the field that featured, over the last three and a bit days of the Test, 228.5 Australian overs straight. We had our chances to win, but dropped critical catches and, on a flat pitch against quality batting, we paid heavily. Any cricketer who says he's enjoyed every moment of his career either has selective memory or is a liar, because I can guarantee that after 200 consecutive overs in uncomfortable temperatures and in front of a sparse but parochial Rawalpindi crowd, the fun factor wasn't registering. The 'whingeometer', though, was off the scale, especially because the arch-villain, Salim Malik, batted sublimely for 237, displaying his velvet touch, precise placement and stunning timing. Every run was graceful but, after the offer he had made to our guys during the first Test, also extremely irritating.

A few days later, Malik and I had a brief conversation after I scored 59 not out in a handsome Australian victory in a one-dayer at Multan. While I was walking off to greet my ecstatic teammates, Malik sidled up alongside and said, 'Why are you so unkind when all of your team-mates are so nice?'

I didn't dignify his claims with a comment, but thought to myself, *Look in the mirror, arsehole.*

It's a given when you've been fielding for many, many overs that the 20-minute tea break seems to be over in the blink of an eye. The last five minutes are consumed with attempts to lift yourself out of the quicksand of delirium that has engulfed you. If I ever felt myself slip-ping into this mode, I'd either have a shower and put on a fresh set of whites, or scroll through the inspirational tapes in my memory files to find an appropriate image to snap me out of the abyss. It might be as simple as looking forward to a meal that had been organised after the day's play or to a movie I was keen to see, or perhaps recalling part of a phone conversation between Lynette or the kids and me, or even a childhood experience. It was real mind-over-matter stuff, because physically we were exhausted but there was only one choice: to take the remaining wickets or stay out there longer. In a funny sort of way, I used to privately measure myself up against the rest of the guys. I didn't want to show weakness, and although I did my share of complaining, ultimately I wanted to lead the way, be assertive when I walked from the change rooms, and make an effort to be upbeat. It's not an easy thing to lift when the team really needs you, but to me the response offered in such situations is a clear window into a person's strength of character. Positive talk and good body language are easy when things are running smoothly, but much rarer when the chips are down.

For Mark Taylor, this tour represented a tumultuous entry into the leadership of Australian cricket, but his even temperament in public and in game situations provided such a solid base that he had the ability to treat those dual impostors – adulation and criticism – with equal con-tempt. He knew the truth usually lay somewhere in between. I'm sure there were times during the two-month tour when he would have liked a disguise – which, quite appropriately, fitted into one of the team's off-field pursuits, the Facial Hair Competition. Each player dipped into a hat to extract a piece of paper detailing his task for the next two weeks of touring life. Options such as a thick Rod Marsh moustache, a Merv Hughes handlebar, an 'Abraham Lincoln', a goatee or a pencil-thin handlebar were all considered reasonable outcomes, with the most cursed assignment being the full beard. Tubs actually jagged that one, but he ended up liking the result so much he later used it as a fashion statement in Oz.

A fortnight later, as I peered into the mirror, I thought my full goatee didn't scrub up too badly. However, those sentiments weren't exactly shared by the lads when the judgements were handed down at the awards ceremony later that day. When I landed back home, shoulder all strapped up with less than a month to the first Ashes Test, the 'beard' was gone.

22

As confused as the Poms

As far as seasons go, the 1994–95 one – involving a Test series against England and a very commercialised one-day tournament featuring two Australian teams because Zimbabwe weren't considered market-able enough to sustain a tri-series – was hardly memorable.

The entire Ashes campaign was probably best summed up by the outcome of the very first delivery, which sped to the point boundary from the flashing blade of the always amped-up Michael Slater. I never missed the start of a Test with Slats in action, because the energy he generated meant there would invariably be fireworks. This time his opening salvo was an important psychological boost for us, and the Poms didn't at any stage of the series have the momentum going in their direction. Also helping us was the fact that the English selectors hadn't been able to work out whether to go for youth or hardened professionals, and ended up going for a blend. However, in 41-year-old Graham Gooch and Mike Gatting, 37, they had two guys who were past their best and holding back talented youngsters, even if I did admire their professionalism, playing record and work ethic. So long as the passion and skill remain, age has never been an issue for me, but in my opinion Gatting didn't meet these criteria any more and Gooch was just clinging on. Both had led their country and been influential players over a long period of time, and much about their achievements and longevity was to be admired, but the harsh truth was that we were glad they had been picked.

Another England batsman from the series, Graeme Hick, had as much talent as any player I ever came across, yet he never made the impact in Test cricket most thought he would when he started. He was a colossus at the crease, particularly in his youth in Zimbabwe, when he regularly carved up touring international sides. Hick was unlucky that the English media had hailed him as 'the best since Bradman' and saw him as the man to restore national pride after serving a seven-year qualification period. County cricket attacks, which are largely innocuous after an initial onslaught, placid pitches and small outfields were too easy for Hick's prodigious talents, but they were also a dangerous impediment to his development, because any technical weakness went largely untested. Similarly, prior to his Test debut his capacity to overcome hardship was never called upon. It soon would be.

Curtly Ambrose made Hick's life a misery on his debut for England in 1991, when the 'Antiguan assassin' locked his image onto his scope and dismantled Hick's mind and wicket with clinical efficiency. You could almost see Curtly's hunger intensifying with each glowing Hick tribute, and by the time 'Let's play ball' came around, he was like an Alsatian with a rag doll. Then, three years later, just as it appeared as if Hick's liberating gifts were about to re-emerge, in stepped England captain Michael Atherton to extinguish the flame. As far as exerting your authority at the wrong time and not knowing your own players well enough, Atherton's decision to declare before tea during the fourth day of the third Test, in Sydney, when Hick was 98 not out, must rate as a major blunder. Either it was imbecilic batting or no message had been forthcoming, because there was no urgency from Hick as the milestone and the time for the tea interval converged. A captain must always look beyond personal milestones for the benefit of the team, but in Hick Atherton had a potentially great player who hadn't scored a Test century against Australia and was in urgent need of a confidence boost. One more over and he might have been a totally different player for the rest of his career, but sadly for him, he never did make a hundred against us and his self-belief never matched his gifts. Significantly, Hick's fellow players seemed disheartened by the coldness of the declaration and we sensed the tension it caused. In his misguided belief that to show tunnel vision in the search for victory was a virtue, Atherton overlooked the very secret to team success: effective man-management.

We, too, had a player of immense natural gifts who most assumed would follow the path to distinction. Michael Bevan did just that in the one-day games as a 'Pyjama Picasso', creating masterpiece after masterpiece to the point that his genius became mundane when people were spoilt by his continued brilliance. In the nets, he was a guy to admire: he would literally invent strokes to fuel his search for greatness and his desire to attain new levels of excellence. Prior to his Test debut he was fearless, uninhibited and purposeful at the crease in all forms of cricket, and to those in the know a long and fulfilling career in the five-day game appeared a given. His only danger was himself, because he was a very harsh judge and expected nothing less than complete success, so failure wasn't contemplated. But perhaps even more damaging was his eternal quest to better his game. I believe improvement is an ongoing process. When I thought I couldn't keep going forward, then it was time to give it away, but there are times when for peace of mind you must be satisfied with what you've got and where you're at. Bevo tinkered with his methods at the wrong time. I vividly remember him during 1994–95 asking me about playing the short ball and then listening to him saying that he wasn't sure about hooking. I told him I believed it had to be a personal choice but I appreciated him sounding me out, though not convinced he was clear in his own mind as to what to do. I loved the thought of helping others and playing a guiding role, but in this case all I could give Michael were my reasons for not hooking and how it had worked for me. Obviously Bevo hadn't resolved the issue by the time the series got under way, because he got himself in a hell of a tangle over the short ball on a number of occasions and after three Tests was shown the door by a ruthless selection panel. Sometimes as a cricketer you've got to know when to 'stop and smell the coffee' and just enjoy your own game. Self-assessment for international players is a tough road if it's a constant one. Too much of it can arouse the monsters within that manipulate the mind and leave the inquirer muddled in his convictions.

Replacing Bevo in the Test team was another exceptionally talented batsman. Greg Blewett would distinguish himself with back-to-back centuries in his first two Tests, achieved with such ease and grace that the 'potential greatness' tag was quickly slung around his neck. It was strange for me to line up alongside 'Blewey', because along with the rest of the Panania–East Hills Under 10s I'd watched his dad, Bob, play for SA on one of my first visits to the SCG. Greg had almost too much talent, which allowed him to dominate most attacks. But he did have a technical flaw when facing deliveries that swung in or deviated from off to leg, in that he often left an inviting gap between bat and pad. Unbelievably, having scored those centuries in his first two Tests, he only scored two more in his next 44 Tests, despite often looking as if he belonged and was heading for a highly successful career.

Blewey was like many others who couldn't align their talent with results, largely because of rollercoaster emotions and wayward form fluctuations that prevented stability. Perhaps being a big fish in the small pond that is Adelaide didn't help Greg's mindset, because I'm sure as soon as he became a Test star his status and profile would have increased overnight. Lack of discipline and a lack of self-belief are two negatives that seem attracted to each other and end up using each other as crutches to lean on. Blewey had a touch of both, but I always enjoyed his company and the aggressive way he played his cricket. It's just a shame he didn't quite attain the levels he could have.

By the time the Ashes series was over, the team was on the ascendency and had gathered enough momentum to feel confident about our chances of capturing the elusive Frank Worrell Trophy in the upcoming series in the Caribbean. I was also edging towards the dubious honour of securing the most Test nineties in the history of the game. It was a statistic I didn't enjoy, but in the overall scheme of things there are much worse things to be claimed. My 99 not out made during the fifth Test, in Perth, was my sixth Test ninety, two short of the then Test record held by the West Indies' Alvin Kallicharran.

Falling one short of 100 is torment enough, but to be not out as well left me with a hollow pain that inhibited my sleep over the ensuing couple of nights. At the non-striker's end was my brother, running for the injured Craig McDermott, and in his desire to get me to tri-ple figures Mark backed up aggressively but anticipated a single that wasn't quite there. I sent him back as quickly as I could, but already knew what the outcome was: death by a centimetre as Graham Gooch removed the bails with Mark diving back in vain. Watching the scene unfold was harder to take than being told that Santa Claus wasn't real.

Proving how much cricket is a game of psychological mini-battles is the joy a fielding team can get out of preventing an opposition player achieving a milestone. Somehow a dismissal such as this seems like a victory and acts as a catalyst even though it may not resemble anything remotely like that in terms of the overall state of the game. Likewise, the deflation the individual dismissed can feel and the knock-on effect it can have on his teammates can get out of proportion. I was certainly not a happy camper as I strode back into the spacious WACA change rooms. In the confines of a team environment there's a time to talk and a time when peace and quiet are advisable. The cold silence of our dressing-room was shattered by my 'Look out, the helmet's coming!' I needed to discharge my frustration, so I let it rip a good 5 metres through the air before it clipped the underside of the door frame and then bounced a couple of times on the floor tiles of the shower room. Following it in, acutely aware I was carrying on like a pork chop, I picked up the severely dinted fibreglass cap and its mangled grill, cra-dled it and wondered how a potentially joyous occasion had turned into such a debacle. I must have wandered around aimlessly in the shower area for a couple of minutes trying to pull myself together before I gathered enough courage to get back amongst it, and over-come the embarrassment of disfiguring my helmet and altering the mood of the camp.

Searching for that extra run consumed my semiconscious sleep pat-tern that evening. *Why didn't I take that easy single to wide mid-off? How come I smashed that long hop straight to point? Why didn't I just go over the infield on 99?* Instead, I was condemned to the record books as only the second man after Geoff Boycott to remain undefeated one short of a century in a Test match. The sun did come up the next morning, the newspapers still said I was one short, and the anguish had partially subsided to the point where comprehension of world events was at least registering on my radar.

History of a different kind was being created in the one-day game. Zimbabwe were the second overseas team in the World Series, but they weren't considered to be good enough to pull any sort of crowd or create sufficient revenue, so an Australia A team was included as the fourth team in the competition. In theory, this was a real coup for the ACB and Channel Nine, the long-time holders of TV rights to Australian cricket, because all Aussies love an underdog and here we had the next-best group of cricketers trying to take down the elite. The only Australians who didn't like the idea were, quite obviously, us – the members of the high-achieving 'first team' squad.

While we were all under pressure, the captain probably had the most to lose, with his reputation as a leader and his own position under scrutiny. Wanting to have a unified approach as far as the Test and one-day teams were concerned, the selectors had made a deal with Tubs that guaranteed his selection in the one-day side for at least the first 12 months of his Test captaincy. It sounded like good practice, but it did create a difficult precedent that was to cause consternation down the track. Deals such as this are done to create solidarity and give confidence to the group, but they also cause resentment among those trying to force their way into the side, because one less position is available and an elitist attitude percolates through the ranks. While batting for Australia A, Matt Hayden chipped Tubs during a tense encounter and in the process gave us all an insight into the potential problems of Australia v Australia A matches. Normally such banter is considered part of a one-day international match, but here it was coming from a guy who wasn't considered good enough to be in the top side. Mark took exception, deeming that Matt was showing a lack of respect. I could see both sides of the argument, but knew that if I was in the Australia A team I would have been letting the top boys have both barrels, reminding them I was around and didn't want an 'A' next to my team name. Both Australian teams made the finals, and in the end we snuck home, winning two tight games. I remained unbeaten in both, proving that experience does count in the big occasions, even if these fixtures weren't recognised as official one-day internationals.

Another bizarre episode was the commercial for Ansett Airlines that Mark Taylor and I filmed during the season. Ansett being a board sponsor meant we didn't receive a cent for our efforts. Activity such as this was covered by our all-encompassing contract, which wasn't as rewarding as many thought. Normally, sportspeople in these situations are handed very average scripts – because they can't act and the client generally doesn't really care about the sportspeople's reputation so long as they, the client, get some exposure. Ansett were looking to make inroads into new markets and we were their mouthpieces. No one had bothered to tell us that we had to learn fluent Cantonese in 30 minutes, but this was the designated task. Thankfully my lines weren't too taxing, but Tubs had to phonetically reproduce whole sentences, which he did to his enormous credit. I can still hear the phrase I had to deliver with a quizzical look: 'Gay pil gar!'

What those words exactly meant I'm still not sure. I was as confused as the Poms, who had come to Australia with high expectations but too many negative memories, which ultimately curtailed their ambitions. Now it was our turn to jettison the emotional and physical scarring many a West Indian team had handed out to us. Our true worth as a team was about to be revealed.

23

A certain type of loneliness

The elderly woman at the check-in lounge in Sydney didn't exactly recognise our potential when she commented on our new pinstriped blazers, 'Which school do you lads go to?'

A day later, and the tone of the tour was set during an overnight stopover in London, when a team meeting was called. Captain Taylor stressed that the Windies had everything to lose and we had nothing to lose, and that we had to play our natural games instead of worrying about what their bowlers might do to us. Not since early 1980 had the West Indies juggernaut been stopped by anyone, and Australia hadn't tasted success against the giants of the Caribbean since 1975–76, so the task at hand was acknowledged as being the Everest of cricket. But we believed the time was right to ascend the final peak, which had eluded us so narrowly back in Adelaide on Australia Day in 1993.

The Caribbean will always be special to me. I love the attitude of the people, their laid-back lifestyle and the way they respect those who have a real go at things. Not surprisingly, right from ball one in 1995 I was switched on, in tune with the excitable atmosphere around the ground, lapping up our opponents' love of a contest and positive outlook on life. A 96-ball 117 retired against Barbados was the start I was searching for, because it allowed me the luxury of relaxed practice sessions instead of the difficult task of correcting faults or finding satisfaction in the level I was at.

Crowds in the Windies have a quick wit, cleverly disguising their version of the truth in sharp humour. Here are a few of my favourite crowd comments.

About Brian Lara: 'He's the best in the world . . . and on Mars too!'

On Mark Waugh: 'He drives like a lady, but he's got no brains.'

About Warney's zinc cream: 'Hey man, you look like an Indian with that face mask on.'

Glenn McGrath's physique copped a hiding: 'McGrath, you're so skinny you need steroids.' And his bowling copped this: 'Well bowled, McEasy!'

The 'shazam' knuckle engagement was a sign that you had their respect. Any time one was extended my way, I met it with the full impact. I knew that if the fans were showing me their view of my worth, then their cricket team would more than likely be of a similar view. I felt ready for the battle and confident that a big series was imminent.

However, it was not all smooth sailing. Either through good fortune or naivety, I'd never before really had to deal with an issue evolving back home while I was on tour. So, when a month into the tour we were in Barbados and Lynette had to go into hospital for an operation to remove her tonsils, I waited with some trepidation to learn about the outcome. I was sure it would go well, but there was a large dose of helplessness about the predicament I was in, and some guilt that I couldn't be there to assure her everything would be okay.

Being on tour is like being cocooned in a soundproof booth: the importance of anything outside the tour is almost invariably diluted. I should have recognised more acutely the life-altering incident Lynette went through during the 2002 South African tour. She saw the tragic cot death of a very close friend's young boy, and had to notify the husband and comfort the wife. She called me in a distressed state, but I didn't fully comprehend the magnitude of the situation. Of course I was devastated at the horrific news, but because of my focus as an international cricketer, touring life continued next morning while Lynette grappled with grief, overwhelming sadness and nightmares without the support she deserved and needed from her husband.

Lynette actually went into hospital for her tonsilectomy on the opening day of the first Test. By this point, the confidence we'd had at the outset of the tour had been frayed somewhat by a 4–1 drubbing in the one-day series, but in all honesty we had set our sights on the stuffed Mickey Mouse doll and not the plastic keyring. The double loss of our spearheads, Craig McDermott and Damien Fleming, prior to the first Test further tested our conviction and again emphasised how quickly things can change. During the just-completed Australian season Brendon Julian had been relegated to 12th man for WA, so he was something of a surprise choice to replace Flem, and found himself taking the new ball in a Test match. In order to let guys relax more in the days leading up to the game, the squad's final team meeting was for the first time moved from Test-match eve to the night before that, and that was commonsense – if you needed to have a serious session 24 hours before the match, then you were in trouble and highly unlikely to solve the problem you felt needed fixing. It was also a positive considering the intensity and length of this particular preseries get-together. I concurred thoroughly with our departing words: 'Let's treat their tail-enders with no respect. Let's bounce them upon their arrival at the crease, to show them we mean business. We'll be the ones doing the intimidating this time around, but we must never lose a grip on things. We must follow up this greeting with controlled aggression, to then get them out.'

★

The opening session of the first Test was one of the most spine-tingling I was ever involved in. The crowd was in shock and we couldn't believe what was unfolding, either, with the scoreboard attendants cluttering the metallic name plates onto the 'used' pile down below with unexpected regularity. At 3/6, with Stuart Williams, Sherwin Campbell and Richie Richardson back in the pavilion having faced 14 balls from Brendon Julian and Paul Reiffel between them, the scene was surreal. But we hadn't banked on the most courageous counterattack I ever witnessed. Carl Hooper, in a premeditated all-out assault, charged Warney, hitting him out of the already crumbling rough outside the right-hand batsman's leg stump and over the top on either side of the wicket. It was fearless, brilliant batsmanship that rendered his partner, the genius Brian Lara, a mere passenger by comparison.

Warney would later say that Hooper was the hardest of all batsmen to bowl to when he was on the charge. He would leave his crease late and without any obvious giveaway signs. Quickness of feet and sweet yet brutally efficient stroke play were Hooper's trademarks, and it took Shane a lot of postgame videotape analysis and careful attention to crack his code. Eventually he concluded that when Carl moved his eyes down to look at his stance and back again, as most players do, he wasn't going to charge; when he employed the fixed stare at the bowler, he was about to jump out of the blocks. Even then, though his system had been discovered, it still required subtle modification to nullify Hooper's aggression.

By lunch, Lara and Hooper had put together 110 runs at better than a run a minute, provoking the steel bands and conch-shell blowers into continued wild celebrations. Soon after, with Lara on 65, Julian bowled – and I could never have imagined what a profound effect the outcome of one delivery would have on my career. A wide half-volley was smashed straight to me in the gully, and I clutched at the chance with hard hands, unable to take it cleanly. As the ball bobbled out, I made a further two attempts to gain control, and when my right arm landed on the ground, the ball simultaneously bounced off my wrist before I grabbed hold of it, clumsily but safely. Lara rightly waited for confirmation from me and the surrounding fieldsmen that the catch had been completed before departing. Everyone in the near vicinity agreed it was out, but at the end of play Simmo hit me between the eyes when he said, 'What are you going to say to the media?'

Stunned, I replied, 'About what?'

Video replays had cast doubt on the legality of the catch. From some angles, it appeared that the ball might have touched the ground before I took control of it. I had been carved up by Michael Holding, among others, on television, while Viv Richards threw his weight around in the morning papers, all but calling me a cheat. I was angry at their enthusiasm to dissect my integrity, especially as some of my critics hadn't exactly been angels when they'd been playing. All I could do was say to myself, *You've done nothing wrong – stay positive*, and find a way to use the criticism to my advantage, in the way a sewage-treatment works can ultimately extract drinking water from effluent.

My senses must have been aroused by the controversy, because when we replied to the Windies' 195 I got a very real insight into extra-sensory perception. I was batting with Mark, and as Curtly Ambrose was running in to bowl I 'saw' my twin being caught behind, sparring at a good-length ball. It was as if his fate was sealed and he was power-less to alter the sequence of events I had been delivered. I was spooked by the clarity with which I had foreseen what happened. This kind of thing would occur sporadically throughout our careers, but only from me and never from Mark. When I told him what I'd seen, he simply asked, 'Why didn't you tell me?'

The outcome of this three-day entertainment extravaganza – a win to us, by 10 wickets – was beyond our wildest expectations. The home team had previously lost only two of 30 Tests played in Barbados, and never to Australia. Making our win even more meritorious was the fact that our coach was in hospital with a blood clot in his left calf, but still his influence had played its part in the mindset we took into battle.

Before the Test series Simmo had called a meeting, at which he asked us to respond to three questions: 'Why haven't we been playing as well as we can? What can you do to improve your performance? What sacrifices are you prepared to make?'

Following on from our loss in the one-day series, it was the wake-up call we needed, and gave us a clear focus as to what was required. Our game plan was simple: bowl line and length to frustrate them into playing big shots, and make every chance count. From the batting side of things, the virtues of patience and having your own battle plan were emphasised, while an overall resilience was needed to front up to any situation that may present itself. We had a solid battle blueprint cen-tred on discipline, an area in which we believed the West Indies might be deficient.

Three days of cricket later, a night on the *Baja Queen* swigging rum with a dash of Coke around the idyllic setting of Barbados was the perfect way to celebrate our win. The feeling was best summed up by Tim May after two hours of cruising the crystal-clear blue waters: 'Hey, when is this boat going to move from the docks?'

★

Cricket, more so than many other sports, gives you a glimpse of the inner workings of the people involved, purely because there is so much time to observe and form opinions. It may be as simple as the animation a cricketer shows, the way he moves in the field or the gestures he makes when among teammates. Often the signals are subtle, and sometimes you can argue about what they really mean, but for me seeing the fearless Richie Richardson coming out to bat in a helmet for the first time in his career during the second Test, in Antigua, was an insight into his decaying technique and an omen that change was in the wind. I had never imagined this guy backing down and protecting his natural instincts artificially, but here he was, the captain, taking a step back. Not that he wasn't entitled to, but his team's aura of invincibility was slipping, in our minds and in their actions.

Of course, this didn't mean they were going to lie down. In fact, the last nine overs of day two bordered on being savage, with Ambrose and Walsh peppering Slater and Taylor in unrelenting fashion. Slats' pregame statement, 'The West Indies attack holds no fear for our batsmen', was countered by Amby replying, 'Slater is going to have 19 ambulances waiting for him when he goes into bat this match.' The positive sign for us was that the boys from Wagga Wagga didn't back down, even though a swag of icepacks were needed at the end of the day's play. Our spirit was unbroken.

In previous series the Windies could, seemingly at will, turn a game around by upping the tempo and creating panic via fear. But we had learnt the art of intimidation from previous batterings and weren't about to back down this time. In fact, our desire to retaliate had grown in intensity. We knew their quicks hated copping 'chin music' (bouncers around the face) when they batted, but until McGrath started handing out this unpalatable medicine we couldn't match our talk with action. The courageous part wasn't the bowling of bumpers, but the recognition on Glenn's part that by making himself Enemy No. 1 he also made himself a target for retribution. For him to face up to that must have been terrifying, because his skill level with the bat was akin to a featherweight taking on Muhammad Ali – and pain was a logical outcome. In the second innings of the first Test Walsh had tried to cover his nerves and intense dislike for the short stuff by clowning around and amusing the crowd. We knew we'd touched an open wound.

I did, too, when asking Tubs and Slats to pose for a photo while they sat in the Antigua dressing-room with icepacks all over them after their tussle with Walsh and Ambrose. It was the only time in all my photography moments inside the privacy of the team rooms when I thought, *Bad move*. The boys were still very much on edge, high on adrenaline and in 'battle' mode. I took one photo and then put my camera away.

I scored 65 not out in our second innings – my second half-century of the series – and knew something big was brewing. I just needed to trust myself and not force the issue and a big score would come. I'd done the hard work in the nets, increased my fitness levels and mastered the art of switching on and off when required, so the foundations were solid. All I needed to do was be patient. Meanwhile, the third Test, in Trinidad, loomed as one of those games you live for as a player – the series was on the line, and we had a chance to slay the giant and determine exactly where we were at as individual cricketers and as a team.

David Boon's great resilience, legendary toughness and profession-alism were rewarded with his 100th Test cap at the third Test, but his joy was short-lived upon arriving at the Queen's Park Oval in Port of Spain, Trinidad. The wicket was excessively grassed, bright green and alarmingly moist to prod. If you push a finger at a prepared pitch there shouldn't be any give at all, but on this occasion it resembled hardened plasticine. A nightmare awaited the loser of the toss.

Batting at No. 5 normally gave me enough breathing space to watch the first couple of overs before donning the creams and preparing my batting gear, but once I learnt Mark Taylor had called incorrectly, intui-tion told me to fast-track the process. Habitually, once a wicket fell I would put on my protector (which wasn't the traditional, flatter cricket design but like that of a bike rider or baseball player, with a deeper cup, solely because I had decided that the impact of a blow to that area would be distributed better by such a shape. My relatively flimsy thigh guard was made of foam, which gave a more natural feel as it hugged the body shape and didn't protrude; the fact that it smarted more when I was hit was a sacrifice I was willing to make. Most guys used a thigh guard bolstered by fibreglass, while the enigmatic Carl Hooper bat-ted with nothing more than a handkerchief in his pocket. Carl does, though, have thighs a body-builder would kill for).

When the second wicket fell, I switched from taking in bits and pieces to immersing myself in the on-field action. The book or news-paper I might be reading was discarded and I preferred my personal space, or at least to disengage from the conversations going on around me. It wasn't a total blockout, but the guys knew my mind was elsewhere. I was searching for fielders who were trying to make an impact, and for those who were sluggish, working out who I might be able to take on. I enjoyed studying the opposition's body language, in particular trying to gauge the captain's disposition and the mood of his bowlers. Watching closely allowed me to gauge the tempo and momentum of the match, which would give me a headstart when I got out there, in terms of getting into the flow of the match. I wanted to hit the ground running, not walk out in a semi-dazed state hoping for success, as I'd done early in my career. I now expected success. A thorough preparation, together with a sensible routine, certainly helped manage nerves and ease tension as I began the unpredictable wait.

On this day, it wasn't long before I made the walk from the players' pavilion, past the old cycling track that runs around the outside of the Queen's Park Oval beyond the boundary, into a cauldron of animosity. We were 3/14. A chorus of 'Tief! Tief! You're a tief, man!' accompanied my quickened gait to the middle. The 'thief' tag was a reference to the controversial catch that had terminated the dig of local legend Lara in the first Test. Trinidad nightlife was something I hadn't been seeing much of after an intrusive late-night phone call before the Test in which an anonymous caller suggested, 'Don't go out at night, man. If I see you on the street, you're dead, man!'

I was acutely aware that this was going to be a test of character just as much as of skill, but I was comforted by an inner sensation that told me I was the guy to take them on. The hostile reception followed me all the way to the crease, where I joined forces with David Boon, a bloke who was never big on mid-pitch dialogue, generally keeping it very simple with lines like 'Well done, keep it going' or 'Keep working hard.' So I knew it was a difficult pitch when he said, 'Jeez, it's doing a bit here.'

It sure was. Ambrose and Walsh were as close to unplayable as you could get, combining extravagant sideways movement off the seam with venomous exaggerated bounce that made survival demanding and stroke play foolhardy. At the end of each over, we would walk down the pitch and clearly see the ball indentations from the previous six deliveries: little oval-shaped pot marks, a couple of shades lighter green, where the excess moisture had been compressed out.

Initially I was in survival mode, leaving as many balls as possible and defending with a short backlift and soft hands to deaden the impact. I was heartened by the second ball I faced, which I avoided cleverly with a precise movement, instilling in me the belief that I was switched on for the task at hand. A confidence-filling stroke doesn't have to be an attacking one out of the middle of the bat – it can be a solid defensive shot or an artfully dodged bouncer, but it must be executed with validity. We needed a partnership, and the best way to get that was to ride out the storm, wait for the pitch to dry and look to attack the men who replaced Ambrose and Walsh – the unrelated Kenny and Winston Benjamin, who might have been quality bowlers but thankfully were not all-time greats like the Windies' front men.

Curiously, Courtney Walsh never really troubled me like he did many others. I knew he was one of the best quick bowlers around, combining pace, skill, stamina and courage with a hatred of losing a one-on-one battle with the batsman. However, I didn't mind his angled deliveries, finding solace in the fact that he would eventually stray onto my legs or ribs and that I had the technique to get him away. Left-handed batsmen hated his bounce and angles, never sure what to leave and what to play, and such was Walsh's quality he was always asking the difficult questions. Any flaw in a batsman's make-up was cruelly exposed.

To me, Curtly Ambrose was the supreme fast-bowling machine. He moved with the ease and grace of a champion athlete across the ground, was beautifully balanced and coordinated, and could blast you out with pace if needed or revert to a strategic assault. As well, he owned the trait everyone wants but few possess: the gift of being able to shift into that extra gear when needed. His calling card when he thought he had you plumb lbw was a double clap of the hands that was as reliable as the umpire's finger going up. He detested singles off his bowling, believing the prey had escaped his clutches.

The icing on the cake for Amby was his imposing physical presence – legs like stilts, arms that never seemed to end and pouting lips
that looked like they'd been stung by a swarm of bees. When he stood
a couple of feet away giving me his Clint Eastwood glare, I had the
feeling he could take me down at any stage but still wasn't quite sure
which of his weapons he would employ to do the job.

Ambrose, like me, was a man who had plenty on his mind, with many
in the media questioning his commitment to the team after the first two
Tests, in which he'd taken three wickets. There were suggestions he was
past his best and not playing with his usual intensity. Something had to
give, and when it did, an everlasting image was born.

As soon as quicks see encouragement from a pitch, the intensity
levels immediately lift, and on this minefield we were trying to avoid
being detonated. For a batsman to survive and ultimately score runs
on this type of pitch he must have a component of luck, because it
is only a matter of time before a ball either beats the outside edge
or brushes against it. Luck favoured me early on, especially against
Ambrose, who cut me in half with one delivery and then forced me
to jab at the next ball as it deviated away from the outside edge. With
each play and miss, he would pull up just in front of me and glare; it
was if he thought I was purposely taunting his efforts.

For me, a volcano of emotions was brewing: frustration at my inability to get on top of the situation, anger at the booing that had greeted
my arrival at the crease, irritation after a restless night's sleep and now
Amby's bloody stare. A steepling bouncer that flew harmlessly over
the top of my head was almost a relief, because it didn't pose a danger,
so when I saw Ambrose staring intently from close quarters I snapped
back at him, 'What the fuck are you looking at?' This was a clear case
of the mouth beating the brain to the punch. It *was* what I was thinking, but saying it took even me by surprise. It was pure instinct, as my
survival mechanism took over; I wasn't going to just stand there and

cop physical intimidation while he was making a mockery of me with the ball and his gestures. It was fightback time. It was also, realistically, my last resort to get some impetus into my innings.

Ambrose was clearly stunned, most likely because no one had ever been stupid enough to employ such an aggressive measure against him. Furthermore, respect is very important in the Caribbean, and when you swear directly at someone you are not showing them respect. In this culture, profanities are rarely heard.

Amby countered my bar-talk bluff by saying, 'Don't cuss me, man.'

Commonsense should have told me to leave it at that. But I needed to have the last say, to get all the anger out, clear my thoughts and start afresh. Unfortunately, nothing inventive or witty came to mind, rather another piece of personal abuse: 'Why don't you go and get fucked.'

Curtly's eyes were spinning and the situation had rapidly escalated to the point of total ugliness. Thankfully Richie Richardson stepped in, grabbed his great bowler by the wrist with both hands, and attempted to yank him away 'tug of war' style. Of course, Amby didn't want to back down and walk away, and I was also past the point of no return. We needed to show the Windies it was our turn to dictate proceedings, and that we weren't afraid to get in their faces and get our hands dirty. Ego plays a healthy role in this type of stand-off situation; neither of us was willing to lose face by backing away. I was totally unsure what to do if he lunged at me, because I'm certain he would have made light work of me even though I had a bat in my hands. I kept saying to myself, *Don't move, don't move. Look tough, stay focused. He'll have to go away.*

Eventually he did. However, as he ran in to deliver his next ball, I braced myself for an Exocet missile at the throat. That would be his way of winning the battle. He put in the big ones, striding out to full pace before letting go an absolute scorcher of a bouncer that reared alarmingly off a shortish length and crushed my top hand against the handle of the bat, directly in front of my grill. Such was the venom in the execution that I was a foot off the ground at the time of impact. Again Amby was there, menacingly staring me down, but this time my lips were sealed. I'd already smashed the wasp nest open; there was no need to go back and trample on it.

For many players, getting involved in a confrontation is a death sentence for their performance as it consumes their thoughts. The guilt and embarrassment often lead to a loss of clarity, as most players can't compartmentalise and move on. I didn't mind this clash with Amby because I knew I could forget about it after using the altercation as motivation to do well. I never minded being the villain, because it set me up against the rest – a scenario that turned me on. Obviously, being the bad guy had the same effect on Curtly, because he finished this innings with 5/45 from 16 overs, while I scrapped, slogged, scampered and stroked my way to one of my finest Test knocks: 63 not out in a team total of 128.

At the end of two and a half days, the game was over. We had been crushed by a proud cricketing dynasty, but at least I could console myself with the fact that I'd scored the only 50 in a game totally domi-nated by the bowlers. Emphasising how tough it was for batsmen, I learnt that the game's official Deloitte ratings system measured my 63 not out against high-quality bowling in tough conditions as being equivalent to scoring 204 against an average attack on a good pitch. One of their representatives told me that if I scored 200 not out and the West Indies' Jimmy Adams failed twice in the fourth and deciding Test in Kingston, Jamaica, I'd become, in Deloitte's eyes at least, the world's No. 1 batsman – a fact I didn't entertain again. But nor did I forget it.

★

The consensus among the critics was that the mood of the series had changed abruptly, with the home team now in the ascendancy. Perhaps naturally, we were downcast. I will never forget, though, the manner in which the shocking sights on television of the Oklahoma City bomb blast, with the haunting image of a firefighter carrying a dying baby from the rubble, offered the reality check we needed to put things in perspective.

Bob Simpson certainly didn't hold anything back during an impromptu meeting of the batsmen the day after the Test concluded. I clashed with him more than once, most notably over his view that we were soft and not expecting enough of ourselves. Simmo backed his comments up by pointing out that no one had made a century during the series and it was about time someone not only scored one but then went on to make a big hundred. I countered by saying, 'It's not as if we aren't trying. They have four excellent quicks at us constantly.' That day he and I agreed to disagree, but the more I thought about it the clearer it became that the coach was right. The situation confronting us was not frightening, but as challenging and exciting as we'd ever been exposed to. This was the time to make all the sacrifices, the thousands of hours of training, the years of preparation, the moments of tough self-analysis worthwhile, by excelling in the ultimate examination.

Our final session before the series decider was as intense as an actual Test match. This was what Mark Taylor and Simmo wanted, and when Tubs had a new 'Kookaburra' bounce off his grill during his net session, we all knew we were ready. My prematch Test routine was pretty much down pat by now: a haircut, a massage, a swim, pasta and a movie, before taking a Voltaren (anti-inflammatory) pill the night before, followed by a shave on the morning of the game. Athletes often mention 'tapering', which, if it's done effectively, means peaking, physically and mentally, at the right time. I always wanted to wake up on a Test-match morning without any aches and pains, looking and feeling sharp and being energised and excited about the match ahead. It was almost as if I was convincing myself that I'd never been better prepared and I'd given myself the best chance to excel. Tricking the mind by conditioning it is all part of the knowledge that comes with experience. Watching the senior players prepare can be an invaluable learning tool for younger players to draw upon.

Meanwhile, the groundsman at Sabina Park in Kingston was actually trawling the pitch like a tiler to smooth it out. Pitch preparation in Jamaica is different, we learnt, because of the soil in the wicket square, which has a high clay content that needs to be moistened, then baked like a cake to produce a highly polished, marble-like surface. The end product was a gleaming surface in which you could actually see your reflection. For consistency, pace and bounce it came close to matching the greased-lightning pitch at the WACA.

A roommate can alleviate homesickness: he provides a listening ear and is a buddy to team up with. But it can also have its downside, especially if one roomie is a batsman and the other is a bowler. On day one, our bowlers performed exceptionally well to dismiss the West Indies just before stumps for 265, and assumed that the batsmen would at least be able to bat throughout the second day. Once this notion had gained peer-group impetus, the lads felt comfortable engaging in a more relaxed environment, generally somewhere near a bar. I was keen to get an early night, so I left my bunk buddy, McGrath, to his socialising with the message that I'd leave the door ajar because we only had one key. A couple of hours later I instinctively awoke and sat bold upright, chilled all over with goose bumps. I could hear a rustling at the foot of my bed and caught a glimpse of someone crawling on all fours across the floor.

'What the hell are you doing?' I shouted.

The startled intruder, who I think was searching for a couple of souvenir freebies, stumbled an improvised reply: 'I'm a security guard . . . I saw your door open . . . I just came in to see if you were okay.'

Never again did I leave the door open and never again did that guy work at that hotel.

★

A couple of hours of distracted sleep wasn't the ideal preparation, but not for the first time I discovered that nothing else counts once you take centre and devote your thoughts to the duel ahead. Just as I was contemplating what I was going to have for lunch, Slats finally won the battle to get himself out. His innings had been exhilarating theatre, with top edges, mistimed hooks and brilliant audacious shot-making, but quite obviously (except to the batsman) the outcome was inevitable. In many ways, that's the beauty of a free spirit like Slats – his attitude remained firm and the opposition were always under pressure to counter his tactics. The only drawback is the high expectations that such a style of play brings with it. People want action, and they don't appreciate a guy like Slats grinding it out through a tough period or neatly placing the ball into gaps in the field. They prefer batsmanship that disorientates the opposition and sets the tone for the day ahead. Slats was often a match-winner and occasionally a frustration – mainly to himself, because as teammates we accepted that such high-risk batting would lead to disappointments. More importantly to us, he created winning opportunities for the side.

By 1995, at the fall of a wicket I was consistently trying to get onto the park as quickly as I could. I wanted to catch the opposition unawares as they celebrated their success and enjoyed a drink from their 12th man. Many times I would be asking for centre while my opponents were still in a huddle, and by doing so believed that I had gained an advantage without them even knowing. I had claimed ownership of the stage for battle, which gave me a chance to dictate proceedings. The alternative was to casually stroll into the middle, to be surrounded by a fielding group already in their positions and a bowler at the top of his mark ready for the confrontation, and feel under siege without a ball being bowled. Straightaway, a batsman is at his most vulnerable, so it made sense to give myself every opportunity to make it through this acclimatisation phase. My approach also bought me some time, which allowed me to do my stretching and gardening of the pitch at my leisure, gave me sufficient time to get my bearings regarding field placements. It meant that by the time the bowler was moving in for his first delivery to me I'd steeled myself for the battle ahead. Taking the time to get it right at the start is often a forerunner to what lies ahead.

My best moments as a batsman came when I had no extraneous thoughts in my head. It was about having a clear focus, concentrating wholly on the next ball and playing it as best I could. It was simply total engagement, almost to the point of being oblivious to anything else except that little red ball – a certain type of loneliness that I found extremely peaceful and opened up the possibility of entering the much-sought-after 'zone'. Successful players not only become absorbed in the contest, but more importantly can also dispose of dangerous self-doubting messages.

It's very difficult to know why or explain how one ball can give you an inkling that it's going to be your day. In Port of Spain it had been the second delivery I received; here, it was a first-ball bouncer that could have caused me a lot of trouble if I hadn't been sharp. Instead, I was immediately comforted by the ease with which I handled it. At 3/73 chasing 265, the game was poised for a defining moment and Mark and I recognised that our partnership was the key to the outcome. The Windies attack, as always seemed to be the case, revolved around a quartet of pace bowlers with a part-time spinner (although Carl Hooper was good enough to take over 100 wickets in both Tests and one-dayers in his career), and on this excellent batting wicket, once we adjusted to the constant short stuff, the sameness of the assault worked to our advantage. It was important that we capitalised on this.

Gradually, over by over, the chat in the field began to diminish as our assertiveness increased. When a fielding team drops its intensity levels the pendulum begins to swing, presenting an opportunity for the batsmen to take up the slack. Further deflating the Windies was the turning point of the whole match, a dropped catch by keeper Courtney Browne that had flown low and quickly to his right off my outside edge, catching him so much by surprise that the chance bounced off his wrist. Any time I got a reprieve, I felt obliged to knuckle down and make the most of my good fortune; anything less than a hundred wasn't an option.

During this partnership Mark and I conversed at the end of every over – short messages of reassurance such as 'Keep working hard', 'Don't relax now', or 'They look like they're beginning to tire.' Occasionally our competitive natures would surface with statements along the lines of, 'I can't wait to have a bowl at that guy when it's his turn to bat' – meaning 'I'm going to bounce him and see how he likes it!' By the end of the day we had assumed control of the game and the Waugh twins had lived out a backyard dream by peeling off centuries and combining for a double-hundred stand. Because of all that happened over the next two days of the Test, Mark's innings would not get the kudos it deserved. It was one of the best two or three digs of his career in terms of influencing the outcome and the crispness of his stroke play, not to mention the unflappable temperament he exhibited.

For me, being 110 not out overnight was a great position to be in, but trying to get any sleep proved virtually impossible as I lay contemplating the achievements of the day and the possibilities for tomorrow. I knew that the key to making the very big score I craved was concentration, and that the key to concentration was to move through various stages of awareness. As I moved towards my double century on day three, the years of fine-tuning my mind and learning the art of concentrating allowed me to strengthen my resolve, while the Windies visibly wilted. For me, there is no better feeling in sport than seeing the opposition fall apart under pressure and know that you contributed to it. Between deliveries I totally tuned out and switched off from the intensity of the game. The bowler beginning his run-up was the signal for me to move into 'semi-awareness' mode, watching but not being absorbed by the action. At the precise moment the bowler took his last stride before delivery, my switch was flicked and the senses aroused to full capacity. If I struggled to reach the level I desired or felt distracted, I would revert to an old technique of talking to myself, saying things like, 'Watch the ball! Concentrate!' Or my favourite: 'Now!' I really enjoyed the task of lifting into a state of total absorption and then letting go two seconds later. If I did this correctly, I could bat all day but only had to concentrate intensely for around 20 minutes. In doing so, I could stay relatively fresh.

A change of clothes and a shower during the intervals made a significant difference, not only aesthetically but by galvanising my attitude, and I kept eating bananas for an injection of energy. I could have batted for a week. Tiredness wasn't a factor: it was totally wiped away by enjoyment and a sense of achievement. Milestones are important to all players, as they are the only reasonable way to compare yourself to cricketers of other eras. After more than 400 balls and nine hours at the crease, I summoned up enough vigour to scamper an all-run four with my trusted good mate, No. 11 Glenn McGrath, to reach 200 and fulfil a treasured cricketing ambition.

It was a wild celebration from the healthy contingent of Aussie supporters at the ground. Most of them were fuelled by Cockspur rum and cooked from a long day in the sun. After acknowledging the crowd and my team members, I was caught unawares by a young girl who planted a kiss on me and amused by a didjeridu player standing next to a guy bouncing a Sherrin footy on the square. However, nothing prepared me for the arrival of a former Test teammate. A forceful slap on the back caught my attention and I couldn't believe my eyes when Greg Ritchie said, 'Well played, you're a legend.' The fumes of the Cockspur had the same effect on me as smelling salts on a knocked-out boxer. I sprang to life, catching the comments of Richie Richardson, 'Hello, Fat Cat, what are you doing here? You should know better.' Greg would later cop a bit of grief over his actions, especially as he was leading a tour group, but I was genuinely touched by his gesture.

The victory we all desired so much came late on day four and was shared with former players who'd never triumphed over the cricketing dynasty the Windies had created. Allan Border, Geoff Lawson, Dean Jones and David Hookes were among the jubilant well-wishers to enter the hotbed of celebrations. It was important to recognise the contributions of those who'd gone before us and the part they'd played in where we now were, especially our former captain, who seemed touched to be invited. 'Khe Sanh' bellowed out from the ghetto blaster while I indulged in specially-catered-for Southern and Cokes delivered to me by one of the game's finest raconteurs and genuine good guys, Carl Rackemann.

A little later and without thinking about it, I agreed to do a phone interview with Channel Nine's Ray Martin. I was on the brink of a personality change when the camera was parked in front of my face and a phone shoved in my hand.

'Are you ready to do a live cross with Ray for *A Current Affair* in 30 seconds?' the guy who'd handed me the phone asked.

'Thirty seconds? Yeah mate, sure.' What else was I going to say? No one had told me it was going to be live, or that it would involve pictures as well as words. To this day, I'm not sure whether I got away with it.

About 10 hours later I slumped into the quicksand mattress of

Room 5/200 (good omen: batted five, scored 200), totally exhausted, still fully kitted up. It was a little strange to wake up dressed in my creams, with the baggy green welded tight to my head and my half-spiked cricket shoes still on, but the satisfaction I felt from having seen team and personal goals achieved was tremendous. I knew this Test was my defining moment in cricket.

This was as good as it gets.

24

A new life

Lynette and I had been talking for a while about the best time to try to start a family. The correct answer wasn't easy. With me being away for long periods, our kids would essentially be brought up by a single parent, which troubled us both, but the other option was for me to give up cricket, which was our livelihood and my lifelong passion. With no guarantees in cricket but believing my career probably had between five and eight years to go, we decided that the time was right.

In the years that followed, the quality of our moments together became the focal point of our long-distance relationship. We always tried to make the most of opportunities to travel to new places at the end of a cricket tour, such as sailing down the Nile in Egypt or driving along the Amalfi coastline in Italy, or to just enjoy the simple things, like catching a movie together or spending time with our families. With her caring instincts and nurturing ways, I knew Lynette would make a fantastic mother, and that her qualifications as a preschool teacher would help, too, while for my part I had always loved kids and was still one at heart. However, we knew we were heading into uncharted territory, that we couldn't hand them back at the end of the day.

The frustration of failure on the cricket field was put clearly into perspective when positioned against the absolute and utter anguish Lynette and I experienced when we were told our first pregnancy had ended in a miscarriage. Neither of us knew what to say as we left the medical centre; an ultrasound was supposed to show us the miracle of life, but instead it left us shattered by life's absence. I was hurting more than I'd thought possible, but I knew the pain was more acute for Lynette, who had for so long been a cricket 'widow' and was now being denied the chance to start our own family. I struggled to find the right words. 'I love you' and 'It's going to work out in the end' were about all I could manage when the shock engulfed us.

Some things in life happen when you least expect them to, and it was just a couple of months later that the pregnancy-test stick turned blue again. A new life was beginning.

Meanwhile, the Deloitte ratings had a new-found validity in my eyes as I sat proudly as their No. 1-ranked batsman. If you were to ask any player what they think of the ratings system, their response will be a clear indication of how they are going at the time. Those in good form agree it is a fair and reliable system, while the guys struggling dismiss it as inaccurate and riddled with flaws. No. 1 was a position I occupied for more than three years, and not surprisingly this was a period when my concentration and mental toughness reached levels that no one else could match. It was during a post-Test get-together in the Sri Lankan dressing-room, after I'd scored back-to-back hundreds in 1995–96, that I realised the method and excellence with which I was playing were influencing others. Sitting among a group of five or six of the Sri Lanka team, I was barraged by questions about why I was scoring so many runs and how I was doing it. One particular question struck a chord, probably because I'd never heard it before or remotely expected it: 'Do you meditate or do yoga?'

'No, why do you ask?'

'Because you look like you get into a trancelike state when you are batting and that nothing is going to break your concentration.'

This was one of the finest compliments I could have wished for from an opposition player.

It was a rare conciliatory moment in a summer of cricket that was filled with animosity and controversy, and as far as uniting cricket globally goes it was pretty much a disaster. Before the Sri Lanka matches we played three Tests against a very formidable Pakistan team, but that series was overshadowed by continuing speculation about the activities of Salim Malik. The first story involved his delayed arrival in Australia; he didn't link up with his team until a couple of days after they had landed, as he waited until the Pakistan cricket authorities cleared him (for the time being) of any untoward activity before heading for Oz.

We knew Malik was expecting us to 'tee off' in his direction, but we also knew he was still a key player for them with his experience and class, so we went the opposite way and decided to say absolutely nothing. Not a word was uttered to him during the tour, and I'm sure that caused him plenty of confusion and messed with his mind, as it was designed to. During the first Test, in Brisbane, fate took charge of proceedings when he split the webbing on his left hand while fielding and was unable to bat in Pakistan's first innings. This was followed up by a second-innings duck at the hands of Shane Warne, one of the guys he'd tried to bribe.

We wanted to play well, not only to rectify the infamous Test result in Karachi, but to maintain our new position as the game's premier side, and by winning the first two Tests decisively we went a long way towards achieving that goal. By this stage of my career, my confidence as a batsman was at its zenith, scoring runs had become a habit and the hunger to keep on batting was burning within. The years of self-doubt and treading water had taught me to never waste good form because down the track there would be, in all probability, a form slump where runs would seem harder to find than a television remote control. So, because my 112 not out in the first Test wasn't my most fluent innings, it didn't invigorate me in the same way other hundreds had. I could never rate a century that was made by giving a chance as highly as a mistake-free one. The perfectionist in me strove for the consummate performance, not the flawed one.

My second Test century of the summer came in Melbourne during the Boxing Day Test, but it went almost unnoticed because of other events that consumed the match. As controversies go, the seven no-ball calls for throwing by umpire Darrell Hair of Muttiah Muralitharan was as big as they come. A stunned silence greeted the first call. In our dressing-room, most of us did not know whether it was for a front-foot indiscretion or for perceived throwing. However, with each subsequent call the reason became apparent and the embarrassment to Murali grew ever more acute. It was difficult to watch someone being slaughtered in front of a world audience: surely it didn't have to get to this point, where potentially a career was being forever altered?

Hair and Murali would both need strong support networks to deal with the ramifications of this carve-up. Hair would subsequently be relieved for many years of umpiring Sri Lanka, and Murali became gun shy about touring Australia. It was a clear case of the authorities not being proactive and working together. The issue of whether Murali threw, which had invoked various strong opinions in cricket circles for some years before this Test, should have been settled long before this onfield soap opera, with consultation and precise testing procedures being utilised. Instead, Murali became a pawn in a battle of wills between Sri Lanka captain Arjuna Ranatunga, who would never back down even if he knew he was wrong, and an obdurate Fred Flintstone lookalike, Darrell Hair. To his credit, Hair stuck to his guns, calling it as he saw it, unlike other umpires who privately agreed with Hair's stance but publicly dodged the tough calls. One ump who did this was Hair's partner for the Boxing Day Test, New Zealander Steve Dunne, who apparently backed down from supporting Hair only when the incident blew up on the field. After Hair's no-ball calls the wily mind of Ranatunga returned fire, switching Murali to Dunne's end where the off-spinner bowled an additional 32 overs without further problem. It was a farcical situation that split opinion, even among the members of the Australian team, some of whom had privately questioned the validity of Murali's action. The trouble was that no one could prove their suspicions, because his method of delivery was unique and so unusual that even to debate it was provocative.

I was a fence-sitter, at times thinking, 'This guy is dodgy', and at other moments thinking, 'This guy's a freak.' He is the David Copperfield of cricket, blurring illusion with reality, delivering with a rubber wrist and bent elbow that allows prodigious turn and lets him impart widely varying rotations on the ball. Batting against Murali is the ultimate challenge, with the ball reaching you a split second later than you envisaged, as if he's bowled two balls and you needed to focus on the second one. He controls the ball as if it is attached to a string, enticing then withdrawing, probing before striking, each delivery a mini-battle for the batsman to overcome. Murali possesses a very even temperament and a cool clinical demeanour that belies the infectious smile and grotesque facial contortions he unknowingly manufactures at the point of delivery. He is also focused and driven, always looking to extend his repertoire – which eventually included his own invention, the 'Doosra', a ball that defies convention and turns from leg to off even though out of the hand it looks like a conventional off-break. In the end, one can only marvel at his unsurpassed record, his ability to adapt and his pride in playing for his country, which almost single-handedly keeps them a competitive unit. He is great for world cricket. And a better human being you would struggle to find.

The Australian team's relationship with Sri Lanka became very strained, culminating with our opponents refusing to shake Mark Taylor's hand after being beaten 2–0 in the finals of the one-day series. There were a number of on-field incidents, most of them in the second final in Sydney, with Glenn McGrath and Sanath Jayasuriya exchanging heated words and Ian Healy telling Ranatunga that he couldn't have a runner just because he was unfit.

There was a difference of cultures that neither team wanted to recognise or embrace. We considered them the experts at manipulating the press and, at times, bending the rules, while they saw us as being demeaning and abusive towards them. In truth, the two teams probably weren't that different, but the stubborn streak that impedes harmony blighted us both.

My one positive achievement from that acrimonious one-day series came in Melbourne, when I posted my first limited-overs international hundred in a game against Sri Lanka. However, only one shot stands the test of recollection: a charged on-drive for six off their left-arm opening bowler, Chaminda Vaas. I do, though, remember the pressure

Dave Gilbert (top left), Greg Matthews (in sunglasses) and Greg Dyer join me on an elephant ride up to the Jaipur Fort during our 1986 India tour.

The backdrop to this unusual team photo in New Delhi in 1996 is a monument erected to honour Mahatma Gandhi's epic 'Salt March' of 1930. Back, from left: Errol Alcott, Stuart Law, Paul Reiffel, Glenn McGrath, Jason Gillespie, Adam Gilchrist, Damien Fleming, Peter McIntyre, Brad Hogg. Front: Ricky Ponting, Michael Bevan, Geoff Marsh, Mark Taylor, Cam Battersby (manager), Ian Healy, Mark Waugh, me, Michael Slater.

The imposing view from a light tower at Eden Gardens, Calcutta, in 1998. The lack of a safety rail doesn't seem to worry our team-sponsor liaison officer, Ray Phillips.

McGrath in his element outside the Amber Fort at Rajasthan. It was payback time for me, as Pigeon had earlier delayed taking my photo when the roles were reversed.

All aboard the Patiala Express. Geoff Marsh, Michael Slater, Paul Reiffel and Ricky Ponting kill time on what turned into a six-and-a-half-hour marathon.

Incognito at the Taj Mahal during the 1996 World Cup.

Village elders watch the local fishermen head off for a day's work at Visakhapatnam.

An aerial view of the largest and best known of the 'dhobi ghats', or washing sheds, that are unique to Mumbai.

The laundry is being sorted at the dhobi ghat. I was taken by the colours and mood of this scene.

A father and daughter at work. I love the girl's innocent smile.

A remarkable show of religious faith on the streets of Old Delhi, 1998. These young men were proud and happy to have their photographs taken.

On the banks of the Ganges, capturing what for many people in Calcutta is everyday life.

A grotesquely deformed young beggar looks despairingly up at Glenn McGrath and me, after we've opened the window to our hotel room in Calcutta to get some fresh air at the start of the 1996 World Cup tour. The memory of this poor man's utter helplessness lingers in my mind.

Mealtime at Udayan – the rehabilitation centre in Barrackpore, Calcutta, built for children whose parents suffer from leprosy – consists of rice, dhal and chicken, finished off with a mango. Incidentally, this girl is a fantastic dancer.

Street kids of Lahore, in Pakistan, photographed in 1998 while I was out on the streets with Gavin Robertson.

valve being released at finally reaching three figures. One-day batting at five or six in the order, where I usually came in, isn't about big scores – the number of runs isn't important, the outcome is. That said, whether the assignment be a run-a-ball 20 or offering support for a rampaging partner, the challenge was always there.

Unfortunately, the end of the Test series was hardly the end of the animosity between the two countries. Further trouble was brewing, with Australia due to play its opening match of the 1996 World Cup in Colombo. For the first time, the Cup was to be staged in three countries: India, Pakistan and Sri Lanka. A number of players, including McGrath, Healy, Warne and McDermott, received death and bomb threats. McDermott's was particularly concerning, as a bomb threat was posted to his home, after which the matter was handled by the Federal Police. The team also was notified of a fax that had been sent to the ACB's office in Melbourne, claiming we'd be greeted by a suicide bomber upon our arrival in Colombo. We knew Sri Lanka was politically very unstable, in the throes of an often fiercely fought civil war. We needed to talk through the issues immediately.

Three days before the Adelaide Test match, Denis Rogers, the ACB chairman, and Graham Halbish, the CEO, assured us that we would be afforded the same security arrangements as a visiting head of state. There would be one bus for the players and another for luggage, and security guards would stay with us 24 hours a day. The team would be given its own floor at the hotel, with that floor and the ones above and below secured by armed guards. Team lists would be checked off regularly to make sure the right people knew where we were at all times. All incoming calls would be screened and all practice sessions supervised by security guards. *Jeez, what is the game coming to?* I thought. Previously the word 'sport' had been synonymous with enjoyment. Halbish, as the CEO, obviously had to keep an eye on cricket's bigger picture, and after listening to our concerns he countered, 'If you decide to pull out of that first game, it will take at least 10 years to rectify the situation.' This 'situation' we took to be relations between Australia and Sri Lanka.

We left the meeting content with the levels of protection being offered, although feeling slightly snookered by the fact that the implications for the game appeared to outweigh concerns for our own safety. But two days after the Adelaide Test our positive outlook was shattered by the repulsive news that a massive bomb had been detonated by a suicidal maniac, killing more than 100 people in the precinct adjacent to what was scheduled to be our hotel. The images on television and in the papers meant that we were now faced with a very real situation instead of threats. For the first time, I seriously contemplated whether touring was worth the risk, particularly as I was only months away from becoming a father. The feeling in the squad that we shouldn't go was backed by the Department of Foreign Affairs, who warned people off visiting the country. To everyone's great relief, we now had a politically sound argument not to go. The ICC didn't see it that way, though, and we – like the West Indies, who also refused to play in Colombo – had to forfeit our match against Sri Lanka rather than play it elsewhere. This, of course, jeopardised our chances of progressing in the tournament, but no one in the Australian team cared – firstly, because our safety was the priority and secondly, because we were still confident we could make it through the preliminary stages despite giving our rivals a game's start.

One cricketer who wouldn't be with us on the subcontinent was David Boon. The Adelaide Test had been the farewell for Boonie, one of Australia's best No. 3 batsmen and a man with a serious cult following. His emotional pregame address, where he announced it was to be his final Test, was obviously extremely tough to deliver and showed us all how much he valued the honour of playing cricket for Australia.

Whenever I think of Boonie, I see Swampy Marsh alongside him. They were inseparable, always rooming together, complementing each other with different interests, habits and backgrounds, both with an enormous passion for cricket and their families. I can still visualise what it was like in their room at 6 a.m., with the lingering diffused light of half a dozen cigarettes permeating the room, Boonie still half-asleep while a stark-naked Swamp lunged forward, Gray-Nicolls bat in hand, mimicking a perfect forward defence. Swamp loved companionship and was totally against the proposal to give guys single rooms on tour. He wanted someone to talk to. Boonie, on the other hand, enjoyed the solitude of reading a novel, often much to his best mate's frustration. On one occasion Swamp warned his roomie that if he didn't refrain from reading, his book would have an untimely accident. Sure enough, a few days later Boonie awoke to find his paperback was now a 100-page jigsaw puzzle.

They were very much a part of Australian cricket's renaissance, leading the way in attitude and professionalism. They often set off for training an hour before the rest of us to practise against net bowlers and talk cricket with Simmo, who had a profound influence on both. Boonie and Swamp represented the 'typical Aussie bloke': tough, uncompromising, exponents of mateship and revellers in a team environment. At team dinners Swamp used to amaze me with his eating techniques, devouring everything with minimal wastage. Chicken wings were pulverised, bones and all, and oranges eaten like apples, a habit that always gave me a shiver when his teeth sank into the rind.

Boonie loved the simple things: a cold beer (not that Swamp was averse to one either) and a 'blue' steak. He used to say, 'Drag it by the horns through the kitchen and that'll do me.' He was a man's man. Together, they were the heart and soul of many an Australian team and it was ironic that when Boonie called it quits his great mate Swampy was part of the selection panel. Boonie's final act as an Australian player was the perfect way for him to leave the game – standing atop the dressing-room table leading the team in 'Under the Southern Cross I Stand', proudly flanked by his anointed successor, Ian Healy. Boonie had been leading us in this anthem, sung after Test-match victories, since the mid-'80s. It was extra-special enough to warrant a rare third verse, instead of the usual two, and then it was over. Another member of the family was gone.

★

I don't consider myself a religious man, probably because religion wasn't a major influence in my life when I was growing up. However, I certainly admire those who commit and follow through on their beliefs and there was one woman I wanted to meet if I got the chance. She was born in Algeria as Agnes Gonxha Bojaxhui but became known as Mother Teresa and was a remarkable woman who lived by her vow to give wholehearted free service to the poorest of the poor. It is almost beyond comprehension that anyone could give themselves totally to others, with no consideration for personal success or mate- rial possessions. I had read about her devotion to providing dignity and comfort to the destitute and dying in their gravest hours of need, and I wanted to see her in person and experience her aura. The News Limited cricket writer Robert Craddock remembered a player profile I had done for his column that asked which person I would most like to meet. My answer had been Mother Teresa, and soon after we arrived in Calcutta for the World Cup opening ceremony, Robert made a couple of phone calls to arrange a meeting.

   The early-morning cab ride through Calcutta was worth the effort of responding to a 5.30 a.m. wake-up call. We wound our way around the City of Joy while it, too, awakened. Rickshaws full of schoolchil- dren dashed down alleyways, pulled along by scrawny, sinewy men whose age bore no resemblance to their weathered appearance. Animals roamed the streets in a leisurely fashion, oblivious to the dangers of technology, as homeless kids wearing barely a stitch of clothing ran playfully, dodging street vendors, trucks and cows, while workers carried their tools of trade and produce, seemingly precariously perched atop their heads, to the markets. The place was buzzing, and so was I.

After a short trip our animated driver said, 'We're here.' Looking around, I thought, *Sure, pal – we're lost and this is as good as anywhere to dump a few tourists.* I was accompanied by the team's liaison officer and award-winning photographer Trent Parke, both of whom looked equally dismayed. Then the driver said, 'Down there', and pointed towards a tiny side street.

On the wall hung a sign: 'No photography or video cameras allowed.' But proving that playing for your country does have privileges, arrangements had been made for one photograph to be taken. I instantly felt uncomfortable with my status as we were escorted up two flights of concrete stairs by one of the sisters of the Missionaries of Charity. We entered a room that reminded me of an old school classroom, with wooden shutters running horizontally the full length of one wall and open doors opposite, to find that mass had already begun. The floor space was almost totally taken up by the tightly bunched sisters, all clad in pure white cloth with dashes of blue, sitting serenely as the morning sunshine burst through the slats of the shutters, radiating piercing beams of light across the top of their bowed heads. It gave them an angelic appearance. I stood there, not knowing the correct protocol, in the midst of tourists from all over the world.

Moments later, the sisters rose one by one to receive their communion. Their faces reflected a wide variety of ages and races, which to me was tangible confirmation of their faith and beliefs. In what seemed like no time, the service appeared to end, yet the woman I had come to lay eyes on was nowhere to be seen. Then, suddenly, from my position in the walkway just outside the open doors, I saw our liaison officer drop to his knees and assume the prayer position. Spinning around to see what had caused this affirmation of faith, I almost bumped into a hunched-over sister who stood not more than five feet tall. All around me people were praying, many in tears, while I stood gazing inquisitively at this incredible person. Our liaison friend gathered enough composure to gain Mother Teresa's attention and introduced me as a member of the touring Australian cricket team. She replied with a polite, 'Hello,' while I managed a nervous, 'Pleased to meet you.' And then she shuffled off to meet the overwhelmed devotees who were visibly in awe and quite clearly experiencing one of the moments of their lives.

Just when I thought my fleeting encounter was over, Mother Teresa came back towards us and begun handing out what looked like pieces of paper. It was extraordinary to be in the presence of someone who exuded such a calming influence; she truly had a magical aura about her. Yet she had the common touch. I noticed that she walked with some difficulty. Her hands and toes were badly mangled and deformed by the ravages of arthritis, and she was permanently bent over, reflecting her age of 75 and the sicknesses, including three heart attacks, that had plagued her in recent years.

Her face was wrinkled and weathered, yet soft and welcoming, and she radiated a tremendous inner strength and sense of compassion. I tried to take in as much as I could, knowing full well that we wouldn't cross paths again and that I wanted to be able to recount to my grandkids what this experience was like. She then walked towards me, stopping within a metre and extending her hand. 'Here,' she said, 'have one of my business cards.' And then she was off back to her compound, disappearing behind the linen curtains that concealed the entrance. It was over, but she left a group of people mesmerised in her wake and I, for one, felt eternally grateful to have shared a few precious seconds with her. The card read: 'The fruit of silence is prayer, the fruit of prayer is faith, the fruit of faith is love, the fruit of love is service.'

All I could think of on the taxi trip back to the hotel was the total and utter devotion she had to improving the lives of people around her. Throughout those few hours, playing cricket was forgotten and I gained a clearer perspective on what life is really all about: helping those who are less fortunate.

For 12 days after the team arrived in India we found ourselves in limbo, not really knowing where we were going and which hotels we were staying in, and with no guarantee of practice facilities. Visakha-patnam, the location for our first World Cup match, against Kenya, was hardly a major cricket venue. As such, it wasn't exactly the place to prepare for the premier event in world one-day cricket, so we moved between Calcutta and Bombay. The opening ceremony in Calcutta was perilously close to a debacle, with the laser show nulli-fied by an unexpected windy night that saw the wire-mesh backdrop swing wildly in the breeze, eluding the laser projection. Adding to the occasion, the announcer mixed up the UAE and South African teams and almost forgot the Sri Lankans. However, the goodwill and spirit of the people could overcome any mishaps, and India went into the frenzied, fanatical mode that so defines this nation of more than one billion people.

Never was this better captured than in our game against India in Bombay. One of the problems of modern cricket is that there are a large number of one-day games that have no obvious reason for existence other than to boost the coffers of the respective cricket boards. For that reason only, many uplifting or inspirational segments of play have been lost over time. But listening to the crowd urge on Sachin Tendulkar after he lost two early partners in their quest to chase down our respectable total of 258 was enough to know that this was one such special occasion. After a shaky start, Sachin came to life during one over from Glenn McGrath, in an assault that left everyone in the jam-packed stadium, including me, with goose bumps. The atmosphere was charged and the crowd gelled together as one animated mass. A savage pull shot that defied the textbooks and made our fielders as useful as the moulded-plastic green figures found in the toy game 'Test Match' ignited the worshippers. It was followed by a remarkably improvised hook shot off the front foot that only a man with an eye like a dead fish would think of playing. Indian batsmen often ride the wave of goodwill from the crowd, which seems to grant them immunity from mistiming and poor placement while empowering them with bucketloads of courage and intent. Two balls later, we were all props in his final act of carnage for the over, standing helplessly as he unleashed a scorching cover drive that was met on the downswing with a deafening roar from the crowd, who knew instinctively what the outcome would be.

It was game on, and we needed the cool heads of experience to slow things down. Otherwise we risked being swept away in the euphoria of the occasion. A mixture of luck and composure altered the course of the match when Mark Waugh had Sachin stumped after he premeditated the wrong ball and charged a wide. It was icing on the cake for Mark, who had earlier played a gem of an innings to compile his second hundred in as many matches. This crucial win was perfectly capped off back at the Taj Mahal Hotel when a strikingly good-looking woman passed by us in the foyer and asked, 'Had a good game today, boys?'

'Yeah,' was all we could manage: it's not every day Demi Moore compliments you on your work.

A quarter-final in Madras against a well-drilled and solid-looking New Zealand side was our reward for successfully getting through the preliminary matches. This was to be a night where Mark Waugh showcased his skills by scoring an unprecedented third century in a World Cup tournament, leading us to a six-wicket victory. It was also one where, after twisting both ankles in separate incidents, I had to engage mind over matter to avoid embarrassment and appear weak by walking off to get treatment. The surging waves of pain were bearable until Tubs walked up and said, 'I think it's time for you to have a bowl, Tugga.' There was only one option: grit the teeth and get through it, which I'm sure all quick bowlers have to learn to do to be a success. Bowlers are the brickie's labourers, while batsmen are the interior designers, and I'm sure most bowlers evolve only when they realise they don't bat very well. How else could you explain someone wanting to constantly stress his body and then wake up every morning feeling like a 60-year-old?

This match taught the team a valuable lesson, in that no opposing player should ever be taken for granted or dismissed as not being a potential threat. Lee Germon, a surprising choice as the Kiwis' captain and confrontationist, and the evergreen Chris Harris were passed over in our team discussions as batsmen who wouldn't cause us any harm; we quickly moved on to the obvious threats of Stephen Fleming, Nathan Astle and Chris Cairns. Germon and Harris then went out and played the innings of their careers in a partnership that nearly put the game out of our grasp.

The semi-final against the Windies at Chandigarh was always going to be a dangerous proposition, with Curtly Ambrose, Ian Bishop and Courtney Walsh leading the charge. And so it was, especially after we found ourselves floundering at 4/15 after nine overs. Cool heads were needed, and in Michael Bevan and Stuart Law we had two guys who could assess exactly what was required. Thanks largely to what amounted to Test-match batting, we ended up with an ugly but effective score of 207. From there, we had the belief but they had Brian Lara, and it took the best ball of my life to alter the tempo of a match that was quickly sliding away from us. The Windies had reached 1/93 from 23 overs. It was the last ball of my spell, bowled from around the wicket, and I was willing myself as hard as I could, straining every muscle in search of an extra yard of pace to get us back into the game. The delivery landed in that minuscule patch of pitch, the 'area of uncertainty', where a batsman isn't really sure whether to go forward or not, and then it darted off the seam to clip the top of Lara's off stump. Neither Brian nor I could believe what had transpired. I had reached my zenith as a bowler.

Even with the loss of their flawed genius, the Windies still held the upper hand. Captain Richie Richardson joined Shivnarine Chanderpaul and they were still together with nine overs to go, needing only 43 with eight wickets in hand. Up stepped the ice-cool McGrath and Warne, the antidotes to pressure, and then Damien Fleming, a class wicket-taking swing bowler whom the Windies disliked primarily because they weren't proficient in their footwork. Crucially, Chanderpaul went trying to slog McGrath, and along with him went the Windies' composure. Instead of relying on their batsmen to do the job they sent out tail-enders Roger Harper and Ottis Gibson to try to blast their way to the total. Temperament is the fundamental element when you're under intense pressure, and that is exactly why they shouldn't have sent in hit-and-miss batsmen who were much more likely to be influenced by the delicate game situation. Harper and Gibson were both dispatched with ease, as was Jimmy Adams, who a year earlier had been ranked the No. 1 batsman in the world but was now enduring the batting 'yips'. Like Ian Baker-Finch hitting his drive out of bounds on the football-field-wide first fairway at St Andrews, Jimmy couldn't get comfortable with his grip and stance, and this had a domino effect on the rest of his game. Six for 183 became 7/187 when the coolest man ever to lace on a cricket boot, Keith Arthurton, had his thermostat tampered with and froze on the spot, slogging wildly as if the gods were going to gift him the victory.

By now, the biggest danger to our winning was ourselves. We were hyped and animated, with the adrenaline zipping around like a Scalextric race car and threatening to overload our thought processes. After Bishop fell to Warne, 10 runs were needed from the last over, to be bowled by Fleming. Richie Richardson was on strike. It was a genuine 50/50 situation until Richardson hit a lofted four that realistically should have ensured their victory. Acquired knowledge told us all that the next ball was the definitive one and that we needed a wicket. Lack of communication cost the Windies dearly when Richardson called Ambrose through for a poorly thought-out single. Even if it had been successful, the run would have put the onus on the No. 10 batsman to finish the job. Instead, it was all over next ball, when Walsh tried to seal the win with a homer over left field – a shot which was slightly ambitious considering he'd left a dressing-room full of bright lights to walk into the darkened surrounds of the arena, then out to the middle where the lighting was okay but strangely different to most other venues. The light pylons were lower than usual so as not to inconvenience the aircraft from the nearby military base.

The sound of ball crashing into timber sent us into a frenzied romp around the infield as we valiantly tried to haul in Flem, who had taken off like a looter with a television. Once we rounded each other up, the pent-up emotion exploded, with guys screaming at the top of their lungs, none of it making much sense because it was a combination of all the nervous energy unleashed and a sense of disbelief that we had pulled off one of the most amazing escape acts of one-day cricket history.

Surely, we felt, we were destined to win the final now. Even Amby wished us well during the handshaking at the conclusion by saying, 'Well played. Don't waste it now, man. Go all the way!'

It didn't work out that way. Our problems started the following morning when our patience was severely tested at the airport by security overkill due to the plane flying from Chandigarh in the north of India to

Lahore in Pakistan. We went through so many security checks that our boarding passes and luggage tags were completely covered and I wished I'd extracted my protector from my cricket bag and inserted it to ease the distress caused by the overeager metal-detector brigade. Errol Alcott did balance the ledger when a disbelieving inspector insisted that our physio show him how one particular suspicious-looking piece of equipment worked. Seconds later he had two electrodes placed on either side of his palm and the switch was flicked, making his hand spasm violently and confirming it was indeed an electromagnetic pulse machine.

By the time we arrived in Lahore that evening we were already a day in arrears of Arjuna's boys, who had beaten India in the first semi-final the day before. The Sri Lankans had settled in comfortably for the biggest event in their country's sporting history, while our preparations were still somewhat confused. Playing on the subcontinent requires continued patience and an ability to adapt and be flexible. I'm not sure whose fault it was, but both teams turned up to train at roughly the same time when there were only enough facilities for one, and since we'd arrived second it was decided that we had to wait our turn. Then our management informed us just before our team meeting that there was an official dinner to attend, which was just what we all wanted the night before a World Cup final. These dinners inevitably become a bureaucratic bullshit-fest, with the guys getting 'picked off' one by one and being obliged to engage in mindless small talk when we should have been relaxing and preparing for one of the biggest games of our lives.

Our team meeting was conducted in the manager's room, with guys sitting on coffee tables and television stands, or stretched out on the floor, not exactly conducive to information retention. Fortunately, after playing the Sri Lankans so often in the previous six months, the need for a lengthy analysis wasn't there. We stressed the importance of keeping the bowling in and around off stump, because Sri Lanka's batsmen sweated on width that allowed them to free their arms and thrash it away. We also needed to use changes of pace to upset their rhythm. Intensity and attitude in the field were our key indicators, we stressed, as was the need to build momentum via partnerships with the bat. 'Cashing in' during the last 10 overs of our innings rounded off our simple game plan.

The next morning we awoke to leaden skies, having had our sleep interrupted for part of the night by the sound of heavy rain. In our wisdom, only manager Col Egar, coach Bob Simpson and captain Mark Taylor went down to the ground at the usual time, as the word was out that there was going to be a late start at best. But then, within half an hour, the boys were summoned from their beds and told to get down to the ground in a hurry because the game was starting on time. We managed to gather ourselves and catch two separate buses for the 15-minute trip to the ground, but some damage had been done. It was quiet and pensive on the bus I was in, which was understandable when you consider that the next seven or eight hours had the potential to change a cricketer's life.

The toss was of interest only to the statisticians, because the Lankans were desperate to bat second and rely on their strength – a lengthy, experienced batting line-up – to get them home, while we always liked to bat first and make the running under Tubby. We would soon learn that in this instance we were probably wrong to be so entrenched in our ways. Our lack of pregame planning and reluctance to do that little extra bit of homework came back to bite us. We should have known that a heavy dew came in after sunset at this time of year, which would make the outfield greasy and negate our attack when the leather ball became swollen and the seam diminished. It would also hinder Warney, who would be unable to grip the ball with his usual authority. We should still have been able to overcome this impediment, but our opponents displayed a greater sense of urgency and hunger, best exemplified by our substandard performance in the field, where we spilled maybe half a dozen chances. It was a day full of mishaps, which included a power failure that blacked out the stadium and delayed the start of the Sri Lankan run chase, a courteous handshake that Tubs extended to Pakistan prime minister Benazir Bhutto at the presentation ceremony but was rejected out of protocol, and the winning captain and the trophy he so desired trampled on by an overzealous media and security contingent as they set off for their victory lap. For us, it was almost a relief that it was all over. A tour that began with a forfeit ended meekly for us, though anyone who could rummage through this loss and learn from it would ultimately benefit.

After New Zealand's innovative tactics of using an off-spinner to open the bowling in the 1992 World Cup, the next new strategy had been eagerly awaited. It was never going to come from our camp under Bob Simpson and Mark Taylor, who had faith in our tried and tested formula: being energetic, hustling the opposition and paying close attention to things such as running between the wickets, forming partnerships and eliminating basic errors. We believed that our consistency would overcome any innovative strategies used against us, and we were nearly proved right.

A surprise packet did come, and it was again a host nation responsible for it, with the Sri Lankan batsmen, led by the pocket dynamo Romesh Kaluwitharana and the more experienced, highly skilled and sweet timer of the ball Sanath Jayasuriya, attempting to blast out of the blocks in the first 15 overs. A lot of attention was directed their way throughout the tournament and a fair amount of credit for their ultimate victory attached itself to this partnership. However, upon closer analysis, maybe the link between their triumph and their openers wasn't as clear-cut as it was reputed to be.

The Sri Lankans qualified for the quarter-finals through a mixture of exciting, energetic play and the gratuity of two forfeits. Then a victory against a fairly lethargic England preceded failures by the top order in the semi-final and final. It was the middle order, most notably Aravinda de Silva, who did the job for them. However, the hype kept snowballing and ultimately it was the concept of attacking during the first 15 overs, when the field was up, that left such an indelible imprint on the tournament. In reality, the successful blockbusting opening to Sri Lanka's one-day innings didn't consistently occur until after the World Cup, and the strategy wasn't totally new anyway, when you consider that, for example, Ian Botham opened the batting for England in the 1992 Cup.

What is undeniable is that the Lankans must be recognised for having the courage to back a relatively untried formula on cricket's biggest stage. Their bravery was well rewarded and their vision was one that other teams would use as a blueprint for future success.

25

Family time

Whether it was directly associated with our loss or not, I don't know, but the major fallout from the World Cup was the exit of coach Bob Simpson. The big surprise was his replacement – Geoff Marsh, who had never coached cricket at any level. It was one of those moves that would end up either being inspired or backfiring on those who had fast-tracked him into the role.

Simmo was always open to being replaced if the team's results didn't match his uncompromising ways. It was his nature to give as good as he got, which meant that people willing to hold a grudge would always have ammunition stored to fire back at him if circumstances allowed. People invariably have an opinion about Bob and it's generally very strong. He was the only truly genuine 'coach' I came across during my career, in the sense that he could technically evaluate all facets of my game and correct deficiencies. Simmo helped develop my cricket more than any other person, while his wife, Meg, was a mentor to many of the players' partners and always there to support Lynette. Back in 1987, when Lynette and I were 21, Simmo planned a holiday for us that involved driving around Europe and staying in budget accommodation. He couldn't help us enough. Travelling was his other passion, and as with cricket he loved to impart his knowledge.

The total absence of a farewell to Simmo from the ACB after he lost the coaching job, an event that would acknowledge his unique contribution to the game, was a disgrace. We, the players, should have stepped into the breach to rectify this mistake. At the time the focus was on our World Cup loss, not the bigger picture that Simmo had had such an influence in developing. From out of the abyss in the mid-'80s, he left the twin legacies of increased professionalism and a winning culture, which were to be the hallmarks of future Australian teams.

The five-month break from international cricket that followed the World Cup final came at exactly the right time for me, as I had an appointment with the surgeon's knife. Throughout my sporting days I had suffered from muscle cramps and excessive fluid build-up after any repetitive exercise. Running on soft turf for more than one lap of the ground caused my lower back and legs to 'blow up' and spasm, while any type of weight-lifting was impossible once the fluids filled the worked-over areas. After exhaustive testing involving probing needles surely better suited to bringing down elephants, it was revealed I had 'compartment syndrome', which arises when a muscle becomes too big for the fascia (the tissue covering the muscle, like the skin on a sausage) that surrounds it. To release the particularly acute pain that this would cause in my lower legs as blood flow to the muscle and nerves was stifled, I was opened up from the knees to the ankles. The fascia was sliced apart, allowing the muscle to protrude but also, importantly, releasing it from the stranglehold it was in.

While I was in hospital I had a lingering groin problem treated as well. An obturator nerve decompression was corrected in an operation that basically involved the doctor sticking his finger in and wriggling it around to free up the congested area and alleviate the pain I experienced while playing. It was a good two to three weeks before I could walk normally again, but the searing pain – that had at times necessitated taking four Panadeine Fortes to allow me to bowl – was gone. The downside was deformed-looking lower legs that have permanently protruding muscle masses, which provided much mirth among my teammates.

My lead-up to the '96–97 season was hardly normal. Rather than the usual net sessions on dodgy SCG practice wickets, which damaged more than developed, I was attending birthing classes. Out went the search for a perfect outswinging ball and in came an understanding of a forceps delivery. *Wisden* was flicked for *What to Expect When You're Expecting*, as I gathered as much knowledge as possible to ensure I could be of use during the business end of proceedings. After the eight-week instructional course I had information overload and knew more than I needed to, especially about what could go wrong. For me, having a baby wasn't as simple as I'd imagined, and as Lynette's bulge grew bigger so too did the horror stories that everyone seemed to delight in telling me.

At just after midnight on July 31 an anxious voice pierced the darkness of our bedroom. 'Stephen, I'm having contractions.' I don't think I've ever moved so fast. On went the light as I stumbled frantically to find the pen and paper that would document, as we had been told to do, the time between contractions. When they quickly increased to five minutes apart we were on edge with anticipation as we drove off to hospital. It's hard to describe the feeling that comes what the realisation that you are about to bring into the world a child who you are going to be responsible for shaping and influencing. There is a sense of fulfilment and in my case also the excitement that came with knowing that the birth would be one of the highlights of my life.

Baby Rosalie arrived, but only after a mighty struggle with the umbilical cord, which was not only wound around her neck but also lassoed around her wrist. Every time a contraction came her breathing was strangled, so that every piece of 'intervention' we'd learnt about in class but said we wouldn't need came into play. Lynette and I still can't believe how hard a midwife needs to pull to extract a baby with forceps. I thought for sure we had a baby with a misshapen head and an extra-long neck; instead, we barely had time to look at her, as she was only momentarily placed on Lynette's chest before being whisked away. Rosie was a bluish-grey colour and hadn't cried; we were emotional wrecks without our baby girl to cradle. Those couple of minutes before we heard the cry of life were excruciating, a time when we would have traded in everything we owned for a healthy baby. Cricket didn't matter; the frailty of a newborn and the preciousness of life dwarfed everything. Life would never be the same again. The unconditional love I experienced looking at Rosie's tiny frame, her complete innocence and that distinctive smell of a newborn head had me smitten.

I think most first-time parents would concur when I say the scariest part of parenthood is when you walk through the front door at home and say, 'Well, what do we do now?' You're on your own, away from the midwives and nurses, with this little human being who is totally reliant upon you. And there's no textbook to follow. I had a couple of weeks to come to terms with this, to just start to get used to our new life, and then I was out the door, en route to Sri Lanka. Leaving Lynette for a tour was always tough, but we both knew it was part of my job and had to be done. This time, exiting through customs and hearing our three-week-old baby crying, knowing she'd be so physically changed the next time I laid eyes on her, was an ordeal I found hard to deal with unemotionally, as I'd trained myself to do as a protection system.

For me, the best way to overcome homesickness was to find time each week on tour to pull out my family photo albums and immerse myself in them, reflecting on the memories before packing them away and getting back into the flow of cricket. I needed to keep in touch with my emotions, but I also needed to do my job and that was to play cricket for Australia. Later on, with the arrival of Austin and Lillian and the tripling of missed experiences, Lynette put my mind at ease by saying, 'I'm happy for you to keep playing as long as you commit to it 100 per cent, because if you don't, you're not only wasting your talents, but you're taking with it family time.' Her advice ensured that each game away from home had extra meaning for me, and partially explains why my away record was superior to my record at home.

Finding ways to stay in the minds of your children can take innovative thinking. The obvious method is via a phone call, but kids can't grasp the concept of you being on the other side of the world. The closest Rosie ever came to getting this notion was when she said to me, 'When we go to bed, we send the sun across to you.'

Of course, bedtime stories are a terrific way to bond with your kids. I used to buy a couple of Dr Seuss books during our stopovers and send them back home, together with a dictaphone tape of me reading about green eggs and ham and the likes of Marvin K. Mooney to be played in my absence. Telling my kids that there was only a set number of days left before I came home was as clear to them as reading a camera instructional booklet, so we needed something that was 'hands on' to explain it to them. I would order from the local florist the equivalent number of balloons to days left and the kids would pop one each morning so they could visualise the days becoming less and less. When the last balloon was popped, they knew the old man was on his way home. Leaving small gifts and lollies in hiding places around the house was something the kids looked forward to as well, and each time we spoke on the phone I'd give them hints as to where they might find them. This was useful until I lost the scrap of paper that detailed their hiding places. Months later, decaying chewie or melted chocolates would be discovered behind picture frames and under windowsills. Rosie used to love giving me a send-off gift so I wouldn't forget her, which might include her favourite book, a ribbon she'd worn in her hair or her best-loved soft toy.

On my first tour as a dad, I packed an unwashed baby singlet that had Rosie's scent all over it. The anguish I felt at having to leave so soon after her birth wasn't alleviated at all by a comment from an embassy official at the high commissioner's welcome party in Colombo: 'Why are you guys here now? Nothing's changed since you boycotted the World Cup.' This was not the information we had received before we left Sydney, and I hoped we were not being used as a political tool to 'make up for' our earlier forfeit and appease the cricket world. We should have smelled a rat, though, when the originally scheduled five-week, two-Test tour was condensed into a three-week dollar-driven extravaganza devoted solely to one-dayers. Cricket officialdom had compromised and we players were the pawns in the game.

Catching a decoy bus to the ground, with the window curtains drawn and special-forces soldiers armed with AK47s patrolling the aisles, didn't exactly have us in a relaxed mood upon arrival. This was on top of the rule that kept us all within the confines of our hotel for the entire trip, with absolutely no exceptions, making us all feel like we were on some kind of parole. The only player who didn't seem to mind this embargo was my roomie, Paul 'Pistol' Reiffel, who was always a huge fan of the hotel room becoming a 'bat cave' (stay in bed with the curtains closed, get room service and watch television). The only time he emerged from the sheets was for sustenance, bodily functions and cricket activities. Instead of a weekend with Bernie, it was three weeks with Pistol! As far as tours go, this was the pits and I couldn't wait to get home and see the family. I'm sure I wasn't alone among the team in regularly saying to myself during these 21 days of imprisonment, *What am I doing here? This isn't remotely enjoyable.*

After Sri Lanka, we were home briefly and then away again. A one-off Test in Delhi didn't give either India or Australia a chance to assert any authority or conclusively prove they were a dominant team. The only people to claim any sort of victory in the end were the members of the Indian Cricket Board, who sent us on what amounted to a wild-goose chase by programming our only lead-up game in a town called Patiala, a supposedly lovely 'four-hour' train trip into the 'countryside'. Six and a half hours later, and without catching so much as a glimpse of the countryside due to the densely stained windows clogged by years of pollution and minimal maintenance, we arrived at our 'five-star' hotel. Not exactly. There was no hot water, we had sandbag pillows, the eating areas were unhygienic and a musty, 'wet socks and kerosene' stench invaded our nostrils and overpowered everything else.

The match, against a Board President's XI, was played on a raging seamer that even Queensland would have been embarrassed to roll out, a totally inappropriate pitch on which to prepare for a Test match most likely to be played on a spinning track. The sure thing was confirmed when we strolled out two days prior to the Delhi Test to view a pitch resembling a dry outback creek bed, with mosaic cracks covering the entire 22 yards. It was a masterpiece, expertly concocted by the groundsman to take advantage of an Australian side that was missing Shane Warne and thought to be susceptible to quality spin bowling. Not a blade of living grass could be located, only rolled-in clippings that would surely perish in the intense heat. This would be a real test of mind over conditions, and anything less than total clarity of thought would be exposed.

In the first innings I meekly surrendered to the conditions. With our lead-up match useless, and having not played in a Test match since late January, the dark inner voice returned. I allowed entry to it, the gobbler of good thoughts, and out to bat a dead man walked. Further, the safety blanket, my red rag, had been inadvertently left at home, and the sanctuary of our dressing-room and viewing area was poorly policed, with a constant steam of intruders disturbing the peace. This meant that I watched way too much of the action on television prior to my innings, which tends to exaggerate the complexities of the pitch because of the numerous replays and camera angles on offer.

I was distracted, agitated and unable to extricate myself from the malaise. Predictably, the end result was a big fat zero, followed by plenty of contemplation: how the hell was I going to turn my fragile state of mind around for the second dig, when conditions would be considerably worse than on day one? The answer, of course, had to come from within, but I did consult others as well and had the most extended conversation I'd ever had with Allan Border, who was in India for the launch of the Border–Gavaskar Trophy, the new prize for India–Australia Test cricket. 'Play straight, occupy the crease and sweep,' AB said.

I also spoke to the person who knew me best and was quite often the most perceptive – Lynette. She reminded me of my mantra: there was no position so hopeless that it could not be regarded as a challenge and so turned into a positive force. My resolve was further strengthened the next morning when Glenn McGrath cheekily informed me that Ian Chappell had told him over a drink at the bar that he, McGrath, had looked more like a batsman in the first innings than I had. For some reason this really pissed me off, probably because the comment came from a guy I'd looked up to in the backyard battles of my youth as we listened to Alan McGilvray call the game on the radio. Now Chappell was constantly sniping from the sidelines. His sarcasm added fuel to the fire and heightened my desire to stand up and be counted. It culminated in one of my proudest works of unfaltering concentration and watertight defence, as I scored 67 not out against the maestro of powdering surfaces and uneven bounce, Anil Kumble. Not only did I repel a tailor-made attack, but I had exorcised the demons of the first dig purely through will and desire. It further confirmed to me that the toughest battle to win is the one going on between your ears.

The tour as a whole was a real wake-up call for the side, in particular for the one-day squad, who lost five games out of five in a lethargic showing. New coach Geoff Marsh went to town when talking to journos, questioning our commitment and lack of pride and ending with: 'One area I've been disappointed in is their training. I think they train like millionaires instead of getting down to business. These guys are professional cricketers, but they've lacked concentration in the nets.'

What Swamp said might have been fair enough, but the forum in which he chose to air his thoughts was questionable. The first point of call for criticism should be face to face, not via papers that are read by millions. I'm sure Swamp was just trying to exert some authority in his new position, but it didn't sit well with the guys at the breakfast table, who felt a little betrayed by his absolving himself of responsibility for our results.

The fallout from the tour was harshest on Michael Slater, who was told of his sacking from the Test side by selector Steve Bernard at the end of a day's play during a Shield match at Bankstown Oval after we returned to Australia. His piercing shriek of 'No!' resonated around the ground, and the way he sped from the carpark left no one in any doubt as to what had happened and what our debonair opener thought of a judgement the selectors had made just three Tests after he'd scored a double century. Heals also came under heavy fire from respected journalist Mike Coward, while Tubby's back injury, which had forced him out of the tour of Sri Lanka, was still causing some concern. However, as usual Mark had his thoughts well organised and believed the next three series – at home against the West Indies and away tours to South Africa and England – would be defining ones for the team. Planning ahead and having vision were his strengths, with Test matches clearly the priority. In Tubs's view the one-dayers were necessary, but he knew that he and his team would be judged by five-day play.

Over the next 12 months the selectors would get themselves into a pickle on a regular basis under the new leadership of Trevor Hohns. Anyone in a position of authority needs to make some adjustments to find the right balance, but at this time we were often wondering whether the selectors were planning for the longer term or just looking for quick fixes. Ricky Ponting was cast aside one match after making 88 batting at three against the Windies, while Paul Reiffel would later miss selection in the original Ashes touring party after being on the wrong end of some peculiar selection decisions in South Africa. Little faith was shown in Matt Hayden, even after he made his first Test century against the Windies in Adelaide and then played an innings of real character in Perth against a marauding four-man pace attack while all others meekly surrendered. Three months later, 'Haydos' wasn't good enough to claim one of the nine batting spots (10 if you count second keeper Adam Gilchrist as a batsman) in a ridiculously lopsided Australian squad for England.

26

Raising the bar

When I think back to the 1996–97 home series against the West Indies, the personal memories are not all that positive. First up, I re-tore my groin during the opening Test, overexerting myself after charging in to bowl at Jimmy Adams. I was hyped up with emotion at the time, having just taken my 'bunny' Carl Hooper's wicket, but knew straight away that I'd need weeks, not days, of total dedication to get back. In the end I only missed one Test – the second in Sydney – but, having made it back into the side, I managed in Adelaide to get out to the worst ball of my career – a long hop from Shivnarine Chanderpaul that I could have dispatched anywhere. Eventually I selected a spot in the near vicinity of Hooper, who intercepted Halley's comet with consummate ease.

The displeasure I experienced after that dismissal wasn't eased by the serve I received during the fifth Test, in Perth, at the hands of the Windies' 15th man, Patterson Thompson, who had obviously cashed in on the team's KFC tour sponsorship after realising he was superfluous to his side's playing requirements. As I walked out to bat, the big fella, fresh from delivering drinks to his team, strolled past me and said, 'They're going to fuckin' kill you, man!' *Thanks very much for the newsflash, buddy*, I thought, *but why don't you mind your own business and concentrate on nailing another of the Colonel's buckets of fried chook?* As it turned out, they didn't get much of a chance to enact his plans, as my brief stints at the crease in this fifth Test totalled nought and one.

Getting forward to elite fast bowlers such as Courtney Walsh, Curtly Ambrose and Ian Bishop on an unpredictable pitch required enormous courage and a healthy dose of good fortune, especially after we watched in horror a short-of-a-length ball from Ambrose not fly through nose-high but crash into Greg Blewett's stumps after not getting more than 5 cm off the ground after pitching. In this fifth Test, Walsh was so encouraged by a WACA pitch that had, after days of baking in extreme temperatures, broken into hundreds of miniature plates each bordered by yawning gaps, that he ignored a hamstring strain, got off the physiotherapist's bench and took 5/74 bowling off half his normal run-up.

Waiting as their fast bowlers approached the crease, the crevices took on an even more sinister look. They seemed incredibly wide and in precisely the right areas for the bowler, so I felt sure they'd come into play. The trick was to take them out of the equation and play each ball on its merits, as if you were batting on a surface as flat as a table-top. In reality, though, batting on this wicket was akin to being a wildebeest crossing a swollen African creek bed, knowing that eventually a submerged crocodile will eventually sink its fangs into your flesh. Admirably, late in the game No. 9 Shane Warne and No. 10 Andy Bichel delayed the inevitable, adding 56 for the ninth wicket out of an innings total of 194. This so irritated Amby that he decided to go around the wicket and purposely overstep the line to try to inflict pain and suffering on Warney and 'Bic' during a 15-ball over that was both cowardly and dangerous.

It was a series that was played extremely hard, though at times not in the best spirit of the game. It was always going to be highly competitive, as both the players and fans in the Caribbean assumed we'd just 'borrowed' the Frank Worrell Trophy. Tempers and emotions boiled over on a fairly regular basis. The first flashpoint came during the second Test, when Brian Lara stormed into the home dressing-room having been – in his opinion – dudded by Ian Healy when given out caught behind for his third straight failure in the series. The video replays did show the ball bubbling out of Heals's gloves for a second, but no one else gave the out decision much thought at the time. Still in his whites, Lara made a beeline through the members' bar before belting on our door. A disbelieving Geoff Marsh took his succinct message: 'Tell Healy he's not welcome in our dressing-room.'

Not for the first time against our arch-enemies of the era, pre-series ambitions for a cordial environment between the teams were blown out of the water by a single incident. To me, it was always only a matter of time before these friendly gestures came unstuck, as massive egos, hard-nosed competitors and a condensed itinerary combined to form an explosive cocktail that was inevitably going to discharge at some stage. Once Lara overstepped the boundaries by putting his personal grievances ahead of the teams' goodwill, the mood altered dramatically. The animosity was at its sharpest during the fifth Test, in Perth, when Lara went into bat belatedly to support one of the young batsmen, Robert Samuels, who was in his first year as a Test cricketer and was experiencing the customary testing-out period at the top level. I didn't believe we were over the top with our chatter, but Lara was keen to make a lasting impression within his ranks and went directly to the press, accusing us of unfair tactics. At the same time, he tried to absolve himself of any blame even though at the end of the Windies' first innings he had returned as a runner for the injured Walsh and immediately tried to cause trouble. He was doing a 'Ranatunga' – giving as good as he got on the field, but divulging only half the information to the media afterwards.

Ian Healy and I were the two guys who often got mentioned when sledging controversies arose, and again on this occasion we came in for some flak. We were certainly talkers on the field and saw ourselves as being the lifters of spirits and motivators during flat periods of play. We could be prickly at times and in the opposition's face and we would always stand up for our teammates, which put us in the firing line and also got us into potential trouble with the authorities. The perception was that we could sledge with the best of them, but for me it was never more than gamesmanship and occasionally brinkmanship, and in Heals I had a willing and able ally. There were occasions when I thought other guys in our team could have taken more initiative to lift the team during periods of staleness, but they weren't inclined to get involved. Each to their own, but sometimes you have to get out of your comfort zone to benefit the mood of the team.

Heals had been under some pressure coming into the series, but he lifted like the true warrior he was, smashing 161 not out in his home Test, the first of the series, to silence the doubters, and go on to average nearly 60 for the series. Having his back against the wall was the type of situation he thrived on and probably privately sought, to draw out the fighting qualities that best defined him. I always found his roguish charm infectious and his larrikin ways very Australian. On the 1993 Ashes tour we swapped identities for a radio interview back to Australia, with me carrying on about how well I was gloving them and he how sweet he was hitting them. We must have been convincing, for there were no reprimands to deal with later.

It was a series where we retained the Frank Worrell Trophy but also one in which our captain began an unfortunate run of poor form. Throughout this, Tubby's captaincy was never questioned and, in fact, helped delay the deluge of questioning he eventually had to face. He was a skipper who knew how to press the right buttons of his players and never shied away from making tough calls during a match. Communication, particularly during the many one-on-one off-field chats he instigated, also helped form a strong bond between himself and his players; even if we didn't always agree with him, he left no one in any doubt as to his expectations of each player and of the team.

Mark was a man of strong convictions who enjoyed the power base that a captain is afforded. In Geoff Marsh he had the perfect coach to work with, a laid-back guy who offered support more than vision. As an all-rounder, more often in one-dayers, I would sometimes be frustrated at what I perceived to be a lack of trust from Tubby in my instincts as a bowler to have an extra over to finish off the job, or when I had a gut feel a wicket wasn't far away. It appeared he didn't quite understand it from a bowler's point of view, which was understandable considering he didn't roll the arm over very often. We'd agree to disagree – occasionally he'd get it wrong, but regularly he'd make the correct change at precisely the right time, proving his cricket brain was of the highest order.

To his credit, he never let his batting slump dilute his leadership, which must have taken enormous self-discipline, because he was prone to the odd outburst – especially on the golf course, where his language

and length of club-hurling were distinguishing attributes. Tubs successfully managed to tread that fine line between being one of the boys and
being a guy whose every move was scrutinised by the board, though
he had an advantage, in that the powers-that-be thought he was the
best thing since sliced bread and were happy to give him some extra
leeway. The patience of both the administration and his teammates was
pushed to the limit during what became a prolonged batting slump,
but throughout Tubs amazingly kept it all together, at least from the
outside.

Unfortunately our home season ended in a kind of disarray, with the
one-day team missing out on the Carlton & United Series finals for
the first time since 1979–80 and a chorus of journalists and ex-players
stirring the debate about Mark's right to be in the side. I believed he
needed to be given time to recapture his form, because at any given
period someone will be out of sorts and one of the marks of a great
side is its ability to nurse someone through until that player recov-
ers. Later, though, as Tubs's run of outs continued during our tour
of South Africa that was inserted between the Windies Tests and an
Ashes series in England, it started to affect morale and threw out the
balance of the team. At that point, it became a matter that needed serious attention.

The South African team of 1997 was a world-class side that was going
to stretch us in every facet of the game. The build-up to the first Test
in Jo'burg was intense, with the locals talking up their chances; with
a bowling attack featuring the likes of Allan Donald, Shaun Pollock,
Brian McMillan, Lance Klusener, Jacques Kallis, Paul Adams and
Hansie Cronje in their ranks, they had every right to believe they
could win.

Bowled first ball by Devon Malcolm in Adelaide in 1994–95. There were any number of English medium-pacers I preferred facing to the ultra-quick Malcolm.

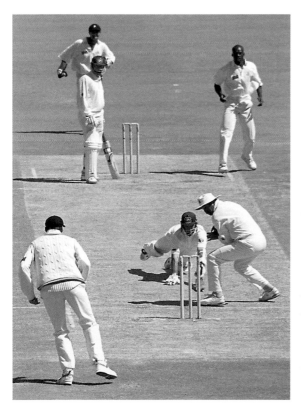

Mark Waugh, running for No. 11 Craig McDermott, is run out by Graham Gooch at the WACA in the fifth Test of the same summer. I'm the batsman at the other end. The verdict went to the third umpire, but I knew intuitively that I was about to become the second batsman in Test history to remain unbeaten one short of 100.

This was one of the most important catches of my career, taken as I ran towards the midwicket boundary to dismiss West Indies keeper Junior Murray at Bridgetown, 1995.

The confrontation in Port of Spain. I wasn't going to back down and neither was Curtly Ambrose, until his captain, Richie Richardson, stepped in to drag him away.

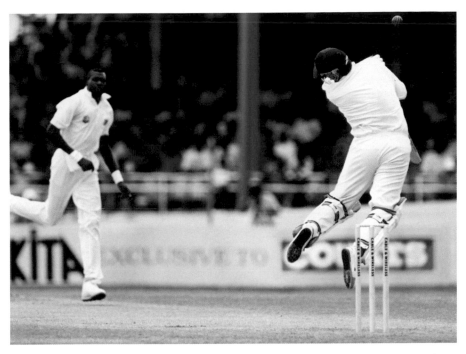

Curtly's response to our altercation was to try to remove my head from my shoulders.

I scored my first Test hundred against Pakistan at the Gabba in 1995–96, but it was an innings of how many, not how.

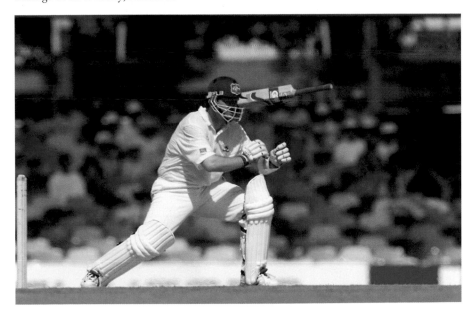

This photograph, by the award-winning Trent Parke, of me batting in the nets at the WACA is one of my favourites.

Meeting Mother Teresa in Calcutta in 1996 was one of the most unforgettable moments of my life.

We've just made the 1996 World Cup final, after completing an amazing win over the West Indies at Chandigarh. From left: me, Damien Fleming, Mark Waugh, Mark Taylor.

Silly mid-off Mark Butcher frantically avoids an off-drive during the first of my twin hundreds at Old Trafford in 1997.

Ian Healy (front left, wearing his baggy green) leads the Australian team in song at Headingley in 1997, after we won the fourth Test.

Three images from my camera, each of a famous cricket moment.

Mark Taylor enters the dressing-room at Edgbaston in 1997, having scored the hundred that saved his career.

The Australian team celebrates in Hobart in 1999–2000 after Adam Gilchrist and Justin Langer scored superb fighting centuries to win a Test against Pakistan that most thought was lost.

Matthew Hayden in the home room at the WACA in 2003, having just established a new world record of 380 for the highest score made by a batsman in a Test match.

With Lynette, 17-month-old Rosalie and the baggy green on New Year's Eve in 1997, at our team hotel in Sydney, preparing for my 100th Test match.

Big occasions generally reveal a team's true colours, with many a contender metamorphosing into a pretender in the cauldron of heightened emotions and intense engagement. As a team, we loved the 'world's best' title being disputed and the opposition talking up their chances, while we calmly tapered our preparations before exploding out of the blocks. A three-match Test series is often decided during the very first session. Win that and you generally win the first day, and more often than not that puts you in a position to take the first Test. Rarely does a side lose a series after winning the opening Test, so it's crucial to get the ascendency quickly and then allow the domino effect to occur.

In this case, we absolutely murdered them by an innings and 196 runs, their biggest Test loss in 47 years. Greg Blewett and I batted from tea on day two until lunch on day four in a chanceless partnership of 385, then the 11th-highest in Test-match history. It was a dream pitch to bat on, true in pace and even in bounce with a lightning-fast outfield, which meant big runs to anyone who could muster up the concentration. Blewey and I hit it off as a combination, enjoying the odd laugh but keeping each other focused and hungry enough to never be satisfied. In my mind I had captured a real sense of tranquillity at the crease that gave me a profound focus at the same time. I was at a place all elite sportspeople strive to reach, yet aren't sure how to, and find extremely hard to reach again.

It was a real benchmark victory for the team, which now knew its capabilities; in the future, anything less than what we'd achieved here would be seen as a backward step. To me, this win was a forerunner to future success, not necessarily because of our planning or preparation, but because we could no longer hide behind the veil of being *potentially* a great side. The bar had been raised. Mind you, so had the celebration factor, with straight shots of Southern Comfort and Jack Daniel's being skolled on a two-hour trip to Sun City. Thanks to the ample measures that 'Barman Bic' was administering in between his bottle-juggling and ice-tossing exhibition, we fell out of the bus upon arrival. It was rumoured that one player left his 'trollies' behind on the bus when he checked into the hotel, but I was in no state to back up this assertion as I was lucky to locate the lobby. I did, however, force myself to get up at 5 a.m. the next morning to check out the game park next door. Only Glenn McGrath was keen or able-bodied enough to make the trip with me.

After expecting so much and coming up disastrously short in Jo'burg, the locals produced an underprepared pitch for the second Test, in Port Elizabeth, to negate our skill on flat pitches where hard work and all-round skills make a crucial difference because there is no assistance from the conditions, and also to benefit their strength: pace bowling. Our selection was, in a word, dreadful. Paul Reiffel was again left out in favour of a seventh batsman on a track that was tailor-made for his precision line-and-length seam bowling. Two spinners, one of whom (Michael Bevan) was basically a part-timer, backed up the quality of Glenn McGrath and his new fast-bowling partner, Jason Gillespie, so we were a quick bowler short. Bevan had been taking wickets, most notably 10 in the Adelaide Test against the West Indies and six in the first Test of this series, and it is accepted by all that to keep a winning side intact is generally a good policy, but the murmurs of discontent regarding the protection of the captain were beginning to gather momentum. Many people believed that Bevo was only kept in the side to bolster the batting, which was being weakened by Tubby's continued struggles at the top of the order.

Often, unsuitable pitches provide memorable matches because both teams are less reliant on pure skill and much more vulnerable to the 'rub of the green'. So it was here, with the teams drawn closer together, but fortunately my brother played an innings of equal magnitude to his 126 in Kingston two years before. Here, chasing 270 on a pitch on which we had been bowled out for 108 in the first innings, Mark guided us to within sight of victory and changed plenty of perceptions – such as that he was always 'casual under pressure' – by the manner in which his innings was constructed.

At the end of day two South Africa had been 0/83 in their second innings, a total lead of 184 on a bowler-friendly pitch. A little less than two days later, Heals capped off a remarkable comeback by lofting Cronje for six over backward square leg to win the Test under excruciating pressure. We all leapt for joy, wildly embracing each other with Swamp and Tubs clamped together for what seemed an eternity, which signified how much this victory meant to them. I was ecstatic for Heals, who had carried a heavy burden since the Karachi Test of 1994. In my mind, if he thought he was responsible for that loss, then he had won us this one. My first words as the team greeted him at the boundary ropes were, 'That's Karachi gone, mate.' I hoped the win and his six had exorcised the demons that were, but shouldn't have been, residing in his mind.

An away series win against such quality opposition was always going to lead to a massive celebration, and for five hours we maintained the rage, headlined by a Hayden–Gillespie pantomime in which they mimicked a hunter and his conquests in the African wild. Resplendent in white zinc and Vegemite, the boys went off in search of a kill and came home victorious; needless to say, they were Australia and their fresh 'kill' was the Proteas. A rousing rendition of 'Under the Southern Cross' led by a highly charged Heals (who hates a celebration) was declared by many as 'the best ever'.

Playing an upcoming third and final Test didn't really register in our minds, which may have contributed to our dismal showing and a fourth instalment, after England in 1993, Pakistan in 1995–96 and the

Windies in 1996–97 of what was becoming known as the 'dead rubber syndrome'.

Fronting up for another Test so soon afterwards was always going to be a big ask after such an emotionally draining match. Lack of sleep, a sense of the job being completed and the physical aches and pains from back-to-back Tests, on top of the fact that South Africa's pride had been hurt, added up to a big assignment. Then, prior to the Test, the selectors announced that Matt Hayden, Justin Langer and Matthew Elliott would not be staying for the seven-match one-day series that would follow the Test. It hadn't occurred to us that new players would be coming in and others would be leaving. To say the timing of this announcement was ill judged would be a gross understatement.

Adding to the mix was some atrocious umpiring from South Africa's Cyril Mitchley, who was partially deaf in one ear, and England's Mervyn Kitchen, who looked frightened to back himself. Inevitably, trouble materialised on the final day, when a loud-mouthed employee of one of South African cricket's sponsors, Nando's, escorted Heals up the steep and seemingly endless steps to the change rooms high in the stands at Centurion Park, all the way shouting abuse and taunting him to retaliate. Our vice-captain was already seething from a shocker of a caught-behind decision, and finally the toys came out of the cot. Into the air went his Kookaburra bat, through an opening and into our viewing area. It was a moment of madness that would ultimately give the selectors an easy way out when they dramatically stripped Heals of the deputy's job for the Ashes tour. The two one-day games that he was suspended for seemed a very harsh penalty, but the open secret going around was that there were a couple of players in each side who had asterisks next to their names in the match referee's book. If these players stepped out of line they were going to be made examples of. Unfortunately for Heals he was a targeted one. I was also on that 'naughty boys' list.

I was actually really pleased with the way I performed in that Test, combining near-perfect execution and unwavering concentration while many others got fatigued. Mind you, one over from Donald left me no option but to survive any way I could. I was struck five balls out of six, including one flush on the protector that was a guaranteed laugh all round for everyone except me. All I could think was, *Did anything that might not have been securely tucked in as it should have been get squashed?* There's no greater trepidation than nervously checking out the damaged region and praying your first sight isn't blood. It was an over that saw me cop one riser flush on the forearm and a couple on the gloves, and culminated in a thunderbolt that crashed into my ribs. The pain from being struck in this area is about as intense as it gets. The initial burning sting as the capillaries are crushed against bone and burst is followed by a pulsating ache, which slowly retreats to a throbbing, dull pain that gnaws away at you. I could either let the sensation take control by thinking about how much it was hurting, or see each impact as a badge of honour that reinforced the fact that nothing was going to worry me. I enjoyed testing my pain tolerance, almost willing it to hurt more so I could counteract it just as strongly with the notion that this was as good as my opponent could give: *If that's the most you can damage me, then I'm in charge out here.*

Donald was a class act, mixing express pace and an excellent cricket brain that enabled him to plot, as well as plunder, batsmen's deficiencies. He was a genuine superstar, but when I looked into his eyes in the real, raw moments of heightened battle, I believed he wasn't quite as mentally strong as his reputation suggested. Maybe we are all a bit like that, but I had an inkling that he knew I was on to him. At least, that's what I told myself.

I remember a South African television commentator interviewing me after the game. 'Jeez, we felt sorry for you copping that over from AD,' he said.

I couldn't help it when I replied, 'Don't ever feel sorry for me. That was one of the most enjoyable overs of Test cricket I've ever played.'

It was Test-match cricket the way I loved it – genuine one-on-one warfare, with no place to hide and everything on the line.

★

Dark clouds were gathering, not as a result of our loss in the third Test but over the continued poor form of our captain, who was on the verge of being outvoted on a selection panel consisting of himself, coach Geoff Marsh and vice-captain Ian Healy over whether he should be in our one-day starting XI. However, the intervention of ACB chairman Denis Rogers, who arrived in South Africa straight after the Test series, put an instant stop to the notion. Showing enormous faith in the captain is a trait I admire, but in this instance the board's distinct lack of belief in the other candidates was grating and short-sighted.

Heals' suspension created an awkward situation, in that if Mark was left out of the one-day team – as his poor form demanded – then the captaincy would be rotated between Tubby as Test captain, presumably me for the first two one-dayers, then Heals when he came back into the side – and this was finally offered as the reason Tubs stayed on as one-day captain for those first two games. When Heals came back, Tubs sat out game three reputedly because his back was troubling him, and this added to the confusion within the team as to what was really going on. The issue finally came to a head before the fourth game of the best-of-seven series, when Mark Waugh was ruled out through injury and the choice as his replacement came down to either Tubs or the new whiz-kid, Adam Gilchrist, who was a relatively unknown quantity at the time. I'm not sure how the idea was eventually sold, but 'Gilly' ended up getting the nod and Tubs didn't play again during the series.

To everyone's great credit, team spirit and morale stayed solid and we won one of the best one-day series I ever played in 4–3. Personally, I couldn't have achieved much more on the tour, winning both the one-day and Test-match player-of-the-series awards and then the ultimate honour, the captaincy, for the last one-dayer in Bloemfontein, which we lost convincingly. However, I did manage to smite Allan Donald for a six straight back over his head during a defiant 91 from 79 balls.

The absolute privilege of captaining your country should never be diluted, but I did experience a sense of believing it was almost a token gesture, with Healy and Taylor sitting it out with niggling injuries and the match having no bearing on the outcome of the series. It was a one-day international where guys who hadn't had many opportunities played, which further emphasised the low-key nature of the game and underlined the belief many people held that limited-overs cricket was the commercial arm of the game and could be tinkered with and cheapened while Test matches had to be shielded from such undertakings.

27

A culture forever changed

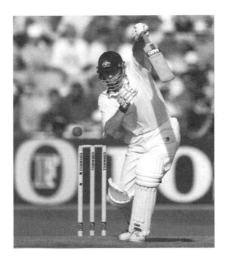

There are very few occasions in life when you inwardly leap for joy at the sound of your mobile phone going off, but if it means a few minutes respite from the serious business of shopping with your loved one, then it's pure bliss. Fresh from digesting a crash course in women's clothing lines and agitated by the complete lack of seating facilities available for taking a breather, we had ventured up to the children's department when chairman of selectors Trevor Hohns stunned me with the news. 'You're the new vice-captain for the tour to England.'

My immediate response was, 'What about Heals?' My first call as Australia's new VC was to the outgoing one. I knew he'd be devastated at this undeserved demotion. He'd been a fantastic sounding board and a perfect link between the players and the squad's hierarchy. And then there was the great pride he displayed in his role. All I could do was say how sorry I was that it had to happen this way. Sometimes, as a professional sportsperson, you've got to cop it on the chin and move on, and that's exactly what Heals vowed to do. Resilience was always one of his strong suits, and this sudden turn of events would test this trait out to the max.

There was no doubt that the change had been made in case Mark Taylor's form didn't improve and the need for a new captain arose. Clearly, I *was* the next in line for the captaincy, and the selectors believed I needed to assume the vice-captaincy immediately to satisfy protocol if a change at the very top was deemed necessary. I appreciated the support, but wondered why they couldn't just make the move as a clean, crisp swap if it was required, and at the same time leave Heals alone. I also pondered how this would affect Mark Taylor's psyche, knowing he was basically on his last warning and that the next slip-up would be terminal. It was a major gamble by the selectors in terms of how it was going to affect the mechanics of the team as a unit, and could have been disastrous had we not all been really good mates.

The pretour get-together in Sydney took on extra importance for the squad because of the line of questioning we knew we'd cop from the voracious Fleet Street press on our arrival at Heathrow. The media training session the board put on gave us an insight into what to expect and how best to answer and deflect questions. 'Bridging' is a technique used expertly by politicians and now it was to be put into action by us. Bail-out lines included, 'But what's more important . . .', 'The real issue here is . . .', 'That may be so . . .', 'Our role is to . . .' and 'Perhaps we've already dealt with that, can we move on?' The whole point of giving an interview, we were told, is to get your message across or to emphasise the point you want to make, rather than getting diverted or sidetracked into a line of thought or point of conjecture you don't want to participate in. After a couple of hours we could have sold ice to Eskimos; it was time well spent and a lesson I never forgot.

The landscape of professional cricket was changing rapidly and Geoff Marsh wanted to be at the forefront of these modifications. He saw part of his role as being a facilitator to many other specialised people who would eventually form a nucleus around the players. It was a concept that Swamp's successor, John Buchanan, would expand and streamline. The newest member of the squad was a full-time fitness advisor named Steve Smith, an ex-navy diver who was as tough as nails and pound for pound as strong as any man alive. He was also the fastest walker on the planet, conning us into going for a leisurely 'stroll' at his pace, which was to me a brisk run. The goalposts had moved and from this point match fitness alone wasn't enough to sustain anyone. Out went the Four'N Twentys and in came sushi and energy bars, as 'Smithy' made us aware of how we needed to prepare our bodies and also of what went into them. Boonie's exploits would never again be challenged and a culture was forever changed.

To mark the shift to greater professionalism we moved away from the garish pin-striped blazer to a business suit with a stylish tie, chosen with the aid of the team's fashion consultant, Ian Healy. It was only a small change, but I certainly noticed a shift in attitude from carefree to being aware of our responsibilities just a little more. Symbols are important to organisations, because they make team members feel unified and that they all stand for something. This Ashes tour was serious business, and though we all hoped there would still be time to party, we knew it could come *after* we had been successful.

An early sign of our new approach came at the first official media conference, which took place at our new home away from home, the Westbury Hotel in London. The acclaimed interviewer and cricket lover Michael Parkinson was in the chair, and he best summed up what was expected to transpire when he said, after opening up the floor for questions, 'Let the bunfight begin.' However, our ready-made answers, combined with a bit of improvisation, repelled the poisoned arrows and the tour was off on a positive note.

Being the new vice-captain provided one immediate lurk – having a single room instead of sharing, which is a big deal when loved ones call and you have to rely on the good nature of your buddy to take a walk or make an extended trip to the toilet. Squaring the ledger was the fact that I was now a tour selector, alongside the captain and coach, and facing the very real possibility of dropping a good mate who, six years earlier, had been a groomsman at my wedding. The bottom line was that we all wanted to see Tubs score runs and squash the speculation that was seemingly seeping into every conversation. The three-match one-day series came and went in the blink of an eye, over before we could find any worthwhile rhythm. Tubs stepped down after the second game, before Geoff Marsh and I had got around to discussing again the captain's place in the side. I'm not sure what was more gut-wrenching – the demoralising losses, or that uneasy silence at the selection meeting until the obvious question came out.

My second foray at the helm was again unsuccessful, with a young upstart named Ben Hollioake dazzling all comers with an astonishingly effortless ease about his game that had people thinking of a young, right-handed David Gower. Tragically this was to be Ben's cricketing highlight, as he passed away in a motor accident in 2002 at the age of 24.

★

A 3–0 loss in the limited-overs series was painful but, as is the case with the one-day game, the impact only lasted a few days as players, fans and commentators forgot who did well and what actually happened. But given our indifferent performances and the conjecture over the make-up of our Test side, the county fixtures now had their status dramatically lifted. During one of these matches we had the chance to catch up with one of the game's real characters, who also happened to be the best keeper I ever saw. Jack Russell of Gloucestershire is also a gifted portrait and military artist, and he extended an invitation for dinner at his gallery during our match against his county. Jack, who on the field looked like the straw man from *The Wizard of Oz*, could best be described as an eccentric recluse, with routines and intricacies that you'd think would be enough to have him committed to an institution. His playing gear looked like he'd flogged it from a museum, and each morning he eats a bowl of Weet-Bix that has been soaked in milk for 12 minutes; for the rest of the day he exists on baked beans, rice, potatoes, jaffa cakes and digestive biscuits, and an excessive amount of milky tea – never less than 20 cups per day. Jack is a man who guards his privacy so closely that it is rumoured no one knows where he lives. Teammates and workmen have been known to be blindfolded a couple of kilometres away from his home to protect its whereabouts. Further emphasising the legend is his wish for his hands to be embalmed upon his death. Who says there are no characters left in the modern game?

Cricket, because of the length of tours and the manner in which teams are often confined for long periods in the change rooms, draws unusual traits out of its participants. Because of the level of introspection it allows, it cultivates self-doubt and exaggerates differences between teammates and opponents. All the successful teams I've played in have been dominated by people willing to see past others' faults and appreciate their strengths.

As far as the conundrum over Tubby's form was concerned, it felt as if nothing much changed in the lead-up to the first Test, in Birmingham, except for the little-known fact that we as a selection committee had agreed that if Mark's form didn't improve during the Test then he would stand down. This verdict not only made me extra-nervous for him, it also put me on edge, knowing that I'd be the one to take over. However, with hindsight, there were some signs that things were slowly turning for him. In the second innings of our last game before the first Test, against Derbyshire, the county's overseas professional, our former colleague Dean Jones, dropped Tubby early on. If that chance had been taken, and it should have been, Mark's confidence levels would have been at an all-time low; instead, he ground out an innings of 63 during a couple of hours at the crease. It wasn't a great innings, but gradually foot movement returned, along with some authoritative body language. It was almost as if he was learning to bat again.

Tubs got some help from his batting partner Justin Langer at one stage when, in frustration, he told Justin, 'I just can't fuckin' play!' As only teammates can do at certain times, Justin snapped him out of the mire he had immersed himself in by retaliating this way to his captain's comment: 'That's rubbish. Of course you can play. You know that. Just watch the bloody ball real close, stick in there and it will come.'

At the conclusion of the game, with the water trickling out of the barely satisfactory showers as we attempted to wash out the shampoo, Mark caught my attention. 'Tugga,' he said, 'do you think I should play? Am I still good enough?'

'Yes, you should. Just back yourself. Don't force it.'

A day and a half later, on the eve of the first Test, Tubs was still in turmoil, for D-Day was imminent. Another brief conversation at the breakfast table went as follows: 'Don't worry too much about the outcome and remember, whatever happens is meant to be,' I said, trying to offer some reassurance.

'I'll just try to really enjoy the game, and not put too much pressure on myself,' Tubs replied.

The coach tried to lighten the mood on the bus during our 10-minute trip to the ground on Test-match morning by showing us video highlights of our recent series wins against England, with snippets of the Don and other Aussie greats thrown in. His presentation was capped off by another look at the remarkable Kieren Perkins' 1500-metre triumph at the Atlanta Olympics. However, our subdued mood was hard to alter and was reflected on the scoreboard at lunch, where we were placed precariously at 8/54. It was a situation we never recovered from.

The only real ray of sunshine came from the captain, who after failing to reach 50 in his previous 21 Test innings, dug deep into his own chronicles to produce a Taylor special, full of concentration, calculated shot selection, detachment from the goings-on around him and a brooding intensity on getting the job done. Ours was a highly emotional viewing room when he reached three figures because we had all been through a small part of the ordeal he'd encountered. We so admired his resilience and courage to turn things around. As he sat in his chair in the chaotic confines of the grossly undersized Edgbaston change room, he just reclined back, sipped a sports drink and stayed silent. His face said it all: *Thank God I did that. The pressure's off. Now I can relax!* It was a sentiment I certainly echoed.

Touring life for me was about to change radically with the arrival of Lynette and Rosalie, and Lynette's parents Phil and Ethel. Already in the UK was my mother, Beverley, and her partner Darryl, and it was extremely comforting knowing that the foundations of my success were here to support me.

For the first time, though, I experienced the anguish of my child not being entirely comfortable when they set eyes upon me. The six weeks that had gone by since the team had left for England meant baby Rosie was initially and unusually coy in my presence, but as soon as I started to smile at her and make physical contact it was as if a light had been turned on as she recognised her old man. The next half an hour more than made up for the lost time as we bonded by playing games, mimicking sounds and settling into the confines of a hotel room. The room we found ourselves in was so small that we had to forfeit that week's wages to upgrade, so Rosie could go exploring on her hands and knees in a more appropriate setting. Families were more welcome than on previous tours, though there was still no real support structure in place. Things such as getting to and from airports and to grounds and seat allocations still left a lot to be desired.

Such was my hectic lifestyle now that I had to dash off the day before the Lord's Test to have a root canal and crown filling finished – a job that had spanned three countries, Australia, South Africa and England, over a period of five months. Life in the fast lane required adaptation, flexibility and an ability to just go with the flow, because there was no such thing as a regular doctor or dentist or a schedule to see your accountant or financial planner. Everything revolved around cricket.

In the dentist's chair I was able to ponder the special nature of Lord's Cricket Ground and the euphoria that goes with an Ashes contest. With the Poms a Test up, it was primed as potentially a grand occasion. Unfortunately, rain robbed everyone of the chance of an outcome, wrecking all of the first day and most of the second and fourth, but it did allow enough play to see the technically gifted but temperamentally flawed Matthew Elliott concoct a quality first century in international cricket that gave the indication he'd be the man to play at least 50 Tests. Sadly things didn't turn out that way by a long shot, as Matty was prone to serious bouts of self-doubt and a tendency to let injuries rule his thought processes. Much is expected of professional cricketers, yet many are very insecure. Teammates are valuable in such situations, but not always available. Their own game might need fine-tuning and they might not be aware of the onset of a dark mood in a comrade. Throughout my career I certainly had moments of self-doubt despite the fact that I consider myself to be mentally strong, with a fierce will to make the most of my abilities. I can understand how tough it might be for those not as driven or resilient as me. If only 'Herb' could have commandeered his gifts and suppressed the lurking little inner voice that ate away at his confidence and distracted him. If we'd had a sports psychologist travelling with the team or a regular mentor to coax players like him along, Matty would have been a perfect candidate.

As to my contribution to this Lord's Test, just when I thought I had the game covered and only good times lay ahead, I was brought down to earth with a shattering jolt: lbw first ball. Having bowled England out for 77, I was wondering how many we were going to need before declaring and was thrown slightly out of kilter when Shane Warne was sent in before me to have a slog. There was no need for an inquisition to pinpoint the reasons for my downfall. It was obvious to me that I didn't have a clear head, which probably explained my rushed routine and lack of intent. I had paid the price of a wandering mind. *What a bloody waste*, I thought as I brushed past the startled MCC members on the way back to our room. Many of these men would never see me play again, and most probably wondered if I had actually participated in this one!

Ducks are a guaranteed room clearer, with the other guys unsure as to the dismissed player's reaction. One thing they don't want to risk is saying the wrong thing. Comments like 'Bad luck, pal' or 'You couldn't do much about that one' or 'You'll get 'em in the second dig' sound hollow and don't really soothe the bubbling anger, so most players just disappear and wait for the tempest to pass. As a globe-getter of some experience – I managed to tally 22 in my Test career – I never quite knew what my reaction was going to be. There were times when I'd sit in my gear rueing my bad fortune at getting an unplayable one early on, or perhaps I'd curse myself for making such a meek offering or showing a lack of application. A dodgy decision would necessitate a long hot shower or a forceful repacking of my kitbag followed by an animated pace around the change room. In such circumstances I could never complete a task, whether it be watching the game on television, eating a piece of cake, signing the team's souvenir autograph sheets, sitting on the balcony or opening a pack of chewie that I realised one minute later I didn't want. It was like an itch I couldn't scratch. Eventually the anguish would subside and a clearer picture emerge, but failure was not just a scoreboard thing – in those blurred moments, I felt personally inadequate as well.

Two months after the second Test, I discovered the life diary of our most loyal supporter, Luke Gillian, a.k.a. 'Sparrow', which centred around his budget travels, wedged behind the padding on the inside of my left leg guard. He had given it to me to review as I made my way back to the change rooms after the pregame net session, just as a storm shower materialised. Wanting to preserve his memoirs from the rain, I inserted the notebook in my pads before carrying them back to my 'coffin', where it was forgotten. For the life of me I couldn't work out what I had done with his precious cargo, and was racked with guilt until, at the end of the series, just when I was about to give my gear away, to my everlasting relief I spotted the frayed edges of his work protruding from the side of my front pad. I figured we were even when, a few years later, I gave him one of my playing shirts from our victorious 1999 World Cup tournament.

To ambitious sides, rain delays are more than a nuisance, while they are a godsend to unmotivated ones. However, if you have to choose a venue for a break in play due to inclement weather, Lord's is the place because the change rooms are massive, secluded and very accommodating, with comfortable lounges. As the rain fell in 1997, each guy had his own way of passing the time. Warne, Taylor, Elliott and Bevan swiftly commandeered a table and had a game of five hundred up and running almost as soon as the umpires confirmed play wouldn't be commencing. Blewett and Ponting, as the team's gun golfers, set about ordering a couple of sets of new sticks to complement the numerous sets they had back home, while Gilchrist tested his ball-juggling skills with a soccer ball. Next to Gilly was that frustrated rock star Michael Slater, who was strumming and singing not exactly in tandem, but with unbridled enthusiasm. Paul Reiffel completed the task of signing 50 team-autograph sheets next to Mark Waugh, who was watching the nags and dishlickers do their business on the racing channel.

The team's ultimate 'Julio', Brendon Julian, lay prone devouring a novel, while fellow fast bowler 'Dizzy' Gillespie immersed himself in a cricket journal. In startling contrast, our No. 1 pace man, Glenn McGrath, was salivating at the size of a wild pig's tusks in *Guns & Game* magazine. Justin Langer was tapping on the keyboard of his personal computer, detailing the events of the day for his daily 'Postcards' report for the ACB's latest innovation, a 'web site', while Ian Healy never needed a second invitation to tidy up his gear and whiten his boots. Michael Kasprowicz was extolling the virtues of some unknown grunge band to anyone who would show even the slightest interest, while I got stuck into writing my latest tour diary. The one constant was always the physiotherapist, Errol Alcott, who had a never-ending stream of patients benefiting from his healing hands and insightful observations.

England escaped with a draw, so we made our way to Manchester one down with four to play, for a Test I described to a startled journalist as 'the most important of our careers'. In truth, that was the attitude I tried to take into every Test, because it led to a hunger that would in turn give me the best chance to seize the initiative when the moment invariably presented itself. And I always thought that, at worst, this might be the last Test I ever played, so I didn't want to leave anything in the sheds.

★

Walking up the steps to the dressing-rooms at Old Trafford, I became aware that I was much more contemplative than usual before the start of play in a Test match. Usually I'd observe and take in what was going on around me without really soaking it up, until I found the need to get animated during the warm-ups. No matter how profitable the previous year has been in terms of runs scored, as soon as a successful sequence hits a submerged log a batsman suffers a distinct swing in confidence. In this instance I was coming off a first-ball 'gozzer' and knew that the pitch was going to suit the seamers, and suddenly I was fearing the worst before the game had even started. Just as rapidly, I remembered how Bob Simpson broke his Test century hoodoo here back in 1964 – six and a half years, 51 innings and 15 fifties after his debut – and went on to get a mammoth 311. This was the imagery I needed, for it planted the seed that if I wanted something badly enough there was nothing anyone could do to stop me getting it. Little signs often came to me, such as visualising 100+ next to my name on the scoreboard during warm-ups, or Lynette, who has amazing intuition, telling me 'Today is going to be your day'. If it the message was positive I took possession of it and kept on reinforcing it until it almost became a given.

I'd known since early that morning that the wicket was a 'green top'. In modern cricket, before the team gathers together for a brief chat and a stretching routine, everyone makes their way out to the pitch to assess how it's going to play. It ensures that your first sighting of the playing surface isn't during the actual game. It's a peace-of-mind thing, a routine that provides comfort and helps you feel that you've covered every base. The only guy I played with who never looked at the pitch before a game was Jason Gillespie, who says, 'It doesn't affect how I'm going to bowl, so why let it play a role in my preparation?' At the other end of the scale was Matthew Hayden, who wanted to become one with the pitch and get grounded by sitting in a guru-like pose at one end as he imagined himself batting. Matt often cut a solitary figure out in the middle as the rest of us packed away our gear at the end of a training session. Perhaps this pregame check is more significant for batsmen, who expect to see a flat surface promising plenty of runs. Mostly it's productive, because that's what they generally find, but as soon as an extra shade of green materialises or any sign of dampness, softness, dryness or cracking is visible, the talk among the run-scorers becomes animated, with conspiracy theories tossed around.

What confronted us 90 minutes before starting time at Old Trafford was a heavily grassed pitch with enough dampness to cause alarm, particularly for the side batting first. Then, at around 10.25 a.m., 35 minutes before the first delivery, Tubs sidled up to me in the change rooms and said, 'Tugga, I think I'm gonna have a bat if we win the toss.' I thought he was taking the mickey, but a follow-up punchline didn't materialise. Instead, he adjusted his collar and checked his blazer in front of the mirror, then headed off to meet England captain Mike Atherton for the walk out to the middle.

Captains, at times, can be real tormentors. The players know that whoever gets interviewed first by the television commentators has won the toss, and nine times out of 10 everyone in the squad knows what the plan is. However, if they don't, everyone looks for a hand signal to discover what they are about to do. No such signal came this time, so when Tubby returned and announced he'd won the toss and elected to bat, disbelief swept the room. On the surface his decision appeared foolhardy and a massive gamble, but he had backed his gut instinct reasoning that if we could get through the first day relatively unharmed, the pitch would deteriorate and allow Shane Warne to take control of the fourth innings. A captain needs to see the bigger picture, like a chess player planning ahead, with each move culminating in the decisive one at the appropriate moment. Initial moisture in the surface means that quick bowlers, with their full-spikes, will gouge out pieces of turf in their delivery strides and follow-throughs, leaving the wicket uneven with divots and bare patches of pitch that are ideal for spinners to aim at. With the pitch worn in this way, the amount of turn is unpredictable and the bounce is variable, doubly so for a guy like Shane, who imparts massive revolutions to the ball.

Waiting to bat as the next man in seems to go hand in hand with the urge to have a toilet stop; to my mind, it's the best cure for constipation there is. Trying to manage this as quickly as possible between overs is a curly one, particularly as you're all padded up. I was trying to come to terms with this dilemma when I heard the piercing hometown roar that meant only one thing – I was in. Getting out onto the field as quickly as possible was truly a test of my composure and a chink in my usual pattern. Fortunately, experience kicked in and told me not to rush. They can't start the game without two batsmen.

With our first-innings score at 3/42 and the ball moving alarmingly sideways and upwards, I was called upon to leave the hot, stale air of the change room and walk into a chilly breeze that flared the nostrils and prodded the senses. I always preferred a bite in the air to a humid, trance-inducing atmosphere, because not only did it make me feel alive, it made me stretch and limber up to get the blood flowing. Facing Darren Gough, Andy Caddick and Dean Headley was going to be a searching examination on this pitch, but my priority as I went through my setting-up routine was to survive until the wicket settled down and the ball lost its shine and hardness. The 'blood loss' had to be stemmed if we wanted to stay in the series, and this gave Matt

Elliott and me the focus we needed to start altering the momentum. Like any batsman, I was keen to get off the mark early and always considered it a real bonus to do so with the first ball I faced. Though, when you think about it, it's quite ridiculous the amount of tension that is released just by going from nought not out to one not out. Experience helps overcome these mind games, but at Manchester in the first week of July 1997, even after 11 and a half years at the top level, I still couldn't help but feel relieved that I was off and running.

To me, 'luck' is an overrated term, as everyone has what can be described as 'good luck'. Quality players profit from let-offs, while 'unlucky' ones don't make the most of their opportunities. People never describe a guy who scores 20 after being dropped on 10 as lucky, but if that same batsman goes on to get 120, he is seen as fortunate. A Caddick full toss that I lost against the backdrop of a red-brick pavilion – because the sightscreen was too small – hit me flush on the lower part of my pad and intuitively I awaited the dreaded raised finger. But after a few seconds I sensed that while the umpire thought it was probably out, he wasn't 100 per cent sure. I said to myself, *Switch on, You've dodged a bullet. Make the most of it.*

It was a crucial incident. We were teetering on the edge of collapse in a make-or-break Test, and the Poms knew, as did I, that this was the type of pressure situation in which I thrived. I was aware, too, that there is nothing that provides a better perspective of the true difficulty of the situation in front of me than occupation of the crease. For the first few deliveries it seemed impossible to survive, let alone score runs, but as I was able to adjust and settle the whole scenario suddenly seemed much more friendly.

Quickly it became obvious to me that the English team couldn't let go of that line-ball decision that had gone against them, which led to a lack of discipline and a move away from how they should have bowled to me. The short stuff increased, which to the spectators' eyes appeared menacing and intimidatory, but it was a blessing as it allowed me to duck and weave and rarely look like getting out. The dangerous length was a fuller one, which would have allowed the pitch to do the damage through the inconsistency it was volunteering. With each bouncer the bowlers' energy eroded further, and with each over safely negotiated, the pitch dried out some more and became easier to survive on. It was a waiting game, with patience the number-one priority in my mind. If I could frustrate them by not buying into their confrontational tactics, I knew they would eventually be drawn into bowling where I wanted them to: either straight, which gave me scoring opportunities through the leg side, or short and well outside off stump as they tried to entice me into cutting some wider deliveries.

Once my plan was set in motion and the mind slotted into the groove, the rest of my game sprang to life and gradually I assumed control. Presenting an extra challenge was the consistent loss of teammates at the other end, but at the fall of each wicket I felt my confidence grow because I sensed they were focusing much more on the new batsmen than on me. The key in such a situation is to instil belief in your partner so that, while the opposition is being aggressive as they try to get rid of the tail as quickly as possible, the tail-ender (who often is a batsman of some ability) can make the most of the increased scoring opportunities. Inevitably there are plenty of fieldsmen in catching positions, and if a wicket doesn't fall quickly the bowlers become frantic and no longer work to a plan, which means loose deliveries present themselves.

In these circumstances, I found that a sure sign we were getting on top was my new partner outscoring me. As soon as that happened, confusion would be so entrenched in the minds of the opposition captain and his bowlers that they wouldn't know which way to turn to address the problem. A 'senior' batsman taking a single from the first ball of an over and thus putting the 'junior' partner in the firing line may seem selfish to some, but I always saw it as showing respect for a colleague. This plan of action, which entrusted responsibility to your partner, was one I believed was most likely to get a player to rise above his stereotyped position. At Old Trafford, after Shane Warne fell for three to make it 7/160, I found a willing ally in Paul Reiffel, who was clearly a talented batsman but who often played not to his ability but to the number next to his name. Like many down the batting order, all he needed in order to prosper was a dash of inspiration and a touch of encouragement. Once Pistol started to take advantage of the attacking fields, the dilemma for Atherton was whether to continue to focus on the No. 9 or revert to a more normal line of play, giving us both the same level of attention. Approaching stumps we were still together and had reached a competitive score rather than a potentially disastrous one.

Attitude has always been the key driver of my game, which is why I turned down three chances to leave the field after being offered bad light by the umpires. I did so for two reasons: we were beginning to dominate, and I was fast approaching a century. With two scheduled overs remaining and all five light indicators brightly illuminating the scoreboard (normally it's three lights on and you're off the field), and with the umpires conferring once more, I took the unusual step of asking Atherton who was going to bowl out the day. As soon as he told me it was to be the off spin of Robert Croft and the medium pace of Mark Ealham, I motioned to play on. Amid the gloom, Croft served up an inviting short and wide one and I pinned the ears back and pierced the offside field to complete one of my best ever hundreds. The sense of satisfaction was intense, because I'd beaten the pregame blues, crafted on a difficult wicket an innings of quality that altered the course of the match, and executed it in front of my family and also in front of Peter and Iris Greenalgh, the exceptionally generous couple from Bolton who'd volunteered to billet Mark and me 12 years earlier on our first trip abroad.

It was close to a perfect day, and it was capped off when I returned to my hotel room that night. Usually it would have been empty, but instead Rosalie was climbing all over the furniture in the confines of an area that didn't provide enough obstacles to keep her fully occupied. It was wonderful to be able to switch back from the all-consuming confrontations of a Test to our nomadic lifestyle and experience a sense of 'normal life'.

Like most babies, Rosie was irritable when her routine was interrupted, and as she grew more restless Lynette volunteered to sleep on the sofa bed with her in an attempt to pacify her. That would have been the easy solution, but I wanted as normal a family environment as we could muster, and if that meant Rosie crying intermittently and me being woken up spasmodically it was a price I willingly accepted. It could be frustrating at times, but it also meant the family dynamics were sort of back to normal and that was comforting. In fact, the most difficult aspect for me was keeping up with my diary writing, which I not only enjoyed because of the 'release factor' it offered, but also because I found the discipline required seeped into other aspects of my life. Writing a diary from the confines of a minuscule bathroom as I perched atop the closed toilet seat was hardly a stimulating setting and many may say it was appropriate for the quality that emanated from my pen, but I forged on, seeing it as just another challenge to be taken head on. Compartmentalisation was becoming an ever more important tool of survival for me. I had to provide regular reports to Triple M radio and conduct interviews for the Channel Seven News sports report. Often, with the TV camera looking at me, I found it hard to keep a straight face, but I saw this work as another life experience, and as such something I needed to stay sharp and alert for.

The residual effect of scoring a hundred is that muscles you didn't even know existed now ache. As well, there is a tiredness that comes after the adrenaline rush of the previous day's events drains away.

And, of course, there is what every cricketer likes to see – positive write-ups in the newspapers. I had all of these, plus a massively swollen right hand that resembled an inflated dishwashing glove. The sesamoid bone (which forms the 'V' between your thumb and index finger) on my right (bottom) hand had been jarred continuously during the innings to the point that it was so angry and inflamed I wasn't sure batting was going to be possible the second time around. My bat handle wasn't the usual round shape, but an oval one that suited my slightly unorthodox grip and allowed me to play with a freer swing of the arms through the line of the ball. The only trouble with this shape is that it has to be handcrafted, and with this particular bat, which I used for the first time in this innings, there was a slight ridge on the curvature that kept on banging into the bone with each impact of ball on bat, causing the damage.

For all this, it was a comforting feeling knowing I already had a hundred. But I wanted more, and on the third day of the Test my troublesome hand gave me the focus I needed to harness my powers of concentration. 'Beware the injured player' is a phrase every cricketer should take heed of, because often it rings true. In order to compensate for the inconvenience of basically batting one-handed, I had to lift every other facet of my game to restore equilibrium.

Batting on will and desire can sometimes be enough. I was in battle mode, blocking out the pain and dismissing any potential threat, totally divorced from things such as the fieldsmen encouraging the bowlers or the England supporters shouting from the stands. It was another of those rare days when I was experiencing the steel-trap state of mind that goes under the name of 'being in the zone'. At no stage in the match did I think I was going to get out until the fourth morning, when I let my guard down after completing a century in each innings. I wish I could have bottled all the elements that went into the potpourri of emotions I experienced during that Test, so I could reproduce the way I played then any time I wanted, but the fact is that each innings has its own little challenges.

In the end, confirming that a captain must back his instincts, we won by 268 runs – even though the expectation that Shane Warne would dominate in the game's later stages didn't really materialise (ironically, having bowled superbly to take 6/48 in England's first innings, he came back to the field a little, with 'only' 3/63 in the second). This result further emphasised to me the fact that nine times out of 10 the toss doesn't affect the outcome of the game; it merely comforts you if you win it and strengthens your desire if you don't.

After the game, as I began to shift and sort my spread-out gear into some form of order in my kitbag, I felt complete as a batsman. I had handled all the obstacles, both in my mind and physically, that had been put in front of me and etched my name in the history books as only the third Australian batsman, after Warren Bardsley and Arthur Morris, to score two hundreds in an Ashes Test match. It wasn't long before I was comparing this assured feeling to the way I was thinking 17 days earlier, when I stood motionless under the giant stainless steel showerhead in the away change rooms at Lord's, contemplating a golden duck, oblivious to the drilling force of the jets of water.

Such a comprehensive win, and the manner in which we achieved it, gave us the belief that the momentum had swung well and truly our way. We sensed that the English knew their moment had passed and in the next two Tests they played accordingly.

After the fourth Test, at Headingley, my tour nearly ended abruptly, not from an on-field injury but as a direct result of hero worshipping and the bravado alcohol can coax out of you. The Canberra Raiders rugby league team just happened to be in town and ended up celebrating long into the night with us, and while their level of enthusiasm for our victory was admirable, it was very difficult to compete with. I'm not sure why, but the mere presence of their former captain, Mal Meninga, and the vivid memories of him trampling over defenders from 20 metres out to score got my competitive juices going.

Like a maniac, I imagined myself capable of performing a feat many professional footballers couldn't even contemplate – bringing the big fella down with a head-on tackle. The goal posts were set – two lounge chairs at one end of the bar – with a Foster's beer can acting as a footy in the palm of one of the all-time greats. Almost immediately I realised I'd bitten off more than I could chew, but only brother Mark appeared keen to lend a hand, before a couple more cricketers reluctantly agreed to join us. As soon as Big Mal took his first purposeful step on the beer-stained carpet I feared for my life, and I couldn't help homing in on those huge thighs pumping vigorously in my direction. I knew the outcome was going to be ugly, especially when I discovered that I alone was now the first line of defence, with Mark hovering slightly behind and, like me, no real impediment. I managed to feebly entangle my arms around Mal's waist and for a moment foolishly believed I'd tamed the beast, but the power in his body came at me like the backdraft of an inferno, pulverising my 85 kg frame before he trampled the rest of the team and casually placed the beer over the imaginary line. I knew I was in a spot of bother when, despite the anaesthetising influence of my pregame drinks, I felt my neck going into 'shutdown' mode, stiffening up even before the legend resumed his chitchat at the bar.

There were other humorous moments on this tour, often out in the middle and normally involving byplay and gamesmanship between the teams. Robert Croft fancied himself as a handy batsman and couldn't help admiring the straight six he took Warney for in the fifth Test, at Trent Bridge, when it was replayed on the huge on-ground video screen. England were trying to force the game into a fifth day at the time. As he did after being hit for six, Shane wanted to get stuck straight back into the action in the hope that the batsman's adrenaline would initiate a rush of blood, but Crofty stalled him by staying focused on other things. Our champion leggie called down the pitch, 'Hey, Crofty! Don't worry, mate, you'll be able to see the replay again in a couple of minutes.' As usual, the 'Sheik of Tweak' got it right: Croft, caught McGrath, bowled Warne, 6.

The series was played in good spirits, but proved testing for the batsman as a couple of the Tests were played on substandard wickets. However, our debacle in the final Test could best be attributed to the fact that we'd been on the road for 26 out of the previous 29 weeks and all longed to see what life was like back in our homes. The solace of sleeping on your own pillow and the regularity of waking up in your own bed was something we all longed for. While there may have been some validity in that line of thought, and guys playing five hundred in the change rooms during play wasn't the crime of the year, the fact that this was happening when there hadn't been any card schools during the first five Tests irked me and I said as much to the offending quartet. The role of monitoring moods and team habits fitted comfortably within the vice-captain's job description and I saw it as my duty to voice my disapproval.

Little did I know that within months my leadership skills would be given a much sterner examination.

28

Now or never

A grassy embankment shadowed by the stupendous arch of the steel colossus, the Sydney Harbour Bridge, was the meeting point that signalled for me the start of a battle for players' rights between the ACB and a proposed cricketers' association. This was 1995, more than two years before the fight would reach its climax.

I sat relaxed, with a dictaphone placed between Kimon Taliadoras and myself, as I searched for knowledge as to how our aspirations could best be turned into reality. Two years earlier, Kimon had been a key figure in the establishment of the Australian Soccer Players' Association (since 1999, the Australian Professional Footballers' Association), which had led to a historic collective-bargaining agreement being forged between Australia's top footballers and Soccer Australia in 1994. Kimon was ASPA's inaugural chief executive and, later, president, and as such I saw him as an influential figure who could provide insights into and an understanding of the pitfalls that lay ahead if cricketers were to head down a similar path to the one taken by the footballers.

The success of the footballers furthered our own desire to pursue a better deal for Australia's Test and first-class players. As a group, we felt as if the advancements made by the players who broke away from 'traditional' cricket in 1977 to join World Series Cricket had been steadily eroding. Still prevalent was the old favourite attitude of board members: 'If you don't want to play, there are millions out there who will for nothing.' That was undoubtedly true, but what we wanted was a fair percentage of the revenue we helped generate, and not just an amount that had no formula or reasoning attached to it. We didn't want to damage grassroots development or feather our own nests; this was about our entitlements, about setting up a system for future players to benefit from, giving players some security and making the board more accountable. All of this would, in turn, lead to increased professionalism from the game's administration and hopefully forge a united approach by the board and the players in the future.

We saw the big picture as the players and administrators working and growing together to benefit everyone, but the board blindly believed we were out to erode their power base and make a quick grab for cash. The course was set and the collision a formality. Once the board got wind of our gathering momentum, significant increases were made to a number of senior players' contracts in the hope the folded stuff would buy our loyalty, but once it became obvious this wasn't working the figures came tumbling down at the next assessment of our worth. In three years, my guaranteed money went from $100 000 a year to $200 000, then back to $140 000 as the goalposts kept moving.

By the time of the 1997 tour of England, it was now or never for this group of cricketers. We were sick and tired of rehashing the same old arguments every time we sat down for a meal. We had just retained the Ashes, had excelled on the field in recent years and had a strong unified base of senior players whose influence would be needed to ensure that Sheffield Shield players would align themselves with us. In August of '97, the Ashes squad, plus Tim May, who had retired after the 1995 West Indies tour and a year later become the chief of our own fledgling body, the Australian Cricketers' Association, gathered at our humble abode, the County Hotel in Canterbury, Kent, for a 'boardroom' meeting that would set us on a course of no return. One of the results of this was that I became ACA secretary and Shane Warne became treasurer. In September, Tony Dodemaide and Greg Matthews, as state representatives, joined Tim, Shane and me on a five-man executive. Ian Healy, who along with Tim and me had initiated the process back in '95, remained strong in his support.

'People are going to be shocked if you guys hire me. They are going to say, "Jesus Christ, these guys are serious".' It was at the conclusion of that discussion at Canterbury, and the speaker was a fellow named James Erskine, who was addressing us in a room that lacked air-conditioning in a hotel that could easily have doubled as a weight-loss sauna retreat. Erskine was a brash, smooth-talking, assertive type with a snazzy suit and an imposing résumé that included work with the multinational sports management company IMG. He was a guy

Tim May believed would give us a power base that could make the ACB accountable. Previously, Maysie's negotiations with the board had stalled, as the administrators figured they could brush him away and that the fanciful notions he harboured about gaining cricketers a fairer, more equitable deal would eventually subside.

All up, the meeting at Canterbury lasted 90 minutes. It started with a preamble from Maysie and Graham Halbish, the former ACB CEO who had controversially come on board with the ACA as national director in March, not long after he had been sacked by the ACB following a bitter falling-out with Denis Rogers, its chairman. (Tim's lateral-thinking mind had latched onto the fact that Graham had left the board on less than amicable terms; now that he was available, he would be the perfect acquisition for the cause. It was a move that so infuriated Rogers that during the tour to South Africa in early 1997, he gathered a group of touring journalists to inform them that the ACB would not deal with Halbish. For the next four months Rogers was pretty much true to his word, even though our legal advice reckoned he had no right to act in this way. His intransigence was to become maybe the single most important factor in an increasingly bitter dispute.) Tim then introduced Erskine to the squad, and this experienced negotiator of things such as TV rights, elite player contracts and sponsorship deals gave us 15 minutes about himself and how, if we consented to his terms, he would help us. For the final 20 minutes he fielded questions from the floor.

In introducing Erskine to us at that historic meeting, Tim described him as a world-renowned hard-nosed negotiator, right up there as the best in his field. He continued, 'Erskine is a third party, who will take any personality out of negotiations. His deal also includes bankrolling the ACA. At the moment, we have two elements of income. One of them is player subscriptions that amount to $6000 a year, and let me tell you, that's nothing. The other is distribution from the ACB, with regards to royalties received on team merchandising items. Last year, we received 90-something thousand dollars. This year we'll only receive $30 000.

'The ACB know we have something of a financial crisis, so they can draw it out, then go to court and we won't have any money to fight the battle. This guy will provide all the costs for that battle.

'The biggest negative? Obviously he's not going to do it for nothing. James Erskine's proposal is very much market-place orientated. He will receive a commission on an annual basis for a period of five years.'

Graham told us how cash inflows in Australian cricket had increased enormously. In 1989, the net assets of Australian cricket were $13 million. In 1996, they were $46 million. 'You'll hear about "rainy day syndrome", he said, projecting ahead to when the ACB would try to counter our claims. 'You're all going to get pressure about taking money out of the mouths of the cricket babies, robbing the grassroots and all of that. You'll hear about concerns about the future. When I took over from David Richards there were a number of concerns about the future, about sponsorship, television rights, players' contracts, programming. They've all been satisfied. The rainy day is gone. The rainy day will never come.'

These words were quite ironic, considering Graham had given me the 'rainy day' spiel many times as I sat across the table from him discussing past contracts. At least now the record had been set straight and this guilty card forever dismantled in our minds. Graham then added a warning, something that became an underlying theme for the night: 'The divide-and-conquer approach will occur . . . It will only take one, two, three or half a dozen of you to decide that this isn't really for you and it will all collapse like a deck of cards.'

The battle was certainly about money, but it wasn't only about money. I still have in my possession a single page, ripped out of a pad from the Taj Palace Hotel in New Delhi during our ill-fated tour to

India in 1996, where I wrote down some of the issues I thought were pressing. These included tour programming, mode of travel, quality of accommodation, phone-call allowances and treatment of wives and partners. I wondered how the board determined which players got what contracts and whether players' rights and responsibilities were considered when the board signed deals with sponsors and suppliers. Was the board good at negotiating these deals, and how much did they pay in consultancy fees and percentages to outside companies? In the back of my mind were two quotes from the board's head of marketing, who had said that the Internet was a passing phase and that the Australian cricket team would never be able to secure a sponsor from outside of Australia. This lack of foresight and vision concerned us as a group. The Australian cricket team was entering a new era of professionalism and we wanted the board to do the same. This needed to involve mutual respect and trust between the players and the board, built upon an ambition to be the forerunners in building amicable player–official relations throughout the cricket-playing countries.

Like most of the guys, I wasn't totally sure what to make of Erskine. I admired his bravado and confidence, but expected his brashness, set ways, unfamiliarity with cricket's idiosyncrasies and inability to get players' names right to cause conflict. Making it easier for me to support him coming on board were the twin facts that he could bankroll our battle and that the ACB would have to treat us seriously. Quite clearly, he was also our best option and to delay the task at hand might be to miss the moment completely.

I thought Erskine was ambitious in thinking he could convince other TV networks to bid for the rights against Channel Nine in the future, considering the rock-solid relationship the board and Nine already had. He told us that if his negotiations with the ACB went down to the wire we'd have to be prepared to withdraw our services, but that 'it won't get anywhere near that'. He seemed unaware how keenly board members would protect their right to run the game the way they saw fit. However, when he talked about how Australian cricketers were treated compared to footballers, golfers and tennis players and how transparent other sporting organisations' business affairs were compared to those of the ACB, I agreed with him 100 per cent.

'Think about it,' Erskine said firmly. 'You're in a $40 million business, a $45 million business. Is it unfair that you should get 30 or 40 or 50 per cent of that? Most businesses have to justify what they spend. Has the ACB ever had to justify what it spends?'

He continued: 'Some of you are going to be worried about public perception. I'm not worried about public perception. You guys are the heroes. You guys have made the television ratings. You have one disadvantage over a Greg Norman, because you are a team. That team changes – some of you stay for a long time, some of you don't stay for a long time – and when you are a team it allows other people to divide and conquer. That's why you have to make an unselfish decision here, not just for yourself right now but for people in the future . . .

'I'm not going to go into this unless there is an absolutely unanimous decision to go forward. This has to go forward as a five- or 10-year plan. In 10 years' time, we'll all be having a drink and saying, "ACA now controls cricket in Australia." That is actually what I'm interested in, because I'm a great believer that a professional sport should control itself, and that the players in that professional sport should be masters of their own destiny. Take the ATP tennis. The Professional Golfers' Association. But you're different because you're a team and people pick you off because you are a team.

'You need to have a position of strength.'

During a Q&A, Shane Warne asked, 'What about all the guys playing Shield cricket? What about if all of us decide we are going to withdraw our services and some guys in Shield cricket think they've got a chance to play for Australia?'

Erskine replied, 'The top 70 or 80 players in the country all have to agree, not just the guys in this room. And I would say to you, if all the guys in this room are prepared to do it, but your mates in the Shield sides are not prepared to do it, then don't do it.'

The theme of solidarity kept coming through. Tim and Graham had already been round Australia to see most of the Shield players. Once the next Australian season began, we would do our bit to keep everyone up to date. Back at Canterbury, I asked Maysie if it was the ACA's job to help persuade the Australian public that we were doing the right thing. 'You bet,' Tim responded. 'We're an association and our job is to promote and protect our members. That's what we're here for.'

'The timing couldn't be better, because of what you've just done here,' Graham added, referring to our Ashes win. 'If we're seen to be reasonable and we put it in the right way, and we can demonstrate how the players are taking a very responsible position, what we think will happen is that we'll get enormous public support. The last thing the ACB will want will be to have this issue debated in the media . . . trying to justify the way the cake is divided now would be a tremendously difficult job.' Unfortunately Graham had forgotten the beast he had helped forge, and this was to be a gross misreading of the landscape. The following few months were going to be extremely difficult indeed.

Days later, a meeting was arranged in London to run the whole scenario out in front of John Cornell, a trusted friend of many of the players, including me. John, of course, is a guy who played a key role in the birth of World Series Cricket, and here he helped make sure that the deal to be struck between the ACA and Erskine's company was fair to all parties. We didn't want to be waging a battle on two fronts, and John's concise thinking and calm demeanour allayed our concerns.

★

While World Series Cricket must have shaken their confidence, the administrators of my time seemed to believe they didn't need input from the players. Even after the three years of jousting that took place from 1995 to 1998 and the spot fires that broke out afterwards, this us-against-them philosophy was still simmering below the surface for some board members. I'll never forget Malcolm Speed, the bespectacled, grey-haired, stern-faced, *Thunderbirds* lookalike who became the ACB CEO in May 1997, saying to me when I was appointed Test captain, 'You realise you're on our side now.'

As a 20-year-old making my Test debut, I neither knew nor cared about politics in cricket, nor was I aware of the money that could be earned by playing top-level sport. I just wanted to play and any money I made was a huge bonus. I couldn't quite believe I was making more money than all my mates from school and I didn't even contemplate what the ACB was earning through gate recepts, broadcasting rights, sponsorship and the like. I wasn't really interested in who ran the game, and never mixed socially with the members of the board. They may as well have been aliens from another planet. There were occasionally suits in the change rooms, generally after a good performance, but they hovered around the senior players, the coach and each other, and their connection to me and many others was minimal. They seemed aloof and dismissive while we were, looking back, rude and unwelcoming in our attitudes. Right up until I became captain, with a few exceptions, the players would privately moan when a board member walked in and we would either begin packing our bags or heading for the showers. It was as if a tradition had been built up and neither side wanted to show weakness by compromising with the enemy.

It probably wasn't until after the 1987 World Cup, my first taste of winning on the international stage, that I gave any real thought to the question: 'Are we being fairly compensated for our efforts and achievements?' We received $6000 each as our share of the prize money, a thousand a week, for winning the most prestigious trophy in world cricket – hardly a windfall. At the same time, the ACB raked in a profit of $600,000, an imbalance that was pretty much the norm for cricket governing bodies across the world, all of whom operated as 'closed shops'.

In my experience, any time we made a request to the board to improve things, it was cut off by the first point of call, the team manager, who on tour was essentially a board member, keeping an eye on proceedings and giving very little away. Players weren't considered to be employees, and consequently received no entitlements and no possibility of salary sacrificing, which all board employees benefited from. The fact that we were their primary source of income was irrelevant. We were made to feel greedy and selfish if we put any proposal forward that might benefit us.

When I first played for Australia, the board CEO was David Richards, who went on to work at the ICC. I'll never forget how one of my first one-on-one meetings with him took a turn for the worse from the very first sentence. Without prior consultation or warning, the board had negotiated a footwear deal with the big sportswear company Puma that meant all first-class cricketers in Australia were required to wear Puma cricket boots, in return for what we thought was a measly amount of money that went into the board's general revenue. The fact that some players had existing contracts with other bootmakers was completely disregarded.

'We've got a problem,' Richards said to me. 'Why aren't you wearing the board's official footwear supplier?'

I explained that I had an existing relationship with Dunlop, who had sponsored me for the previous five years. I had another two years still to run on the contract and I owed them my trust and loyalty. You'd think my explanation would have been not only accepted but applauded, for Richards was himself asking for the same values, but his response, wasn't what I was looking for, though sadly it was the one I thought I might hear. 'Well, if that's the way you want to play it,' he said, 'then we'll have to deduct an amount from your contract to make up the difference.'

There was absolutely no recourse, for as players we had no representation, no place to air grievances, and apparently no right to question their wisdom. I walked out with my shoe contract in place but a diminished board contract and a reputation as a troublemaker. I also now realised we were defenceless in a one-on-one situation.

★

The hastily arranged Nehru Cup in India, staged during October 1989, was in cricketing terms a low-key 'politically correct' event, relatively inconsequential in the scheme of things. However, it became something of a catalyst from a players' rights point of view, a starting point for future negotiations.

Having just completed the '89 tour of England, where we'd played in front of packed grounds in games beamed across the world, we knew that the pittance we got was basically wrong. I knew too that the contracts we were obliged to sign carried restrictive clauses throughout. Peter Taylor, for example, was forced into signing a 12-month agreement for $4000 or else he couldn't tour, so he reluctantly put pen to paper to fulfil his dream.

For much of the 1980s Geoff Lawson had been locking horns with the ACB, becoming almost a lone players' advocate for most of his career. Unfortunately, on most occasions his fellow senior players weren't committed enough in their support or willing to ruffle feathers for fear of recriminations later on. Furthermore, Henry wasn't everyone's cup of tea and didn't have that welcoming demeanour that makes people feel totally at ease with your objectives. Further holding his ambitions back was Allan Border, who after the rebel tour to South Africa and the supposed golden handshakes that various players received in response to that situation, couldn't or wouldn't commit himself to fighting for the cause. Without the captain involved, nothing would change. The board knew the simplicity of that fact and kept AB happy with his lot.

A strictly players-only meeting was held in Goa during the Nehru Cup to discuss what action to take. However, news of our clandestine get-together was common knowledge the next day and quickly came to the attention of Graham Halbish, then, of course, the ACB Chief Executive, who in his wisdom called a meeting at Newcastle while a NSW–Queensland Shield game was being played there early in the 1989–90 season. He listened to our grievances and then put across the board's regulation spiel; it was as if all the CEOs had a chip implanted upon reaching that status. They always cried poor, citing a need to look after grassroots cricket and saying they were paying us as much as they could afford. Of course, no proof of such a perilous financial position was ever offered, and besides guessing a rough estimate we were never any the wiser. Part of the story might have been true, but their financial situation was fairly and squarely their fault. Until 1994, when the ACB retook control of the game's marketing in Australia from PBL following a ridiculous deal struck in the early '80s, too much of the game's revenues were going straight into PBL's coffers.

With the retirement of Allan Border after the South African tour of 1994, the 'old school' – as the players of that era enjoyed being termed – had finished and a new breed of senior cricketers who expected more from the board emerged. Over the following years, Mark Taylor was more proactive in regard to players' rights but was still in the awkward position of trying to please both cricketers and administrators, and found it hard to be as unyielding as the troops wanted on occasions. Prior to and during the West Indies tour of 1995, Tubby was part of meetings that were organised to discuss what we should do in regard to our relationship with the board. On the afternoon prior to our departure for the Caribbean, the ACB called a meeting with the players, but it was hardly a businesslike affair. There was no formal agenda to prepare for, but this was something that had never happened before. It was held in the manager's hotel room, with players spread out on the floor, lined up parallel on the king-sized bed or crammed into any available space. It had the feel of a *Brady Bunch* slumber party instead of the serious discussion they had intended.

This was the meeting when the team first became aware as a group of Mark Waugh and Shane Warne's involvement with an Indian bookmaker. On the subject of player payments, Halbish churned out the jargon, the rhetoric going into overdrive on topics such as worker's compensation, sponsorships and player responsibilities. While we were now engaging in a dialogue and were receiving the odd concession, such as business-class airfares, single rooms on tour and decent pay rises for the top few players, we felt we were still a long way from where we wanted to be. After the tour, we as a player group asked Mark Taylor to formally invite Tim May to take the newly created ACA's top job. The board offered $25 000 to get the venture started and we were promised a percentage of merchandising revenue to help keep it alive, but Tim's efforts to have a serious discussion about how much money the players should be receiving were always quickly rebuffed. At the '96 World Cup, the disparity between the prize money and the revenue created by the event was staggering, and with pay television becoming a new income stream in the near future, all major sports, including cricket, were well and truly entering a new phase as highly profitable entities.

By the end of 1996, Tim's patience was just about exhausted, and then Graham Halbish was sacked by the ACB in January 1997. The 'Earl of Twirl' (Maysie, of course, had once been the spin-bowling partner of Warney, the 'Sheik of Tweak') had no second thoughts about turning to a man who had all the ammunition we so craved in regard to board revenue. In April in South Africa, during our tour there, Denis Rogers called a group of journalists together to tell them that his board would have nothing to do with the ACA while Halbish was involved. Not long after, Maysie was introduced to James Erskine, while Malcolm Speed became the new ACB CEO with riding instructions from Rogers that he was to counter our push for improved money and conditions. After our meeting at Canterbury, Halbish and Erskine set up a joint venture called SEL Cricket Ltd to work with Maysie in negotiations with the board.

★

On September 1, 1997, Tim May and Graham Halbish met in Melbourne with representatives from every Sheffield Shield squad to outline what had been heard and discussed by the Test squad in England. At that meeting, Daniel Marsh, who was representing the Tasmanian players, said that Denis Rogers, in his capacity as the Tasmanian Cricket Association chairman, had told a group of players that the TCA would only deal with players individually and not collectively. We had strong advice that Australian industrial laws said he wouldn't be able to adopt such a stance. The gloves were finally off.

The question of whether Australian cricketers could negotiate under the Workplace Relations Act, which had been introduced by the new Australian federal government in 1996, would become the critical issue over the next few months. The Act enabled employers and employees to have appointed bargaining agents work out an Australian Workplace Agreement (AWA) to cover their working arrangements. When negotiating for the making of an AWA, the law protected employees who withheld services in support of their claims, provided they had complied with the requirements of the Act. Our industrial lawyers explained that some unscrupulous employers sought to strip employ-ees of the protection of the Act by refusing to recognise appointed bargaining agents, by pretending not to recognise that their employees were serious about moving for an AWA, or by making an offer outside the procedures laid down in the Act, such as negotiating with unrec-ognised third parties or individual employees.

Once Maysie obtained written instructions from the Test and Shield players that they wanted SEL Cricket to negotiate on their behalf (which he had by late September) and informed the ACB that the ACA would pursue further negotiations under the Act, the board was required by law to recognise Erskine and Halbish as the ACA's negotiators. But they didn't want a bar of that. Instead they went on a media blitz, a proc-ess that began at the official launch of the 1997–98 season, when Denis Rogers decided to ignore the speech that had been written for him and instead launched into something of a tirade against 'the impostor who only has self-interest at heart and no real emotional attachment to the longstanding traditions of the game'. In this instance, Rogers' 'impostors' were Halbish and Erskine.

Three days later, the board revealed how much money its top 10 players had been paid in 1996–97, a move Rogers later called a 'master-stroke', but one I thought defined exactly why we were having a dispute. In my view it was dishonourable, deceptive and a cheap shot, and displayed a lack of loyalty and respect for the players. As he well knew, this tactic avoided the real issue, which was how much money the board had at its disposal to spend on all its players, not just the elite. Rogers did, however, win the first round of the PR battle by having us perceived as ungrateful millionaires by many in the media and a few recently retired players, who echoed his sentiments. For the next six weeks we were on the defensive while the board enjoyed play-ing the 'innocent party' role, but all the while our resolve was being strengthened and we were uniting as one, ready to fight back.

A meeting scheduled for October 22 lasted around 30 seconds before the board walked out, Malcolm Speed claiming that the ACA's log of claims was 'an attack on the fundamental principle of cricket administration'. Maysie conceded that a strike was now a real possibility. A week later the independent auditors Coopers & Lybrand found that the board was, in words straight out of the accountancy handbook, in a 'sound financial position, with a prudent but not excessive level of resources'. The ACB had liquid assets of $13.2 million and the state associations liquid assets of $8.3 million, which the board maintained was, in their words, a 'rainy day fund' to keep as insurance against a wet summer, a desertion by sponsors and other variables they did not define. The figures also revealed that player payments had increased by 106 per cent in the previous five years, which looked good for them as a one-off statistic but simply reflected the way we'd been shamefully underpaid through the late '80s and early '90s.

On November 3, Tim May sent me a fax, part of which read:

> The ACB are attempting to draw us into a situation outside of the protection of the AWA, and as soon as they do that, they will call an Industrial Dispute and the matter will be adjourned to the Industrial Court, where it would most probably sit for the nest two years before being heard. This process also results in the loss of the Protected Action afforded to our members under the AWA. (ie: should the players strike they would now be in breach of contract.)
>
> If you believe everything that you read in the press, the ACB have now changed their stance on Erskine and want to meet under their agenda ASAP. I understand that I am supposed to be receiving a letter from them sometime today. I will keep you informed.
>
> The whisper around the traps is that they have been getting pressure from interested parties to resolve the issue . . .

A meeting was set down for November 12, which both sides kept secret, a sign that perhaps the petty individual squabbles had finished and the real issues were finally going to be debated. There were now two major hurdles. One, inevitably, was player payments, with the ACB refusing to consider the concept of players' salaries being tied to ACB revenue. No counter-proposal or suggestion of a way to move forward was offered other than the patronising idea that the dilemma could be solved via one-on-one discussions. The second sticking point was SEL's proposal to market the game, which the ACB quickly knocked back outright. They were entitled to reject it and the ACA was happy to withdraw it, but in the battle for public opinion some damage had been done. In the proposal, SEL guaranteed the ACB $305 million over five years in return for the opportunity to market the game. The idea had been to demonstrate just how much money could be made from cricket, but after the proposal was made public many journalists seemed eager to paint Erskine as an infidel out to rape and pillage the game, while no one pressed the board about their future business and marketing plans.

In the days following that meeting, a letter from Speed was sent to all first-class players in which he explained the board's attitude. It ended with this: 'You should also note that the ACB has consistently opposed bringing the relationship between the ACB and the players under the Workplace Relations Act. The ACB's opposition to this was confirmed when at a recent meeting the ACB was advised that the reason the ACA sought to rely on the Workplace Relations Act was so that players could take industrial action without the risk of legal action.' That was the crux of the matter: when it came to player payments, the ACB did not want to negotiate with a trade union.

Tim May sent out an ACA newsletter to all members that ended with a plea: 'All our strength, which is considerable, comes from your united support. This is our assurance that we will win and win well, and you will have played a vital and important role in bringing about a set of conditions for which future generations of cricketers will be eternally grateful . . . Don't let them down, don't let yourselves down. Stay with this, together, and you will win and win well.' Maysie is, without really recognising it, a real motivator of men, and during the ACA–ACB war he kept the potential defectors in check with his vision and air of confidence. I have complete trust and faith in him and, while not understanding every intricacy of the negotiations, was totally committed to seeing a deal done that gave us a fair percentage of revenue and some ownership of our livelihoods, as well as an influence on all matters pertaining to the game.

Attached to the newsletter was a form entitled 'Notice of Intention to take AWA Industrial Action'. Tim needed ACA members to sign and return the forms 'as a clear demonstration of players' joint resolve and the need for the ACB to get serious about a proper negotiation'. The vast majority of players from across the country did so in the lead-up to the second Test against New Zealand, in Perth. The idea was that if we officially threatened to strike by serving the signed forms on the board, it would force them to the negotiating table. The form listed the games for which we'd withdraw our services: four one-day internationals in early December.

Then somebody leaked an 'Intention Form' to the board, who passed it on to the media. And all hell broke loose.

We were actually fielding when news of the leak broke. Twelfth man Andy Bichel ran out onto the field during a break in play on the first day of the Test to say that a form had just been shown on Channel Nine. Off the field, Malcolm Speed quickly revealed to the media that he had invited Tim May and senior players to some 'informal' meetings and was 'very disappointed' that the invitation had been declined. 'The ACB is running out of olive branches,' he said. However, the board knew that such informal discussions would seriously weaken the ACA's position under the Workplace Relations Act; it was as if they were desperately seeking out a point of weakness as the game of chess neared a defining move.

The 'wildcard' through this whole affair was Kerry Packer, owner of the Nine Network. At a meeting of the ACA executive and some senior players held in Sydney in late October, Shane Warne had volunteered to keep Mr Packer's son, James, abreast of developments from the senior players' perspective. We had no doubt, given the 18-year relationship between the ACB and the network, that they were getting plenty of perspective from the board as well.

In the United States, elite sportspeople out of contract are often referred to as 'free agents', able to sign with whatever franchise they choose. There was a free agency clause in the log of claims the ACA had handed to the board in October, and the whispers were out that by asking for that we had plans to break away and play elsewhere. Never ever had we discussed any sort of move in that direction; it was ridiculous. Clause 13, buried deep in the document, was about 'Free Agency' and it clearly referred to the movement of players between Australian states. We were trying to protect the rights of cricketers who couldn't get a game with their own Shield team and wanted to further their career by moving interstate. Such freedom of player movement had the potential to toughen up and even out the domestic first-class competition. Yes, it was true that if we didn't sign our new ACB contracts – and we'd been receiving regular requests to do so – eventually the terms of our last contracts would expire and we'd become free agents of sorts, but the current scenario had only come about because the board had refused to come to the negotiating table. There was no hidden agenda. Free agency should never have become an issue. I remember the term 'free agency' being tossed at us by journalists in the foyer of our hotel in Perth, and Shane and I being out of our depth, confused as to what it actually meant.

On the evening of November 20, the first day of the second Test, Gary Burns, director of sport at Channel Nine, organised to have dinner with the four members of the Test team who also had deals with the network – Warne, Taylor, Healy and myself – to clear the air. Once it was clearly established that we weren't the slightest bit interested in forming a breakaway group or competition, the cloak of doubt that had been shrouding us via misinformation about our motives lifted and attitudes changed immediately. Gary went as far as to allow Shane to go on Nine's telecast the next day with an interview in which he put forward our case. Cricket fans finally understood what we were about. I wonder if the board spun that 'free agency' line out there to save face, because early on, when the publicity battles were going their way, we didn't hear about it at all. For most of the time, their line centred around us being greedy, ungrateful bigheads trying to bankrupt or take over the game.

People have also linked our dinner with Gary Burns to the fact that we didn't go on strike, assuming that Nine told us not to go on strike so we didn't. Quite obviously Gary preferred we didn't, because the one-day internationals rated well and advertising deals were in place, but the truth is that his view didn't influence in any way what happened over the next couple of days.

On the second day of the Test, Friday November 21, there were rain interruptions as we took our score from 1/32 to 4/235, during which time a crucial development took place that turned things around, though not in the way that one of the key participants, Denis Rogers, might have imagined. As the players waited for the weather to improve, Rogers met with Mark Taylor one on one. Tubby had been dismissed late on the first day, so it wasn't as if he was waiting to bat. Rogers, as the chairman, thought his persuasive powers in conjunction with the captain's could settle the dispute like gentlemen. The outcome of their meeting was a proposal that the existing contracts scheme continue and the ACA give up its right to negotiate on behalf of the players, while the ACB would give ground when it came to paying more to Shield cricketers. Tubby said he'd go back to the players and try to break the impasse. Straight after play, the captain explained Rogers' offer during a meeting that went a lot longer than we'd all anticipated. By its end, the mood was somewhat confused but no attempt was made to resolve the issue there and then – not least because we had another get-together scheduled for later that night with James Erskine, who had just arrived in Perth.

Not surprisingly, Erskine didn't back away from the strike option. We players knew it was still an alternative, though as always a last resort that we didn't want to enforce unless we felt absolutely convinced there was nowhere else to go.

For Mark Taylor the situation he found himself in was tricky. He wanted an end to the disruption the dispute had caused and needed a close working relationship with the board, but he also needed to be strong in the players' eyes as a guy who was 100 per cent behind our claims. Of course, he couldn't be all of the above and the somewhat clandestine meeting with Denis Rogers, which had had good intentions attached to it, actually jeopardised the whole process, for we had all been made fully aware by Tim May that individual meetings could lead to a breakdown in our bargaining position. Mark's move may well have been proactive, but it also exposed us as a group and was not entirely met with approval, especially as all previous dialogue between the ACA and the ACB had been planned and known to the members.

That night, a day after the Intention Form had been leaked to the ACB, Warney and I were corralled by the assembled media waiting in the lobby of the Perth Sheraton Hotel. We had just walked from the ACA meeting where we met Erskine and where we had resolved that one part of our plan of action was not talking to the media. This decision was a clear error of judgement and left Shane and me looking like fools as we fobbed off inquiries with 'no comment' until the respected journalist Mike Coward piped up with, 'This is preposterous – you can't just walk away.' He was right. We had nothing to hide. We were two players passionate for the cause, who also wanted a swift, positive outcome, but we had to stay loyal to the ACA hierarchy.

Mark Taylor talked again with Denis Rogers on the Saturday, before another players' meeting was called to talk about the latest board offering. Speed and Rogers were so confident of success that they made plans for a media conference that evening to announce the peace, but they had misread the mood. What they expected to be a short players' meeting, with Mark outlining and then gaining approval for his joint proposal, stretched out to two hours, most of which went monotonously around in circles. Finally, a clear, straightforward comment silenced the gathering when Matthew Elliott said, 'Why are we talking about this? Nothing has changed from the start. If we don't make a stand, nothing *will* change', or words to that effect. He had hit the nail on the head, summing up what we were all thinking before the mumbo-jumbo and gobbledegook had confused the real issues.

Twelve pieces of ripped paper were handed out, with only a 'yes' for strike or 'no' for no strike required. Out of a baggy green, under the watchful gaze of Greg Blewett, came seven straight yeses, at which point, obviously, a verdict had been reached. But Greg was committed to his task and wanted all the votes counted, ending in a final tally of 11 in favour and one against. Tubby seemed genuinely disturbed at being rolled and fearful about what the consequences would be, while the rest of us felt a sense of completion. Enough was enough. We'd been pushed to the limit and had decided to risk it all by striking. We then put in a call to Tim May to tell him of our decision. His concise reply to the news altered the history of Australian cricket. 'Don't strike! The momentum has swung our way and we don't need to do that.'

A collective sigh revealed our relief that the ultimate step didn't have to be taken. However, we were also buoyed by our unity and willingness to sacrifice in order to succeed.

Though the board would continue over the following few months to try to regain the initiative and draw out the process, and while James Erskine never really obtained the influence he had envisaged or proposed, the flight to get a collective agreement was now inevitable. Erskine's five-year deal with the ACA would eventually be terminated early and his partnership with Halbish dissolved, but well before that, as early as during the third Test against New Zealand, in Hobart, the board resolved to meet with the ACA in Sydney in the first week of December. The progress out of that meeting was positive, but over the next six months some of the delaying tactics used by the board almost beggared belief, with the dented pride and damaged egos of a few probably stalling the work of other ACB members who'd finally recognised that the ACA and the ACB needed to work together to benefit the game.

For a while in February, rumours of a player boycott for the upcoming Indian tour surfaced, but it was never a possibility in our eyes. Gradually, after such a difficult first year, we came to realise that Malcolm Speed was approachable, honest and tough, a guy who should be respected. Once our agreement was in place, we knew where we stood. In the seasons that followed, an arrangement was established whereby the ACA and ACB would meet once a month to talk through issues – a means of communication previously unheard-of in Australian cricket and a major breakthrough. The players now had a voice that was not only heard but influential, one that led to genuine dialogue between players and officials. ACB staff and members were made welcome in the change rooms and became involved in things like leadership courses with us; generally, the relationship became that of two teams working together rather than being diametrically opposed.

It was in March 1998, eight months after that defining meeting in the steamy Kent hotel room, that we finally signed our new contracts. However, it wasn't until September 15 that the ACB and ACA were able to finally sign off on the first-ever collective agreement, to be known as the 1999 Memorandum of Understanding. Two features of the historic agreement were that the ACB would now contribute $250 000 annually to keep the ACA afloat and an extra $300 000 was made available to players from the state squads. The top players did take a pay cut, but that was money well spent and, with cricketers' incomes now tied to an agreed percentage of the board's revenues, we knew we'd be better off in the long run.

The harder we worked and the more professional the board became, the more the benefits would flow. From 1997 to 2002, the player payment pool would increase from $9.5 million to $22 million. And, we presumed, the huge upward graph in revenue would more than cover the eternal concern of that troublesome 'rainy day'.

29

The challenge of the unknown

'Do you think we need a change of one-day captain?'

The words stunned me with their simplicity and importance. Malcolm Speed had just laid the cards straight out on the table. It was a trait I admired and in Malcolm's case one I would eventually come to respect as we communicated more often in the seasons that followed the ACA–ACB dispute.

My instantaneous reaction was to say, 'You know the answer to that. Why do you want me to say it?'

Malcolm countered by saying, 'We just want to make sure we're going in the right direction.'

With the formalities out of the road, I said, 'Yes, the one-day team is stale and we need to change things around.'

'Good, that's what we thought. That's the feedback we've been getting.'

Really, it was hardly earth-shattering information. Blind Freddy would have known there was a problem, as we had won only one of the last six one-day series we'd contested, been victorious in only four of the 17 limited-overs internationals that Mark Taylor had led us in since the 1996 World Cup, and fallen to seventh in the world rankings. We were flat and uninspired, and a perception had crept in that we weren't as committed to excellence in one-dayers as we were in Test matches. In truth, Tubs would readily admit that Test cricket was where it was at for him, that the one-day game sat below Tests on his list of priorities. This preference had unintentionally created a crumbling at the edges of the team's respect for the shorter game, and was partly to blame for our demise.

Around a month after that conversation with Malcolm, in late November 1997 during the Hobart Test against New Zealand, I received the news from the chairman of selectors, Trevor Hohns, that I was the new one-day captain. Hohns also informed me of the selection panel's desire to pick, for the first time, a specialist one-day team; in effect, to create separate Test and one-day squads. My first priority was to ask that we assemble the best possible fielding side for the one-day team, as I felt this was a crucial facet to dominate in and would win us many games.

The move to separate teams was one I applauded, but one that also caused me instant grief when, during the Test, I found out that my great mate Ian Healy had been axed from the new-look outfit. I wasn't obligated to do so, but I believed it was the right thing for me to tell Heals of his omission face to face, for him to receive the bad news from a mate who cared about him rather than from a member of the selection panel that had just terminated his one-day career. Knocking on his door and sounding the death knell of half his career put my heart rate into overdrive, and I could feel my airways constricting with each second of waiting as I contemplated how I was going to break the news. I knew he'd be devastated, shocked and angry. The moment we made eye contact, he knew bad news was on the agenda.

In Heals' autobiography, he remembers our time in his hotel room this way:

> I remember staring blankly straight ahead at the TV and muttering something like, 'If I'd known averages meant something in this one-day game, imagine the number of times I'd have been not out in my career.'
>
> I got up and grabbed the remote while Stephen sat on the couch. There was a long, huge silence, which he finally broke, saying that he knew how disappointed I must have been. I think he did, too. We talked for a little while, and then he left. I was shattered . . .

I left Heals' hotel-room totally gutted, experiencing a grief associated with separation. I felt our relationship had changed in those torturous two minutes of strained conversation. Confrontation is something I have never sought or been comfortable with, and although this wasn't an argument it gave me a very real snapshot of what leadership is all about: being up front, communicative and honest in what you are saying and doing. While I had been affected by the process, I tried to imagine how Ian felt sitting in his dimly lit room with his room-service dinner half eaten, making calls to his family, telling them of the change in direction his life had suddenly taken.

The separate teams and captains was a totally new concept. I had gained while Mark Taylor had lost, and he struggled to see the sense in splitting up the highest-profile position in Australian sport. At the time I thought it was a move that would work and that the transition would be a smooth one, particularly as there were a few new young guys, like Ian Harvey and Adam Gilchrist, in the one-day squad whose enthusiasm levels would be exaggerated. I was excited at the challenge of the unknown that lay ahead. Mark, on the other hand, had seen his power base halved, future contracts potentially reduced (the board did give players hurt by the new selection policy a bonus payment the following year when everyone adjusted to the new criteria for contracts) and a sense of belonging lost because he would now be coming in and out of the Australian squad. It was totally understandable that he didn't approve of the split, and I was utterly prepared to give him leeway when he aired his views and thoughts. The only time we had any sort of conflict was at the conclusion of the 1998 Test series in India, when Mark rather forcefully put his views forward. Heading home with Heals and a few other Test specialists, Tubby posed a series of rhetorical questions to the media: 'Do we still believe in leadership and the captaincy of Australian cricket, or do we just pick 11 blokes who we think are going to be the best and change them for the next game, and the next? We have to look at the set-up of Australian cricket. I don't think this is a settling process, having two different teams and two different captains.'

To me, those comments devalued what the one-day team was now about and also, to a lesser extent, it was an affront to my captaincy. I also saw them as a plea to unify the teams again, which I couldn't quite understand considering that Tubs and I had a very strong relationship and the separate teams were running smoothly. Even though we lost the series in India, the Test team continued to be a major force while the one-day team was busy building the base for future successes.

★

I'll never forget the first team meeting I held with the one-day team. It was conducted within the hallowed walls of the SCG home change room. Manager Ian McDonald went through the formalities of welcoming the squad and distributing the itinerary and meal allowances for the days ahead before handing over to me. Wanting to make it an intimate affair, I sat atop my 'coffin' (kitbag) surrounded by the guys seated on chairs or spread along the steps that separated the two tiers of the room. In my mind I was very clear about what I wanted and how we were going to do it, but still my nerves had me tied up in knots as I worried about not presenting my ideas succinctly or authoritatively enough.

My ambition was for the team to be a tight unit, with its members always supportive of each other and able to enjoy their personal successes and also that of others and the team. I wanted a strong sense of pride in playing one-day cricket for Australia to develop, which required hard work and a long-term goal. Our aims, I explained, would be to hold the World Cup aloft in 1999 and, before and after that, to consistently be the best side in the game.

To achieve this, I went through a 10-point (subsequently 12) blueprint for success:

1. Stay a strong unit, and enjoy each other's success
2. Play each game as if it's the most important of your career
3. Don't hesitate – always back yourself
4. Never believe the game is lost
5. Aim to be man of the match every time you play
6. Improvise – think on your feet
7. Learn something from every match
8. Do the little things right and the big picture will fall into place (for example: training, talk on the field, backing up the stumps, calling correctly)
9. Enjoy the fact that you're representing your country – have pride

10. The best fielding side nearly always wins
11. Know your own game and what your role is
12. Have fun – have a laugh

On paper these mantras sounded great, and they seemed to strike the right chord with the guys. However, when it came to getting amongst the real stuff on the field, plans are only a guide and on their own don't necessarily translate into victories. My first home season as a one-day captain, against New Zealand and South Africa, wasn't the honeymoon period I'd been looking for; in fact, it almost ended in an early divorce.

While we accounted for New Zealand three times out of four, we lost all our qualifying matches and the first final against South Africa, and my own form was dismal. Six single-figure scores, including three ducks, had me doubting whether I was the man for the job. It was after a crushing loss in Perth that I sat opposite Trevor Hohns in the home team's viewing area and bared my soul. 'If you think I'm not the right guy for the job,' I said, 'then I'm happy to walk away.'

I was searching for affirmation that the selectors had faith in me and that they believed I could and would turn things around. Thankfully, Trevor told me what I wanted to hear and the weight lifted.

A combination of factors had contributed to my self-doubt, mostly stemming from my very limited experience as a captain. My time as the Panania Primary School skipper didn't necessarily translate into a watertight guarantee that I would waltz around and blitz it in the top job. Instead, I succumbed to the first pitfall that many a captain can't seem to avoid – captaincy by consensus. I wanted to please everyone, hoping this would result in team harmony and each player thinking, *Jeez, this guy's great – he's giving me a fair go.* Further, I found it hard to discipline guys I was used to joking around with, good mates who were not used to me being the guy in charge. At the same time, on a personal level I barely knew many of the new players. Ian Harvey was about to make his one-day debut, while Michael Di Venuto, Adam Dale and Andy Bichel were in their first year of international cricket, and even Adam Gilchrist, who had been in the NSW Shield squad in the early '90s and on segments of tours to India, South Africa and England, was something of an unknown quantity to me. These blokes didn't know or hardly knew me, and I had no idea what made them tick. In some ways I adopted a 'suck it and see' approach that required time and patience, but in the results-orientated world we live in, crushing losses and disastrous form had my head fairly and squarely on the chopping block.

After a particularly poor team effort against New Zealand in Melbourne, former Test vice-captain turned commentator Keith Stackpole described me as the worst Australian captain he'd seen. Among his comments was a line that went something like: 'It looks like there are captains everywhere, with no one in charge.' In doing this, Stackpole emphasised to me how important body language is. I could see where he was coming from, because a couple of senior players, in their quest to help me out, had started signalling field changes in a manner that from afar must have looked like a recipe for disharmony and chaos. All that was needed was leadership, which was exactly what I had been chosen for. I rang Stackpole to discuss his views, and afterwards my spirits were galvanised and the captain born. It was a conversation that started with our defensive mechanisms firmly in place, but it ended amicably after we realised that perhaps we'd both overreacted.

Consensus captaincy was out and in came gut feel and intuition. This began with the promotion to opening bat of Adam Gilchrist, taking over from Tom Moody, for the first one-day final. The idea came like a bolt of lightning as I contemplated my second spoonful of vanilla ice-cream with strawberry topping during the break between innings. I felt we needed a spark to get our innings going and just said,

'Moods, I think Gilly should open instead of you, so we can get off to a flyer.'

Being the ultimate teammate, he replied, 'Yeah, sure, that sounds like a great idea.'

With that, it was over to Gilly. 'I want you to open the batting,' I told him. 'Just go out there and play your way, and have fun.'

While we didn't win that game, we did win the next two finals and the series, with a more relaxed leader finding some touch with a couple of half-centuries. Not only did I begin to lead my way, the group responded, and the bond we would later rely on started to form.

On a personal level, my home Test season was enormously frustrating. Falling a boundary short of a hundred twice in three Tests led to many a restless night's sleep and a complex I would have to confront next time I got into the 'nervous 90s'. I had made it an issue, no matter how many times I told myself it wasn't, and needed to find a method to get me through next time. The answer was, as it normally is, very simple: keep on playing exactly the same way and forget about the scoreboard.

The only century I managed was my 100th Test match, against South Africa in Sydney, 12 years after my debut as a mullet-haired, pimple-faced, pretzel-framed fibro boy. Longevity in sport equates to resilience, enjoyment of what you're doing, an attitude that you believe in and portray, and a group of selectors who like your style. It takes character to survive for any length of time, because inevitably failure is a travelling partner and the incubator for self-doubt, and the will to bounce back must be roused again and again. It's a constant battle, but one that has enormous rewards. The desire to fulfil my potential always drove me in the quest to improve. As soon as you become complacent and settled, any dormant potential is extinguished and someone keener will pass you by.

The occasion was marked with the customary plaudits, but also with a brickbat wielded with such force that in my mind it took precedence over all else. It was a story by the well-known journalist Paul Sheehan that tried to disgrace and discredit the Australian team and a number of individuals, including me. If we'd had more spare time following its publication, the matter would have ended up in court. Among other things, he accused me of verbally abusing a young first-grade opponent who apparently worshipped me – an allegation later denied 100 per cent by the club concerned, to the point that they were willing to go to court to support me. Worse still was the disgusting charge that as a team we had tormented New Zealand's Chris Cairns during a game by whispering, 'Choo-choo choo-choo-choo-choo' when he came the crease not longer after his sister's tragic death in a train accident near Christchurch. Chris, like us, was repulsed by this claim and rejected the story outright. It left a sour taste in everyone's mouth. The dilemma we faced as players was that we could make an issue out of the story and take legal action, which would attract massive media attention, or just leave it and have people assume it was true. In the end, we received legal advice saying we'd win any action hands down, but that ideally the writ would need to be served by the captain. He declined because, like the rest of us, he was still involved in the ACA–ACB dispute. What an A-grade goose Sheehan was – we should have cooked him!

Allan Donald ensured my 100th Test was a match to remember by giving me another searching examination and repetitively homing in on the area between waist and chin, intermingled with the occasional forehead-seeking express-paced delivery. In the end he wore me down with the barrage, as I played from the crease in expectation of another short one only to be beaten for pace and hear that ugly timber rattle, followed by the disappointed oohs and arghs from a parochial crowd.

Stupid as it may seem, I took a hint of solace in the pathetic fact that I'd fallen five short of my nemesis, the cursed 90s. But essentially I'd let a chance to mark a celebration slip by because too many thoughts had been occupying my mind.

The following day, Shane Warne's 300th Test wicket came as most things do in his life, with fanfare and a superb piece of timing. The delivery that penetrated the technically brilliant Jacques Kallis was pure artistry. Going around the wicket late in the day, with shadows creeping annoyingly across the pitch and seeping into the batsmen's line of vision, Shane tossed up an enticingly flighted delivery with enough loop to attract the batsman's instincts to attack but subtly infused with enough pace through the air to warrant caution. Adding to the confusion was the fact that the ball was his very sparsely bowled wrong 'un, which snuck between bat and pad like a kid would slip past a teacher on canteen-queue duty. The sight of a bemused Kallis minus his bails, and an exultant bowler with arms aloft, leaning backwards as the boys raced in to smother him, was Warney at his theatrical best. The guy is a genius, the Kasparov of cricket, always thinking one step ahead.

'Dramatic' was the best way to describe the last afternoon of a titanic battle in the third Test against the Africans, at Adelaide, when Mark Waugh stood between a series win for us and a courageous drawn series for our visitors. Like all controversies, there were two versions of what happened and what should have been the outcome, but because the incident was so bizarre, the only solution that could be reached was to agree to disagree.

After being struck on the arm, Mark swished at the air, apparently in annoyance, only to clip the top of the stumps with his bat and dislodge the bails. It was either a form of hit-wicket, even though he wasn't attempting a shot, or, as Mark would later claim, a result of dead arm from the impact that made him lose control of his actions. Either way, he didn't knock the bails off in the process of playing a shot, and consequently the umpires ruled that it was as if it was a dead ball and the 'hit-wicket' occurred outside the time when play was live. The South Africans were livid, and Hansie Cronje expressed his opinion by putting a hole through the umpire's dressing-room door with one of the match stumps on his way to their dressing-room. I could understand his frustration, but if they were honest in their assessment they should have pointed the finger fair and square at the dropped catches that had kept us in the game.

It was a shame the tour ended on such a sour note, because the teams had enjoyed each other's company on and off the field. Shane Warne and Jonty Rhodes, for example, developed a lifelong friendship, proving that opposites in many ways can connect. The two appreciated each other's qualities and traits, and both were superstars in their own right. Sharing a beer at the end of a series is important, as it is sometimes the only chance international cricketers get to see their opponents as human beings. More often then not, we'd hit it off as we all share the same concerns, doubts and, quite often, interests.

Three weeks after that Adelaide Test we were in Mumbai for the first game of a tour of India. This series was seen by the Australian team as one where we could assess our evolution and at the same time cement our spot on top of the world in regards to Test cricket. After that, a one-day tournament, which would also involve Zimbabwe, would give us a real guide to our chances for the upcoming World Cup. We were without the injured Glenn McGrath and Jason Gillespie and had gambled on a not fully functioning Shane Warne, who was fighting a bung shoulder. So the task ahead was formidable, and when news reached us before the first Test that Sachin Tendulkar had been preparing for weeks in his desire to dominate Shane, our antennae tuned in.

Sachin had apparently directed a curator to prepare a turning practice wicket, which he then scuffed out with his spikes to loosen pieces of pitch and dirt on a line and length a leg-spinner would land his deliveries on. Then he asked a group of young leggies to aim at the rough. By the time the first Test arrived he was primed, while we had lost the tour game before the Test and were struggling for form.

Making his Test debut for Australia in Chennai was my great friend (and soulmate in many ways) Gavin Robertson. Robbo, Mark and I went back to the Under 10 days, had been on countless schoolboy tours and had been regular picks for representative under-age sides. Gav was a guy who had the big raps on him as a youngster, the 'gun' batter for whom, when he walked into the nets, everyone dropped everything to watch his all-encompassing stroke-making and elegant style, which we all wished we could emulate. Maybe Gav had had enough of the pretty-boy look and rebelled, because by the time he wore the baggy green cap, Cinderella had well and truly become an ugly sister. He once had the classic textbook technique, but it somehow metamorphosed into a batting stance that resembled a badly constipated individual with a 'headless chook' approach.

This was his second tour with the Australian team, having been with us in Sri Lanka and Pakistan in 1994 when he didn't play in a Test, and it was fantastic to have him around because he and I shared a love of getting out there and meeting the people on the streets. We enjoyed taking photographs and possessed a mischievous, rebellious streak that we coaxed out of each other. At the conclusion of our first team meeting, managers Steve Bernard and Cam Battersby informed us that no one was to leave the hotel without security and advised us to stay in the confines of the hotel unless we went out in a large supervised group. Like many rules, this order only signalled a window of opportunity. Gav and I looked at each other and said, 'Meet you downstairs in five.'

As we walked the back streets, we marvelled at the diversity – the barber plying his trade under a roadside tree, skilfully manoeuvring his cut-throat razor with blinding pace and precision. We watched the street hawker sell to tourists his giant balloons that, incidentally, don't blow up when you try to inflate them (I know – I bought four packets), and experienced the anguish of seeing a beggar with pus-oozing wounds, arms outstretched, desperately hoping for a tattered, grimy rupee note. We followed the path of a group of giggling schoolgirls crammed in the back of a tut-tut, ribbons in their hair, as they headed off for a day at school. The streets were alive and gave us a real spring in the step and, for me, a genuine inspiration to get stuck in and have a go. It was a huge reality check seeing the young man earning a livelihood cleaning debris and skin out of people's ears, or to watch a taxi driver battle his adversaries for the attention of potential customers, in between spitting a stream of red betel juice out the window of his dilapidated 1950s Ambassador car onto the pavement below, staining it forever.

For me and everyone I knew back home, having a bad day at the office would be infinitely better than the greatest day of ear-picking that poor guy would ever have. Seeing the real India and experiencing the vibe on the street confirmed to me that we should all make the most of our opportunities, because many, sadly, don't have that luxury. I'd like to think Gav and I played a small part in broadening the culture of the Australian team by moving away from the confines of five-star luxury. Touring life gave me a chance to extend my horizons and grow as a person; it also had the ability to stunt a man's personal growth if the sheltered, artificial lifestyle dictated his every move.

Robbo must have been inspired by what he saw, because he took 4/72 and contributed 57 batting at No. 10, a startling performance considering he had only played one first-class match in the previous three years. Test cricket can do that to people. Some newcomers go in thinking they have nothing to lose, but just as regularly the latest 'wonderkid' can be swamped by exaggerated expectations. One thing for sure was that we witnessed a phenomenal batting display from Tendulkar, who smashed 155 not out in India's second innings despite having plenty of pressure riding on him. The match was evenly poised when he arrived at the crease, and he'd failed in the first innings. Just under five hours later, we'd been privileged to have a free, up-close-and-personal lesson in how to pulverise an attack on a turning wicket and make it look like you were playing a knock against your brothers in the backyard. We kept on waiting for the mistake to come, especially as he was breaking the golden rule that says you never hit against the spin out of the rough, especially if you're taking the aerial route. And he was doing so against, of all bowlers, the greatest-ever leg-spinner! Sachin had a willing ally in the turbaned Navjot Sidhu, the cleanest and most consistent hitter of sixes against spinners I ever saw. Sidhu used to literally throw himself into the shot with such force that he finished in a front-on position rather than the conventional side-on.

When these two got on a roll it was absolute pandemonium, with whistles, catcalls, clanging bottles and plastic horns making a non-stop cacophony that devoured us like a mini-tornado. In such a situation everything goes into fast motion, with bowlers straying from game plans in their desire to shut the crowd up, but the resultant loose deliveries only add further impetus to the wave of euphoria. At the same time the batsmen become bulletproof, as if they've signed an indemnity form against getting out. A cool head is needed in this scenario, but with such an inexperienced attack we stood back and 'enjoyed' the dazzling shot-making rather than slowing the momentum.

On day five we crumbled in unison with the pitch and a delirious umpire. George Sharp, of English origin and used to infinitely milder conditions, fell ill during the match and the effects of this ailment, combined with the fact that he had to stand in the sun for 30-plus hours ridiculously wearing a tie to satisfy protocol, meant he was so knackered by the end of the Test that decision-making was almost beyond his capabilities. Who could blame him? We players were making elementary mistakes, so it was only natural that he, too, was susceptible.

In the second Test in Calcutta, we were never in the hunt, losing two wickets in the first over of the Test – Michael Slater and Greg Blewett were consigned to history as only the second pair to achieve this dubious distinction. From that moment we were limp, and for one of the very few occasions in my career I sensed we didn't have the will to tough it out. One sight really got my blood racing and that came on the fourth day when, from out on the field, I saw some of our players showered and changed into their civvies as if the game was already gone. I lost my temper, furious that we had given up hope at a time when I was batting on with a torn groin and the end of the day was near. I figured that if we could make it through to stumps, then maybe a natural or man-made calamity might keep us in the series. Maybe I was overreacting, but I can't stand people in sport not believing and not battling on until the very end. Character very often reveals itself in adversity, and I have no time for shirkers or disbelievers. I'm positive our guys weren't that, and perhaps the frustration of butchering a hundred in the first dig – when I'd been on a roll before tearing a muscle, and then got myself out batting with a runner – had me agitated.

I made my feelings known at our 'wrap-up' meeting after the Test, delivering my opinion amid dead silence and with a look of disbelief appearing on a few faces at my uncharacteristic outpouring. I needed to get it off my chest. However, barely a week later the roles would be reversed due to a communication breakdown and a poor judgement call on my behalf. During the third Test, in Bangalore, where Mark Waugh achieved his highest Test score despite fighting a bout of food poisoning, I was asked by David Hookes to do his commentary team a favour. As I was out of the Test because of the groin injury and thus relatively ideal, they wanted me to take a helicopter ride during play, to hover over the ground and conduct an interview about the game. Initially I didn't see any harm in the idea, and asked Cam Battersby for permission to take the chopper ride during the lunch break. He had no problem, so after congratulating Michael Kasprowicz on his gutsy five-for, which had put us in a winning position, I headed off for the supposedly quick car ride to the chopper. However, after two minutes I had that sickening sensation in the gut, and my worst fears were realised when the driver informed me that it was a 45-minute trip to the heliport.

For the next two hours my mind was consumed with the thought, *How could I let this happen? This is exactly what I nailed the boys for just last week!* Sure enough, when I finally returned during the tea interval I got the silent treatment. The lesson was well digested, especially after the lads emptied my wallet at the next team's fines meeting. The issue for me wasn't about doing the wrong thing, because technically I hadn't: it was about consistency. I vowed never again to let myself be taken advantage of by a media interest during the course of the match, or, for that matter, after play.

After we won this dead-rubber Test we all knew what it was like to be a Pommie cricketer. It was a heartening victory, but not as satisfying as doing the job in the heat of a 'live' battle. It was definitely a character-revealing win, achieved in terribly hot conditions and after Tendulkar scored another big hundred in India's first innings, but in all seriousness we hadn't got close when it counted and deep down that irked us all.

The one-day players arrived in India during this Test, and for the first time we had the overflow of limited-overs 'specialists' holed up in the same hotel and at times sharing the dressing-room with the Test team. Having so many people around was awkward and not conducive to concentration. For seasoned professionals like Ian Healy and Mark

Taylor, the situation must have exacerbated their sense of rejection and their embarrassment at not being considered good enough to play one-day cricket (though in time this line of selection would become the norm and not the exception). That the boys could rise above all this to win the Test, with Tubby making an unbeaten hundred on the final day, spoke volumes for their pride and determination.

The triangular limited-overs series represented a growth period for the one-day team that culminated in a courageous win against the hosts in the final, in Delhi. Just as it appeared we were certainties for victory in that game, news filtered through that the promised prize money had been withdrawn for no apparent reason other than the obvious – that we were about to collect the cheque. A cheap-and-nasty trophy is probably still residing in the cold, dimly lit change room in Delhi, but the fact was that we had bonded as a unit during the tournament; the climb to our Everest, the 1999 World Cup, was under way. Geoff Marsh had actually drawn a mountain peak on a sheet of butcher's paper, placing 'base camps' along the way. This was what we later came to call the 'pyramid of success'. The first camp was a win over South Africa in Australia; the next was the series in New Zealand in February, which we'd squared 2–2; and now this one. The ascent was on, with our ultimate goal being to peak at Lord's in June '99.

My leadership was evolving with each game and I found that players not only needed but wanted discipline and direction. For example, a game against Zimbabwe in Ahmedabad was one we should have won easily, but we got ourselves into a difficult situation through sloppy, uninspiring, unprofessional play and only woke up when it was nearly too late to retrieve it. Instead of a round of backslapping and congratulatory handshakes after the win, I launched into a tirade that ended with the line: 'Show me you want me to be captain, or let's get another one.'

My frankness must have struck the right note, because we promptly went on a winning run of six straight games, having lost four of the previous five. Even though we lost the final of the Sharjah Cup, which followed the matches in India, standards had been established and now everyone knew what was expected. The sounding-out and getting-to-know-one-another periods were over, while the job of man-managing each of my players was taking shape.

In the Dubai desert, Tendulkar overcame, among other things, a delay in play due to a sandstorm to create back-to-back masterpieces and steer his team to tournament victory. In doing so, he earnt an extra bonus from the Indian Cricket Board, who obviously had surplus funds after dudding us 10 days before. Being the captain and knowing the guys felt ripped off, I fronted Raj Singh, as he was India's top board man there. 'So you guys *have* got prize money – it just depends on who wins as to whether or not the winners get it.' Unfortunately my satisfaction at stepping up to the plate for the boys was tempered when I was asked by ACB chairman Denis Rogers to please explain why I had burnt the bridges between India and Australia that had taken 12 years to mend. A letter of apology was hastily sent off and a lesson digested – that anything I did as captain would have consequences. But I still knew that the right thing to do is to always back the players if you believe in the cause, and stand for something or else fall for everything.

30

Udayan

On the 1998 tour the City of Joy, Calcutta, certainly didn't live up to its billing for us from a cricket point of view. However, it became a catalyst for my involvement in charity work, a development that was very much a turn of fate. A letter pushed under my door on the evening after we had been beaten by a large and convincing margin ensured that my life would never be the same again.

The anguish of defeat, especially if you have failed individually, is heightened when you walk back into your hotel room afterwards and contemplate the outcome with only your thoughts as company. So after four days of complete annihilation at the hands of a marauding Indian outfit in the second Test, at Eden Gardens, I wasn't really looking forward to the night ahead as I wearily entered my 'portable' home that had bags strewn all over the place and clothes spread in all directions cloaking the predictable basic furniture and appliances. Such organised chaos had become something of a trademark of mine, though I knew where everything was because it was always visible. On the carpet sat the letter. I thought it would most likely be either from an autograph seeker or a request for a donation, or even someone asking me to sponsor a family to Australia, but instead I was immediately touched by its contents and legitimacy, and felt compelled to reply.

Hours earlier, Shamlu Dudeja, the chair of the Calcutta Foundation, had been sitting in a hospital ward attending to her critically ill husband. On the television set, the Indian side was dominating Australia but Shamlu's husband's favourite player was hanging in despite a groin injury that had rendered him incapable of extending himself beyond the bare necessities of survival. Shamlu herself was immersed in an article that had appeared in the local *Telegraph* newspaper about one of the Aussie players who had expressed an interest in helping underprivileged children. It was then that she sensed fate was telling her something and consequently penned a letter inviting me to go out and have a look at Udayan, a rehabilitation home for children whose parents suffer from leprosy.

At the time, 250 boys were being looked after at Udayan, but no girls. Because they were seen as future breadwinners, boys were being given preference. The Calcutta Foundation wanted to build a girls' wing to complement the present intake, but just as the project was about to go ahead, the required funds had failed to materialise. Now they needed to think laterally, and this was where I came into the picture. Shamlu hoped I'd be prepared to give the project some profile and commit to some fundraising activities. The day after I read her letter, on what would normally have been the fifth day of the Test but was now a free day for me, she and I drove for an hour behind a police escort vehicle that looked like it had come straight out of a Dick Tracy cartoon to the village of Barrackpore, which is located on the outskirts of the metropolis. Udayan itself was peaceful, with open spaces, well-planned buildings, surrounding rural villages and a harmonious ambience that infiltrated all who were housed there. The children were playful, mild-mannered and appreciative of their environment, with a variety of learning opportunities presented to them each day, from violin lessons to tending the chickens and goats to studying on the Internet.

Udayan was an initiative of the Reverend James Stevens, who had come to India as a volunteer after reading an article at home in England about a French social organisation called Brothers to All Men, which served the poor, sick and uncared-for around the world. Years later, on March 25, 1970, he had borrowed an old Volkswagen van from Mother Teresa and gone off and picked up 11 children from the Pilkhana slum made famous by Dominique Lapierre's book *The City of Joy*. Rev. Stevens had to convince the parents of the girls that he wasn't kidnapping their children or converting them to Christianity but rather giving them a chance to have an opportunity at life. Such was and still is the stigma attached to leprosy that if one person suffers from the disease, his or her entire family is ostracised from the community and shunned from socialising, which leads to the children receiving no schooling and the family having no opportunity to earn a livelihood by normal means.

I needed to see the other side, and requested a trip to where these kids had come from so I could get a true indication of how valuable the project was. I'm not exactly sure what my expectations were, having only ever heard jokes about lepers and seen them in movies. Like most people, I was naive and ignorant of the fact that 14 million people worldwide, including four million Indians, suffer from this affliction. It is caused by bacteria, is one of the least infectious of all diseases and is curable with multi-drug therapy, and 95 per cent of people develop a natural resistance to it. But if you have it, life is pure misery, with nothing to look forward to except an existence full of pain in every sense.

I was escorted down a zigzagging corridor that was flanked on either side by ramshackle structures on the brink of collapse, and an easement containing vile green fluids trickling reluctantly off to I don't know where. These actually masked accommodation that ran parallel to numerous railway tracks, home to various animals oblivious to the squalor and transient locals who wandered aimlessly. We turned sharp left, as if to lose our inevitable tailgaters, into a black hole of depression, a place that looked like the marrow of life had been sucked out of it. Then we stopped at a quadrangle of concrete pathways that acted as both a play area for the free-spirited kids and a meeting place for their elders. What caught my eye most were the huts, which were made of a hotch-potch of black plastic, rusted corrugated tin and broken bricks, with rocks on top that were heavy enough to ensure the structures survived during the monsoon season. Inside, the 'living spaces' were eerily dark, with a suffocating staleness of musty air that didn't encourage breathing but rather forced it upon you. Material possessions amounted to a couple of pots and pans and a shared mattress for sleeping, while running water and electricity were a fanciful notion. This was the most basic means of living I had ever seen, with minimal hygiene, limited stimuli and no real hope of escape. The people who lived there were trapped due to no fault of their own, but by the circumstances into which they'd been born.

Through an interpreter, I asked a mother of three whose hands and feet had been ravaged by the disease and whose exposed weeping wounds symbolised her 30 years of misery as a pariah of society, 'What do you look forward to in life?'

The startling answer perfectly summed up her tormented soul: 'Nothing.'

Another mother came out from inside the hovel and, once she knew we were there to help, got out a comb and began to show us how she could tend to her daughter's long hair even though her missing fingers left her with only mitts to manage the task. Another began knitting in the close vicinity. Small things to us are major achievements for someone who has so little to hope for. The pride on that mother's face was unforgettable.

The children had obviously been hardened by their circumstances, but they still retained the vibrancy of youth without having the innocence that was appropriate for their ages. This was understandable, as many were already the only member of their families bringing in any income. Begging was the art they'd learnt, and they'd been practising it from as early as they could entice money out of others. I was horrified to learn that girls as young as seven or eight had to resort to selling themselves as a way of supporting their families. It was this knowledge that left me feeling I had no alternative but to help in any way I could. Magnifying this horrendous situation for me was the fact that my daughter Rosalie was only 18 months old; I struggled to comprehend the notion that kids had to endure this type of existence. Right there and then, I said to Shamlu, 'Let's do something for the girls. We've got to give them the same opportunities as the boys.'

It didn't take long for the locals to find out what was going on. The day after my first visit, a picture appeared in a prominent local paper featuring me in among a group of leprosy sufferers. This was basically taboo and pricked a lot of consciences as to what was happening in their own backyard. The project already had a life of its own and I knew it was a lifetime task I wanted to be a part of. I saw my role as being the vehicle through which funds could more readily be accessed through sponsors, donations, fundraising evenings and personal endorsements, and to strive to increase awareness of the magnificent work of Rev. Stevens.

With land available at Udayan, the task was to raise enough money to establish infrastructure so there could be an initial intake of girls. This was partially achieved through a dinner and memorabilia auction, which was supported by many of the Aussie team. It's amazing what you will do if you believe in a cause, and somehow I found myself singing 'New York, New York' on the night in front of 200 stunned onlookers. I should have charged them *not* to listen.

The original concept of asking people to sponsor a child at Udayan has since been abandoned, because it was found that the money was better utilised in a communal way, and the dejection a child felt if she wasn't sponsored while others were was in conflict with what the place is all about. Initially, however, I did sponsor a young girl called Lakhi Kumari, and have since watched her grow from being crippled physically and emotionally through polio and from being born to parents who have leprosy into a contented young teenage girl who now participates in dance, has learnt to play musical instruments and does well at school. She didn't smile for her first six months at Udayan, but now revels in being in the middle of 80 or more other girls from similar backgrounds at Nivedita House, the wing built for them. I felt an immediate connection to Lakhi from the first time I was told about her, as my grandmother Ella May Waugh, who is still alive today, was struck down with polio at 19.

I'm continually amazed at the goodness of the human spirit and the desire most people have to help those less fortunate than themselves. After seeing a special that Channel Nine's *A Current Affair* did on

Udayan, a generous Sydney couple took it upon themselves to find 300 sponsors to pay for 300 beds and pillows and some play equipment for the kids. When the fold-up beds arrived, the excitement was at fever pitch, for none of the children had ever slept in a bed, let alone owned one. Over the last seven years, medical students have travelled from Australia at their own expense to help out, medicines have been donated thanks to OPAL (Overseas Pharmaceutical Aid for Life), schools have raised money to buy books and toys, and one woman in a nursing home has donated her life savings to the girls at Nivedita House.

For me, Udayan has been an enriching experience that continues to develop today. When I visit I see lives irrevocably changed for the better, past students returning to volunteer their services, gracious kids enjoying proper meals for the first times in their lives and children regaining their innocence as they play the way they have a right to do. It uplifts and inspires me to see the goodness of the human spirit and the way it can come back to life with a little bit of encouragement.

To have parents swathed in bandages come out of their slum dwellings and push their girls towards me or the workers of Udayan, begging us to take them, is heart-wrenching but immensely satisfying. It means they have faith in the rehabilitation centre and know that it is a chance for their kids to break free from poverty and enter a society that would otherwise shun them. Rev. James Stevens is a rare man indeed, capable of giving love to everyone and making sure each child believes they are special while also ensuring that the most crucial link – that of the child to the parents and vice versa – is not only maintained but strengthened. For a slum-dwelling child, education is a wonderful gift because it enables them to realise the dream of a better life, fills their parents with a sense of pride and provides much-needed self-esteem. The children visit home on weekends and holidays, with the parents often saving for months to celebrate the homecoming with a nice meal and gifts. Because of one man's vision and courage, their world is a better place – and I, for one, am thankful our paths have crossed.

Each time I walk through the gates of Udayan I feel a sense of belonging that has helped shaped me into the person I am today and given direction to where I'm heading. I'm forever grateful that we lost that Test back in 1998 – not because of losing, but because we did it with a day to spare.

31

Anything is possible

The very instant I got wind that cricket was to be played at the 1998 Commonwealth Games in Kuala Lumpur, I knew we had to send our top team and not the A team that was being proposed. The chance to mix with some of the elite of the sporting world in an environment ripe for learning, not to mention the chance to watch the action live and be part of a 439-member Australian team, was in my eyes the opportunity of a lifetime. It turned out to be one of the best two weeks of my sporting career and in some small way I'd like to think we added to the Games experience by bringing to the Aussie contingent a sense of team and mateship that was infectious.

The strangest thing about our participation was the expectation by some that we would be elitist, like the American basketball dream team at the Olympics, and stay outside the village. It couldn't have been further from the truth. Every second night during the Games we'd send out invitations to different sections of the Australian squad to join us for a few drinks in our dormitories. This was something that hadn't been done before within the Games environment, and it was well appreciated. We revelled in the dynamics of having a few guys to each apartment – except perhaps for my brother Mark, who couldn't believe the day's newspaper wasn't outside the front door when he opened it on the first morning. Handwashing clothes, and gathering breakfast from the food hall and bringing it back for each other was like going back in time to a school excursion. It was one big adventure, and I didn't want to miss a thing. However, our identification passes only gave us entry to the track events and the cricket. If we wanted to see any other event we had to either pay full price or beg for a ticket. We weren't too proud to choose the latter, but then Gav Robertson and I managed to persuade the team manager, Perry Crosthwaite, to give us a letter of accreditation to go to the swimming one night. So off we went in our green-and-gold face paint to cheer on Kieren Perkins, Ian Thorpe, Grant Hackett and Sam Riley, among others.

The problem of how to get in for the next three nights was easily solved by a stroke of liquid paper and a change of date, until Robbo left the letter in his cricket bag and a leaking floor ruined it. Plan C now came into effect: pretend we're competing. It was an audacious move, but with the team uniform on, our hair slicked back with water and goggles around our necks, we walked up to the official entrance for competitors and said, 'We're swimming. Sorry – we've lost our tags.' The officials were very helpful, pointing us in the direction of the swimmers' change rooms. Of course, this was not where we wanted to go, and the situation became a little tricky when we found ourselves walking past swimmers making their way out onto the pool deck for the next event. As discreetly as we could, we strode along the tunnel to the pool entrance, skirted around the judges, who were assuming their positions, and skipped over the barrier to join the Aussie team in the stands. Robbo and I became so committed that, besides the parents of the two Aussie girls competing, in the synchronised swimming we were the only people there to cheer the girls on.

For us, shorts were banned at the mess hall at meal times because our variously shaped bodies didn't quite match the toned frames of the elite athletes. Maybe that explained why we were the only ones eating the newly released blueberry Cornetto ice-creams on offer around the cafeteria, and why we got quizzical looks as we carried off a couple more to munch on back in our rooms. I gained a greater appreciation of and respect for the track-and-field and swimming competitors when I saw their immense discipline with regard to diet, preparation and avoidance of anything that may lead to trouble, such as changing sleep patterns, alcohol consumption and hanging around cricketers for too long. Cricket was essentially an exhibition sport, but the way in which we lost to an under-strength South African side in the gold-medal game hurt me, because some of our guys had switched into party mode and believed it was a given that we would win. I wasn't upset with the silver, but I was aggrieved at our lack of professionalism.

It was a critical lesson to all the guys – that each opportunity gone is one you can't get back – and the fact that it was well learnt is why the team became such a great big-match side. While the Games matches didn't receive official accreditation as limited-overs internationals, they were at times worthy of such status. In fact, the 100 not out I scored against India on a turning, wet track against Anil Kumble would go close to being in my top 10 innings.

Curtly Ambrose was playing for Antigua, and facing him on a wicket that was deemed so unstable that the New Zealand-born curator brushed it with wood glue before the game so it would stay together, was a long way from social cricket and a real test of courage. The 'cosmopolitan' nature of the competition for me was best summed up by the Canadian No. 8 batsman who took centre against us and said, 'Don't hurt me, guys – I have a newsagency and pizza shop to run next week.' Unfortunately for him, the first ball he received crashed into his ribs and sent him to the deck, collapsing 'chair-style'. There would be no hurling of newspapers or tossing of pizza bases next week – only ice packs and stories of stout resistance to his mates. It was friendly but competitive, and the Englishmen who didn't play because their counties wouldn't let them participate were the real losers, especially as Manchester, the host of the 2002 Games, didn't include cricket in its charter.

During the closing ceremony, our disappointment at not winning gold was tempered somewhat by Kieren Perkins, who walked over and said, 'You guys have been great for the whole team. Your enthusiasm and energy reminded us all that we shouldn't take anything for granted, and that the Commonwealth Games is a special event.'

That it was. I wished we could do it again.

★

The minibus came to a sudden halt, with dust flying out from behind the back wheels as we stopped at the designated checkpoint where we were to pick up our extra security and local tribesmen to ensure a safe passage up the fabled Khyber Pass. It was a world away from the Commonwealth Games closing ceremony, but in its own way just as exciting. We wound our way up the steep pass seen so often in movies, with barely enough room for two vehicles to slide by each other without holding their breath.

At the peak the view was stupendous, with the barren, uninviting territory of Afghanistan intimidating us by both its look and its reputation – that once you were on their turf the rules changed. Our hosts for the day, the famed Khyber Rifles, took us down to their shooting range to let off a few rounds and show us their extraordinary skills, while we proved that as marksmen we would be laughable opponents. Life here seemed harsh and tough with little room for weakness.

Attitude is everything. With a good one anything is possible, while with a bad one life is laden with excuses. In Pakistan in 1988 the battle had been lost without a ball being bowled; this time around, we saw every setback as a challenge to be taken head on.

A dry cracking surface complemented by four spinners had been a fatal combination for us a decade earlier, but this time around we not only foiled Pakistan's well-laid plans and specifically tailored pitch in Rawalpindi but managed to stun them with a win by an innings and 99 runs. After the home team had been dismissed for 269, Michael Slater and I put on 198 for the fourth wicket to steer us out of a potentially difficult position and in doing so expose our opponents' lack of match planning. The Pakistanis fully expected us to roll over and cave in, but the moment we grabbed the initiative they had no fallback position and their famed infighting and Keystone Cops approach kicked in. Slats, at his peak, was a brilliant player of spin, combining lightning-fast and uninhibited stroke play with always giving bowlers every indication that something had to give. When he was on song his natural gifts more than compensated for his bravado. At the other end, I decided to take the high ground and try to dictate terms, regularly sweeping wrist-spinner Mushtaq Ahmed off the stumps. It was a gamble that paid off because he, along with their usually outstanding offie Saqlain Mushtaq, seemed to lose focus and began to bowl at me and not against me. In contrast to most others, who looked for wrist position to detect subtle changes, I tended to pick the spinners through the air and off the pitch. Frustration took them away from their strengths of consistency and applying pressure and into areas of impatience, whereupon I seized on most of the loose offerings.

Saqlain was like a cockatiel out in the middle, chirping away with the regularity of Dustin Hoffman in *Rain Man*. 'C'mon, Wassy – you are the best, you're number one in the world,' he'd squawk every time Wasim Akram had a sweat-infused ball in his hands. Saqlain was a real goer and I respected his desire to always compete, but surely he could have changed his lines occasionally. The repetition was enough to send his own mates mad. Pakistan were a hard team to monitor, because one minute they appeared to be bickering and the next they were best mates, and often their quicks would be wolves in sheep's clothing, waiting for a batsman's complacency to set in before letting the wild beast spring to life.

There are days as a batsman when no amount of runs is enough. On this occasion my shot selection and concentration were faultless, so when, first ball after lunch on the third day, I tried to sweep a part-time spinner out of the rough but got a top edge to be dismissed, I instantly knew I'd blown a chance to take my innings to another level. I was fresh mentally, had the bowlers at my mercy and had a full session to cash in on as they wilted in the oppressive temperatures. Sitting slumped in a lounge chair under a creaky ceiling fan, wet towels draped around my neck and sipping on a cold Pepsi rimmed with rust stains, I reflected on a commanding innings that had ended meekly, which to me is a crime. In other words, I was soft. The steeliness had left me first ball after lunch and I'd paid the price, which hurt. As always, time is the healer of all things, and 15 minutes later I allowed myself to comprehend the level at which I had played and what we were about to achieve. The following day Ian Healy made it a guaranteed hangover by breaking Rod Marsh's world record for the most Test dismissals by a keeper when he caught Wasim Akram off 34-year-old Colin Miller, a guy who had played first-class cricket for nearly 13 years before making his Test debut in this match as a quick-cum-spinner.

During our time in Rawalpindi, Heals wanted to prove that his watch had been stolen overnight from on top of his kitbag by someone who had access to our rooms. His plan was to set up the thief again. Sure enough, the bait was taken the following night and the new world-record holder's theory was confirmed, but he was now two watches down and proving that longevity doesn't necessarily equate to commonsense. Bad luck also awaited him in the shoe department. An emergency SOS was sent to his sponsor, Puma, to express-freight a new pair of half-spikes to replace his worn-out pair. To his relief, the new boots turned up on the eve of the Test. However, joy immediately turned to devastation once the tissue paper was unravelled to reveal a stinky old well-worn pair of sandals, lovingly signatured with a blackened imprint of the previous owner's footprints. The expression on Heals' face was surely the inspiration behind MasterCard's 'priceless' advertisements.

From the diplomatic outpost we ventured back to the Pakistan–Afghanistan border town of Peshawar for the second Test. This time, the only thing missing from the pitch preparation was a bucket of white paint to mark the lines down the middle, for this was an absolute road. It was billiard-table flat, concrete hard and bereft of any grass and signs of cracking. In short, it was a batsman's paradise; someone was going to 'fill their boots', as Graham Gooch would say.

I had my selector's cap on when, the day before the game, I knelt down to examine the strip for any possible signs that it might fall apart later in the game. Any hint of potential wear and tear might influence the make-up of the team. I thought Swampy Marsh, who was next to me, was doing much the same thing, but then he worriedly said, 'I can't see Tubs getting too many. What are we going to do if he fails here?' Not wanting to go over old ground, we both agreed to just see what happened. What did happen was truly remarkable and further confirmed that Mark Taylor was one tough nut, capable of excelling under pressure and lifting to levels very few could aspire to. Scoring 300 in the backyard would ensure seniority over one's brothers for life; Tubs did all that in a Test match and then went on to equal the immortal Don with 334 not out. He did try with all his might to sneak past the great one, but much to his chagrin hit the last couple of balls of the second day straight to fieldsmen.

The declaration the next morning came as a shock to me because at breakfast I had sat opposite Mark and to me it seemed that he was inclined to bat on for a further 40 minutes. In the end, I'm sure he made the right call, because we needed time to conjure up a victory, and being equal with Sir Donald ensured a longevity of remembrance for his remarkable feat. If anything, we probably should have called it quits late the evening before and had a crack at a weary opening pair who would have been mentally fatigued after nearly two days in the field. Of course, that's easy for me to say. When you're 290-odd not out and unlikely ever to have the chance to conquer 300 again, the lure of creating history must be overwhelming.

Mark played from memory, executing precise driving that was reminiscent of his brilliant debut Ashes series in 1989 (when he scored 839 runs at 83.90), along with his trademark pull shot off balls pitched almost on a good length. The one thing his innings proved was that the old adage 'Form is temporary, class is permanent' always comes true. At the other end, Justin Langer had an instant when he must have thought his Test career was over. In the Rawalpindi Test a first-ball duck, lbw, had put his position in the side into the 'perilous' category. Here, in a carbon copy, Lang missed the first one, again falling over himself and getting his head position and balance all out of sync. There surely must have been only one conclusion, but somehow West Indian umpire Steve Bucknor saw a reason to spare him, and the rest is history – Lang's first Test-match century. The 'pardon' and the consequent release of pressure unburdened the pent-up West Australian and changed the entire destiny of his career. It's hard to put what happened down to luck or justice for the rough ones he'd copped in the past, but to me it was a reward for all the dedication, hard work and selfless team commitment he'd provided from the bench in previous years. I firmly believe that karma plays a major role in life and that you reap what you sow. In Justin Langer, the evidence is there before our very eyes.

Inevitably, given the wicket, this match was drawn, as was the third Test, in Karachi. Although we were a little negative in setting Pakistan 419 to score on the last day of the series, I could fully understand Tubs's reasoning, for we had everything to lose and the hosts didn't really deserve the luxury of being gifted a chance to escape with a win. This was Australia's first victory in a Test series in Pakistan for 39 years.

The one-day series that followed was a watershed one for us, as we won 3–0 on foreign turf against a very formidable opposition. It was here that I had the vision that limited-overs cricket is all about making every ball count equally. A batsman having a few 'sighters', just to get his eyes adjusted, or a bowler rolling the arm over and 'loosening up' for his first two or three balls could potentially lose his team the match. Each ball has to have a priority stamp on it. In a 50-over innings there is no time to waste, particularly when you are batting and have guys like Tom Moody, Brendon Julian and Damien Martyn at Nos 7 and 8. We had enough talent to be proactive with the bat from ball one and create instant pressure on opponents who would, if we were successful, quickly be under siege. It didn't have to be the big shot – it might be an aggressive single, backed up by assertive body language; but whatever it was, it had to be done with purpose. I figured that at least two or three out of eight batsmen would hit it off each innings and the rest could chip in, and if this occurred, more than likely we'd have an imposing total. Wickets in hand during the last 10 overs was still seen as our launch pad for mayhem, but it wasn't to be a period that required any more hustle that then previous 40. In Adam Gilchrist, Mark Waugh, Darren Lehmann, Ricky Ponting and Michael Bevan a core group at the top of the batting order had evolved to complement the bowling line-up led by Glenn McGrath and Shane Warne, and with each step the likelihood of Australia winning a second World Cup increased.

The biggest breakthrough came in our third victory, because we not only won a game chasing – which many opposition teams thought to be our weakness – but in doing so we achieved a record 50-over run pursuit. Of course, there was again no prize money, nor was there any sign of a trophy to mark the series, which infuriated the team more than anything – surely someone could have had the decency to conjure up a symbol for the series – but instead, the authorities were showing their hand, treating the players and the one-day game with contempt. Little wonder there were some who strayed and decided to earn a few dollars by other means from limited-overs international cricket. Although *nothing* should ever have led to that outcome, it did provide an excuse.

Further proof that the players' professionalism had outstripped that of management came with the amateurish organisation of our flight from Karachi to Dhaka in Bangladesh, for a mini World Cup staged straight after the Test series. A 4 a.m. wake-up call barely shook most of the guys out of their self-imposed comas, but when we boarded our plane we discovered that the flight path had us routed via Dubai, a couple of hours in the wrong direction. What should have been a two-hour flight was now a six-hour marathon. Our co-manager, Steve Bernard, could only claim, 'I couldn't do anything about it.' Funny, though, that the Pakistanis caught a direct flight an hour after ours, and little wonder that we failed miserably in our quarter-final against India, especially as we were obliged to complete a sponsored coaching clinic between the time we landed in Bangladesh and the start of what proved to be our only game. For us, it was more like a hastily arranged social fixture than a small-scale World Cup.

★

Ricky Ponting is a prankster of the highest order at times. I still recall his larrikin streak on his first overseas tour, in 1995, as a fresh-faced, goatee-wearing cocky upstart from the back blocks of Mowbray in northern Tasmania. 'Punter' was seated next to me on the plane and generously offered me some mouthwash from his business-class toiletry giftbag. *Nice gesture, young fella*, I thought to myself. *This kid's got respect . . .* and then I realised a jet of foam was engulfing my yawning mouth. The little smartarse had stitched me up with shaving foam and had a cheesy grin more mischievous than that of the Luna Park entrance. I had to admire his nerve and ingenuity.

Three and a half years later, in Pakistan, Ricky's cheek wasn't so well received. Alcohol can be a catalyst for trouble; when it is combined with frustration the mixture is dynamite. Michael Slater was never in the David Boon class for drink consumption. He was well known as 'Sybil', a man with numerous personalities. Unfortunately for me, I copped the brunt of an aggressive one as we gathered to celebrate our series win at the American Club in Karachi.

With a couple of Coronas relaxing and controlling the conversation, Punter began to tread on touchy ground as he told Slats he was always going to get out in the 90s because he started slogging whenever he got there. What started as a friendly chat with humorous banter soon escalated into a potentially bruising encounter, so being the vice-captain I tried to diffuse the situation with a half-hearted laugh and a suggestion they change the subject. With glazed eyes, Slats switched his focus, calling me a range of adjectives and suggesting that I, above all people, should know the pain of getting out in the 90s. On that count he was right, which is exactly why I had intervened. But the grog was firmly in charge. Only a right hook or a toilet break was going to diffuse the situation, and since I'd only ever thrown one punch in anger outside of brotherly spats in my life, I headed for the urinal. I was expecting him to say sorry on my return, but instead I was told, 'You're a coward.' So instead of rejoining the group, I walked straight out the door and headed back to the hotel, utterly devastated and with a sour taste in my mouth, at a time when the team's achievements were peaking and the memory of our disastrous '88 tour was all but eliminated.

To Slats's credit, a handwritten apology was forthcoming in the morning, but somehow a line had been crossed and our relationship was never the same.

32

Moving on

There was something about Ian Healy as a cricketer that lifted the passion levels of players on both sides when he strode to the crease. The opposition saw him as a prickly customer who appeared vulnerable, but they also knew from past experience that he could alter the course of the match with his hustle and vibrancy. I always became energised by his enthusiasm and willingness to roll up the sleeves for a good old-fashioned stoush. Decent partnerships between us were fairly frequent because we enjoyed each other's company and fed off each other's competitive nature. There was a level of comfort he brought along with him; it was always 11 versus two rather than a fielding team versus two individuals. My game invariably freed up and became more attacking, which coincided with our objective to put the pressure back on the opposition.

It was intriguing to watch the England team in Brisbane for the first Ashes Test of 1998–99 entangle themselves again in Heals' web of deception. His unorthodox approach looked ungainly and risky at times, but it did entice the English attack to be overly aggressive in their belief that a wicket was only a matter of time. Instead of using patience to wear Heals down – which we always believed was his breaking point as a batsman – they bowled short, wide and full in the hope he'd mishit one, and once he got on a roll, runs always came quicker than anyone appreciated. Together, we took the game away from them with a stand of 187 and a century next to each of our names. Another factor was the Poms' poor fielding, which again proved a decisive difference between the two teams as opportunities were missed at defining moments. A botched run-out by their paceman, Alan Mullally, who somehow got himself between the incoming ball and the stumps and broke the bails prematurely, was an early let-off for me that took the air out of their sails.

To me, this English team lacked match awareness and the self-belief that would allow them to lift in the big moments that present themselves during a match or series. They would trot out well-worn lines such as, 'It's only a matter of time, lads' or 'Keep working – the chances will come'. Both were true, but also hardly enlightening or inspirational – merely a means to an end. We eagerly sought such opportunities. Often when we were fielding you would hear a 'Let's seize the moment' call as one of us sensed that we were at a crucial juncture of the match. It was a line we took from a speech by legendary Australian Rules football coach Kevin Sheedy, which had been organised a couple of seasons before by Geoff Marsh, who was keen to initiate a cross-fertilisation of ideas from various sports to stimulate our thoughts and inspire ideas we might use in a game situation.

On the final day at the Gabba, a sea of golfball-sized hailstones dropped from a sky blacker than a serial killer's heart, just when Stuart MacGill was starting to bamboozle, dashing our victory ambitions. Stuey had come into the side for the Tests in Pakistan because Shane Warne had undergone a shoulder operation, and was taking advantage of the Poms' weakness against leg spin, a flaw that existed through the late '90s and beyond thanks in large part to the psychological torment Warney had inflicted upon them in previous series. MacGill would take 27 wickets in four Tests during the summer, but we had to wait until Perth to go one-up in the series, when a superb display of quality swing bowling by one of the best exponents of the art (alongside Terry Alderman) I ever played with, Damien Fleming, prised apart the English order in both innings to ensure a lopsided win. Flem has shoes the size of Ronald McDonald, a warped sense of musical taste that extends from heavy metal and grunge to his ultimate idols, Kiss, a wise-cracking sense of humour, and a gift for producing wicket-taking deliveries. Besides Shane, he was the guy in our team most likely to conjure up an unplayable delivery when least expected. Injuries and, to a lesser extent, an oscillating temperament prevented Flem fulfilling his enormous potential. Then, in Adelaide, Justin Langer took on the man-of-the-match role, scoring 179 not out from the No. 3 position. Fleming, MacGill and Miller all took key wickets, and in the process emphasised how much our success was a team effort.

By the late '90s, the Boxing Day Test had become an annual pilgrimage, something Lynette and I and other cricketing families all looked forward to. Making it extra-special for us in 1998 was that little Rosie now fully appreciated the magic of Santa's sled and how much it could hold. I had become used to the 'three-family Christmas' scenario – one celebration with my side of the family, one with Lynette's, and a third with the team. Briefly, we had to share our day with the media, too, and while this was an intrusion we respected it as something that had to be done to maintain a working relationship with them. I'm sure the cameramen and reporters would much rather have been with their families, so we all put on the public face, parading the kids out for 20 minutes as if they were our Santa gifts, before resuming normal activities.

The 1998–99 Test was one where I batted commandingly, but because of an error of judgement on my part I would ultimately bear the burden of an Australian loss. My first-innings hundred was technically near perfect until MacGill, batting at No. 10, came to the wicket. It was the first time I'd batted with him and I decided to throw caution to the winds, winding back the clock to my schooldays as I blazed away at anything and everything. With my score on 98, I even played a rare hook shot to a steepling bouncer. The stroke was more like a tennis serve than anything, but it got me two runs down to deep backward square and the exultation I experienced was nerve-tingling. I knew Darren Gough would try to keep me off strike with only one ball remaining in the over, and the obvious choice was the high bumper through to the keeper. I set myself for the hook, which was a dangerous move as it is an instinctive shot and not easily premeditated. I got a fair piece of it, but launched it close enough to fine leg to have to pray it would land safely. As I ran down the wicket I willed it to deviate from its set path, which, thankfully, it did, landing just out of reach of a labouring Angus Fraser. The very instant the ball hit the turf and I dashed back for the 100th run I was washed over with complete joy and satisfaction that I'd scored a century against the odds, which always made reaching three figures extra-special.

The ovation from the 40-odd thousand people present was unforgettable. It was a humbling moment for me as I stood with arms aloft, because I realised what a remarkable thing it is to bring such emotion

out of a crowd, and that I had the power to do it. It was doubly exciting this time because when Stuey came to the crease the hundred was
something I hadn't really contemplated; I was more concerned with
simply getting a first-innings lead. We ended up adding 88 for the ninth
wicket, Stuey making 43, and finished the innings 70 runs ahead.

On the fourth day, the first having been entirely lost to rain, we
appeared headed for a certain victory at 2/103 chasing 175, when Mark
Ramprakash produced a stunning one-handed catch that not only
removed Langer but had a knock-on effect that dramatically changed
the mood of the game. Making up for lost time because of the open-
ing-day wash-out meant each remaining day was scheduled for seven
hours, an extra 30 minutes being added to the start and finish, and
England's slow over rate meant play was extended even further on
the fourth afternoon. With their bowlers tiring badly and the clock
well past seven o'clock, I opted to exercise my rights and ask the
umpires for the extra half-hour the rules made available if a result was
imminent. I believed we were on the verge of winning as, while we
were seven wickets down, we needed only 14 more runs and debutant
Matthew Nicholson was coping assuredly at the other end. Further
making me feel correct in my assessment was the disbelief of England
captain Alec Stewart when the umpires agreed to my request for the
additional time. He complained bitterly about what he considered to
be the already ridiculous length of the session.

It would end up a marathon of more than three and a half hours, and
for me the climax was shattering. When Nicholson was caught behind
off Dean Headley we still needed 14 to win, and the fatal tactical error
came next over. As Stuart MacGill had played so well in the first innings,
I decided to show faith and back him to do the job. Ideally, I planned to
steal a couple of twos to gaps in the deep-set field and then look for a
one or blast a four from the last couple of deliveries in the next over, to
be bowled by Darren Gough. Adrenaline pumping, I clipped the first

ball and set off madly in search of two, but in my haste misjudged the pace I'd hit it and the intuition of the fieldsmen. I quickly realised that the second run would be suicidal. Instantly, my gut reaction told me that the fact I was now off strike was trouble, but I tried to quell my uneasiness by thinking about the resilience Stuey had shown in the first innings. However, within three balls my worst fears had materialised, with a bowled and an lbw leaving us losers by 12 runs and me 30 not out. The satisfaction of having batted so well was immediately overtaken by the pain of an unexpected loss and a misguided gamble that had blown up in my face.

It must have been pure bliss for a guy like Ian Chappell, who always sweated on my blunders and reported them with an 'I told you so' mentality. He labelled me 'selfish' on Sydney radio, which for a cricketer is tantamount to being accused of treason. To me his words seemed like a well-planned move, just when the question of who would succeed Tubby as Test captain was being considered. Chappell was a big Shane Warne fan and Shane, just back from his shoulder surgery, was the only real alternative to me as the new leader.

To say Chappell's criticism irked me would be an understatement, though I knew that, like anyone, he was entitled to an opinion. I don't mind the fact that he criticised me – in fact, I would much rather someone make a judgement than not – but I have always felt that a critic must either be constructive or base his comments on fact. I couldn't help but think about the reasons he was so down on me. It might have been that I praised the work of Bob Simpson, who was his sworn enemy, or that I didn't spend hours in the bar drinking and regurgitating old cricket stories. Or perhaps he wasn't keen on the coincidence of me being, like him, the older brother and combative in nature. Or maybe he didn't like the fact that I refrained from playing the 'macho' hook shot. Whatever it was, his was a personal attack, which came from a guy I didn't know and who certainly didn't know me. It was something I had to live with, and when I realised he was never going to cut me much slack, I decided anything he said that was positive would be a bonus and the rest just cast aside.

We ended up winning a tight fifth Test match in Sydney, largely because of a glitch in the third-umpire technology. It appeared Michael Slater had been run out, but the only side-on video replay was obscured and a conclusive view from other cameras of what had happened at the bowler's end couldn't be found. So Slats survived, although circumstantial evidence would clearly have had him given out, and he went on to score his third century of the series in a one-man-band showing that saw him carve out 66.85 per cent of our second-innings total of 184. His knock ended up being the difference between a 3–1 or a 2–2 scoreline for the series and, considering the enormity of the decision, I was impressed by the way England handled the setback.

For our captain, there were mutterings that this may have been his last Test. There were mixed signals – he wore his baggy green to the presentation ceremony, which at the time seemed very sentimental, but then ended his speech by saying, 'See you next year.' We as team-mates (and I as a good buddy) had no idea what was going on inside our leader's head.

There were only three months between the finals of the Carlton & United Series one-dayers and our first World Cup game. We satisfied ourselves that we were on track by winning nine out of the 12 matches in the triangular series, culminating in a thumping 162-run victory in the second final against England. I only played in two of the matches, missing the remainder because of a hamstring tear, with Warney taking over as captain. Afterwards a 20-man squad was picked, from which the selectors would choose the final 15-man squad for the Cup. I was astounded not to see Tom Moody's name in that first list and immediately called Trevor Hohns. To his credit, Hohns listened to my reasons for wanting Tom included – that I believed the seaming wickets in England in May and June would lead to a conventional World Cup with more Test-like cricket being played on varying pitches that would examine techniques a lot more closely than the cloned batting paradises of the subcontinent's one-day variety, and that I wanted seasoned campaigners who could handle pressure. Moods was certainly that: his bowling loomed as ideal, and his fantastic team ethic and ability to help build camaraderie were added attractions. He was a guy I trusted and the type of confidant that all captains need to have around.

★

In early February 1999, the lead story of a news bulletin confirmed the retirement of Mark Taylor from international cricket and my heart skipped a beat as I struggled to concentrate behind the wheel of my Commodore. The next week would be full of people, from board members to journalists and newspaper polls, telling me I was a sure thing to be the next Test captain, but I wasn't prepared to accept it as a given, particularly as Shane had handled the job so well during the Carlton & United Series. Our captaincy styles were vastly different, and while his outgoing manner and animated gestures on the field earnt him plenty of admirers, in my heart I believed I had plenty to offer, too. After more than 13 years playing at the top level, I had developed my game and mind to a point where I knew I could make a real impact and take the team forward.

Eventually, on February 11, 1999, I was told to hop on a plane to Melbourne in preparation for the announcement the next morning of the 40th Australian Test captain. This made for a nervous night's sleep as I wondered whether the board members had changed their mind since I'd been informed on the quiet a few days earlier that I had the numbers. I was actually alone watching *Sesame Street* when the news finally came through, for no other reason than Rosie loved the show and it was part of her morning routine and, without me realising, mine as well. A phone call from the chairman of the board, Denis Rogers, gave me the news I'd been waiting for: 'Congratulations, Steve, you're the new Australian Test captain. We'll see you at the board's office in one hour for the press conference.'

Life-altering news takes time to sink in, presumably because the news itself battles for ascendancy over the shock factor. The first person I called was Lynette, and then, in what seemed like no time at all, I was proud to be sitting at the press conference, bang in the middle, in front of all the microphones, ready to be introduced as the captain. But when it came to the big moment, I wasn't sure whether Rogers was milking the suspense or if he had just plain forgotten my name as he stared into my eyes for what seemed like an eternity. It was an interesting start!

My immediate goals as the new leader were for the team to continue to play in an aggressive manner, avoid defeats in 'dead rubber' Tests, improve our success rate when chasing in the fourth innings and, where possible, hold on for a draw in matches that we had been losing. At the same time, I was prepared to risk losing if I thought it gave us a chance of winning, and I wanted my teammates to realise their potential and ambitions.

My first 'joint venture' as the full-time captain was a five-month trip away, starting with a tough assignment in the Caribbean, followed by the ultimate one-day test: the World Cup. My on-field start, though, was very low key. Not many Test captains begin their reign as a substitute, but I was the drinks waiter in the first tour game as a precautionary measure to ensure my torn hamstring fully recovered. Before that, the thought of my initial address to the team caused me a degree of anxiety, because I wanted to make an impact but at the same time didn't want to reinvent the wheel. I have found that there are normal nerves and another version that is twice as hard to overcome, and turns up when you are talking to guys you know intimately. When I tried to begin, I thought the words were going to be shut off by a voice box that was tightening and a swarming invasion of hot cells that threatened to overwhelm my system. In the end, my debut address would have been marked as passable rather than historic; I was glad it was over and the preparation for battle could begin.

I hoped the team understood the style of captaincy I believed I could deliver. I wanted to see everyone playing their natural game and being in control of their own situation. I wanted each player to think of himself as a vice-captain, always proactive in his thinking, able to offer advice and, above all, willing to take responsibility for his actions. I envisaged us becoming the benchmark team, which opponents would describe as 'the most professional, most relentless and toughest we've ever come across'. Pride in one's own performance and enjoyment of each other's success would lead to character and bonding, and we had to be aware of the two dangers that could threaten our plans. Complacency and poor preparation had been directly to blame for our losses in recent times, such as at the Oval in 1997 (complacency) and in Delhi a year before that (poor preparation), and we knew they needed to be ticked off our checklist before each game. I wanted to take people on a journey and get them to believe in themselves and in what we were trying to achieve. Empowerment by infusing self-belief was the mantra I wanted to create.

I knew that all successful sides have a certain 'X factor' that comes from each individual giving more than he takes. We believed we could foster that set of beliefs in the individuals who made up the team, something I explained in one-on-one meetings with each of the players. As a follow-up, I gave each of the guys a single page that outlined my expectations for that player. This is what I gave Jason Gillespie:

Dizzy,

- Enjoy the tour – your time is now.
- Work with Pigeon [McGrath] to establish the best opening bowling combination in world cricket.
- Controlled aggression coupled with 'in the corridor' bowling will take wickets in the Caribbean.
- Use your intimidating body language on the Windies batsmen – they don't like it.
- Set the tone for their tail-end batsmen – go for their jugular – get personal, then get them out!
- Work on your batting – you are capable of getting good partnerships going, which could be very important.
- Keep the intensity up at fielding practice – take it into the game with you.
- Be the man – make it your series.
  Play well,
  Tugga

As a way of preparing me for my future as Australian captain, my first tour as Test captain would prove perfect. Every possible emotion was expressed, difficult issues had to be confronted and a range of challenges overcome. Right at the start, it was quite a shock to hear two-and-a-half-year-old Rosie speak into the phone and say, 'Love you, Daddy, miss you . . . Mummy and Daddy . . . baby!' It wasn't the usual way to find out that a tin lid was on the way, but I was ecstatic when Lynette confirmed the news. Four months later, it would be a weird feeling to see her stomach, which had been flat on my departure, past half-term on my return home. It was as if there were two Steve Waughs, one the jetsetting international cricketer and the other Joe Average from the suburbs, and I had to oscillate between them. One day I'd be mixing with a rock-and-roll legend and the next I'd be back home changing a dirty nappy. It was surreal at times and the adjustment was challenging.

After rolling the Windies for 51 in the fourth innings of the first Test, in Trinidad – their lowest Test score – and seeing Brian Lara cop the wrath of a blood-hungry, baying media, I thought to myself, *This isn't too bad a job, being captain of such a great team.* It brought back memories of playing for Panania–East Hills Under 10s, when we used to rely on two 'gun' bowlers and the rest of us fielded for them. In this case, only McGrath and Gillespie were called upon, which was somewhat ironic as most of the press talk before the game had been about the fact that we were going into the Test with just two quicks and two leg-spinners, in Shane Warne and Stuart MacGill. My first observation as a winning captain was that I was at least three drinks behind the rest of the team by the time I was done with the post-match television interviews, countless radio requests and a full-on press conference, and had completed a match report on the umpires. When I did get back to the change room, the biggest celebration going on among our guys was occurring in McGrath's corner, as he re-enacted his pull shot of Ambrose, defying logic and belief, on his way to a then career-best 39.

I found that the focus of my game had changed. The duck I made in the second innings didn't have anywhere near the same impact on me as it would have had a few months earlier, as the nurturing and protective instincts that were part of being captain kicked in. I now had 10 guys, plus the reserves and support staff, to keep in harmony and on a clear path to the same destination – to be No. 1 in both forms of the game. Being a 'together' unit was of paramount importance to me and I encouraged that objective in any way I could. The idea of reading out an inspirational quote or 'phrase for the day' started when I asked our new fitness trainer and all-round good guy, Dave Misson, to give us a lift at the conclusion of his stretching routines. 'Misso', as he invariably did, took my request right on board and even went a step further. The next morning he delivered a poem, and a tradition had begun. In the following years no one ever knocked back the chance to have a turn at motivating the boys, and on occasion players spent hours putting together their piece of work. Simon Katich proved exceptional in this regard during the 2001 Ashes tour, when he spent many hours watching from the bench. His eye for subtle exchanges and byplay came across in his subsequent writings, which also gave a glimpse of his make-up. My intuition told me the guy was a natural-born leader.

Captaincy seemed to soak up my spare time like a sponge. More often than not I found myself short of a decent warm-up and with little or no time to work on what I needed to do to 'switch on'. Strange as it may appear, the toss of a coin sometimes gave me a mild anxiety attack. On a number of occasions I actually went blank, mesmerised by the rotation of the heads and tails, before snapping out of it just in time. 'Heads' was always my call, in contrast to Mark Taylor, who was a 'tails' man in recognition of his surname.

When I became captain I had to ask the delicate question of whether I would alienate myself from the rest of the guys or try to continue as I had in the past. I aimed for the latter, but the meetings I had to have with team management, board members, match referees, selectors and others, plus dealing with internal disciplinary issues, inevitably led to a distancing of relationships between me and the other players. A captain can tell he's skipper the moment he sits down to a team dinner at a restaurant and the chairs on either side are vacant for longer than they would have been in the past. Teammates are careful not to be seen as the captain's favourite and I found that they tended to give me a little extra space until the formalities and stiffness dissipated. Conversations as 'one of the boys' became less frequent, tales of nights out and what time the lads got in were censored, and I was left slightly out of the loop. I'd been through plenty of years when the shoe had been on the other foot, so I knew how it all worked, but I'd never stopped to think about the ramifications of all this from the captain's perspective.

What I needed was a strong lieutenant. In Warney, as vice-captain, I had a good mate with a sharp cricket mind and a desire to form a strong partnership, but what he sometimes couldn't do was tune into the mood of the side. Often he stayed indoors, avoiding the public due to his enormous popularity, and he didn't eat anything you'd find served at a restaurant, so he didn't spend a lot of time with the guys socially. All this meant that I was left a little unaware of how the team was functioning off the field.

We went to Jamaica for the second Test buzzing after our blitz in the opening game and fully expecting to drive the nail in hard. I had one of the strangest sensations of my whole career when I walked out to toss with Windies captain Brian Lara, as he was being booed all the way out to the middle and back. As we parted ways after I had called correctly, we shook hands and I said, 'Play well.' He replied, 'This is the last time I'm gonna have to put up with this shit.'

'This guy's fragile and ready to offload the captaincy,' I told my team as soon as I got back in the room. However, we would have been well served had we listened to Justin Langer, who popped his head up and said, 'Just be careful, we've heard that from him before.'

On day one, my old, reliable batting partner, Glenn McGrath, had guided me to another century before I cost him yet another fifty when I fell for exactly 100 (or at least that's the way he tells it). In truth, he had gone from being comedy value as a batsman to a usable commodity, and to his great credit was now capable of being part of a partnership. He would play his 50th Test match during 1999, by which time his Test batting average was over six. After 20 Tests, it had been 2.23. All he'd needed to improve, like most tail-enders, was an investment of time and concentration on a few basics. Generally bowlers have a poor practice ethic when it comes to batting, primarily because they never get a decent hit as there are no bowlers left at the end of the session to service them. I wanted to change that and at least give them an opportunity, because I saw it as vital for the lower half of the order not only to support the top order, but to frustrate the opposition. Glenn had been going about his practice the wrong way around, playing millionaire champagne shots with only coins for soft drinks in his pocket. He needed a base to launch his potentially expansive repertoire and that meant learning how to defend. Once he grasped the notion that most attacking shots are just an extension of being in a good position, which you get into while defending correctly, the penny dropped. I emphasised one key phrase to remember in the nets, 'Don't drop the baby.' What this meant was that the natural arc of an arm-swing when playing straight is the same motion as rocking a baby, and the moment he played across the line his left arm fell away. Hence the call that would often resonate in his ears during a session: 'McGrath, you've dropped the baby.'

I always had two other theories on his batting. Firstly, I teased that he was actually a natural left-hander. Then I'd tell him he was a frustrated genius, because before practice he'd always pull out a single stump and never miss when the guys bowled to him. Was the bat too wide for his natural eye? Thankfully, 'Pidge' has a gentle nature without a six-stitcher in his hand, because a lesser man would have snapped at the constant stream of sarcasm that came his way. I was as guilty of this as anyone, at one point advising him that when his next bat contract came up, he should speak to every manufacturer and hold them to ransom by asking for five grand or else he'd use their bats. He could have made a fortune.

We missed a golden opportunity on a good batting track to take control of the second Test, but still had command at the end of that first day, with the Windies playing tentatively and with a real brittleness to be 4/37 at stumps chasing our 256. However, on day two they produced a remarkable form reversal that saw us go wicketless, with Lara and Jimmy Adams forming an alliance of contrasting styles that showed no signs of vulnerability. With our leg-spinners struggling to make an impression against the left-handers, our options were limited, with only two genuine quicks to call upon if neither Warne nor MacGill could break through. At this time, so soon after his operation, Warney was only partly match-fit, and Stuey too focused on making the spinning spot his. They were two very different personalities, with varying interests, and while they both bowled leg spin, they operated on different terms out in the middle. Shane loved a chat about field settings and potential ideas, while Stuart didn't concern himself with placements and tactics; he just wanted to bowl. Warney worked over a batsman, sniffing out a weakness and always on the lookout for negative body language or a sign that the player was hesitant. Stuey just went for it, turning and bouncing the ball as hard as he could muster.

One was subtle, the other a sledgehammer. They were like two magnets with opposing fields: no matter how hard they tried to connect, they just couldn't link together. It was amusing at times to see how they worked over an umpire, and unsurprising as to the reactions they got. Warney would often half-heartedly appeal, knowing full well the ball was missing the stumps, and on the way back to his mark, past the umpire, he'd inquire, 'Just going down [leg side], was it?'. To which the umpire would say, 'Yes, Shane, I think it was.' The process might be repeated again with a different query, which would help build up a cordial relationship. Of course, when Warney eventually got one on line he'd let rip with a vociferous appeal and the umpire had little choice but to concur.

'Magilla', on the other hand, had a very different approach to dealing with the white coats. A turned-down appeal would often see him hold back future appeals, as if to say, 'You got it wrong, buddy, and now I'm not even going to give you the chance to stuff it up again.'

One of Stuey's most famous quotes came in a Shield match for NSW after he had a number of close calls refused and was about to start a new over. The umpire tried to initiate a spot of small talk to ease the tension, but was hit straight between the eyes with the bowler's reply: 'Your job is to count to six and hold my hat, pal!'

Lara finished with 213, a brilliant innings highlighted by his extra-ordinary precision, with the ball flowing off his blade. He had torn the heart from our chest too easily and in our second innings past frailties resurfaced as we meekly surrendered to lose by 10 wickets. Losing a session shouldn't be terminal, but for too long it seemed that when we did so it meant a heavy defeat. No one seemed able to cauterise the blood flow and it was something we had to overcome. More match awareness and an ability to absorb advice and learn lessons from past mistakes were needed if we wanted to address the problem.

Coach Marsh reacted exactly the same way as his predecessor and mentor, Bob Simpson, would have done, by calling a centre-wicket practice for the next morning. In cricketing talk this is known as 'bad boy nets', and as the captain I agreed to the measure, not because we'd lost but because of the way in which we went down. Contrary to what was sometimes written by commentators, losing in itself was never an issue for me; it was only ever a problem if I felt we hadn't given it every-thing. After all, someone has to lose in a 'two-horse race' and I was brought up to always shake my opponent's hand, give him credit and then move on to the next challenge. I can't understand tears or indi-viduals moping around after a defeat; such responses are a sign that you have regrets about the way you prepared or put in, and that is some-thing I could never understand. Giving everything and losing wasn't the result I hoped for, but as long as I could sleep at night, comfortable in my effort and that of the team, then I could move on easily.

Press conferences are usually fairly predictable, with most ques-tions leading to a couple of quotes needed to slot around the story or angle for the day. I eagerly anticipated stimulating and thought-provoking inquiries, and would have been happy to move away from cricket clichés into more analytical and meaningful answers, but, disappointingly, clever questions rarely came. There were times when I'd walk away from a press conference and say, 'Jeez, I've given them some pearls of wisdom there,' only to see the predictable mundane wrap-up in the following day's papers. I know the journos had editors in their ears, but surely just occasionally they wanted to rebel.

It was a former Test cricketer, Windies fast man of the late '70s and early '80s, Colin Croft, who got my ears to prick up at the press conference after the resounding loss in Jamaica. 'Why didn't you bowl when you won the toss?' he asked me. 'You had just bowled them out for 51 and mentally they would have struggled to front up again so soon.' It was a valid point, although at the time I was sensitive to his forthright view and didn't fully recognise the rationale behind it. Upon reflection, I realised I had chosen to bat primarily because we had two spinners who I believed would influence the game in the fourth innings, but had McGrath and Gillespie gone right at them we would have stepped on their throat and kept them down. Putting myself in my opponent's shoes was something I never again forgot to do. Generally, I felt I knew what they didn't want to do, and that gave us a big advantage.

Both teams went to Barbados for the third Test full of hope, and together we played one of the all-time great matches. Both captains passed 150 in one innings in the same match, but it was Lara's cool head and presence under pressure that guided his team home by the barest of margins. He was mobbed all the way off by ecstatic spectators who knew they'd witnessed something special, while for us it was so mentally draining and physically debilitating that we just sat in the rooms, slumped in our chairs, almost oblivious to the surging crowd directly outside our open windows.

I was immensely proud of McGrath, who bowled 44 overs in intense heat, the last dozen purely through will and competitive instinct, and Gillespie, who showed incredible courage and resilience to come back after lunch and bowl with back spasms. But in all honesty, it was too few doing too much. Close losses happen for a reason, but it's not bad luck – it's a warning sign that something isn't quite right. This time, for us, it was some guys playing with injuries, others not being as professional as they should have been off the field, and a couple of blokes not lifting enough when their form was down.

Four days earlier, at the start of the Test, batting had been a real gun-slinger stand-off affair, with Curtly Ambrose bowling like a dream on a seaming track. At 3/46 we were in serious 'Barney Rubble', with Ambrose leaping into the crease like an uncoiled spring, unleashing unplayable thunderbolts one after the other. I survived purely on acquired knowledge and lack of ego, because I couldn't lay my bat on many of the balls delivered by this perfect bowling machine. Fortunately it's amazing what a bit of sun and a 40-minute lunch break can do to alter the nature of a pitch, and we found batting much easier after the chicken jerky, rice and black-eyed beans, our staple diet for the tour, had been consumed. A quick outfield, outrageously small boundaries and a baked, rock-hard wicket saw Ricky Ponting and me tear into their attack, which had peaked in the first two hours. In the end, though, it wasn't enough – not even my 199 which saw me enter another '90-something' club (as the fifth man to be dismissed one short of 200 in a Test match) – but to be honest, falling on that score didn't particularly bother me. However, falling behind in the series 1–2 with only the Test in Antigua to come and the realisation that I had to deal with a major issue within the team certainly did.

★

Being the boss has many privileges, but with leadership also comes the duty of sometimes having to distance your emotions so as to make the correct decision. Sitting in the team room with fellow tour selectors Geoff Marsh and Shane Warne prior to the fourth Test, we were faced with a situation that all three of us knew was potentially volatile. In our search for clarity and an objective view, Allan Border, a member of the selection panel in Australia (but not a selector on the tour), came along to oversee the proceedings. Having taken just two wickets in the first three Tests, and with the two leg-spinners bowling in tandem proving largely ineffective during the series, Shane knew his spot was up for debate. I had flagged it to him at an official function the day before, but knew he'd be desperate for one more chance. At the meeting we all had our say, with Geoff and I agreeing that Shane wasn't 100 per cent fit and that we needed to change our line of attack by letting the multipurpose Colin 'Funky' Miller use his away-from-the-left-handers offies. Hopefully, we argued, this would cause the Windies batsmen to rethink their strategies. Warney put up an emotional argument that included some very valid points, but when it came to summing it all up, AB agreed that the tough call had to be made.

Shane then asked for one more quick hearing to further his case for inclusion. He pointed out that he had never ever let the team down and firmly believed he could lift himself in the deciding Test. I certainly didn't doubt him, but my gut feel was still to drop my vice–captain, even though we all knew he was a legend of the game. I kept on asking myself, *What team is going to give us the best chance of winning?* To me, Shane wasn't in that starting XI. However, AB was obviously impressed by the stirring words because he changed his opinion and plumped for Shane, but by this time it didn't matter, because Geoff and I had had our say. Warney, to his credit, handled an extremely tough situation stoically and, while I was feeling his anguish, I also experienced a heavy load being lifted. Warney then departed, and I was surprised to hear AB turn to Geoff and me and say, 'Yeah, you guys are right – you made the right decision.'

The last Test was a gutsy win by us, with the tough-as-teak Justin Langer pulling out a trait that would come to define his career – the ability to accumulate runs in adversity and when the team needed them most. The pressure valve of our team had been released with Shane not being there. This isn't meant to be unkind, but when a great player is for some reason unable to achieve what he's used to achieving, players begin to tread on eggshells around him in an attempt to not make his life harder then it already is. A new freedom showed in our play and I'll never forget the hook shot by Colin Miller off Ambrose that took off like a rocket out of a milk bottle on cracker night, hit in front of square and landing in the jail situated outside the ground. Such was the shock to the hometown hero that those impressive lips of his curled up at the ends for a split second in admiration. Of course, his comeback was always going to be extra-special. A thin-edged attempted pull missed Funky's helmet grill by a whisker before bouncing once on its way into the sightscreen behind the keeper, and the balance of power was restored.

So the series was shared, we retained the Frank Worrell Trophy and, as far as getting out of a series with a draw was concerned, I was pleased. However, I also knew we'd blown a genuine chance to win an away tour, which was never easy to do, and in assessing matters afterwards it was clear some things had to change. What I saw as a drinking culture was affecting more members of the squad than I had initially thought and the way that we were tending to socialise in the same groups had unhinged what should have been the joker in our pack: togetherness. As captain, I felt slightly let down by my most senior professional, Ian Healy, who was struggling to come to terms with the approaching end of his career and for the first time in his cricket life had let his discipline and work ethic slide. It was as if our partnership against the Poms at the Gabba had happened a few seasons earlier, rather than just a few months. Mark Waugh had an average tour and didn't get involved enough in the running of the team, while some younger guys followed the leads and erroneous ways of others. I felt betrayed when later I discovered that secret pacts had been made by some of the guys to stay out past curfew, and I vowed to monitor things and take action more swiftly in the future. I needed to man-manage better and get feedback from the guys on a more regular basis, and I also required the coach and team manager to impose their pow-ers of authority when it came to team discipline.

In my experience players look for and need guidance, but it can be a fine line between imposing too many rules and not enough. In an ideal situation, which I was aiming for, team members would know the dif-ference between right and wrong and be responsible for their actions. My job, and that of management, was to make sure the players knew what was acceptable and what wasn't, while always fully realising that it was unreasonable to expect the guys never to make mistakes, so long as those mistakes weren't repeated.

Wasting opportunities and talent is a sportsperson's greatest crime. As I pondered the way the tour had gone to this point, I couldn't understand how some of the guys were allowing blurred ambitions to compete with those sparked by a dream.

33

The power within

There's no doubt my first series as a Test leader was very eventful. It also provided the perfect grounding for future years, as it showed me what was required to be a success: hard work.

It may have been the icing on the cake to be the big C, but I needed to have a defining influence on the ingredients to make sure the cake was cooked properly. After making a duck in my first Test as captain, I played well enough in the final three Tests to be, along with Brian Lara, a standout performer with the bat, and in doing so I was able to alleviate the pressures that had so strangled my predecessor. The write-ups Brian and I received after scoring hundreds in Jamaica and Barbados proved that stereotypes are almost impossible to break down once established. Brian's innings were 'dashing, debonair' affairs, full of 'audacious stroke play' that 'thrilled' the crowds, while mine slotted easily into the 'gritty, determined, back-to-the-wall' theme. The reality was that my hundreds were made from fewer deliveries than Brian's, but no one was willing to base their thoughts on reality, preferring the perception. Such typecasting does annoy many players and I know that brother Mark certainly didn't appreciate the 'casual, soft dismissal' tag that, in the media's eyes, was often dangling around his neck.

The one-day series that followed the Test matches ended in a 3–3 draw, with a tie thrown in for good theatre. The competition for places in the two Australian teams ensured that both line-ups were a little flighty and inconsistent, and towards the end of the tour controversy overtook the action on the park with a calamitous finish to the Guyana one-dayer and then a near riot in Barbados.

In Georgetown we needed six to win from the last over, which was to be bowled by part-timer Keith Arthurton. I was on strike and 67 not out, entitling us to favouritism, but I hadn't banked on a few good yorkers and a quicker ball that I missed, so by the time the last ball was due we needed three to tie and four to win. It seemed as if every member of the capacity crowd was lining the boundary, all 'in the blocks' ready for the start of a 100-metre sprint. As soon as I mishit the ball to deep midwicket they were off, and so were Shane Warne and I on pretty much a lost cause. But then, after completing two runs and turning blindly for an impossible third, I realised Arthurton had the ball in his hands at the non-striker's end, near where the stumps had been before they were souvenired by members of the crowd. Seeing a ray of hope, I went for it, lunging desperately at the crease line at the precise moment a spectator clipped me from side on as he attempted to swipe my bat. It was absolute anarchy, with people running in every direction, police atop white horses, umpires missing in action and seemingly no way to get off the field.

In the aftermath, I managed to convince match referee Raman Subba Row that the ball had still been live when I turned for three, so a tie was the only fair outcome. That was good for us, but not so well received by the crowd, who had remained on the ground ready to celebrate. I then had to make my way in darkness across to the other side of the oval to reach the team bus. That walk, amid calls of 'We gonna kill you man!' and 'Waugh, you're a tief!', remains one of the most uneasy minutes of my life.

Life didn't get any easier in Bridgetown, where local hero Sherwin Campbell got tangled up with bowler Brendon Julian in mid-pitch, tumbled over and was run out. After checking BJ's version of events and getting confirmation from the umpires that the collision wasn't intentional, I assumed Campbell would accept his dismissal in the right spirit. On the contrary, it only took a few indecisive gestures from him as to how he'd been hard done by for the field to be instantly covered in bottles, food and anything else the locals could grab hold of. Normally the mood mellows after a couple of minutes, but this time it appeared a full-scale revolt was on the cards. I had an obligation to protect my players, and eventually I issued the order, 'Let's get out of here while we can.'

Just as I was about to get off the field and into the safety of our change room, I looked up and saw the anger in the members' faces and experienced the gushing airflow of a flying object brushing past the left side of my head. It was so close it almost felt like the glance of someone's palm, but when I heard the bottle thud into the turf, my immediate reaction was anger and I felt intense disappointment at the stupidity of the guy who had thrown it. I later found out that the villain was a distinguished member of the community, an architect of some renown.

With play suspended, an emergency meeting was called between the captains, coaches, managers and match referee to work out a plan of action. My mind had already been swayed by the time we gathered, because our manager, Steve Bernard, had said to me, 'I think we had better get back on. The local police commissioner has told me if we don't, they can't guarantee your safety.' In the end we had no choice and basically handed the Windies the win, because their target was severely reduced. The events in these two games left an ugly taste in the guys' mouths; the stance I had been taking for a while – that it was only a matter of time in cricket until we saw an incident akin to the awful moment when tennis champion Monica Seles was stabbed – was gathering credibility.

When I woke the next morning, I was looking forward to our next destination, the World Cup. Instead I was stunned by the news that I was about to be sued by the Barbados Commissioner of Police, who had taken offence at my comments at the postgame media conference when I echoed the words uttered to me by our manager at the height of the fracas. Unfortunately the commissioner himself hadn't been at the game, and it was the person filling his role who had made the statement I attributed to him. Two years later the ACB paid an out-of-court settlement to appease the dinted ego of the main man. No one was the wiser, nor was there a winner.

After nearly 10 weeks of head-spinning stuff in the Caribbean, we could finally focus on the big prize: the 1999 World Cup. However, as we set off, bound for England, I couldn't help but look back on my visit to Trench Town, a tough suburb on the outskirts of Kingston, and think how lucky I was and what a great life I had the good fortune to be living.

Trench Town is a tough place. One of the first things I learnt was that in previous years around 1000 people had perished in a gang-related war. The local soccer field was the neutral piece of turf in town, the only place where killing wasn't allowed. Being with the respected locals was a white man's safety valve – I'm sure that Justin Langer and I would have found it tough to leave if we'd just stumbled into the area on our own. But, while scarred by the violence, the locals loved their cricket, so instead of fearing for our lives Lang and I moved freely and engaged in animated discussion with them.

The streets had a desolate, wild-west feel about them, but still children skipped down dilapidated roads in front of decaying blocks of flats with the same zest for life that young people do anywhere in the world. The bright-eyed innocence of kids is universal, until they are corrupted by the environment and attitudes that surround them. I couldn't take enough photographs, with the locals keen to display the entry and exit marks of their gunshot wounds, the elongated machete gashes, and tools of their trade hanging out of their trousers. A young boy burst into tears when he saw me, and his mother had to explain that it was the first time he'd seen a white man. I left impressed by the human spirit, glad I hadn't been born into such an angry lifestyle and amazed that it could have produced a man capable of influencing a whole generation: Bob Marley.

Not surprisingly, the first press conference upon landing at Gatwick Airport for the World Cup on the way to our base at Cardiff revolved around Warney. 'How did he react to being dropped?' 'Is his shoulder okay?' 'Will he have a successful World Cup?'

The guy is the media's dream – everything about him makes for good print. In May 1999 the jury was out about his form, but he loved the big stage and had an uncanny and legendary knack for timing his great performances. He also loved touring the UK, where he felt at home. Indeed, being on tour in England was comforting for many of us, not least because we again had Tony Smith as our baggage handler – in 27 years of looking after touring teams, he never lost a single bag – and a bus company with the same driver as our previous Ashes tour. Familiarity breeds confidence and avoids the stiff settling-in period that can inhibit the first week of a tour. I always made a point of trying to get to know the 'staff' around the team, as I appreciated that it must have been an intimidating experience for them to make the first move. Once they settled in, they became part of the group that formed the 'one per centers' that gave us an advantage.

I'd been somewhat spooked by the lack of discipline in the Windies and our casual approach at the Commonwealth Games, and considered our greatest danger to be ourselves. It was with this in mind that, after consulting with Geoff Marsh, I laid down guidelines in regard to hours kept and alcohol consumption. 'Up to midnight is your time,' I explained, 'after that it's cricket time.' Exceptions were to be made on the days when we played, and the evenings after games were a time for having a drink. I didn't want to put a total ban on drinking, because we'd always played hard and celebrated and the guys needed to be able to let off a bit of steam at some stage.

The new rules seemed a good idea, but a few days after they were introduced my trusted shop steward, Tom Moody, informed me after a restaurant meal, 'The boys aren't too happy about the restrictions. You might have to revisit that line of thought.' The last thing I wanted was dissent in the camp or a clique of renegades developing, so I relented and instead put the onus on the individual to be responsible and asked teammates to look out for each other.

I also recognised we needed a spark to get us going and thought there was no better way to do that than to give ownership to the team and start our own little tradition. I sought out our long-time scorer, Mike Walsh, to draw up a chronological list of all the men who had played one-day internationals for Australia. I wanted every member of the current squad to be aware of their position in Australia's 28-year limited-overs history. I was the 90th of 139 Australians to have played one-day international cricket to that time, while the coach, who had debuted two games after me, was No. 91. The list complete, I sent Moods off to get corresponding numbers embroidered on our caps, to give out at the team meeting before our first game, against Scotland at Worcester. The big fella thumbed through the Cardiff Yellow Pages before securing the services of a knitting dynamo of a grandmother. Trouble was, despite a commendable 48 hours of hard labour, the figures she sewed on were big enough to go on billboards, creating a look that didn't quite hit the mark; we had to call in a professional to finish the job. For me, the numbers worked; for the first time in my career I felt a part of one-day cricket history. No longer would I just hand the cap away at the end of a tournament as if it was just another piece of merchandise, and when the caps were presented to the guys I could tell straightaway the piece of ownership they'd been given was worthwhile. It was as if each player's place in history was assured. This was a link to the past and also to the way of the future, and the practice has since been adopted by most sides in both forms of the game.

Back to Shane Warne. In the lead-up to the Cup, he couldn't keep out of the papers. Already, the *News of the World* tabloid had caught him having a smoke in the Caribbean when he was supposedly promoting a product that helped you quit the habit, and then he slipped the boot into Arjuna Ranatunga in his weekly column in *The Times* broadsheet. There were moments when I thought Warney must have loved controversy, because he either sought it or was unaware of his ability to sell newspapers.

One welcome addition to our squad for parts of this tournament, on a needs basis, was sports psychologist Sandy Gordon. His role was to ask the players questions no one else would ask, gain feedback, offer suggestions, put strategies into place and see things from an outsider's point of view. Geoff Marsh and I had been strong advocates for Sandy to play a part in our preparations, especially for overseas tours, where potential problems such as homesickness, staleness, personal problems and personality clashes can affect individuals and break down the team unit. Cricket, we knew, is a game that obviously requires talent, but when the talent is equal, as it so often is, the formula for success comes from strength of mind. In my view, the emphasis on physical fitness and practice, at the expense of mental fitness, was very lopsided. Cricketers need to work on their pregame and match routines and on visualising what they are trying to achieve, to learn by asking each other questions about strengths and weaknesses, and to share insights about doubts and fears. There is a wealth of information stored within us all, and it's a great shame if it stays locked away, never to be used for the benefit of others. My hope for the World Cup was that Sandy could extract some of that stored knowledge and give the team a clearer route to the success we were all trying to achieve.

After 11 weeks away I needed to keep busy to quell the pain of missing Lynette and Rosalie, and I vowed to myself to get stuck in and make being away from my family worth something. I didn't know whether this was going to be my last World Cup and I didn't want to die wondering. Strengthening my intent was the guilt associated with being away while Lynette suffered horrendously with morning sickness. I remember feeling so helpless as she told me how, while she knelt down and vomited into the toilet each morning, Rosie would rub her back and say, 'Mum, are you okay?'

I tried not to be consumed with thoughts of home, but couldn't help but wonder how much Rosie had grown up. Had her physical appearance changed? What had she learnt? How much did she miss her daddy reading her the bedtime stories? Would she run and jump into my arms in five weeks' time? Simone Warne was also pregnant, and like me Shane was 'going solo' for the entire trip; agonisingly for both of them, he would be away for the birth of his second child.

While we were making plenty of headlines, the South Africans had an innovation that split the cricket experts. Coach Bob Woolmer had proposed, with captain Hansie Cronje's blessing, that Cronje wear an earpiece on the field so they could discuss tactics on the go and pass on relevant information to each other. To me, this was against the spirit of the game and a slur on Cronje's captaincy credentials. A leader must be able to think on his feet, improvise and follow his instincts; allowing someone else to get into my head in the heat of battle would have been confusing and, in many ways, demeaning. In any case, it was banned after one game.

Our campaign began in a haphazard way, with atrocious outfielding and a flatness about our play that suggested we were either tired or tense. Although we beat the Scots by six wickets, after the game, for one of the few times in my career, I aired my dirty laundry in public. I knew public criticism had the potential to break down a unit, especially if someone embellished an angle I provided, but on this occasion I had to let the players know how disappointed I was. I wouldn't do it again, at least not before I'd had a chance to discuss my grievances with the team. The topic of our inept fielding came up again a couple of days later, when Michael Bevan and I went out for a bite to eat. While he is an intense introvert at times, Bevo can reveal pearls of wisdom when you unlock his intellect. He is a deep thinker, but this time around his message was simple: 'We're putting too much pressure on ourselves. Let's seek enjoyment and relax a bit.' Perhaps we had been too focused on winning the World Cup and bypassed how we were going to get there.

Despite cigars all round, a convincing loss to New Zealand in our second game made for a subdued celebration for the birth of Jackson

Warne. By this point, my mind was churning as I sought answers as to why we were so lethargic. Before the tournament began, I had decided to use our best two swing bowlers, Adam Dale and Damien Fleming, with the new ball because we were using Duke balls, which had high seams and swung more. My hope was that they would strike early and then the opposition batsmen would be confronted by the world's best pace man in Glenn McGrath. It was an unashamed copy of tactics used by the South Africans, who had deployed Allan Donald in the same manner and been very successful. However, my move lasted only one more game before we decided to go back to the tried and trusted formula of strike power up front. In that third game, a tight loss to Pakistan, positive signs did emerge, but our dream was dying along with the fading light in which the game ended. It took a sly kick from Shoaib Akhtar (or, as we called him, 'B-grade Actor'), as I attempted to slide in and turn for two late in our innings, to awaken the raw fighting spirit within me. Akhtar's action was a cheap shot that caught me by complete surprise. As discreetly as I could, I walked with him for a few steps before saying, 'Every dog has its day.' He just puffed out his chest and kept on walking.

We'd had a very open and honest meeting before the Pakistan game, during which a few players had got some issues off their chests and cleared the air. The solution was, as it generally is, very simple: we needed to support each other and be more patient in our cricket. Even though one-day cricket is frenetic by nature, there is still a vital need, if you want to govern the course of the match, to identify the right time to increase your risk-taking and when to hold back.

There was, however, one disturbing line of questioning that was troubling me. It came from respected ABC commentator Tim Lane, who stopped me for a quick chat before the training session on the day leading up to the Pakistan game. Tim didn't pull any punches, asking, 'Is there a feud between Shane and you?'

This proposition totally blew me away, so much so that I called Warney over as he departed from the dressing sheds to refute the claim, which he did. I learnt that the story had been publicised by a source 'close to the team', which I was later told was apparently New Zealand coach and 'loader of bullets' Steve Rixon. I had no problem with Shane other than I had been forced to drop him from the Test side, which for me was ancient news, but the old saying 'Where there's smoke, there's fire' gnawed away at me. Was there a problem? If so, I needed to confront it and find a solution. When I brought the general issue up of player discontent at the pregame team meeting, all I got were vacant looks and full support.

Inspiration comes from all sources and in varying guises, and during this World Cup I had back-to-back experiences that played a big part in our eventual turnaround.

A quick beer, 20 minutes before closing, with Adam 'Chippen' Dale and Damien Fleming in a deserted Leeds pub led to a mini bowling group being formed, the objective of which was to develop a clearer pattern for our bowling. Various options were put forward, including breaking down the innings into four clearly defined segments: 0 to 15 overs, 16 to 25, 25 to 40 and the last 10, which are the most crucial as they can either set up the opposition's platform (if they are batting first) or bring them home for a win. 'Let's get back to bowling the yorkers, mix our pace up and stop the boundaries,' we decided, 'because those last 10 overs have been killing us.'

The second inspirational experience came as I sat watching TV and having a room-service club sandwich and a Coke in Durham the night before our game against Bangladesh. I marvelled at Manchester United coming back from 1–0 down with two minutes of injury time left against German champions Bayern Munich to score two goals, make the improbable happen and win the Champions League final. Right there and then I lifted, realising that it was only willpower we needed to steer us out of trouble. As captain, I had to lead the way. Deep inside, I wanted and knew I was going to play a part in something special.

The night before our crucial match against the West Indies, Mark and I received the shocking news that our paternal grandfather, Edward, was seriously ill with cancer and not expected to live much longer. My memory immediately flashed back to the jar of jersey caramels he used to let us dip our eager hands into when we visited Dad's parents every couple of weeks, and the 20-cent coins he and my grandmother would slip into our palms – we thought we were rich. It seemed like yesterday that his father, our great-grandfather, and he were pushing us down the hill at Earlwood in a handmade billycart. I wondered if they had ever thought Mark and I would get where we were today. Way back then, I doubt it!

My grandfather preoccupied my thoughts, but also on my mind was the World Cup points table. The organisers had come up with a complicated formula in which the top three teams in each of two groups qualified for the second round – what they called the Super Six. The Super Six was structured so that the teams involved would play a 'round robin' format, with the top four going through to the semi-finals. However, rather than the teams from the first-round groups playing each other again, their first-round matches against *each other* – but not the other first-round matches – would be taken into account when calculating the Super Six rankings. If Pakistan and New Zealand went through with us, we'd be starting the Super Six series with no points. This set up a scenario where we had to defeat the Windies in our final first-round match to go through, but ideally not beat them too badly, so they, rather than New Zealand, would qualify with us. Adding a double-jeopardy element was the fact that if we ended up on equal points with either of the co-qualifiers from our group at the end of the Super Six matches, then the early losses would be used again as a countback mechanism to split the tie.

It's hard to devise a foolproof system, and the flaw in this one meant that, after dismissing the West Indies for just 110, once we got close to victory it was in our best interests to slow down our run rate to help the Windies out. Bevo and I dawdled our way to the last 20 runs in 20 overs of unappealing, boring cricket, but I felt we owed it to each other to give ourselves the best chance of winning the tournament. This was one step along the way. I knew I'd cop a blast at the postmatch press conference and in the subsequent days, but I was steadfast, if not a little hot-headed, when I said, 'We're not here to win friends, just the World Cup.'

Three days later we were in London – at Buckingham Palace to be precise. A meeting with the Queen on your birthday isn't something you would ever expect, but the Waugh boys exchanged conversation with this most pleasant lady whose love is for horses and corgi dogs, not cricket. Talking to her was relatively easy, as she reminded me of my grandmother, which broke down the mystique somewhat.

Two moments remain etched in my memory from that day. Zimbabwe's Murray Goodwin somehow got himself detached from his team when the formal introductions were being made, first to Prince Philip and then to the Queen, and he found himself tacked onto the Windies squad. The Prince reacted with, 'You don't look much like a West Indian!' to which Murray dryly replied, 'No, but I wish I was hung like one.'

The second event focused on our scorer, Mike Walsh, who, unbeknown to most of us at the time, almost created a royal incident. The following evening, on the team bus, a video was paraded high in the air. 'Watch this, boys,' proclaimed someone who'd had a sneak preview of the tape, 'you're going to have a good laugh.' As Mike had been last in line, none of us had seen the calamity 'live'. Upon being called to meet the Queen, Walshy had got his foot tangled on the royal red carpet, then caught his shoe on its lip and been thrown forward, head first, for a couple of steps before he pulled up just in time, regained his composure and said, 'Ma'am, nice to meet you.' 'Walshy', in his clumsiness, had nearly 'Mr Beaned' the Queen. By the 30th replay our stomach muscles could take no more.

Despite our best endeavours, New Zealand's emphatic victory over Scotland in their last first-round match meant we did go through to the Super Six in last position. We had to win at least two but most likely all three of our games against India, Zimbabwe and South Africa to make it to the semi-finals. First up, a match against India on the bounciest track in the UK, the Oval, filled me with hope as the flat-track maestros don't enjoy extra pace and bounce. Another positive was the ploy we introduced of giving each player their opposite number to analyse and then report back and present their views at the team meeting. This innovation ensured that every member of the squad had ownership of the team's plan, and it also made everyone accountable and attuned to the impending task.

As I'd done at the start of the West Indies tour, I gave each player a single page that outlined my thoughts on his respective role. I added a catch phrase that I believed was a key point for that player. For Tom Moody, it was 'Be decisive'; for Mark, 'Back your instincts'. For Paul Reiffel, I thought 'Believe in yourself' was appropriate. At the bottom of each player's page was the same message:

> Every sacrifice we make is a down payment on the acquisition of the World Cup.
> Play well,
> Tugga

For me, this summed up how we were going to achieve our ambition.

★

Big kid Glenn McGrath always loves a challenge. However, on the beach at Colombo in Sri Lanka, this was as far as he got.

Matthew Hayden forces a smile while perched on the edge of a 226-metre (741-foot) drop at the Kaieteur Falls, located near the borders of Guyana, Venezuela and Brazil.

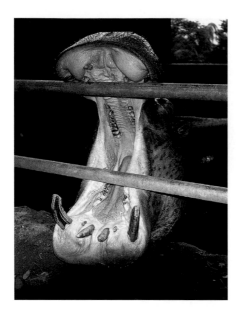

This hippo (LEFT) at Guwahati Zoo in the far north-east of India seemed to be on the lookout for a wayward child, while this camel (RIGHT) just wanted to race in the Dubai desert.

The plains of the majestic Serengeti in Kenya are simply spectacular.

On the train to Victoria Falls, with Stuart MacGill and Justin Langer proudly wearing hats they've acquired from fellow passengers such as the woman standing in the doorway.

Andrew Symonds and I take in the breathtaking views from Table Mountain in Cape Town.

Lynette and me with a tranquillised lion moments before a tracking device was attached to it, at Pilansberg National Park, near Sun City.

This is the effect the mere sight of a white man can have on a child in Trench Town, Jamaica.

A young boy poses in front of a mural of Trench Town's favourite son, Bob Marley.

During our 2002 tour to South Africa we visited Robben Island, the island prison in which Nelson Mandela was incarcerated for 27 years. I'm standing in front of one of the large pictures of inmates that sit on the walls as a reminder of past crimes.

Aussie all-rounder Shane Lee has snuck into a team photo of Maasai tribespeople at Masai Mara Game Reserve in Kenya.

The dazzling colours impelled me to capture this image.

A tribal elder counts the US dollars he has received after selling some souvenirs.

A moment of reflection at Gallipoli. Note the mixture of slouch hats and baggy greens.

As a tribute to the Anzacs, we tried to recreate the brave game of cricket eight diggers played on Shell Green during the Allies' evacuation.

Shane Warne examines the willow at Gunn & Moore's old bat factory in Nottingham during the 1997 Ashes tour.

Friendly faces at Dhaka in Bangladesh during our brief trip there for the mini World Cup of 1998.

Street life near the entrance to the checkpoint at the Khyber Pass.

Members of the famed Khyber Rifles took us to their training grounds in the mountains bordering Pakistan and Afghanistan.

Schoolgirls full of life skip in front of derelict buildings in Trench Town. The rawness of where they live doesn't appear to worry them.

Meanwhile, these seemingly happy, innocent kids are eager to check out my camera.

Our momentum kept building towards the business end of the tournament. I felt we were beginning to peak and that a winning vibe was definitely in the air. If we could overcome South Africa, the media's clear favourite, in our final Super Six match (which it turned out we had to), I knew we'd go on and win it all, and I was sure that deep down South Africa feared us as their real dangers. It wasn't all smooth sailing, though, because I had to cope with a distracted and somewhat distant vice-captain who was apparently on the verge of retirement. His bowling in the first two Super Six games had been ineffective, and psychologically he was at an all-time low. The morning after our Lord's victory against Zimbabwe, Dave Misson took us for a recovery session through Hyde Park in London to get rid of the excess lactic acid that can lead to stiffness and soreness and to clear our heads, and it was during this long walk that I linked up with Shane to have a chat about how he was feeling. I sensed a man in desperate need of support and cheering up. His head was in a pickle, a fact that had been further confirmed by Sandy Gordon when he informed me that Shane *was* causing some friction behind the scenes over the captaincy. He was lonely, hurt, annoyed and frustrated, and quite frankly sick of the media attention. He just wanted to be Shane Nobody for a day to get his bearings back.

It had been a tough 12 months for him, with his shoulder surgery, the 'bribery' allegations, the captaincy debate after Tubby's retirement, his axing from the Test side in the Caribbean, the cigarette photo in Barbados, the Arjuna article that caused a stir, the birth of a child while he was away, the intrusive media and the sometimes abusive crowds. Through it all he'd been playing with a shoulder that was sore and not fully recovered.

The instant we walked back into our hotel in London after our deep and meaningful chat, I asked Moods to pass the word around: 'Keep Warney up and look after him in the next couple of days.'

We'd all been there, at the doorway of despair, and a good team will recognise a member's personal struggle and lend a hand. Subtly, I tried to involve Shane more in discussions and team tactics, which were strengths of his. However, ultimately he had to give more to the cause and only he could muster that. Knowing Shane well, I believed he would lift in the definitive games because of who he was: a champion competitor who loves everything being on the line and the result being dependent on him. Shane needs constant support, encouragement and reassurance that he is the man, and at the 1999 World Cup that played a big part in getting him going. He loves to be loved. For the rest of us, it was in a way comforting to know that even a legend needs to battle the dark forces occasionally, that no one is exempt from self-doubt.

So it was up to Leeds for the match of the tournament: a duel with South Africa. The night we arrived, I had a chat with Trevor Hohns regarding who might be the 25 players nominated for contracts leading into the new season, which led to an open and frank three-hour discussion about how, if the results didn't meet expectations, a change at the top of the one-day team might occur. I took this to mean that had we not qualified for the Super Six I would have been gone, and that if we failed to reach the semi-finals I was in trouble. It was good to know where I stood, but still I was a little shocked at how cutthroat the selectors' attitude was. Again I said, 'If you don't think I'm the guy, then let me know and I'll step aside.' It was an honest comment, though I genuinely believed I was the right guy.

History shows that Australia's next two games were among the greatest ever played. Gilly set the scene by reading an anonymously written poem at the end of our warm-up:

Believe in yourself and in your plan
Say not 'I cannot', but 'I can'

The prizes in life we fail to win
Only if we doubt the power within.

★

It was a day I'll never forget, a day when all the years of throwing away my wicket in the slog overs, of not really achieving what I wanted to as a one-day batsman, came together at exactly the right time. In a way, the story actually starts at the pregame meeting. The very last comment came from the king: 'If anyone hits the ball in the air in Herschelle's direction and he catches you, don't walk straight-away because he has a habit of "show boating" and he might drop it in the process.' With a hint of scepticism, someone said, 'Good point, Warney,' and the meeting was over.

At 3/48 chasing South Africa's 272 on an up-and-down pitch against a quality attack, it was all on the line. When the third wicket fell, which meant it was my turn out in the middle, that familiar surge of gut-wrenching anxiety and heightened arousal that follows the loss of a wicket hit me like a freight train. This was it – the point of no return. Failure meant a flight home and, in all likelihood, the end of my one-day career, and it was this hovering guillotine that activated the spirit within. I didn't want it to end this way after 13 and a half years in limited-overs international cricket. The job wasn't done yet; there was unfinished business.

Saying this was the easy part. The reality was coming out to a fired-up attack who were well in charge on an unpredictable pitch, and a yapping Herschelle Gibbs saying, 'Now it's your turn, let's see how you handle the pressure.' If I'd answered him truthfully, I would have said, 'Good point. I'm nervous, my heart's racing, my palms are sweaty, but you're going to have to kill me to get me out!' He was well within his rights to enter into a bit of gamesmanship, as we had questioned his temperament during his innings by asking rhetorical questions such as, 'I wonder why Herschelle isn't in the Test team?' Though he had scored Test runs against other teams, he'd struggled against us in the past, so we'd answer ourselves: 'He mustn't be very good at concentrating.' Or: 'I can't believe he's not in the Test team – he must be a bit soft.' You could say our talk backfired, because this gifted timer of the ball, a man with a god-given talent only a few possess, carved us up for a majestic 101, using our barbs like Popeye would a can of spinach.

To Ricky Ponting and me, the situation we faced was fairly obvious: 'Let's build a partnership, but cut down the risks against their strike bowlers before unleashing against their spinners and all-rounders.' A meagre 22 runs were taken from the next 10 overs, by which point the game was close to slipping away. Risks needed to be taken: 82 came from the next 10, and I knew we'd worked our way back into the game when Hansie Cronje swore at me. That was a rarity, and a clear sign he was on edge. The game's equilibrium had shifted.

I was in complete battle mode, to the point of being arrogant, but still tactically aware as to whom to single out. Cronje was a tough leader and a fine cricketer, but he could be broken down under the blowtorch of pressure and it was with this in mind that I said to him, as he walked back to bowl his first delivery, 'I'm taking you down today.' His smile turned to fury as the game changed during his spell. I was on the edge, juggling a fine line between self-belief and pretentiousness, but in my own way I was also trying to convince myself I could do what needed to be done. Like learning your times tables at school, the more you say something to yourself, the easier it becomes. I was taunting myself to get on board and knuckle down, and every time I got a reaction from the opposition, my intent strengthened.

With my score on 56 a miraculous event occurred. Proving that Shane Warne's gift of intuition and eye for body language are generally spot on, Herschelle Gibbs played out Shane's prediction in front of a huge worldwide audience when his attempt to complete a simple catch went horribly wrong. He knew straightaway he'd stuff up. A desperate Cronje tried to convince the umpire his fieldsman had controlled the ball even as Gibbs walked away in embarrassment. When we crossed paths mid-pitch, I couldn't resist a jibe in our ongoing verbal battle. 'Hey, Herschelle,' I said, 'do you realise you've just cost your team the match?' My mouth was well ahead of my brain and almost out of control, but I still knew this moment was the turning point of the game. Here was a chance of a lifetime that needed to be grabbed onto; such was my focus that I now felt destined to see it through.

When I was on 91, I played the greatest shot of my career. It happened by impulse – an extremely high-risk slog-sweep hit of their opening bowler, Steve Elworthy, that sailed miles over the longest boundary as I lay prone in an ungainly position after swinging myself off my feet. There are few greater joys than seeing a ball launch off your bat so well that it's not a question of whether it's a six but rather how far will it go. There's a minute area on the bat which, when found, doesn't vibrate in your hands as you connect with the ball but rather just allows it to become one with the timber for a split second before it catapults off into the stratosphere. It's pure bliss for the batsman, a rare moment of perfection.

With 4.2 overs remaining and Australia needing 26 to win, Michael Bevan was caught by Daryll Cullinan. At the end of that over, with us needing exactly a run a ball, I was joined mid-pitch by my old mate Tom Moody, who said simply, 'What do you reckon?' This was no time to hesitate, so I just said, matter-of-factly, 'We've waited 15 years for this situation. Let's just do it.'

Do it we did, and the postmatch celebration indicated that we weren't going to waste such a fantastic comeback. We were on a roll. The Cup, I believed, was there for the taking.

★

No one could have known that this spine-tingling affair would actually be topped by a game with even greater theatre and more fluctuations only four days later. Again playing South Africa but this time batting first, at 4/68 from 17 overs I found myself in a situation not dissimilar to the one we'd been in at Headingley. This time, though, there were moments when I felt mentally fatigued and needed to pep-talk myself back into the current state of affairs. Bevo and I decided early in our partnership to aim for 220 as a score that would give us a fair chance of victory, so ending up on 213 was a good outcome after our potentially disastrous start.

My team talks before entering the field of play were generally brief, as I believe that lengthy sermons can sometimes distract players at a time when they are entering their own little worlds of preparation – and the one I gave before we went out was no different, but Shane's emotional words that preceded our walk onto the field clearly signalled that if we didn't win he'd be hanging up his boots. He was passionate and fired up for the duel and his emotional plea for a big performance further charged the atmosphere.

At 0/48 off 12 overs, I needed to break from tradition and take a gamble, and in Warney I had a bowler capable of turning a match on its head. He started by dismissing Gibbs with his second ball, a delivery very similar to the Mike Gatting 'Ball of the Century' from 1993, and as I was fielding nearby I was the first to be hit with the pent-up force that he'd suppressed in his system. He was so fired up and animated that it took a wall of players to stifle his forward thrust. His drive and will were literally scary, but he sparked life into others who were tensing up under the South African onslaught and got us back into the game. His three wickets in eight deliveries, as South Africa slumped to 3/53, not only put us back on an even keel but also undoubtedly affected the confidence of the remaining batsmen in the viewing rooms.

The game was well and truly on. For every single ball of that innings

I was aware that one wrong field placing or a poorly timed bowling change could cost us the game. This was without doubt the most testing time of my captaincy – this whole World Cup campaign, which had begun two years earlier, was at least in part dependent on my calmness and ability to think clearly under pressure. The responsibility lifted me, because I knew that not everyone in the game could handle what was being played out and that I had a real chance to influence the result. In some ways, being fully occupied was probably a blessing, as idle moments can make a fieldsman think too much about an outcome. It was in this scenario that one of our safest catchers, Paul Reiffel, spilled two chances, one of which altered the status quo significantly. With South Africa nine down, the second-last ball of the 49th over, bowled by Glenn McGrath, was a low full toss that Lance Klusener smashed to long-on. The match was ours until Pistol slightly misjudged the ferocity of the shot and palmed it over the crossbar, goalie fashion, for six. With a camera undoubtedly focusing on my facial expression, I managed to refrain from letting any emotion out – firstly, to not rub salt into Pistol's wounds, secondly, to not look like a goose, and thirdly, because the match was still there for the taking.

A single from the final ball left Klusener, who was yet to mishit a ball in the tournament, on strike for the final over, to be delivered by Damien Fleming. South Africa needed nine to win. The plan was simple: fire those yorkers in and give him a single. All the infielders stayed as far back as they could, on the circle, while the five outfielders patrolled the boundary ropes.

Flem was our best yorker bowler, but Klusener was in the same frame of mind as Warney had been and he smoked the first two balls with pure brute force through the covers for blistering fours that never looked like being cut off. Our only chance now was to break his concentration and rhythm, to slow up the pace in the hope this might alter the groove he was in. My only option was to bring the field in to stop the single and hope for a catch or a run-out, while Klusener no doubt had another four in mind. And now, in the defining moments, he proved he was fallible after all, as a mishit drive presented Darren Lehmann at mid-on with a straightforward run-out opportunity – but he stiffened up under the crushing weight of a berth in the World Cup final and missed from short range, with No. 11 Allan Donald way out of his ground. *Shit! That's it – our last chance gone. We'll need a miracle now.* Amazingly, neither Donald nor Klusener instigated a mid-wicket conference to discuss a plan for the next three balls, and neither did we! Everyone was going in blind, hoping fate would be kind, and then it happened – a yorker that the batsman miscued again, this time to Mark Waugh who flicked it backhanded, indoor-cricket style, to Flem, who was hovering around the stumps at the bowler's end. Donald, still dazed after the confusion of the previous ball, dived back into the crease and lost his bat in the process while a rampaging Klusener was running to the same end.

It was then that the slow-motion button kicked in. Donald scrambled up from the ground, turned and began to run without his bat to the striker's end for what would have been the winning run. At the same instant, Flem took the 'wild throw over the keeper's head' out of the equation by executing a classic underarm delivery down the pitch into the match-winning hands of keeper Adam Gilchrist. Flashes of the team's tenpin-bowling night out the week before suddenly flickered in my mind. Fate was on our side.

Klusener kept on running, aware the game was lost, while a dejected Donald trudged back to pick up his bat. We ran around like prison escapees, not knowing who to grab, totally overcome with excitement. I knew the match had ended in a tie, but wasn't sure if we'd qualified for the final. The only thing I was sure of was that we'd escaped, and then I heard Bevo yelling, 'We're in! We're in!' Our Super Six win at Headingley, which meant we had finished higher than South Africa in the Super Six table, had suddenly become doubly important.

Once the on-field backslapping concluded, a replay of the final over came up on the monitor in our dressing-room. It was an eerie sensation watching those last four balls again. I was still nervous; had it really happened? Were we going to win? It was like watching a live game that didn't involve us and over whose ending we had no control. Then a massive cheer went up as soon as Gilly whipped the bails off!

I don't think I've ever seen such a crestfallen individual as Hansie Cronje when he and I waited to be interviewed by Ian Chappell after the match. He was zombie-like and barely acknowledged my words: 'No one deserved to lose such a great game.' Actually, no one did on the scorecard, but the fact was we were off to Lord's.

I was later told by Bob Woolmer, who left the South African team after the tournament, that they never had a post-mortem on the result. Some would say they needed to, for it seemed there were unresolved issues that would plague them at the next World Cup, when again they crumbled under pressure at precisely the wrong time.

Our game plan for the final was simple: play the way South Africa would. I'd spotted a statistic that showed that Pakistan had lost the last 13 times they'd played South Africa. Why? Because Wasim Akram's team hated persistent, consistent, ruthless teams who could expose the Pakistanis' inconsistency and volatile moods. If we could exert consistent pressure, I reasoned, they would crack and give us plenty of opportunities. We also had the extra incentive of making sure they were going to face up to the bribery allegations that had been rumoured might dissipate if they won the final. We wanted to play our best game ever, and to do that we left our pregame team meeting with the words, 'Don't forget to enjoy it and have fun.'

Making it through to the final meant I had to come good on my promise to provide the team with a pregame poem, a commitment I had made at the start of the tournament. With no 'home team', the two sides had to agree or toss on which room they wanted, but there was no problem as our lads were keen to occupy the 'away' room and the Pakistan squad preferred the bigger 'home' room. Considering Australia's great record in Test matches at Lord's (12 wins and just one loss in 26 Tests between 1899 and 1997), the away room was a good-luck charm in our eyes. A delayed start due to rain reminded me of the 1996 World Cup, but this time we were ready to the point of warming up in sprinkling rain while the opposition waited inside for the skies to clear. We didn't want to disrupt our routine or alter our attitude to influences outside our control.

A little more than 18 months after I had assumed the one-day captaincy and set our goals, we played the ultimate game when it counted most. We hardly bowled a bad ball, fielded brilliantly from the moment Mark took a spectacular diving catch at second slip to dismiss the Pakistani opener, Wajahatullah Wasti, and never allowed Pakistan to settle with the bat. It was machine-like, with every field movement, bowling change and tactic coming off. For me, an easy guide as to whether the guys were switched on to the task was if I didn't have to signal twice to get someone's attention when I wanted to make a fielding change. Further to that, I knew we were really on song if I made a deft hand signal for a slight alteration in the field and the guy in question picked it up without the batsman realising. All these things happened on this memorable day.

After steamrolling Pakistan for 132 in 39 overs, we flew up the pavilion steps and entered the Lord's Long Room to raucous applause. I got the shock of my life when I saw former Australian prime minister Bob Hawke standing directly in front of us with a beaming smile. He was yelling congratulations and calling the lads by variations of their nicknames: 'Well done Punto, Gillsey, Waughsey,' he quipped as we high-fived him on our way past the cigar-smoking, cucumber-sandwich-eating brigade. Surely we were home now, 'Hawkey' never gets it wrong! And from the sixth over, when Gilly snapped out of his form slump and cut Shoaib Akhtar for six over third man, the match slipped away from Pakistan with ease.

A considerable amount of effort, especially by Swamp, and to a lesser extent myself, was put into helping Gilly in the lead-up to the final, because for the first time in his international cricket life he'd been out of nick with the bat and unsure how to reverse his run of poor form. In nine innings in the tournament he'd scored only 170 runs, 69 of them against Bangladesh. He had become noticeably more subdued than we'd seen him before, and as the keeper and heartbeat of the side we needed his spirits to lift. Like all champions, the bigger the occasion the more probable it was that he would be able to find something, and that he did. As he struck each boundary, the group gathering on the famous Lord's balcony increased, filling it to capacity, as did our contentment. It's a fantastic feeling sitting side by side with your mates as you enjoy the benefits of hard work and planning and ultimately lift the World Cup, which became a reality when 'Boof' Lehmann cut Saqlain Mushtaq behind point for four. In the ensuing minutes, no one could tell me that one-day cricket wasn't as important as Test cricket.

A song in the centre of Lord's, where Punter, from atop Tom Moody's shoulders, recited the poem he'd written and used a few weeks before, was followed by a three-verse version of 'Underneath the Southern Cross I Stand'. Then we had an all-night party back at the team hotel that doubled as Glenn McGrath's bucks night – or at least that was the excuse I used to demolish a couple of B52s that tumbled down my throat with alarming ease as I held grimly onto the 18 kg World Cup with my aching left arm. But then a phone call unexpectedly summoned Mark and me away from the festivities.

It was 2 a.m. when the shattering news of our grandfather passing away hit us between the eyes and ended our celebration. We headed off teary-eyed to our rooms, almost unable to comprehend all that had happened in the previous 24 hours. I was basically devoid of thought, unable to concentrate on any issue long enough to make sense of it. Many lives had been changed and one close to us had ended, thankfully in one sense because the savagery of the cancer had taken away the very essence of who our grandfather was.

Winning the World Cup ensured stardom for the members of the squad, at least in the short term. Our profiles skyrocketed overnight, which was especially fantastic for the guys who were used to being in the background. For the Waugh twins, though, it caused immediate pain. Carrying our grandfather's casket as pallbearers with Dean and Danny and our father, Rodger, who was understandably numb after minutes earlier laying his dad's favourite possessions on the coffin, we carefully walked down the stairs outside the church in Ballina on the NSW north coast, to be hit by the flash bulbs of a press photographer who'd been sent on an errand by his editor. It was difficult to ignore, and I knew the photographer didn't really want to be there and that it was part of the reality of being high-profile sportspeople: we were public property. For me, just five months into the job as Test *and* one-day captain, and now a World Cup winner, this scrutiny was something, more than ever, I was going to have to come to terms with.

34

The Holy Grail

Our next assignment was always going to be a testing one: a tour to the slow-turning tracks of Sri Lanka. Before we departed, a camp in Brisbane gave us a chance to sharpen our skills, and perhaps most importantly to have a session with Sandy Gordon, 'Mental Skills for Performance Management'.

We were handed a questionnaire, the answers to which Sandy and Geoff Marsh would use as guidelines to understand each player better.

A whole raft of topics were covered and, like any concept, some guys really enjoyed the stimulation of thinking about their cricket, while others, such as brother Mark, thought it to be more hocus-pocus then science. I certainly didn't see any harm in the clarity and positive rein-forcement Sandy's work provided, but I could also understand how others wanted to keep things simple and just play. The best aspect of it all was that the results were made available and you could take or leave them.

First question: 'How can I best help you the cricketer/performer?'

My answer: 'Constructive help is always appreciated. Likewise, posi-tive reinforcement is needed by all the players, even the senior guys.' I felt that sometimes we'd tended to gloss over the great players in the side. The first example that came to mind was Ian Healy, whose pol-ished performances we became used to and almost took for granted. The truth was that Heals, like anyone else, loved to be told he was doing an outstanding job and probably didn't hear it enough. My mental goals for the season ahead were to stay hungry and focused for each game and to get myself in that zone of intensity and desire that leads to success.

The one-day series in Sri Lanka began ominously with 'Waltzing Matilda' blaring out of the ground's loudspeakers as our 'national anthem'. Then, as part of an 'opening ceremony', the captains of the three teams involved in the competition – Sachin Tendulkar (India), Sanath Jayasuriya (Sri Lanka) and I – had to ignite a cricket-themed cauldron with a flaming torch. Later I was told that Sachin nearly lit up my backside when I brushed past him. Our run of 11 straight limited-overs international wins was ended by the hosts in the final. Arguably the biggest positive for us coming out of the competition was the sight of Ricky Ponting and newcomer Andrew Symonds patrolling the inner circle like two sharks would a home aquarium: everything that moved was vulnerable. However, for me the cricket was overshadowed by the announcement that our beloved coach,

Geoff Marsh, was to step aside to spend more time with his family. It was a decision that shocked me, but the tragic news of his best mate passing away while we were on tour made Swamp redefine his priorities and family was now by a long way top of the list.

Geoff was one of that rare breed who can occupy a position of power yet still be your mate. He had a real passion for the game and knew exactly when to say the right word at the appropriate time. Plenty of times he'd just walk up and say, 'Well done' or 'You're moving your feet well' or 'Great shot', which to me, when said at the right time, make up the one per centers that enter the X factor category. He was a fitness fanatic who could have a laugh at himself, which was good because he needed a thick skin when questions like this were asked whenever his girth expanded: 'What bra size are you, Swamp?' and 'Did you swallow a sheep in the off-season?' With his pride on the line, he'd then embark on a maniacal regime where he'd be running around hotel gardens at six in the morning, monitoring all his foods, wearing the treadmill out and pinching his stomach every five minutes to see if one of his rolls had disappeared. A fair-dinkum Aussie character, he loved the camaraderie of sharing a beer and a story, and no one appreciated the honour of playing and coaching his country more than he did. I'll never forget Swamp walking back to the pavilion at Lord's after we'd sung our team song out on the pitch after winning the World Cup. He turned around and with an impish grin said, 'Tugga, it doesn't get any better than this.'

The Test series offered a chance for us to solidify and gel as a unit, hence our motto for the three Tests: 'Back to basics'. This was a tour where guys had the opportunity to put their hands up and say, 'Look at my attitude – I'm here for the long stay.' Or at least that's what I hoped. The three 'Ps' that had sustained us for the best part of a decade – Patience,

Partnerships and Pressure – were the pillars on which we had built our reputation, but ones that we might have taken our eyes off in the West Indies. Also on my radar screen was the team's spirit. I wanted a genuine, not manufactured, effort to be together and I wanted the guys to respect the team rules (which had reverted to the midnight curfew and drinking rules), which had flexibility but needed acceptance by all if they were to have an impact. I was searching for the right balance and hoped that by being hard early the benefits would come later, through self-monitoring.

What I found immediately was a casualty bed in Colombo Hospital alongside Jason Gillespie, on just the second day of the series. The first morning of the opening Test, in Kandy, was a disaster, with the game essentially lost by lunch with careless soft dismissals leaving us precariously placed at 7/61. A wet tissue would have offered more resistance than we mustered, as our long-standing weakness of having not an occasional bad session but a rare terminal one resurfaced. About two-thirds of the way through the first session of day two, I acted on a hunch to move from midwicket to 45 degrees behind square in the quest for a catch off Colin Miller's bowling to Mahela Jayawardene. Sure enough, next ball Jayawardene went for the full-blooded sweep but top-edged it high into the air – a spiralling chance over my left shoulder that required a delicate balance between sprinting and keeping an eye on the ball's flight path. Just as I went to link my hands with arms outstretched for the catch, I lost the ball in the sun; I found it a moment later, but in that blinding millisecond I'd miscalculated my finishing point and had to lunge to take the offering. Instead of feeling the worn leather nestle into the soft fleshy part of the palm, I experienced the numbing pain of my head feeling like it had been poleaxed by a Mike Tyson knockout punch. In that fleeting moment, I couldn't work out what had happened. How could such a brilliant piece of captaincy and inspiration go so horribly wrong?

As I lay prone, I thought to myself, *Shit, this isn't going to be good. Have a feel around and assess the damage.* My first concern was that I couldn't see: everything was blurry. Then, while fumbling around, I noticed my nose wasn't where it was supposed to be. I'm not sure whether or not I was knocked out for a few seconds, but the first person to talk to me was Errol Alcott. 'Hooter' later told me he went for the medical kit as soon as the ball went into the air and was out the door by the time Jason Gillespie and I collided like two downed helicopters.

My first words to him were, 'Hoot, I can't see.'

'Don't worry, it's only the blood in your eyes,' he countered.

It's funny what comes into your head in these situations. My main concern was for my wife, who I knew would be watching the coverage live back home, so my next line was, 'Cover me up so Lynette doesn't see the blood.'

Minutes later, back in the change rooms with blood streaming down the back of my throat and oozing out of a gaping laceration where a bone had penetrated the skin, I was thinking, *I'll be back for tomorrow's play. The doctor will be able to straighten it up and away I'll go.* The next thing I saw was Dizzy being carried in on the shoulders of our reserves, and in my shocked state I said, 'What the hell are you doing here?' It hadn't registered that he, too, was seriously injured; indeed, with his broken leg and other injuries he would ultimately pay a much higher price than I did for not calling for a high ball, which is one of the first lessons any coach gives to his team in junior cricket. Further confirming I was in shock was my insistence on getting a photo of the smashed 'Lionel Rose', which a pale-faced Dave Misson reluctantly took as he winced at my ugliness.

We endured the short trip to Kandy Hospital in a beat-up old minivan that doubled as an ambulance and was piloted by a young man very inept at handling a steering-column gearstick. Each grinding gear change that jerked us forward was met with an agonising moan from Dizzy, whose condition was obviously quite serious. But if we thought the hospital would bring relief we were sorely mistaken. We were escorted to a waiting room where we were bombarded by a horde of cricket-loving autograph collectors wielding flashing cameras.

It was tough to muster up a smile with blood streaming out of a nose that belonged to a face I couldn't feel. Dizzy, meanwhile, was slumped in his wheelchair battling waves of nausea and throbbing pain. The local specialist had a quick look and a prod at my nose and said, 'No problem, we'll just put a local in and move it back into place.' Thankfully, Errol's father was a doctor and his acquired knowledge was enough to tell him that it might be prudent to investigate further. An X-ray, which was later souvenired by hospital staff, revealed a multitude of broken bones, a compound fracture and a septum bent at a 35-degree angle. Jason's X-ray revealed a clean break in his right tibia, and 10 weeks later a crack was also found in his right wrist.

After this initial consultation it was time to fly down to Colombo for further treatment, but not before a subsequent disaster nearly took place when the back door of the minibus was almost slammed shut by the overzealous staff with Jason's leg still protruding from it. The ever-alert Errol spotted the danger and intervened to save the day. Thanks to Sri Lankan captain Sanath Jayasuriya, our trip was by helicopter. His connections in the military soon had an army chopper ready and we were thus able to avert a four-hour road trip. The last image I saw before undergoing a two-and-a-half-hour operation was a conglomeration of smiling Sri Lankan doctors saying, 'It's Steve Waugh! It's Steve Waugh!' and my last thought, as I felt the cool sensation of the anaesthetic sliding down my arm, was *I hope this turns out better than I'm anticipating.*

Back in our private room we looked a sorry sight, me with a Hannibal Lecter face mask and Jason wearing a hip-to-toe plaster cast. To make matters worse, on the TV the team were slipping towards a crushing defeat and we weren't allowed to eat for another two hours.

Dizzy rather dryly turned to me and said, 'Hey, Tugga, I don't think you're going to make it back for tomorrow's play.' His slight sarcasm would badly backfire later that night when he was in a distressed state because of his total reluctance to have a painkilling needle and I buzzed the male nurse to see if there was any way to stop the big, menacing, tough quick's constant moaning. It began with the startling snapping sound of a pair of latex gloves being pulled on as the nurse instructed Jason to roll over and bend his knees up for a quick fix. As he did so we made eye contact from our closely aligned beds, and in those fleeting seconds I saw pure helplessness and total resignation emanating from his eyes. Dignity was about to be taken away. In a moment of rebellion the suppository popped out, but its escape was only temporary; needless to say, Dizzy's phobia of needles was cured in those intimate moments, which provided me with a laugh amid all the gloom.

The next 11 days were a race against the clock if I was to be passed fit for the second Test. In those desperate days I listened to my inner voice, which said, *Follow your instincts as a captain. Don't do it by consensus – lead by example.* Each day was a battle as I awoke to a splitting headache, blurred vision and wobbly balance, but I knew there was no way I was going to or could afford to miss the Test. By game day it felt like I'd had only 10 Southern and Cokes the night before instead of the 20 it had felt like the day after the collision – which might lead some people to think that I shouldn't have played, but when I look back on my Test captaincy career, getting on the park as quickly as I did was the start of Steve Waugh as a leader. As it turned out, the remaining two Tests were rendered useless by the monsoon season, so for Geoff Marsh it was a tame finale to his highly successful coaching stint.

From Sri Lanka we headed to Zimbabwe, a historic leg of the tour because it included the first-ever Test between the two countries. It was here that our record-breaking Test winning streak began, and in my mind it all started with a train trip from Bulawayo to Victoria Falls that was the idea of the team's socialite, Stuart MacGill. The trip shaped as a schoolboy adventure, with 15 stops in a 36-hour marathon along rickety tracks and ending at the entrance to one of the natural wonders of the world. The train trip wasn't compulsory, but a party of 11 shared a life experience that bonded us much tighter than we could ever have imagined. Listening to the Eagles singing 'Tequila Sunrise' in the middle of the wilds of Africa, our heads out the window as we gazed at the multitude of crystal-clear twinkling stars in the cool, crisp night air, with that distinctive African smell, was invigorating and head-clearing. I remember being mesmerised by the brightness of Venus against the pitch-black night sky as our music box churned out 'You're So Vain' by Carly Simon while I twirled a glassful of Amarula (an African liqueur) and crushed ice. Pure bliss.

Not everyone appreciated our music, including a man from Malawi in the next compartment who requested a tune from Creedence Clearwater Revival and was eventually given a guernsey from Stuey's extensive collection. A hat-acquiring competition was thought to be as good an idea for a laugh as any, so each of us had to beg, bribe or buy another passenger's hat on the trip. I offered a departing mother $10 for her tartan-checked, red-rimmed mad-hatter lookalike, an amount she was so pleased with that she wanted to give me her daughter's cap as well. But I figured the baby in the backpack sling needed it more than I did, so I respectfully declined. This welcome break from the monotony of airport check-ins, mundane flights and structured days gave us the opportunity to be regular guys for a while and have some good old-fashioned fun. I'd come to recognise that recharging the batteries was a critical area for me; the short break without cricket on my radar did me the world of good.

In the Test, I scored 151 not out, and although it wasn't my best innings it did underline the fact that scoring runs and being consistent had become a habit. During the Test and the three limited-overs internationals that followed, we managed to have a lot of fun – including setting nine slip fielders at the conclusion of a one-dayer, watching Colin Miller alternate between pace and spin in the same over depending on whether the batsman was left- or right-handed, and on one occasion me bowling with Shane as temporary keeper in the quest to run out a batsman who was taking guard outside his crease. We all enjoyed our cricket except for Heals, who couldn't settle. He was tormented by his impending retirement, which he hoped would begin after the opening Test of the upcoming Australian summer, against Pakistan at his home ground, the Gabba in Brisbane. Sadly, a tough call by the selectors meant that dream never materialised, and a great mate, brilliant player and for a long time the heart and soul of the side was gone. The 'drummer in the band' had left the building.

Our workmanlike victory in the Test at Harare, achieved against a handy side, was a base from which bigger things could be achieved. Back-to-back series against Pakistan and an emerging Indian team were matches where we needed to really up the ante. I wanted my attitude to be infectious and decided to issue the team a challenge internally and on the public record by saying there was no reason why we couldn't win all six home Tests. My reasoning was quick and simple: we now had a team philosophy where there would be no place for tame draws. Someone had to win, and I didn't expect to lose. It helped that the team was bristling with talent, but more than that, I wanted to instil a belief that we were a unit who could be whatever we wanted to be.

This was a new era in many ways, with this positive attitude being pushed to the forefront, Adam Gilchrist taking over from Heals as keeper, and a completely different style of coach, in the form of the analytical, thought-provoking John Buchanan, coming in to stimulate the players' minds (Allan Border had filled in as coach in Zimbabwe). I was a big wrap for 'Buck', having watched him mould the Queensland side into the best Shield team in the 1990s and been especially impressed by the way he had helped to change their culture by working away diligently in the background. I saw him as a 'performance manager' more than a coach, in that he would address a variety of issues, many not necessarily cricket related, and would endeavour to have each player prepared for his cricket with a clear mind so that the actual playing side would be easier. With Buck and me on a similar wavelength, both of us wanting to provoke, stimulate and challenge the members of the team to be the best they could possibly be, we set about putting a healthy work environment and a strong framework in place.

There was no doubt as to the skills of the squad, and I wanted all of them to be on show. Consequently I saw that a major chunk of my captaincy role was to empower players by reinforcing positive messages and providing opportunities. I realised that some of my ambitions were big asks, but reasoned that unless you put players in situations they are not used to, they will not grow as cricketers. Buck was keen to get to know the guys as human beings and not just cricketers, and on our first tour, to New Zealand in February–April 2000, he got each of us to stand up and talk on three things: something about Australia, something we were passionate about and something that would enlighten our teammates. At first the lads were very sceptical, thinking they'd landed back in school and had an assignment due, but it worked. Andrew Symonds talked about the Australian coat of arms and Matty Hayden waxed lyrical about the virtues of fly fishing, while Michael Slater passionately told us about the history of his beloved Bon Jovi. Damien Martyn gave us an insight into his personal experience of Cyclone Tracy, the awful storm that wiped out Darwin in 1974. Colin Miller, as expected, came from left field to discuss the legend of the Loch Ness Monster, while lessons in guitar-playing came from the brothers Lee and, on a serious note, Patrick Farhart extolled the virtues and influence of multiculturalism in Australia. We discovered more about each other and what made us tick, enabling us to definitely grow closer as a group, even though some of us might have nodded off during Haydos's exhaustive explanation of the angling art.

Near the end of the New Zealand tour, Matty came into the Test XI in what was effectively his 'debut' match for the second half of his career. In the previous six years he'd played seven Tests, scoring 261 runs at 21.75. Things would change dramatically in the seasons that followed. I've always believed a debut is special, an event to savour and reminisce about later. It was with this in mind that I set out from the start of the 1999–2000 season to lift the experience for new guys by inviting ex-players to present the latest baggy green on the morning of the debutant's first Test. Watching the emotion in Bill Brown's face and the pride he displayed in handing over caps to Gilly and fellow debutant Scott Muller was a wonderful few minutes we all shared and made us appreciate the link between now and the past. Bill, who made his own Test debut back on the Ashes tour of 1934, is a baggy green icon who represents all that is good about playing for your country. He is humble, self-effacing and respectful, proud to have been afforded the honour of being an Australian Test cricketer, and a man who always looks for the positive in people.

Buck set the tone for his tenure as Australian coach at the Gabba by sticking up a large sheet of butcher's paper inside the door of our change room that carried the words:

> Today is the first Test of our journey to the Invincibles.
> Let's make the ride enjoyable and attainable.

My initial reaction was that you can't steal the title given to Bradman's 1948 Australians. However, I couldn't help but admire his ambition for the team, and although I wasn't quite so bold, I did agree with the belief that the talent and experience in the team meant there was nothing to stop us becoming a squad capable of special things.

★

My lead-up to the first Test was confused somewhat by the fact that Lynette was already four days overdue with our second child when the five-day game began. We had talked through the options and in the end decided that we'd let nature run its course instead of having the baby induced. Each day of the Test I prayed that the bub would be happy not to make its way into the world just yet, and it wasn't until 36 hours after the conclusion of the game – comprehensively won on the back of Michael Slater's lightning feet and slashing blade, in tandem with Damien Fleming's quality swing bowling – that a new life began. Seeing the crown of a baby's head at first glance is to panic at its walnut-like appearance, but seconds later, when air is expelled from the miniature lungs and the tiny lips quiver, you become blissfully unaware of what the rest of the world is up to. The miracle of life is the best relief you will ever know. Baby Austin ensured that the Waugh name would continue, and guaranteed me a buddy to watch the footy with and give me negotiating power with the remote control. He was a little porcelain doll that I couldn't quite believe I'd helped create. I was so grateful I'd seen him enter the world, and, as with Rosalie, I was instantly smitten.

As far as sporting wonders go, the catch taken by Mark Waugh in the second Test, in Hobart, to haul in a late cut from Inzamam-ul-Haq must be right up there with the most freakish of them all. That the catch turned the tide of a match that was drifting hopelessly out of our reach only added to its greatness. It was an effort that needed remarkable anticipation backed up by incredible hand–eye coordination. And it occurred in a game in which we witnessed one of the great Test-match partnerships, between Justin Langer, who was under enormous pressure to perform, and Adam Gilchrist. The duo put on 238 in the fourth innings to win the impossible against an attack that had nearly 1000 Test wickets to their credit.

No one moved in the change rooms for hours during this amazing stand, as the runs-required total slowly came down and I carried on Allan Border's tradition of tossing a 'worry' cricket ball from hand to hand and made everyone stay in the same seats throughout. It was a win that as a team we'd talked about but were never sure we could actually achieve. But once the winning runs were hit, we elevated ourselves to a different level, where anything was possible.

This Hobart Test was the match that I feel established the virtue of what became one of the trademarks of my captaincy: backing my players to the hilt. Faith and support are almost everything a talented guy needs in a team environment. Lang had been copping a bagging from the critics before the game, which I believed to be not only unfair but unwarranted, so I came out swinging, saying, 'He's the best man for the job. He's Australia's best No. 3 and I want him in the side.'

On the other side of the coin was new boy Scott Muller, the unfortunate recipient of the infamous 'Can't bowl, can't throw' line during the second Test that apparently came from the soon-to-be-famous 'Joe the Cameraman', a Channel Nine employee who claimed his off-the-cuff comment had been picked up by his camera's microphone. At first Shane Warne was seen as the culprit – an extraordinary mix-up, the likes of which had not occurred before and won't occur again. Being the captain, at the conclusion of the match I tried to rouse Scott out of his depression by constantly ringing his phone and then, when I didn't get an answer, smashing on his hotel door for 10 minutes to try to get him to come out and celebrate with the team. But his gentle nature and fragile sensibilities had quite obviously been damaged beyond repair. It was a shame that this was to be his last Test and that both he and Shane ended up carrying psychological wounds that bogged them down for a long time after. As a team we wanted to support both guys, but they were big boys who had to somehow find peace by themselves and get over it.

True colours are best displayed when facing adversity, and Ricky Ponting showed all his class in scoring a majestic 197 in the third Test, in Perth, which helped set up a dominating victory for us. Punter had made three successive ducks before this innings, including a pair on his home turf at Bellerive, but at the WACA he confirmed that his battle-hardened mind would be around for a long time to come. I am always fascinated to watch how a guy handles a pressure situation. Some players become animated, some train extra hard, some withdraw – but the true greats keep their self-belief, trust themselves and continue to work away, knowing that if the foundations have been established, good form will come. I had described Ricky as 'the future of Australian cricket' after his good series in Sri Lanka a couple of months earlier, and I was now certain it was a fair call. This guy had ticker, and plenty of it.

Speaking of character, a quick who took seven wickets in the Perth Test, Michael Kasprowicz, along with one of his Queensland contemporaries, Andy Bichel, are to me classic examples of guys who are willing to lay it all on the line for the betterment of the team. In a warped way, both probably suffered during their careers because of their generous and giving natures. Whenever they were involved in line-ball decisions at the selectors' table, it was perceived that they would take a demotion in the right spirit and better than the other candidate. They never did whinge or drop their bundle, and both played a major role in setting the benchmarks of character and building the pyramid of success the current Australian side continues to maintain.

India came and went, a mentally fragile team meekly led by a reluctant captain, Sachin Tendulkar. Their defensive attitude and preoccupation with existing meant they were there for the taking. Thinking purely about survival is only one step away from experiencing defeat, and if you start from such a diminished point the odds are you'll finish exactly where you fear going. India had us in trouble on the first morning of the series when we stumbled to 4/52, but in a tactical move that would influence the outcome of the whole series, the innocuous floaters of Sourav Ganguly greeted Ricky Ponting and me after lunch. We got our eyes in and went on to add 239 for the fifth wicket, thereby completely changing the impetus of proceedings. My 21st Test century was my first against India and meant I was the first person to score hundreds against eight Test-playing nations. It was a significant achievement for me as it reflected consistency and an ability to score runs in varying conditions.

In between the first and second Tests against India I had a rare game for NSW and was mesmerised by the pure artistry of a young quick named Brett Lee. Like Warney years before in Zimbabwe, I knew straightaway this kid was special; he had that twinkle in his eye that belied a killer streak, and on the pacy WACA pitch he was lethal. The guy was a match-winner. I caught up with selector Geoff Marsh at the conclusion of a match in which Lee had broken Jo Angel's forearm, terrorised Damien Martyn and Adam Gilchrist and bowled the quickest spell I'd ever seen, and said quite simply but half-jokingly, 'Swamp, pick him or I'm out, pal. This kid's raring to go. Don't waste him – the Indians will hate him!' It was purely a case of letting Lee loose and watching our fragile opponents fold, and when it happened in the Boxing Day Test, from my view in the gully it was thrilling stuff. Seeing terror in a batsman's eyes is bliss for a quick, and for a captain there's no better feeling than to know you have a weapon who can intimidate top-order batsmen and finish off the tail purely by the length of his run-up.

The third Test of the series, in Sydney, was Mark's 100th and the first Test of the new millennium. I wanted to mark it with something special. Like most good ideas, this one was there right in front of me, in a magazine – the famous, enduring, black-and-white set-up photograph of Victor Trumper, Australia's great batsman of the twentieth century's first decade, stepping out to drive. It wasn't the artistry of Victor's cover drive but the 'skullcap' he was wearing that struck me. A plan was set in motion and then approved by the ACB chairman, Denis Rogers, but when it came to unveiling the finished product at a team meeting two days before the Test, I was very unsure as to how it would be received. New caps, replicas of those worn by Joe Darling's team during the 1901–02 Ashes series, had been produced to mark the start of the new century, with my ultimate hope being that the same process would be repeated another 100 years on. The caps were slightly smaller than the current Australian cap, more rounded, with a velvet finish, marginally darker and bearing a different coat of arms, but they were, in essence, still the baggy green. And thank God, the guys loved 'em.

It was a proud moment for me to watch my brother lead the team out onto the SCG at the start of his landmark Test match, and an amazing feeling to flash back to the backyard Tests of our youth and then realise that we'd both played 100 Tests. No one would have thought it possible in the days when we had to abandon games because we couldn't get a ball out of Mum's flowering bird of paradise, riddled as it was with spider webs that neither of us had the mettle to take on, or the razor-sharp pampas bush that also made retrieval a test of courage. I could still see Mark unable to get back over the picket fence at Waverley Oval during an Under 15 Green Shield representative match for Bankstown. A six had been struck out of the ground and then rolled down a hill onto the road, ending up 50 metres away. Mark, being the closest fieldsman, went to retrieve the 'cherry' but climbing up against the slope and his lack of height as a 13-year-old meant that he couldn't make it back onto the field until reinforcements came along. He also distinguished himself by pushing the sightscreen off its hinges at Rushcutters Bay Oval during one of our early first-grade appearances, and I'll never forget the hair-dye kit that went horribly wrong and gave him a burnt-orange, 'been to Mecca' shade instead of the blond Ian Botham look he was after.

Mark had the rare talent as a cricketer to turn a game with bat and ball, and that's before you consider his gifts as a catcher. He had a good cricket brain and a simple yet logical outlook that shaped his cricket and defined him as a player. His longevity proved to the doubters that he was tough, mentally and physically; he had a record of resilience that he'd often quote and attribute to not overtraining. One of his favourite lines about going to the gym or on a road run was, 'You don't take a Rolls Royce out on a country road every day – you only use it for the big occasions.'

His 100th Test ended in another emphatic victory, as we swept aside India after I asked for the extra half-hour on the evening of day three, a period which highlighted their muddled thinking and lack of fight, especially when a comical run-out ended the match in the last over of the day. It was almost a relief for them not to have to turn up the next morning – not so much because getting to day four would have saved the game (it wouldn't have), but because, much more importantly, displaying some fight would have shown they had spirit and an aptitude for battle. Clearly, they did not. I came away from the series convinced that until such time as India identified players with steel and a strong leader, they would always be pushovers away from home. Fortunately for them, in time these harsh lessons were digested.

One of the most important things to come out of the summer from our perspective was that the 'dead-rubber syndrome' had been put to bed with two emphatic third-Test victories and a new attitude within the squad that every Test was equally important. We'd come to realise that it all boils down to personal pride and mental toughness in these perceived lesser-value games. One thing we had to consider was that in such matches someone might be playing for his spot, making his debut or experiencing his last memories as a national representative. As a captain during this home season, I was comfortable with the way I followed my gut feel, often throwing the ball to part-timers in search of a breakthrough, once elevating Gilly from No. 7 to No. 4 in the batting order and twice breaking convention (or the 'Australian way') by sending the opposition into bat. The old saying 'When you win the toss, you bat nine times out of 10 and the other time you think about it and then bat' is, in my view, about as realistic as telling kids not to pull faces because if the wind changes they'll stay like that. I also really enjoyed inviting or letting teammates invite guests of the calibre of tennis champion Pat Rafter, ultra-marathon runner Pat Farmer and members of the '48 Invincibles to our pregame dinners and into our change rooms. (The person who had the greatest impact was a 'Bali survivor' who I originally met on the set of Andrew Denton's TV chat show, *Enough Rope*, in September 2003. Peter Hughes inspired us with tales of survival and how the Aussie spirit surfaced in the most terrifying conditions. He spoke of the horror of being in the Sari Club that night and the force of the Paddy's Bar bombs, and showed us the wounds from his life-threatening ordeal. Peter made us contemplate how lucky we were to be born Australian and how we needed to never take things for granted and to appreciate our mates. He spoke of the uniqueness of Aussies and how we stick together in times of need, and after three hours of talking and answering questions we were ready to take on anyone. The unfortunate 'anyone' was Zimbabwe, in a badly lopsided Perth Test where Matt Hayden eclipsed the highest individual Test score, no doubt inspired by the words 'Make the most of every day'.)

The triangular one-day series that followed the Test began in a laughable way with the 'toothless tiger', the ICC, suddenly chang-ing a ruling that Shoaib Akhtar was banned from playing until he completed a course of remedial work on his sometimes jerky action when he pitched the ball short. At the very last minute before the opening game of the competition was about to start, then ICC presi-dent Jagmohan Dalmiya of India overruled an expert panel and gave the Pakistani quick a reprieve, his logic being that in one-day cricket Shoaib wouldn't bowl any bouncers because under the rules at the time they were deemed no-balls. Just 45 minutes before play, umpires Steve Davis and Daryl Harper came knocking on my door, seeking permission for Shoaib to be allowed to play even though he'd be late turning up. He was still in the air at the time, flying to Brisbane from Perth, where he'd been working on his action. I have no idea why the umpires or, more correctly, the match referee didn't make a stand themselves rather than dumping the hot potato on me. Our team had been picked and planned on the basis that Shoaib wasn't going to play, and if I objected now I'd be branded unsportsmanlike and probably racist, while if I said it was okay I'd be going against the original ICC ruling and hampering our own chances of winning the game. It was a hassle I didn't need or appreciate, and the day–night ended with us being beaten and me suffering a first-ball duck at the hands of . . . Mr Akhtar.

The rest of the series went smoothly, insofar as we won nine straight. However, with each day the challenges of captaincy were preparing me for life after cricket. After yet another unruly crowd caused a stoppage in Melbourne when Ganguly forgot to ground his bat, the big screen of the MCG couldn't display the sharpness needed to pick up that piece of laziness, so the Indian contingent in the stands saw a conspiracy. I was at the stage of being totally sick of the imbecile element that continued to ruin too many matches on the excuse of an alleged mistake by the umpires. It was only a matter of time before

I'd lead a team off the park to get the players' view across. This time, though, I put my diplomat hat on and sat beside the police chief at the postgame media conference and backed him up with a couple of well-prepared answers. Constantly being in front of the camera and dealing with a range of issues not necessarily directly related to the team but that could impact on them was part of the job of being Australian captain. I came to reflect that the job also meant that I was now expected to know something about everything, as if my intelligence had all of a sudden increased in accordance with my stature.

With life moving so quickly, there were periods of time when I didn't get to see my extended family or touch base with my roots. It was no one's fault – there just didn't seem to be time to chill out and do the normal, average, everyday things all my non-cricket mates were doing. I still had a core group of friends from junior sporting days and high school who kept me grounded and saw S. Waugh the person, not the Australian cricket captain, and I found the time I spent with these people liberating. Thus it came as a real honour to have the pavilion at the ground where my senior career began, Memorial Oval at Bankstown, named 'The Stephen and Mark Waugh Grandstand'.

As an aspiring youngster, I'd been rapt to get my name in the 'Best of the Day' section of the sports pages of the local rag, *The Torch*. Life had changed beyond belief.

Things such as filming TV commercials became a fact of modern cricket life for players once they established themselves in the Australian side. Here, Warney felt fine in his Hawaiian shirt and beach gear, but I'm not so sure that Wagga Wagga native Tubby Taylor or the twins from Panania were quite as comfortable.

A surreal scene. I turn blind for the third run that would tie the game as the fans charge on to the field at the end of the one-day international at Georgetown in 1999.

Three images from the latter stages of the 1999 World Cup.

A slog-sweep for six off South Africa's opening bowler, Steve Elworthy, during my hundred in the Super Six match at Headingley.

Shaking hands with South African captain Hansie Cronje after our win in that game, which confirmed our place in the semi-finals.

With Australian coach Geoff Marsh in the away dressing-room at Lord's, in the corner I always occupied, after we defeated Pakistan in the final.

On-field celebrations after South Africa's Allan Donald was run out to leave the semi-final at Edgbaston tied and giving us a place in the final.

The Australian team forms an emotional circle minutes after our decisive win in the final at Lord's.

The problem at Kandy in 1999 was that neither Jason Gillespie, running in from deep backward square, nor I called for the ball – we were both focused on the catch, the sun was in my eyes for an instant and the result was a smashed nose for me and a broken leg and wrist for Dizzy.

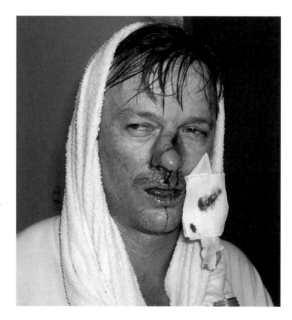

I'm not sure what it says about my state of mind at the time, but I insisted that fitness advisor Dave Misson take a photograph of my nose in all its gory, before we set off for hospital to get the thing straightened.

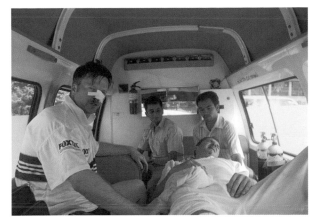

With Dizzy in the minivan that took us to hospital in Kandy. My fast-bowling mate was doing worse than I was; every bump in the road was agony for him, and our driver managed to find as many as he could.

With former Australian Test batsman Bill Brown, as fine a gentleman as you could meet, in Hobart in 1999–2000.

My mate Mathew Dean, who has inspired me with his ongoing fight against serious illness, with some Test-match souvenirs and my 2000 diary, *Never Satisfied*. The cover image of the book features the 'Victor Trumper caps' the Australian team wore for the first Test of the new millennium.

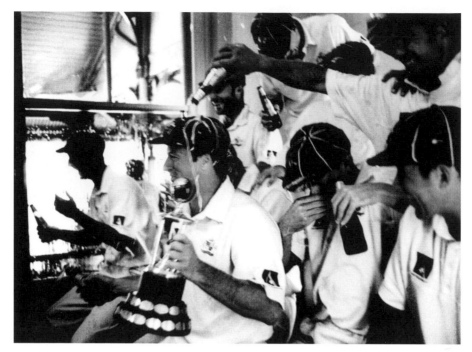

The beer is flowing in Sydney in January 2001 after we won the fifth Test against the West Indies, our 14th consecutive Test victory.

Windies captain Jimmy Adams and Matthew Hayden relax on the sodden carpet in the SCG rooms at the end of the series as Justin Langer looks on.

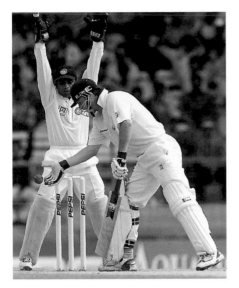

This brain explosion at Chennai in 2001 left me as only the second Australian in Test history to be given out 'handled the ball'.

We were only 69 runs from retaining the Ashes in 2001 when I badly tore my calf muscle. Jock Campbell (left) and Errol Alcott were soon on the scene.

Following the Ashes tour, I signed a lucrative bat contract with the Madras Rubber Factory, who also had Sachin Tendulkar and Brian Lara as clients. Among the promotions the three of us did together was this go-kart race at Navalur, south of Chennai, in 2003.

The Australian cricket team's 'brains trust' during most of my time as captain. From left: Steve Bernard (manager), Errol Alcott (physio), me, John Buchanan (coach), Jock Campbell (fitness coordinator), Patrick Farhart (physio).

The body language says plenty. None of us – chairman of selectors Trevor Hohns (left), ACB CEO James Sutherland or me – wants to be at the media conference where my sacking as one-day captain is announced.

35

From good to great

During the second final of the 1999–2000 one-day series, Ricky Ponting severely damaged his ankle sliding into the boundary as he tried to prevent a four, which in time would see the ICC make boundary ropes compulsory to prevent a repetition of such an injury. A bit more than a week later we were in New Zealand minus Ricky, which was a real blow for the side because he had been in magnificent form.

However, his absence did give someone else a rare chance to

experience the ultimate in-house honour – to lead the boys in the team song. This is an elite club, with only David Boon, Ian Healy and Ricky doing it regularly during my career, and I became the newest recruit when Punter phoned, inviting me to take on the role. Of course I was thrilled, but having to live up to the volcanic eruption of a Boon, a neck-vein-bulging, face-about-to-explode Healy rendition or the brooding ferocity of the pent-up dynamo that was Ponting had me slightly nervous as I pondered my debut.

We'd arrived in New Zealand to the usual low-key media intrusions that came with touring the rugby-mad country, but I still expected a few fireworks after Shane Warne's departing one-liner at the Sydney Air-port 'presser'. We had discussed beforehand our tour objectives and the conservative yet confident message we wanted to get across, and as the media gathered in front of us Warney and Buck took their customary places beside me. Invariably the questions were fired at the captain – the vice-captain and coach may as well have been body doubles – and for a while things followed their usual course: a couple of simple pat answers, then a question about a tougher issue like ground security before it eased up again, and finally a statement about my hopes and aspirations for the team and a request for a scoreline prediction. Just as I was about to get up and make my exit, a last-ditch question came Warney's way: 'Shane, what do you think of New Zealanders?'

This was an inquiry that warranted a one-liner if ever I'd heard one – just a general response that would maintain cordial relations. How-ever, Shane went for the backyard-barbie talk and said, 'Really, they're all just frustrated Aussies.'

You can always tell what the lead story will be in the next day's papers by the way the heads go down and pens fire into action after a particular comment. All I could see in front of me were the tops of heads. Warney, as Warney often did, stood up, turned to me and said, 'That was easy, no problems there' while a car crash piled up in our rear-view mirror. Not long into the tour, after that little diplomatic 'crisis' passed, Shane's real-life soap opera had its next episode when two teenagers took a photograph of him smoking in a non-smoking stadium and threatened to sell it.

For a while it felt as if we were fending off plenty of off-field bouncers, including Buck's first of many 'missing team notes' sagas, which saw our team plans mistakenly slipped under a journalist's door. Over the years we would be accused of purposely planting material that was harmful to our opposition's state of mind, but I can honestly say it was just Buck. He's a man who is so attentive to detail that as a coach at the ground he documents every ball he sees, always thinking ahead, but who at the same time is notorious for leaving books on buses and video cameras on planes. He would hand notes to the concierge at the team hotel and assume they'd get it right in regard to team members' room numbers.

On this occasion it did work extremely well for us, with the weaknesses of the New Zealand players being splashed across the newspapers. Chris Cairns was summarised as 'fragile – a good frontrunner, but lacks confidence if you get on top of him'. Craig McMillan's dossier said, 'A good confident player, but prone to silly mistakes.' It must have been embarrassing for them. We escaped this time, though on later occasions when team notes fell into the wrong hands we would pay for such an absence of professionalism and lack of attention to detail.

The Australian one-day team was playing exceptional cricket in the latter stages of a run of 29 games that included 26 wins, a tie and just two losses. Through my time as captain I became a big supporter of the 'rotation' selection policy, which had been tried with success among the bowlers even though there had been some resistance to the change, as guys with natural competitive instincts sought to protect their position. But to me the benefits were obvious. Giving first-team players occasional games off even though they were fit, which became known as rotating, would ensure longevity and freshness, give guys a chance to recharge their batteries, and by giving game time to 'fringe' players better prepare them for future competitions.

Trying to convince batsmen that rotation was a good thing was even more difficult than it had been for the bowlers, as most saw someone else treading on their turf and possibly excelling to the point where they might even take over their position as being too big a negative against the overall bigger picture. To me, though, if a premier football side like Manchester United and many American sporting teams could rotate players, than I couldn't see why cricketers should see the concept as something sinister.

Initially the Australian selection panel back home saw the merits in such a line of thinking, but in New Zealand it was the tour selectors – captain, vice-captain and coach – who had the say; and, when it was all said and done, it was the captain who called the shots. So I promoted Damien Martyn to open the batting in the last one-dayer, in Auckland, when we were on track to achieve Operation Blackout, as we called it, referring to the legendary All Blacks. After a wash-out in Wellington, we'd won the next four games. Damien needed to move outside the 'Golden Wing lounge', as John Dyson would say, of the middle order, which more often than not involved scoring quick runs late in the innings. I knew from personal experience that playing the same role time after time could stunt development and that the key to improving one's game is to accept challenges that often catch players unprepared but are at the same time stimulating. Marto duly peeled off 116 not out and batted through the innings while the rest of us capitulated to 191. Of course, the press blamed the loss directly on the rotation system and most likely some of the players did as well, but I wanted a squad full of players who could lift and play unaccustomed roles when required. Down the path to the next World Cup, variety and flexibility would be paramount.

We required men of vision rather than those who reacted negatively at the first sign of failure. In my mind, Marto's century in a new role gave the team an added option, was a breakthrough for him as it was his first century for Australia, and created a healthy, competitive in-house working environment.

During this tour, at team meetings I'd occasionally throw around the concept of what it takes to go from good to great. The catalyst for me was the dedication shown by Patrick Farhart, the long-time NSW physiotherapist filling in for Errol Alcott, who got me back on the park two days after I severely twisted my ankle in a one-dayer at Dunedin. Pat put in two 15-hour days of intensive treatment to give me a chance of making the starting XI for the following match, which I managed to do.

Eventually I made the notion of 'good versus great' a key discussion point at a get-together, and we concluded that while talent, skill, passion, discipline and respect for ourselves and the opposition were all factors, what we also had to do was:

- raise the bar of expectations
- identify and overcome barriers in our way
- get to know each other better
- be honest with ourselves and our teammates
- be ruthless
- enjoy each other's success
- champion things we do well.

These principles would form the foundations of a blueprint for success we were developing as we moved forward; our ambition was that they would remain as a legacy for future Australian sides to emulate and improve on as time went by.

Creating our own fun on tour has always been the Aussie squad's strength, and on this tour the social team of Gilly, Haydos and Warney came up with a concept that saw each player pull a colleague's name out of a hat and then set out to buy the worst shirt they could find for that person – and then we'd all go out on a team night wearing the piece of clothing we'd been presented with.

Plenty of shopping was done in Dunedin's St Vincent de Paul and Salvation Army stores, but the bargains came at a cost because the next morning we woke to a headline in the local newspaper: 'Aussie Cross Dressers!' It transpired that Gilly had been overheard mentioning that a particular ladies' frilly blouse looked like a good buy, which was enough information for a local spy to call up a radio station that then ran a piece about our weird sexual preferences, and this in turn led to the newspaper story. We laughed it off, happy to recall the catwalk disaster of the evening: John Buchanan's black tank top and rub-on stomach tattoo, skilfully selected by Brett Lee.

★

Looking back over the cricket we played from late 1999 to 2001, the most underrated and understated Test series victory was definitely our 3–0 whitewash of the Kiwis. It came at the end of a period when we had been playing for 20 of 22 months straight, and we came back from perilous positions in each of the three matches. Above all else, players such as Damien Martyn, Colin Miller, Adam Gilchrist and Brett Lee emerged and improved, while they and others – most notably Justin Langer – displayed enormous character.

Going into the last day at Eden Park in Auckland, a rectangular ground made for rugby union, with the pitch diagonally placed to give it a baseball-diamond feel, we were a 50/50 chance at best to record Australia's first Test win there in 23 years. New Zealand needed 130 runs to win with five wickets in hand, and in a gut-instinct move I went for off-spinner Miller ahead of Warne to open the bowling for the day, alongside Glenn McGrath. Shane had begun the Test needing five more wickets to overtake Dennis Lillee as Australia's highest Test wicket-taker, and though by this fifth morning he had four of them, he appeared distracted by the attention his chase was getting. As well, Colin had already taken three wickets in the Kiwis' second innings. Funky was everyone's hero – a guy who reinvented himself by turning from medium pace to off spin and who kept a contagious enthusiasm and love for the game that saw him savour every minute he played. He was a throwback to players of previous eras who enjoyed a beer, dressing-room banter and touring life, not to mention an infatuation with outrageous hair colourings. What he had in common with his spinning partner was a diet from hell, matching Shane's bread rolls slathered with butter and tomato sauce with his own speciality sand-wich: cheese, chips, ham and a Kit-Kat all squashed together.

We lifted under pressure, with the 'robotic' McGrath squeezing the life out of the New Zealand batsmen with unyielding accuracy and an imposing body presence that set the standard for everyone else to aspire to. I'm convinced that will is the No. 1 attribute needed for achieving success. On this day I so desperately wanted to get into the action that I convinced myself the ball was coming my way; if it wasn't, I wanted to make the batsman think, *Don't hit it near him – he's ready to hurt us.* Two catches did come my way and I was never going to miss them, for I was in the fielding equivalent of the zone: I wanted and expected every ball. The match finished on a perfect note when I brought Shane back to get the record out of the way. This doesn't mean I was or am trying to diminish his great achievement, but I wanted to free up his mind for the next Test. Soon the last man in, Paul Wiseman, had been caught Gilchrist, bowled Warne, and it was time for 'Underneath the Southern Cross'. I dragged the new record holder up on the bench with me and arm in arm we ripped into the team song as former coach Geoff Marsh and Ricky Ponting listened in on two of the boys' mobile phones.

Consistently winning alleviated a lot of the potential staleness that could have come with playing nonstop cricket. Before the second Test, Buck got us all to write down what we wanted to achieve, and he jotted down the responses on a sheet of butcher's paper that he hung on our dressing-room wall for the entire match. It was a clever move that also involved our support staff, who played a crucial role in our success. Doing this meant we were all committed *and* accountable; the process meant we'd had to think about our game and then follow through. We had pledged our loyalty to the cause, and to renege would be tantamount to treason. Asking people to live up to their statements can be a powerful motivator, especially when they are there for all your mates to read.

To score 151 not out was, of course, a significant outcome for me, one that reinforced how important a normal lifestyle and family are to being and staying centred. Having to change a nappy as the contents oozed out the sides required a defter touch than that needed for a late cut, but it was a strangely welcome task at the end of a long, hot day in the field. With Lynette, Rosalie, new son Austin, in-laws Phil and Ethel, and father Rodger all in town it was in many ways just like a home match and business as usual, without the extra media, ticket requests and distractions. Being away from home yet having the family along was the best combination possible, but only in the short term. The kids needed their routine, and hotel life certainly wasn't conducive to that.

A win in the second Test, at Wellington, elevated us into history as we went past Warwick Armstrong's 1920–21 side, which won eight Tests in a row. To mark the occasion, I invited every member of the touring party to get up on the table and recall a favourite memory of any one of our nine wins and then recite one verse of our team anthem. Matt Hayden, though not yet back in the starting XI, gave us his thoughts on why the baggy green is so special, then Lang got up and gave everyone a rap individually, while Dave Misson and Pat Farhart told us how proud they were and what it meant to them to play their part in our victories even though they couldn't get amongst the action. For me the highlight was Damien Fleming, who ripped off his entire kit and delivered his message stark naked, though from our position directly below, it was tough to concentrate on or recall exactly what he had to say.

Besides that enduring image of Flem, I also can't get a tune out of my head that is indelibly etched alongside the victory. It was from a bargain-basement CD called *Country Favourites*, featuring gems such as 'The Gambler' and 'Coward of the County' by Kenny Rogers. In its own way, that CD is a piece of personal memorabilia like a stump or a team shirt. The song that keeps playing in my head is 'Try a Little Kindness', by Glen Campbell, probably because each time I snuck it into the music box someone would yell, 'Get that crap off!' It isn't about the quality of the tune (which I still reckon is okay), it's about the period of time the song represents for me and the memories it brings back. Similarly, Joshua Kadison's 'Jessie' reminds me of the 1995 Windies tour and Midnight Oil's 'Beds Are Burning' immediately makes me think about the 1987 World Cup. Music was important to me on tour and I'd regularly take my mini stereo system away with me so I could chill out. At night it was important to drift off to sleep peacefully, and it was here that Barbra Streisand, Enya and classical music did the trick.

One other item I valued above all else on tour was my own pillow. Being unable to sleep because my hotel pillow had the consistency of a sandbag or was so bulky it gave me a jammed-up neck the next day was potentially career-damaging, and easy to avoid. Some of my prized possessions are probably just junk to others – an empty caviar jar from the restaurant after we beat the Windies in 1995, a hollow tube that held the cigar I attempted to smoke after winning the 1999

World Cup, the cheap plastic trophy I received for finishing third in a go-kart race with teammates during the 2001 Ashes tour, or the coin from my first Test-match toss. They all have a story associated with them and bring back memories of the incidents that made my career.

Further adding to our postmatch celebration was the fact that my good mate and Aussie icon John Williamson was in town and agreed to drop around and sing a song or two. I was half-joking when I pleaded with him to put on a mini-concert, but he ended up giving us an intimate two-hour performance in the team manager's room, with my favourite, 'Galleries of Pink Galahs', capping off a magical evening. By the end, I had an inkling that even Flem might have been converted from his preferred Metallica rawness to the class of some true Aussie ballads, but perhaps that is drawing too long a bow.

★

The third Test was our 13th in eight months. I was very keen to finish on a positive note, but as captain and a tour selector I had to make one of those career-changing decisions I didn't believe should have been my responsibility. Despite all his natural talent, Greg Blewett just didn't seem able to get going and looked out of sorts at the crease. It was obvious he didn't enjoy having to struggle for runs and scratch around, and I sensed it was almost a relief when I gave him the bad news – but I was annoyed that, as had happened in the West Indies, it was me who had to make the tough call on a teammate instead of the selectors, who appeared to be absolving themselves from the big decisions. One international career ended with Blewey's demotion, but another took off like a shooting star as Buzz Lightyear's long-lost twin, Matthew Hayden, began a period of excellence rarely seen in the game.

Our confidence as a unit had soared so high that at 5/29 in our first innings, in reply to New Zealand's 232, no one blinked an eyelid.

Everyone had faith that someone would put their hand up and turn things around. It was an unspoken code, a comforting notion that had engulfed the team, along with a fierce determination and pride to create our own little niche in the history of the game. We had set our sights on the record held by Clive Lloyd's West Indies team of 1984 of 11 straight Test-match wins, and nothing was going to stop us from realising that dream. Again, this feat wasn't spoken about much; our focus was on the process and the 'now' moment. The downside to such unreserved confidence is the danger of slipping over the edge into complacency, which happened during the Kiwis' second innings – they fell to 6/130, but then Chris Cairns led a fightback that meant we were facing a potentially awkward fourth-inning chase – and led to me giving the guys a rare rev-up, something I only did when I thought we were getting carried away. This feeling that the job was already done might have shown itself by a lack of purpose between overs, talking about future tours instead of worrying about the current state of affairs, discussions about commercial endorsements, or simply tardiness in being ready to go back on the field at the scheduled time for a restart.

Generally it would come down to having pride in what we were doing and working for each other. After winning our 10th straight on the back of Justin Langer's quick-fire 122 not out, I caused a kerfuffle in the press box by declaring Lang to be the best batsman in the world at the time and also saying that the current side could compete with any team that had ever played the game. This, of course, translated into headlines that said I'd described the team as the best ever, which stirred up a hotbed of debate.

To win so many in a row we must have been doing something right. Winning at Test level requires an ability to handle pressure for sustained periods at a time and more consistently than your opponents. You have to seize the moment before it presents itself, which comes back to being able to recognise when that moment is upon you. You have to know when to retreat and stem the damage, and when to up the intensity as you sense weakness in your adversary. Each team member must know his game and prepare accordingly, with bowlers generally tapering off leading into a big game while batsmen tend to up the tempo. The captain has to pull together 10 different individuals with contrasting personalities and character traits and get them all going in the same direction by treating them equally but differently. He also has to keep the team's reserves energised and filled with a sense of being part of the big picture. He must build morale in a way that leads to everyone believing in each other, even when those outside the team have doubts, and empower players to get outside of their comfort zone to fulfil not just their obvious potential, but also to awaken dormant skills they might not even know about. He has to strive to continually improve his own game by recharging the batteries, clearing the mind, improving physical fitness to strengthen the body, and maintaining technique to ensure consistency, while also massaging and suppressing egos that may otherwise cause damage to the karma of the team. No one can rest on their laurels – the hunger has to be real and the intent clear.

Cricket teaches you a lot about yourself and provides a forum where you can grow as a person, if you realise your opportunities. The game exposes you to many different scenarios and situations that not only affect matches and your career, but later on in life may lead you in a certain direction or influence your judgement. The winning team is not necessarily the one with superior talent. A successful unit features a combination of people, each of whom is mature enough to take responsibility for their actions and decisions, and strong enough to live by them.

36

Flesh and blood

The Sydney Olympics of September–October 2000 provided me with a life highlight when I was afforded the honour of running down George Street in the city with the Olympic flame the evening before the opening ceremony as an estimated 500000 people lined the streets. At one point, however, it almost went horribly wrong when I stumbled on a speed bump while engaging with the crowd and nearly set my 'running aid', the person who was jogging with me, ablaze.

It's difficult to explain, but the moment the flame was actually passed to my torch and I alone became responsible for its continued journey was quite remarkable. For me, the flame is a symbol of all that's good in sport, so holding the torch aloft was as awe-inspiring a sporting moment as I've ever experienced. The day will live with me forever, especially because my 'pass-off' was to Australia's then oldest-living Olympian, Mrs Edie Payne (nee Robinson), who was in a wheelchair and accompanied by her grandchild. Mrs Payne, who in 1928 had become the first Australian woman to compete in an Olympic track event, was so emotionally overcome with the honour that as we were transported to our assigned places she began crying, which in turn set off a chain reaction among everyone in our minibus just minutes before the eyes of the world were upon us. I was honoured to hand the flame over to such a remarkable woman and terribly saddened to hear of her death just a few weeks later.

The ICC Knockout, a sort of mini World Cup, was our 'bogey' tournament. In 2000 it took place in Kenya in the days straight after the Games, and from our perspective was again derailed by an unconventional but brilliant piece of tactical batsmanship by the little maestro, Sachin Tendulkar. He charged the quicks one minute and backed away the next on an excellent pitch that heavily favoured the bowlers, and so invigorated his teammates that they sent us packing with an element of ease. At least this time we had the option to visit the Serengeti National Park in Kenya, an opportunity most of us took up with relish. Michael Bevan, though, decided to hang around a tired hotel and catch a few rays instead. I often wondered how someone like Michael would look back on an outstanding career and not be able to correlate his achievements with any cultural or learning experiences. Surely it was worth the effort of packing a bag to see a pride of lions rip into a bloodied carcass, follow a cheetah as it strolled the plains on the lookout for a fresh kill, or be mesmerised by the sheer beauty of nature? But I guess part of being in a team is accepting that it is made up of diverse characters with assorted tastes. To judge too harshly would be to see everything through your own eyes, but sometimes the rationale for such behaviour escaped me.

One of the more intriguing spectacles of my first tour to India back in 1986 was the mongoose-and-cobra show that took place outside the Pink Fort at Jaipur. Facing the West Indies without Curtly Ambrose was like watching that show knowing the cobra had been defanged; the element of danger was gone. Maybe not surprisingly, then, our home series against the Windies in 2000–01 was a tame one, its one-sided nature only emphasising the Windies' decline and our ascent. At the end of the 5–0 drubbing I sat in my regular locker seat at the SCG and thought, *That wasn't how Test-match cricket is supposed to feel.*

From the very first morning of the series, our opponents showed their lack of intent. Glenn McGrath was allowed to bowl wherever he wanted without any concerted force against him and predictably he cleaned up, taking 10/27 for the match – figures you only dream about. Maybe only in the third Test, at Adelaide, did the Windies ever look truly competitive, so there was no real sense of satisfaction for us except that of a job accomplished. I hated the lack of spirit they showed, their meek surrender, the scarcity of confrontation. Except for the heart and soul of Courtney Walsh, the talent of Brian Lara and the pluck of captain Jimmy Adams, they were spineless and not much better than an outfit in Sydney first-grade cricket. It's the *way* you win – the blood, sweat and tears that go into a hard-fought victory that invigorates me, not the demolition of a non-believing foe. On a positive note, though, we still had to go out there and complete the task, and we managed to remain unbeaten through the summer, in

Tests and one-dayers, even though Shane Warne missed the entire Test series and Jason Gillespie, Brett Lee and I were also missing for part of the season because of various injuries. Our strength was the sum of the parts, which to me was vital, because while we would always have the brilliant individual feats, our solidarity came from consistency. If our opponents couldn't see an opening, then our collective spirit could overwhelm them.

My mid-season 'disguised blessing' came along again: this time, a grade-three tear (the worst category) to a glute muscle in my left buttock. I actually suffered the injury six weeks before the discomfort reached the point where not even a couple of painkillers could mask the sharp pain I felt with each forward lunge. So it was off to rehab and a few days at the beach house. Once more I was indebted to the sacrifices of NSW team physio Patrick Farhart, who surrendered his own Christmas holidays to help me rehabilitate as quickly as possible.

As in the past, I came back with a clear mind and renewed vigour, and posted my 23rd and 24th Test centuries. The first of these, in the Boxing Day Test at the MCG, featured a trip to the dentist before play on a morning when I was set to resume on 98 not out; the second, in Sydney, was marked by my most embarrassing dismissal in Test cricket. I was sick and tired of the Windies leggie Mahendra Nagamootoo constantly aiming into the scuffed-up rough way outside leg stump – a purely defensive tactic – and in my frustration and contempt I lashed out with my left foot to kick the ball away, only to see it bounce off the inside of my leg and cannon back onto the stumps. Treat the game with a lack of respect and it will always come back to bite you.

Throughout the series I stressed to the guys how I wanted them to ward off the threat to success: complacency. As a unit, we discussed and dismissed the let's-have-one-because-we-always-have-one concept of the nightwatchman as outdated and, in many ways, illogical. Why send a guy in who has less chance of surviving, and protect a guy who would and should thrive on the challenge of batting out the last few overs of the day? We also decided to increase the tempo at which we played the game, on the basis that if we succeeded we would disorientate the opposition and provide entertainment for the crowd. I could feel myself growing as a leader and, as far as the team went, the all-round package was blossoming. Any chance I could, I tried to praise the guys. I raised a few eyebrows by saying publicly that Matthew Hayden would end his career by doubling his then Test batting average of 24, which I thought was logical considering he had always murdered Sheffield Shield attacks, averaged 70 in first-class cricket at the grassy Gabba, and had the desire within. Matty just needed a match to light that fire and get things going.

The one guy in the Windies camp I felt sorry for was Jimmy Adams. A finer human being you wouldn't find, but Jimmy knew his head was about to be lopped off. I doubt whether any captain could have altered the result of the series, such was the decline in his team's overall culture and attitude. He always enjoyed a drink and a chat in that rich, laid-back Jamaican accent, but as he and I sipped a beer after the series, lounging on the SCG dressing-room carpet covered with spilled alcohol and sweaty footprints, we both knew he'd played his last Test. The pain of continued loss and the realisation that his batting had lost its vibrancy were in his eyes.

They say books pick you and not the other way around, and it was during a transit stop at Hong Kong airport that I found what I didn't know I had been looking for. The tour to India promised to test us to the limit, and to prevail we needed one thing above all others: the right attitude. Instinctively, my hand reached out for the yellow spine of a title in the self-help section, which turned out to be a gem. A heading at the beginning of one chapter jumped out because it was so in sync with what I wanted; it was as if it had been written just for the team: 'Attitudes are contagious! Is yours worth catching?'

I was keen to set the scene for what I believed would be our toughest challenge yet, and at our first team meeting I stressed that I wanted us to be, mentally and physically, the toughest team India had ever played, the hungriest and most uncompromising side they'd ever seen, the closest-knit, most determined unit they'd ever come across. I also wanted us to be positive, self-assured and aggressive, and have the strongest body language and most intimidating aura they'd ever encountered. Above all, I wanted us to believe we could win from any situation and focus on the things we could control.

The initial press conference was a little strange without Warney, who during the 2000 off-season had used all of his 'Get out of jail free' cards with the board and been replaced by Adam Gilchrist as vice-captain. About the only prickly question that came up was related to a quote attributed to the new Indian skipper, Sourav Ganguly, who had apparently claimed that we'd only beaten 'weak' teams during our undefeated run. I couldn't let this opportunity go through to the keeper, and replied, 'Strange that one of those teams was India.' This was the beginning of an ongoing verbal battle between Sourav and me that belied an underlying admiration for each other; in the glare of the public eye, the gloves were off. I saw Sourav as elitist, a bloke who made a few rules for himself in his exalted position and who thought the world revolved around him. He was also constantly bickering over the nature of pitches and trying to influence the groundsmen in India. To me, this wasn't too different from match fixing, because captains who try this on are attempting to alter the conditions in collusion with a force they shouldn't be tampering with. It's a groundsman's job to prepare a pitch to the best of his ability, then hand it over to the players for them to adapt to the conditions. That's why it's called a 'Test';

it's supposed to challenge you, not appease your wishes. At the same time, I saw in Sourav a committed individual who wanted to inject some toughness and combativeness into a side that had often tended in the past to roll over and expose a soft underbelly, especially when touring life and certain events in cricket matches took them away from the cosiness of what they knew they could control.

A mighty shadow was cast upon the series two days before the opening Test with the passing of Sir Donald Bradman at the age of 92. The whole of India appeared to be in mourning, with every second person saying, 'Sorry' to me after the news came through. This was testament to his greatness, for he never toured India with an Australian team. One of the most vivid memories I have is of a couple of hours I spent with the Don at his Kensington home in Adelaide in August 1999, thanks to Malcolm Speed, who arranged the visit. Sir Donald was still incredibly sharp-minded when I met him. He held strong opinions and had an engaging manner that demanded attentiveness on my behalf. Initially, I kept thinking, *Wow, I am face to face with the legend! What would it have been like to have lived his life?* More than 50 years had passed since the end of his playing career, yet he was still getting 300 to 400 fan letters a week and was replying to every one of them.

The first thing that struck me about our meeting was the simplicity of his house, which had a red-brick exterior and an interior that was simple and uncluttered. There was no memorabilia or trace of his status, except for a portrait hanging above a fireplace. He had been escorted downstairs by a nurse who remained out of sight for the meeting, and we were joined halfway through by his son John. Sir Donald's attire was neat and, while he was physically diminutive, he exuded a dazzling aura; I felt secure in his company. I learnt that his health wasn't as good as he wanted, but his conversation was engaging and knowledgeable. He loved the modern game and was glowing in his praise of one-day cricket. I had a million questions to ask him, but time seemed to evaporate. 'If there's one thing you could change about the game today, what would it be?' As quick as a flash he replied, 'Get rid of the front-foot [no-ball] rule. Go back to the back-foot rule.'

'What were you like as a captain?'

'I was ordinary.'

'Why were you so much better than everyone else?'

'I wasn't – they just didn't realise their full potential.'

Eventually his modesty abated somewhat, but he still seemed to me to be a guy who just wanted to live a more normal life than he was ever afforded. I did get the strong impression that he was sick of being ripped off by people seeking his original playing gear for future profit, and others who made a trade out of his signature. Not one item had survived among his family members, but thankfully the Bradman Museum, at Bowral in the southern highlands of NSW, where he had lived as a young boy and teenager, ensured that not all the memorabilia was being used to make a profit. I was struck by his politeness and goodwill, and realised that he *was* flesh and blood after all when he signed a copy of his classic coaching book, *The Art of Cricket*, but found it genuinely hard to do because of his arthritic, gout-riddled hands.

We were in Mumbai when Sir Donald passed away, and I was asked by many people whether or not the first Test should be postponed. I replied, 'Sir Donald wouldn't have wanted that. We should play the series in the spirit he would have liked to have seen.'

It was a mere ten seconds before the coin was flipped in the opening Test that I made up my mind to trust my instincts and bowl first. It was a move against the grain, and unexpected, probably on a par with Mark Taylor's decision to bat first at Old Trafford in 1997. On the downside was the fact that we'd be batting last on a turning pitch against two frontline spinners and Tendulkar's vastly underrated leggies. (When Ganguly and I exchanged team sheets on the way out to the middle to toss, I noticed India had included two spinners and not three, which further tempted me to bowl first.) I genuinely believed, however, that we could take the game out of India's reach before the fourth innings by being proactive and bowling first. I had a number of reasons for thinking this, including the fact that they weren't Test-match battle-hardened, having played only Zimbabwe and Bangladesh in the previous six months, and would be underdone against our class attack. They had also failed in all six innings against us in Australia in 1999–2000 and had barely healed wounds that in my mind could be reopened under pressure. By having to bat first they wouldn't be able to ease their way into the series but would have to front up and face the music. The overriding factor, though, was that we had won 15 Tests in a row. That statistic meant we'd bowled out the opposition on 30 consecutive occasions, so we knew how to get the job done.

When we bowled India out for a modest 176 in their first innings I thought I'd done the right thing. However, with us at 5/99 in reply, the game was poised for one team or the other to assume control. What followed was an awesome display of courageous batting as, in total defiance of the textbook, Matthew Hayden and Adam Gilchrist scored astonishing centuries. Against sharp turn and exaggerated bounce they swept, heaved and hacked across the line through a couple of hours of continuous batting highlights that were breathtaking to watch. Haydos and Gilly dictated the tempo and kept backing themselves, which I'm sure shocked the Indian spinners, who must have thought subconsciously after the fifth wicket had fallen that the end of the innings was only a matter of time. Instead, we finished with a first-innings lead of 143.

What also was only a matter of time was Michael Slater being involved in an incident. With his marriage apparently in trouble, Slats was struggling to find a clear direction and had strayed from his normal means of preparation. Greatly exacerbating the problem was the fact that no one in the touring party was trained to handle personal difficulties of this nature. I tried my best to keep things under control, even speaking to Board officials about getting professional help, but with everyone's lives being so busy and the guy in question denying there were any problems, life went on. Slats' personal issues were brewing, however, and unbeknown to me at the time he was also suffering a medical condition that was related to an injury he'd suffered at the Australian Cricket Academy many years before and required ongoing medication.

During India's second innings, Rahul Dravid scooped one out in Slats' direction at midwicket, but it was difficult to see whether the catch had been made. Slats claimed it, but the days when any fielder's word was taken as true were gone and umpire Venkat referred the matter to the third umpire, who gave the benefit of the doubt to the batsman. Slats saw this as his integrity being questioned, and the time bomb ticked its final second. He blew up at the perceived injustice, and his personal stresses spilled out in a messy tirade that involved finger-pointing and an out-of-control plea for justice. It was the last thing I wanted to see, particularly as we'd regularly talked about our on-field behaviour and wanted to change the long-held perception of many that we were 'ugly'. Slats' performance was unacceptable and selfish, as he let his personal emotions overrule the team's ethics and standards. I was torn between physically pulling him away – which may have led to real ugliness – or yelling at him to get out of there. I opted for the latter, but my order fell on deaf ears and I was left holding the baby. As his friend and the captain I was willing to wear the consequences to a certain extent, but if I had my time again maybe I would have risked manhandling him out of the confrontation.

One of the problems with such an incident is that when it happens it's over very quickly – in this case around 30 seconds – but with continuous replays, many of them in slow motion, reality gets distorted and the ramifications grow. The bottom line was that I was in charge of the team and on this occasion, in trying to protect a guy on the edge and manage the situation in the best way possible, I was derelict in my duty to protect the image of the game.

The match referee, Cammie Smith from the West Indies, showed sympathy by letting Slats off with a censure and a severe warning. It was a decision we welcomed, but one that put into question yet again the inconsistencies of the system when penalising players who stepped out of line. This was an area Tim May, as ACA boss, and I had often talked about. We believed there needed to be a uniform penalty for clearly defined breaches so that everyone knew the consequences when they did the wrong thing, and therefore couldn't claim bias when they were punished. On this occasion, after handing down his compassionate verdict, Cammie Smith clearly stated to Slats, Buck, manager Steve Bernard and me that the matter was closed and not for public discussion.

The Test ended in a stunning 10-wicket win for us, even though for a long time it seemed the game could go either way. We had the knack of winning. Straight afterwards, Slats went on Australian radio to discuss the Test. The 'incident' came up and he said he'd done nothing wrong. Cammie Smith was so incensed by this that he immediately informed us that Slats now had a one-Test ban for his comments. It took an emergency meeting a few days after the Test, at the Taj Hotel in Kolkata, to sway Cammie from making Slats the first international cricketer to miss a Test due to a suspension earnt in a Test match. Steve Bernard and I argued that such a ban would be a stigma Slats would have to bear for the rest of his playing days and that his behaviour had been out of character. Slats remained unrepentant and felt hard done by, and I'm sure he was only saved by our pleading and well-conveyed sentiments. Cammie eventually changed his mind and issued a one-match ban suspended for six months and a loss of half a match fee. It was as good a result as we could have imagined, yet Slats didn't then thank the referee for his leniency or us for our efforts. He just left the room without uttering a word.

★

Away from the cricket, the opportunity to see at first hand how around 750 million Indians live in poverty drew me in, as always. I wanted to view their lives warts and all and understand how, without material possessions and wealth, these people keep their spirits up and have such a positive outlook on life. During our time in Mumbai on this tour, John Buchanan, Justin Langer and I took the chance to visit a local program that counsels and provides shelter for kids whose parents are sex slaves in the notorious red-light district. They were such happy children, with radiant smiles that belied their one-way ticket to future troubles. The area they came from is run by the local mafia, and while I felt safe that day surrounded by the adoring kids, I suspected that nightfall would bring out the rogue element. Colin Miller went one step further, spending half a day with a fishing community, living as a local, sipping tea in their basic shacks made of scrap metal and bricks.

However, not all contact with the locals ended in mutual admiration as our relatively wet-behind-the-ears coach was stung for a couple of hundred dollars. Looking inconspicuous in his Aussie training gear with a video camera documenting every move of the street life, he was offered a chance to see a unique tourist site. The con involved taking him to a temple where a burial was supposedly happening. At the ceremony's conclusion there was a need to pay for the materials used to cover the body, and Buck agreed to put up the cash. Quickly another deceased family member was whisked out, which meant they needed double the donation. Buck later admitted he never actually saw a body, only the extended hand of his 'guide'.

John and I strongly supported the idea of the guys learning from each other in order to increase mental strength while acquiring knowledge. Often, we'd get one of them to address the team on a cricket subject, followed by a question-and-answer session. A topic such as batting in the last 20 overs of a one-day innings would be covered by Michael Bevan, bowling in the last 10 overs by Ian Harvey, or anticipation in the field by Mark Waugh. After seeing Gilly and Haydos play out of their skins in the first Test we all wanted to know more about the so-called 'zone'. Gilly began by saying it was an 'out-of-body experience' where he felt in total control and not threatened. To get there he needed the peace of mind that only came with knowing he'd done the work beforehand. His personal secret was to start the innings thinking he was 20 or 30 not out already – this way, he'd feel more relaxed and calm, having, in his mind, jumped that nervous starting period. He believed that the key to staying in the zone was communication with his partner, as it kept him focused. (It sounded like ground-breaking stuff. The only trouble was that Adam either forgot it or it didn't work, because the next two Tests produced an overseas dialling code for him with innings of 0, 0, 1 and 1, to sink his theory, at least in the short term.)

Glenn McGrath stated that his trigger was to visualise his next over from fine leg, with the key being 'What do I want to do with the ball?' Shane said he needed to go through his own checklist the night before and, when he was in action, think about what shot he wanted the batsman to play and not worry about the possible consequences. Each time we held such a forum the information gathered was invaluable, and the process further confirmed to me how each team is a collection of minds, all of whom have something vital to add if they are given a chance. In cricket, the best coaches are without doubt a player's teammates, and if a team can self-monitor, most problems can be fixed before they become endemic.

After three days of the Kolkata Test, we buzzed around the change rooms at Eden Gardens imagining what the celebration was going to be like after we won our 17th Test in a row and a series victory, the first by an Australian team in India since 1969–70. All we needed to do was break the Rahul Dravid–V.V.S. Laxman combination early on day four and the possibility of a spare day loomed. We knew not to be *too* overconfident, but with Sachin out and our proven track record, surely 'True Blue' and 'Khe Sanh' would get a run in the next 48 hours. A customary bottle of Southern Comfort lay safely under my chair, ready to enhance the festivities.

Much later on, during the evening after the fifth day, the Southern was opened but it went down to drown the sorrows. India had performed a miracle on day four, with Laxman playing the innings of his life in tandem with the 'brick wall', Dravid, as we toiled away for absolutely no result. As that day wore on it appeared their bats were widening with each boundary and its accompanying thunderous roar, while our hopes were whittled away by a combination of delirium and desperation. I had enforced the follow-on after bowling India out in only 58 overs for 171, leaving them a deficit of 274. It was a decision we discussed as a team, but I was extra-keen to keep them pinned down and keep the momentum going. Previous to this, I had crafted a century at the ground I like to call the 'Lord's of the subcontinent'. It was an emotional hundred, with my close connections to Udayan and the fact that Australia's cricket renaissance had begun here back in 1987 with our unexpected World Cup win.

On the morning of day five I told the guys, 'If we are forced into fighting for a draw, let's do everything we can to achieve it. If that means not scoring or letting a long hop go through to the keeper, we must do that.' However, we ended up losing the Test after being only three wickets down at tea and needing an impossible 223 to win. In hindsight, I should have addressed the team again to reinforce our plan, to make sure everything was doubly clear. Obviously it wasn't, as sixes were flying into the crowd and all manner of shots were being played. The two who best followed through on our plan were the last pair, Glenn McGrath and Michael Kasprowicz, who stuck together for over half an hour before the familiar raised finger went up after an lbw shout, for the fifth time in the innings.

Some observers have said the umpiring was dubious on that final day, but I tend to disagree – all our guys were fairly given out. However, there were a couple of poor decisions both ways throughout the Test, with the most critical being the full toss that struck Venkatesh Prasad, the Indian No. 11, on the full when they were 9/140 in the first innings. He was given not out, which allowed Laxman, on 37 not out and playing for his career, to cut loose at the other end and end up with 59. That extra time in the middle might have played him into form, because, having batted at six in that first innings, he came in at No. 3 in the second and made his historic 281. It was an important call that went their way, but in all my time in sport rarely has one decision influenced the outcome. We were beaten by a more resilient force than we'd expected and paid the price for our careless approach with the bat.

The match, which was watched by an estimated 400 000 people, was memorable for many reasons, including some lighter moments that broke the tension during those five days. In our first innings, Jason Gillespie and I added 133 for the ninth wicket and we both needed to change our gloves fairly regularly to make sure the bat handle wouldn't slip out of our hands. Halfway through our stand, Dizzy nearly lost his focus completely when he peered down at his new gloves and saw a Glenn McGrath autograph on the back of each one – payback for a previous infringement when Pigeon had taken delivery of a new set of gloves, pads and bat and Dizzy had kindly decided to moniker them free of charge to inspire him. This was 'Dumb and Dumber' doing some of their best work for the amusement of the rest of us.

I was learning more and more that being on tour as a leader invariably involved dealing with issues before they became major problems. I have always believed in the policy of praising in public, criticising in private. As soon as criticism is out there in the public arena, a different spin can get placed on it and a wedge can be put in the team mechanics. When coach Buchanan in his well-intentioned way questioned Warney's fitness and future place in the side through the media, he may have meant to inspire, but all he did was alienate. This ploy may have worked when Buck was in charge of Queensland, working with a lower-profile player on the way up who might have found such a public challenge motivational, but in Shane he picked his mark poorly. It was Buck's first real blunder as coach, and after 24 hours of mulling over the situation I organised for the three of us to get together and work through it. Shane saw it as a cheap shot that should have been discussed face to face, and the coach admitted that would have been a better plan.

Also brewing in the background on this tour was a Buchanan–Bernard feud that at one stage had them dealing with each other through intermediaries. Buck was always going to ruffle a few feathers with his strong opinions and way of doing business, which was 100 per cent full-on and at times inflexible. His great strengths were his vision and proactiveness, but at the same time, if you didn't entertain his ideas you could get left behind. As Buck tried to move in a different direction to the one Steve preferred, our manager felt like his authority and place in the pecking order were being challenged. It was a clear case of the 'old school' clashing with a new wave of change and neither wanting to give ground. Egos are not exclusive to players and the existence of a disruptive support group will often be reflected in a team's results. It was a distraction I didn't need and one they had to sort out, which they did after the tour.

★

Going into the deciding Test in Chennai, we vowed as a batting group to take their spinners on and be aggressive rather than perish playing meekly. The turbaned Harbhajan Singh had taken 13 wickets in the second Test, in part because we played too often from the crease with hard, low hands instead of either advancing down the pitch to dominate, or going back and creating more time and space to improvise some shots. The hesitation was killing us, and Harbhajan's unusual bounce, which was mixed with his sharp, turning off-breaks and a cleverly masked 'mystery ball' that went straight on, made him an especially dangerous proposition for the first 20 minutes of an innings. Being more superstitious than I liked to admit or recognise, as soon as we arrived at the M.A. Chidambaram Stadium I made a beeline for the exact seat Dean Jones had sat in during his epic double century back in 1986, hoping some of the magic would be residual. I could still picture his gaunt appearance, and a face that didn't belong to him with a distant, vacant gaze that suggested he was on the verge of losing his faculties. I sensed we'd need a similar effort from someone if we were to end up on the right side of the ledger.

By the end of day one we'd flayed their attack to be 3/326, with Matthew Hayden again batting with supreme confidence and sweeping the spinners from all angles and to all parts of the ground. Matty's strength was his sense of strategy. He'd wear down the opposition attack before launching into the spinners in courageous fashion. Once that assault was accomplished, his confidence levels would carry him upwards and onwards. The key to his audacious sweeping was his technique in getting his front leg in line with the ball, which helped him also to align his head and kept him balanced.

Haydos's mastery of the turning tracks was in stark contrast to Ricky Ponting's struggles. Punter just couldn't seem to coordinate his movements and for the first time in his life looked ungainly at the wicket. I knew he was in dire straits mentally but banked on him fighting his way through and, furthermore, we were loath to drop a guy until every possible opportunity had been offered to him. The tour itinerary also made it tough to replace him, because his natural replacement, Damien Martyn, had played very little cricket over the preceding four weeks. To bring Marto into the side in such circumstances would have been a massive ask. Showing trust in players is something I always stood for, and while it occasionally backfired, the benefits more than made up for the odd disappointment.

The turning point of the match happened early on the second day and saw me become only the sixth cricketer in Test history to be given out for handling the ball. When I missed an attempted sweep, all I could think about was what a wasted opportunity it had been, along with the umpire's response to the half-hearted appeal. A split second later I was startled by Matty Hayden yelling, 'Look out, Tugga!' I reacted instinctively by knocking the ball away with my hand before it could spin back towards the stumps. As soon as I palmed it away to 'safety' I felt that sick feeling in the pit of my stomach that told me I'd stuffed up in a big way, while the joy in the Indians' appeals suggested they knew immediately that they had a free wicket. Mine was the first of seven wickets to fall for 51 runs to let the Indians back into the match. A Tendulkar century put them in the box seat, with a first-innings lead of 120, and was followed up by 'The Turbanator', who terrorised us as he claimed 15 wickets for the Test. Not only did Harbhajan dictate terms with the ball, he backed it up with verbal barrages that would have been big news if we'd been giving instead of receiving. The opposition players who did well against Australia during my career were the ones with a combative spirit, who weren't submissive but rather enjoyed the gamesmanship and unrelenting pressure. The guys who had a go and stuck it back in our faces had a much greater chance of triumphing. This was especially true during my final four years of Test cricket and remains so today.

Chasing 155 to win, India were cruising at 2/101 before they suddenly realised they were about to complete one of the all-time great fightbacks in Test history and began to crack under the strain of such an achievement. A breathtaking catch by Mark Waugh off a Colin Miller long hop saw a disbelieving Laxman trudge off and lift our spirits to the point where, when Sairaj Bahutale was dismissed for a duck three balls later, we had our noses in front at 7/135. Nerves become stretched in the frantic last overs of a tight one-day contest, but when a crucial Test match is on the line, all the senses are on red alert. This is truly a time for self-convincing. You must *want* the ball to come your way, you must be eager to get under that steepling chance, and you can't afford to entertain the thought of being the guy who might stuff up the match-defining chance. I loved the transparency of knowing what I had to do, but I had also experienced the hollowness of cracking under pressure. A reflex catch was everyone's preferred option in the field, because a skied ball gave you a moment to reflect on the gravity of the situation, the crowd's expectations and the probability that your team-mates were already running in your direction, ready for a celebration.

The victorious side in a 50/50 situation is always the one that keeps its cool, the one that reproduces the same quality performance no matter the pressure – and that only comes from having a solid base that is the result of hard work. If you've prepared properly, you can trust yourself. As a captain, these circumstances were the ones I dreamt of, because I knew my decisions could have a real influence on the outcome.

I gambled on Colin Miller and left a gap in the field from extra cover to slip, hoping to entice their last decent bat, inexperienced keeper Sameer Dighe, to cut against the off-spin. Not only did he risk the shot once, but pulled it off twice, to guide his team to a gut-churning two-wicket win. It was courageous batsmanship, which was duly rewarded by his axing from the team not long after in a clear case of a selection panel overlooking a key trait: character. A promising career was curtailed by short-sightedness.

We did dismiss Zaheer Khan with four still needed, but soon after,

Harbhajan eased Glenn McGrath through point for the match-winning runs and the crowd was delirious. So was I, from exhaustion. The tension and fluctuating nature of these back-to-back Tests had mentally drained me and I was almost relieved it was all over. We had given everything and I was proud of our effort, and while the final scoreline read 2–1 to India, I didn't feel as if we'd lost, but, rather, we'd advanced in many ways. Our enjoyment and the way we embraced the culture, our positive play and our competitiveness in all three Tests were vastly superior to how we'd performed on our previous tour to India in 1998. But one element needed fixing: our technique against spin. For Australia to win next time the two countries met on Indian turf would require eliminating risky shots and playing with softer hands and decisive footwork. I wasn't sure whether I'd be there, but like Allan Border with the West Indies, if I wasn't, I liked to think I might have contributed along the way.

During my time as one-day leader, our 3–2 win of a series that began only three days after that dramatic Test series rates just about top of the pile for me. The first challenge was to re-energise the Test players who were in the limited-over squad; equally as difficult was getting the one-day specialists acclimatised to the conditions.

The pitches we played on were dustbowls, at venues that weren't of the quality we'd had during the Tests. On the administration front we were sloppy in regard to communication, with Michael Kasprowicz initially being told he was staying for the one-dayers, then being informed he was going home and being handed the ultimate lack of respect by being asked to return his meal allowances. Jason Gillespie was also sent home without anyone consulting me, as management was sidetracked and lacking its usual professionalism. Playing in satellite cities such as Pune, Indore and Goa meant fanatical crowds who not only packed the stadiums but also congregated in the hotel foyers and booked rooms on our floors just so they could get autographs and photos. Our privacy went well and truly out the window. Often people would walk into our rooms while we were watching a movie or eating a meal, and just stand and stare, so our doors needed careful attention. In the end, it came down to a simple and cheap solution: water pistols.

Elsewhere, the continued petulance of Sourav Ganguly in being late for the toss and then walking off by himself after the event had me really wound up. It also upset match referee Cammie Smith, who called a meeting to tell Sourav to show some respect and be on time. The next day the Indian captain made the point in his own style by turning up early wearing a tracksuit top, just to let everyone know who was running the show. You had to give him 'A' for effort in his attempt to annoy us, and in particular me. It worked to a certain extent, but I wonder at the end of his career what his winning percentage at the toss will be. I hope the coin has the last laugh.

Our victory in the final one-dayer, at Goa, was achieved through a skilful chase on a disintegrating pitch, orchestrated by the maestro, Michael Bevan, in conjunction with the guy I consider to be the most slumbering cricket talent in Australia, probably in the world. Ian Harvey has too many natural gifts to choose from and as a consequence hasn't worked hard enough to polish his gems; instead, they remain uncut and unfulfilled to a certain extent. An example of his ability was his quickness in learning to throw proficiently with both hands – a concept introduced by our coach, who as usual was trying to be innovative and one step ahead. Within months 'Harvs' was equally brilliant from both hands and didn't really see what all the fuss was about. Playing well under pressure had been his nemesis to the time of the series decider. I honestly believed that his innings of 25 would see him flourish from that point onwards, but unfortunately peer-group pressure and a need to fit in as 'one of the boys' too often stymied his destiny.

37

Roads less travelled

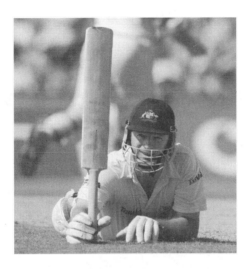

What a contradiction this place is, with its crystal-clear, turquoise waters and strikingly rugged mountain ranges, all shrouded in a serene air of tranquillity. Yet on the very ground on which we stood, a parcel of land no larger than two tennis courts, 6000 men had lost their lives in hand-to-hand combat. Our Turkish guide, whose grandfather had died in combat, spoke eloquently as we sheltered under the sole tree at Lone Pine at Gallipoli, scarcely able to comprehend the courage and bravery shown by both sides in a battle that, in many ways, forged the spirit of two countries. Later we re-enacted the famous image of the diggers playing cricket at Shell Green. Our guide gave each of us a bullet from the battlefield to commemorate the experience and to remind us all of the sacrifices made by those who had gone before us.

To me, 'bonding' is an overrated term normally linked to reminiscing about past escapades with a truckload of grog on board. I've had my fair share of these nights, and while they can create a few laughs and a better understanding of each other, the experience is shallow and soon forgotten. True bonding experiences stand the test of time and become part of you and, most certainly, visiting Gallipoli together on our way to England for the 2001 Ashes tour had a profound effect on most of the squad.

The stopover came about after a chance luncheon between the then head of the Australian Army, Lieutenant General Peter Cosgrove, and me, not long before we were due to depart for England. What was at first just an idea was further developed by the ACB, and led to the team feeling something very special – though for many of us it was hard to put Gallipoli into words. We waited for a couple of days and then each member of the squad stood up and tried to explain what the experience had meant to them. Like many, I was moved by the words of Patrick Farhart, who is of Lebanese descent. He said that for the first time in his life, even though he'd been born in Australia, he felt 100 per cent Australian as he stood among the trenches at the Nek. John Buchanan had worn his father's war medals to Gallipoli, but didn't know why. 'I felt compelled to ring my [18-year-old] son, Michael, and tell him how much I love him, as you never know what might happen tomorrow,' he told us. 'We don't spend enough time telling our family how much we love them.'

★

Instead of the usual 'dragon's breath' air of a cold English morning, this time the first memorable moment of a tour of the UK came in an altogether unexpected fashion before I'd even escaped from Heathrow Airport. The head-down, ask-questions-without-making-eye-contact attitude of the customs official caught me off guard: 'What are you doing here? Are you being paid? Who's paying you? Where's your work permit? If you haven't got one, you're not coming in.'

I had a quick scout around, but I couldn't find the *Candid Camera* crew and began to think this might be serious. Thankfully, the tour manager explained our situation and the tour was off and running.

For 2001, the itinerary was significantly different to previous Ashes trips. This time the tour was basically divided in two parts, with a 10-game one-day series involving England, Australia and Pakistan being the feature of the first month and the five Tests being played during July and August. In the limited-overs tournament, we put to good use the increased unity we had gained from Gallipoli, and dominated our matches. We elevated the aggressiveness in our play and tried to consume our opposition as quickly and ruthlessly as possible. A demolition job on England at Manchester, where we bowled them out for 86 employing Test cricket fielding positions, set the tone for future battles and allowed us to mentally harass a few of their players. I had sensed that their respect for us actually bordered on them being resigned to defeat when I heard their stand-in captain, Alec Stewart, say during an interview following the toss for our first encounter, at Bristol, 'We're just hoping to compete today.' This translated to me as 'We are shit-scared and hope we don't make fools of ourselves today.' Maybe that was a harsh assessment, but I always searched for a guide to the opposition's frame of mind and to me this was a clear sign they feared us.

We steamrolled the Pakistanis, too, in a one-day final at Lord's, taking only 26.3 overs to reach the target set for us of 153 and re-open the wounds from the 1999 World Cup. The Australian one-day team was now a smooth operator running on all cylinders, and I was batting probably better than I ever had in the limited-overs form of the game. Little did I know that I would play only eight more games for my country before, without warning, I'd be shown the door.

Unfortunately, the one-day series finished in a blaze of controversy when Michael Bevan was picked off by a full can of VB as he stood on the Lord's balcony ready to receive his winner's medal. Realistically, he was only a couple of centimetres away from receiving a potentially fatal blow. The stupidity of the act was beyond belief, as was the strength and length of the villain's throw. This brazen act came on the back of a walk-off I ordered at Trent Bridge after Brett Lee's head was narrowly missed by a rocket firecracker that came from an out-of-control section of the crowd. I'd had enough of the lack of security and the administrators' slowness to act despite the increasingly frequent bad behaviour of the 'fans' – which included a young boy being surrounded and then injured by a menacing group of Pakistani supporters at Cardiff, and a security guard being hospitalised after he tried to help the players get off the ground at Headingley. The authorities were living in the dark ages, arguing that letting spectators run onto the field was all part of English cricket's 'village green' atmosphere, never realising that times had changed – we don't watch black-and-white TV or leave the front door unlocked any more.

John Buchanan and I were always looking to stay one step ahead and follow our creed to 'take the road less travelled'. At one point Buck produced statistics that showed that most one-day games finished in the second innings with between five and 10 overs left unbowled, so we decided to go hard and allow our top bowlers to complete their allotted 10 overs early. If needed, part-timers like Mark Waugh and Andrew Symonds would finish the innings off.

Getting the guys to read motivational books provided some humorous moments. *Tuesdays with Morrie* and *Who Moved My Cheese?*

weren't everyone's cup of tea, but they did challenge and provoke. Each player was asked to divulge their thoughts on the books, and in true form 'Simo' replied, 'Didn't read it. Don't read books.' And that was that. Brett Lee was a late call-up to the one-day squad, and I'll never forget the look on his face when he was asked to elaborate on a questionnaire Buck had surprisingly got under the right door, which referred to *Who Moved My Cheese?*, a book that deals with life taking different directions and how we adapt to change. Brett hadn't arrived when the books were handed out, so when he read questions such as 'What new cheeses would you like to taste?' and 'Which cheeses are your favourites?' he thought that either the questionnaire was a hoax or Buck was a sandwich short of a picnic. 'Binger' didn't know or care; he just wanted to roar in and let 'em rip.

The decision before the tour to relieve Buck of his selecting duties had come as a surprise to me and was one I hadn't been consulted on. Rather than the captain, vice-captain and coach forming the selection committee on tour, Gilly and I were to work with the chairman of selectors at home, Trevor Hohns, to pick the sides. I was pleased that Hohns was finally getting involved in on-tour selections, even if it would most often be via a phone hook-up, but disappointed that we'd no longer have Buck's input; in my mind, the change was a direct result of the coach's outburst against Shane Warne in India.

Also altering the landscape dramatically was a new Memorandum of Understanding agreed to by the ACB and the ACA, which ensured that Australian cricket's profits would be distributed in what we saw as an even more equitable fashion than had been achieved with much unnecessary bitterness in 1997–98. The new agreement also contained formulas for distributing revenue related to intellectual property rights, and a player retirement scheme. An unwritten consequence of the agreement – because of both the end result and the manner in which it was achieved – was that players and administrators would now be more professional, accountable and closely aligned. It was a positive outcome and left us believing that the relationship between us and our board was now the best in the cricket world.

A demonstration of the lengths to which the parties had moved together was the appointment of our first full-time tour masseuse. This was an initiative I had proposed during our tour debrief of India. In years gone by, such a suggestion would have received a swift 'No way – that's the physio's job, and it'll make you guys soft.' Now we were told, 'Yes, if it will have a positive influence on the players and their preparation, we'll do it.'

The Australian team was noted for its excellence on the field, but we had a reputation for sledging that I and everyone else involved didn't want as part of our legacy. There had been times when we'd been out of line, but we had actually improved each year with regard to appearances in front of and penalties from the match referees. Still, we needed to continue to improve. With this in mind, I gave a public guarantee that there would be no dissent on the field and we'd play the game in the right spirit. It was a concept that everyone in the squad embraced and that would later be recognised with the Spirit of Cricket Award from the MCC, although some were worried it would affect our mode of engagement when playing. I believed it wouldn't, because we only ever crossed the line when we were out of control. All that was needed for us to maintain our composure was discipline.

With the next Ashes tour not due until the year of my 40th birthday, this was in all likelihood my last one – so I wanted it to be special, not just for me but also for my family. I decided to rent a three-bedroom apartment in London for eight weeks to give Lynette, Rosie, Austin and the in-laws a base, a more relaxing environment and a steady routine. It was also designed to ease the stress of travelling for Lynette, who was heavily pregnant with our third child. I was also in serious need of bonding time with Austin, who was 19 months old when he arrived in England and had known his dad mostly via phone calls and watching cricket and news reports on the television. Having a base less than a kilometre from the team's Kensington Park hotel gave me an opportunity to be physically part of his life and take the place of the Teletubbies as a role model.

During the tour, in keeping with a desire to make family time count, we tried whenever possible to give a player time off if his family came over. I had my four days away before the first Test and made use of them by going to Euro Disney, scaling the dangers of Peter Pan's Flight, taking the Dumbo the Elephant ride and circling the canals of 'It's a Small World'. There are few greater sights for a parent than seeing your kids' faces light up when they spot Mickey Mouse for the first time or marvel at the sight of Pluto's tongue.

Prior to the Test series there had to be another dreaded phone call to a player saying, 'Can I just come up and see you for a minute?' With Damien Martyn in the form of his life, and Justin Langer disadvantaged by not playing one-day cricket and having been unable to capitalise on recent Test-match starts, Adam, Trevor and I decided to make the tough call. There's not much to say and it's not really the time for a lengthy discussion, so I gave it to Lang simply: 'Sorry, I know you'll be devastated but we've decided to give Marto a chance and you're the one who's missed out.'

Lang would later say he didn't know whether to hug me or punch me; I just felt like throwing up. Not until the next day did we chat for any length of time, but even then Lang was in denial and still shocked by his demotion. I did tell him he needed to start making hundreds and that he should start thinking about becoming an opener, as down the track I could see an opportunity evolving for him if our current situation at the top of the order didn't change for the better. He vowed to do whatever it took to get back in the side, but I could tell that deep down he was barely holding it together. It wasn't until near the end of the trip that he offloaded the burden of mental anguish and conspiracy theories that for a while stagnated his fightback.

The day before the first Test we were presented with the newly introduced ICC mace after officially being recognised as the world's No. 1 side. When I think back on our record streak of 16 Test wins in a row, achieved by 20 different players and numerous other squad members with bloodlines as diverse as Polish, Lebanese and Aboriginal, particular images flash to mind, the first four being:

- Colin Miller's brilliant, spine-tingling one-handed pick-up and throw to run out Matt Horne at Hamilton in the third Test of our 2000 tour, which came at a crucial moment. In the field Funky normally had the touch of an Edward Scissorhands
- Ricky Ponting's courage in standing his ground at silly mid-off when Shane Warne bowled a waist-high full toss during the first over of day five in the first Test against Pakistan in 1999–2000. Abdur Razzaq smashed the offering straight into Punter's midriff, again giving us a vital lift
- Justin Langer calling for the 1900 replica cap to replace his helmet as he neared his century against India in our first Test of 2000, at Sydney
- the support staff who clapped us into the change rooms after a courageous but statistically unrewarding effort during the opening session of the third day of the first Test, at Mumbai, in 2001.

These and many other important little moments, when connected, made us harder to break down. Each unselfish act galvanised the spirit and helped raise the bar for the future.

The first Test of the 2001 Ashes series, at Edgbaston, would be my first in England as a visiting captain. It was also a new situation to be without a bat sponsor, a circumstance that had come about largely because I hadn't received any decent offers. Instead of selling myself short, I had decided, in conjunction with the Duet Group, my new management company, to go 'cleanskin' and see what came of the exercise. This gamble paid off handsomely when the Madras Rubber Factory eventually came in with a proposal that more than doubled what I had previously been earning. The entrepreneurial streak I possessed made this type of left-field gamble exciting. I'd always taken a hands-on approach with my business interests and endorsements, including book, clothing and equipment deals, coaching clinics and agreements to write articles for newspapers and magazines. However, the extra obligations as captain meant I needed a full-time management company to deal with the endless requests I was receiving. In modern-day cricket, just about all players have managers, but only the top dozen or so players really need to be managed. The rest either have a guy who is chasing his tail or someone hired only to keep up with the Joneses.

At 9.35 p.m. on the eve of the first Test, my thoughts of a dominating opening day were totally sidetracked by a distressing noise from just outside our room that sounded like someone in serious pain. Upon opening our hotel door, Lynette and I spotted a limb protruding from the doorway five or six down from us. By the time I reached the middle-aged naked man he was barely conscious, and as soon as he said he wasn't hurt much, to my alarm he lapsed into unconsciousness. An ambulance was called by Lynette and paramedics arrived shortly after, but what I'll never forget is the state of his room. A pungent odour emanated from the bathroom, where the full bath was covered with vomit and a smashed bottle of alcohol lay on the floor. An empty aspirin bottle stood on a shelf, there was a splattering of blood on the tiled walls and, chillingly, a pâté knife sat on the edge of the bath. We learnt later that the guy had swallowed 24 tablets in his effort to commit suicide. It was a scene I couldn't let go of. I wondered how a life could end up so skewed and what would drive someone to such lengths. How could I be so invigorated by the promise of great times ahead while this guy was so depressed he didn't want to face another day?

★

What an amazing 90 overs the first day turned out to be, with 427 runs scored and 12 wickets falling in a sure sign that Test-match cricket had changed forever since the less frenetic days of, say, 1985–86. I remembered the old clichés, such as 'Openers take the shine off for the middle-order stroke-makers' or '250 is a lot of runs for a single day's play'. What this style of Test cricket showed was that, contrary to popular belief, one-day cricket didn't erode batting skills – it improved them. Batsmen expanded their repertoires, invented new shots and got into the habit of being positive and proactive in everything they did. A direct flow-on effect was increased scoring rates.

Adam Gilchrist's hundred during our first innings was brought up not by a frenetic single but by guiding an attempted bouncer over the wicketkeeper's head. What an asset to the side Gilly is, coming in at five down and regularly taking the game away from the opposition in the space of an hour. It's a perfect role for him. He often comes in around the time of the second new ball, with no limitations or designated role to stick to, which allows his natural, unaffected style to take the game by the scruff of the neck. I've never seen a guy block a ball harder. Gilly has steel-infused wrists and refuses to defend meekly. Every shot is played with the intent of scoring runs, and the extra arc he creates by holding the bat high in his grip translates into extra speed on the down-swing and more pace for the ball off the face of the bat. He must have an eye like a bald eagle, because he never seems to mistime or leave any balls; each delivery is an offering to be dispatched to his liking. Instead of backing down after an onslaught, he ups the tempo to a new level and demolishes bowlers like the tornado did Dorothy's house. He is the modern-day batting prototype, tackling each assignment with the bravado of an Indiana Jones. As a keeper he is much better than he gets credit for, probably because his batting steals all the headlines. He handles the subtleties of Shane Warne and Stuart MacGill with considerable poise and glovesmanship, and moves silently and effortlessly, rarely missing an offering from the quicks. A great player is one who changes the thinking about how to play the game, and Gilly has done that. He has redefined the role of a keeper/batsman and also singlehandedly affected the outcome of more games than any of his peers.

Gilly's 152, along with a maiden Test century for Damien Martyn (scored in his 12th Test, a remarkable eight and half years after his debut), whose easy manner catches opposing teams on the hop, and my clinically proficient 105, laid the platform for a crushing win, and in the process we took out their captain, Nasser 'Poppadom Fingers' Hussain, who snapped a digit when struck by a Jason Gillespie riser. It was rumoured Nasser's bones were so brittle he'd break a finger playing balloon volleyball.

Winning the first Test in four days gave us a bonus day off that just happened to coincide with the Wimbledon men's singles final, which had been delayed a day due to rain. Down we travelled to London with the baggy greens on top to support Australia's Pat Rafter against Goran Ivanisevic. I was lucky enough to spend a few minutes with Pat in the change rooms before he journeyed out onto centre court. I couldn't believe how quiet the room was, with his entourage calmly wandering about and Pat himself dousing his skin with sunscreen and asking whether I'd seen the State of Origin rugby league score (we both knew Queensland had won, much to his delight). Centre court was packed with Aussies, who broke into spontaneous applause as we took our seats. I quickly saw why tennis players love this place – it is intimate, yet steeped in history. At the opposite end of the court sat

Jack Nicholson, wearing his signature dark shades, just far enough away to tease Warney, who was desperate to meet him. Shane would have also loved to meet his idol, John McEnroe, who strolled past us before the action got under way. We witnessed one of the great finals and in the end Goran lived out his dream, but as a group we admired our man's fight and the way he handled himself in defeat.

Continuing the tradition of having varied guests speak to us before a Test, Justin Langer invited his mate from South Africa, François Pienaar, the 1995 rugby World Cup-winning captain, to speak to us. François's message revolved around four 'Ds': Desire, Determination, Dedication and Discipline. 'Embrace these,' he said, 'and it will lead to Delight.' John Buchanan had a surprise for me on the same night as we wound our way through the back streets of London in a black cab before pulling up at an address in Mayfair. He and I were there in our quest to venture further down the 'road less travelled' and to pick the lateral-thinking brain of one Edward de Bono. One concept I took away from this meeting was that of keeping in a batsman who was scoring slowly in a one-day game. 'Why would you try to get that player out when he's actually doing the job you want him to do for you – limiting the scoring?' de Bono asked.

This was a theory we often joked about but never employed, for fear it would stifle our natural aggressive instincts – the lure of a wicket was too strong to suppress. But if we wanted an edge, maybe this was the one we were looking for. At the conclusion of a deep-thinking and expansive conversation I hopped into a cab with a pulsating migraine, while Buck was on cloud nine. The coach was in his element; he was stimulated by a person who came from the same side of the tracks as he did, a person who challenged set procedures and broke things just so he could reset them differently.

★

With Nasser out for a couple of Tests the Poms needed a new captain, and I couldn't believe my eyes when I read that no one wanted the job. On the same day, three of our guys, Michael Slater, Ricky Ponting and Mark Waugh, had their 'Test numbers' etched for life on their bodies – though unfortunately for Mick, he gave the wrong number to the tattooist. He and Brendon Julian both debuted at Manchester in 1993, and Slats incorrectly thought that the official numbering system was based on whoever batted first and not on alphabetical order. His embarrassment was later minimised when protocols were relaxed and his and BJ's numbers were reversed. The contrast between our newly decorated men and England's non-captains was stark. One group was claiming ownership, the other was avoiding it. The lack of English pride was similarly captured at an official function at the Café Royal in London, where the sentiments expressed by the locals were so one-sided in our favour it was almost fingers-down-the-throat stuff. All we heard was how good we were and how bad the English team was; it was pathetically self-mocking and weak. Why didn't they show a bit of ticker, back their own team and have a go? Their negativity appeared to be a form of protection for when things went wrong. Sport to Australians is more about 'Let's show 'em', a way to be recognised and respected on the world stage. Aussies appear hungrier and less accepting of mediocre performances than many other nationalities.

Not surprisingly then, we gave England a bath at the home of cricket. We celebrated in the dressing-room with our partners and kids, a move that, if they'd known about it, would have caused a dramatic decline in numbers of the 'egg and bacon' members (so named because of the colour scheme of their ties) through heart attacks. Attitudes can be hard to change, especially when they are linked to tradition, but as a side we wanted to involve our families because they played a key role in our success. A happy family man was a more contented player who could focus better on his game.

Meanwhile, Rosie Waugh had a thrill when she received a reply to a letter I had given to one of the Queen's ladies-in-waiting when the monarch met the teams on the first day of the Test. The critical question 'How many dogs do you have and what are their names?' was answered in a pamphlet detailing the profiles of each of Her Majesty's corgis, but the answer to the query on whether or not she eats Coco Pops for breakfast is still a mystery. My nerves about not making a mistake when introducing the team members weren't made any easier by Damien Fleming, who mouthed the words 'Don't forget me this time', in reference to my '99 World Cup faux pas.

The lead-up to the third Test, at Trent Bridge, was highlighted by another document being misplaced by our management, this time a dossier put together by John Buchanan that extolled the virtues of fifth-century Chinese warrior and philosopher Sun Tzu, and detailed his 'nine situations on the battlefield'. Buck wanted us to draw some parallels with Sun Tzu's interpretations of such diverse situations as 'Dispersive Ground', 'Contentious Ground' and 'Ground of Intersecting Highways' among others. Quite frankly, we were relieved that the media got hold of the memo so they could translate it for us. As usual, Buck had gone to extraordinary lengths to challenge us, which was part of his role, but two things often made his assignments hard: we needed the intellect to pull them off, and we struggled to read his minuscule handwriting. He should have handed out a magnifying glass with each document.

As coach and captain, Buck and I had a simple relationship: I never meddled in his theories, ideas and concepts, and he never interfered with the way I ran the team. All decisions on the field were mine, though of course we would discuss them when we needed to, and the simplicity of the way we worked and the space we maintained between us made for a smooth ride. In general, Buck and I had the same principles at heart: challenge the team, make them responsible for their actions, create a relaxed working environment and get them to realise their full potential.

As professional sportspeople we were well aware of our obligations to look after our sponsors and did so without question. Often, though, we'd be astounded by the amount of wrong gear we were sent and how it almost invariably didn't arrive in time for the start of a season or tour. And always, we heard the same excuse: 'Time got away from us.' However, when something like a player wearing a logo on the wrong sleeve meant that the main sponsor didn't get the exposure they were entitled to, the board came down on us like a ton of bricks. It didn't matter that they'd printed the logos incorrectly, so that a right-handed batsman had the logo on his right sleeve as he faced the bowler rather than his left; all the board wanted was to be the good guys as far as their corporate contacts were concerned. One particular letter from the ACB's general operations manager to Steve Bernard after a few of us wore the 'wrong' shirts during a Test on this tour read, in part: 'We are paying these guys hundreds of thousands of dollars and it's about time they accept their responsibilities as professional sports-men and understand that the only way they can be paid the way they are is because of the support provided by sponsors.' Even though we had made giant leaps in our relationship with the board, there were times when they went back to their militant ways. We found com-ments like that a bit rich, especially when injured players going home midway through a tour had to hand back their training gear before they left because management said there was only so much money in the sponsorship budget.

A few days after the second Test I was back to being a bachelor on tour after the family headed home. Lynette was only eight weeks away from delivering baby number three and I wanted our child to be born an Aussie, not a Pommie. A week later, the experience of wearing Victor Trumper's Sheffield Shield winner's medal from the

1903–04 season around my neck (fulfilling a promise I'd made to the medal's owner, former NSW Cricket CEO Bob Radford) lasted an entire one ball when, after turning the first delivery behind square leg, I hit the deck feeling as if I'd been struck in the left calf with a cannon ball. During my first couple of steps, I tried to convince myself that it didn't actually hurt and was just a spasm or cramp. But three-quarters of the way down the pitch I knew it was serious, with my calf 'grabbing' and then stabbing in waves of excruciating pain. To be carried off on a stretcher is humiliating, especially when you're captain and about to retain the Ashes, and with self-pity and anger bubbling to the surface, the sight of an eager press photographer waiting at the gate for an 'anguished look' from me led to a token act of frustration. With all the force I could muster, I spat out my wad of chewing gum, which slapped into the poor guy's camera lens and stuck there, smack-bang in the middle, obscuring his picture. The comfort of that small victory was soon lost in my despair at the extent of the injury. A 5 cm × 5 cm tear in my lower left calf had also caused a breaking point higher up in the muscle, where a 2 cm rip had occurred. The prognosis: a three- to six-month lay-off. *Bullshit. That can't be right.*

But I could barely wiggle my toes. The news of our retention of the Ashes came via a phone call as I sat in a wheelchair in a deserted hospital room, which wasn't what I had in mind as the winning captain in one of the world's most revered sporting contests. Back in the rooms hours later, the celebration was tinged with sadness for me, for I thought my tour was as good as over. I didn't want to be a burden, just hanging around, so in my mind it was QF10 for me.

During a phone conversation late that night, however, Lynette dramatically revised my opinion. 'You're the captain, they need you and you should be there at the Oval to accept the trophy,' she said. It was the lift I needed to get back on track. Instead of packing my bags, I initiated a 19-day recovery program that involved up to 10 hours a day of physio and exercises to try to get back on the park before the tour was over. That I did so was a triumph for hard work and the magic hands of Errol Alcott, who realigned the damaged fibres and kneaded away the scar tissue manually for four to five hours per day. It was at times torturous, but I was inspired by the responsibility of leadership and the need to set an example, and also by the belief that it was my obligation as a professional sportsperson to get back as quickly as I could.

In moments of despair I'd often use people who had inspired me to galvanise my spirits. A young boy from Geelong by the name of Mathew Dean, who wasn't expected to survive open-heart surgery on the day he was born, endured over 60 operations in his first 10 years, and suffers migraines 20 times more powerful than the average, was my motivation to do the hard work. Each time I began to wane in the rehabilitation phase, I thought of his courage and refusal to let any ailment get the better of him.

During my recovery we lost the Test at Headingley through a mixture of hard luck due to rain, allowing England back into the match, and a phenomenal innings from Mark Butcher that stole the game away. As touring captain it was tough to watch, but I had no problem letting Adam Gilchrist make all the decisions. He was the match captain, and I didn't want to infringe on his instincts and was aware of the need to back his judgement.

Days later Gilly and I, as selectors, had to concur when the ordinary form and negative attitude of Michael Slater could no longer be ignored. Technically Slats was permanently on the move at the crease, which caused his balance to be poor and his head position to be out of line, and his backswing was exaggerated and loose. In his prime, Michael had a pristine technique that was tight in defence and expansive in attack, but the longer this series went on the more he was 'going fishing' outside off stump, a dead giveaway of poor form. Just as concerning was him missing a bus to training and numerous reports of his lack of professional behaviour. A rebellious streak had taken over, causing his teammates to tread on eggshells around him. Excuses impeded reasoning, and the fault was always someone else's. It was time for a change. Gilly and I were in total agreement, but we knew it would be tricky communicating our concerns to Trevor Hohns on the other side of the world.

The result was an animated three-way phone hook-up, with the chairman of selectors pushing for a stay of execution, suggesting there was no need to make a change at this time. Besides, he added, the selectors had only picked two opening batsmen for the tour. This was red-rag-to-a-bull stuff and I countered strongly, 'You aren't here! The change needs to happen and it should be now, not in a few weeks' time at the start of our home season. Secondly, you guys didn't pick an extra opener, not me. And in Justin Langer we have a guy who will do a great job.'

In the end, it was 2–1 against Slats. With hindsight I might have been a little assertive in my views, but I knew, as did most of the guys, that the change would be in the best interests of team harmony.

Telling Slats was the toughest part, and next morning I asked Steve Bernard to come with me to back me up when we talked about the disciplinary issues and make sure it went okay so we could all move along as a group afterwards and be in harmony if the press tried to make an issue of the decision. But the meeting didn't last long, with a shocked Mick getting up and exiting the room with, 'You can all go and get fucked!'

The situation didn't get much better at training later that day when I thought it was appropriate that the team learn of Slats' axing direct from me as a sign of respect to him and to clear the obviously edgy atmosphere. But halfway through my attempt, Slats cut me off and said, 'Come on, Tugga, tell them the real reason why I got dropped.'

To which I replied, 'If you'd bothered to stay and hear me out [this morning], you would know.'

Thankfully, Lang jumped in and settled things down with a heart-felt spiel on how we should never take the baggy green for granted because we never knew when we might be wearing it for the last time. That was the last we saw of Slats for the session – he walked off and went back to the team hotel.

One of the first things I did when I saw the new board CEO, James Sutherland (Malcolm Speed having moved on to the chief executive job at the ICC in July 2001), during the following Australian season was to propose that the method of selecting Australian teams should be the same away from home as it was in Australia. Domestically, the selection panel picked the side after consulting with the captain, but on tour the captain, vice-captain and whoever was the 'touring selector' (in years past this had been a senior player, then the coach, and was currently the chairman of selectors) made the call. I argued that one selection committee making all the decisions, home and away, would create greater stability and confidence throughout the squad. Having a player as a selector could potentially divide the team, and with the selectors now being paid they should also be accountable. It was a big ask for, say, me and Gilly to tell a teammate he'd been dropped and that his income was consequently going to be cut by 75 per cent. The game was now a business, and critical decisions such as selections needed to be based totally on clear thinking and made by those who were a step back from the coalface.

Lang plays his best cricket under the most intense pressure, and at the Oval he responded with a century. Likewise, I generally played my best cricket when there was something to prove, whether in support of a cause or in response to a criticism or an injury. When I was wait-ing to bat this time, I'd never been more nervous and was constantly thinking, *What if my calf tears in taking off for a sharp single? That would leave the team at a considerable disadvantage.* Thirty runs into my dig I did twinge a muscle, this time in the middle of my calf, which led to an extra strain on other muscles unaccustomed to the workload. A buttock strain soon followed and, with my options running out, I told my batting partner at the time, Mark Waugh, 'Don't take too many tight ones – I'm struggling and I'm gonna have a slog.'

However, once I got to 100 I said to myself, *Why throw it away now? Keep going.* By this stage Nasser was employing 'in/out' fields that made for long, easy singles to the outfielders, and a fairytale had materialised – an unbeaten century in a winning Test where the Ashes were presented to me as the victorious captain. In fact, we didn't receive the actual Ashes – we were handed a replica Waterford crystal trophy that in its own right was dazzling. But we wanted the real thing. When they didn't materialise, we improvised and made our own, pouring kerosene over the four bails used in the Test and setting them alight, giving us our own 'Ashes'. It was the start of a marathon celebration in the Oval change rooms that culminated in a comical nude lap of the ground sometime around midnight.

38

Games within the game

One week I was the Ashes-winning captain; the next, that joy was a distant memory as I lay awake at night badgered by a constantly throbbing leg with its own heartbeat that was eventually diagnosed as DVT (deep vein thrombosis). It required six weeks of complete rest and daily self-administered injections to the stomach before I could resume playing. It was a stressful period, with a baby on the way, not knowing when I'd get the all-clear, and carrying the emotional baggage connected with Slats' axing in England.

Lillian Mary Opal Waugh arrived nine days after the horrors of September 11, and her beauty left me speechless. I was so mesmerised by her minute flawless features that I was unable to call anyone on the phone for 20 or so minutes as I shed a tear and held many more back, in keeping with the Aussie macho thing and the way I'd been brought up. Lilli came into the world with a rare form of reflux that saw her too often literally choking on a vicious, clingy substance that would stop her breathing and never allowed her to sleep for more than an hour at a time for the first 12 months of her life. Lynette deserves a medal for her unconditional love and resilience in seeing the problem through. It's not until you can't get solid sleep that you realise it is the fuel that enables you to function properly.

My preparation for the three-Test series against New Zealand that started Australia's 2001–02 international season was confined to one innings for my beloved grade club, Bankstown, but an assured 84 against Fairfield had me believing I hadn't missed a beat and everything would be business as usual. Once back at the top level, I walked straight into all the things that as captain I came to associate with the first Test of a home series – any number of meetings, functions, sponsor commitments and, because of all that, hurried team training sessions.

The most important get-together revolved around developing a planning schedule for the 2003 World Cup. This meeting was attended by, among others, the captain, vice-captain, chairman of selectors and coach. We talked about where we wanted to be during this 'warm-up' phase, how we were preparing, what the likely make-up of the side would be, plus any other issues relating to the one-day squad that needed to be discussed. Just to make sure we were all on the same tack, I asked if I was still the man they had in mind to lead the side in the Cup, as the tournament dates were getting too close for the selectors to be making major changes. I was assured that I was the guy they wanted to lead the team.

Everything was going along nicely, though I did have to deal with something of a storm in the newspapers. 'Are you going to keep on favouring Brett Lee in selections?' This loaded question had come from the new whiz-kid on the journalistic block, Jon Pierik from News Limited, as he sought a story in the lead-up to the New Zealand series. Pierik owned a half-smile, half-smirk that made me want to let Brett bowl half a dozen deliveries at him without a helmet, but I knew a headline when I saw one coming and instead gave him a straight bat. With a dozen or so of the media contingent encircling me at the start of a practice session for NSW, I just wanted to answer nicely and get some much needed net practice in, so I said, 'No, Jon, that's not the case. Everyone's in contention for a spot and it may well come down to whoever is in the best form or even who looks the best in the nets in Brisbane. Brett, like all the bowlers, is a chance of playing, but the only certainty at this stage is me, because I've been named captain'.

I thought to myself, *Well done – good diplomatic answer, nothing controversial. No chance of a stitch-up job there.* Wrong! The screaming headline on the back page next morning read, 'Waugh says he can't be dropped'. Welcome to the ever-changing world of journalism, an evolution that was in some ways understandable. In the past, action from matches was the focus for press writers, because the next morning's papers were the first port of call for readers; for many people, this was the closest they would get to the action. But in today's technically enhanced world, with extensive coverage on television, ball-by-ball analysis on the Internet, digital photography and blanket radio commentary, the actual on-field action isn't new for newspaper consumers: it's old news. Replacing the action nowadays are writers' personal insights into players' minds, behaviour and lifestyle. Nothing is private and everything is fair game.

I'd like to think I had a good relationship with the media in my time as captain. There was a mutual respect between me and most reporters. I always believed it wasn't healthy to build up too close a relationship with any particular reporter, because that would alienate others and eventually cause grief. If they were good at their job, they needed to be impartial. I respected the work ethic of guys like Robert Craddock, Phil Wilkins and Malcolm Conn and enjoyed the articles by feature writers such as Peter Roebuck, Mike Coward and Greg Baum – not least because they rarely went to press conferences, which meant they made their own observations and weren't influenced by the few quotes from that group environment that usually made up the bulk of the stories the following day.

Each journo has quirks and idiosyncrasies that distinguish him from the next. 'Crash' Craddock would feign the 'gibbering sidekick' routine, asking questions with an innocence that disarmed the player and belied Crash's nous on what would make good print. I always found him professional and very likeable, but I also knew he wanted to break a story – and, like a gypsy getting inside a tourist's coat pocket, he'd use all his acquired tactical acumen to prise information out of you. I enjoyed the jousting and stimulation he and many others provided, and in a funny sort of way enjoyed locking horns with them.

Roebuck, a devourer of Shakespeare by night and modest county cricket attacks in his playing days, had been my captain back at Somerset in 1987 and 1988, and had the advantage of having played first-class cricket and being able to see the little pieces of byplay that went on out in the middle. His alert eye often homed in on and detected variations in body language, routine and behaviour. Quite often, Peter's writing provided me with an extra set of eyes I could trust. Just occasionally, though, I would have appreciated a departure from his favourite line about my expression on the field, which was 'old stone-face'. I guess it could have been worse.

As a cricket journalist, you have to enjoy your own company or that of a beer. It is lonely and at times unappreciated work, with no real back-up or support on arduous away tours, where deadlines are hard to work alongside. In my experience, most players tend to give journos the cold shoulder, and even after years travelling together on the circuit, little is known about or shared with them. Rather cruelly, many were thought of as only having a job because of us. We cynically believed that most of them wouldn't have known a googly from a flipper, dressed as if they were regulars at Lowes annual Christmas sale and would have been candidates for the captaincy if a nerds' team was being selected. The truth is that they were more astute packers of luggage than us. They were often family men, driven by delivering quality stories that would make a difference, and we shared many common worries, including lapses of form, homesickness, the need to be appreciated and fears about job security. Crucially, we needed each other. At times in my career, we both neglected that fact.

Experience used to tell me that at each press conference the first couple of questions would be nice and easy, to get me in a relaxed frame of mind. With the guard lowered, the controversial or dangerous questions came in. Often I knew which phrase or word the media were after to fit the story of the day, and I needed to sense the tone of a question and the ramifications of my answer before jumping in. For example, a relatively simple question like 'Have you got Tendulkar's measure after his last few scores of 0, 1, 38 and 0?' and a confident reply of 'Yeah, I believe we have' could translate into the headline: 'Waugh says Tendulkar is finished'. A good-looking reporter with a short skirt or revealing cleavage would occasionally be sent out to entice an interview on a touchy subject in the hope that such 'eye candy' would lead me to drop my guard. It was a game within the game and I enjoyed the interaction, the altercations, the stimulation and, in most cases, the friendship. And when it all boiled down, I had actually been a cricket journalist myself since 1993, writing books and articles on a regular basis.

This crossover between cricket and writing did cause some angst, with many of the players having columns ghosted by overworked journalists whose wages were much less than the cricketer's. I don't agree with players putting their name on a column when they haven't written it themselves because, for one, it's not their work, and two, they can offload responsibility if 'their' words go down badly. I only ever used a ghost on the rare occasion that a deadline made it physically impossible for me to write the column I was committed to, such as when a day's play was extended because of rain interruptions.

★

The first two New Zealand Tests in 2001–02 were dominated by the weather, while the third was a memorable game that ended with both sides claiming they'd won the bout on points. The Brisbane and Hobart washouts still featured top-quality batting from our engine-room boys Matt Hayden, Justin Langer and Ricky Ponting, but the middle order fell away, victims of a lack of intensity and the dead atmosphere out in the middle. After sitting for hours on end in the stale air of a viewing room, then walking out with 300 or 400 runs already on the board and the guy at the other end 100-and-plenty not out, I found it hard to get into the rhythm of the game. The edginess and fight for survival I thrived on was non-existent and I just couldn't seem to elevate my game. I was flat and lethargic with the bat and paid the price with scores of three and eight, missing my only opening in each match. For some peculiar reason, playing the Kiwis didn't stoke the fire like other sides and I never played my best cricket against them. I don't really know why, because they were always competitive. Usually I had my eye on the next tour, or perhaps I was looking too much at the outcome and not at what was in front of me.

In what was the most generous declaration of my Test captaincy career, I set the 'Black Caps' 284 runs in 57 overs at the Gabba, and came within one shot of losing the Test when Chris Cairns was caught on the boundary with a New Zealand victory in sight. I didn't mind the fright, though, as it kept us alert and made us really work on that final day. It was only the third draw the Australian Test team had been part of since I'd taken charge – the other two being rain-affected matches in Sri Lanka in 1999 – and broke a run of 23 Tests with a result. This sequence reflected my dislike for wasting five days on a draw and the fact that we were prepared to risk losing if our tactics increased our chances of gaining a victory.

Throughout the series the Kiwis adopted the ploy of totally leaving Glenn McGrath's bowling alone, refusing to play a shot against him. To a lesser extent they did the same thing with Shane Warne, hoping they could drag us into days four and five and exploit a theory that we were vulnerable late in a Test. It was an admirable and quite clever tactic – as a high percentage of our games had been ending early, we couldn't be sure if it was a fair call or not. Stephen Fleming's boldness in the first Test, when he declared their first innings at 199 runs behind in the hope of engineering an exciting fourth-innings run chase, didn't extend to the second, when on the last day I offered to forfeit our second innings if he first declared his, leaving them needing 316 in a bit more than two sessions for victory. Rain would have the final word anyway, but clearly in these situations they enjoyed the odds being heavily in their favour and preferred smaller targets with fewer overs available. Who could blame them, when it seemed they saw a draw as being an above-par result?

However, with the series on the line in Perth, they began playing the most aggressive Test cricket I'd ever seen them play. Four batsmen scored hundreds against us for the only time in my career. Then, when we were 6/192 in reply to their 534, an unlikely Australian batting hero emerged in Shane Warne. Warney has more talent with the bat than he's ever fully realised, but understandably he's always wanted to bat without the intense concentration he demands of himself with the ball. When he did settle in and take it one ball at a time instead of wanting to be 50 not out without doing the hard yards, he was much better than your usual No. 8 batsman. His 99 here was a vital contribution, but the shot that led to his demise will always haunt him. Realising that he was just about to stick the flag into the summit of his Everest of batting, the floodgate of nerves opened as the thought of scoring a century for Australia began to asphyxiate him. A nondescript delivery from left-arm spinner Daniel Vettori, whom Shane had dealt with comfortably all innings, had 30 years on the public-speaking circuit hanging on its outcome. A clip off the legs for one turned into a lofted chip as Shane's muscles contracted in unison with his quickened heartbeat, and the outcome was disastrous: a simple catch in the outfield and a dream shattered. I'm sure Shane would have swapped 100 wickets for that one extra run. As his teammates we felt enormous sympathy for his near-miss, because we knew how much he craved that Test-match hundred.

Negative comments about us not going for the runs on the final day of the series proved how much we had changed the expectations of our supporters and the media. We'd needed 440 to win from 110 overs, including 371 from 93 overs on the final day – a chase I don't think had ever been seriously attempted in a Test in Australia – but when we fell 59 runs short with three wickets in hand it was deemed a disappointment. It was flattering that people expected so much, but at times their hopes for us were impossible to live up to, even with the gifts of Adam Gilchrist, who nearly created yet another miracle in the last session.

South Africa came to Australia in 2001–02 spruiking a title fight, with ex-players such as Mike Procter, Kepler Wessels and Barry Richards saying we were too old, had lost our work ethic and were ready to crumble. But by the end of the first day's play of the series, the smokescreen had cleared. We quickly learnt that the South African team didn't really believe the prematch publicity, with the usual talkative, exuberant, tight-knit unit appearing to be subdued and reactive. Without the livewire Jonty Rhodes to talk them up in his perplexing Afrikaans accent and to inspire them with his sixth sense of anticipation and freakish ability to unravel himself off the ground, spring to attention and create opportunities in the field, they lacked spark. Jonty was the heart and soul of their team and without him they were vulnerable.

So, too, following my innings of eight in the first Test, was the palm of my right hand. After mishitting a slog sweep in the quest for quick runs, I took out my anger with an open-palmed shunt of my locker in the dressing-room and in my petulance didn't spot a protruding hinge. The sharp edge of metal bit into the flesh, opening up a nasty little gash next to the drumstick of my right thumb. The claret came gushing out as I stood there dumbfounded by my stupidity. Sheepishly I called out, 'Hooter, I need you!' A doctor was called and not 10 minutes later I was signalling a declaration with four well-hidden stitches in the palm of my dominant hand. A crushing Australian win followed, underlined by the new breed – Hayden, Langer and Martyn, who all made centuries – leading the charge with the bat. The dynamics of our team were changing, with the Waugh brothers no longer having to be relied upon to contribute heavily. That pressure of expectation was something I'd always enjoyed.

Our relentless stranglehold further exposed our non-believing opponents in the second and third Tests, and they were crushed almost to the point of surrender. Their renowned hard man with the Clint Eastwood glare, Lance Klusener, lost his normally dry, wise-cracking humour and wandered around meekly before going home and bypassing the last Test. In contrast, we were like a school of sharks looking for another kill, especially after all the hullabaloo in Adelaide when Brett Lee bounced tail-ender Nantie Hayward to the point where he was backing away and trying to bat from off the prepared pitch. Some people say Brett's bowling was unsportsmanlike, but I disagree. To me, being fully professional and earning large amounts of money mean you have an obligation to work on all facets of your game, and for a tail-ender that includes batting. There are no secret pacts between the quicks any more, where they don't bounce each other; it's common knowledge that everyone is fair game. By making an example out of Hayward, their bowling spearhead, and having him look cowardly, we inflicted significant psychological damage on both him and his team. We wanted to expose them. It was hard but fair, and set the tone for future matches. I made no apologies for our tactics then and would do the same again.

My battle with Hayward in the Boxing Day Test epitomised why I loved Test-match cricket. It was one on one, with neither of us giving an inch and neither prepared to back down. I'm amazed that the guy didn't kick on and become world-class, because he had genuine pace and the stamina to back it up. I saw him as South Africa's equivalent of England's Devon Malcolm, in that a collective cheer went up in the Australian camp whenever his unpredictable raw pace was overlooked for an honest line-and-lengther.

Hayward was in my face from ball one, with a bombardment of short stuff that included a couple that flew off a ridge in the pitch and took the shoulder of the bat and a piece of finger on the way. I knew the storm would eventually subside, but I needed the help of the short-leg fieldsman, Boeta Dippenaar, who grassed two simple chances to make me think it was going to be my day. My first 20 runs were gathered through nothing more than willpower and a survival mechanism developed over 30 years of playing cricket, but from 20 to 90 my game clicked into action. I never looked like getting out until Marto called me through for a tight single to the Rhodes protégé, Herschelle Gibbs.

Out of the corner of my eye, I knew it was going to be a photo finish considering the acute angle Gibbs had taken to the ball and his renowned agile movement. In desperation I dived full length into the crease in unison with keeper Mark Boucher breaking the stumps. Boucher's eagerness to remove the bails made me immediately suspicious, and I knew that the third umpire would be called to adjudicate what had been a close call – not least because the umpires had been advised to use the video replay whenever *any* doubt existed. During the previous day's play, South Africa's off-spinner, Claude Henderson, had been quite obviously run out but umpire Darrell Hair had gone to the third umpire to confirm the thought he shared with us: 'I'd better make sure just in case, but he's out!' Good move, 'Big D'; it's not worth the trouble to get it wrong when the technology is available.

In my case, while the South Africans went into an animated celebration, I looked up to watch the expected replay on the big screen and thought, *Jeez, these guys are confident*, as Darrell walked towards me saying, 'That's out.' *Fair enough*, I thought, *but let's see what the replay shows*. I couldn't believe what was happening when the ump reaffirmed, 'You're out in conjunction with a raised finger.' Stunned, I said, 'What about the third umpire? Aren't you using it?'

'No, you're out.'

The delay I caused must have looked ugly, but I honestly thought I was awaiting a verdict, not avoiding one. It was inconsistent umpiring, and especially annoying considering I'd been between Darrell and the stumps, obstructing his view. Ironically, the video showed that the bails had been broken prematurely, but as I was the captain and expected to set standards and maintain values, I was a condemned man at the match referee's meeting. Not even O.J. Simpson's attorney could have got me off, and a $4000 fine after tax and a headline that included the term 'Bad sport' capped off an incident that should never have happened. I'm the first to admit that at times I have loitered and shaken my head in a show of disappointment at an umpire's verdict, but in this case the headline that questioned my sportsmanship was way over the top. A line of thought that the press were trying to push my buttons was starting to eat away at me, and that wasn't healthy.

Hayden and Langer continued to grow in stature as individual Test cricketers and as an opening partnership in Sydney, with another hundred each and a fourth stand of over 200 in just 11 innings together. 'Nature Boy' and 'The Philosopher' were fused at the hip and delighted in their joint achievements, celebrating more for partnerships than individual milestones, in behaviour that sent out a strong message that this Australian team was a unit based on partnerships and not on egos or individual brilliance. Seeing both these guys realise their ambitions gave me enormous satisfaction, akin to a parent at a child's graduation. I felt I'd played a part in their development, having shown the faith and support they both craved.

It was also rewarding to see Damien Martyn come back after so long in the wilderness and be so professional in his work ethic and so grounded in his temperament. Marto is a standout example of how people need guidance to mature and to make the most of their natural gifts. Watching him in total command as he reverse-swept his way to a classic hundred at the SCG was to watch poetry in motion. He is a guy who likes a low profile, loves a latte, sticks religiously to a low-carbohydrate diet, and allows only a select group of friends into his circle to become close mates. In cricketing terms, he is a rarity: a gifted player who learnt how to work hard and metamorphose. For that, he should be very proud.

★

Trevor Hohns and I, while not always agreeing, had a healthy and honest relationship in that we listened to each other and took on board what each other said. For example, initially 13 players were picked for the first segment of the 2001–02 VB Series, but on my insistence, because Matt Hayden was in the form of his life, Trevor changed the squad and included Haydos as its 14th member. Looking back, that might have been one too many, making things hard to manage. We also discussed the controversial rotation system and it was all systems go.

Precompetition meetings with the match referee, umpires, team managers and coaches (and often vice-captains) were usually done and dusted in 10 minutes, with the emphasis on how the skippers were responsible for anything and everything. Before the VB Series, though, our get-together ended in absolute chaos, with Hanumant Singh, the match referee, explaining that a bumper rule introduced by the ICC in 2001 meant that any delivery that bounced above head height would be a no-ball and would thus constitute a free hit for the batsman. Umpire Darrell Hair disagreed and said if a batsman hit such a delivery and was caught, he'd be out. The impasse was resolved by the officials asking Stephen Fleming and me, the captains in the opening match of the tournament, to make a judgement for the summer – without even consulting a representative from South Africa, the third team in the competition. That the implementation of a new rule had come to this was nonsense, and in my eyes further eroded the ICC's credibility.

When we got on the field against the Black Caps, we managed to snatch defeat from the jaws of victory. Needing 65 runs from 22 overs with six wickets in hand, we were complacent and very poor in terms of our match awareness. I genuinely believed the performance was a one-off and not worth overanalysing. The new blight on the game, crowd trouble, surfaced once more as a group of MCG spectators lost control. There is no doubt that a one-day crowd is vastly different from that of a Test match. One-day fans want action, feel a need to interact more and like to have a say in what's going on. It's more of a mob mentality, where 'hunting in a pack' holds an attraction. Consequently, when one bloke feels bored or aggrieved he has no trouble finding partners in crime. By contrast, a Test-match crowd is made up of many 'regulars', whose habitual behaviour often goes to the point of sitting in the same seat year after year and going to the same day of the Test each season. It's a ritual more than a spectacle. Most Test-cricket aficionados love to immerse themselves in the unfolding plot and study the action as closely as possible, taking enormous pride in predicting the outcome.

David Boon happened to be the 'selector on duty' for game two and I fully expected him to adopt a relaxed approach to our lazy loss in the competition opener. (The way things worked, the selectors picked the team by a phone hook-up, with at least one of the panel required to be at the game to consult with me as captain before the toss.) At the conclusion of my spiel to Boonie, which was based around the original concept of rotating players to give opportunities to all in the squad and ensure freshness, the 'Keg on Legs' unexpectedly pulled out a piece of white paper that had a contrasting line-up to the one I thought we were going with.

'Mate, we don't think this rotation thing is a good idea.'

I didn't really know what to say, except, 'I thought we'd decided to go that way?' It seemed one loss had put paid to any faith in that system. But, more than that, as I look back now this was the first sign that change was in the minds of the four selectors – Hohns, Boon, Allan Border and Andrew Hilditch. After all, though rotation had never been a locked-in policy, we had actually played 28 consecutive matches with different teams, never once replicating the starting XI from one game to the next.

Two more losses in consecutive games had the bloodhounds out, with the usual suspects sniffing a blood trail. David Hookes, who, remarkably, seemed to have access to inside information on a regular basis, commented as he had played – aggressively – and was as opinionated as ever. He called me 'the worst player in the team', in part because

I wasn't bowling any more. I thought it was a harsh assessment, but that was Hookesy: no grey areas and, if possible, create a headline. It wasn't the first time I had disagreed with Hookesy, who I'd played alongside in my first Test, and came not long after he'd accused me of picking Brett Lee purely because 'Bing' was from NSW. When I fronted David on that one he came back with, 'I don't really mean it like that.' Whatever side people took in regard to his opinions, they were generally thought-provoking and out of the box and stimulated debate, which was healthy for the game when there wasn't an agenda lurking in the background.

In the meantime, I had my work cut out getting Mark Waugh and Brett Lee a stay of execution from a selection panel that seemed to be wilting under the heat generated by our idle start to the series and a hounding media. I pleaded for patience and a belief in the current squad, because I knew we could turn it around; hard work and conviction would see things improve. Two straight wins over South Africa were followed by a loss to New Zealand, who had planned well for the series and caught a few of us off guard with unorthodox field placements and well-executed bowling plans.

It was a pregame selection meeting in Sydney, on the day of what turned out to be our second loss to New Zealand, that started tongues wagging. The ridiculous aspect of this rumour was how far it was from the truth. As usual, as we inspected the wicket, Trevor and I talked about the make-up of the starting XI and the state of the pitch, among other things, and our conversation continued as we walked off the ground. Without really noticing, we were three-quarters of the way off the ground and still in conversation mode. Spending quality time and getting privacy in a busy change room can be near impossible, so we decided to stop and chat in the solitude of the vast expanse of the SCG. This action was misconstrued by sections of the media as an animated chat that bordered on an argument, so next morning at the airport I was asked by a reporter, 'What about the feud between you and Trevor Hohns?'

I said, 'There is no feud.'

Next day, instead of a headline saying 'Waugh confirms feud with Hohns', the word 'confirms' was jettisoned in favour of 'denies' and the story had another two or three days' life.

I never thought Trevor and I were feuding, but I found it increasingly hard to convince the various selectors at each venue that things were on the improve and a little bit of patience was all that was needed. Before the third-last game before the finals, in Adelaide, Andrew Hilditch was on duty. He reinforced the doubts they had about Brett and Mark's continued selection. I really thought they were overreacting and that they just needed to relax and let the team settle into its work. Making sure there wasn't a hidden agenda, I again checked their thoughts on the leadership and was heartened by the line, 'There's no problem at all. We are very happy with your position.' Considering I'd played Test cricket with Allan, David and Trevor, and against Andrew at Shield level, I assumed they'd be able to tell me face to face what was in their thoughts and be assured that we were all on the same track. However, our views didn't seem aligned, particularly before the last one-dayer, against South Africa in Perth, a game we needed not only to win but to play well enough to claim a bonus point if we were to squeeze into the finals.

Not surprisingly, then, it was agreed that our best option in Perth was to pick seven batsmen and try to post a massive score, and then, to get the required bonus point, bowl them out cheaply enough that our run rate for the game was at least 1.25 times that of our opponents. Allan Border called me aside during the practice session before the game to tell me that Darren Lehmann would play and also to encourage me to bowl a few overs as we were a specialist bowler down. Not long after, John Buchanan sidled up to me to ask how I felt about batting seven and bowling. The second part was no problem, but the batting bit was news to me. Obviously it needed clarifying. I took the chance to invite AB out to the middle of the WACA to have a closer look at the pitch and discuss his thoughts. I learnt that the selection panel did indeed want me to bat at seven. But in my view, having the captain batting at seven was certainly not the right thing to do in a do-or-die game, and eventually Allan agreed. He would have argued exactly the same way if he had been in my position.

In the end, under pressure we played an adventurous brand of cricket that was a clear indication of our true colours. While we missed out on the finals on a countback after all three teams finished level on the points table, the future looked promising. It was with this in mind that I went along to the postgame media conference in a relatively buoyant mood, but it quickly turned sour when all they wanted to know was why we hadn't made the finals and what were the ramifications of our failure to qualify. Question after question focused on selection, which was unfair because I wasn't a selector. The more the same questions came out, the shorter my answers became. I was in a no-win situation with television cameras capturing every move, a stand-in ACB media liaison officer just sitting back and not controlling the environment, and journalists firing questions from all sides. The shotgun-style inquisition was relentless and unending, and by the time I had answered some questions for the fourth and fifth time I was mentally drained with very little wick remaining. In keeping with a succession of run-ins in a home season of frustration, I mumbled to Pat O'Beirne, the ACB media man, 'They're a bunch of cockheads!' It turned out the AAP 'cockhead' had a set of highly efficient ears, and unbeknownst to me he quickly sent my throwaway line down the wire to papers across Australia. I'd created another fish-and-chip wrapper. It was a careless mistake and one I shouldn't have made, especially as 12 days earlier at a press conference I had jokingly whispered, 'I bet they didn't find anything' about the results of an MRI scan on a head injury to South African paceman Steve Elworthy, who had been hit by a McGrath bouncer. The joke was old, in reference to quicks being a little slow on the uptake, and my timing was poor. The comment was inappropriate and because it was overheard I copped some criticism. That matter was cleared up with me making a few apologetic phone calls, which were well received. I knew that my position of authority came with added responsibility – a point I shouldn't have neglected.

Without fully recognising it, I was in a conflict with the media boys that I couldn't win and should have left alone. My form in the middle was mediocre, my relationship with the selection panel was workable but not close, and on the home front, baby Lillian had that terrible reflux while Austin was suffering mysterious nosebleeds that had us fearing that something was seriously wrong. I felt under siege, with nowhere to turn. Being the way I am, I internalised it all and didn't divulge my anguish to anyone. Being self-sustaining gave me freedom to be my own man and not give in to the politics or the system, but when things got tough it meant taking a lot on board and bottling up my emotions. There had been a time when it nearly became too much: during the Test against New Zealand in Perth, on the third or fourth morning, as I sat in my room contemplating my situation. I was lonely, sick of being away from the family, tired of the media intrusions and negativity, pissed off with my own form and struggling for inspiration. The normal indestructible brick wall came tumbling down during a phone call to Lynette. I let all my pent-up emotions gush out and bawled like a baby, not exactly sure why and unable to control it, but the relief was immediate. Even before the tears had dried I began to feel better and the familiar wave of optimism swept over me. But, as I was to understand later, when a career is winding down, the moods fluctuate. I had to come to terms in my own mind with the fact that the end of my cricketing career was approaching and I couldn't go on forever.

Sometimes, in the artificial confines of my four-walled jazzed-up cell, I felt incredibly cut off from the real world, eating bland club sandwiches full of left-over fatty bacon from the breakfast buffet, while watching movies that had come out nine months earlier at the flicks. It was heart-wrenching at times to hear the kids say, 'Daddy, we want you to come home today. We miss you.' I felt like a part-time dad, and the introspective moments always seemed to coincide with a failure on the field.

The one person who could always lift me was Lynette. She knew which buttons to press and made me feel as if I wasn't alone but working as a partnership, that things would work out if I kept on rolling up the sleeves and enjoying the challenge. I believe the secrets to my longevity were that I knew how to compartmentalise and had other interests, an excellent network of close friends, a strong family framework and a fierce desire to compete. I'm sure every cricketer goes through torment at some stage but many don't have a system in place to cope. Underneath all the glitz and glamour, the harsh reality is that occasionally it can get too much. Of course, for most of the time playing cricket for your country is one of the world's great adventures and we were getting rewarded handsomely to do a job we loved, one we never imagined we'd get paid for when we first picked up a bat. In all fairness, the odd depressing times are a small price to pay, though when they come they can take you a long way down.

Missing out on the one-day finals meant I had a couple of unexpected days off at home, but the peace they brought was shattered by an out-of-the-blue phone call from Trevor Hohns. 'Tugga, we're going to make some changes to the one-day team,' he said. 'We just hope you'll accept them in the right spirit.'

I put the phone down, turned to Lynette, and said, 'They're going to drop me.'

I really hoped my gut feeling was wrong, so I immediately got on the blower to John Buchanan to see what his view was on the overall picture. He told me I was the right man to lead the team and that I had his support. I hoped I was overreacting and seeing things that weren't there, but deep down, niggling away, was the notion that the selectors had already kissed me goodbye.

For the next few days, however, the old saying 'No news is good news' rang true. I went to Devonport with NSW for a one-dayer against Tasmania, and heard nothing more on the issue until I reached for the morning paper at our digs. One quote from an interview with Allan Border stood out as if written in bold type: 'Darren Lehmann is a good captaincy candidate for the one-day team.'

Coming from an ex-captain and legend of the game, the comment lacked respect for my position and should have been kept in house. It was also a fair indicator of the selectors' thinking, for AB generally had the role of prepping the public before any changes came to fruition. His status and credibility as an all-time great meant that he could 'break the ice' with the press and public, making it easier for controversial decisions to be accepted.

Trevor Hohns was in Devonport and appeared agitated when he knocked on our viewing-room door some way into our run chase for victory. He asked for five minutes of my time, but as I was next in I couldn't simply dismiss my responsibilities to the team and be diverted away as if it were a local pub match. 'Okay', he responded, 'we'll catch up tomorrow in Melbourne.'

That catch-up meeting, on the day of the Allan Border Medal presentation, began with the line, 'Do you want to talk about Test-match cricket or one-day cricket first?'

'Test matches,' I replied.

Plans for the upcoming South African tour were discussed, including selections and future directions. Everything was straightforward and expected.

Now for the one-dayers. 'We've decided to go in a different direction and you are not part of that plan.'

Even though all the clues had indicated this possibility, I still hadn't really expected it to happen. I was in total shock and didn't show any real animation. Instead, I sat calmly while Trevor explained that he didn't see me as one of Australia's top six one-day batsmen. There really wasn't a lot to say or be said; the decision had been made. After 325 one-day internationals in a little more than 16 years, it was over.

I was in the unusual position of knowing how both of us were feeling, having been in Trevor's shoes on many occasions. I had always said to him, 'If you think you can improve the side, then you've got to do it', so in principle I didn't have a problem with the decision. However, I did have an issue with the lack of man-managements skills involved in letting me know about it. Surely, after so many years playing and being the captain of a side that had been ranked No. 7 when I took over and was now No. 1, at least one phone call or conversation letting me know how the selectors saw the bigger picture would have been nice. In business, people get warnings along the way in the hope they can rectify or turn things around. In sport, you get a tap on the shoulder and a goodbye. The clinical efficiency of my dismissal stung me most, because as a player I had always given everything, mixing passion, pride and loyalty, yet I never received the courtesy of a warning that more was needed. As a batsman, I honestly believed the previous 12 months had seen my game develop and improve, and Buck's charts said that I was the biggest improver in the team in regard to strike rate during that time. I fully realise selection is not just based on statistics but also on gut instinct, but I felt cheated that they had strung me along to within 12 months of the 2003 World Cup and then terminated my career without so much as one discussion.

As soon as the door shut behind a relieved chairman of selectors,

I got on the phone and called home. Lynette helped put things into a clearer perspective by saying, 'Things happen for a reason. It mightn't be clear right now, but it will work out in the end.' I hoped that thought would be enough to sustain me for the remainder of the day and the awards ceremony that night.

It was ironic that straightaway I had to go downstairs to listen to the Bradman of radio, Alan Jones, give a motivational speech to the squad and board members. He was doing so at my request and among his subjects was selection. The focal point of his speech was his belief that it is more important to know when *not* to make changes for change's sake than to make changes. I sat there in a detached state, as if my umbilical chord had just been severed, pondering the ramifications of what had just transpired.

My gut instinct was to make the decision public as soon as possible. I knew it wouldn't stay in house for too long, even with the most admirable intentions. The selectors and board wanted to keep it under wraps until part way through the Test series of South Africa, but I believed that it would be destabilising to announce such a major change midway through a tour, and that the process of waiting for the sacking to be announced would eat away at me. My news sense was proved correct when on the morning after the Border Medal, Radio 2UE's breakfast announcer, Steve Price, had the inside information from his cricket contacts in Melbourne. What was supposed to be a month-long secret was out in 12 hours. My idea of a quick formal announcement was now not only important but a necessity.

Two days later I found myself sitting between Trevor Hohns and James Sutherland at a media conference at the SCG. I appreciated how tough it was for them, but I also couldn't help feeling that they seemed like chaperones rather than work associates. I vowed to fight hard and to give it all to regain my place in the one-day squad, but I also knew it would take a minor miracle to force my way back in, especially as

I'd only have a maximum of three one-day games in domestic cricket in 2002–03 to make my case before a preliminary squad for the World Cup was chosen.

Twenty-four hours later, after receiving a massive swell of goodwill from a cross-section of people, I was at Sydney Airport ready to leave for the return leg of the South African Test series. It had been an emotional farewell at home, with so much having happened in such a short space of time. Austin and Rosalie actually found it amusing to see Dad on television and the back of every newspaper over the previous couple of days, and Rosie had even begun calling me 'Steve Waugh' as she'd heard it so much at school. The best way I could explain my axing to the kids was to say that Daddy was now captain of the white team, but someone else was captain of the yellow team.

39

Slow torture

I was determined to be upbeat and wanted to socialise with and be nourished by positive influences, infectious personalities and driven people. I didn't want to wallow in self-pity or be distracted by daily debates as to the rights and wrongs of selections, and was glad I could escape what had become the fishbowl of Sydney and immerse myself in a difficult assignment on foreign turf. But no matter how hard I tried for the next five weeks, something had been ripped out of my guts and I couldn't totally bluff myself into believing everything was in equilibrium. I was denying that I was in denial. The autopilot system was in place and tasks at hand were completed competently, but throughout my time in South Africa my emotions were simmering in the background and diluting the enjoyment I usually felt when I was at the crease.

Champion players and great teams have the tools not only to cope with distractions but to turn them around and actually use them to inspire. Our performance in the first Test, at Johannesburg, was a faultless one as a team and we won by an innings and 360 runs, losing only seven wickets in the process and handing the South Africans their second-heaviest loss ever. Our batting was out of this world, starting with Matthew Hayden, who made a seaming, bouncy pitch look placid by continually driving on the up with controlled brutality. I was simply in awe of his methods. He demanded respect merely by the way he was strutting around and intimidating bowlers through the savagery of his clean hitting. Damien Martyn continued his development and rise into the peripheral ranks of being a great player, while Adam Gilchrist played with a rage that was unstoppable. Every shot Gilly played was a slap in the face for a scurrilous rumour involving his family that had been circulating via email. Upon reaching 200, with his punishment of the home team finally dealt out, he collapsed emotionally and cried. It was a unifying moment for the team, as we'd all felt his anguish, and confirmation that this guy was headed for absolute stardom.

Our build-up to the game had also been hampered by the news that Shane Warne and Brett Lee had been involved in a plot to hold the ACB to ransom. An alleged incident involving a schoolgirl on the Gold Coast was the source of this problem, but it ended with the complainants themselves facing criminal charges. It was never boring being part of a team full of superstars, with off-field issues cropping up on a regular basis, but this Australian team was a unit that thrived on distractions and used them to galvanise the spirit of the group.

The only downer to arise from our dominant batting display, which saw us take 652 runs off a quality attack in 146 overs, was the reaction of the Jo'burg fans. I was spat on during my walk back up the 'gangway' from the field to the dressing-room, while Marto copped a couple of beers over his helmet and down the back of his shirt when he was finally dismissed for 133. Revenge was ours after three days, when Punter led the team song at the exact point where Marto and I had copped our barrages, and back in the dressing-room we enjoyed a 'ceremony' in which our complimentary but now worthless days four and five admission tickets were set alight.

The intent and purpose that we displayed in the field had been predatory and remorseless, so intense and concentrated, that it was reminiscent of the great Windies team of the early 1980s. In my mind, we'd played the perfect Test; no team could have touched us when we were producing that quality of cricket. The best part about the victory was the way the team raised the bar when it had to, with each player setting a standard to which he expected his mates to aspire.

When challenged, we always thought it best to target the opposition's captain or their most prized weapon, and in Jacques Kallis South Africa had an outstanding technical batsman with an impressive shot-making ability. As soon as he arrived at the crease, Kallis was terrorised by a succession of yorkers and bouncers from Brett Lee and meekly perished fending off a short one into the slip cordon. It's a psychological blow for a team to see its most competent player getting a workover, and Kallis's demise set the tone for the rest of the Test. We not only beat them with skill on the scoreboard, we crushed their spirit and minds.

The writing was on the wall for South Africa going into the second Test, in Cape Town, when the veteran Daryll Cullinan, who'd been recalled to the side, pulled out due to a contractual dispute. I found it amazing that someone who had apparently been keen to return to the side would now walk away over money. Cullinan's withdrawal was a major disappointment for his nemesis, Shane Warne. Not only was it a shame that we wouldn't get to see them joust again, but we'd also miss out on the banter between the two, which was often amusing and at times clever. Warney would usually greet Daryll with a reference to the fact that the South African was seeing a sports psychologist to conquer his demons when facing the 'Sheik of Tweak': 'C'mon Daryll – let's see if we can get you back on that leather couch again.' Occasionally Daryll would pluck up the courage for a comeback, once countering with, 'Go deflate yourself, you balloon', and another time saying sarcastically, 'Looks like you've been eating all those pies again.'

It was intriguing to watch such a competent player as Cullinan crumble because of another man's mere presence. His footwork dissolved along with his desire to be combative, while his body language signalled complete submission. In contrast, Shane launched into action, increasing the tempo with assertive gestures, verbal interrogation and extra intensity, and bowling with a controlled rage that enabled him to impart extra revolutions on the ball. Often, I'd be focused on how these two were dealing with the subplot they were involved in and wonder why Daryll didn't just take him on and at least go down fighting, rather than being pummelled, because against everyone else he was a class act with the bat. We would have respected him more if he'd taken up the fight and put the pressure back on us, and in a strange way Shane would have enjoyed that provocation much more as well.

Back home, baby Lillian racked up a Cullinan by rolling over for the first time in her efforts to get mobile, which didn't help the niggling homesickness pangs I was experiencing. However, a long walk along the beach at Port Elizabeth helped to refresh the mind and invigorate the soul. The familiar sound of kids laughing as they frolicked, skipping over the incoming waves, combined with that magical smell of a salty sea breeze to energise the spirit, had me upbeat for the challenges ahead.

Having time alone always played an important part in my capacity to refresh and reassess, and two of my favourite places to do that were in the solitude of a cinema, where my thoughts could be taken away by the escapism of a movie plot, or a stroll around a zoo, where I could marvel at the raw power and beauty of various creatures that moved and behaved in their own unique way. Forgetting for a while about how my weight transferred as I played a cover drive or why a journalist was hounding one of my players was something that had to be done if I was to remain fresh and clear-minded.

The lure of the big occasion always draws out stars, and in his 100th Test Shane Warne bowled 98 overs and took eight wickets in an epic man-of-the-match performance. Typically with Warney, it wasn't a simple tale – he came to me five minutes before the toss to say he had a slight twinge in his hamstring and wasn't sure how it was going to hold up. Quite possibly he was struggling, but I felt he was trying to conquer his nerves by putting barriers in front of himself so he could then try to get over them.

Having a reputation for being mentally tough can have enormous advantages, because opponents respect and admire that trait and will put you on a bit of a pedestal, while teammates also hold you in higher esteem. But equally, because of that air of invincibility, people can skim over the fact that the mentally tough individual also needs a support structure. Being a guy who could compartmentalise well gave me an advantage in that I didn't allow emotion to rule or distract my thinking to the degree it affected others. Once an issue had been recognised I either dealt with it immediately or was able to put it in its place until it could be attended to later. On the rare occasions when something couldn't be clearly categorised, it had the potential to slowly eat away at me. My form lapse was bothering me, but I was too proud to let it be known that I was struggling with it. My way of fixing the problem was to work extra hard in the nets, to make sure I had all the bases covered and had given myself no reason for future regrets. But right now it wasn't so much my cricket that was holding me back as the internal turmoil that emanated from being dropped. I had made a vow to myself to fight back and just accept the selectors' decision, but in the rush of being demoted, then having to hold a press conference 48 hours later, before embarking on a major tour 24 hours further on, I hadn't actually had a chance to grieve and distil all the information I needed to absorb. It was as if my system had been short-circuited, which prevented me from escaping the darkness that had descended upon me.

It was the perceptive mind of Stuart MacGill that picked up my self-doubt. As I walked back from the practice nets before day five of the second Test, he said, 'You know, you've got nothing to prove to anyone.' I was grateful for this discreet show of support. In my quest to get among the runs I was trying too hard and tensing up instead of just letting it happen in conjunction with clear concentration. It wasn't as if I wasn't paying attention; it was more that my mind wasn't attuned to the task at hand because I was cramming too many thoughts in at once.

Be positive! I'd be saying to myself. *If it's there to hit, don't hold back. Watch the quicker one. Let's get off to a flyer. Make it your day.* It was all good healthy reinforcement, but in the past when I'd played at my best, all I'd been thinking was, *Be sharp and alert and trust your instincts.* Once there is more than one thought fighting for your attention, the chances of a loss of focus and of straying away from the basics are increased. Ninety-nine times out of 100 a batsman loses his wicket when he has been dwelling on the past, looking to the future or muddling the present. Clear, simple thought is the very essence of successful batsmanship, and I had forgotten it and was paying the price. A double failure, bowled both times at the hands of a left-arm wrist spinner whose action was best described as 'a frog in a blender' – Paul Adams – confirmed for me that I was too concerned about the outcome and not enough about the process. To further emphasise that my concentration was slipshod, before this game I don't think I'd ever been dismissed by exactly the same ball twice in a match.

At the same time as my batting remained below par, the battle was bringing the best out of us as a team and I couldn't have been happier with my decision-making and proactiveness as a captain. Another outstanding victory was built around the platform of creating and executing half-chances in the field, and our display confirmed for me a long-held belief that the confidence levels of a team run parallel with the attitude shown in the field, while quality catching is a direct offshoot of concentration. A feature of this match was how Ricky Ponting's stature as a player and leader continued to expand, culminating in the six he hit to win the series and take him to a century. It was the perfect finish to a stunning fifth consecutive mauling of the Africans.

The only time we had our momentum interrupted was on the night of day one, when our departure from the ground was delayed for 90 minutes while sniffer dogs scoured every inch of our bus in response to a phone call that had been placed to the ground with the message: 'The Australian team will be eliminated tonight on their way home.' Though nothing came of the threat, it was a very subdued and relieved team that alighted from the bus at our Cape Town hotel that evening.

Winning means celebration and, in contrast to most of my career, wives and partners now joined us for a drink in the rooms afterwards. We all looked forward to the team song, but were at the whim of the orchestrator, Ponting, as to when and where we would sing it. The picture-postcard backdrop to the Newlands ground in Cape Town is Table Mountain, and it was there that Punter decided we would carry on the festivities, thanks to the generosity of the owner of the mountaintop restaurant, who allowed us to have sole use of his establishment after official closing time was called. Not only did we sing together under the stars overlooking the dazzling beauty of the Cape Peninsula, we were allowed to travel up and down the almost vertical slope on the roof of the cablecar, attached only by safety harnesses. The sight of Matt Hayden, draped solely in an Aussie flag, looking headlong into the breeze with arms aloft as he leant over a railing in the famous pose adopted by Leonardo DiCaprio and Kate Winslet in *Titanic*, was unforgettable.

A Channel Nine *60 Minutes* crew, headed by reporter Peter Overton, flew to Durban to do a feature on why this Australian team was such a great unit. The only other time the current-affairs show had come near the team in my experience was back in 1988 during our ill-fated tour of Pakistan, and the memory of that stitch-up job and the fact that most of the guys wanted any insights from the change rooms, team meetings and private conversations to remain sacred almost cancelled out the positive effects of the 'feelgood' story the program wanted to create this time. They were given only limited access into what made the team tick, because we wanted to retain an element of mystique about life in the baggy green army and for it to remain special for those who would enter the fray in the future.

If there was a sympathy card that had exempted me from criticism after my run of failures in Test cricket (two half-centuries in 11 innings since the Oval in August 2001), the credit had run out and I was fair game to the cricket analysts leading into the third Test, in Durban. That bloody little weakling of negativity, the doubting voice, had reappeared with all-consuming force for the first time since the early '90s, and now threatened to destabilise and rule my batting. The pillars of my foundation had been invaded by the white ants, and I hated how the thought of failure was causing me anxiety, disturbing my sleep and gnawing away constantly at my self-confidence. No matter how hard I tried to squash the feelings they kept coming back, like a rogue mosquito under the cloak of darkness in a confined room. Cricket played with a stressed mind is slow torture, as the game is 90 per cent waiting, and I realised that I had to turn this situation around or I would perish through failure and a lack of purpose at the batting crease. For the first time I seriously considered retiring, and I told Lynette exactly that as we spoke on the phone one night. When she called back an hour later, she had roped in the in-laws to take care of the kids, booked a plane ticket and was about to pack her bags. She recognised the mood behind the words and knew we had to talk it through face to face.

When I needed it most, my close mate Matt Hayden recognised that I needed to have a chat and offload some of the emotional baggage. The distant sound of crashing waves and a strong breeze infiltrated the hotel room as we sat, feet crossed and legs extended to rest on the windowsill, and gazed out at the deep blue ocean. Occasionally there was eye contact, always mutual respect, as we had a lengthy discussion that meant a lot to me, more than anything because Haydos had the compassion to know that I needed a reassuring voice.

Lynette's arrival immediately lifted my spirits and gave me added incentive to make a worthwhile contribution with the bat in the third Test, if for no other reason than the fact that she had put me ahead of the needs of our three young children. She advised me that I should end my career on a high note and not during a slump, and deep down I knew she was right, but to do that I needed time in the middle. I felt my will strengthening, but still went into the game undecided as to whether or not it would be my last.

★

Our team meeting going into the Test was a debacle. It ended when I said, 'That's it, no more, we're all wasting our time. Let's go!' I knew I was speaking on behalf of all the lads, who had persevered and showed unending patience with the team's computer-analysis system, which over a number of years had not worked and on the rare occasions when it had, had never been user friendly. The popular myth about our side was that we were dependent on statistics and detailed analysis, but I bet we used less computer-generated data than other teams. While the computer is definitely a valuable resource, we actually preferred to back our own judgements and assumptions, only using it to back up or dispel a line of thought we might have about an opposition player. I certainly relied heavily on my ability to spot technical deficiencies and fragile body language, and had built an archive of personal data to detect a weakness and deploy a plan to capitalise on it.

I doubt the computer could have saved us in this match, as the physical and mental demands of having to take 40 wickets in back-to-back Tests spread over just 11 days took its toll, as did the reality of the Test series having already been won. It appeared that the batsmen's minds were either on the trip back home or the upcoming one-day series. I scrapped my way out of the mire to some degree, top-scoring with a disjointed 42 in our disappointing second innings, and though my batting was definitely still scratchy my effort convinced me that the desire was still there. Even under the most trying of circumstances, I could still lift when I had to.

The realisation that my life had irrevocably changed came when I had to bid farewell to the one-day guys at our end-of-Test-tour get-together. My limited-overs termination had coincided with the initiation of other players into that fold, again proving that no one is bigger than the game. Cricket will always survive and prosper no matter who departs. But still a piece of me wanted to be the wide-eyed Shane Watson, whose whole cricketing career was in front of him.

On the last night of my tour I sat between him and the new one-day captain, Ricky Ponting, both about to embark on their new journey. The simple advice I gave Ricky was to be sure that he made time for himself, keep his game in order, be his own man and follow his gut instincts. To Shane I suggested he simply enjoy the experience and not change his game just because he'd reached the next level.

The following day Lynette and I were inhaling the putrid odour of warthog intestines that had been dragged through waist-high scrub in the Pilanesberg wildlife sanctuary next to Sun City Resort, in an attempt to entice the lion population to come out of hiding. The waft of the carcass impaled on a tree, combined with the distress call, blaring from a portable loudspeaker, of a warthog being attacked, had nature's kings converging from every angle in their stealthy, effortless style. Their striking body structures and the grace and camouflaged speed at which they travelled had us thinking how incomprehensible it is that they are an endangered species. We were fascinated by our guides attaching a new satellite tracking device to them to learn more about their behaviour.

A complete and utter break from thinking about cricket was exactly what I needed. The handbrake had been released, the air smelt fresher, the sun was more invigorating and life was ready to be sampled again. By the time we returned to Australia I had decided that when it all came to an end it would be on my terms, that I would be playing well and, hopefully, that people would be asking, 'Why has he retired?

40

My way

An unexpected honour for the Australian cricket team came when we won the Laureus Award for the best sports team in the world for 2001. We had been nominated alongside Champions League winners Bayern Munich, the all-conquering Ferrari Formula One motor-racing team, France's Davis Cup heroes and the Los Angeles Lakers NBA team. Being announced as the winners of one of sport's equivalents of the Oscars was easy compared to making a speech to a huge worldwide audience and a front row in the Monaco ballroom that included the likes of Sean Connery, Morgan Freeman, Michael Douglas and Catherine Zeta-Jones, not to mention Michael Jordan, Nadia Comaneci and Mark Spitz among those in the row behind. The four members of the team lucky enough to be there – Shane Warne, Glenn McGrath, Ricky Ponting and me – felt like gatecrashers who should have been asking for autographs, even though the honour and value of the recognition for the team and the game of cricket didn't escape us. It was a major breakthrough for cricket in its quest to be a global sport, and very significant purely for the fact that most of the judging panel were uneducated about the game.

Unfortunately, our subsequent interview with an Italian news crew didn't exactly have the people of Italy trading in their soccer boots for a cricket bat. It was a debacle, with the language barrier leading to a series of misinterpretations and what we thought were dead-end questions culminating in a request for a song. The first tune that came into my head was 'Underneath the Southern Cross I Stand', which, when we sing it in the dressing-room after a win, ends in an expletive. As captain, I tried to defuse the bomb by getting in first and changing the words of that line, but I truly stuffed it up when I jumped in one line early. It must have gone down a treat in the lounge rooms of Rome, with three Aussie superstars looking at their skipper, stunned at his stupidity. A long night of celebration ended when the big fish took on a couple of tiddlers as he departed the flash post-function party. On our way to the exit, Lynette and I were trampled by an invasive cordon of bodyguards who had encircled His Airness, Michael Jordan, in an uncalled-for show of strength that ensured our feet were firmly back on solid ground.

That back-down-to-earth feeling was reinforced at the annual non-negotiable, negotiable contract meeting with the ACB, where I learnt that I'd gone from being ranked the No. 6 one-day player in the country to one who couldn't make the top 20, and that my Test ranking had slipped to No. 8. Add these two assessments together and I was now the 13th-ranked player in Australian cricket, with a 50 per cent pay cut, though still deemed good enough to be the Test-match captain.

The cutthroat nature of modern sport demands results and rewards success, and this is reflected in how much a player is paid. In measuring a player's quality it tends to forget about longevity, loyalty and the influence he has on his teammates. As a leader and a guy who had completed a decade of success, I thought the No. 13 assessment by the board lacked a human touch. It was as if my ranking had been determined solely by a computer that was concerned only with age and recent results. There was dialogue between the parties at the handing over of the contracts, but the chances of them having a change of heart were nil, because the money for each ranking had already been allocated. All you could really hope for was that 12 months down the track, things might change, but the length of a contract was the truest indicator of your prospects. A one-year deal was either a warning to pick up your game or that age was winning the battle, a two-year one was comforting and meant you were a wanted commodity, while a three-year contract was the Holy Grail: you were the chosen one.

If one episode for me underlined how much the relationship between players and the board was one-sided before the ACA–ACB partnership was established, it came during a season when Graham Halbish was the board CEO. Being told what I was getting each year without consultation never sat well with me, and neither did the way my queries about certain clauses in the contract were never followed up, as if they didn't really matter. I wanted to see if the professionalism they demanded of us would be reciprocated, and when it wasn't I sat on my unsigned contract for nine months until someone finally twigged that it hadn't been returned. It wasn't about the money so much, because that was never going to change: it was the lack of respect and the board's inability to have any meaningful dialogue about playing conditions that irked me.

I wanted to somehow influence the selectors to reconsider my World Cup chances, but after South Africa there was no cricket scheduled for me until October, and that was in a series against Pakistan to be played at neutral venues in Sri Lanka and the United Arab Emirates, which would feature exactly no one-day cricket outside the three Tests. My offer to lead an Australia A side on their trip to South Africa for a series of one-dayers was rejected, and these circumstances left me no other option than to find an English county side if I was to get some meaningful practice in. A deal with Kent County Cricket Club was done, and I resolved to try my best not to get dragged into the various debates that would inevitably come about my future. All I wanted was to concentrate on playing the next ball to the best of my ability and enjoy each match, especially as my career was closer to ending than starting.

Before I headed to Kent, though, I had business and charity trips to India to enjoy. More and more, India was a place I bonded with. The girls and boys at Udayan were full of optimism, content with their new sense of belonging and grateful at being afforded opportunities every kid should have to make the most of their talents. Lynette, on her first trip to India, fell in love immediately with the children at Udayan, while a visit to a hospital for leprosy sufferers was gut-wrenching, with many incomprehensible sights as hundreds of patients lined up on basic beds, sitting forlornly with haunted eyes staring into a black hole of no hope. There was no stimulation for the patients via television or technology, very little interaction on a personal level, only one wheelchair available to be shared by 100 sick people, each day highlighted only by a change of dressings and bandages. It was a place doing its best with limited resources, but as much as anything it was a 'holding pen' for those facing a slow, torturous death with decaying minds and bodies. One particularly frail elderly lady caught our eye as she huddled in her pyjamas at the end of her bed, her hands and wrists swathed in bandages. She weighed no more than 25 kilos and had been abandoned by her seven children. The poor woman hadn't seen a visitor for years and had no reason to live, with each meaningless day merging into the next. Lynette and I sat down next to her, and like a lost kid she grabbed onto us with a strength that belied her tiny frame. Not only would she not let go of us, she kissed Lynette with a tenderness that suggested she was desperate to feel human again.

Communication was impossible through words, so Lynette showed her our family photos, which she immersed herself in and wouldn't let go of. It was as if she'd drifted off to some imaginary place where everything was okay again. For a few minutes she wasn't abandoned or riddled with such a cruel disease. The pain and emotion on her face were heartbreaking, especially because they came from the way she had been ostracised by her family purely as a result of a disease that had attacked her through no fault of her own. She never had a chance.

Eventually we had to leave her to the isolation and mind-numbing environment she was in, which was so sad. I remember looking back and seeing her frail silhouette slowly vanishing into the abyss of darkness that had become her constant companion and feeling incredibly guilty for the fortunate life I have. At least we'd allowed her to dream for a moment that the world isn't such a bad place.

My four weeks with Kent gave me a snapshot of why English cricket had been in the doldrums for such a long time but also exposed me to the belief that it wouldn't be long before they'd be back as a force. I found a reticence on the part of county teams to take a gamble and be prepared to lose a game in order to force a win. It was endemic not only in my team but also in those I played against, but I was encouraged by the notion that with just a little bit of guidance this learnt caution would dissipate. Contrary to popular opinion, county cricket gives players an excellent grounding for Test matches, with quality play to be found among some mediocre stuff. It is tougher knowing that to be successful you have to play to your own standards rather than relying on being stimulated by the duel that confronts you. For players to succeed they have to lift above peer-group pressure and mediocrity of others and be resilient when the form declines or when the packed itinerary makes rectifying problems difficult. But I guess looking for the easy option or a short cut is understandable given that continuous cricket provides endless opportunities and can diminish the real hunger needed to progress.

On my first day in the field I got a whiff of the mentality of some of the guys when I was offered some extra-strong mints from a teammate, which I thought was a nice gesture to make me feel welcome. Seconds later, as I crunched into a chalky coin-sized lozenge, a startled voice said, 'What the hell are you doing? Don't chew the mints!'

'Why not? They taste pretty good, pal.'

'You're wasting them. You're supposed to suck 'em and then use the saliva to polish the ball. It's the best ball shiner available.'

'Piss off, mate, I'm eating mine,' I said. It was the last free mint I was offered. Even though it was all the rage on the circuit, surely if a mint was that important then it was a sign that all wasn't well. It was also a source of amusement for the lads to regularly tease me about how good the mints tasted during play, while I chewed on my gum. In the overall scheme of things it was minuscule, but it did provide an insight into their thought processes and how their priorities can be distorted. Kent were an ambitious team who had the perennial tag of 'nearly men', and maybe it was a culmination of these little things that held them back when it really counted.

For me, the runs took a while to come, but a last-up 146 at my good-luck ground, Headingley, gave me renewed enthusiasm that I could convert starts into hundreds and show everyone I was right in believing I could always improve and hence continue to be a force at the top level.

Only two weeks later, I was pondering the thought that sometimes it doesn't matter what your mindset is, the opposition can be just too good. When in the mood, with the right conditions, Pakistan's Shoaib Akhtar was as close to unplayable a bowler as I ever faced, and that's exactly how it was for the supposedly not-as-sharp-or-with-sufficient-reflexes Waugh brothers during the Test in Colombo, as we came and went in a flash. A wickedly reverse-swinging old ball in the hands of the world's quickest bowlers was dynamite. Having to repel a hat-trick is made tougher by the simple fact that it is hard not to focus purely on that thought. Here, the difficulty was magnified further when I looked up from my batting stance to see the signature backward head tilt and hair flick that signals the jet-propelled start of the bowling approach of a man who literally sprints in and hurls the cherry at you as fast as he can.

I always found the best way to avoid being mesmerised by a long run-up was to avoid looking at it until the last portion of it was upon me. For the hat-trick ball I knew what was coming: a late, in-swinging full-length ball aiming to trap me lbw or spreadeagle the timber. To counter this plan, I kept saying to myself, *Keep the backlift short, play straight and just get bat on ball.* At the point Shoaib unleashed his 90-plus-miles-an-hour Exocet I snapped to myself, *Now!* to launch my concentration, which was enough to scunge an inside edge first ball but not enough to prevent the next one getting through my 'French cricket' style of defence and send me back to sit alongside the previous shot duck, brother Mark.

Was I getting too old? Were the doubters right? Or was it just because I'd left my red hankie back in Australia? There were too many questions, and only one answer was needed to support me: I had to keep trusting myself. I had to earn the right to continue in Test cricket through good preparation and attention to detail, not by looking for luck and excuses. In a way I was fortunate to be the captain because my mind was kept occupied with decision-making, whereas Mark must have been agonising over his lack of runs as he stood at second slip, leading to him dropping two catches he'd normally have taken standing on his head.

This Test was one of the tensest I was involved in, and it finished in our favour shortly after I took the new ball on the final day, when Pakistan needed 74 runs to win with five wickets in hand. It was a gamble, not least because Warney had taken four wickets in the innings, but instinctively one I knew should be taken even though there was no consensus among the guys. Making what turned out to be the right strategic move was enormously satisfying and to a degree filled the void of my empty return with the bat. But I knew no matter how many right reins I pulled as captain, the bottom line of runs on the board had to be rectified. And soon.

The on-ground thermometer had the mercury at 58°C, making my lost toss a potentially ruinous one. The Sharjah pitch is renowned as a batting haven that metamorphoses into a spinner's paradise – but for the Tests of October 2002 this was true only for those left standing in a heat so oppressive and dangerous that spectators refused to turn up to be roasted alive. I knew we needed early wickets to lift the spirits, but the sight of Brett Lee's face turning crimson after he'd sent down just two overs and him saying, 'If I bowl another over, I'm going to die' wasn't promising. Glenn McGrath lasted 18 balls before letting me know, 'I'm cooked. Can't bowl another one', while our iron man, Andy Bichel, whose unluckily intermittent selection spurred him on to stirring feats whenever he did get on the field, walked down to fine leg after six straight overs and just kept going to the change rooms, for an ice bath and half a dozen bottles of water to extend his existence.

Thankfully, the Pakistanis' two innings totals mirrored the temperatures: 59 and 53. This was a totally inept display of embarrassing batting against Warney, who just kept mixing his pace up and catching them flat-footed and empty-headed. My misery with the bat continued when I was fired first ball in the sort of umpire's mistake that so often happens when you are struggling. There's no doubt that deflated energy levels and an obvious lack of confidence make you more vulnerable, not only to your opponents, who tend to lift as you struggle, but also to umpires, who find it easier to give you out. It's almost as if they are putting you out of your misery sooner rather than later.

Like Haydos had in Durban, Lang knew the hurt I was experiencing from my continued run of failures, and he positioned himself next to me on the bus back to the hotel for a bit of a chat. Again, it wasn't so much the words he said but the fact that he had considered how I was feeling and took time out to try to make a positive difference that meant so much to me. With a knowing look, he said, 'Mate, it's a lonely old life, isn't it?' Ironically, I'd said a similar thing to him 12 months before during the Ashes tour, when he'd missed the first four Tests. Such can be the life of a professional sportsperson.

This had been my 150th Test, and one of the most bizarre, lasting one minute less than 12 hours. I knew that with another failure in the next Test my tally would be complete at 151. In the days before the match Mark and I became the target of taunts from the Pakistan coach, Richard Pybus, who said we were past it, which was a bit rich considering his side had just been annihilated. I noted that Mark didn't appear to be too angered by the comments, which concerned me as he normally hated negative press. The four years of constant inquisition about the bookie affair had worn him down and the game was no longer fun for him, or the adventure it used to be. On the outside Mark always seemed casual and unfazed, but underneath he was affected just as much as anyone and probably suffered more than most through a lack of confidence when out of form.

Inspiration came from different places going into this last Test, with a guided tour of HMAS *Arunta*, a warship that was in dock in Dubai preparing for possible conflict in the Persian Gulf, that allowed us to mingle with the men and women of the Australian Navy. Lynette and Rosalie flew over for a week and helped me to relax in the lead-up to the game, with Lynette simply saying: 'Play it with spirit.' This struck a real chord with me, given that the Test began just days after the Bali bombing that cost so many lives, many of them Australian. We were aware of the many heroic tales of mateship and survival in the aftermath of that devastating blast. Lang again helped me when he showed me an article he had written about me a few years before that featured valuable lessons like 'Trust yourself' and 'Do the things that made you what you are'. Buck, Gilly and Haydos added words at the right time and a quote I'd found in *One Step Ahead,* a book by the World Cup-winning coach of the Australian rugby team, Rod Macqueen, had neon lights around it: 'Whenever I find myself confronted by adversity in any situation, my first thoughts are to fight back.'

The way in which I strode to the middle with positive intent and the assured manner in which I moved around the crease with authority instantly gave me the high ground and a sense of control. The Pakistan captain, Waqar Younis, then did me a huge favour by saying, 'Let's send him out in style, fellas. Let's make his last Test finish with a duck' before I'd even scratched out my centre. I returned fire with, 'Not today, buddy.' The trusted red rag was back, having been couriered over by my family, and a quick glance down at it gave me instant security and comfort. Maybe the reason I did so well in such pressured circumstances was the absolute and crystal-clear simplicity of the moment. I had two choices, one easy, the other hard, and since I'd often said I'd rather do it tough because the satisfaction if you're successful is much greater, I thrived in this delicate setting.

Lynette and Rosie were scheduled to leave after day one, and at stumps I was 33 not out. I really wanted them to be there for the second day, but my wife already knew the outcome, saying, 'You'll get a hundred', before catching a taxi to the airport and flying home. She left me with part of her 'wife factor': positive thoughts.

In fact, I became the first man in Test history to reach a hundred with back-to-back sixes. I did so while wearing the baggy green cap, and with no batsmen left in the shed – a script you'd die for as an Australian batsman. All the collective goodwill swept over me and carried me through. I'd needed courage to keep believing, and getting these runs confirmed that it was the down time and periods of introspection, often endured away from the action, that could cripple my performance. Once I was finally able to immerse myself in the action with a positive outlook, the pure enjoyment of winning one-on-one battles took over.

My ninth Ashes series began in eerie fashion. Mark was absent, having been dropped after playing 128 Tests, 108 of them with the two of us alongside each other. It was almost a given that we travelled, played and spent our sporting lives together, but now, after a 12-year operation, the Waugh twins had been separated. It felt strange to look around me as I walked onto the Gabba for the first Test and not be able to find him there.

A few minutes earlier, Nasser Hussain's worst nightmare had eventuated when he won a toss he'd desperately wanted to lose. His decision to bowl first wasn't a bad move on face value, and I would have chosen that option, but it wasn't right simply because of how it was implemented. Sending the opposition in has to be an attacking move, to try to exploit the conditions or to interrogate the opposition batsmen, but in this case England did so as a means of working themselves into the game – a conservative start rather than taking the initiative. Rarely, if ever, has the first session of an Ashes campaign begun without one bouncer being bowled in anger. It was tame, lame stuff that allowed Matthew Hayden and Ricky Ponting to take the match beyond England's reach after just two sessions of play and set the mood for the whole series.

Ours was a near-faultless performance and we won decisively by 384 runs. The only downside was me as captain missing out in each innings to start the 'When are you retiring?' circus again. This time there was no brother to share the insatiable attention of the media and I knew there was only one way to kill the story: score plenty of runs, starting next innings.

In between the first and second Tests I peeled off a spectacular 135 for NSW against South Australia and my net form was sparkling, but the nonstop speculation about my place in the side was distracting and mentally fatiguing. I came out swinging in Adelaide, making 34 from 40 balls before I thought, *Now you can relax, you've done the hard work*, and promptly expired to the medium pace of Darren Lehmann's brother-in-law, Craig White. It was a real opportunity wasted, and with not too many such chances left the disappointment was acute. The sand in the eggtimer was tumbling fast. I needed the quality innings I felt was imminent to materialise on the pitch and not in the practice nets or in my mind.

Leading into the third Test, at the WACA, I predicted, 'Blood will be spilled on the world's quickest pitch and courage will win the day.' It would be a prophetic comment when late in England's second innings their big promising quick, Alex Tudor, who'd once scored 99 not out in a Test, couldn't fend off a Brett Lee bouncer and the ball penetrated the gap between his helmet peak and grill to expose his left eye socket and eyebrow. I had probably the best view in the house at bat-pad and could clearly see the terror in Tudor's eyes at the precise instant he knew he was going to get smashed. The whites of his eyes enlarged as the body strained to pass on vital information to the brain about what needed to happen and the consequences if it didn't. When it became obvious that contact was unavoidable, he reeled his head backwards in the hope of taking a glancing blow and not flush-on. With the sickening sound of leather against skull he stumbled to the ground, where he frantically tried to rid himself of the unhelpful helmet and attend to his damaged face. It was one of those moments where bravado and banter cease and the welfare of the injured takes total precedence. As soon as Alex grabbed at his eye the ruby-red streaks appeared, trickling down the white fingers of his batting gloves and onto the insignia of team sponsor Vodafone on his white shirt. I was genuinely concerned for his eyesight as he writhed around on the ground, moaning in pain, and so too thankfully was his good mate and Surrey colleague, Alec Stewart, who held his hand and reassured him that everything would be okay.

It's moments such as this that make players realise that cricket isn't the be-all and end-all. When someone's well-being or health is in peril, all the talk and bluff amount to nothing and you often see the real character in a person come through. I know Brett Lee has a reputation as a tearaway quick who doesn't mind hitting the odd batsman, but when he saw blood he turned deathly pale and could barely utter a word. He kept on asking Alex, 'Are you okay, mate?' I can't recall any cricketer ever feeling a sense of satisfaction or achievement when a batsman is seriously hurt; every emotion is about hoping the guy will be all right.

The day before, I had scored 53, another excellent platform, but this time I could at least comfort myself with the fact that I was dismissed by probably the ball of the match, from Alex Tudor, a bowler whose natural delivery slants in, except for the odd unplayable one that defies the laws of physics and shapes away. Sure enough, he produced such a gem and it made me wonder why this guy couldn't cement a regular spot in the England XI. Having a high pain threshold is a vital attribute for a successful quick; if you expect to feel 100 per cent right before each game then you may as well take up lawn bowls, because it's hardly ever going to happen. The resilient fast men almost desensitise their bodies to pain by learning to block it out and play through it, while the 'injury-prone' ones let the niggles grow into problems by paying them too much attention. Perhaps Alex fell into the latter category.

An unexpected call from Trevor Hohns on the day before the Perth Test to meet him downstairs for a chat proved to be beneficial in terms of knowing where we stood. A little less than 12 months earlier, Trevor had been pilloried in some quarters for dropping me from the one-day squad without giving me any prior warning suggesting such a move was on the agenda, or any guidance as to how I might attend to any perceived problems. This time, thankfully, the lines of communication were open. I appreciated his honesty and how tough it was for him to sit opposite me, a former teammate, after years of having a working relationship on selection issues, and give it to me straight. We talked about how well the team was playing (we'd won 11 Tests out of 12 going back to the start of the South Africa Tests of 2001–02) and his belief that there was a strong need to plan for the succession, because the team was ageing. I was all for that idea, but why rush things when the team was at its zenith and no one was demanding immediate inclusion? The batsmen knocking on the door for Test selection, such as Martin Love, Michael Bevan, Greg Blewett and Simon Katich, were hardly inexperienced and, when selected, would easily assimilate into the team. I knew I couldn't continue forever, but I also knew I had more to give. Indeed, right at that moment I truly felt I had something special left in me. In a perfect world I had my eye on the upcoming Caribbean tour, because it meant I'd have been through a 'full circle' of tours, having started my reign as Test captain with the drawn series of 1999. And, a long way off in my sporting life, the so-called 'final frontier', the next Test series in India scheduled for the second half of 2004, was a challenge everyone in the Australian squad had in the back of their minds.

I let him know that a big score wasn't far away and that my momentum was going in the right direction, which he acknowledged. He also argued that if that was the case then maybe the fifth Test, in Sydney, the last of this Ashes series, might be a good place to finish. I wasn't sure. All I wanted to do was be in control of my destiny, end my career playing excellent cricket and know when the time was right to exit stage left. I left the meeting accepting that two more Tests without runs would make the decision easy for all concerned.

It was an amicable, mature exchange, which I thought left nothing unsaid from either party. So I was distressed to read a quote from the chairman in the media shortly afterwards: 'At the moment, Stephen has our support until the Sydney Test. The decision is then up to him whether he wants to continue or not. If he does, he will be judged on form like any other player.'

I responded by telling reporters, 'I've never asked for a guarantee, nor did I want a guarantee. After 154 Tests, I didn't want any favours or expect them and I take offence to the suggestion that I asked for a favour.'

Maybe Trevor was trying to put a lid on the debate by issuing a firm statement, but it had the opposite effect, doubling the pressure on me going into the Boxing Day Test. The story was deemed so newsworthy that my life was no longer mine.

The actual cricket in the Test series was so one-sided that only 10 days' play were needed before Australia had retained the Ashes for the eighth consecutive time. In the first three Tests we scored 1796 runs for the loss of 34 wickets compared to England's 1313 runs for the loss of 57 wickets, and to a hungry press contingent there weren't too many stories coming from such a thrashing that would be capable of selling a paper. The only other story that was gathering momentum was the one about my opposite number, who as the losing captain was in the firing line with many travelling journos suggesting his time as skipper might be about to end. To Nasser's credit, he stood firm and committed himself to the remainder of the series rather than looking for excuses, which maybe he could have done given the loss of bowlers Simon Jones, Darren Gough and Andrew Flintoff through injury and the continued unpredictability of Andy Caddick, who seemed just as big a mystery to the Poms as he was to us. Nasser's style as captain was very hands-on, and it was clear he enjoyed the power and influence the job brought him, which in many ways was what his team needed, because for too long they'd lacked drive and belief against Australia. He wanted that to change, and was trying to do so by forcing them to confront situations.

However, at times he went over the top with his badgering of bowlers, appearing to be more of a nuisance than a help. He was constantly in their ear, holding up the game and instructing them what to do. When Steve Harmison, a young quick on his first Test tour, got the 'yips' in Perth and couldn't work out which foot to launch his run-up from, it precipitated a collection of stuttering and ungainly approaches to the wicket. His captain swamped him with over-the-top attention, rather than offering a quiet word or perhaps granting him a reprieve down to fine leg. There are times as captain when you need to be discreet to be kind, not big-note yourself as the saviour.

Captaincy is about empowerment, about making your players

responsible for their actions and, in turn, accountable. It's about treating everyone equally but differently by recognising there are varied characters and personalities who need to express their individual flair and instincts inside the ultimate team vision. It's about setting an example and not expecting anything of your players that you aren't willing to do yourself. It's about mentoring and at times protecting individuals, and taking on their problems so that the team will benefit. You must recognise mistakes and not be above criticism, and be prepared to swallow your pride in order to move on. Crucially, it's about seeing the good in people and focusing on the positives and the things you can control. It's making sure your time management is spot on and that you continue to earn your place in the side. At times for me it was about being an advisor, psychologist, mate, mentor, mediator, selector, mouthpiece and politician. Above all, it was about being me and doing it my way.

41

The perfect day

During the break between the third and fourth Ashes Tests I had time to go back and captain NSW in a Pura Cup game against Victoria (the Sheffield Shield had been renamed after its new sponsor, Pura, in November 1999). Here, I could relax away from the scrutiny, have a decent hit-out and view the progress of the country's up-and-coming talent, and it was an enjoyable experience. However, it was difficult in one way because I felt like a rookie each time I came back, as I didn't really know the guys because we hadn't had a lot of time together. The connection was loose in terms of getting a handle on their temperaments, character and ability to handle pressure situations, so all I could do as a leader was show faith and back them to the hilt. Unfortunately, that sentiment wasn't shared by Blues coach Steve Rixon, who called an impromptu meeting involving myself, the selectors and Cricket NSW's CEO, Dave Gilbert. After the opening formalities, Steve argued that the guys felt intimidated and that a change of captain may be in order. Not only had he not briefed me or those assembled before the meeting, but astoundingly he didn't have any real reason to call my position into question. It was quickly established that I had the full support of the selectors and the CEO, which was not really surprising given that they had basically begged me to be the first-choice captain at the start of the season. I concluded the meeting by saying, 'I'll do the job I was chosen for and we are going to go on and win the Pura Cup and the ING [one-day] Cup. Thank you and goodbye.'

In the end, this disagreement turned out to be the best thing that happened for NSW. I assumed more control in the way we trained, cut down the monotonous pregame meetings that had become a regular feature of the team's preparation, and gave players chances to move out of their comfort zones. Maybe Steve Rixon knew me too well, knew that whenever I was backed into a corner I'd come out fighting and that I saved my best for such occasions. The lack of respect hurt – we'd always enjoyed a good working relationship – even if the end result was immensely rewarding as we completed the double, coming from challenging positions on the competitions' tables halfway through the season. Australian domestic cricket may be a level below the international game, but the rivalry and competition are just as intense, and with more than 150 Tests to my name I was an enticing target. I always enjoyed the banter, especially when it came from a young upstart trying to impress. A McGrath clone from South Australia named Paul Rofe loved to send a bit of niggle my way, but he missed his mark when he made a wisecrack about my much-publicised bat contract with Indian firm MRF, just loud enough for me and a few surrounding players to hear as I stood in semi-concentration mode at the non-striker's end. Rofe thought he'd pulled off a purler when he chirped up from mid-on with, 'Let's get this Kashmir willow [cheap wood] bat out of here, boys.'

'Hey, Rofey, the contract for that Kashmir willow would buy your house,' was my response. I knew it was a winner when the bowler had a giggle to himself, while Rofey managed a bit of a smile in an admission he'd been gazumped.

The length of a cricket match and the amount of downtime leads to players often having to amuse themselves, largely by way of humour. One of the most memorable sledges I heard during my career involved my younger brother Dean, who played for NSW and captained teams in both NSW and South Australia. The bowler was a guy called Richard Stobo, an old-fashioned quick whose no-frills attitude and dress sense saw him wear lawn-bowls whites with belt loops around the waist. Richard had been a regular teammate of Mark and me in junior rep cricket and was a straightshooter of a guy who never appeared to get flustered. However, his patience came to an abrupt end when Dean played and missed a fourth consecutive ball during a first-grade clash at Bankstown Oval. In total exasperation, he exclaimed, 'For Christ's sake, you must have been adopted.'

It was the kind of humour I'd been brought up to play with and against. On occasions for Australia, if we had two batsmen of equal ability in the lower order, it would normally be the man with the higher score to his name who went in first, or perhaps the highly scientific game of 'Rock, paper, scissors' would decide the outcome. I knew I'd need plenty of that spirit if I were to save my career over the following two weeks. The coat-tuggers were multiplying, their whispers gathering impetus, and I had only Test cricket to focus on as I contemplated the possibility that I was about to play my final Boxing Day Test. The last semblance of an outside chance to make a fifth World Cup had died in early December when I was deemed not good enough to make a preliminary squad of 30; 'encouragement awards' rather than genuine rankings had been handed out. While I knew I was a long shot to make the final team of 15 – realistically only a rough chance if injuries occurred in large numbers – I was annoyed at the red line that had been put through my name. To me, it was un-Australian to snuff out a dream, especially as AB had kept saying, in relation to my chances, 'We're happy to be proved wrong.' Well, it's tough to prove anything without being given a chance.

The media were having a field day. I can still remember a journalist knocking on the front door of the family's holiday house and asking to do a story. I told him I wasn't interested, that I saw no point in inflaming the situation, to which he responded, 'But we'll do a sympathetic piece.'

I couldn't believe my ears. 'Why the hell would I want sympathy?' I replied. 'I just want to relax and spend a few days off with the family.'

One year earlier, this journo's newspaper had started a campaign to have me sacked as Australia's one-day captain, and now they wanted to be the good guys. One Sydney newspaper, the *Daily Telegraph*, was supporting me, the other, the *Sydney Morning Herald*, seemed to be attacking me, and I was the meat in the sandwich, the name to get a headline to sell a story. It didn't actually matter whether the issue was relevant or newsworthy; as long as my name was controversial it meant sales. Often, I'd make a statement at a press conference and the next day it would be interpreted differently by the two papers, which was very frustrating. However, on reflection I shouldn't have taken it so much to heart. It wasn't really about me – it was a story and tomorrow it would be forgotten. Unfortunately, as I found in 2002–03 and AB discovered in 1994, when you're the nation's cricket captain you feel as if everyone is hanging on every word written about you and, even worse, believes every word written about you.

By the time the Boxing Day Test arrived, my only concern was getting out there and mixing it with the Pommies. At 3/265 on the opening day, I entered the concrete coliseum to rapturous applause. My heart skipped a beat as I glanced skyward to adjust to the bright light that contrasted so markedly with the artificial illumination in the underground, dungeonlike MCG change rooms that held us like transit passengers at an airport. I took a deep breath, twirled the shoulders in succession and steeled myself to be strong, positive and assertive. The spring was in the step, the mind was strong, the tension was stimulating and I wanted confrontation. And Nasser obliged. The England captain recalled his quickest bowler in Harmison to the crease and then proceeded to give Justin Langer an easy single to a spread-eagled field to get me on strike. It was a cheap-shot ploy that Darren Lehmann would use against me the following year in a Pura Cup game and on both occasions it had the same result: raising my intensity levels to the point where I was one step away from imploding but exactly where I needed to be to funnel all my willpower.

It was Under 10 stuff by Nasser, intended to take the piss out of me and let his quick have his way with me. All I could think was, *Don't get involved in a slanging match that's out of your control, because that's what he wants you to do so your concentration will be deflected into a wasteland.* But I needed to let off some steam and, importantly, do so decisively. 'You smartarse prick!' seemed to cover that objective pretty well. Then I took guard and tried to pull things back together. Sometimes, though, no matter how hard I concentrated or how noble my intentions were, a force too strong obliterates the best of plans. Just as Harmison was about to soar into his delivery stride, I gambled on defusing his probable bouncer by simultaneously charging forward and stepping away to the leg side, to flat-bat him over cover.

It was probably the gutsiest shot of my career, with the potential to make me look cowardly and inept if I missed it. To me, it was about respect; if their plan was to humiliate me, then I wanted to counterpunch as quickly as possible. It was dangerous, though, because whenever ego becomes the prime motivator, emotion rules over commonsense and usually equates to disaster. This time, judging by the stunned looks I got from the English players, the gamble paid off, and after having risked all I decided to get back into the groove, knuckle down and go with the flow. A breezy 62 not out at stumps had me well placed for the hundred I craved, but next morning a ball from Craig White that I assumed would go on with the angle held its line, and the faintest of edges ended an innings I thought was destined for bigger things.

The aspect about cricket that kept me invigorated and entranced for so long was the fact that I continued to learn about myself and be amazed at how each day turned up a life lesson. During my innings, I was like a bear that had been woken from hibernation. My midpitch conversation with Lang went like this: 'Why haven't I been doing this? Why haven't I been backing myself?' With so many distractions, I'd neglected the approach I'd tried to pass on to every cricketer I'd played with. I'm not sure how many other people felt the same way, but I knew I was back, still as good as anyone when my mind was focused.

Not that too many others thought so after my bizarre cameo in our second innings. Ever since the head-on collision with Jason Gillespie in Kandy in 1999, I had suffered migraines at fairly regular intervals. These ranged from just bad headaches to severe pain plus blurred vision, vomiting and, in extreme cases, trouble with balancing.

We were two wickets down chasing a small total of 107 for a fourth straight victory when all the symptoms of a migraine attack hit me with full force. Next ball, before I could grab the attention of our new No. 6, Martin Love, to swap positions in the batting order, Damien Martyn was dismissed for a duck. The roar of the travelling England supporters, the 'Barmy Army', echoed through the underground chamber and infiltrated our change room seconds before the image of the dismissal came up on our television set. *Take a deep breath and snap yourself out of it* was my immediate thought, but as soon as I hit the outside air the heat and humidity turned everything fuzzy, at the same time igniting that hot rush down the oesophagus that indicates carrots have a date with the deck. The whole debacle was a blur and I'm amazed I lasted long enough to make 14, for each ball was played through a fogginess as if I was wearing a smeared pair of sunglasses. I survived a caught-behind situation where I glanced one off the face of the bat but no Englishmen saw or appealed for it until the replay came up on the giant screen. This ignited the Barmy Army and brought a belated shout from Hussain that was 30 seconds too late.

Maybe it was going to be my day. I pinned the ears back next ball and smashed it 'through' the cover region, only to see Nasser take a screamer and generously guide me in the direction of the change rooms. But amid the commotion no one noticed the no-ball call from the umpire, so I saddled up for another crack. I repeated the dose next ball, this time playing my shot of the year to totally deflate their spirits. Four overs later, my misery was ended by Sky TV's back-up-satellite-dish-in-disguise, Andy Caddick, a bowler who had all the ammunition to be the equal of Glenn McGrath and more, but who lacked that little something special to reach the greatness he was capable of.

Throughout this demanding summer I had many people help me out with words of advice, including some from our deep-thinking coach, who penned a letter after the Adelaide Test that made a big impact on me. It concluded by saying:

You play best when you are angered, you have a cause, you are showing opposition/people they have got it wrong, you have purpose, whether that is self-directed, team-directed, or both. If you have not got this sorted in your mind, then these last Tests will be difficult. You do not have to go out of your way to have teammates, people, etc., like you, because it is the last time you will play with them or be seen. You already have that, plus huge respect. Be remembered for who you are and how you have always played your cricket: aggressive, uncompromising and demanding of excellence.

The days leading up to the Sydney Test seemed centred solely on my impending retirement. Though my teammates never asked me, they probably thought it would be the last time we played together. The truth is I hadn't decided either way. I preferred to stick to the plan in my head that read: *Don't put a finishing date on it or else you'll play accordingly. Just let it happen.* That relaxed state of mind came through at the pre-Test press conference, when an off-the-cuff question produced an instantaneous reaction: 'What's been the most defining moment of your career?'

'Well, perhaps it will happen in this game,' I said contemplatively, without imagining the outcome.

★

Just before tea on the second day, I sat in the players' balcony of the home change room at the SCG, next in to bat and with a million thoughts racing around in my head. The capacity crowd was here to see a traditional Ashes battle, but with the series decided I could feel the eyes and expectations of the masses firmly on me. The tide of goodwill was astounding, with people having yelled out to me on the trip down to the ground stuff like, 'I've driven 12 hours straight from Broken Hill to see you bat. Good luck!' From my perspective, it was overwhelming, largely because I felt I owed the fans something in return for their dedicated support. Some fans know no bounds in their loyalty: one man asked me to sign his wrist one day, which I did, then he came back later that day to show me how the tattoo had come out. I've had children, pets and car numberplates named after me and a young Indian boy acquired 'Tugga' for a middle name, which will confuse his mates later in his life. A girl from Orange in NSW sent me copies of her life diaries for the 20 years I was a professional cricketer and has sent the entire Waugh family gifts for Christmas, birthdays and anniversaries, never missing one. Such blind faith can be overlooked amid the hectic lifestyle that overtakes a sportsperson's life, but as I sat there with the pads on, experiencing the immense kindliness of the crowd, I fully grasped how important the game is to so many people and how important the fans really are for us.

I found it hard to focus on one thought, fluctuating between *Don't make a duck* and *Jeez, it'd be great to peel off a hundred.* The longer I sat there the more the dark forces seemed to gather, until I said to myself, *Take it easy. Just enjoy the experience.*

I saw immediately that a Justin Langer top edge off Andy Caddick had a trajectory destined for the hands of England opening bowler Matthew Hoggard at fine leg, and rather than wait for the obvious I velcroed on my gloves, picked up my helmet and was up out of my seat and already down the players' race leading out onto the field when the catch was completed. I wanted to reach the middle before the emotion of the moment swamped me and distracted my senses too much, and also to send a subtle message to the Poms that I was ready for action. I wanted to stake ownership on the middle. The roar was tumultuous as I passed Lang, already almost halfway to the wicket. I noticed people standing in the aisles and cheering as loudly as they could, in a show of support that made me incredibly proud and humbled by its intensity.

Nasser Hussain went for the captain's weapon of choice, the psychological interrogation, and promptly threw the ball to his white West Indian, Steve Harmison, to try to ruffle me up. But that initial over passed without anything too memorable occurring, except for an amazing cloak of tranquillity that engulfed me. Then a clip off the toes behind square leg off Hoggard shortly after raced to the boundary and I was beginning to believe that this day was meant to be. I'd entered the coveted zone and felt like the scenes had been written for me with only one condition attached to them: concentration.

Throughout the last session I was sharp on my feet, alert to scoring opportunities and back in sync with my greatest attributes: quick wrists and ball placement. I was loving batting, feeling the same joy that was there when I thought I'd reached my summit in scoring 28 as a seven-year-old for Panania–East Hills Under 10s at Smith Park 30 years earlier. The ecstasy of knowing that a shot is destined for the boundary, the sweet sensation of a perfectly timed stroke as it pings off the blade and the power of piercing the gap and winning the duel over the bowler still stimulated me. Media personality Andrew Denton had paid for the privilege of being the assistant coach for the day, with the money going to the Malcolm Sargent Cancer Fund for Children, and part of his role involved helping to bring out the refreshments at the drinks break during the final session, when I was 47 not out. All he could say to me was, 'Don't be home before six', which was sound advice from a man who had nearly been decapitated by an Adam Gilchrist off-drive during the morning's warm-up when he did the big no-no: walking out of the nets without watching the next ball.

Coming into the last over of the day, to be bowled by off-spinner Richard Dawson, I needed five to complete the Cinderella story and make 100. In what everyone thought was a magnanimous gesture to give me a chance to complete the hundred, Gilly had let the last ball of the penultimate over of the day go through to the keeper, but the truth is he thought it was the last ball of the day and was ready to walk off and look forward to tomorrow. As the field changed over, I received an unexpected pressure-valve release from Alec Stewart when he asked, 'Do you write your own scripts these days?' Not only was this the ice-breaker I needed, it in some way acted as confirmation in my mind that the hundred was meant to be. As I hunched over in preparation for the first delivery I kept telling myself, *Stay patient, don't force it, it will happen.* This thought, thankfully, outweighed an urge to slog-sweep a six.

After respecting three decent deliveries, I needed to force the issue more than I'd anticipated or wanted to, and an improvised shot off the back foot past cover point initially had me thinking we'd run four, as the nearest fieldsman, Caddick, had a lot of ground to cover. As I turned for two, my vision of a four was never going to materialise, but I also knew if any batsman was capable of finding a single from the very next ball, then that man for the big occasion, Gilly, would sniff it out.

That he did, thanks to the generous field set by Hussain, who seemed to want to see the scenario played out to the full. The next minute or so went in slow motion, as Nasser went for the art of gamesmanship by conducting a long conversation in the guise of tactical planning with Dawson, more than likely chatting about that evening's restaurant of choice, thus making me wait. I was aware of the crowd and their phenomenal support, but their cheers seemed muted or muffled as I stood intently, not really thinking about anything, almost detaching myself from the events going on around me. I reached for the security blanket, the old, worn, ragged red cloth, wiped the sweat from under my helmet peak and eyeballed Hussain as he walked back to slip. As the bowler began his run-up, I didn't have any doubts about the outcome – not only did I feel positive, but the collective vibe of 40000-plus spectators was with me and gave me comfort.

Let it unfold, react to the opportunity, don't force it . . .

The delivery was a quicker ball on a line outside off stump, apparently intended to catch me playing across the line as I swung a slog sweep over midwicket, but I saw it in a flash and just released the arms and locked in the wrists. I didn't really even bother to follow its path, because it was fence-bound the instant the ball connected with the heart of the blade. Out of habit I ran the length of the pitch, totally oblivious to my batting partner, whose attempted high-five came to nothing. It was a massive relief to have waited until the very last moment to convince everyone else that I wasn't just talking a good game when I said I could still do it.

The next hour or so was a period I wish everyone could experience just once in their life: the ovation from the crowd, the appreciation from the opposition, the encore demanded by the spectators who stayed at the ground, the joy of family sharing the occasion, and the total and utter contentment I experienced sitting in front of my locker surrounded by teammates who didn't really know what to say. It had been a boyhood dream to hit the last ball for six ever since the 1974–75 season, when on television I saw Doug Walters hit Bob Willis for six at the WACA. To do something like that, passing 10 000 Test runs and equalling the Don on 29 Test-match centuries, added up to the perfect day in cricketing terms.

I'm constantly amazed at the stories I hear from people about what they were doing when that last ball from Richard Dawson was bowled. Twin brother Mark had left the SCG to make sure he got to Harold Park Paceway in time for the first, while at the Stony Creek races in country Victoria the nags had to be taken out of the barriers so the punters could watch the last ball on the on-course televisions. Only in Australia!

The Test itself ended in a 225-run loss, a result that came largely because of the superb batting of the best English opener I played against, Michael Vaughan, who also happens to be the only guy I've ever seen succeed after Glenn McGrath made his annual declaration of intent upon the opposition's key batsman. Vaughan, unlike others, took Glenn's challenge head on during this series and gave back as much as he copped. For all of us, Australian and English alike, it was a welcome sight, and a trait that needed to be seized upon. For guys like Nasser Hussain, Alec Stewart and Andy Caddick, however, the dream of wresting back the Ashes had vanished. Their careers, like mine, weren't far from finishing up.

42

My last overseas tour

After the euphoria of the hundred in Sydney, control of the debate about my future was by and large back in my hands and not in those of the headline grabbers or the selectors. I was given plenty of time by Trevor Hohns to let him know whether or not I wanted my international career to continue, and I intended to use that time to make sure that my head was clear and the reasons for my eventual decision were right.

In the days before the Pura Cup final, Lynette said, 'If you want to keep going, we'll be there to support you.' They were the words I needed to hear, for within me was a calling to complete the job I had started four years earlier when I debuted as a captain in a drawn series. It was this unfinished business that lured me, and I was also enticed once again by the rustic charm of touring the laid-back Caribbean, where the fans are among the most passionate. There's something very basic and raw about the facilities there that reminds me of my junior cricketing days, and I love the varying sights and smells that the culture of each island provides. It's a tour that conjures up magical images, delivers adventure and guarantees fond memories. I wanted to be a part of the odyssey again.

The 2003 World Cup came and went without me, and also without Warney, whose hard work in rehabilitating from a shoulder injury suffered during the Australian season was spoilt by a simple yet costly mistake. Many found it hard to believe he had taken a diuretic simply to help his appearance, but as a long-time teammate and good friend, I knew his desire to lose excess fluid was only an extension of the sun-bed tan, streaked hair and whitened teeth Shane regularly indulged in to help him look sharp and young. Sadly for him, the pill he swallowed was on the sport's banned list because it had been used by others as a masking agent for illegal drugs, and the world's greatest leg-spinner was suspended for 12 months. However, one man's loss is another's gain, and in Brad Hogg, a part-time 'postie' and, to me, the best left-field selection made by the panel under Trevor Hohns's leadership, Australia unearthed one of its players of the tournament. He and Andy Bichel starred in what was essentially a team triumph. After speaking to Ricky Ponting on the phone prior to the match, I listened to the World Cup final on the radio as I drove back from the NSW Central Coast. Many thoughts were running through my head, but more than anything I was proud of the guys and their professionalism as they destroyed India by a big margin, and pleased that I had played my part during the three years of lead-up work and pushed for a rotation selection system that had its payday in the end, and a style of cricket the masses enjoyed watching.

The Caribbean campaign began with Glenn McGrath getting one of those dreaded late-night calls from home. Errol Alcott woke me at 5 a.m., asking me to meet him and Pigeon, and I learned that Glenn's wife, Jane, had been diagnosed with breast cancer. While Glenn hadn't fallen apart with the news, he was in shock and desperate to get home, and as quickly as possible he was on the first flight back to Australia. I assumed he wouldn't be back, even though he bravely assured us that as soon as it was all clear he'd rejoin the tour. By the time I was back in my room I was already thinking about the alternatives now that our two bowling greats weren't on the tour. Warne and McGrath had been pillars of strength, the wrecking balls capable of containment and incision, worth two bowlers each.

In the days leading up to the first Test, in Guyana, my gut instinct told me that five bowlers might be a good option on what looked like a flat, lifeless pitch and against a side that was more superior in the batting department than in their bowling. Having Adam Gilchrist batting at six was hardly a concern, and with the all-round capabilities of Bichel and Hogg there would still be some run-scorers in our lower order and endless options when we were in the field. I elected to open the bowling in the second innings with two wrist-spin bowlers, Hogg and Stuart MacGill – one of the few times that has happened in Test history. Using the extra bowler and at the same time keeping everyone's appetite for long spells in check proved to be a demanding exercise, but the need to take 20 wickets on a featherbed was overwhelming and the new formula worked as well as I could have hoped.

The policy of having a member of the Australian selection committee in attendance before the Test, to liaise with me and get the inside mail on tour before reporting back to Trevor Hohns so that the selectors could pick the team, didn't work in Guyana. David Boon was still in the air as I chatted to Trevor on the phone on the day before the Test, but, perhaps fortunately, we were thinking along the same lines, which meant that the desperately unlucky Martin Love missed out. Martin had waited nearly 10 years since his first-class debut for a chance to make his first Test appearance, which he had finally done very effectively as a replacement for the injured Darren Lehmann during the 2002–03 Ashes series. Now, with Darren back but Damien Martyn out after badly breaking a finger during the World Cup, the door had been kept open, only for our decision to play five bowlers to take his chance away. I was aware that this would alter his career, but I had to push for the side I thought was best equipped to win the Test, and Martin was just plain unlucky with his timing. The match was effectively won in the first session when we had the Windies in disarray at 5/53 in the first 16 overs. It seemed such a long time ago that Richards, Haynes, Greenidge and Richardson were mauling us; in contrast, the current crop seemed to think they were as good as their predecessors, but quite obviously had only half the talent.

If I were to choose a place to get medical assistance during a tour of the Caribbean, Guyana would be my last pick. This beautiful nation, blessed with abundant natural resources, is now racked by corruption and crime and resembles a third-world country that has been plundered by greedy leaders. The medical centre I found myself in during the Test after I badly split the webbing on my left hand between the index and middle finger, was as horrific as the outfield that had caused the injury. All around the waiting room sat people with wounds of varying severity, many the victims of knife attacks. Strangely, their alarming calmness suggested the scene was an everyday occurrence. Half a dozen stitches and the same number of needles later, I was back fielding with a hand as numb as if I had slept on it for hours. Justin Langer, meanwhile, was playing with technical perfection in scoring 146 and 78 not out to guide us to a convincing victory that was diluted somewhat by terrible umpiring.

There are occasions in Test cricket when a player freezes in the spotlight and totally cracks because of the intense pressure, but it is rare to see an umpire retreat so much that he is incapable of giving a decision. During this match, Asoka De Silva, a Sri Lankan umpire whose reputation was solid, became so negative that he wasn't even entertaining lbw shouts and didn't seem capable of answering any inquiries about his reasons for saying someone was not out. He was, quite clearly, stale and, like many players constantly on tour, in need of a break. Indeed, because of the need for two neutral umpires from the ICC panel to officiate at every Test, he was actually travelling more than the teams. At this time there was increasing debate about using technology to decide lbws, but I was and remain strongly opposed to this concept. To me, Test cricket is unique because it lasts five days, a result isn't guaranteed, and the human element and the potential for mistakes from players and umpires adds to its beauty. People love to discuss the controversial decisions because it makes them feel intimately involved with the game. To take away the human element would be to 'Americanise' the game, slowing it down through the unnecessary re-viewing of replays, which in turn stops the flow and momentum of a match. I'm a big believer in the notion that good and bad decisions will eventually cancel each other out, and for that reason alone am loathe to change the dynamics and very essence of the game.

Our victory in the second Test, at Port of Spain in Trinidad, was achieved through real toil in the home team's second innings. I set the Windies 407 to win with plenty of time to get them, and we'd lost only four and three wickets respectively in our two innings. I wanted a result and the only way to get it was to risk defeat, but with five bowlers I believed we had the options to cover any onslaught from our opponents. My impact on the match came down to knowing when to declare, orchestrating bowling changes and setting appropriate fields, after I didn't face a ball, claim a wicket or take a catch. It was a 'Mike

Brearley' performance, as Lang enjoyed telling me later, recalling the successful England captain of the late '70s and early '80s who averaged 22 with the bat in Tests, but a blessing in disguise as my hand was tender and tight with the fishing-line-width stitching still in place.

★

In the third Test, I snuck past the Don with Test century number 30, scored at one of my favourite grounds, Kensington Oval at Bridgetown, Barbardos. (The scale of this achievement is put in perspective by the fact that I took 107 more Tests than the legend had to score one more century.) The ground is in many ways a ramshackle venue, with harsh wooden seats, archaic stands and an irregular shape, but it has atmosphere and charm that come largely from the vibrant, energetic and knowledgeable crowd. When the Windies were at the height of their powers this was an intimidating venue, but not so much now, as the team continued its slide backwards and also partly because the authorities have decided that spectators are no longer allowed to bring musical instruments to the game.

The character of Bridgetown has softened over the years and its appeal has somewhat diminished, but I still love the place. Our win here was one of the best victories I was a part of, in terms of courage and of following through on a plan with unwavering attitude and commitment. To bowl 244.5 overs straight was a Herculean effort from our bowlers, performed on a pitch that was uncharacteristic for the Caribbean in that it didn't bounce above hip height and the pace off it was annoyingly slow. I enforced the follow-on even though we'd already bowled 128.5 overs in the first innings, because I believed we didn't have time to bat again and then force a win, and I realised we had an extra specialist bowler to share the load. I asked everyone to work together, focus on each ball and never at any stage let up in the field, no matter the scoreline. Patience and perseverance would win the day, but we had to be tough. I wanted the fielders to lead the way and show the bowlers they weren't doing it alone. That we achieved all this and won the game was the ultimate team effort and was duly recognised when we stayed out in the middle after the final wicket fell to sing 'Underneath the Southern Cross' in a tightly packed scrum that was full of sweaty underarms and gaunt faces. For a captain, the win was as good as it gets, because I'd asked for more than perhaps I was entitled to and the guys had never at any stage questioned the wisdom of my thinking.

This Australian team was a unit capable of anything, and as the guys' 'father figure' I felt like they'd just had their 21st birthdays and the world was now theirs to conquer. It was a thought I pondered during a late-night walk along the beach with Lynette, who after my four tours to the Caribbean had finally made it to this paradise on the other side of the world. We sat there on a bank of sand built by the previous high tide, a full moon shimmering across the water surface and the mesmerising crashing sounds of the waves making clear thinking easy. I turned to Lynette and said: 'The time is right. I feel as if I've gone about as far as I can as a leader, and I miss the family too much now. This will be my last overseas tour.'

It wasn't a planned conversation, which made the decision all the more certain in my mind. I think Lynette knew before I did that it would be my last tour, because she'd organised for the kids to pose for a photo at our front gate in the morning shortly before I left for the airport, something she'd never done before. And each of the kids had given me a soft toy for good luck to hang off my backpack: Austin handed over a moose, Lillian a rabbit and Rosalie a bear, which I believe brought me good luck and certainly gave me comfort each time I looked at the dangling bodies entwined with each other. Each time I carried the backpack a little piece of my family came along for the ride.

The downside to such a spirited performance as the one we

provided in the third Test was the brutal physical drain on the bowlers. This is where I have a real issue with back-to-back Tests, because it disadvantages the team that has played well or won the first of the two games – you have to take 20 wickets to win, and that can take time and a superior level of fitness and intensity, which usually means it is the victors who are the more fatigued of the two sides at game's end.

Of course, in the lead-up to the fourth Test we insisted there would be no excuses. Early on the third day, with a 240-run lead and 10 wickets in the shed during our second innings, we were unbackable favourites. However, as Langer and Hayden were building another double-century opening partnership, the rest of us were all thinking the same thing and we were caught daydreaming by an inspired spell from the West Indies' most notable underachiever, Mervyn Dillon, a quick bowler who, when he had his act together, didn't lose much in comparison to his legendary predecessors. Unfortunately for Dillon and his team, such days were a rarity. Then, having been set 418 to win, the wallowing genetic gifts of the Windies batsmen all came to life in unison and swamped us with a collective brilliance that must have made their supporters question what had transpired during the previous nine straight hidings they'd suffered against Australia.

We couldn't quite find the answer in our hour of need. We were always a wicket away from achieving equilibrium and two from dictating terms. I kept on attacking and calling on my trusted strike weapons to take the crucial wicket that would precipitate a collapse. Looking back, I probably should have given Andy Bichel more of an opportunity, but the 'five specialist bowlers' theory that had worked so well to this point in the series became something of a hindrance here. While my instincts were saying, *Stick with the guys you think*

Lynette and me among the smiling faces of the kids of Udayan.

Three street scenes
from Pakistan.

A family sells
nuts and spices
on the sidewalk.

A range of non-
refrigerated chickens
hang by hooks awaiting
a hungry customer.

A wide variety of
vegetables and other
produce is available
at this market stall.

Fisherwomen from the Kerala Coast, in India's south-west, sort the morning's catch.

A trader in Jaipur shows off his exotic range of spices.

Three barbers ply their trade on the sidewalk in Delhi.

In India, many people have to think outside the square to make a living. Here, an 'ear cleaner' goes about his business.

A carpet seller and his granddaughter in Pakistan. This is another of my favourite photos, as it captures one wise face that has clearly experienced much in life, and another full of innocence.

This time, it's the smiles that say it all: a loving Indian grandmother and her grandson.

Tragically, the criminal underworld on the subcontinent can manipulate situations and leave beggars such as this poor woman being forced to use children to survive from day to day.

Not even leprosy can stop this woman knitting with some skill for her healthy daughter.

A broken ankle added to this woman's distress, but couldn't fracture her spirit.

Serving a meal to the children at Udayan. To Lynette's right is Shamlu Dudeja, the woman who first got me involved in the project.

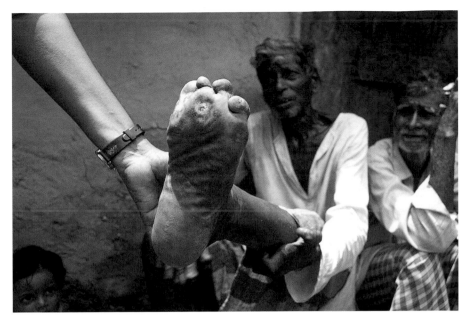

Unfairly, this man has become an outcast because he suffers the ravaging effects of leprosy.

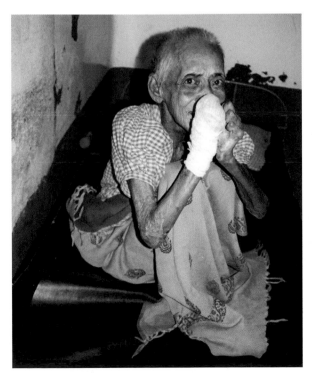

This woman has also been tortured by leprosy and abandoned by her family. When Lynette and I met her in 2003, she so craved human attention that she grabbed hold of us and wouldn't let go.

School's in at Udayan,
July 2003.

With Lakhimi Kumari, a
young girl we personally
sponsor. Both her parents
have leprosy and she con-
tracted polio at six months,
but nothing can counter
her courage and spirit.

I'm always touched by the girls' affection, and
the positive impact Udayan has on their lives.

will make the breakthrough, I felt pressure to make changes to give everyone a go. Instead of Bic I opted for McGrath, who on returning to the tour had come back into the side for the third and fourth Tests. I went that way because of his imposing record in these situations and his skill at taking wickets using his presence, body language and precision. But it was a move that was based more on past miracles rather than the medium pace he was delivering here – a product of him missing half the tour and also the fact that he hadn't fully recovered from the injuries that had restricted him during the recent Australian season. Glenn had been picked on reputation and not on his fitness or state of mind, and this contributed to a substandard performance that, when delivered by an all-time great with exceedingly high expectations who was extremely stressed by his wife's health problems, meant a time bomb was ticking.

During his late-afternoon spell to Ramnaresh Sarwan I sensed the telltale signs that the kettle was on the boil – the right arm reaching across to tug at the collar of his shirt above his left shoulder blade, thus obscuring his mouth, meant he was dissecting himself or the batsman. The question I had to ask myself was straightforward: *Is he worth one more or is it time to try someone else?* Loyalty to a guy who had invariably lifted when we needed him doused my worries about his anxious state, and I made the call to give him one more over. My encouraging words were the ones that had inspired Glenn in the past, but when he delivered the last ball of another unsuccessful over, his emotions boiled over, resulting in a sledge a lunatic would have cringed at: 'What does Lara's cock taste like?' Why that question came out not even Glenn could fathom. Quick as a flash, young Sarwan barked back, 'Why don't you ask your wife?'

Well, the dog was off the leash, launching a machine-gun offensive that essentially had nothing to do with Sarwan, who was merely the vehicle for Glenn to vent his spleen. As this was happening, I was more concerned with organising a bowling change so I missed most of the altercation, which must have looked horrendous on television during the slow-motion replays, but in real time was over in about 10 seconds. What I did see at the end of the tirade was a couple of our guys backing McGrath up and Sarwan standing his ground. To my mind it was a dummy spit and not the first one the big quick had been involved in throughout his career. I told him to settle down as I walked past him, and, with reluctance, he did.

Perhaps I could have done as Richie Richardson did with Curtly Ambrose at Port of Spain in 1995, and I may well have done so if I'd seen the initial altercation and heard the toilet dialogue, but I wasn't fully aware of all that transpired until I saw the replay on television. I knew then that the toys would be flying out of the cot and in my direction. Confirmation of this came just a couple of hours later when James Sutherland contacted me demanding answers, not only for his personal benefit but also to cover his bases before the next day's onslaught from the media. Glenn was apologetic but couldn't really comprehend the bunfight he'd created. It was a foolish act that jeopardised the team's reputation and, of course, his own, and to a degree that of his leader. We'd talked at length about taking responsibility for our own actions, but in this instance ego and frustration had got in the road. I understood his concern for Jane's health and we all felt his pain, but this was a complete brain explosion that went a large way to camouflaging the enormous goodwill and good spirit the series had been played in.

Critics were able to use the images of the McGrath–Sarwan clash and earlier confrontations between Brian Lara and a number of Australian fieldsmen, including me, to conclude that the 'ugly Australians' were back. Not for the first time, on the second day of this Test Lara had stepped up to play the victim, trying to use his team's underdog status to his advantage. As he strolled through our slip cordon on his way to take centre he picked a blue with Matt Hayden, a ploy we were well aware of and had talked about. Our fear was that if we bought into it he would use it to motivate himself, focus on the job at hand and fight back. Lara is a good player against average bowling sides and a great one against formidable attacks, but when harassed into a corner by his own brinkmanship or if he's targeted, he elevates himself into a genius.

Often he would initiate a conversation by being assertive and confrontational, to give himself a cause. I sometimes did the same thing when I was batting. Here in Antigua I loomed as a promising target early in his innings. Out of the blue, as he stood regally waiting for the next delivery, he slammed me for not walking during our first innings. I couldn't let this little upper cut go unrewarded, and countered by saying words to the effect of, 'At least I'm consistent. I just don't walk when it suits me.'

Round one was a draw, but I thought I had him on the canvas soon after when a massive appeal by us for a caught-behind was denied by the umpire. I thought I'd remind him of our previous chat: 'Told you so, you only walk when it suits you.' Well, Brian must have been taking the same pills as Glenn McGrath, because it seemed an alien took control of his being. The next 10 seconds went like this, with Lara screaming 'Shut up!' as Waugh shot back, 'Told you!'

'Shut up!'

'Told you.'

'Shut up!'

'Told you.'

He then walked my way and stood two inches from me, quivering as he said, 'C'mon, let's go, let's get it on right now!'

I'm no boxer, and players should never forget that the eyes of the sporting world are on them. Umpire David Shepherd gave us both an appropriate stern word and the battle resumed.

Three days later, the Windies blazed their way to an amazing victory that filled the Caribbean with hope – something the cricketing world needed. By the time a smooth Cockspur and Coke slid down our parched throats, Brian and I were hugging each other, exchanging shirts and telling each other how good we were. I'd always got on well with him and had a number of 'deep and meaningfuls' with him, dating back to when he was the West Indies' 12th man throughout the 1991 Tests against Australia and continuing on this tour, where he felt ostracised by the fans. He is charming, vulnerable, endearing, moody and impossible to work out at times, and endlessly fascinating. Contrary to reports, this 2003 series was the most pleasant I'd seen between the two sides, with regular sharing of cricket information and advice in the change rooms at the end of play.

Quite a few of the young Windies boys idolised our guys. The young Barbadian paceman Tino Best knew Brett Lee's every move and mimicked many of his mannerisms. On finding out he'd been selected to make his Test debut in front of his home crowd, Tino excitedly rang Brett at 7 a.m. to give him the good news, which was thoughtful but one and a half hours before Binger's usual wake-up call. Marlon Samuels took a shine to yours truly and was always asking questions and looking for insights. Before the Test in Barbados I don't think I'd ever walked out to bat in a Test match to be greeted by the opposing 12th man with a comment like this one: 'Good luck today, I want to see you get a hundred!'

From just about the first time I played against Marlon, in the 2000–01 series in Australia, he'd say, 'Hey man, give me some of your red rag, I need some luck.' Eventually I gave in and cut him a sliver of the tattered cloth, which he now carries out to bat each innings. I had to laugh when he scored a quickfire hundred against India and instead of raising his bat held aloft the red rag between his thumb and index finger, to the bemusement of all those watching, who had no idea what he was doing.

Upon our arrival back in Australia, the fallout from the McGrath incident hadn't finished just yet. The introduction in 2001 of a leadership course conducted at the Victorian Police Academy had been seen as a positive step in the education of cricketers in a variety of areas. I'd been to the initial intake in 2001 and found it an extremely valuable tool in learning about man-management and conflict resolution; we listened to speakers such as Australian Olympic Committee president John Coates, AFL coach Kevin Sheedy and Lieutenant General Peter Cosgrove. Why it had taken two years to repeat a process we all raved about is a mystery, but after our time in the Caribbean, with the board believing the team had an image problem, we reconvened. Afterwards the players, as a group, decided to put in place our own code of conduct, finalising a process that had really been evolving over the previous couple of seasons. We wanted to make it clear to everyone in the squad exactly what was acceptable, what wouldn't be tolerated and how we should carry ourselves. I wanted us to be remembered for all the right reasons and to be the leader in all facets of the game. Being a team that prided itself on innovation and being proactive, we wanted this code to be a blueprint for all junior teams and possibly for international teams, too. The players could no longer hide behind lines like, 'I wasn't sure about that' or 'I didn't know that would happen'. It was all down on paper and every player contracted to the board signed off on its contents.

In my view, self-regulation is the strongest way of ensuring that discipline and behavioural standards are maintained within a group, because everyone then has an input into expectations and takes ownership of them. There is a twisted appeal in breaking rules set and enforced by others; in such circumstances, people can't help testing things out just for the sake of it. For a leader, a secret to good governance is to be prepared and able to enforce rules when necessary, but until such time as that happens you need to encourage individuals to take responsibility as they head in the direction you want them to go without suffocating or stifling their own ambitions or personalities.

43

Hooked for life

The 2003 version of the annual contract meetings were held just before the inaugural Australia–Bangladesh Test series, to be played in Darwin and Cairns during the Australian winter. My meeting was attended by James Sutherland, Trevor Hohns, Michael Brown (the ACB's cricket operations manager), John Buchanan and my manager, Robert Joske. It was a meeting that had to happen, and I went in with modest expectations after being ranked the 13th most important player in Australia during the previous year's negotiations over a one-year contract. I thought the length of that deal was probably fair enough, but still somewhat galling considering the team manager had been given a three-year guarantee after a performance that I considered steady at best.

As it turned out, my surge from 13th to 12th in the rankings was merely cosmetic, but nevertheless a pleasant move and in complete contrast to the ambush that lay in waiting. Contract talks completed, out of the blue I was told by the chairman of selectors, in a statement that was then backed up by the coach, that there were one or two players unhappy with my captaincy. This was the first time I'd heard any such rumblings and I didn't appreciate the coach divulging his perceptions in this forum, especially when he'd had six weeks in the West Indies and a further two months afterwards to let me in on the issue. Further annoying for me was that no reasons, no issues, no clarity and no names were put forward, meaning I had absolutely no idea what the problem was or, in fact, whether there was a genuine concern.

I was never naive enough to think that it was always smooth sailing as a leader and that everyone liked me all the time, because a good leader will invariably ruffle a few feathers whenever he makes a tough call. I didn't have to be loved, but I needed to be respected. The fact that a couple of players weren't ecstatic with the lie of the land was pretty much a normal occurrence; certainly, both AB and Tubs had had players unhappy at times, but it was all part and parcel of team dynamics. As long as issues are addressed swiftly and aren't allowed to fester or spread, then no harm is done. To be told there was an issue without any confirmation or reason was mystifying and incredibly frustrating. The only way for me to investigate was to call a couple of guys in the team whose opinions I trusted and ask them to fill in the gaps in the story. Nothing whatsoever emerged, however, which was a relief but did nothing to ease my concern as to why the matter had been brought up. When I thought about it, the positive news wasn't surprising, as Australia had just won a series in the Caribbean for only the second time in 30 years, and had done so without Shane Warne for the entire series and without Glenn McGrath for the first two Tests. In doing this, we'd become the first team in history to win three Tests in one series in the Caribbean. In the end I decided to let the matter go and concentrate on the upcoming cricket, on the basis that the complaints that had been heard were no more than off-the cuff comments that had been given too much credibility by a few people who were possibly looking to cause trouble. Sadly, though, a link had been taken out of the chain of trust between Buck and me that day, and the flow of information between us and bouncing of ideas off each other that had once been so relaxed never proceeded with the same ease again.

The experiment of playing winter Tests at new venues was welcomed by the players but detested by the Nine Network, whose ratings suffered at the hands of a visiting team who were no better than most of the first-grade teams running around Sydney. As Test matches, these ones were statistically enhancing but in reality more of an exhibition, with tutorials in the change rooms afterwards. I'm all for the expansion of the sport, but Bangladesh's rushed elevation to Test status reeked of political manoeuvres and did nothing for their cricketers' confidence or for the game's credibility. Personally, back-to-back hundreds proved to me that my concentration remained spot on and the mental toughness was still evident, but little else.

Matthew Hayden came to me after missing out on the teddy bear's picnic, looking for an insight into how to cash in against inferior teams. I often found that scoring runs against a weaker side could be more demanding mentally than succeeding against top-liners, because the competitive streak that normally lifted me wasn't there. Personal pride and the ability to play in the present were the traits that needed to be aroused. The answer I offered Matt was, 'Respect your opposition and show respect to yourself and play the next ball to the best of your capabilities.' I took on the attitude of challenging myself to never take an outcome for granted and to enjoy and appreciate the effort needed to concentrate totally.

I also enjoyed the question-and-answer sessions that took place after each day's play. The Bangladeshis' quest for knowledge indicated that they would eventually make it through to the other end and be competitive in international cricket. One guy who caught my attention during his brief but positive stays at the crease was Test cricket's youngest centurion, Mohammad Ashraful, who surprisingly didn't have a bat sponsor. During a brief chat about my MRF bat he indicated how much he liked the look of my gloves, so I said to him, 'You score a fifty in the next Test and they're yours.' Obviously the thought of a decent set of mitts played heavily on his mind, for a pair of ducks awaited him in Cairns, but as I felt partly responsible for his demise I still handed over the much-sought-after items.

No one's reputation or status was enhanced more during the two Tests than our 12th man, Andy Bichel. The task of letting a player know he'd be missing out on the action was without doubt the toughest I experienced as a captain. I always endeavoured to let the 12th man know as soon as I could that he'd been demoted, so that everyone could relax leading into the match. Generally I did this at the last practice session, and nine times out of 10 it came down to a choice between two of the bowlers. For that reason, the captain became the prime target for the duelling contestants to have a final 'shootout' at as they strove to impress. Once a decision was reached by the selectors, I would head in the direction of the relegated guy as discreetly as possible, but as soon as he saw me coming his way there wasn't much need for many words. All I could offer was 'Be ready when the next chance comes around' and 'Keep working hard'. In Cairns, it was a particularly bitter pill for Bic to swallow as his family had travelled up for the occasion and a plethora of soft wickets were to be had but, as usual, he just said, 'I understand. I'll keep working hard in the nets. If you need anything I'll be there – and good luck, champ!'

The guy was a dream team man with quality and character in abundance. Further confirming his selflessness was the advice he gave fellow fast man Brett Lee during our sluggish start to the second Test, when the visitors went past 150 with only one wicket down on a green, seaming pitch. Instead of escorting the drinks cart onto the field, Bic headed off in the direction of Bing to give him a few tips in the hope of rectifying a couple of technical hiccups that had caused him to fall away in his action. Soon we were back on course for a predictable win, but the victory was outshone by one man, whose attitude genuinely showed he could put aside personal ambitions for the good of the side and, even further, do so in a manner that could jeopardise his own cricket future. That type of act ensures that no one in a team slips into complacency, for to do so would be to let down not only yourself but also the team. And much worse than that, not to put in is to show no respect for the 12th man who hasn't got the opportunity.

Respect for the baggy green cap goes without saying, and my love of what it stands for and the memories it created for me make it my most prized possession.

My wish for its future is simple. I'd love nothing better than for my great-grandkids to pick it up, finger the frayed felt, recoil slightly at its musty odour, ask why the kangaroo has all but vanished, inquire about the faded brown stains on the inside (blood from that collision with Jason Gillespie) and then try it on and have their dreams ignited by its magical powers. The line that best summed up the baggy green for me was penned by a journalist who wrote that when we walked out onto the ground wearing our caps we 'looked like 11 prize fighters entering the ring'.

When I was playing, the baggy green was more than a symbol that its owner had been inducted into an elite club. It lifted our spirits, gave us an aura and indicated to the opposition that we were a tight unit who would take a lot of breaking down. As captain I felt enormous pride looking over my shoulder to see behind me a line of caps in various stages of ageing. As the years rolled on, my cap disintegrated around the peak line and separated along the crease, giving it a ragged appearance. This led to a ridiculous amount of debate as to whether or not it should be retired, but I never contemplated replacing it just because it had aged. I saw the stains, tears, fading and fraying as badges of honour, each imperfection telling a story. To trade it in would have been a betrayal. I loved the fact it had character and was flawed, because that meant it was full of memories.

I also didn't want to disrespect it by letting it fall completely apart, so in 2002 I compromised and had it steam-cleaned and patched up. The underside of the peak was turned over and placed on the top, replacing the torn piece, while some new fabric was attached to the underside. It was the equivalent of minor plastic surgery that appeased the antagonists and ensured my baggy green would make the entire journey with me.

★

After I scored successive unbeaten centuries in Darwin and Cairns, a proposed chat that Trevor Hohns had wanted to have straight after the series didn't materialise until many weeks later, just before the start of a two-Test series against Zimbabwe scheduled for the start of the 2003–04 season. Quite clearly the selectors were looking at succession planning – as they should, considering it is part of their charter and a responsibility they must take on. Trevor and I agreed we'd take it series by series, which in reality was no different from how it had been in the recent past, but quite obviously with me now at 38 years of age the issue was becoming more relevant with each year.

Following on from the thoughts I'd had in the Caribbean about not touring again, the obvious choice for a finish line was the upcoming New Year's Test in Sydney against India. The two Zimbabwe Tests would be over by mid-October; the India matches were due to begin in the first week of December. The next Test series after that would be in Sri Lanka, beginning in March, so I expressed a desire to Trevor that, form and fitness notwithstanding, for the SCG to be my ultimate place to retire. It wasn't long before James Sutherland was on the phone wanting to know when the announcement would be made, and for the *Sydney Morning Herald*'s Peter Roebuck to be following up a leak he had been given. After the ding-dong battle of the previous 12 months, it seemed that, in Sydney at least, the *Herald* had the inside running on the hot mail about the make-up of the Australian team while the *Daily Telegraph*, which had mounted a strong campaign for me and against the selectors, was shut out.

The decision to make an announcement early went against my grain, for the simple fact that I'd always wanted to finish without too many people knowing, to just walk out without any fanfare. I subscribed to the Carl Rackemann school of thought, which is, 'You don't make a statement to let everyone know you're debuting, so why should you have to declare your intention to finish?' If it had been that simple I could have been a contented man, but I knew the bloodhounds would be sniffing around, and with plenty of loose lips and attention-seeking sources in the mix, I needed to be proactive. Also swaying my judgement was the inevitable relentless questioning about my retirement and the destabilising effect it would have on the team, especially if I failed once or twice early in the summer.

Once my mind was made up to make an announcement as soon as possible, I was relieved and eager to get it over and done with so everyone could concentrate on the demanding series against India and so I could finally let my family know that the constant absences from home would be ending. I knew the time was right for many reasons, including my good form over the previous nine months, the fact that the finale would be in Sydney in front of my family and friends, finishing against the team I'd first played against 18 years ago – and, most significantly, because of a comment Rosalie had made at the dinner table: 'Daddy, I don't want you to go away any more.' As soon as she said that, it was as if a weight had been removed from my shoulders. There was no need for me to worry about how my retirement was going to be perceived by the various spin merchants. The reason was pure and simple: the time was right, and I knew it in my heart.

The designated day, November 26, duly arrived. I practised my speech in the lounge room in front of a confused audience made up of four-year-old Austin and two-year-old Lillian, who would have much preferred to be watching the Hi-5 spectacular that had just been terminated by the remote control. Austin had only one question for me about the whole episode: 'Does it mean finishing all cricket, even with me?'

The day ahead was one I both dreaded and couldn't wait for. I wasn't sure how I'd handle it emotionally, as it wasn't something I'd done before; perhaps the realisation of it actually happening would hit me between the eyes. I wanted to announce it without anyone holding my hand or delivering a spiel that wouldn't add to the moment, so for that reason I notified the people who needed to know only a couple of hours before the press conference was to begin. I didn't see not involving Cricket Australia (the ACB's new name as of 2003) as a snub; I simply believe there are some things in life you just have to do yourself.

As it turned out, I probably didn't need to sweat on or rehearse my opening paragraph half a dozen times, for the prepared speech came out naturally, albeit shakily to begin with. Walking away from the throng hand in hand with Lynette through the members' bar at the SCG, it felt like the handbrake had been released and equilibrium had been restored. Life had taken a turn in another direction and I couldn't wait to see where it was going to take me.

First up, though, was my desire to finish on a positive note, and part of this quest involved me being as innovative and proactive as I could. I began specialised sprint work in conjunction with the team's fitness trainer, Jock Campbell, and one of Australia's finest-ever all-round track-and-field athletes, Peter Hadfield. Finding a new challenge provided a spark that left me invigorated. Each fitness session came and went with an improvement and by the time the team convened in Brisbane for the first Test against India I felt sharp, alert and five years younger. I knew the hunger was still there, not because it should have been or because someone had made a positive comment, but because I wasn't taking the easy option or looking for a short cut. This realisation had come during an extra sprint session that Jock had pencilled in for me. The culmination of the 90-minute routine was 20 sprints, each of 30 metres, at the end of which I was struggling for breath but happy to have finished the assignment. After the final sprint was executed with that extra burst of energy that goes with completing an arduous task, I was retrieving my tracksuit top and car keys when I began to wonder if it had been lap number 20 or only 19. I didn't think I'd miscounted, but my conscience wouldn't let my walk off without making sure. It was a mini-battle that had to be won, my own little test to see whether or not I still wanted to tackle the tasks ahead. It was inconsequential in fitness terms, but a real barometer with regard to my attitude, and by lining up for the extra sprint I answered my own interrogation.

Unfortunately, my retirement announcement and the fact that Ricky Ponting was quickly named as the future captain didn't have the effect I'd envisaged. Instead of diluting the attention paid to my every move, the media's preferred option of dissection brought an intense focus on how the now 'farewell' Tests would pan out. I was humbled by the interest but overwhelmed by the snowball that had been set in motion. I was also concerned that the team's focus might be distracted, which was ironic considering that minimising the distractions had been a major factor in deciding how I would handle things.

★

If I thought the cricketing gods were going to be kind to me as a gesture to my longevity, that illusion was swiftly shattered during two calamitous overs before the luncheon interval on the second day of the first Test, at the Gabba. A mix-up as I was striving to scamper a third for Damien Martyn, which led to Marto being run out, didn't look good live, nor did it improve on the endless replays. For some critics it represented just the tonic they needed to bring me down a notch or two as I began what they perceived as a long goodbye tour. Down at pitch level, the run-out was caused by a combination of my eagerness to get into the flow of the game through aggressive running, a line-ball call by me and a couple of steps towards me by Marto that had me committed to go for that third run. Afterwards Marto and I accepted that it was just one of those things and that we needed to move on to issues that lay ahead.

I didn't expect to have my integrity questioned at the press conference that evening as I sat passively copping cynical remarks and questions that implied I was a serial offender when it came to confusion that led to my partner being run out. Making the day a total write-off for me was the fact that two balls after the run-out I was dismissed for nought, which confirmed my place behind Glenn McGrath and Shane Warne as Australia's No. 3 collector of Test-match ducks with 22. I'm pretty sure none of the first 21 was as memorable as this particular ill-fated episode. A short rising ball from their left-arm quick, Zaheer Khan, jumped venomously off a moist, green-tinged pitch and stung me hard on the knuckles before narrowly eluding a diving keeper and eventually spearing off down to the fine leg boundary for four. All I could think was, *Close call, lucky four, it might just be your day.* It was then I became aware of squeals and animated finger-pointing from the fieldsmen, and realised that a bail had been dislodged. In the space of a few seconds I had dodged a bullet but copped the rebound, and all I could do was wait for the third umpire's decision and trudge my sorry butt off to eat a lunch I didn't taste or need.

It was a humiliating dismissal and I couldn't work out how it had happened. I'd played the same shot a thousand times before in Tests and never trampled on my stumps. The thought of a final campaign, the enormous emotional energy I'd expended in the lead-up and my burning desire to do well had accentuated my every move and not only put me on edge but obviously my batting partners as well. My short stint at the crease was akin to a hyperactive kid's reaction after pouring a can of Coke down his throat. It was a low moment, walking off with my dream turned to a horror flick so quickly and so unexpectedly. My mind was bereft of any meaningful objectives for the next hour or so as I replayed the moment, searching for a glimmer of hope to inspire me to forget what had happened and move on. However, the slate was wiped clean the second I realised that the only way to put my misery to good use was to will myself to turn my state of mind around.

I had to say to myself, *Don't be soft – find the mongrel within and just get out there and get stuck straight back into the action.* I was proud to get 56 not out in our second dig with the eyes of the world on me. Marto was unbeaten on 66 when I surprised everyone by declaring late on the final day of what had been a rain-interrupted Test, setting India the unlikely target of 199 from 23 overs. He, like me, was happy to sacrifice an opportunity to get a hundred to make India sweat out a short onslaught while we sought to weaken a couple of their top-order players before moving onto the second Test. In my mind, I also entertained the long shot of a miraculous win when no one expected any chance of a result. A captain can make things happen if he instils belief and plants the seed of hope. Of course, the chances of a win were one in a million, but those odds were enticing enough to make sure I at least acknowledged them.

Of concern was the fact that for the first time in 22 Tests we had conceded a first-innings deficit, a precursor to our struggles to get wickets in the remaining three Tests without the great Warne–McGrath combination. The niggling injuries to the back-up ensemble didn't aid our pursuit of victory, further softening our ability to make inroads into a world-class batting line-up and seeing us spend an unaccustomed amount of time chasing the ball around the park.

Despite a masterly batting display from Ricky Ponting in the second Test, at Adelaide, and our remarkable effort of scoring 400 runs on the opening day, we were revisited by the ghosts of Kolkata when V.V.S. Laxman and Rahul Dravid put on 303 for the fifth wicket after India had fallen to 4/85 in reply to our 556. Rahul's batting was poetic, with flowing follow-throughs that capitalised on exceptional footwork and a rock-solid base. His head was like the statue of David, allowing for perfect balance and easy hand–eye coordination. We'd formed a mutual respect that had started back in 1998 with a long dinner conversation about cricket, when he'd quizzed me endlessly about the mental side of the game. Rahul wanted the edge that would elevate his game to the next level, and at the Adelaide Oval he completed the journey. As an opponent I respected his professionalism, and as a friend I admired his balanced views and the way he treated people from all walks of life equally.

Unfortunately, despite the free lesson these two batsmen gave us, we failed to adhere to the basics and recklessly handed the match to

India on a platter, which earnt us John Buchanan's wrath. Buck's inti-mate, incisive written thoughts provoked debate not only within the team but also among the general public after they again unintentionally fell into the wrong hands. Buck had every right to explore avenues he thought were problem areas, especially after I'd chatted to him at the conclusion of day four about our flat attitude and reactive play, and I expected we'd address these concerns next morning. This Buck did, but the stinging nature of his comments, which included the statement that our lack of focus was 'un-baggy-green, soulless and immature' and that we were more concerned with 'deal-making, sponsors, Tug's farewell to Adelaide, the choice of helmets, what the media is saying about you, domestic games after this Test match', in my opinion pushed the bounds of fairness. It would have been much more beneficial if these criticisms had been delivered face to face, not slid under hotel-room doors just as the boys were about to nod off. They were tough to swallow, but a coach must say what he feels without worrying about hurting anyone's pride or ego, so I had to admire Buck's conviction, if not his method.

We also had to recognise that this wasn't the usual soft-underbelly Indian touring squad, but rather a hardened force forged by Sourav Ganguly, their feisty leader, who saw his own reputation being gouged out by the outcome of his team's duels with Australia. Not helping us was the fact that no Test in this series was played at the WACA, where the bouncy pitch meant a virtually guaranteed victory for us, and that we encountered the flattest, lowest Adelaide pitch I ever played on, a surface the Indians could have played on blindfolded. With only two Tests to go, in Melbourne and Sydney, we faced the imposing task of countering a team who were known as excellent front-runners and who wanted desperately to dispel the notion that they were worthless away from home.

★

Soon the annual pilgrimage to Melbourne for the Boxing Day Test was under way, with the family and mountainous amounts of luggage – including bags of presents that Santa had dropped off early, and many more presents for teammates' kids – in tow. It was both strange and comforting to know that a normal Christmas awaited us next time around. Even Christmas had had to fit in around cricket for all the years of my career, and it seemed every other celebration or family get-together had to be slotted in around tours or commitments to the game, too. It was a price we were willing to pay as a family, and in the overall scheme of things it was accepted as a given.

By 2003–04 the Boxing Day Test had become like a true 'home' Test match, with the ACB generously paying airfares and organising apartment-style living quarters for us that gave the children room to move and a more familiar environment and allowed us to take along our nanny, who had entered the fray when Lillian was born. Entertaining three kids with walks along the Yarra or morning swim sessions at the hotel pool alleviated me of the dual stresses of clawing our way back into the series as a team and the *EDtv* script my life had become.

Our struggles with the ball didn't abate on day one at the MCG, as Virender Sehwag's cavalier batting technique was more than compensated for by his unorthodox attacking style, which shies away from keeping the ball on the ground. Sehwag is an exceptionally dangerous player in that he looks vulnerable and likely to get out at any time but behind that exterior lies a remarkable talent capable of tearing apart attacks and reputations. He answers to no one, refuses to be intimidated and has abundant self-belief, which allows him to play with a clear head and a simple formula. He's a role model for the KISS – keep it simple, stupid – method of play and a breath of fresh air for cricket. However, with a free spirit comes a proneness to self-destruction, and with the score at 3/311 and his personal tally at 195, Sehwag smashed a Simon Katich full toss down the throat of our new opening bowler,

Nathan Bracken, who was fielding on the deep midwicket boundary, to precipitate a major collapse that gave us the opening we craved.

The next day, Ponting's extravagant and deceptively powerful stroke repertoire threw India's attack off balance for the second Test in a row as he completed back-to-back double centuries. This guy is the complete package, having converted his natural gifts into a polished product through dedicated practice, an inquiring mind and a hunger for runs, all of which help separate the good from the great. Punter combined with Matt Hayden in a double-barrelled assault that left the bowlers shell-shocked and with no respite because it went against the normal basis of partnership, where one batsman is passive and the other aggressive. Instead of a pit bull terrier and a labrador playing ball, the guide dog had been replaced by a Rottweiler. I came in with the score at 4/373, an increasingly familiar situation, as the top order had again dominated, and I found myself the target of an attack trying to salvage credibility by charging in against a fresh batsman with the second new ball. Shortly after, through a combination of an error of judgement on my part and a bouncer that didn't rise as high as I'd banked on, I had only my arm to stop potential broken ribs. I braced for the impact.

When you're hit by a cricket ball, you know straightaway whether or not it's going to cause any damage. On this occasion the dull sound I heard as the ball slammed into the outside of my elbow alerted the pain sensors that this was a nasty one. Not wanting to show too much concern or to give the bowler a victory, I matter-of-factly pulled back my sleeve to see an egg-sized lump filled with blood. This wasn't what I'd hoped for, and neither was the fact that I couldn't exert any pressure on Errol Alcott's finger when minutes later he instructed me to squeeze it as hard as I could. I was now confronted with a predicament all batsmen fear: the real possibility of having to desert my post because of pain and injury. A final attempt to grab the bat and play a couple of air defensive shots gave me a sharp, debilitating pain, so off I went, not knowing if this was my final scene as an Australian player. Soon after, I was in a medical clinic wishing I'd been a regular churchgoer in return for one small favour: that the X-rays would show no break. It was crazy now to think that as I sat there I had made my mind up that even if it showed a crack I was going to play. No doubt, if that had been the case I wouldn't have played, but when something you treasure is about to be taken away you cling for dear life to protect it. My heart was in my mouth as the X-rays were illuminated against the fluorescent backdrop and the specialist calmly said, to my utter relief, 'There's no break.'

That well-used and trusted friend, the room-service bucket of ice, played a valuable part over the next couple of days as I battled against invading blood that threatened to track into joints and unwanted spaces and cause pain and stiffness. Not even a pressure bandage nor the pain inhibitor Panadeine Forte gave me a realistic chance of making runs on my return to the crease. My forearm blew up to a size Popeye would have been proud of, and the arm had all the life of a newly attached transplanted limb. I didn't have the power to get a ball off the square without worrying about the shooting pain that surged down my arm with each shot. I finished with 19 from 69 agonising balls, hardly my most memorable Test innings.

It was as if fate was saying, 'I know you really want to leave on a special note, but you're going to have to earn it.' Through a combination of stage fright on the part of India – who, when they realised all of a sudden that their dream of winning a series in Australia was possible, promptly baulked at the importance of such an achievement – and our inbred fighting quality, we decisively won the Test despite having been in serious trouble before Sehwag got himself out on day one. It was the type of victory I loved: a real character test where there was no place to hide, where individual players had to find something special within themselves to inspire their teammates to emulate their actions. One man alone can't sustain a comeback, because eventually the chain of action will be broken when the slack isn't taken up. A successful team is one whose collective will can manipulate the crucial moments in their favour by never giving up. We went to Sydney intent on winning the series, while my gut feeling told me India would be happy with a draw.

The Sydney Test, my 168th and final Test appearance, presented me with myriad emotions. I was relieved that I was reaching the end, but unsure what I would feel walking off for the last time. I was apprehensive about the outcome for the team and myself, at peace with the decision, and swamped by the media hysteria and the public's incredible show of support. In many ways, this game was a carbon copy of my first Test, except now I had nothing to prove and I knew my teammates well enough to call them by their nicknames.

The years of my cricket career had blurred and I was undecided if they had gone quickly or slowly, which was a reflection of the profession. The day, month or year was irrelevant; it was just play well this game and then worry about the next one, and so on. There were times when I boarded planes not having thought about the tour until I settled into my seat and contemplated the battles ahead. Regularly, the guys would eat together at a restaurant and have two or three guesses as to which day of the week it was.

Yet there was always something special about drifting off to sleep the night before a Test. The unknown that lay ahead teased, enticed and lured me. There were many sleepless nights, some through the adrenaline rush that comes with success, some with the anxiety that apprehension breeds. I loved the fact that anything was possible, that here was another chance to lay the heart and soul on the line. The great thing about cricket is that failure is inevitable, but coming back from it is the very core of the game and what it is all about.

As I lay alone with my thoughts on the eve of my last Test appearance, I decided I just wanted to go out and enjoy myself and play good cricket. In the end, it was that simple.

Lynette too was retiring from the game, and although she had not physically competed, she had performed the infinitely harder task of experiencing emotions in a more heightened way because the solutions were out of her control. My wife could watch, impart wisdom and give balance and perspective, but ultimately only I could change the result. Today a goodbye kiss at our front door and an 'Enjoy the day' once again kept it simple and appropriate, and then she was off to the phone to organise the 40-something guests a day who were coming to our corporate box, most of them long-time supporters – people who had always been there for us through the good times and the bad, and who don't need to be named because they know who they are.

The trip to the ground was memorable because of the buzz that had formed in and around the SCG. Pubs were already full of fans knocking back their first cold one for the day, while parents held their children by one hand and carried a bag or Esky in the other as they headed for the turnstiles and a day of bonding. People had been queuing since 5 a.m. in the quest to sit in their favourite seats and a sea of souvenir red hankies, given out by the *Daily Telegraph*, were waved at me as the team threaded our way through the masses into the change rooms. I felt proud to be acknowledged by so many yet embarrassed by all the attention, and in my reflective mood I noticed again the real passion and love of the game that so many diehard fans possess. I also realised that many of the crowd had shared 18 years of emotion with me and had been a big part of my life with their support and loyalty. They had seen me grow up, evolve, succeed, fail, excel and disappoint and I guess they must have felt like a little piece of them was retiring, too.

It was a morning of heightened emotions, beginning with the national anthems being played as the teams lined up in front of the capacity crowd. I was aware of the many banners that bore my name and the replica hankies fluttering about, but it was holding the baggy green over my heart for the last time that made me realise more than anything how fortunate I'd been to represent my country so many times. Singing 'Advance Australia Fair' while lined up alongside your mates is a totally unifying experience, and knowing it wouldn't happen again like this intensified the moment. As I scoured the ground, focusing on the majesty of the charming old Members Stand with its green corrugated roof, quaint architecture and remodelled but still old-fashioned clock defying the trends of a sterile digital age, I could relate to that old saying, 'You don't know what you've got till it's gone.' The SCG lost much of its beauty when the Hill and many of the stands made way for a mismatch of concrete structures, yet on this day it still held a magical quality, as if all the events and images that had occurred there had been trapped inside and were floating around, creating a special atmosphere that flared everyone's nostrils and awakened their senses.

Accolades and gestures take on extra significance when they come from teammates, because respect from within the inner circle has to be earnt. Ricky, as vice-captain, had told me to wait inside the change room while the team made its way out onto the field after I lost the toss, and a guard of honour greeted my arrival. I didn't really know what to do except shake everyone's hand and thank them. The genuineness of this moment uplifted me and made me feel proud to be their leader, but as we were about to find out, the opposition had plans to ruin the party. Early on we were our own worst enemies, dropping chances and taking a 'wicket' off a no-ball as we squandered the initial assistance the pitch offered us. It was a false start that paved the way for more than two days of misery, with Laxman excelling against us yet again and the batting maestro, Sachin Tendulkar, clinically accumulating runs, eliminating extravagance and controlling his tempo, shot selection and mind to produce a faultless classic.

I had learnt over the years that when great players start by concentrating on their defence and technique they have ambitions to stay for the long haul, so when Tendulkar let scoring opportunities pass by in preference to sizing up the pace and bounce in the pitch, the signs were ominous. When things were running smoothly I'd regularly have suggestions coming from many directions, but with India at 7/700 the ideas had well and truly run out and I was given a final taste of one of the more deflating things a cricket leader can face. One thing I hated as a captain was waiting for the opposition to declare, because it meant they were in total control and dictating terms. There was no doubt our attack struggled in this Test and that was nothing to be ashamed of, but it was frustrating that the cutthroat nature of modern-day sport meant that we fielded four bowlers in Sydney who each carried niggling injuries into the game for fear that if they'd revealed all before the Test their chance may have slipped by.

Eventually it all came down to the last day of the series, after four days of bat dominating ball, with us needing what would have been a world-record fourth-innings score to win. We were flattered that there was talk of a run chase, which was a reflection of our long-held attitude of always going all out for a win, to only rein in our pursuit as a last resort. Our plan this day was to bat as normally as possible until tea and then reassess, with the view of having a dash at the unlikely win if we had seven or eight wickets left. Unfortunately for us, we kept losing a wicket just as we had visions of hauling in the 443 runs needed. About two-thirds of the way through the middle session, I made my way to the crease in much the same manner as I had against England 12 months before, catching many in the crowd by surprise with my speed. The applause was constant and this time around I soaked it up, savouring every second, speechless at the people's enthusiasm and generosity of spirit. My sense of serenity as I took centre was so strong it was scary. I literally felt as if I was back in the school playground about to have a bash with my buddies. Thankfully, the boldness of youth snapped me into game mode when India's 18-year-old keeper Parthiv Patel chirped at me with a sly, 'Let's finish it off with a slog-sweep.'

That quip was music to my ears. Firstly, it engaged me into a chat, which I never minded, and secondly, it had come from a young pup. The art of good banter is to come back quickly and with something that hits the mark. Quite calmly, I swung around and said to his face, 'Listen, mate, how about showing a bit of respect? When I played my first Test, you were still running around in nappies.' The muffled chuckles of the in-close fieldsman and the half-defeated smile from the instigator of our conversation signalled that the battle was on, but also that humour could have its turn as well.

While the keeper reminded me of my debut as a 20-year-old, I played out most of my last innings with Simon Katich, a guy who I see as ready-made to fill the role I occupied for so many years. I can see his fire within, his quiet brooding intensity and love of a challenge against the odds. 'Kato' thrives on competition and has the ability to lead others. A snapshot of his attitude had come to light during his first fitness session with the NSW team at the start of this 2002–03 season, after he had transferred from WA during the 'off-season'. At a preseason camp we were given a rock-climbing exercise best suited to guys with thin wiry builds who could scale a vertical face with their lightweight frame. Kato managed to get three-quarters to the top before he seized up and was unable to climb any further. For the next 40 minutes he clung on by his fingertips, unable to progress but steadfastly refusing to back down. It was a glimpse into his make-up and why he is a future Australian captain. Leaders must make players better because of their presence and make them want to share the journey. Simon Katich, in my mind, would do that.

Kato and I batted aggressively for a couple of hours, and in the latter stages of our partnership considered making a dash for the target, but as soon as we went on an all-out attack, half a dozen guys were stationed on the boundary. Needing 12 or more runs an over we required a miracle, but Sourav wasn't willing to play ball and the match began to die a slow death. By this stage I was into the 60s, and having received such phenomenal crowd support I decided to have a go at reaching the ton as a way of paying back the crowd and finishing on a personal high. The plan was simple: attack the relatively inexperienced left-arm spinner Murali Kartik by trying to slog-sweep him to the shorter boundary, and milk ones and twos off the more accomplished Anil Kumble, whose quicker leg spin, when dumped into the rough, was virtually impossible to dominate. Proving that even 168 Tests isn't an antidote for a hot head, 20 runs short of fairytale No. 2 I felt the old rush of blood and threw the plans out the window. My last shot as an Australian batsman was a mistimed slog-sweep off Kumble that Tendulkar calmly accepted close to the boundary rope at deep square leg.

My walk off the ground was surreal, with Indian players running up to congratulate me and the capacity crowd standing as one. I was pleased and satisfied that I'd helped save a Test, glad we hadn't lost the series and humbled by the attention. It wasn't until I saw Adam Gilchrist come out the gate that I suddenly said to myself, *You bloody idiot, we might lose the game because of that reckless shot!*

All I could manage to Gilly was 'Sorry, mate' as we passed each other. In typical fashion, he responded, 'Don't worry, you've got nothing to be sorry about.'

Three balls later I did, though, because Adam was stumped and the game was well and truly back on. This is the beauty of cricket and why it has had such a hold over me for more than 30 years. No battle is ever lost until the last ball. It is always an adventure – nothing is ever guaranteed, and if you want something badly enough and are prepared to work at it anything is possible. I loved the challenge of trying to alter and steer the course of a match and impose my will and desire on it. Thankfully, on this occasion we held on, which, while not quite the perfect finish, did represent something of an accomplishment in that by hanging in and gutsing it out we'd drawn a Test match that we might well have lost. One of the goals I had set out to achieve as a captain when I was first appointed was to help make the Australian team capable of doing precisely that.

Cricket had given me many cherished memories, but to be carried around the SCG on the shoulders of my teammates, with an Aussie flag draped around my neck and the crowd going berserk, was as good as it could possibly be. To then be greeted by Lynette, Rosalie, Austin and Lillian on the ground was to know I was blessed, and lucky to have a supportive and loving family who'd sacrificed so much to allow me to fulfil my dream.

Hours later, with the crowd gone, I walked back out onto the hallowed turf and inspected the pitch for one final time. With me were Lynette and the legendary Barry 'Nugget' Rees, a bloke who is special in every way. Jason Gillespie had organised for Nugget to travel from Adelaide to cheer me on in my final Test.

From a humble beginning dusting tennis racquets at the Rowe & Jarman sports store 30-odd years ago, Nugget has become part of the very fabric of Test cricket at the Adelaide Oval. He is renowned for his humble, kind and gentle nature and exemplary manners. He is a beacon of goodness, loved by all. Today he proudly wears the baggy green cap given to him in 1962 by former Test star Norman O'Neill, having proudly supported South Australian and Australian teams for the best part of 50 years, looking after the players' needs, running errands and regularly standing on a table to recite motivational messages to the teams. So one-eyed is Nugget's support of Australia that he was eventually made to wear batting gloves to muffle his enthusiastic clapping.

Now, as I surveyed the worn and dusty footholes and cracks that meandered along the entirety of the pitch, I saw Nugget play an imaginary defensive shot with the same dreams I had harboured as a kid. It had been a long journey from the uneven lawn of the backyard in Panania to the playing field of the SCG, one that had taken me to opposite ends of the emotional spectrum and to all corners of the globe in a quest for fulfilment. The game had questioned what I was about and who I'd become, and provided a crash course in life's lessons.

I was born with cricket in my blood and I'll die that way. I'm sure of that, because even today, each time I drive past an oval and notice a game in progress, I'll slow down to make certain I see the bowler deliver the ball with enthusiastic anticipation to a batsman who has equally ambitious aspirations, as the fielders hover with intent.

There's nothing like it, the excitement of the unknown. Once it seduces you, you're hooked for life.

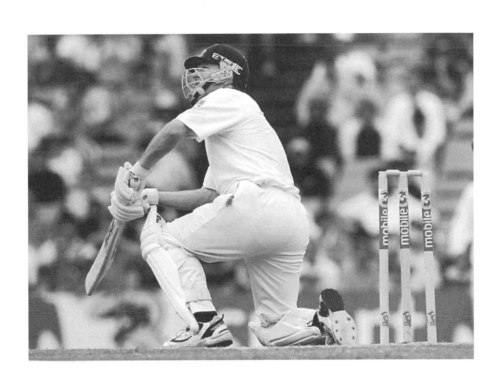

Life on the road provides enduring and contrasting images, such as (LEFT) when we were able to burn the now unnecessary tickets to the last two days' play after beating South Africa by a record margin at Johannesburg in 2002, and Adam Gilchrist's exhausted face (RIGHT) after a gruelling flight to the Caribbean 12 months later.

The Australian team in casual mode after the Test against Zimbabwe in Perth in 2003. Clockwise from bottom left: Glenn McGrath, Andy Bichel, me, Ricky Ponting, Justin Langer, Damien Martyn, Adam Gilchrist, Darren Lehmann, Matthew Hayden, Brett Lee, Jason Gillespie, Shane Warne.

The Barmy Army vents its collective spleen after I am finally dismissed on the last day of the fourth Ashes Test of 2002–03, at the MCG. Their abuse did nothing for my migraine.

To help sell their pies in 2002–03, Vili's added this message to their product after I was left out of a 30-man preliminary squad for the 2003 World Cup: 'You're 5 for not many chasing 250 in the World Cup semi-final. Who do you want at the crease? Pick Steve Waugh now!'

The cover drive that sealed my 'perfect day', Sydney, January 3, 2003.

The fans on what used to be the SCG Hill share in my 'last ball of the day' hundred in my final Ashes Test.

Before the Windies tour in 2003, Lynette organised a family shot with Austin, then aged 3, Rosalie, 6, and Lillian, 18 months, at the front gate on the day of my departure.

The Aussie team on the
pitch at Bridgetown in
2003, after one of the
gutsiest victories I was
ever involved in.

Earlier in the tour, during
the first Test, at Georgetown in Guyana, I split
the webbing between my
middle and typing fingers.
I wondered if the 'fishing
line' used for the job
really needed to be
this thick.

With members of the
Bangladesh team in the
dressing-rooms in Cairns
after the two-Test winter
series in 2003.

There are three things that stand out for me when I think about the day I announced my retirement from international cricket.

One is the time I spent rehearsing my speech in front of an enthusiastic audience of two: Austin and Lilli Waugh.

Then there was the feeling of some trepidation as I walked into the media conference.

And finally there was the smile Lynette couldn't lose after the timing of my career's end had been confirmed.

More and more as my career moved towards its conclusion, I wanted my family to be a part of my cricket life.

Rosie does a cartwheel on the MCG while Lilli and I look on.

The kids have posed for the obligatory press photographs on Christmas Day 2003, and now it's time for the presents.

Austin practises his golf swing at the Gabba.

News Limited photographer Phil Hillyard took a series of family shots before my farewell Test. This is one of our favourites.

My successor, Ricky Ponting, gives me a friendly pat as I run through a 'guard of honour' at the start of my last Test.

As we made our way around the SCG after my final Test had been drawn, the press were keen for another group Waugh shot. Lynette and I were thrilled with the way the kids handled all the attention.

Walking off my home ground after one last walk to the middle, with Lynette and the legendary Nugget Rees.

MY LIFE WITH STEPHEN
by Lynette Waugh

When I was a young girl in my primary school years I had a fascination with the airport. I would often ask my parents to take me there and I even remember visiting my Auntie Gloria, who sold flowers from a fancy white wrought-iron cart in the departure area. I left my only worldly possession, my first watch engraved with my name, jammed into the coin slot of a Space Invaders game – a result of trying to push a stuck coin in – at the airport. I recall leaving that day drowned in sorrow. Little did I know that my connection with the airport, and my rollercoaster ride of happiness and sadness when I visited it, would become a major part of my life some 10 years later when I met Stephen.

My first serious encounter with Stephen was at a school dance in a community hall at Milperra, in Sydney in 1983. I was 17 years old and Stephen was 18 years old and we had both just finished our last year of high school. I was at the dance with some friends from East Hills Girls High School. I have a vague recollection of meeting him through our friend Richard Lane on that night, but it wasn't one of those introductions that I thought was going to change my life. Stephen, on the other hand, can recount every small detail about me – who I was with and even the dress I was wearing that night. At the traditional Year 12 muck-up day, where the boys' and girls' schools take to battles against each other armed with items of mess and mischief like cold spaghetti, water and flour bombs, talc and tomato-sauce bottles, I remember him dousing me with a bowl full of spaghetti. But I missed him trying to impress me there, too! Later that week I received a phone call at home from someone named Stephen asking me to his Year 12 formal. I still didn't remember him. 'Stephen who?' I asked.

Stephen would probably say that persistence finally paid off or that it was third time lucky. My reasoning was a fair deal simpler. Going to the boys' school dance was a really big social event, especially if you attended a girls' school like me. I, like Stephen, was reasonably shy; I'd been keen on another Year 12 boy but an invitation from him was clearly not going to come my way. When Stephen called me from a public phone box and asked me to go to the dance with him, it wasn't like me to accept an invitation from someone I didn't know. I'm not sure if I was just caught up in the excitement of teenage life or of having a date for the formal, or whether it just felt right to take a chance on this stranger who had entered my life.

So, our first official date was the 1983 Year 12 Formal Dinner for East Hills Boys School at the Camerlang Lounge in Padstow. As a date, Stephen did everything right. He was on time, had a corsage for me and even wore a jacket, which impressed me, even if it was worn over an apricot-and-white-striped shirt. Our date was a great success. I liked him a lot, and at last he had made an impression on me. There was an instant friendship between us. He was very likeable and easy to be around. He wasn't a show-off teenager eager to impress his mates. He was rather quiet and shy, but also funny. The only concern I had was on one of our early dates when a friend and I had to wait in the car while he went into his friend's house to change. They were absolutely ages returning, and when they finally emerged two unhappy girls greeted them with, 'Where have you been?'

'Watching cricket,' was the reply. A one-day match was on TV.

'I hate cricket,' I said.

'That's the end of you,' he joked dryly.

How ridiculous, I thought, *he must be joking*. Thankfully, this didn't prove to be a setback.

We spent loads, if not all, of our free time together. It was a very steady friendship. Looking back now, I'd say there was a real connection between us. It wasn't that we fell madly in love but that we seemed to walk slowly into it. We just seemed to be on the same path. It was a wonderful time in our lives – we had great dreams ahead. As teenagers leaving school and choosing a career path, it felt like our adult life was beginning. Life was fun. We shared in each other's excitement of what we were going to do in our lives. I had chosen to be an early-childhood teacher and was hoping to get accepted into college. Stephen, on the other hand, had never really expressed exactly what he wanted to do. He had outstanding HSC marks of 305 and I encouraged him to enrol in college to make use of his excellent results.

I wasn't aware of his ultimate dream until a dinner at my parents' home. With my parents, Ethel and Philip, my sister, Sharon, and a visiting cousin and his wife, we were enjoying the meal when the conversation turned to what we would be doing after leaving school. I was so excited about teaching and rambled on for ages. Stephen sat quietly waiting for his turn. 'I want to play cricket for Australia,' he said, and the conversation at the table went silent. Nobody knew exactly what to say, so nobody said anything. I can't imagine what Stephen thought. I remember thinking that I knew he played and liked cricket a lot, but playing cricket as a job? Well, that's not really a job, is it?

Even knowing it wasn't what he really wanted to do, with encouragement from myself and another school friend, Stephen decided to enrol at Milperra Teachers College. I thought this would be an excellent back-up in case the cricket thing didn't work out. But while I was just about bursting with excitement about beginning college, Stephen was strangely quiet. To his credit, he gave it a go, even if it was only for a day.

I come from a family comprising only one sister. Cricket, or any sport other than tennis or netball, wasn't part of our vocabulary or interest. It was, however, the droning sound that came from my grandad's TV all summer when we visited him at Patonga Beach, on the central coast of NSW, for four weeks every year. Sharon and I couldn't wait for Grandad to disappear over the hill into Gosford for 'Pokie Day' so we could take possession of the TV.

After meeting Stephen and spending a summer with him, and seeing how serious he was about this cricket ambition, I realised I would have to take an interest and learn something about the game. And so began my cricket-watching days at the age of 17. I would travel with him and his brother Mark to grade cricket, and later to NSW and Australian Under 19s games. I remember grounds at Manly, Drummoyne and Newcastle. I remember long days alone, often as the only spectator. I remember counting down the overs – calculating how many were left in a day's play to work out how many balls remained. Overall, what I remember most is boredom.

I would sit and watch. He always seemed to be batting, all day sometimes, which I would later learn meant he was doing really well. But at the time I would just wish he would get out so he could come sit with me. I would later learn that meant he would probably not be very happy because it would mean he'd gotten out. How was a girl ever going to fit into this cricket world?

We had been dating for 12 months when Stephen received an opportunity to play cricket in England. We had grown incredibly close over that past year and our relationship was very important to both of us, but so was our desire to achieve our career goals. I was well into my college course, doing really well and loving it. His career was beginning to take direction so it was important that he go to the UK. The separation of five and a half months was never going to be easy, but we had a great friendship and both believed that keeping in contact was very important. Neither of us could afford the costly phone calls, so letter writing was our main form of communication. My connection to the airport resumed at this point, and the rotation of 'drop off, pick up, tears and smiles' began on the day I saw him off on his first trip to England in 1985.

I missed him dreadfully. We'd got used to seeing and speaking to each other every day and now suddenly he was gone. I'd always kept diaries (and still do to this present day), so I just decided that I would write my journal in letter form to him. I wrote to him every day he was away and posted a letter to him weekly. He corresponded to me regularly as well, often sending back photos and newspaper clippings. Our letter writing became a special part of our relationship that lasted his entire career. It was definitely love by correspondence. When Stephen began playing for Australia we still couldn't afford the phone calls, so the letter writing continued and we both loved it. We've exchanged unusual items in letters over the years. A flower he picked and pressed in a letter from his first trip to the UK is now framed on my bedside table; I have a coin he found on the beach in the West Indies; our first baby Rosalie's ultrasound photo went via post to him in India. I even sent Easter eggs to him in the subcontinent; they arrived smashed into pieces. The children have always written to him when he's away, too. When faxes became available they would fax him drawings and I would fax him tracings of their hands and feet to show how much they'd grown. I've a lovely collection of correspondence between Stephen and myself from many years. It holds a very special place in my heart.

★

Entering the Waugh domain was an experience in itself. I was the first girl to do so. One teenage girl among four sports-mad boys was a bit like trying to mix oil and water. I quickly learnt that the best policy to adopt was silence, somewhat staying invisible. This was an environment completely immersed in masculinity. The fact that a girl had appeared never seemed to make a ripple in the testosterone-deep waters of the Waugh household. One drawback as a girl was that I was never asked what I wanted to watch on TV – it was sport, sport, sport and more sport, with a bit of *Kingswood Country* thrown in. Sport so dominated the TV that a cricket bat leant up against the on/off switch to ensure it stayed on.

Stephen's parents, Bev and Rodger, did everything possible to make me feel welcome and I did feel welcome. Bev would always make sure that I was served a cup of tea with a slice of Sara Lee cake first when I was there, even though the boys hovered impatiently nearby waiting for theirs. I enjoyed my visits to the Waugh home – they were fun and interesting times and gave Stephen and me some wonderful memories that we still laugh at today, like my first meal with the family. The dining-room table was a large, pine, rectangular one and seemed enormous to me, a lot different from the small round one in my home that sat four people intimately. The Waugh table never seemed to fit into the room quite right. It dominated, which suddenly seemed appropriate when I came to realise how important food was to an always-hungry family of four boys. If you were one of the last two to the table you had already drawn the short straw because the two chairs against the wall were an absolute squeeze to get into, and once you got into them there was no getting out, as you were trapped by the gas heater at one end and the back of the lounge at the other. So the first rule of survival for meals was never to be late to the table if you wanted the best seats. There I was, seated in one of the good seats for my first meal with the family very excited but very quiet too. The TV was on and the conversation little. Bev had cooked the meal of the day: steak and vegetables. The plates had barely touched the table when there was a flurry and a clash of forks with food going everywhere. Next minute, a piece of steak was flicked from Stephen's fork and plonked right onto my plate. 'You can't hang back here – get it while you can,' said Stephen, stating what seemed to the second rule. It was an eating frenzy. I just kept thinking, *Oh my gosh, where am I?* There was this frantic pace to meals, every meal, as if they'd not eaten for a week. Along with the unbelievable speed they could eat, was the noise – the sounds of chomping almost drowned out the TV.

The only dilemma I couldn't really resolve in visiting the Waughs' was the toilet. This was 'Boys' Zone' in big red flashing letters. Bev, as mothers do, just made the best of a bad situation. I mean, she was outnumbered by males five to one – but I wasn't as easygoing as that yet. On visits, I would hold off or hold on for as long as humanly possible because I knew what would greet me on a toilet stop. I mean, did these boys ever flush? When it became desperate, I would send Stephen on a scouting mission to the loo to flush it. Only then was it safe to enter.

Bev was a busy mum, and between working, playing squash and keeping house she had long given up trying to get any of the boys to contribute to the household chores. She would leave lots of notes on the kitchen bench requesting rubbish to be taken out or washing to be hung out, but I don't recall too many requests being acted on. I remember one summer Rodger, Bev, Dean and Danny headed to Ballina for a holiday and that meant Mark and Stephen were home alone. I caught up with Stephen after a week and I just couldn't believe the state of the kitchen when I walked in. Instead of washing up at the end of each meal, they'd literally used every bowl, plate, cup and piece of cutlery in the house. It looked as if a crowd of people had visited for a meal – it was hard to imagine that two people alone could generate such a disaster. All I could think of was what Bev would say if she returned home to such a mess, so I began the enormous clean-up task. The plates had been there so long they were stuck together; I needed a knife to get them apart.

Combining cricket life and our relationship was, as I imagine it is for anyone who has a partner immersed in a demanding career, the ultimate balancing act. The obstacles were numerous and often seemed endless. We were always conferring and modifying our relationship and lifestyle to meet the restraints caused by Stephen's cricketing career. For us, these obstacles were just challenges and I am content to say that after 22 years together, none of them were relationship-ending ones. For me, it was just that I loved Stephen. I valued our relationship and knew we had something pretty special and worth working on. Rather than working against cricket, I welcomed the challenges it threw at us. Stephen always made it clear to me that as much as he was passionate about cricket, he was equally passionate and committed to me. He's a very balanced person and strives to have his life reflect this. He has amazing commitment to our children and to me, and makes sure in his planning that the work he does is balanced with time for us. In his early days as a cricket-playing father, his absence from an active parenting role, and missing those special occasions like birthdays, school concerts and baby milestones, hurt him more than missing out on a hundred.

The obstacle of separation was probably the hardest and became more complicated as Stephen's cricket career marched on. His early ACB contract was for a low $6000 per year, plus match payments, and while I had the freedom to travel, coming straight from college meant I didn't have the finances to do so. In 1986–87 I went on a crazy and exhausting timetable of cleaning offices in the very early hours of the morning and then doing casual teaching blocks during the day. It was a desperate effort to save enough funds for airfares and accommodation so we could be together. When we couldn't avoid the separation, then it was love by correspondence and late-night phone calls again. I was just glad to hear his voice. As we became more financially secure I began to travel for small blocks of tours, often using up Stephen's entire tour fee, but spending that time together was always worth it. The energy and enthusiasm we generated for each other and from the places we were in were enormous. It was the memory of these times together that sustained me through the lonely months apart.

When Rosie was born on July 31, 1996, it became even more important to us that we be together. Whenever the cricket calendar allowed we'd fly to meet Stephen somewhere, everywhere. In Rosie's first 24 months she'd had 25 flights. Luckily for us she was a fantastic little traveller. She, like me, has had such wonderful life experiences through travelling. Her first birthday was celebrated on an Ashes tour in England; she's ridden a camel in the desert; she and her younger brother, Austin (born on November 11, 1999), have climbed the Eiffel Tower; she's written to and received a letter from the Queen of England; she's celebrated her second birthday with Mickey Mouse in Florida; and she's sat on the 'footsteps' of the Giant's Causeway in Northern Ireland.

Travelling with Rosie on our first overseas trip, for the 1997 Ashes Tour, was a shock to both of us, though. It was a very testing time and required a modifying of family and cricketing life. Stephen had been living alone in a hotel room for nearly two months. There was no baby timetable to follow and no baby crawling around the floor getting into his gear. Our arrival, though welcomed, was definitely a shock to his unstructured living arrangements. But it was just another obstacle we acknowledged, managed and overcame. While Rosie slept in a portable cot in a small hotel room, Stephen wrote his tour diary in the bathroom – with the vanity as his desk and the toilet his chair. It wasn't a perfect scenario but it worked for us.

Austin's arrival didn't slow us down. Six weeks after his birth, we were all in Melbourne for Christmas and the Boxing Day Test match. This was followed by a trip to New Zealand six weeks later, then many interstate trips, and a UK tour in 2001. Like Rosie, he was a great baby to travel with and Stephen loved having the children around; it gave his life the balance he craved. I had the luxury and total support of my parents, who'd travel with me to help out with the children. I was so grateful for their help because they gave me the opportunity and confidence to travel and be united with Stephen as a family.

Sometimes, the overwhelming urge to be together resulted in some questionable choices by me. One was a decision to travel to the UK for the 2001 Ashes tour with two children aged four and 18 months while I was seven months pregnant. What was I thinking? It was a long and uncomfortable flight, and I needed injections prior to each leg to avoid blood clots. We decided to forgo the difficulties of hotel rooms and instead rented a lovely apartment with my parents, 10 minutes from the team hotel in London – a wise decision that resulted in a wonderful trip for us all.

As time marched on, Rosalie started school and our family grew. Lillian was born on September 20, 2001. It was the beginning of a difficult period in our personal lives, as Lilli, at 10 days old, was diagnosed with chronic colic and severe reflux, which saw her inhale her stomach secretions and at one point stop breathing for nearly three minutes. She was put permanently on a respiratory monitor and began weekly visits to the paediatrician. Her pain was terrible and her crying intense, and it was incredibly stressful for us all. We opted for the non-drug path of treatment for her, and carried her around upright the entire day with only catnaps for a break. The dynamics of our family changed dramatically. I would be up all night with Lilli until she crashed at around 5 a.m., then Stephen would be up at 5.30 a.m. with Rosie and Austin. It was simply exhausting for everyone.

To make matters worse, I was diagnosed with Graves' disease in August 2002. After 18 years with Stephen, I had developed this tremendous sense of independence about everything in life – I'd helped supervise the building of our house, survived three bushfires and saw no reason why I couldn't manage a baby with reflux and two other children under five alone as well. Stephen, knowing me as well as he does, tried to be my voice of reason. He quietly pointed out that he would be beginning the Australian season in the next few weeks and that I would need help. For so many reasons, I didn't want to acknowledge that I couldn't cope any more and being as private as we were, I knew I would have to open up a part of our life to someone else. In the end it was one of the best life decisions we made because our dear friend Lorinda Small entered our lives, not only making our lives easier but enriching and delighting the children. From the day she joined our family she was always our friend, never our nanny. She was a special presence in our lives.

When you have a partner who's absent for sometimes eight months a year, year after year, it can become easy to dwell on the heavy heart that accompanies his departure. Stephen and I would often speak to each other about how the times apart were only steps to another part of our life and how in the scope of our lives it only represented a small part of it. We tried to make the time apart a positive thing – play great cricket. For me, making the time apart a positive was easy, but I can never say I liked it. It was the part of Stephen's job I hated the most. You may get used to it, but you never like it.

His absence drew others into our life, people who helped our family function – people like my mum and dad, who in their retirement gave their time to keep us company, to be the Mr and Mrs Fix-It when I needed odd jobs done, to offer emotional support and love during the long months alone. I can never say enough to thank them for the contribution they made to our family, and Stephen acknowledges, as do I, that without their presence in our life he probably wouldn't have been able to play for as long as he did.

On the days when I simply had nothing left physically or emotionally to give the children, my mum and dad would turn up and become the heartbeat of our family. One of my greatest joys since Rosie was born has been watching the amazingly strong and loving bond the children have developed and shared with Mum and Dad, who have touched every part of our lives. It was not uncommon to have one of the kids, especially Austin, cry for Nannie and Pa after my parents had stayed and cared for them for a few weeks while I joined Stephen on a tour. They are so tightly woven into the fabric of our life.

As well as my parents, sister Sharon and close friends from the children's school would pour energy and love into me and the children. The contribution they made to our family eased the difficulties of having a partner regularly away for long periods of time.

In the beginning, simply being a cricketer's partner was a handicap in itself. For me, those early years were the darkest and unhappiest of Stephen's career. I was new and young but already I felt the chill from being around the team. It wasn't an environment that welcomed women. You so wanted the team to win, but a part of you didn't because you knew it would mean that your partner would be locked away in a dressing-room for hours, followed by a long celebration out on the town and then a day to recover. You would often return after cheering and sweating over your partner's success for seven hours to an empty hotel room. It was pretty deflating.

The banning of wives and girlfriends from the start of the Ashes tour, and then from all hotels until the last Test, was to my mind cruel and thoughtless. It left partners, wives and families alone in an overseas country with no resources to fall back on but each other. Even though I appeared to support the decision publicly, because I didn't want to ruffle feathers or jeopardise my partner's career, behind the scenes it was a complete disappointment; neither Stephen nor I liked it. Long-term partners and wives couldn't even enter team-hotel foyers, but single players could – and did – meet girls on tour and take them into the hotel. As the years went on the captaincy changed, but the compatibility between family and cricket only improved slightly. It just made no sense to have unhappy husbands in one hotel and unhappy wives in another; it just didn't seem to help team harmony.

Stephen would talk to me about an idea he had to include families more in team life and touring. Of course, I didn't object. I know that under his leadership and with coaches Geoff Marsh and John Buchanan – two other men with a strong sense of family – the move to include families began. Partners were invited into team dressing-rooms at the end of winning Tests and one-day matches. Suddenly, winning gave me a wonderful new feeling. I enjoyed it. In 2000 I was welcomed into the SCG dressing-room for the first time. Stephen had now been playing for Australia for 15 years, yet this was my first dressing-room and the first time I had ever celebrated a win at a ground with Stephen!

After that, there was no looking back for wives and partners. We were invited to join the players whenever they wished. Arrangements were made under the Memorandum of Understanding negotiated by the ACB and ACA for 'partner visiting periods' on away tours, with the cost covered by the ACB. It was a welcome and much appreciated initiative. Touring conditions for partners and wives are now outstanding, and distance and separations are no longer the obstacles they once were.

I made use of my first visiting period on the 2001 Ashes tour and then again on the West Indies tour in 2003. That time in the Caribbean, with all but a few wives present, was the happiest team environment I had ever been part of. I'm sure the team's continued success came about in part because of this harmonious environment. Along with the way Stephen played the game and what he achieved on the field, I'm equally – if not a touch more – proud of him for the vision he had for families in cricketing life.

★

I never really saw myself as having a public life; rather, I just had my own life and Stephen had the public life, which I was part of from time to time. He and I are both fiercely private people. I had no trouble saying no to media requests. I never enjoyed being interviewed; it just made me feel so uncomfortable. I never felt that I'd done anything particularly special except sit and watch my partner play sport. When our children were born it seemed to create interest, but I'm not sure it was newsworthy. While I was in the labour ward at hospital, some journalists were ringing to see if 'the baby' had arrived yet.

After Rosie was born, Stephen hated being separated from her. He wanted to spend every precious moment with his new daughter. He wanted ours to be the first faces he saw through the airport arrival gates. We tried it for a while, but the jostling and shoving from the media to snap a picture just got too much for an anxious mum and dad with a precious little parcel to protect. After a while it became obvious to us that Rosie was affected by it, too. As I passed her over to Stephen at the airport, not only was she trying to process and remember her dad after several months apart, she had to deal with dozens of bright, popping flashbulbs. She would go emotionless – she almost appeared stunned. This method of leaving and homecoming was simply not going to work for us. While Stephen recognised he had a responsibility to be available to the media, we felt that our children didn't. They never asked to have such a public life and we kept them away from it as much as we could.

During the time leading up to Stephen's final Test we were flooded with requests from the media for us and the children to do stories. It was impossible to ignore all of them, and we arranged for our photo to be taken on the SCG at the conclusion of the last day. As a family, we sat down together, even with Lilli, and asked the children if they wanted to have a photo taken. Stephen and I tried to prepare them for what it might be like – lots of people, lots of noise, and lots of 'Look at me' being shouted at them. I was so proud of how the children handled themselves and amazed at their calmness and cooperation; it was as if they'd done it a million times before.

The last 12 months of Stephen's career were a crazy cocktail of stress, disappointment, anger, excitement and calmness. After he scored his fabulous hundred at the SCG in 2003, I quietly mentioned to him that maybe this would be a wonderful time to retire, that it couldn't get much better then this. The home season had been long and hard, and he had been in the papers daily for months and months. It was tiring and frustrating. He simply wanted to play cricket and leave the politics alone.

The idea of retirement was never something we dreaded – it was a part of our lives we were looking forward to. Everything Stephen had been working for, the decision to delay having our children until the later part of his career so he would be around for the majority of their life, enduring all the long and numerous separations, was to prepare and help us in post-retirement life. He loved playing cricket, so losing interest in the game and not wanting to play or train were never going to be signals to him to retire. He was driven to succeed as a captain and a player; he never lost the desire to perform or improve. He always remained highly motivated.

The decision to retire, like the way we led our life, like the way Stephen played the game and captained the team, wasn't complicated or complex, and it was realised long before the home 2003–04 season. Quite simply, it was what felt right for our family. Stephen had been playing cricket now for a very long time and he just wanted to do something else. We'd talked a lot after the Sydney Test of 2003. He'd been dropped from the one-day international team during the previous season and was determined it would be different next time.

Leading up to the West Indies tour the children were disappointed to learn that he would be going away again. It seemed particularly hard for Rosie, who wanted her dad around more. On the day he departed, we always had a going-away ritual we would do at the front gate. It's a black wrought-iron gate and the children would climb on top and hang over the edge. Stephen would go along and kiss them one by one, sometimes even a second time, but this time through the openings of the railings. He would always say, 'See you clowns later.' This always left the kids with a giggle in their hearts and a smile on their faces as their dad drove away. I don't know if it was because of our conversation or just a feeling I had, but this time I wanted a family photo of us at the gate before he left. I knew in my heart this would be probably be his last overseas tour, unless he changed his mind while he was away. It had been a really long time since I'd snapped a departure photo – over a decade, in fact – but this time felt it was a special occasion and I wanted to capture it forever.

Stephen wanted me to travel to the West Indies to join him on his last overseas tour. With the help and support of Mum, Dad and Lorinda, I was able to join him in Antigua and Barbados. It would be the longest time I'd ever been away from the children and it was difficult for me to go. I wanted to be with and support Stephen, but I also wanted to be with the children. It was one of those times when you wished you could split yourself in two.

When I arrived in Barbados it was the happiest Stephen had ever been to see me. I knew this time together was going to be special and life-changing. We were walking along the beach the first night when he told me that he was sure he wanted to retire and felt Sydney at the start of the new year would be the ideal spot and time. He simply wanted to walk off the ground on the last day and announce to the team in the dressing-room that it was over, he was finishing here and now. He didn't want any fuss or bother, didn't want to distract from the team. I told him I couldn't really see it happening that way. For one, the media would focus on him during the upcoming home series one way or another. He wasn't getting any younger and the talk of retirement had been an undercurrent for a long time. He also needed to talk to the selectors, as they had a responsibility to plan ahead.

Stephen and I were the only two involved in the decision. We consulted no one. There weren't any long conversations about it, just a decision and the acknowledgement that both of us thought it right.

He'd hated the 'one-day dropping' press conference. This time, he would take ownership. It would be a message from his heart delivered at a time and place best suited to him. He followed protocol not wishing to offend anyone. On the day he made the announcement, a letter of retirement was sent in the early morning to the ACB. A press conference was called and the announcement was made. Prior to leaving for the SCG, he telephoned family members to let them know he had decided to retire and would be making his announcement today. He then practised his speech over and over, with the children as an eager audience. It seemed entirely appropriate that, as I watched and filmed him doing this, the first ones to hear him deliver his speech were our children and me. I won't hide the fact that I was bursting with happiness about the news. We could see nothing but positives for us and our children in his retirement.

Ever since the decision to retire had been made in the West Indies, I'd had this quiet excitement about the year ahead. I remember swimming with Kellie Hayden, Matthew's wife, in Antigua on our last morning there. She was chatting about the year ahead, the tours coming up and asked me about travelling to India. I so wanted to tell her, but Stephen and I had decided that keeping it to ourselves would shield family and friends from the intense media scrutiny that would inevitably come if the decision was leaked. After the announcement, when friends and family said they'd had no idea it was coming, they were being truthful.

In response to Kellie's question about India, I made a general comment about it being so far off it was difficult for us to look that far ahead. I remember her shocked look and her saying something like, 'Don't talk like that. I couldn't ever imagine you and Stephen not being there.' I remember thinking that maybe everyone wasn't going to be as chuffed as me about the announcement.

In fact, people's reactions were so mixed. Stephen and I seemed to be reassuring everyone that this was great for us. People congratulated us, hugged us and cried in front of us. Me? Well, I did apologise to Stephen before I left the house that day.

I recognised the sadness of the occasion, in that his cricket would come to an end, but I told him I'd been waiting for this day for such a long time and rather than cry all I wanted to do was smile. By the end of the day my cheeks were aching from endless smiling, like they do on your wedding day. I just kept smiling – I couldn't help it. It just kept bubbling up from inside.

Stephen has never – even as a baby, I'm told – liked a lot of attention, so the 2003–04 season was always going to be a challenge. We just rolled with the momentum of it and tried to enjoy it. By the end of the final Test, in Sydney, it was by far the most exciting and unbelievable experience for us, even if the children remained virtually oblivious to it all. I'd ask them if they wanted to see Daddy play, and occasionally they did, but mostly they wanted to play with their cricketing friends down in the players' creche. However, I did ask them to watch Daddy walk out onto the field on the first day and to be there when he left the field on the last day. They really enjoyed this, and Lilli still talks about all the flags for Daddy that day.

As I stood outside on the last afternoon soaking up the atmosphere, I couldn't have imagined missing this for anything. I would have stood on a box under the blazing sun just to see Stephen play for the last time, just as I had after driving down to Melbourne to watch him in a Test for the first time. Nothing could've stopped me.

We had a great box given to us by the SCG Trust. With Stephen's then manager, Robert Joske, and his assistant, Zoe Burgess, we organised 46 tickets for family and friends for a day. It was a huge task that went relatively smoothly. We had some fantastic friends as guests during the Test and it was a wonderful time. Stephen's cricketing life had gone a complete circle – the end now linked with the beginning. He had started his career against India; now he was finishing against them. Like me, his dad had driven alone all the way to Melbourne to watch him in his first Test. Now I was standing next to Rodger, and he, my parents, and great friends Gavin Robertson, Chris Madden, Brett Pike and Todd Crameri all had tears in their eyes.

It was a special moment that saw us all united in our support and friendship for Stephen and his cricket career. We awoke the next day to a new life. There was no feeling of sadness, just complete joy.

Since Stephen's retirement I've been asked a lot about my life now, and about my life then. People have asked whether the sacrifices have been worth it, or had I missed the opportunity to pursue my own career. I have absolutely no regrets. I believe that life sets its own path. I followed mine. I've always just aimed to do my best at anything I've tried my hand at. During Stephen's career I think I've been a good companion, an interested listener, at times an accurate advisor, a loyal friend and a devoted mother.

I often think of Nicholas Sparks' *The Notebook* when I wonder about my life's gifts and successes. Unlike Stephen's cricket career, which can be valued by runs and wickets, I'm reminded: 'I am nothing special, of this I am sure. I am just a common [man] with common thoughts, and I've led a common life. There are no monuments dedicated to me and my name will soon be forgotten, but I've loved another with all my heart and soul, and to me, this has always been enough.'

For this, I am blessed and thankful to you, Stephen. At the end of it all, I'm the luckiest one. While many have shared in your career, now that it is all over and they're gone, I'm left with the best part – you, the man I first met 22 years ago, fresh and enthusiastic to head down a new path in life together. Life really is wonderful. I may never stop smiling.

CAREER RECORDS
by Geoff Armstrong and Ian Russell

Stephen Rodger Waugh

Born 2 June 1965
Twin of Mark Waugh (128 Tests, 244 limited-overs
internationals between 1988–89 and 2002)

N.B. See page 764 for a key to the abbreviations
and symbols used in the section

1. Test cricket

Steve Waugh's Test debut: 26–30 December 1985 v India at Melbourne,
scoring 13 and 5 and taking 2/36
Final Test match: 2–6 January 2004 v India at Sydney, scoring 40 and 80 and taking 0/6

The Australian Test team, 1985–86 to 2003–04

Steve Waugh's teammates (70)

108 Tests with Steve Mark Waugh; *101* Ian Healy; *96* Shane Warne; *89* Glenn McGrath; *85* Mark Taylor; *79* David Boon; *70* Ricky Ponting; *69* Justin Langer; *67* Michael Slater; *65* Allan Border; *49* Adam Gilchrist; *48* Matthew Hayden; *46* Jason Gillespie; *44* Greg Blewett; *43* Craig McDermott; *42* Merv Hughes; *40* Geoff Marsh; *37* Dean Jones; *36* Brett Lee; *35* Damien Martyn; *33* Paul Reiffel; *29* Stuart MacGill; *23* Bruce Reid; *21* Tim May; *20* Damien Fleming; *19* Matthew Elliott, Andy Bichel; *17* Greg Matthews, Terry Alderman, Colin Miller; *16* Michael Bevan; *15* Michael Kasprowicz; *14* Darren Lehmann; *11* Greg Ritchie; *10* Tim Zoehrer, Geoff Lawson, Peter Sleep, Peter Taylor; *8* Mike Veletta, Tony Dodemaide; *7* Ray Bright, Trevor Hohns, Carl Rackemann; *6* Greg Dyer, Graeme Wood, Brendon Julian; *5* Wayne Phillips, Dave Gilbert, Martin Love, Simon Katich; *4* Greg Campbell, Tom Moody, Jo Angel, Brad Hogg; *3* Chris Matthews, Mike Whitney, Gavin Robertson, Brad Williams, Nathan Bracken; *2* Peter McIntyre, Simon Cook, Scott Muller; *1* David Hookes, Bob Holland, Simon Davis, Dirk Wellham, Shaun Young, Paul Wilson, Matthew Nicholson, Adam Dale

Team performance, by 'segment'

Years	Tests	Won	Lost	Drawn	Tied	Win%	Loss%	Draw%
1. 1985–86 to 1988–89	26	4	7	14	1	15.38	26.92	53.84
2. 1989 (Eng) to 1991 (WI)	18	8	2	8	–	44.44	11.11	44.44
3. 1992–93 to 1994 (SA)	21	10	5	6	–	47.61	23.80	28.57
4. 1994 (Pak) to 1997 (SA)	24	13	7	4	–	54.16	29.16	16.66
5. 1997 (Eng) to 1998–99	22	10	5	7	–	45.45	22.72	31.81
6. 1999 (WI) to 2001 (Eng)	28	21	4	3	–	75.00	14.28	10.71
7. 2001–02 to 2003–04	29	20	4	5	–	68.96	13.79	17.24
Total	168	86	34	47	1	51.19	20.23	27.97

Notes
1. For this table, to illustrate how since 1985–86 the Australian Test team has increased its win rates and reduced the number of draws it is involved in, Steve's career has been separated into 7 segments: 1. from his Test debut to the eve of the 1989 Ashes tour; 2. from the '89 Ashes series to Steve's dropping from the side; 3. from his return to the team to Allan Border's final Test; 4. from Mark Taylor's first Test as captain to the eve of the 1997 Ashes tour; 5. from the Ashes '97 series to Mark Taylor's final Test; 6. from Steve's first Test as captain to the end of the 2001 Ashes series; 7. from the 2001–02 Australian season to Steve's final Test.
2. The figures above do not include the 21 Tests Steve missed because of injury or non-selection during his career. Including those Tests, the totals change as follows:

Tests	Won	Lost	Drawn	Tied	Win%	Loss%	Draw%
189	97	37	54	1	51.32	19.57	28.57

3. At 31 March 2005, Steve's 86 Test victories remained the most Test wins in any player's career. Other players to play in 60 Test victories at this time were Shane Warne (75 wins), Mark Waugh (72), Glenn McGrath (72), Viv Richards (63) and Desmond Haynes (60).

Steve's appearance 'milestones'

Test	Series	Versus	Venue	Notes
50	1993	NZ	Christchurch	26th Australian to play 50 Tests
100	1997–98	SA	Sydney	3rd Australian to play 100 Tests
150	2002	Pak	Sharjah	2nd player to play 150 Tests
156	2002–03	Eng	Sydney	Equalled Allan Border's world record
157	2003	WI	Georgetown	New world record

Notes

1. Border and David Boon were the 2 Australians to precede Steve to 100 Test appearances. On his retirement, 7 Australians had appeared in 100 Tests: (in order of achieving their century) Border, Boon, Steve Waugh, Ian Healy, Mark Taylor, Mark Waugh and Shane Warne. Glenn McGrath played his 100th Test in October 2004.
2. At 31 March 2005, the 10 cricketers with the most Test appearances were Steve Waugh, Allan Border, Alec Stewart (133 Tests), Courtney Walsh (132), Kapil Dev (131), Mark Waugh (128), Sunil Gavaskar (125), Javed Miandad (124), Shane Warne (123) and Sachin Tendulkar (123). Thirty-one men had played 100 Test matches: 8 Australians, 7 Englishmen (Stewart, Graham Gooch, David Gower, Michael Atherton, Colin Cowdrey, Geoff Boycott, Ian Botham), 7 West Indians (Walsh, Viv Richards, Desmond Haynes, Brian Lara, Clive Lloyd, Gordon Greenidge, Carl Hooper), 4 Indians (Kapil Dev, Gavaskar, Tendulkar, Dilip Vengsarkar), 4 Pakistanis (Javed Miandad, Wasim Akram, Salim Malik, Inzamam-ul-Haq) and 1 South African (Gary Kirsten).

Steve Waugh: Batting and fielding

Series by series

Series	Versus	Tests	Inn	NO	Runs	HS	100	50	Avge	Ct	Results
1985–86	Ind	2	4	–	26	13	–	–	6.50	–	–DD
1986	NZ	3	5	–	87	74	–	1	17.40	2	DDL
1986	Ind	3	4	3	59	39*	–	–	59.00	2	TDD
1986–87	Eng	5	8	1	310	79*	–	3	44.28	8	LDDLW
1987–88	NZ	3	4	–	147	61	–	2	36.75	3	WDD
1987–88	Eng	1	1	–	27	27	–	–	27.00	–	D
1987–88	SL	1	1	–	20	20	–	–	20.00	3	W
1988	Pak	3	5	–	92	59	–	1	18.40	2	LDD
1988–89	WI	5	9	1	331	91	–	3	41.37	3	LLLWD
1989	Eng	6	8	4	506	177*	2	1	126.50	4	WWDWWD
1989–90	NZ	1	1	–	17	17	–	–	17.00	–	D
1989–90	SL	2	4	1	267	134*	1	2	89.00	2	DW
1989–90	Pak	3	4	–	44	20	–	–	11.00	1	WDD
1990	NZ	1	2	–	50	25	–	–	25.00	–	L
1990–91	Eng	3	4	–	82	48	–	–	20.50	2	WWD– –
1991	WI	2	3	1	32	26	–	–	16.00	1	– –DL–
1992–93	WI	5	9	–	228	100	1	–	25.33	5	DWDLL
1993	NZ	3	4	–	178	75	–	2	44.50	1	WDL
1993	Eng	6	9	4	416	157*	1	2	83.20	5	WWDWWL
1993–94	NZ	3	3	2	216	147*	1	–	216.00	1	DWW
1993–94	SA	1	2	–	165	164	1	–	82.50	1	– –W
1994	SA	3	4	1	195	86	–	2	65.00	3	LWD
1994	Pak	2	3	–	171	98	–	2	57.00	2	LD–
1994–95	Eng	5	10	3	345	99*	–	3	49.28	3	WWDLW
1995	WI	4	6	2	429	200	1	3	107.25	6	WDLW
1995–96	Pak	3	5	1	200	112*	1	–	50.00	1	WWL
1995–96	SL	2	3	2	362	170	2	1	362.00	1	–WW
1996	Ind	1	2	1	67	67*	–	1	67.00	–	L
1996–97	WI	4	6	–	188	66	–	2	31.33	2	W–LWL
1997	SA	3	5	1	313	160	1	2	78.25	3	WWL
1997	Eng	6	10	–	390	116	2	1	39.00	4	LDWWWL
1997–98	NZ	3	5	1	130	96	–	1	32.50	4	WWD
1997–98	SA	3	5	–	238	96	–	2	47.60	1	DWD
1998	Ind	2	4	–	152	80	–	1	38.00	2	LL–
1998	Pak	3	5	1	235	157	1	–	58.75	1	WDD
1998–99	Eng	5	10	4	498	122*	2	2	83.00	–	DWWLW
1999	WI	4	8	1	409	199	2	1	58.42	1	WLLW
1999	SL	3	3	–	52	19	–	–	17.33	1	LDD
1999	Zim	1	1	1	151	151*	1	–	–	1	W
1999–00	Pak	3	4	–	58	28	–	–	14.50	3	WWW
1999–00	Ind	3	5	–	276	150	1	1	55.20	4	WWW
2000	NZ	3	6	2	214	151*	1	–	53.50	4	WWW
2000–01	WI	4	6	1	349	151*	2	–	69.80	–	WW–WW
2001	Ind	3	5	–	243	110	1	–	48.60	4	WLL

Series	Versus	Tests	Inn	NO	Runs	HS	100	50	Avge	Ct	Results
2001	Eng	4	5	2	321	157*	2	–	107.00	2	WWW–W
2001–02	NZ	3	4	–	78	67	–	1	19.50	3	DDD
2001–02	SA	3	4	–	141	90	–	1	35.25	–	WWW
2002	SA	3	5	–	95	42	–	–	19.00	1	WWL
2002	Pak	3	4	1	134	103*	1	–	44.66	4	WWW
2002–03	Eng	5	8	–	305	102	1	2	38.12	2	WWWWL
2003	WI	4	4	1	226	115	1	–	75.33	1	WWWL
2003	Ban	2	2	2	256	156*	2	–	–	–	WW
2003–04	Zim	2	2	–	139	78	–	2	69.50	3	WW
2003–04	Ind	4	7	–	267	80	–	2	44.50	–	DLWD
Total		168	260	46	10927	200	32	50	51.06	112	

Notes

1. In this table, 'Results' in the far right column are for Australia in the Tests in which Steve played; '–' indicates a Test in which he did not play.
2. Steve is Australia's 335th Test cricketer. Immediately before him on the chronological list of Australian Test cricketers are Merv Hughes, Geoff Marsh and Bruce Reid; straight after are Simon Davis, Tim Zoehrer and Chris Matthews.
3. The most runs Steve scored in a calendar year was 993, in 14 Tests in 1999, average 49.65.
4. In all, Steve missed 21 Tests between his first and last Tests, as follows:

Series	Versus	Tests	Reason	Results
1990–91	Eng	4th, 5th	not selected	DW
1991	WI	1st, 2nd, 5th	not selected	DLW
1991–92	Ind	all five	not selected	WWDWW
1992	SL	all three	not selected	WDD
1993–94	SA	1st, 2nd	injury: hamstring	DL
1994	Pak	3rd	injury: shoulder	D
1995–96	SL	1st	injury: groin	W
1996–97	WI	2nd	injury: groin	W
1998	Ind	3rd	injury: groin	W
2000–01	WI	3rd	injury: buttock muscle	W
2001	Eng	4th	injury: left calf	L

5. Steve won 14 'man of the match' awards in Test cricket: the first in the second Ashes Test of 1989, at Lord's, when he scored 152* and 21* and took 1/49 and 0/20; the last in the first Test against Bangladesh at Darwin in 2003, when he scored 100*.
6. He was named the Allan Border Medallist for 2000–01. This award, given to the Australian cricketer of the year as voted by players, umpires and the media, was inaugurated in 1999–2000, when it was won by Glenn McGrath. Other winners to 2004-05 were Matthew Hayden, Adam Gilchrist, Ricky Ponting and Michael Clarke.

Centuries (32)

Century	Test	Versus	Venue	Series	Inn	Pos	Score	Min	Balls	4/6	Result
177*	27	Eng	Leeds	1989	1	6	4/273	308	243	24/–	Win
152*	28	Eng	Lord's	1989	2	6	4/221	329	249	17/–	Win
134*	35	SL	Hobart	1989–90	3	7	5/253	234	177	14/–	Win
100	47	WI	Sydney	1992–93	1	3	1/42	269	207	5/–	Draw
157*	56	Eng	Leeds	1993	1	6	4/321	405	305	19/–	Win
147*	61	NZ	Brisbane	1993–94	2	6	4/277	380	281	15/–	Win
164	62	SA	Adelaide	1993–94	1	6	4/183	380	276	19/–	Win
200	76	WI	Kingston	1995	2	5	3/73	555	425	17/–	Win
112*	77	Pak	Brisbane	1995–96	1	5	3/213	366	275	7/–	Win
131*	80	SL	Melbourne	1995–96	1	5	3/219	329	252	11/–	Win
170	81	SL	Adelaide	1995–96	1	5	3/96	421	316	13/–	Win
160	87	SA	Jo'burg	1997	2	5	3/169	501	366	22/–	Win
108	92	Eng	Manchester	1997	1	5	3/42	241	174	13/–	Win
116	92	Eng	Manchester	1997	3	5	3/39	383	270	10/–	Win
157	104	Pak	Rawalpindi	1998	2	5	3/28	392	326	15/1	Win
112	107	Eng	Brisbane	1998–99	1	5	3/106	330	232	13/–	Draw
122*	110	Eng	Melbourne	1998–99	2	5	3/98	315	198	13/–	Loss

100	113	WI	Kingston	1999	1	5	3/46	251	165	11/1	Loss
199	114	WI	Bridgetown	1999	1	5	3/36	507	377	20/1	Loss
151*	119	Zim	Harare	1999	2	5	3/96	434	351	18/–	Win
150	123	Ind	Adelaide	1999–00	1	5	3/45	402	323	17/–	Win
151*	127	NZ	Wellington	2000	2	6	4/51	413	312	23/–	Win
121*	131	WI	Melbourne	2000–01	1	5	3/101	362	237	14/–	Win
103	132	WI	Sydney	2000–01	2	5	3/109	300	239	9/1	Win
110	134	Ind	Calcutta	2001	1	5	3/214	305	203	11/1	Loss
105	136	Eng	Birmingham	2001	2	5	3/134	245	181	13/–	Win
157*	139	Eng	The Oval	2001	1	5	2/292	312	256	21/1	Win
103*	151	Pak	Sharjah	2002	1	5	3/233	294	191	13/2	Win
102	156	Eng	Sydney	2002–03	2	5	3/56	182	135	18/–	Loss
115	159	WI	Bridgetown	2003	1	5	3/292	311	229	8/1	Win
100*	161	Ban	Darwin	2003	2	5	3/184	200	133	10/1	Win
156*	162	Ban	Cairns	2003	2	5	3/132	411	291	17/–	Win

Notes

1. In this table, 'Score' is the team score at the start of Steve's innings.
2. Steve was Australia's 97th Test centurion. Australia's Test centurions from numbers 94 to 100 are Geoff Marsh, Dean Jones, Mark Taylor, Steve Waugh, Tom Moody, Mark Waugh and Ian Healy.
3. The 2 centuries at Manchester in 1997 were in the same Test. On Steve's retirement, 3 other Australians had scored centuries in each innings of the same Test against England – Warren Bardsley in 1909, Arthur Morris in 1946–47 and Matthew Hayden in 2002–03, all left-handed openers.
4. Steve's highest score in the fourth innings was 80 versus India at Sydney, 2003–04, his last Test innings.
5. The most Test centuries for Australia is Steve's 32. Next best as of 31 March 2005 was Don Bradman (29 hundreds in 52 Tests), Allan Border (27 in 156) and Greg Chappell (24 in 87). The world record was 34, shared by Indians Sunil Gavaskar (125 Tests) and Sachin Tendulkar (123 Tests).

Nineties (10)

Ninety	Test	Versus	Venue	Series	Inn	Pos	Score	Min	Balls	4/6	Result
90	22	WI	Brisbane	1988–89	3	4	2/16	167	250	9/–	Loss
91	23	WI	Perth	1988–89	2	6	4/167	202	142	11/1	Loss
92	30	Eng	Manchester	1989	2	6	4/274	203	174	7/–	Win
98	67	Pak	Rawalpindi	1994	1	6	4/323	242	188	10/–	Draw
94*	69	Eng	Melbourne	1994–95	1	6	4/100	265	191	5/–	Win
99*	72	Eng	Perth	1994–95	1	5	3/238	288	183	12/–	Win
96	97	NZ	Perth	1997–98	2	5	3/71	213	161	10/–	Win
96	99	SA	Melbourne	1997–98	1	5	3/44	264	188	9/–	Draw
96	111	Eng	Sydney	1998–99	1	5	3/52	202	171	10/–	Win
90	144	SA	Melbourne	2001–02	2	5	3/267	174	156	12/–	Win

Notes

1. As at 31 March 2005, the most nineties in Test cricket is 10 by Steve (8 dismissals, 2 not-outs), then 9 by Michael Slater (9 dismissals), 8 by West Indies' Alvin Kallicharran (7 dismissals, 1 not-out) and 7 by India's Rahul Dravid (6 dismissals, 1 not-out).
2. Steve's 99 not out at the WACA in 1994–95 ended with the dismissal of No. 11 Craig McDermott, who was run out while using Mark Waugh as a runner.

Batting and fielding, by opponent

Opponent	Tests	Inn	NO	Runs	HS	100	50	Avge	Ct
India	18	31	5	1090	150	2	5	41.92	12
New Zealand	23	34	5	1117	151*	2	7	38.51	18
England	46	73	18	3200	177*	10	14	58.18	29
Sri Lanka	8	11	3	701	170	3	3	87.62	7
Pakistan	20	30	3	934	157	3	3	34.59	14
West Indies	32	51	7	2192	200	7	9	49.81	19
South Africa	16	25	2	1147	164	2	7	49.86	9
Zimbabwe	3	3	1	290	151*	1	2	145.00	4
Bangladesh	2	2	2	256	156*	2	–	–	–

Note: As at 31 March 2005, only 3 other players – Gary Kirsten (SA), Sachin Tendulkar (Ind) and Rahul Dravid (Ind) – had scored centuries against all 9 Test opponents.

Batting dismissals, by opponent

Opponent	Inn	NO	RH	Ct	CWk	C&B	B	LBW	St	RO	HW	HB
India	31	5	–	8	5	–	4	6	–	1	1	1
New Zealand	34	4	1	11	7	1	3	6	–	1	–	–
England	73	17	1	22	12	–	16	5	–	–	–	–
Sri Lanka	11	3	–	3	3	–	2	–	–	–	–	–
Pakistan	30	3	–	6	7	2	4	5	3	–	–	–
West Indies	51	7	–	17	17	–	5	4	–	1	–	–
South Africa	25	2	–	7	10	–	5	–	–	1	–	–
Zimbabwe	3	1	–	1	–	1	–	–	–	–	–	–
Bangladesh	2	2	–	–	–	–	–	–	–	–	–	–
Total	260	44	2	75	61	4	39	26	3	4	1	1

Notes

1. The 2 innings that ended 'retired hurt' were both in the fourth innings of Tests (third Test v New Zealand in 2000 and third Test v England in 2001) subsequently won by Australia.
2. Exactly 100 different bowlers dismissed Steve in Test cricket. The bowlers who obtained Steve's wicket most often were Curtly Ambrose (WI) 11; Andy Caddick (Eng) 10; Ian Bishop (WI), Kenny Benjamin (WI), Devon Malcolm (Eng), Angus Fraser (Eng) and Darren Gough (Eng) each 5.
3. The slow bowlers to get Steve's wicket most often were John Bracewell (NZ) and Anil Kumble (Ind), each on 4 occasions.
4. David Richardson (SA) was the keeper to dismiss Steve most often (9 occasions, all caught). Carl Hooper (WI) caught him in the field most often, on 4 occasions.

Batting and fielding, by 'country'

'Country'	Tests	Inn	NO	Runs	HS	100	50	Avge	Ct
Australia	89	140	20	5710	170	15	30	47.58	55
New Zealand	10	17	2	529	151*	1	3	35.26	7
India	9	15	4	521	110	1	2	47.36	8
Pakistan	8	13	1	498	157	1	3	41.50	5
England	22	32	10	1633	177*	7	4	74.22	15
West Indies	14	21	5	1096	200	4	4	68.50	9
South Africa	9	14	2	603	160	1	4	50.25	7
Sri Lanka	4	5	–	83	31	–	–	16.60	3
Zimbabwe	1	1	1	151	151*	1	–	–	1
United Arab Emirates	2	2	1	103	103*	1	–	103.00	2
Total overseas	79	120	26	5217	200	17	20	55.50	57

Notes

1. Forty-three venues hosted Steve's 168 Tests. Outside Australia, the most Tests Steve played at one ground was 4, at each of Birmingham, Bridgetown, Lord's, Nottingham, Port of Spain, the Oval and Wellington.
2. The most runs Steve scored at an overseas venue was 397, in 3 Tests at Old Trafford, Manchester (average 99.25). He scored 396 runs at Kensington Oval in Barbados (average 79.25).
3. Steve averaged over 100 in Test cricket at 7 venues: Centurion, Delhi, Kingston, Leeds, Lord's, Rawalpindi and Sharjah. In 3 Tests at Headingley, Leeds, Waugh averaged 338 (3 innings: 177*, 157*, 4).

Batting and fielding in Australia, by venue

Venue	Tests	Inn	NO	Runs	HS	100	50	Avge	Ct
Melbourne	17	30	6	1284	131*	3	6	53.50	4
Sydney	17	25	1	1084	103	3	7	45.16	6
Brisbane	17	26	4	915	147*	3	5	41.59	10
Adelaide	15	26	2	1056	170	3	4	44.00	13
Perth	15	21	2	843	99*	–	8	44.36	20
Hobart	6	10	3	272	134*	1	–	38.85	2
Darwin	1	1	1	100	100*	1	–	–	–
Cairns	1	1	1	156	156*	1	–	–	–

Batting by career 'segment'

Years	Tests	Inn	NO	Runs	HS	100	50	Avge
1985–86 to 1991	44	67	11	2097	177*	3	13	37.44
1992–93 to 1998–99	67	110	23	5116	200	14	27	58.80
1999 to 2003–04	57	83	12	3714	199	15	10	52.30

Notes

1. Steve's career is divided into these 'segments' to compare his batting from his Test debut to his omission from the side in 1991 (this segment includes the 2 Tests Steve played in the West Indies in 1991), to his batting from his return to the side in 1992–93 to his final Test as vice-captain in 1998–99, to his batting while Test captain.
2. Steve's total figures before he became Test captain:

Years	Tests	Inn	NO	Runs	HS	100	50	Avge
1985–86 to 1998–99	111	177	34	7213	200	17	40	50.44

Batting 'milestones'

Milestone	Series	Versus	Venue	Score	Test	Inn no	Avge
1000 runs	1988–89	WI	Melbourne	42	24	37	30.93
2000 runs	1990–91	Eng	Melbourne	19	41	62	38.51
3000 runs	1993–94	NZ	Brisbane	147*	61	92	41.80
4000 runs	1994–95	Eng	Perth	80	72	111	45.03
5000 runs	1995–96	SL	Adelaide	61*	81	125	50.52
6000 runs	1997–98	NZ	Perth	96	97	151	49.43
7000 runs	1998–99	Eng	Melbourne	122*	110	174	50.20
8000 runs	1999–2000	Ind	Adelaide	150	123	194	50.84
9000 runs	2001	Eng	Birmingham	105	136	216	51.24
10000 runs	2002–03	Eng	Sydney	102	156	244	49.91

Notes

1. In this table, 'Score' is Steve's final score for the innings in which he passed the particular milestone; 'Avge' indicates his career batting average at the end of the particular innings.
2. Steve was the seventh Australian to score 6000 Test runs, after Don Bradman, Neil Harvey, Greg Chappell, Allan Border, David Boon and Mark Taylor. He was the fifth to 7000, after Chappell, Border, Boon and Taylor, and the second to 8000, 9000 and 10000, after Border.
3. At 31 March 2005, 4 other players had scored 10000 Test runs: Border 11174 in 156 Tests, Sachin Tendulkar (Ind) 10134 in 123 Tests, Sunil Gavaskar (Ind) 10122 in 125 Tests and Brian Lara (WI) 10094 in 112 Tests.

Batting, by position in batting order

Position	Inn	NO	Runs	HS	100	50	Avge
No. 3	8	–	252	100	1	1	31.50
No. 4	7	2	196	90	–	1	39.20
No. 5	143	23	6821	200	24	30	56.84
No. 6	78	16	3098	177*	6	15	49.96
No. 7	19	3	543	134*	1	3	33.93
No. 8	5	2	17	12*	–	–	5.66

Highest partnerships

Stand	Wkt	Partner	Versus	Venue	Series	Inn	Score	Result
385	5th	Greg Blewett	SA	Jo'burg	1997	2	4/174	Win
332*	5th	Allan Border	Eng	Leeds	1993	1	4/321	Win
281	5th	Ricky Ponting	WI	Bridgetown	1999	1	4/144	Loss
260*	6th	Dean Jones	SL	Hobart	1989–90	3	5/253	Win
250	4th	Darren Lehmann	Ban	Cairns	2003	2	3/132	Win
239	5th	Ricky Ponting	Ind	Adelaide	1999–00	1	4/52	Win
231	4th	Mark Waugh	WI	Kingston	1995	1	3/73	Win
208	5th	Allan Border	SA	Adelaide	1993–94	1	4/183	Win
207	4th	Matthew Hayden	Zim	Perth	2003–04	1	3/199	Win

Stand	Wkt	Partner	Versus	Venue	Series	Inn	Score	Result
203	6th	Greg Blewett	Eng	Perth	1994–95	3	5/123	Win
200	5th	Graeme Wood	WI	Perth	1988–89	2	4/167	Loss

Notes
1. In the previous table, * indicates an unbroken partnership; 'Score' is the team score at the start of the partnership.
2. Steve's highest partnership at Sydney: 190 for the fourth wicket with Mark Waugh v England, 1998–99.
3. His highest partnership against Pakistan: 198 for the fourth wicket with Michael Slater, Rawalpindi, 1998.
4. His highest partnership against New Zealand: 199 for the fifth wicket with Michael Slater, Wellington, 2000.

Century partnerships (64)

Opponent	2nd	3rd	4th	5th	6th	7th	8th	9th	Total
New Zealand	–	–	2	2	2	1	–	–	7
England	–	1	5	4	4	1	–	1	16
West Indies	1	–	4	6	2	–	–	–	13
Sri Lanka	–	–	1	1	2	1	–	–	5
South Africa	–	–	1	3	1	–	–	–	5
Pakistan	–	–	1	3	1	–	–	–	5
India	–	–	3	3	–	1	–	1	8
Zimbabwe	–	–	2	–	–	–	1	–	3
Bangladesh	–	–	1	1	–	–	–	–	2
Total	1	1	20	23	12	4	1	2	64

Notes
1. The headings '2nd' through to '9th' indicate the wicket for which the partnerships were completed. Steve never opened the batting for Australia, and was never involved in a century partnership for the 10th wicket.
2. Thirty-four of these partnerships were in Australia (including 8 each at Adelaide and Sydney).
3. Of the 26 partners involved in these partnerships, the most were shared with Mark Waugh (9), Ricky Ponting (7), Ian Healy (6), Allan Border (5) and Greg Blewett (5). The most century partnerships with one teammate for one wicket is 7, for the fourth wicket, with Mark Waugh.

Highest partnership for each wicket

Wkt	Stand	Partner	Versus	Venue	Series	Inn	Score	Result
2nd	118	David Boon	WI	Sydney	1992–93	1	1/42	Draw
3rd	197	Mark Waugh	Eng	The Oval	2001	1	2/292	Win
4th	250	Darren Lehmann	Ban	Cairns	2003	2	3/132	Win
5th	385	Greg Blewett	SA	Jo'burg	1997	2	4/174	Win
6th	260*	Dean Jones	SL	Hobart	1989–90	3	5/253	Win
7th	147	Merv Hughes	Eng	Leeds	1989	1	6/441	Win
8th	114	Damien Fleming	Zim	Harare	1999	2	7/282	Win
9th	133	Jason Gillespie	Ind	Kolkata	2001	1	8/269	Loss
10th	43	Glenn McGrath	Ind	Kolkata	2001	1	9/402	Loss

Fielding 'milestones'

Catch	Series	Versus	Venue	Test	Batsman	Bowler
First	1986	NZ	Wellington	3	Bruce Edgar	Greg Matthews
50th	1994	Pak	Rawalpindi	67	Mushtaq Ahmed	Craig McDermott
100th	2001–02	NZ	Brisbane	140	Adam Parore	Brett Lee
Last	2003–04	Zim	Sydney	164	Mark Vermeulen	Brad Williams

Notes
1. Steve was the seventh Australian non-wicketkeeper to take 100 catches, after Bob Simpson, Ian Chappell, Greg Chappell, Allan Border, Mark Taylor and Mark Waugh.
2. He took 107 catches off 32 bowlers (including himself), the most being off Shane Warne (16), Merv Hughes (11), Glenn McGrath (8), Brett Lee (7), Tim May (6), Craig McDermott (6), Jason Gillespie (5) and himself (5).

Steve Waugh: Bowling

Series by series

Series	Versus	Tests	Overs	Runs	Wkts	Best	5w	Avge	SR	ER
1985–86	Ind	2	18	69	2	2/36	–	34.50	54.00	3.83
1986	NZ	3	36	83	5	4/56	–	16.60	43.20	2.30
1986	Ind	3	35	130	2	1/29	–	65.00	105.00	3.71
1986–87	Eng	5	108.3	336	10	5/69	1	33.60	65.10	3.09
1987–88	NZ	3	75	169	2	1/2	–	84.50	225.00	2.25
1987–88	Eng	1	22.5	51	3	3/51	–	17.00	45.66	2.23
1987–88	SL	1	28	47	4	4/33	–	11.75	42.00	1.67
1988	Pak	3	78	216	2	1/44	–	108.00	234.00	2.76
1988–89	WI	5	139	472	10	5/92	1	47.20	83.40	3.39
1989	Eng	6	57	208	2	1/38	–	104.00	171.00	3.64
1989–90	NZ	1	–	–	–	–	–	–	–	–
1989–90	SL	2	6	6	–	–	–	–	–	1.00
1989–90	Pak	3	3	13	1	1/13	–	13.00	18.00	4.25
1990	NZ	1	–	–	–	–	–	–	–	–
1990–91	Eng	3	38	90	1	1/7	–	90.00	228.00	2.36
1991	WI	2	35	90	–	–	–	–	–	2.57
1992–93	WI	5	58	162	3	1/14	–	54.00	116.00	2.79
1993	NZ	3	41	71	2	1/15	–	35.50	123.00	1.73
1993	Eng	6	32	82	2	2/45	–	41.00	96.00	2.56
1993–94	NZ	3	18	41	1	1/10	–	41.00	108.00	2.27
1993–94	SA	1	24	30	4	4/26	–	7.50	36.00	1.25
1994	SA	3	77.5	130	10	5/28	1	13.00	46.70	1.67
1994	Pak	2	30	78	1	1/28	–	78.00	180.00	2.60
1994–95	Eng	5	–	–	–	–	–	–	–	–
1995	WI	4	24	62	5	2/14	–	12.40	28.80	2.58
1995–96	Pak	3	16	40	1	1/18	–	40.00	96.00	2.50
1995–96	SL	2	19	34	4	4/34	–	8.50	28.50	1.78
1996	Ind	1	13	25	1	1/25	–	25.00	78.00	1.92
1996–97	WI	4	25.1	63	1	1/15	–	63.00	151.00	2.50
1997	SA	3	8.3	20	1	1/4	–	20.00	51.00	2.35
1997	Eng	6	20	76	–	–	–	–	–	3.80
1997–98	NZ	3	15	30	4	3/20	–	7.50	22.50	2.00
1997–98	SA	3	31	74	2	1/12	–	37.00	93.00	2.38
1998	Ind	2	12	38	–	–	–	–	–	3.16
1998	Pak	3	20	41	1	1/19	–	41.00	120.00	2.05
1998–99	Eng	5	11	28	2	2/8	–	14.00	33.00	2.54
1999	WI	4	5	19	–	–	–	–	–	3.80
1999	SL	3	–	–	–	–	–	–	–	–
1999	Zim	1	4	17	–	–	–	–	–	4.25
1999–00	Pak	3	5	20	–	–	–	–	–	4.00
1999–00	Ind	3	–	–	–	–	–	–	–	–
2000	NZ	3	7	20	–	–	–	–	–	2.85
2000–01	WI	4	–	–	–	–	–	–	–	–
2001	Ind	3	–	–	–	–	–	–	–	–
2001	Eng	4	–	–	–	–	–	–	–	–
2001–02	NZ	3	–	–	–	–	–	–	–	–
2001–02	SA	3	–	–	–	–	–	–	–	–
2002	SA	3	3	16	–	–	–	–	–	5.33
2002	Pak	3	–	–	–	–	–	–	–	–
2002–03	Eng	5	25	43	2	1/2	–	21.50	75.00	1.72
2003	WI	4	24	76	–	–	–	–	–	3.16
2003	Ban	2	5	4	–	–	–	–	–	0.80
2003–04	Zim	2	17	43	–	–	–	–	–	2.52
2003–04	Ind	4	31	82	1	1/35	–	82.00	186.00	2.64
Total		168	1300.5	3445	92	5/28	3	37.44	84.83	2.64

Note: The most wickets Steve took in a calendar year was 19, in 8 Tests in 1988, average 37.78.

Five wickets in an innings (3)

Analysis	Test	Versus	Venue	Series	Inn	Change	Result
21.3–4–69–5	10	Eng	Perth	1986–87	3	1st	Draw
24–5–92–5	24	WI	Melbourne	1988–89	3	1st	Loss
22.3–9–28–5	64	SA	Cape Town	1994	3	3rd	Win

Note: In this table, 'Analysis' indicates overs–maidens–runs–wickets; 'Change' indicates order of bowling (for example, '3rd' change is the fifth bowler used in the innings).

Bowling, by opponent

Opponent	Tests	Overs	Runs	Wkts	Best	5w	Avge	SR	ER
India	18	109	344	6	2/36	–	57.33	109.00	3.15
New Zealand	23	192	414	14	4/56	–	29.57	82.28	2.15
England	46	314.2	914	22	5/69	1	41.54	85.72	2.90
Sri Lanka	8	53	87	8	4/33	–	10.87	39.75	1.64
Pakistan	20	152	408	6	1/13	–	68.00	152.00	2.68
West Indies	32	310.1	944	19	5/92	1	49.68	97.94	3.04
South Africa	16	144.2	270	17	5/28	1	15.88	50.94	1.87
Zimbabwe	3	21	60	–	–	–	–	–	2.85
Bangladesh	2	5	4	–	–	–	–	–	0.80

Notes

1. Steve's 92 Test dismissals were achieved as follows: 28 caught (including 6 by Allan Border and 4 by David Boon), 24 caught behind (14 by Ian Healy, 4 by Tim Zoehrer, 4 by Greg Dyer, 2 by Wayne Phillips), 23 lbw, 12 bowled, 5 caught and bowled.
2. Batsmen most often dismissed: Carl Hooper (WI) 6 times; Hansie Cronje (SA) 4; Chris Broad (Eng), Mike Gatting (Eng), Brian McMillan (SA) and Jonty Rhodes (SA) each 3.

Bowling, by 'country'

'Country'	Tests	Overs	Runs	Wkts	Best	5w	Avge	SR	ER
Australia	89	738.3	1947	58	5/69	2	33.56	76.39	2.63
New Zealand	10	84	174	7	4/56	–	24.85	72.00	2.07
India	9	60	193	3	1/25	–	64.33	120.00	3.21
Pakistan	8	128	335	4	1/19	–	83.75	192.00	2.61
England	22	109	366	4	2/45	–	91.50	163.50	3.35
West Indies	14	88	247	5	2/14	–	49.40	105.60	2.80
South Africa	9	89.2	166	11	5/28	1	15.09	48.72	1.85
Sri Lanka	4	–	–	–	–	–	–	–	–
Zimbabwe	1	4	17	–	–	–	–	–	4.25
United Arab Emirates	2	–	–	–	–	–	–	–	–
Total overseas	79	562.2	1498	34	5/28	1	44.05	99.23	2.66

Bowling in Australia, by venue

Venue	Tests	Overs	Runs	Wkts	Best	5w	Avge	SR	ER
Melbourne	17	134	426	17	5/92	1	25.05	47.29	3.17
Sydney	17	97.5	244	5	3/51	–	48.80	117.39	2.49
Brisbane	17	127.1	337	10	3/76	–	33.70	76.29	2.65
Adelaide	15	170	380	11	4/26	–	34.54	92.72	2.23
Perth	15	161.3	456	10	5/69	1	45.60	96.90	2.82
Hobart	6	43	100	5	3/20	–	20.00	51.60	2.32
Cairns	1	5	4	–	–	–	–	–	0.80
Darwin	1	–	–	–	–	–	–	–	–

Note: The most wickets Steve took at one overseas ground was 5, at Cape Town (all in the one innings, in 1994). He took Test wickets at 16 overseas venues.

Bowling by career 'segment'

Years	Tests	Overs	Runs	Wkts	Best	5w	Avge	SR	ER
1985–86 to 1991	44	679.2	1980	44	5/69	2	45.00	92.63	2.91
1992–93 to 1998–99	67	495.3	1125	45	5/28	1	25.00	66.06	2.27
1999 to 2003–04	57	126	340	3	1/2	–	113.33	252.00	2.69

Note: Steve's total figures before he became Test captain are:

Years	Tests	Overs	Runs	Wkts	Best	5w	Avge	SR	ER
1985–86 to 1998–99	111	1174.5	3105	89	5/28	3	34.88	79.20	2.64

Bowling 'milestones'

Wkt	Series	Versus	Venue	Test	Batsman	How out
First	1985–86	Ind	Melbourne	1	Ravi Shastri	cwk Wayne Phillips
50th	1993	Eng	The Oval	58	Graham Gooch	c Allan Border
Last	2003–04	Ind	Melbourne	167	Rahul Dravid	c Damien Martyn

Note: Two batsmen were dismissed caught Waugh, bowled Waugh in Tests (as distinct from caught and bowled Waugh), and both fell to Mark Waugh's bowling: England's Mark Ramprakash at Perth in 1994–95 and Indian captain Mohammad Azharuddin at Chennai in 1998. Mark, as at 31 March 2005 the world-record holder for most catches in Tests by a non-wicketkeeper, never took a Test catch off Steve's bowling.

Steve Waugh: Captaincy

Steve Waugh as Test captain (Australia's 40th Test captain)

Opponent	Tests	Won	Won%	Drawn	Lost
West Indies	12	9	75.00	–	3
Sri Lanka	3	–	0.00	2	1
Zimbabwe	3	3	100.00	–	–
Pakistan	6	6	100.00	–	–
India	10	5	50.00	2	3
England	9	8	88.88	–	1
New Zealand	6	3	50.00	3	–
South Africa	6	5	83.33	–	1
Bangladesh	2	2	100.00	–	–
Total in Australia	29	22	75.86	5	2
Total overseas	28	19	67.85	2	7
Total	57	41	71.92	7	9

Notes

1. In this table, 'Won%' indicates win rate (percentage of Tests won relative to Tests captained).
2. To 31 March 2005, Australia had played 665 Tests, winning 303 (a win rate of 45.56 per cent), losing 176, drawing 184, with 2 tied. As at 31 March 2005, 13 men had led Australia in at least 20 Test matches:

Captain	Years	Tests	Won	Won%	Tied	Drawn	Lost
Joe Darling	1899 to 1905	21	7	33.33	–	10	4
Bill Woodfull	1930 to 1934	25	14	56.00	–	4	7
Don Bradman	1936–37 to 1948	24	15	62.50	–	6	3
Lindsay Hassett	1949–50 to 1953	24	14	58.33	–	6	4
Richie Benaud	1958–59 to 1963–64	28	12	42.85	1	11	4
Bob Simpson	1963–64 to 1978	39	12	30.76	–	15	12
Bill Lawry	1967–68 to 1970–71	25	9	36.00	–	8	8
Ian Chappell	1970–71 to 1975	30	15	50.00	–	10	5
Greg Chappell	1975–76 to 1983	48	21	43.75	–	14	13
Kim Hughes	1978–79 to 1984–85	28	4	14.28	–	11	13
Allan Border	1984–85 to 1994	93	32	34.40	1	38	22
Mark Taylor	1994 to 1998–99	50	26	52.00	–	11	13
Steve Waugh	1999 to 2003–04	57	41	71.92	–	7	9

3. Again at 31 March 2005, leaders across the cricket world with 20 or more appearances as captain and win rates exceeding 50 per cent were (win rates listed if not in above table): Steve Waugh, Don Bradman, Michael Vaughan (Eng: 24 Tests/15 wins/62.50 win rate), Lindsay Hassett, Mike Brearley (Eng: 31/18/58.06), Bill Woodfull, Viv Richards (WI: 50/27/54.00), Shaun Pollock (SA: 26/14/53.84), Mark Taylor, Hansie Cronje (SA: 53/27/50.94).

4. Of Australian captains who have led Australia in more than 5 Tests (as at 31 March 2005), only 1920–21 captain Warwick Armstrong (8 wins from 10 Tests) and Steve's successor Ricky Ponting (10 wins in 13 Tests) have a win rate above 71.92 per cent.

Players captained (27)

54 Tests with Steve as captain Justin Langer; *51* Ricky Ponting; *49* Adam Gilchrist; *48* Glenn McGrath; *41* Matthew Hayden; *40* Mark Waugh; *38* Shane Warne; *37* Jason Gillespie; *36* Brett Lee; *30* Damien Martyn; *27* Michael Slater; *21* Stuart MacGill; *16* Andy Bichel; *15* Greg Blewett; *11* Colin Miller; *10* Damien Fleming, Darren Lehmann; *8* Ian Healy; *5* Martin Love, Simon Katich; *3* Matthew Elliott, Michael Kasprowicz, Brad Hogg, Brad Williams, Nathan Bracken; *2* Scott Muller; *1* Adam Dale

2. Limited-overs international cricket

Steve Waugh's limited-overs international debut: 9 January 1986 v New Zealand at Melbourne, taking 1/13
Final limited-overs international: 3 February 2002 v South Africa at Perth, scoring 42 and taking 0/26

The Australian limited-overs international team, 1985–86 to 2001–02

Steve Waugh's teammates (75)

214 LOIs with Steve Mark Waugh; *160* David Boon; *151* Allan Border, Ian Healy; *149* Shane Warne; *148* Michael Bevan; *137* Dean Jones; *125* Glenn McGrath; *117* Geoff Marsh; *112* Adam Gilchrist; *111* Ricky Ponting; *110* Craig McDermott; *95* Mark Taylor; *84* Paul Reiffel; *83* Damien Fleming; *82* Peter Taylor; *72* Damien Martyn; *69* Tom Moody; *65* Simon O'Donnell; *61* Bruce Reid; *58* Darren Lehmann; *48* Greg Matthews; *45* Andrew Symonds; *42* Tim May; *41* Terry Alderman; *39* Simon Davis, Stuart Law; *35* Ian Harvey; *34* Michael Whitney; *33* Merv Hughes; *32* Michael Slater, Shane Lee, Brett Lee; *29* Matthew Hayden; *28* Jason Gillespie; *26* Greg Blewett; *24* Greg Ritchie; *23* Greg Dyer, Carl Rackemann, Andy Bichel; *22* Tim Zoehrer, Adam Dale; *21* Tony Dodemaide; *20* Mike Veletta; *15* Brendon Julian; *14* Wayne Phillips, Dave Gilbert, Dirk Wellham; *13* Gavin Robertson; *12* Michael Kasprowicz; *11* Greg Campbell; *10* Paul Wilson; *9* Michael Di Venuto; *8* Geoff Lawson; *7* Ken MacLeay, Justin Langer, Brad Hogg; *6* Nathan Bracken; *5* Graeme Wood, Brad Young; *3* Ray Bright, Anthony Stuart, Stuart MacGill; *2* David Hookes, Glenn Trimble, Glenn Bishop, Andrew Zesers, Jo Angel; *1* Jamie Siddons, Phil Emery, Matthew Elliott, Jimmy Maher, Brad Haddin, Ryan Campbell, Brad Williams

Team performance, by opponent

Opponent	LOIs	Won	Won%	Tied	NR	Lost
New Zealand	60	42	70.00	–	2	16
India	53	31	58.49	–	1	21
Pakistan	43	25	58.13	1	–	17
England	30	16	53.33	1	–	13
West Indies	50	25	50.00	1	1	23
Zimbabwe	14	14	100.00	–	–	–
Sri Lanka	24	17	70.83	–	–	7
Bangladesh	2	2	100.00	–	–	–
South Africa	47	22	46.80	2	–	23
Kenya	1	1	100.00	–	–	–
Scotland	1	1	100.00	–	–	–
Total	*325*	*196*	*60.30*	*5*	*4*	*120*

Note: These figures do not include the 32 LOIs Steve missed during his LOI career because of injury or non-selection.

Steve's appearance 'milestones'

LOI	Series	Versus	Venue	Notes
50	1987–88	NZ	Melbourne	Equal 13th Australian to play 50 LOIs
100	1990–91	NZ	Melbourne	3rd Australian to play 100 LOIs
200	1996	SL	Colombo	2nd Australian to play 200 LOIs
273	1999	SL	Colombo	Equalled Allan Border's Australian record
274	1999	Zim	Bulawayo	New Australian record
300	2000–01	WI	Melbourne	3rd man to play 300 LOIs

Note: Craig McDermott also played his 50th LOI against New Zealand in Melbourne in January 1988. The 12 men to have played at least 50 LOIs for Australia before this game were David Boon, Allan Border, Greg Chappell, Rodney Hogg, Kim Hughes, Dean Jones, Geoff Lawson, Dennis Lillee, Rod Marsh, Jeff Thomson, Kepler Wessels and Graeme Wood. The 2 Australians to beat Steve to 100 LOIs were Border and Jones. Border was the first Australian to play 200 LOIs. Mohammad Azharuddin (Ind) and Wasim Akram (Pak) were the first 2 cricketers to play 300 LOIs

Steve Waugh: Batting and fielding

Series by series

Series	Venue	Versus	LOIs	Inn	NO	Runs	HS	100	50	Avge	Ct
1985–86	Aus	NZ, Ind	12	10	3	266	81	–	2	38.00	2
1986	NZ	NZ	4	4	–	111	71	–	1	27.75	2
1986	UAE	Pak	1	1	–	26	26	–	–	26.00	–
1986	Ind	Ind	6	4	2	111	57*	–	1	55.50	–
1986–87	Aus	Eng, Pak, WI	3	3	–	127	82	–	1	42.33	–
1986–87	Aus	Eng, WI	10	10	3	245	83*	–	1	35.00	3
1987	UAE	Pak, Ind, Eng	3	3	–	42	20	–	–	14.00	1
1987	Ind, Pak	World Cup	8	8	5	167	45	–	–	55.66	3
1987–88	Aus	SL, NZ	10	8	2	199	68	–	1	33.17	3
1987–88	Aus	Eng	1	1	–	27	27	–	–	27.00	–
1988	Pak	Pak	1	1	–	7	7	–	–	7.00	–
1988–89	Aus	Pak, WI	11	10	3	270	54	–	1	38.57	4
1989	Eng	Eng	3	3	–	113	43	–	–	37.66	–
1989	Ind	E, WI, P, SL, I	5	4	1	83	53*	–	1	27.66	3
1989–90	Aus	SL, Pak	9	8	2	104	31*	–	–	17.33	4
1990	NZ	Ind, NZ	5	4	–	72	36	–	–	18.00	3
1990	UAE	NZ, Ban, SL, Pak	4	2	–	98	64	–	1	49.00	1
1990–91	Aus	NZ, Eng	10	9	5	141	65*	–	1	35.25	4
1991	WI	WI	5	5	2	86	26*	–	–	28.66	3
1991–92	Aus	Ind, WI	10	7	2	60	34	–	–	12.00	9
1991–92	Aus, NZ	World Cup	8	7	–	187	55	–	1	26.71	2
1992–93	Aus	WI, Pak	10	10	1	213	64	–	1	23.66	4
1993	NZ	NZ	5	5	1	120	39	–	–	30.00	3
1993	Eng	Eng	3	3	1	41	27	–	–	20.50	–
1993–94	Aus	SA, NZ	9	8	2	141	33	–	–	23.50	2
1994	SA	SA	8	8	2	291	86	–	2	48.50	2
1994	UAE	SL, NZ, Ind	3	1	–	53	53	–	1	53.00	–
1994	SL	Pak, Ind, SL	3	3	–	53	30	–	–	17.66	–
1994	Pak	SA, Pak	5	5	1	153	59*	–	2	38.25	2
1994–95	Aus	Eng	1	1	–	–	–	–	–	0.00	1
1995	NZ	SA, NZ, Ind	4	4	1	81	44*	–	–	27.00	1
1995	WI	WI	5	5	–	164	58	–	1	32.80	–
1995–96	Aus	SL	4	4	1	128	102*	1	–	42.66	2
1996	Ind, Pak	World Cup	7	7	2	226	82	–	3	45.20	3
1996	SL	Zim, SL, Ind	4	4	–	214	82	–	3	53.50	3
1996	Ind	SA, Ind	5	5	–	152	41	–	–	30.40	1
1996–97	Aus	Pak, WI	6	6	–	159	57	–	1	26.50	3
1997	SA	SA	7	7	1	301	91	–	4	50.16	3
1997	Eng	Eng	3	3	–	60	24	–	–	20.00	2

Series	Venue	Versus	LOIs	Inn	NO	Runs	HS	100	50	Avge	Ct
1997–98	Aus	SA, NZ	10	9	1	181	71	–	2	22.62	2
1998	NZ	NZ	4	3	–	112	47	–	–	37.33	1
1998	Ind	Ind, Zim	5	4	–	131	57	–	1	32.75	2
1998	UAE	NZ, Ind	5	5	–	123	70	–	1	24.60	–
1998	Ban	Ind	1	1	–	7	7	–	–	7.00	–
1998	Pak	Pak	3	3	–	40	30	–	–	13.33	1
1998–99	Aus	Eng, SL	2	2	–	20	20	–	–	10.00	–
1999	WI	WI	7	7	1	135	72*	–	1	22.50	2
1999	Eng	World Cup	10	8	3	398	120*	1	2	79.60	6
1999	SL	SL, Ind	5	4	–	67	43	–	–	16.75	1
1999	Zim	Zim	3	1	–	14	14	–	1	14.00	–
1999–00	Aus	Pak, Ind	10	9	2	195	81*	–	1	27.85	5
2000	NZ	NZ	6	5	3	145	54	–	1	72.50	2
2000	SA	SA	3	2	–	53	51	–	–	26.50	1
2000	Aus	SA	3	3	1	161	114*	1	–	80.50	–
2000	Ken	Ind	1	1	–	23	23	–	–	23.00	–
2000–01	Aus	WI, Zim	7	5	1	192	79	–	1	48.00	3
2001	Ind	Ind	5	4	–	93	35	–	–	23.25	3
2001	Eng	Pak, Eng	6	4	2	200	64	–	3	100.00	–
2001–02	Aus	NZ, SA	8	7	1	187	62	–	1	31.16	3
Total			325	288	58	7569	120*	3	45	32.90	111

Notes

1. Steve is Australia's 90th LOI cricketer. Straight before him on the chronological list of Australian LOI cricketers are Simon Davis, Dave Gilbert and Bruce Reid; immediately after are Geoff Marsh, Glenn Trimble and Tim Zoehrer.
2. Australia's games against Australia 'A' and matches at the XVI Commonwealth Games in Kuala Lumpur, Malaysia, do not have LOI status. Steve's record for Australia in these matches is:

Series	Venue	Versus	Mat	Inn	NO	Runs	HS	100	50	Avge	Ct
1994–95	Aus	Australia A	3	3	2	100	56*	–	1	100.00	1
1997–98	Aus	Australia A	1	1	–	4	4	–	–	4.00	–
1998	Mal	Can, Ant, Ind, NZ, SA	5	3	3	215	100*	1	1	–	3

3. Steve played 83 LOIs without missing a match after making his debut. This remained an equal Australian record (with Allan Border, who played 83 in a row between August 1980 and October 1984) until Adam Gilchrist played 99 straight LOIs between May 1999 and January 2001. Steve missed 32 LOIs between his first LOI and his last, as follows ('Games' indicates games missed):

Series	Versus	Games	Reason
1989–90	Pak	1	Not selected
1992	SL	3	Not selected for tour
1993–94	SA, NZ	2	Injury: hamstring
1994	Pak	1	Rested (shoulder strain)
1994–95	Zim, Eng	3	Injury: shoulder
1995–96	WI, SL	6	Injury: groin
1996–97	WI	2	Injury: groin
1997–98	NZ	1	Injury: hip muscle
1998–99	Eng, SL	10	Injury: hamstring
2000–01	WI, Zim	3	Injury: groin

4. The most runs Steve scored in a calendar year was 777 in 21 LOIs in 1996, average 43.16.
5. Australia won 196 and lost 120 of the 325 LOIs Steve played. Five matches were tied, and 4 ended in a 'no result'.
6. Steve was dismissed in the following manner in LOIs: caught 68 times, bowled 63, caught behind 33, run out 27, lbw 18, caught and bowled 12, stumped 8, hit wicket 1.
7. Steve was dismissed by 117 different bowlers in LOI cricket. Curtly Ambrose (WI), Phil Simmons (WI), Saqlain Mushtaq (Pak) and Allan Donald (SA) each dismissed Steve on 5 occasions, the most by any bowler.
8. David Richardson (SA) was the keeper who dismissed Steve most often (6 times: 5 catches, 1 stumping).
9. Steve won 20 'man of the match' awards in LOI cricket: the first against India in Melbourne in 1985–86, when he scored 73* and took 0–16; the last in the first-ever 'indoor' LOI, at Melbourne's Colonial Stadium, in 2000,

when he made 114*. This hundred was the second LOI century made at the stadium, Michael Bevan having reached his century one ball before his captain.

Centuries (3)

Century	LOI	Versus	Venue	Series	Inn	Pos	Score	Min	Balls	4/6	Result
102*	187	SL	Melbourne	1995–96	1	4	2/28	161	116	6/1	Loss
120*	266	SA	Leeds	1999	2	5	3/48	162	110	10/2	Win
114*	296	SA	Colonial	2000	1	5	3/37	180	103	9/–	Win

Notes
1. Steve was Australia's 15th LOI centurion.
2. Steve's only score in the nineties in LOIs was 91, from 79 balls, having come to the wicket at 3/18 against South Africa at Bloemfontein, 1997. This was his first match as Australian captain. In the previous match, at Centurion, he scored 89.

Batting and fielding, by opponent

Opponent	LOIs	Inn	NO	Runs	HS	100	50	Avge	Ct
New Zealand	60	51	12	1088	71	–	4	27.89	20
India	53	45	7	1117	81	–	7	29.39	16
Pakistan	43	40	8	1003	82	–	8	31.34	19
England	30	28	9	666	83*	–	3	35.05	7
West Indies	50	48	8	1114	72*	–	5	27.85	23
Zimbabwe	14	10	2	436	82	–	4	54.50	5
Sri Lanka	24	20	4	433	102*	1	1	27.06	6
Bangladesh	2	–	–	–	–	–	–	–	–
South Africa	47	44	7	1581	120*	2	12	42.72	14
Kenya	1	1	–	82	82	–	1	82.00	–
Scotland	1	1	1	49	49*	–	–	–	1

Batting and fielding, by 'country'

'Country'	LOIs	Inn	NO	Runs	HS	100	50	Avge	Ct
Australia	153	136	30	3165	114*	2	15	29.85	56
New Zealand	29	26	5	679	71	–	2	32.33	12
United Arab Emirates	16	12	–	342	70	–	3	28.50	2
India	39	33	9	918	82	–	6	38.25	15
Pakistan	11	11	2	245	59*	–	2	27.22	3
England and Wales	25	21	6	812	120*	1	5	54.13	8
West Indies	17	17	3	385	72*	–	2	27.50	5
South Africa	18	17	3	645	91	–	7	46.07	6
Sri Lanka	12	12	–	334	82	–	3	30.36	4
Bangladesh	1	1	–	7	7	–	–	7.00	–
Zimbabwe	3	1	–	14	14	–	–	14.00	–
Kenya	1	1	–	23	23	–	–	23.00	–
Total overseas	*172*	*152*	*28*	*4404*	*120**	*1*	*30*	*35.51*	*55*

Note: Seventy-five grounds hosted Steve's 325 LOIs, including 23 different venues in India. He played 16 matches at Sharjah, the most at any overseas venue, and 10 at Eden Park in Auckland.

Batting and fielding in Australia, by venue

Venue	LOIs	Inn	NO	Runs	HS	100	50	Avge	Ct
Melbourne (MCG)	50	45	12	1155	102*	1	7	35.00	20
Brisbane	13	13	4	236	45	–	–	26.22	7
Sydney	44	40	5	740	71	–	2	21.14	21
Perth	19	17	2	349	82	–	1	23.26	2
Adelaide	17	12	6	323	83*	–	3	53.83	1
Hobart	7	6	–	201	79	–	2	33.50	5
Melbourne (Colonial)	3	3	1	161	114*	1	–	80.50	–

Batting, as non-captain/captain

Status	LOIs	Inn	NO	Runs	HS	100	50	Avge
Non–captain	219	199	43	4984	102*	1	29	31.94
Captain	106	89	15	2585	120*	2	16	34.93

Note: Steve captained Australia in the seventh LOI in South Africa in 1997, the third LOI in England in 1997, and then from the first match in Australia in 1997–98 to his final LOI, at Perth in 2001–02.

Batting 'milestones'

Milestone	Series	Versus	Venue	Score	LOI	Inn no	Avge
1000 runs	1987	NZ	Indore	13*	42	38	36.89
2000 runs	1990	NZ	Sharjah	34	93	83	32.32
3000 runs	1993–94	SA	Perth	25	152	134	30.12
4000 runs	1996	Ken	Vishakapatnam	82	190	170	31.24
5000 runs	1997	SA	Bloemfontein	91	218	198	32.46
6000 runs	1999	Ind	The Oval	36	264	240	31.09
7000 runs	2000–01	Zim	Hobart	79	303	271	32.44

Notes

1. In this table, 'Score' is Steve's final score for the innings in which he passed the particular milestone; 'Avge' indicates his career batting average at the end of the particular innings.
2. Steve was the fifth to score 4000 LOI runs, after Allan Border, Dean Jones, Geoff Marsh and David Boon, the fourth to score 5000 LOI runs, after Border, Jones and Boon, the fourth to score 6000 LOI runs, after Border, Jones and Mark Waugh, and the second to score 7000 LOI runs, after Mark Waugh.

Batting, by position in batting order

Position	Inn	NO	Runs	HS	100	50	Avge
No. 3	8	–	228	37	–	–	19.00
No. 4	54	5	1544	102*	1	13	31.51
No. 5	135	25	4117	120*	2	25	37.42
No. 6	71	21	1423	73*	–	6	28.46
No. 7	16	7	257	57*	–	1	28.55

Highest partnerships

Stand	Wkt	Partner	Versus	Venue	Series	Inn	Score	Result
222	4th	Michael Bevan	SA	Colonial	2000	1	3/37	Win
207	3rd	Mark Waugh	Ken	Vishakapatnam	1996	1	2/26	Win
189	4th	Michael Bevan	SA	Centurion	1997	2	3/58	Win
173	4th	Dean Jones	Pak	Perth	1986–87	1	3/70	Loss
164	4th	Allan Border	Eng	Adelaide	1986–87	1	3/37	Win

Notes

1. In this table, 'Score' is the team score at the start of the partnership.
2. Steve's highest (and only century) partnership at Sydney was 102 for the fourth wicket with Ricky Ponting v South Africa, 1997–98.
3. Steve was involved in 21 century partnerships in LOIs: 4 for the third wicket, 11 for the fourth wicket, 4 for the fifth wicket, 1 for the sixth wicket and 1 for the seventh wicket. These 21 stands featured 9 different partners, including 5 each with Mark Waugh and Michael Bevan.

Fielding 'milestones'

Catch	Series	Versus	Venue	LOI	Batsman	Bowler
First	1985–86	NZ	Melbourne	1	John Bracewell	Craig McDermott
50th	1992–93	WI	Brisbane	135	Richie Richardson	Paul Reiffel
100th	2000	NZ	Christchurch	290	Stephen Fleming	Shane Warne
Last	2001–02	SA	Sydney	322	Steve Elworthy	Glenn McGrath

Notes

1. Steve was the second Australian to take 100 catches, after Allan Border.
2. He took 104 catches off 32 bowlers (including himself), the most being off Glenn McGrath (13), Craig McDermott (9), Simon O'Donnell and Shane Warne (each 8).

Steve Waugh: Bowling

Series by series

Series	Venue	LOIs	Overs	Runs	Wkts	Best	4w	Avge	SR	ER
1985–86	Aus	12	53	231	7	2/28	–	33.00	45.42	4.35
1986	NZ	4	35	159	4	1/31	–	39.75	52.50	4.54
1986	UAE	1	6	25	–	–	–	–	–	4.16
1986	Ind	6	46	226	7	2/40	–	–	–	4.91
1986–87	Aus	3	24.5	113	6	4/48	1	18.83	24.83	4.55
1986–87	Aus	10	85	345	15	3/26	–	23.00	34.00	4.05
1987	UAE	3	24	116	2	1/33	–	58.00	72.00	4.83
1987	Ind, Pak	8	62.3	288	11	2/37	–	26.18	34.09	4.60
1987–88	Aus	10	90	381	17	4/33	1	22.41	31.76	4.23
1987–88	Aus	1	10	42	1	1/42	–	42.00	60.00	4.20
1988	Pak	1	8	42	1	1/42	–	42.00	48.00	5.25
1988–89	Aus	11	78	373	8	3/57	–	46.62	58.50	4.78
1989	Eng	3	33	162	3	2/45	–	54.00	66.00	4.90
1989	Ind	5	–	–	–	–	–	–	–	–
1989–90	Aus	9	16	77	2	1/26	–	38.50	48.00	4.81
1990	NZ	5	–	–	–	–	–	–	–	–
1990	UAE	4	29	112	4	2/22	–	28.00	43.50	3.86
1990–91	Aus	10	76	346	7	2/39	–	49.42	65.14	4.55
1991	WI	5	32	153	5	2/25	–	30.60	38.40	4.78
1991–92	Aus	10	80.3	304	16	3/31	–	19.00	30.18	3.77
1991–92	Aus, NZ	8	60.4	277	8	3/36	–	34.62	45.49	4.56
1992–93	Aus	10	82.3	353	9	2/25	–	39.22	55.00	4.27
1993	NZ	5	35.4	173	3	2/27	–	57.66	71.33	4.85
1993	Eng	3	29	151	5	3/53	–	30.20	34.80	5.20
1993–94	Aus	9	61	218	4	2/20	–	54.50	91.50	3.57
1994	SA	8	56	282	5	2/48	–	56.40	67.20	5.03
1994	UAE	3	24	117	2	2/17	–	58.50	72.00	4.87
1994	SL	3	24	81	5	3/16	–	16.20	28.80	3.37
1994	Pak	5	37	144	2	2/35	–	72.00	111.00	3.89
1994–95	Aus	1	–	–	–	–	–	–	–	–
1995	NZ	4	–	–	–	–	–	–	–	–
1995	WI	5	22.3	123	3	2/61	–	41.00	45.00	5.46
1995–96	Aus	4	4	28	–	–	–	–	–	7.00
1996	Ind, Pak	7	31	157	5	2/22	–	31.40	37.20	5.06
1996	SL	4	25	111	3	1/20	–	37.00	50.00	4.44
1996	Ind	5	13	76	2	2/52	–	38.00	39.00	5.84
1996–97	Aus	6	3	24	–	–	–	–	–	8.00
1997	SA	7	5	25	–	–	–	–	–	5.00
1997	Eng	3	7	42	–	–	–	–	–	6.00
1997–98	Aus	10	4	14	1	1/14	–	14.00	24.00	3.40
1998	NZ	4	29.3	126	3	2/46	–	42.00	59.00	4.27
1998	Ind	5	17	97	3	2/42	–	32.33	34.00	5.70
1998	UAE	5	28	171	5	4/40	1	34.20	33.60	6.10
1998	Ban	1	3	23	–	–	–	–	–	7.66
1998	Pak	3	19.2	97	1	1/22	–	97.00	116.00	5.01
1998–99	Aus	2	–	–	–	–	–	–	–	–
1999	WI	7	16.3	66	2	1/13	–	33.00	49.50	4.00
1999	Eng	10	18	92	3	2/8	–	30.66	36.00	5.11
1999	SL	5	6.1	42	1	1/26	–	42.00	43.00	6.81
1999	Zim	3	–	–	–	–	–	–	–	–

Series	Venue	LOIs	Overs	Runs	Wkts	Best	4w	Avge	SR	ER
1999–00	Aus	10	6	22	–	–	–	–	–	3.66
2000	NZ	6	–	–	–	–	–	–	–	–
2000	SA	3	3	18	–	–	–	–	–	6.00
2000	Aus	3	–	–	–	–	–	–	–	–
2000	Ken	1	4	28	1	1/28	–	28.00	24.00	7.00
2000–01	Aus	7	–	–	–	–	–	–	–	–
2001	Ind	5	6	29	3	3/29	–	9.66	12.00	4.83
2001	Eng	6	–	–	–	–	–	–	–	–
2001–02	Aus	8	10	59	–	–	–	–	–	5.90
Total		325	1480.3	6761	195	4/33	3	34.67	45.56	4.56

Notes
1. Steve did not bowl in matches involving Australia 'A' or at the 1998 Commonwealth Games.
2. The most wickets he took in a calendar year was 34 in 24 LOIs in 1987, average 25.35.

Four wickets in an innings (3)

Analysis	LOI	Versus	Venue	Series	Inn	Change	Result
9.5–0–48–4	25	Pak	Perth	1986–87	2	2nd	Loss
10–0–33–4	54	SL	Sydney	1987–88	1	1st	Win
9–0–40–4	242	Ind	Sharjah	1998	2	3rd	Win

Note: In this table, 'Analysis' indicates overs–maidens–runs–wickets; 'Change' indicates order of bowling (for example, '3rd' change is the fifth bowler used in the innings).

Bowling, by opponent

Opponent	LOIs	Overs	Runs	Wkts	Best	4w	Avge	SR	ER
New Zealand	60	294.4	1365	31	2/23	–	44.03	57.03	4.63
India	53	257.3	1267	43	4/40	1	29.46	35.93	4.92
Pakistan	43	168.5	774	20	4/48	1	38.70	50.65	4.58
England	30	188	870	26	3/26	–	33.46	43.38	4.62
West Indies	50	260.2	1128	37	3/31	–	30.48	42.21	4.33
Zimbabwe	14	41	145	7	2/22	–	20.71	35.14	3.53
Sri Lanka	24	103.1	479	16	4/33	1	29.93	38.68	4.64
Bangladesh	2	10	22	2	2/22	–	11.00	30.00	2.20
South Africa	47	144	646	12	2/20	–	53.83	72.00	4.48
Kenya	1	7	43	–	–	–	–	–	6.14
Scotland	1	6	22	1	1/22	–	22.00	36.00	3.66

Notes
1. Steve's 195 LOI dismissals were achieved as follows: 92 caught (including 13 by Allan Border, 10 by David Boon, 9 by Mark Waugh, 7 by Mark Taylor and 5 by both Geoff Marsh and Paul Reiffel), 44 bowled, 30 caught behind (14 by Ian Healy, 6 by Adam Gilchrist, 4 by Tim Zoehrer, 3 by Greg Dyer, 2 by Wayne Phillips and 1 by Justin Langer), 22 lbw and 7 caught and bowled.
2. Batsmen most often dismissed: Carl Hooper (WI) 7 times; Gordon Greenidge (WI) and Kapil Dev (Ind) 4 times; 16 different players, including Mohammad Azharuddin (Ind), Martin Crowe (NZ), Imran Khan (Pak), Brian Lara (WI), Arjuna Ranatunga (SL), Viv Richards (WI), Salim Malik (Pak), Sachin Tendulkar (Ind) and Dilip Vengsarkar (Ind), 3 times.

Bowling, by 'country'

'Country'	LOIs	Overs	Runs	Wkts	Best	4w	Avge	SR	ER
Australia	153	734.2	3147	101	4/33	2	31.15	43.62	4.28
New Zealand	29	110.1	518	10	2/27	–	51.80	66.10	4.70
United Arab Emirates	16	111	541	13	4/40	1	41.61	51.23	4.87
India	39	163.3	807	30	3/29	–	26.90	32.70	4.93
Pakistan	11	76.2	349	5	2/35	–	69.80	91.59	4.57
England and Wales	25	87	447	11	3/53	–	40.63	47.45	5.13
West Indies	17	71	342	10	2/25	–	34.20	42.60	4.81
South Africa	18	64	325	5	2/48	–	65.00	76.80	5.07

Sri Lanka	12	55.1	234	9	3/16	–	26.00	36.77	4.24
Bangladesh	1	3	23	–	–	–	–	–	7.66
Zimbabwe	3	–	–	–	–	–	–	–	–
Kenya	1	4	28	1	1/28	–	28.00	24.00	7.00
Total overseas	172	746.1	3614	94	4/40	1	38.44	47.62	4.84

Bowling in Australia, by venue

Venue	LOIs	Overs	Runs	Wkts	Best	4w	Avge	SR	ER
Melbourne (MCG)	50	231.4	943	25	3/26	–	37.72	55.60	4.07
Brisbane	13	74	329	12	3/31	–	27.41	37.00	4.44
Sydney	44	187.1	829	30	4/33	1	27.63	37.43	4.42
Perth	19	127.5	571	22	4/48	1	25.95	34.86	4.46
Adelaide	17	84.4	342	8	2/30	–	42.75	63.50	4.03
Hobart	7	29	133	4	2/28	–	33.25	43.50	4.58
Melbourne (Colonial)	3	–	–	–	–	–	–	–	–

Bowling, as non-captain/captain

Status	LOIs	Overs	Runs	Wkts	Best	4w	Avge	SR	ER
Non–captain	219	1306	5855	172	4/33	2	34.04	45.55	4.48
Captain	106	174.3	906	23	4/40	1	39.39	45.52	5.19

Bowling 'milestones'

Wicket	Series	Versus	Venue	LOI	Batsman	How out
First	1985–86	NZ	Melbourne	1	Jeremy Coney	cwk Wayne Phillips
50th	1987	Pak	Lahore	46	Salim Malik	c Craig McDermott
100th	1991	WI	Bridgetown	110	Viv Richards	c & b
150th	1994	SA	Bloemfontein	164	Eric Simons	bowled
Last	2001	Ind	Vishakapatnam	310	Ajit Agarkar	lbw

Notes

1. Steve was the third Australian to reach 100 LOI wickets, after Dennis Lillee and Simon O'Donnell (Craig McDermott took his 100th LOI wicket later in the same match in which Steve achieved the feat).
2. Steve was the ninth player and the second Australian (after O'Donnell) to reach the 1000 runs and 100 wickets 'double'.

Steve Waugh: Captaincy

Steve Waugh as LOI captain (Australia's 13th LOI captain)

Opponent	LOIs	Won	Won%	Tied	NR	Lost
South Africa	20	8	40.00	2	–	10
England	5	3	60.00	–	–	2
New Zealand	20	11	55.00	–	1	8
India	20	13	65.00	–	–	7
Zimbabwe	9	9	100.00	–	–	–
Pakistan	14	11	78.57	–	–	3
Sri Lanka	4	2	50.00	–	–	2
West Indies	12	8	66.66	1	–	3
Scotland	1	1	100.00	–	–	–
Bangladesh	1	1	100.00	–	–	–
Total in Australia	40	25	62.50	1	–	14
Total overseas	66	42	63.63	2	1	21
Total	106	67	63.20	3	1	35

Notes

1. To 31 March 2005, Australia had played 590 LOIs, winning 358 (a win rate of 60.68 per cent) and losing 209, with 7 tied and 16 ending in no result. As at 31 March 2005, 16 men had led Australia in LOIs, as follows:

Captain	Years	LOI	Won	Won%	Tied	NR	Lost
Bill Lawry	1970–71	1	1	100.00	–	–	–
Ian Chappell	1972 to 1975	11	6	54.54	–	–	5
Greg Chappell	1975–76 to 1983	49	21	42.85	–	3	25
Bob Simpson	1978	2	1	50.00	–	–	1
Graham Yallop	1978–79	4	2	50.00	–	1	1
Kim Hughes	1979 to 1984	49	21	42.85	1	4	23
David Hookes	1983	1	–	–	–	–	1
Allan Border	1984–85 to 1994	179	108	60.33	1	3	67
Ray Bright	1986	1	–	–	–	–	1
Geoff Marsh	1987 to 1990–91	4	3	75.00	–	–	1
Mark Taylor	1992–93 to 1997	67	36	53.73	1	–	30
Ian Healy	1996 to 1997	8	5	62.50	–	–	3
Steve Waugh	1997 to 2001–02	106	67	63.20	3	1	35
Shane Warne	1998–99 to 1998–99	11	10	90.90	–	–	1
Adam Gilchrist	2000–01 to 2005	8	7	87.50	–	–	1
Ricky Ponting	2002 to 2005	90	71	78.88	1	4	14

2. Again at 31 March 2005, LOI leaders across the cricket world with 20 or more appearances as captain and win rates superior to Steve (win rates listed if not in above table) were Ricky Ponting, Clive Lloyd (WI: 84 LOIs/64 wins/76.19 win rate), Hansie Cronje (SA: 140/99/70.71), Mike Gatting (Eng: 37/26/70.27), Marvin Atapattu (SL: 35/23/65.71), Viv Richards (WI: 105/67/63.80) and Shaun Pollock (SA: 91/58./63.73).

Players captained by Steve Waugh in LOIs (36)

104 LOIs with Steve as captain Adam Gilchrist; *103* Michael Bevan; *99* Mark Waugh; *86* Ricky Ponting, Shane Warne; *68* Glenn McGrath; *63* Damien Martyn; *58* Damien Fleming; *55* Darren Lehmann; *45* Andrew Symonds; *35* Tom Moody, Ian Harvey; *32* Brett Lee; *30* Shane Lee; *17* Paul Reiffel; *16* Adam Dale, Andy Bichel, Jason Gillespie, Matthew Hayden; *13* Brendon Julian; *10* Paul Wilson, Michael Kasprowicz; *9* Gavin Robertson; *7* Stuart Law; *6* Nathan Bracken; *5* Greg Blewett, Michael Di Venuto, Brad Young; *3* Stuart MacGill; *1* Ian Healy, Justin Langer, Matthew Elliott, Jimmy Maher, Brad Haddin, Ryan Campbell, Brad Williams.

The World Cup, 1987–1999

Steve Waugh's World Cup debut: 9 October 1987 v India at Madras, scoring 19 not out and 2/52
Final World Cup match: 20 June 1999 v Pakistan at Lord's

Australia at the World Cup, 1987–1999

Year	Venue	LOIs	Won	Tied	NR	Lost	Finished	Champion
1987	Ind, Pak	8	7	–	–	1	Won	Australia
1992	Aust, NZ	8	4	–	–	4	Fifth	Pakistan
1996	Ind, Pak, SL	7	5	–	–	2	Second	Sri Lanka
1999	Eng	10	7	1	–	2	Won	Australia
Total		33	23	1	–	9		

Notes

1. The first World Cup was staged in 1975, the eighth in 2003. The ninth is scheduled to be played in the West Indies in 2007.
2. Australia forfeited its scheduled match against Sri Lanka at the 1996 World Cup, after declining to travel to Colombo.
3. Australia's tie in the 1999 tournament occurred against South Africa, in the semi-final at Birmingham. Australia qualified for the final because it had finished above South Africa on the 'Super Six' table that determined the semi-finalists.
4. Steve did not miss a match for Australia at these World Cups.

Steve Waugh at the World Cup

Cup	Inn	NO	Runs	HS	100	50	Avge	Ct	Overs	Runs	Wkts	Avge
1987	8	5	167	45	–	–	55.66	3	62.3	288	11	26.18
1992	7	–	187	55	–	1	26.71	2	60.4	277	8	34.62
1996	7	2	226	82	–	3	45.20	3	31	157	5	31.40
1999	8	3	398	120*	1	2	79.60	6	18	92	3	30.66
Total	30	10	978	120*	1	6	48.90	14	176.1	814	27	30.14

Notes

1. Steve is one of 2 Australians to have appeared in 4 tournaments, after Allan Border (1979, 1983, 1987 and 1992). Javed Miandad represented Pakistan in 6 Cups (1975–1996). In 1999, Steve became the first Australian to play in 2 World Cup-winning teams (joined in 2003 by Ricky Ponting, Adam Gilchrist, Darren Lehmann, Michael Bevan and Glenn McGrath). He was also the first Australian to play in 3 World Cup finals.
3. Steve's 33 World Cup matches remains the most for Australia. Most appearances: 38 by Wasim Akram (Pak).
4. Most World Cup runs for Australia: 1004 by Mark Waugh in 22 innings, 998 by Ricky Ponting in 27 innings and 978 by Steve. Most World Cup runs: 1732 by Sachin Tendulkar (Ind) in 32 innings.
5. Most World Cup wickets for Australia: 45 by Glenn McGrath, 32 by Shane Warne, 27 by Steve, 27 by Craig McDermott, 26 by Damien Fleming.
4. Steve's 120 not out against South Africa at Headingley in 1999 was the first World Cup century by an Australian captain.

3. First-class cricket

Steve Waugh's First-Class debut: 7–10 December 1984 v Queensland at Brisbane, scoring 31 and taking 0/34
Final First-Class match: 4–7 March 2004 v Queensland at Sydney, scoring 65 and 9 and taking 0/13 and 0/8

New South Wales

1. Steve was the 390th cricketer to play first-class cricket for New South Wales. He was one of 4 men to make their Sheffield Shield debuts for the Blues in 1984-85, the others being Imran Khan, Greg Dyer and Wayne Seabrook.
2. NSW won the Sheffield Shield 5 times during Steve's career, in 1984-85, 1985-86, 1989-90, 1992-93 and 1993-94. The Shield was renamed the Pura Cup in November 1999, and NSW won the competition for the first time under its new name, with Steve as captain, in 2002-03. He played in the Shield final in 1985, 1990 and 1992 (when NSW lost in Perth), and the Pura Cup final in 2003.
3. Steve was named the winner of the inaugural 'Steve Waugh Medal', awarded to NSW's player of the season, for 2002-03.

Batting and fielding

Team	Status	Mat	Inn	NO	Runs	HS	100	50	Avge	Ct
Australia	Tests	168	260	46	10927	200	32	50	51.06	112
Australians	Tour games	66	88	16	3858	161	14	15	53.58	35
Australian XI	In Australia	2	3	1	206	100*	1	1	103.00	3
Australian XI	Zim 1991	2	2	–	130	119	1	–	65.00	3
NSW	Shield/Pura Cup	85	147	14	6609	216*	22	24	49.69	83
NSW	Other matches	8	12	1	337	88	–	2	30.63	10
Young Australians	Zim 1985	1	1	–	30	30	–	–	30.00	–
Somerset	County	19	30	9	1654	161	8	5	78.76	24
Kent	County	4	6	1	224	146	1	–	44.80	3
Ireland	v Aust. A, 1998	1	2	–	76	45	–	–	38.00	–
Total		356	551	88	24052	216*	79	97	51.94	273

Notes

1. Steve scored 5 double centuries in first-class cricket:

Score	Team	Versus	Venue	Season
216*	NSW	Western Australia	Perth	1990–91
206	NSW	Tasmania	Hobart	1994–95
200	Australia	WI	Kingston	1995
202*	NSW	Victoria	North Sydney	1997–98
211	NSW	Victoria	Melbourne	2002–03

2. His highest score at the SCG was 170, for NSW v Victoria, 1987–88.
3. When Steve hit his highest first-class score of 216*, he was also involved in an unbeaten fifth-wicket partnership of 464 in 407 minutes with Mark Waugh. At 31 March 2005, this remained the world record for a fifth-wicket partnership and the highest partnership for any wicket in Australian first-class cricket.
4. Mark Waugh's final first-class batting average was 52.04. The twins finished their first-class careers on the same day, against Queensland at the SCG in March 2004, and going into the game, Steve's first-class batting average was 52.01, Mark's 51.98. Steve then scored 65 and 9, Mark 11 not out and 72. Mark's highest first-class score was made in the same match in which Steve made his highest first-class score. Mark's final first-class batting figures are as follows:

Mat	Inn	NO	Runs	HS	100	50	Avge
368	591	75	26855	229*	81	133	52.04

5. At 31 March 2005, the most centuries by Australian batsmen in first-class cricket (including matches for non-Australian teams) were Don Bradman 117 in 234 matches, Mark Waugh, Steve Waugh, Greg Chappell 74 in 321 matches, Allan Border 70 in 385 matches. Bradman (28 067 at 95.14) also had the most first-class runs by an Australian batsman, followed by Border (27 131 at 51.38), Mark Waugh, Greg Chappell (24 535) at 52.20, Steve Waugh and David Boon (23 413 at 44.01).
6. Steve was named one of *Wisden's* 5 cricketers of the year for 1989, after his season with Somerset in 1988 in which he scored 1314 first-class runs at 73.00, including 6 centuries, and 716 runs in one-day matches at 59.60, with 2 centuries. He became the first Australian since Somerset's Bill Alley in 1961 to be named one of the Almanack's cricketers of the year after a season in county cricket. Two years later, Mark Waugh was one of *Wisden's* cricketers of the year after his second season with Essex.

Bowling

Team	Status	Mat	Overs	Runs	Wkts	Best	5w	Avge	SR	ER
Australia	Tests	168	1300.5	3445	92	5/28	3	37.45	84.83	2.64
Australians	Tour games	66	407.2	1320	50	4/71	–	26.40	48.88	3.24
Australian XI	In Australia	2	27	90	2	1/31	–	45.00	66.00	3.33
Australian XI	Zim 1991	2	27	21	2	2/2	–	10.50	66.00	0.77
NSW	Shield/Pura Cup	85	922.4	2617	85	6/51	2	30.78	62.90	2.83
NSW	Other matches	8	55	127	2	2/24	–	63.50	165	2.30
Young Australians	Zim 1985	1	20.5	85	2	2/57	–	42.50	62.50	4.08
Somerset	County	19	135	408	14	3/48	–	29.14	57.85	3.02
Kent	County	4	3	15	–	–	–	–	–	5.00
Ireland	v Aust. A, 1998	1	6	27	–	–	–	–	–	4.50
Total		356	2904.4	8155	249	6/51	5	32.75	69.99	2.80

Note: Steve took 5 wickets in an innings 5 times in first-class cricket:

Bowling	Team	Versus	Venue	Season
5/69	Australia	Eng	Perth	1986–87
5/50	NSW	Tasmania	Sydney	1987–88
5/92	Australia	WI	Melbourne	1988–89
6/51	NSW	Queensland	Sydney	1988–89
5/28	Australia	SA	Cape Town	1994

Captaincy

Team	Status	Matches	Won	Drawn	Lost
NSW	Sheffield Shield/Pura Cup	22	10	3	9
NSW	v Western Province	1	1	–	–
Australia	Tests	57	41	7	9
Australians	Tour games	19	9	9	1
Total		99	61	19	19

4. Important limited-overs matches ('List A')

(The Association of Cricket Statisticians and Historians defines and records 'List A' limited-overs matches as tour and tournament matches between national/state/county/province/zone teams, including domestic limited-overs competitions.)

Batting and fielding

Team	Status	Mat	Inn	NO	Runs	HS	100	50	Avge	Ct
Australia	LOIs	325	288	58	7569	120*	3	45	32.90	111
Australia	v Australia A	4	4	2	104	56*	–	1	52.00	1
Australia	Comm. Games	5	3	3	215	100*	1	1	–	3
Australians	Tour games	12	10	3	230	86	–	1	32.85	1
Australia A	v West Indies	2	2	–	68	56	–	1	34.00	–
Australian XI	Zim 1991	3	3	1	236	116*	2	–	118.00	4
NSW	Domestic	55	54	10	2269	131	5	13	51.56	19
NSW	Other matches	3	3	1	46	24*	–	–	23.00	1
Young Australians	Zim 1985	5	5	–	112	42	–	–	22.40	1
Somerset	County	17	16	3	750	140*	2	3	57.69	7
Kent	County	5	5	1	159	59*	–	2	39.75	2
Total		436	393	82	11758	140*	13	67	37.80	150

Notes

1. NSW won the Australian domestic limited-overs competition 8 times during Steve's career, in 1984–85, 1987–88, 1991–92, 1992–93, 1993–94, 2000–01, 2001–02 and 2002–03, and Steve played in at least 1 match in each of these seasons. He played in 4 finals, in 1987–88, 1990–91, 1991–92 and 2002–03.
2. Steve's limited-overs matches for Australia A were against the West Indies in 1995–96 and 1996–97, both times when he was coming back from injury.
3. Steve's 3 List A matches for NSW that were not part of the domestic limited-overs competition (McDonald's Cup from 1984–85 to 1987–88, FAI Cup 1988–89 to 1991–92, Mercantile Mutual Cup 1992–93 to 2000–01, ING Cup 2001–02 to 2003–04) were against Wellington in Wellington (NZ) in 1984–85, against the West Indians at Lismore (NSW) in 1991–92 and against an England XI at Sydney in 2002–03.
4. Steve's highest score in List A limited-overs matches was 140 not out for Somerset v Middlesex at Lord's, 1988. His highest score for NSW was 131 v Queensland, Brisbane, 1992–93

Bowling

Team	Status	Mat	Overs	Runs	Wkts	Best	4w	Avge	SR	ER
Australia	LOIs	325	1480.3	6761	195	4/33	3	34.67	45.55	4.56
Australians	Tour games	12	46	213	8	3/38	–	26.62	34.50	4.63
Australia A	v West Indies	2	10.4	42	–	–	–	–	–	3.93
Australian XI	Zim 1991	3	21	95	4	2/52	–	23.75	31.50	4.52
New South Wales	Domestic	55	184	853	34	4/32	1	25.08	32.47	4.63
New South Wales	Other matches	3	15	84	1	1/37	–	84.00	90.00	5.60
Young Australians	Zim 1985	5	43	186	5	2/42	–	37.20	51.60	4.32
Somerset	County	17	62	302	8	2/16	–	37.75	46.50	4.87
Kent	County	5	10	74	2	2/6	–	37.00	30.00	7.40
Total		436	1872.1	8610	257	4/32	4	33.50	43.70	4.59

Note: Steve's best bowling was 4/32 for NSW v Victoria, at Sydney, 1990–91.

Captaincy

Team	Status	Matches	Won	Tied	NR	Lost
Australia	LOIs	106	67	3	1	35
Australia	v Australia A, 1997–98	1	1	–	–	–
Australia	Commonwealth Games	5	4	–	–	1
Australians	v Middlesex, 2001	1	–	–	–	1
Australia A	v WI	2	2	–	–	–
New South Wales	Domestic	23	15	–	–	8
New South Wales	v Touring teams	2	1	–	–	1
Total		140	90	3	1	46

Key to words, symbols and abbreviations

* = not out (unless otherwise indicated)
4/6 = fours and sixes
4w = 4 wickets in an innings
5w = 5 wickets in an innings
Ant = Antigua
Aus = Australia
Avge = average
B = bowled
Balls = balls faced
Ban = Bangladesh
c = caught
C&B/c&b = caught and bowled
Can = Canada
Ct = caught
CWk/cwk = caught behind
D = draw
Eng = England
ER = economy rate (runs conceded per over)
HB = handled the ball
HS = highest score
HW = hit wicket
Ind = India
Inn = innings (which innings of a Test OR total
    number of innings)
Inn no = innings number out of all Steve's innings

Ken = Kenya
L = loss
LBW/lbw = leg before wicket
LOI(s) = limited-overs international(s)
Mal = Malaysia
Mat = matches
Min = minutes
NO = not out
NR = no result
NZ = New Zealand
Pak = Pakistan
Pos = position in batting order
RH = retired hurt
RO = run out
SA = South Africa
SL = Sri Lanka
SR = strike rate (balls per wicket)
St = stumped
Test = Test number of Steve's career
UAE = United Arab Emirates
W = win
WI = West Indies
Wkt/Wkts = wicket/wickets
Zim = Zimbabwe

In all tables, 'split' years (such as '1985–86') show that the Test series was played in Australia. 'Whole' years (such as '1986') show that the Test series was overseas, with the exception of the series against Bangladesh played in northern Australia in July 2003.

ACKNOWLEDGEMENTS

My thanks go to everyone at Penguin Books, for believing in the concept and for committing wholeheartedly to the project. Thanks, too, to all the people from the wide variety of photography libraries we consulted while making the book, and also to the many individual photographers who gave me access to their valuable collections.

To Tim May, a great mate and a guy whose opinion is always worth listening to, and to Rahul Dravid, a most respected opponent – your words mean a lot to me and I thank you for your contributions.

I am also grateful to Darshak Mehta, who helped secure three previously unseen photos from Australia's opening game of the 1987 World Cup, and to Russell Box, for his patience while sharing his expertise and knowledge of computers and the wonders of technology that have previously escaped me. And to my wife, Lynette, who diligently collected articles, photos and personal notes over my career, which provided me with a solid base to work from, and my father-in-law, Phil Doughty, for cataloguing 18 years' worth of newspaper clippings.

Lastly, to a guy who offers clear perspective, honest assessment and thorough professionalism. The title 'editor' doesn't do you justice, and without your total support and passion to do the best possible job, the end product wouldn't be what it is. Once again, thank you, Geoff Armstrong. As you always say about yourself, 'You are a legend.'

CREDITS

Unless otherwise credited, photographs are from Steve Waugh's camera or from his private collection. While every attempt has been made to contact copyright owners, the publisher would be happy to hear of any omissions so that we can correct these in future editions.

Facing title page: Patrick Eagar (1989 Ashes series)
Following Chapter 43: David Moir/Fairfaxphotos (Steve's final shot in Test cricket, Sydney, January 6, 2004)
Career records opening page: Getty Images (On the defensive, second Test v. India, MCG, 1999–2000)

Chapter opening pages – captions and credits

Introduction: Final day in Test cricket, Sydney, January 2004
1. A dispute over a dummy, 1967
2. With Mark and the *Daily Telegraph*'s Bob Cooper, 1976
3. First NSW cap, 1984–85
4. Batting for NSW on day of Test selection, December 1985
5. First Test wicket, MCG, Boxing Day Test, 1985
6. First one-day innings, v. India, Brisbane, 1985–86 (Queensland Newspapers)
7. With Allan Border in New Zealand, 1986
8. Fake beard salesman, India, 1986 (Adrian Murrell/Getty Images)
9. Cover drive, third Ashes Test, Adelaide, 1986–87
10. With Geoff Marsh and Allan Border, World Cup final, 1987 (Bob Thomas Sports Photography)
11. Australian team celebrations, first Test v. New Zealand, 1987–88 (Newspix)
12. With Peter Taylor, training camp before Pakistan tour, 1988 (Australian Consolidated Press)
13. Hitting Patrick Patterson for six, Perth, 1988–89
14. With Terry Alderman, Allan Border, Mark Taylor and Geoff Marsh, Old Trafford, 1989 (Patrick Eagar)
15. With fellow 'Blues Brothers' Brad McNamara and Greg Matthews
16. Building the family home, 1990
17. With Shane Warne and Brian Lara, Australian XI v. West Indies, Hobart, 1991–92
18. With Mark on our 28th birthdays, June 2, 1993
19. Blowfly, Adelaide, January 1994 (Mark Ray)
20. Bowling during the South Africa tour, 1994 (Adrian Murrell/Getty Images)
21. With Gavin Robertson in Karachi, 1994
22. With Mark Taylor and our Cantonese masseur, 1994–95
23. Eyeballing Curtly Ambrose, Port of Spain, 1995 (Clive Mason/Getty Images)
24. Bowled for 170, third Test v. Sri Lanka, Adelaide, 1995–96 (Ray Titus)
25. With Rosalie Waugh at Sydney Airport, Sri Lanka tour, 1996 (Gregg Porteous/Newspix)
26. Covered with ice after facing Allan Donald, Centurion Park, 1997
27. Second of twin hundreds, third Ashes Test, Old Trafford, 1997 (Philip Brown)

28. With ACB CEO Malcolm Speed (left) and ACA president Tim May (George Sal/Newspix)
29. Lance Klusener caught, final dismissal, 1997–98 Carlton & United Series (Trent Parke/Newspix)
30. With the Reverend James Stevens (left, at rear) at Udayan
31. Doing your own cleaning, Commonwealth Games, Kuala Lumpur, 1998
32. Hook shot to reach a hundred, Boxing Day Ashes Test, 1998 (Clive Mason/Getty Images)
33. Congratulated by Tom Moody, Australia v. South Africa, World Cup, Headingley, 1999 (EMPICS/PA)
34. Nine-man slip cordon, one-day international v. Zimbabwe, Harare, 1999
35. Ducking a bouncer, fourth Test v. West Indies, Antigua, 1999
36. Meeting IOC president Juan Antonio Samaranch during the Sydney Olympics torch relay, 2000
37. A hundred at the Oval, fifth Ashes Test, 2001 (Philip Brown)
38. With Mark in Adelaide, 2001–02, before the twins' 100th Test together (Nick Wilson/Getty Images)
39. Final media conference as one-day captain, Perth, 2001–02 (Kerris Berrington/Newspix)
40. Acceptance speech at the Laureus World Sports Awards, Monte Carlo, 2002 (David Cannon/Getty Images)
41. A hundred in Sydney, fifth Ashes Test, 2002–03 (Steve Christo/Fairfaxphotos)
42. Face to face with Brian Lara, fourth Test, Antigua, 2003 (Hamish Blair/Getty Images)
43. Family breakfast before the fourth Test v. India, SCG, January 2004

Inserts

Insert 1 – page 8, top: Fairfaxphotos

Insert 2 – page 1, bottom: Newspix; page 2, top: Newspix, bottom: Simon Renilson/Newspix; page 3, both photos: Simon Renilson/Newspix; page 4, bottom: Getty Images; page 5, top: Simon Renilson/Newspix; page 6, all pics: *The Hindu*; page 7, both pics: Patrick Eagar

Insert 3 – page 1, top: Queensland Newspapers, bottom: Getty Images; page 3, top: Getty Images; page 4, top: Newspix; page 6, top: Patrick Eagar; page 8, bottom: Gregg Porteous/Newspix

Insert 4 – page 2, all pics: Gregg Porteous/Newspix; page 3, top: Gregg Porteous/Newspix, bottom: Newspix; page 6, bottom: Newspix; page 7, top: Getty Images

Insert 6 – page 1, top: Graham Morris, bottom: EMPICS/PA; page 2, both pics: Gordon Brooks; page 3, top: Ray Titus, bottom: Getty Images; page 4: Trent Parke/Newspix; page 5, top: Trent Parke/Newspix, bottom: Shaun Botterill/Getty Images;
page 6, top: Getty Images; page 8: Trent Parke/Newspix

Insert 8 – page 1, top: Getty Images, bottom: Gordon Brooks; page 2, top: David White/Newspix, middle: Graham Chadwick/Getty Images, bottom: Getty Images; page 3, top: popperfoto.com; page 5, middle: Getty Images, bottom: Pat Scala/Fairfaxphotos; page 6, top: Trent Parke/Newspix; page 7, top left: Phil Hillyard/Newspix, top right: Brett Costello/Newspix; page 8, top: Andrew Meares/Fairfaxphotos, bottom: Craig Golding/Fairfaxphotos

Insert 9 – page 1: Nigel Wright; page 6, bottom: Nigel Wright; page 8, all pics: Nigel Wright

Insert 10 – page 1, bottom: Andy Bichel; page 2, top: Graham Morris, bottom left: Tim Clayton/Fairfaxphotos, bottom right: Nick Wilson/Getty Images; page 3, top: Tim Clayton/Fairfaxphotos; page 4, top: Gordon Brooks; page 5, middle and bottom: Steve Christo/Fairfaxphotos; page 6, top: Hamish Blair/Getty Images, middle: Angela Wylie/Fairfaxphotos, bottom: Tim Clayton/Fairfaxphotos; page 7, top: Phil Hillyard/Newspix, bottom: Jack Atley; page 8, top: Jack Atley, bottom: Rick Stevens/Fairfaxphotos

INDEX

STEVE
WAUGH
FOUNDATION

There are many people in Australia aged between 0 and 25 who suffer from rare and chronic illnesses that for various reasons don't meet criteria set by charitable organisations. As such, these people are unable to qualify for assistance.

There is a massive void that needs to be filled, and it is in this area that the Steve Waugh Foundation truly believes it can not only make a difference but have a real impact on these people's lives.

If you would like to make a donation to the Steve Waugh Foundation, please contact (+61 2) 9909 0018. Donations made in Australia are tax deductible.

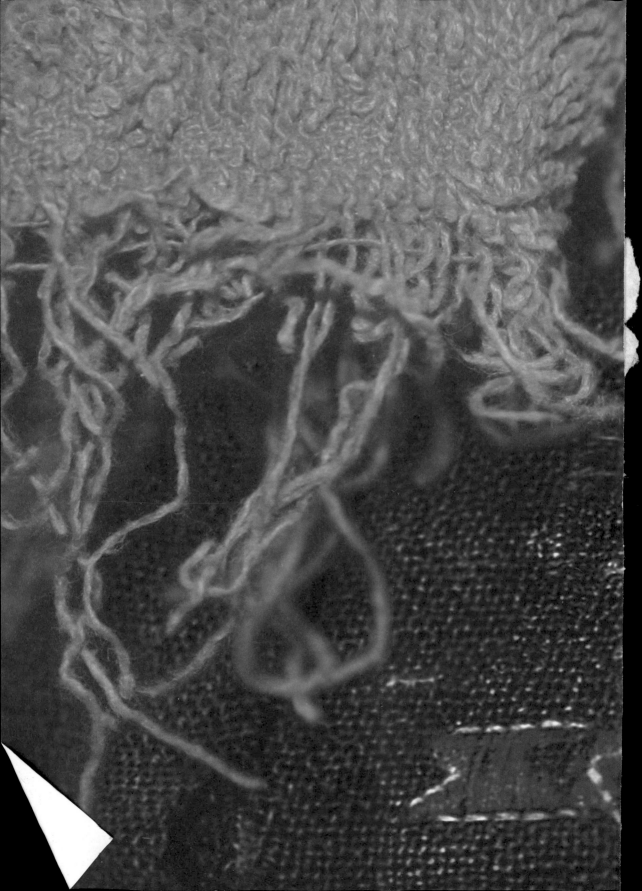